BRUCE H. KIRMMSE is Professor of History
at Connecticut College. As a Fulbright and a
Danforth Fellow, Kirmmse lived in Denmark for several years. He has published numerous articles on Kierkegaard and is the
translator of *Kierkegaard's Psychology* by
Kresten Nordentoft.

KIERKEGAARD

in Golden Age Denmark

THE INDIANA SERIES IN THE PHILOSOPHY OF RELIGION

Merold Westphal, *general editor*

Søren Kierkegaard (1813–55), by Luplau
Janssen, 1902. Although the artist never actually saw Kierkegaard, the portrait is a
very plausible likeness. (Courtesy of Det
Nationalhistoriske Museum på Frederiksborg.)

KIERKEGAARD

in Golden Age Denmark

BRUCE H. KIRMMSE

INDIANA UNIVERSITY PRESS
BLOOMINGTON & INDIANAPOLIS

© 1990 by Bruce H. Kirmmse

All rights reserved

No part of this book may be reproduced or utilized in any form or by
any means, electronic or mechanical, including photocopying and
recording, or by any information storage and retrieval system, without
permission in writing from the publisher. The Association of American
University Presses' Resolution on Permissions constitutes the only
exception to this prohibition.

Manufactured in the United States of America

Library of Congress Cataloging-in-Publication Data
Kirmmse, Bruce H.
Kierkegaard in golden age Denmark
/ Bruce H. Kirmmse.
p. cm. — (The Indiana series in the philosophy of religion)
Bibliography: p.
Includes index.
ISBN 0-253-33044-0
1. Kierkegaard, Søren, 1813–1855—Political and social views.
2. Denmark—Politics and government—19th century. I. Title.
II. Series.
B4377.K5175 1990
198'.9—dc20   89-45419
                                                                CIP

1 2 3 4 5   94 93 92 91 90

For my family

Contents

O

PART TWO: DENMARK'S KIERKEGAARD

Illustrations follow page 247

Preface and Acknowledgments

In the wake of the Enlightenment, the modern world has come to be defined increasingly by the radical restructuring of economic life into a global market economy and by the simultaneous restructuring of political authority into varying forms of representative government. The result has been a marked new emphasis on individualism but, ironically, also an increase in anonymity and in the power and pervasiveness of the institutions of mass society.

During the lifetime of Søren Kierkegaard (1813–55), Denmark entered this new age abruptly and quite self-consciously. Kierkegaard was a keen observer and an insightful critic of the changes he saw around him, and much of his authorship is a meditation on the relation between religion and politics in the changed conditions of modern times. The fundamental characteristics of the era which Kierkegaard saw at its beginning are still with us, indeed more so, and it is likely that they will continue to characterize much of the world for some time to come.

Kierkegaard's reflections on religion and politics are thus of interest, first of all, because they tell us a great deal about Kierkegaard as a thinker and about a nineteenth-century society in a time of rapid transformation; further, to the extent that many of the main tendencies of the late twentieth century are continuations and amplifications of those of the mid-nineteenth, Kierkegaard's insights retain their direct relevance for us today. The present study is an attempt to understand and reconstruct the context of nineteenth-century Denmark in its "Golden Age," and, by situating and examining Kierkegaard's development within that context, to recover Kierkegaard as the historical figure and social critic he was.

No one works alone. Even so apparently solitary an activity as writing a book is essentially a social and cooperative enterprise. The present volume is no exception, and its size and scope have left me happily indebted to many. I am, first of all, indebted to many scholars, not only those cited in the notes, but also to a great number of others, many of whom are named in the bibliography. I am also thankful for the support and encouragement shown by my colleagues at Connecticut College. Similarly, I thank the students who have studied Kierkegaard with me over the past dozen years; I am proud to number them among my most valued teachers.

A number of individuals deserve particular thanks. The hospitality of the late Niels Thulstrup made my work in Denmark more productive, and many conversations with my Danish colleagues Niels Jørgen Cappelørn and Paul Müller helped shape major portions of this book. Both in Denmark and in the United States, the continuing friendship and encouragement of Howard and Edna Hong has been of great value to me. Their careful, steady labor and their broad knowledge of historical and textual materials have set a high standard and have served as an invaluable resource to many who labor in this field, myself included. Alastair McKinnon's friendship and unflagging support have been indispensable, as have his wonderful reference and research tools. Michael Plekon has been a friend and a colleague of the highest order, and I owe much to his comments and suggestions and to his continuing support. R. Francis Johnson, Dean Emeritus of the Faculty of Connecticut College, goaded and encouraged me during the completion of this work. My parents, Herbert E. Kirmmse (now deceased) and Helen E. Kirmmse, read much of the manuscript with care and provided valuable comments. My colleague Garrett Green of Connecticut College read and provided valuable comments on a portion of the manuscript. Portions of the manuscript were expertly typed by Elina Sharp. Diane T. Birmingham was a careful and tireless proofreader.

A number of institutions and foundations have facilitated my work in various ways. Much of the research was carried out with funding from a Fulbright Fellowship, from the Danforth Foundation, and from the American Scandinavian Foundation. The Institute for Søren Kierkegaard Research at the University of Copenhagen provided an excellent environment for my research, which could not have been conducted without the resources of the library of the University of Copenhagen and the Royal (Danish) Library. Additional work was carried out at the Howard and Edna Hong Library at St. Olaf College in Northfield, Minnesota, where Cynthia Lund was helpful in tracking down obscure sources.

I received much assistance in selecting and procuring the illustrations for this book. Here again, thanks goes to the Hong Kierkegaard Library for suggesting a wide range of possible illustrations. Other valuable advice and assistance in choosing illustrations, as well as much else, was provided by Julia Watkin of the University of Copenhagen. The illustrations themselves and permission to use them were provided by: Det Nationalhistoriske Museum på Frederiksborg [The National Historical Museum at Frederiksborg], with the assistance of Kirsten Nannestad; Det Kongelige Bibliotek [The Royal Library], with the assistance of Inger Marie Kromann Hansen; Statens Museum for Kunst [National Art Museum of Denmark], with the assistance of Hanne Westergaard; and the Royal Danish Embassy in Washington, D.C. The dust jacket illustration was provided with the permission of the Statens Museum for Kunst and Det Nationalhistoriske Museum på Frederiksborg. I am grateful to all these institutions and individuals for their help.

Much of the work on the manuscript has been supported by grants from the Connecticut College Faculty Research, Study, and Travel Fund and by the Gift Fund of the Connecticut College Department of History. The publication of this book was supported in part by grants from the Earhart Foundation, the National Endowment for the Humanities, and the Danish Ministry of Cultural Affairs, and with respect to the latter of these I wish to extend my particular thanks to Bent Skou, Minister Counselor for Press and Culture at the Royal Danish Embassy in Washington, D.C.

Finally, I wish to express the deepest thanks of all to my children, Nathaniel and Hannah, who have had to compete with this book for my attention, and to Judith Kirmmse, who has shown endless patience and support for the project. Her editorial eye has been over virtually the entire manuscript, in many places several times, and it is a much better book for her efforts. I thank her for all this and more.

KIERKEGAARD

in Golden Age Denmark

Introduction

O

The history of Denmark in Søren Kierkegaard's time (1813–1855) is first and foremost the history of a rising peasant class, of a revolution in social, political, and ecclesiastical structures and relationships. This fundamental transformation can best be understood as beginning in the agricultural reforms of the 1780's and as reaching its major culmination in the ferment of the 1840's (especially in 1848–49), with the remarkably "abrupt" and permanent transition from a nominally absolute monarchy to constitutional and popular government. Kierkegaard's Denmark also witnessed military defeat and diplomatic decline in the wake of the Napoleonic wars. This was followed by a prolonged period of economic stagnation and commercial ruin for Denmark as a shipping power.

But the early nineteenth century in Denmark was also a period of literary and artistic splendor, of a cultural blossoming in which intellectual, artistic, and ecclesiastical life was dominated by the brilliant writers, artists, and clerics of what is now called Denmark's "Golden Age." All but a handful of these Golden Age luminaries were native-born (or thoroughly naturalized) members of the upper bourgeoisie of Copenhagen, generally stemming from and writing for the families whose fortunes were rooted in the professions (law, medicine, and, especially, the Church), in the more important administrative posts in the absolutist regime, or in the gradually collapsing merchant patriciate. The Golden Age was the collective product of the scions and servants of an elite which was a very narrow and highly urban social stratum. This brilliant elite shone all the more brightly in the first half of the nineteenth century, as if in spite of the fact that the social and economic bases which had enabled it to play a leading role in commercial, political, and clerical affairs were now shattered or severely eroded. The members of the generation of urban aristocrats which produced the Golden Age were the last representatives of their class who could pretend to speak for Denmark as a whole. Genuine economic and social power was shifting away from this thin shell of cosmopolitan urban aristocracy which had been built upon absolutism and maritime commerce. A new society was beginning to burgeon forth from within the old. Power was steadily transferred to a more truly national and democratic Denmark, whose underpinnings would be modern agriculture and whose political and economic center would move sharply away from the capital to the countryside and to the provincial towns where the overwhelming majority of the population lived and created the national wealth. Political, cultural, and ecclesiastical transformations followed in the wake of these social and economic changes.

The remarkable cultural creations of the Golden Age exist as if suspended in a political void. Although the majority of the period's writers and cultural figures did claim to have political views, these almost invariably turn out to be rather empty repetitions of a conservative, aristocratic credo which demanded social hierarchy and respect for the traditional loci of authority—in sum, an insistence upon the suitability of absolute monarchy and social stasis, which was entirely inconsistent with the economic and social transformations which had been set in motion by the peasant reforms. The conservative "politics" of the Golden Age luminaries have in fact a rather comic opera or fairy tale appearance. Hans Christian Andersen was just such an unrealistic Golden Age "conservative" in politics, and the sugarplum vision most Westerners have of "good kings" is probably derived in large measure from Andersen's poetic rendering of the benign notion of absolute monarchy which he shared with his fellows.

The fascinating thing, then, about Denmark in the first half of the nineteenth century is the increasingly evident contradiction between the changing social and economic realities, on the one hand, and the brilliant but blithely "conservative"—apolitical, really—cultural productions of the period, which are still revered under the name of the Golden Age. It is no accident that the middle of the nineteenth century is a great watershed in both the political and the cultural life of Denmark. The end of the absolutist political regime and the emergence into visibility of the common man, the peasant class, is the great punctuation which marks the end of the Golden Age of Danish culture. When the tension between economy and ideology, between act and word, was finally released at mid-century, the Golden Age fairly burst like a bubble, or rather, faded like a dream which was no longer adequate to reality, and after 1860 or so the literature which had so dominated the first half of the century already seemed strangely dated and mannered. It is almost difficult to believe that the great conservative aristocrat of the theatre, Johan Ludvig Heiberg, should have been so contemporaneous with Ibsen as to have prevented his works from being performed. Even in Denmark, the Golden Age writers who are most read today (aside from what is read by literary professionals and in the obligatory survey anthologies of the schools and universities) are those who were outsiders in their social origins or their cultural-political views, e.g., N.F.S. Grundtvig, Hans Christian Andersen, and Søren Kierkegaard.

One of the reasons that Kierkegaard's production holds such interest for modern readers is that his work increasingly leaves behind the apolitical "conservatism" and the social void in which many of his contemporaries wrote and comes to reflect the real tension of his society, a society upon which Copenhagen was losing its grip while the rural "common man" beckoned—a society emerging from elite rule and poised on the edge of the democratic unknown. In his social views, as in other spheres, Kierkegaard came to find virtue in a development which was inevitable, to find freedom, as one always must, in necessity. Kierkegaard's social and political views are often interpreted as being those which were shared by his Golden Age contemporaries, and he is thus depicted as having had no politics at all, or, what amounts to the same thing, as having embraced a nostalgic, traditionalist, and irrational authoritarianism, a misty reverence for hierarchy and monarchy which was completely irrelevant to the emerging social and economic realities of his times. Kierkegaard has thus been enlisted in the Cold War, and his views have been described, on the one hand, as a stout Christian refutation of "the doctrines of political liberalism" which insist upon the "divine right of majorities to govern wrong,"[1] and as a typical irrationalist excrescence of bourgeois society, on the other.[2] The "Marxists" and the "conservatives" both agree in their portrait of Kierkegaard's politics, but merely assign opposite evaluations to it.

But there are major obstacles to assimilating Kierkegaard's view of politics and society to the view which was shared by his elitist colleagues. First of all, it seems indeed strange that Kierkegaard, who fell out with his Golden Age colleagues on practically every important point concerning religion and philosophy, should share their political conservatism and their elitist obliviousness to what was happening in the the society around them. Secondly, and even more damaging, the traditional, conservative interpretation of Kierkegaard's politics always breaks down when it attempts to account for the very remarkable and vociferous "attack on Christendom" which he carried out in the last years of his life. He called for nothing less than the total dismantling of the traditional aristocratic-conservative synthesis known as "Christendom" or "Christian culture," which was the time-honored and comfortable marriage of the "horizontal" element of traditional society and the "vertical" element of religious transcendence, a synthesis in which religion had served as the guarantor of social stability, "moral values," and personal significance. This very Christendom which was the target of Kierkegaard's final authorship was the matrix in which the luxuriant cultural life of the Golden Age had blossomed, and without which it quickly withered.

Thus, if one attempts to see Kierkegaard's political and social views as a conservatism which was essentially similar to that of his cultural colleagues in Golden Age Denmark, the attack on Christendom remains the incommensurable element. Some critics have seen the attack as a deviation from Kierkegaard's earlier writings or as a "slippage," whereas others view it as the result of madness. One commentator has wanted to ease his interpretative burden by wishing that Kierkegaard had died a few years earlier.[3] None of these interpretations of Kierkegaard's attack on the Church wish to view it as connected with his political and social views prior to the attack, or to view the attack as an adequate and logically consistent product of the developing social and political views contained in Kierkegaard's authorship. This latter position is my own view, namely that the attack on Christendom can only be understood intelligently, not as an aberration, but as a response to the social and political developments of Kierkegaard's time. Kierkegaard's attack can be understood as being by and large logical, consistent, and warranted when it is interpreted as an extension of a development of social and political views which were anything other than conservative and elitist and which are better described—for reasons which will become clear in the course of this work—as variants of liberalism and populism.

Far from being the politics of an authoritarian conservative or demented irrationalist, Kierkegaard's politics should be seen as the healthy and enormously fertile and insightful self-criticism of bourgeois liberal society, posited from a radically otherworldly Christian point of view. Precisely because of his otherworldly Christian moorings, Kierkegaard does not feel the need to cling to what is known and personally advantageous in worldly matters—namely, the aristocratic conservatism to which his peers and his social background would normally have led him. Nor does Kierkegaard feel the need to reject what is unknown and threatening in his world—namely, liberalism, democracy, and the age of "the common man." It is a mistake to dwell too exclusively on the attack upon Christian culture which dominated the last phase of Kierkegaard's life, for one then loses the sense of perspective and development which is visible throughout the entire authorship—and especially in the predominantly non-pseudonymous portion which began in early 1846—which was written when political and social issues became increasingly and unavoidably intrusive in the life of the nation.

Kierkegaard, who in personal make-up and in many private matters, tastes, and preferences, was indeed a conservative aristocrat, in the end came not only to resign himself to the age of the common man, but positively to welcome it as the only alternative—risk-filled though it was—to the spiritual suffocation which the continuation of urban elitist Christian culture seemed to guarantee. The great turning point for Kierkegaard, of course, as for his society as a whole, came in assessing the impact of the great changes which took place after the Revolution of 1848, and by the early 1850's his political development was complete. However, he was acutely aware of changing political and social realities well before the visible flare-up in 1848, and his final position can be seen to be clearly prefigured in the most important of his earlier political writings, *A Literary Review* [*En literair Anmeldelse*], which was written in late 1845-early 1846. Kierkegaard's final, "radical" political views, which inform his attack on the Church and which traditional interpretations find so unaccountable and unprecedented, are the fruit of at least a decade of political thinking and writing, a decade which straddles both sides of 1848. One cannot dismiss or discount the attack without dismissing or discounting Kierkegaard as a whole, and one cannot fruitfully interpret this vituperative finale of his career without examining the development of the authorship which preceded it and the contradiction between culture and society which helped give form to the entire development.

In the development of Kierkegaard's social and political views, then, the elitist politics and social vacuum of Golden Age culture served more as a foil than anything else, and Kierkegaard drew his real political nourishment not from the verbal shadow of the cloud of culture which hovered over Copenhagen but from the solid substance of the democratic social revolution which was taking place in the countryside. Therefore, part one ("Kierkegaard's Denmark") of this examination of Kierkegaard's politics will begin with an outline of the history of the period 1780–1850, giving particular attention to agrarian reforms and the rise of peasantry. Attention will also be given to the growth of urban liberalism among the middle classes as well as to the political situation within the Danish State Church and to the events of 1848–49, which were the culmination of 60 or 70 years of change and of a decade of active ferment. This will be our examination of economic and social "reality" to the extent that this can be separated from the high urban "culture" of Golden Age Copenhagen. The second section of part one will then examine several of the principal shapers of Golden Age culture in detail. Part two ("Denmark's Kierkegaard") consists of a detailed examination of the latter portion of Kierkegaard's authorship, which culminated in the attack on Christendom. Kierkegaard's writings will be viewed against the background of the tension between the developing society and the official culture of his time.

An understanding of Kierkegaard's politics should be of particular interest to our own age, first of all because we ourselves are still citizens of the era which Kierkegaard described and heralded and which he ultimately helped through its birth pangs—the secularized and democratic epoch of the "common man," with all its possibilities and dangers. Secondly, and more fundamentally, Kierkegaard's politics hold interest for us in a less time-bound sense, because their substance consists of a rumination upon the separation between what is properly public and what is private—between, on the one hand, the sphere of community and material interests, of instrumental relationships of prudence and utility, and, on the other hand, the non-material sphere of relationships which are ultimate and non-negotiable. In brief, then, Kierkegaard's politics consists of a series of deliberations upon the problem of boundaries, or limits, between politics and religion. That his discussion of the problem took form during a period of transition from a hierarchical to a democratic society constitutes its historical dress, but the problem itself is a problem for all ages.

PART ONE

○

KIERKEGAARD'S DENMARK

1. Historical Background and the Rise of the Peasantry to 1820

O

A. AN OVERVIEW OF 1660–1849

In 1660, after a period of internal division and following a disastrous military defeat in which Sweden took possession of all of Denmark's provinces on the east side of the Sound [Øresund], Denmark became an absolute monarchy. The nobility ceased to be a political factor of any importance, and there were no representative institutions. All sovereignty was vested in the monarch, who generally enjoyed the active support of the urban merchant patriciate. A relatively "enlightened" absolutist-bureaucratic regime ruled Denmark from 1660 until 1848–49, when it was replaced by a constitutional monarchy in which all real power was held by a representative assembly [Rigsdag], which was elected upon the basis of virtually universal (male) suffrage. Throughout the entire absolutist period Denmark remained an overwhelmingly rural and agrarian society, with 75 to 85 percent of the population living on the land. The commercial, professional, and bureaucratic groups which formed the active base of support of the absolutist regime never constituted more than six or seven percent of the population. This support base was almost exclusively urban, and was, further, centered almost entirely in Copenhagen (and in Copenhagen-educated emissaries of high culture, e.g., the local parish pastors). The survival of such a narrowly urban regime depended of course upon the tacit support of the rural majority, the "common man," and the events of 1848–49 thus mark the transfer of power from a narrowly based urban absolutism to a broadly based rural and democratic regime. In the events of 1848–49, Denmark underwent the long-prepared but nonetheless sudden transfer of political power from the "cultured" urban patrician to the "common man"—the peasant—and the shifting of this urban-rural balance thus constitutes the principal theme in the historical study of the period.

The eighteenth century was a time of stability and prosperity for Denmark, whose neutrality in the numerous petty wars of the period enabled the commercial patriciate to bring home enormous profits from the shipping trade, in which Danish ships carried goods to and from the various belligerents. This century of commercial splendor built up and reinforced a high urban culture, and there is a remarkable quantity of first-rate literary production from this period, particularly for the theatre. At the same time, however, this literate urban culture, styled, as were the palazzi of the period, on cosmopolitan rather than local Danish models, reinforced the gap between country and city, between "people" and "culture," a gap which is humorously exploited by the greatest of the eighteenth-century playwrights, Ludvig Holberg, for example, in his *Erasmus Montanus*. It was perhaps as a reaction to its very isolation and provinciality in relation to the great capitals of Europe that Copenhagen developed a highly cosmopolitan, liberal, and enlightened intellectual life in this period of its commercial prosperity.

In the countryside, however, all was not so rosy and enlightened, and the peasants smarted under the imposition in 1733 of adscription [Stavnsbåndet], whereby men between the ages of fourteen and thirty-six were forbidden to leave their holdings. The ostensible reason for this restriction upon mobility was to provide a dependable base for military conscription, for which the great landowners were made responsible, but the practice of course also served to supply the landlords with a fixed source of labor. Adscription was naturally bitterly resented by the peasantry, and, in combination with a number of other ancient rights and restrictions which favored the landlords, it contributed to the destruction of peasant incentive and to the inefficiency of peasant agriculture.

Agriculture was, however, the mainstay of the little country in the long run, since it was the only source of wealth over which Denmark had control. The shipping industry, on the other hand, was dependent on a precarious neutrality which was shattered at the turn of the century in an economic and political catastrophe, thus revealing the fragility of the veneer of urban society, with its palazzi and its "culture."

Happily for the future of Denmark, rural reform had begun before the urban economy became engulfed in disaster, and the government had sponsored a good deal of land reform before its finances were destroyed by war and commercial collapse in the period after 1807. A new, democratic, rural society was launched by the old, hierarchical, urban society before that society became preoccupied with its own misfortunes. In 1784, a cabal of democratic-minded physiocratic reformers seized control of the person of young Prince Frederick (later Frederick VI), who was regent during the reign of his father, the insane Christian VII. Frederick, rescued by these reforming conspirators from the suffocating guardianship of a conservative court faction, happily embraced their plans for a series of thoroughgoing reforms which deeply affected the life of the peasantry. The period of the most profound peasant reforms was from 1787 to 1807, which also saw a steady and continuous rise in world grain prices, a fortuitous circumstance which encouraged many peasants to take advantage of their new opportunities. Thus the reforms were able to finance themselves for the first twenty years, imparting a momentum to the peasant movement which even subsequent price declines and changes of political climate could not arrest.

Diplomatic difficulties with Danish neutrality and a recession of liberal political sentiments at home began as early as 1799, and the period after 1807 was one of increasingly profound economic and diplomatic catastrophe, culminating in the state bankruptcy of 1813 and the loss of Norway in 1814. Both depressed grain prices following the Napoleonic wars and the end of Denmark's greatness as a shipping nation meant that economic recovery during the period 1815–30 was very slow indeed. It was a time of increasingly blind autocracy and bleak reaction in the politics of the aging Frederick VI, once the youthful and idealistic liberator of the peasantry, and it was also a time of stagnation and gloom in the great commercial houses of Copenhagen, which seemed to have lost forever their hopes of greatness.

In the countryside the peasant reform movement slowed but did not come to a complete stop, and with the beginning of the rise in the price of grain, which came in the late 1820's, the peasantry's movement toward economic— and later religious, cultural, and political—independence quickly regained its former vigor. The beginnings of renewed prosperity in the countryside in the 1830's also spelled the beginning of increased economic activity in the towns, though now on a different economic base than the carrying trade of the eighteenth century. This time it was the provincial towns, located nearest to the sources of agricultural goods, which profited most from the return of better times, while once-dominant Copenhagen had to wait longer for improvement and had to content itself with a decreasing share of the total Danish trade.

The 1830's were also marked by the rapid rise of a local Danish liberal movement, centered, as one might expect, largely in Copenhagen, and by a religious awakening and a resurgence of the peasant movement in the countryside. The national question—the question of the political status of the German- and Danish-speaking populations of southern Jutland—also takes its rise in this period which saw the beginnings of liberal political consciousness. In its initial phases, the national question became a burning issue only in the disputed and immediately adjacent areas of southern Jutland—and, significantly, in liberal Copenhagen. It is also in these areas that Danish nationalism found its abiding support in later years. In its more militant and bellicose forms, nationalism, like the liberalism with which it ultimately became linked in the National Liberal Party, remained predominantly an urban, a Copenhagen, phenomenon.

After the death in 1839 of Frederick VI, the grand and autocratic pilot of state, the ferment of the 1830's was succeeded by the open turbulence of the 1840's in which the claims of liberal constitutionalism, various peasant grievances, and the apparently insoluble national question in southern Jutland completely dominated the political scene. In the spring of 1848 all these factors contributed to the explosion which was touched off when the international wave of liberal revolution and conflicting nationalisms reached the shores of the Danish-German state. The immediate results of the explosion were civil war with the German population of southern Jutland and, more important in the long run, a change of regime which gave the liberals their long-desired representative, constitutional government, while the provisions for universal (male) suffrage held out for the peasantry the hope and expectation of eventual popular (peasant) sovereignty. Thus, as a result of 1848, the urban liberals received their war and constitutionalism, while the rural masses received what was ultimately of greater significance, the promise of the age of the common man. And despite liberal second thoughts about it, these hopes and promises of a democratic age were not successfully sabotaged by reaction; Denmark was the only country in Europe to retain permanently the revolutionary changes experienced by so many in 1848. The events of 1848–49 did not merely ratify the temporary ascendancy of the vocal urban liberals; more importantly, they were the constitutional acknowledgment of the long-term rise of the peasantry and the common man. The foundations for the modern liberal-democratic welfare state of today were laid in the broad dispersal of property which took place in the peasant reforms of the late-eighteenth and early nineteenth centuries and which found its political expression in the June Constitution of 1849.

B. THE PEASANT REFORMS

The first and most important precondition for the success of the peasant reforms was the fifty-percent rise of grain prices in the principal reform period of 1788 to 1805, owing particularly to demand from England.[1] Other important contributing factors were the presence of new agricultural techniques and ideas, particularly physiocracy, which was embraced by the handful of well-connected reformers who succeeded in gaining control first of the physical person and then of the personal convictions of Prince Frederick, who, as an absolute ruler and as the nation's largest landholder, had ample means to impose his will.

In 1787, the population of that part of Denmark in which the majority of the population spoke Danish—roughly the boundaries of present-day Denmark—was approximately 750,000, of whom about seventy percent were directly engaged in agriculture. Three-fourths of all agricultural land was incorporated in about 800 estates which, in turn, were owned by only a few hundred estate owners. Crown and church lands made up most of the remainder, with only a small percentage of the land owned directly by the peasants who worked it. However, of the land in great estates, eighty-seven percent was in peasant copyholdings, and the remaining thirteen percent was the demesne, which was cultivated by means of peasant labor dues [Hoveri]. Within the peasant class, land was unequally distributed. There were approximately 60,000 copyholder

[Fæstebonde] families, whose holdings averaged five "Tønder Hartkorn,"[2] and there was an equal, or almost equal number of cottager and dependent [Husmænd and Indsiddere] families who were landless laboring peasants, having at most a few acres or a kitchen garden which came along with their rented dwelling.[3]

Until the late eighteenth century, the landscape still bore the fundamental imprint of the late Middle Ages, and life existed within an elastic frame which included much unused land, woodlands, commons, and wilderness. Typically, peasants lived in small nucleated villages [Landsbyer], and each tenant generally had his share of the better and worse sorts of land, with the result that each tenant presided over many small parcels strewn all over the landscape.[4] In some cases, a peasant might have fifty to eighty separate parcels,[5] plus various haying, forest, and pasture privileges, and this, combined with a number of other venerable rights and restrictions, reduced greatly the efficiency of peasant agriculture under the old system of great landlords, nucleated villages, and dispersed holdings.

Earlier, the peasants paid an average of twenty to twenty-five percent of their harvest in land rents [Landgilde],[6] but this grain obligation had been gradually commuted into the much more onerous labor obligation [Hoveri]. A brief reforming ministry in the mid-eighteenth century had set the limit of labor dues at sixteen days on foot and eight days with a team of horses for each "Tønde Hartkorn" a tenant held, but these limits were soon repealed and remained only as a moral guideline.[7] The old system was thus an inefficient and relatively unproductive means of producing agricultural goods in that, even under the repealed guidelines of the mid-eighteenth century, a typical copy-holder owed eighty days of labor on foot and forty days of labor with a team per year, or more than one-third of his total labor time, and this mass of unwilling (and thus relatively unproductive) labor was squandered on the demesnes which constituted a mere thirteen percent of the nation's arable land. The inefficiency of the old system was further increased by the fact that the landlord could often demand his labor dues at a crucial time when it was much more important for the peasant to plow his own land or sow his own crops. To the inequities and the inefficiencies of the old system must also be added a large number of petty dues and the annoying and demoralizing judicial and disciplinary powers which landlords still possessed in relation to peasants. Further, we must reckon the disincentive of a highly partial evaluation of peasant estates upon death, which often left a peasant's son with a debt rather than an inheritance and which helped break down any impulse to save or to increase productivity. And, finally, the list of burdens upon pre-1787 agriculture and peasant life would be incomplete without mention of the humiliating system of adscription [Stavnsbåndet], touched upon earlier, which was instituted in 1733 as a method of guaranteeing a regular levy of troops by fixing the rural population in its place and placing conscription authority in the hands of the landlord. Sons between the ages of fourteen and thirty-six could be forced to take the vacant tenancies of their fathers, and soldiers could be forced to return to their native district upon completion of their term of service. The original military purpose was soon lost sight of, and the system became increasingly tight and oppressive after 1750, when rising grain prices prompted peasants to attempt to take advantage of their improved economic position by seeking better tenancies elsewhere.

In a system as oppressive and inefficient as that of pre-1787 agriculture, there was a great deal of the sort of mobility within the peasant class which can only be described as "social mobility" with tongue in cheek. Sons, forbidden to leave the district until age thirty-six, would often take a cottage while waiting for their fathers to die or become decrepit, at which time the sons would take over the copyhold. Fathers, burdened with heavy labor dues and knowing that increased productivity, savings, and physical improvements would be taxed off their estates by the unfair assessments of the landlords' assessors at their death, had no desire to invest a great deal of labor in their holdings and were often unwilling or unable to remain on them until their death. Thus, ten percent of copyholders started out as cottagers, and over fifty percent of copyholders, worn out from the burden of unprofitable labor, ended their days by moving back into cottages.[8] Many of these copyholders-cum-cottagers, landless and often aged and infirm rural day laborers, were permanently in arrears and frequently turned to charity and begging. Domestic servants were often considered better off than these peasants.

After their successful seizure of power in 1784, the group of reformers and their young Prince Frederick quickly set to work to implement their policies. In 1785 a commission to reform the agricultural system on the extensive Crown holdings in northern Zealand was established. A uniform and rather generous sort of copyhold was instituted. Many farms were consolidated and reparcelled in a more rational manner [Udskiftning], and peasant houses were moved out to the new locations [Udflytning]. Both labor dues and tithes were commuted to cash payments, which was a great gain for peasants in a period of high and rising grain prices. The only problem with these initial Crown land peasant reforms was the difficulty in getting the better-off copyholders to agree to cede sufficient land to provide a decent base for the wretchedly off cottagers, even though the government was willing to provide cash payment for such cession of land. This problem, as we shall soon see, foreshadowed a lasting problem of the peasant reforms, namely the relative impoverishment of the cottager peasants, who soon fell far behind the copyholder peasants in their economic and social status. Marriage patterns as well as social, political, and religious lines soon hardened to exclude the cottagers from the rest of the peasantry, so that the word "peasant" [Bonde] came to have a political significance only when used polemically, in opposition to the ancient class of estate owners.[9] As we shall see, under any conceivable sort of land reform, the only place from which land for cottagers might have been obtained was the demesnes of the Crown, the Church, and most of all, the great estate owners, but it was out of the question for even the most zealous and liberal of reformers to speak of touching these preserves.

After its initial and successful experiments at reform on Crown lands, Prince Frederick's reforming government established the Great Commission on the Peasantry in 1787. From the very beginning the commission was conscious of producing a document which would be a model not only for Denmark, but for all of Europe, and it was the intention that its deliberations would be published. There was no serious opposition on the commission to major reforms, although there was a significant division concerning the type of peasant agriculture to be encouraged. The minority position cited Adam Smith and wished to see agriculture rationalized on the English model, with a small number of large holdings and a free, dependent rural proletariat. The majority position, much less dogmatic in its liberalism, held that people work most productively when improving their own land, and that a large class of middling property owners was essential to the productivity and social stability of the state. The outcome of the reforms was a more or less unqualified victory for this majority position.

The first of the major reforms was passed as early as the summer of 1787; it provided that the evaluation of peasant estates at the death of the copyholder (and thus the adjustment of debits and assets between copyholder and landlord) must be carried out by an impartial jurist and not by the local sheriff, who was subject to pressure from the landlord. It now became possible for a landlord to owe money to a copyholder's heirs instead of the reverse, which had almost invariably been the case. Frugality and industry now became practical virtues for the peasant.

In June 1788 the next major reform of the commission gave equally profound impetus to peasant independence and industry, namely the abolition of adscription, which was to take place gradually over a twelve-year period. The power of conscription now passed from the landlords to the Crown, and landlords were deterred from grossly alienating their newly mobile peasants. Personal freedom had a great impact on peasant economic behavior and self-esteem, and the balance of rural power was beginning to be tipped in favor of the peasant. Laws of the same period also outlawed many of the more cruel and arbitrary forms of discipline which the landlords had traditionally exercised to keep the peasants in check. In March 1790 another major law forbade landlords to rent farms on one-year contracts and required them to return to the ancient custom of life tenancy where it had been abandoned. Also passed in 1790 was a reform which prohibited a landlord who proved that a tenant was unavailable for a holding from absorbing that holding into his demesne and required him to parcel it out among his other tenants. This was a key victory for those who opposed the English model of large-scale capitalist agriculture, because it prohibited the absorption of the many middling-sized parcels into enormous private farms.

Labor dues, and not property rights *per se*, represented the greatest single political obstacle to reform. In 1799 a law was passed which required all labor dues to be limited to fixed periods, and the state gradually compelled landowners to come to voluntary agreements with copyholders or submit to binding government arbitration concerning the amount of labor dues and their commutation to cash payments. The landlords could not afford to lose their labor supply, and the eventual settlement exempted cottagers from these reforms, as they had been exempted from others, most notoriously those concerning cruel and arbitrary forms of landlord discipline. The cottagers gained virtually no land from the reforms because their continuing existence as a labor force was vital to the continuing existence of the great demesnes and also, as it turned out, a valuable source of cheap labor for the new class of free, "self-owner" [selvejer] peasant farmers [Gaardmænd], which soon took the place of the old copyholder group. The price of the reform which created a stable peasant farmer middle class was the relative impoverishment and social isolation of the large and growing group of landless cottagers.

The reformers had hoped to carry out their reforms with the cooperation of many or most of the great landowners, many of whom had also, like their copyholders, wanted to get on with the business of technical improvements and more rational, intensive agriculture. However, the great landowners lacked the capital for improvements and feared that reform might deprive them of the labor supply with which to cultivate their demesnes. The labor problem was dealt with, as has been noted, by leaving the economic situation of the cottagers essentially untouched (or by actually worsening it), while the landlords could solve their capital problem by selling their legally encumbered copyholdings to their troublesome copyholders. Thus, given the radicality of the changes, resistance to the reforms on the part of the great estate holders was remarkably slight. The relatively small number of important estate owners and the government's control of both physical and moral force made any rebellion futile. The few great estate owners who rebelled were dealt with in the typical absolutist manner, namely the manipulation of prestige: they were fined, stripped of their orders and decorations, and sent into voluntary exile. The enlightened Copenhagen press, never friendly to the landed magnates, gave the government very favorable coverage.

The abolition of adscription, the impartial assessment of peasant estates, the fixing and commutation of labor dues for copyholders, and the prohibition against absorbing vacant copyholdings into the demesne all combined to encourage the great estate owners to sell their copyholdings to their tenants so that they could get on with rationalizing the cultivation of their own lands, the demesnes, and this was precisely the intended effect of the governmental reforms. The government now aided this rapid movement from copyholder to self-owner by establishing a land bank which gave peasants cheap loans for the purchase of their parcels and which assisted in the reparcelling and fencing of peasant holdings and the moving and reconstructing of peasant farmhouses on their new, compact, separate farms which they now owned in fee simple. Thousands of old, nucleated peasant villages were broken up as the peasants reparcelled and purchased their holdings and then took up residence on them. As we shall see, this sudden de-centralization of the ancient form of peasant life led to a sense of isolation which accompanied the newfound social self-confidence and which combined with it to find expression in the religious, cultural, and political self-assertion of the nineteenth century.

Fuelled by the prosperity resulting from high and rising grain prices during the first twenty years of reform, the transition from copyhold to self-ownership was astonishingly rapid. By 1807 about sixty percent of peasant farms had passed over to self-ownership,[10] while 75 percent of the farms on the islands and over fifty percent of those in Jutland had been reparcelled.[11] In 1802, after only fifteen years of reform, about forty percent of Zealand's thickly populated peasant villages and about twenty percent of the entire nation's villages had already been decentralized.[12] This was a social revolution, the effects of which made themselves felt well into the nineteenth century. With the coming of hard times in 1807, this first wave of the peasant movement slackened and even ebbed slightly, but it was followed by a second wave with the return of better times after the late 1820's, creating political and religio-political consequences which we will examine later.

The results of these reforms in terms of productivity are no less staggering. The government offered many prizes, cash incentives, educational programs, etc. in order to encourage the peasants to use new agricultural techniques, plant new sorts of crops, improve their woodlots, and so forth. Better fencing, more compact holdings, more rational rotation systems, the use of green manures, the home consumption of potatoes (which freed grain for the market), and the intangible but powerful goad of being one's own master, self-reliant, and with a mortgage debt to pay off—all these factors help explain the enormous jump in productivity which peasant agriculture experienced. According to where one looks in the country, per acre yields of grain increased from 20 to 40 percent between 1788 and about 1805, and when one takes domestic consumption into account, this meant roughly a doubling of the quantity of grain which the peasant could sell on the market.[13] The fifty percent increase in grain prices in this period, when viewed in conjunction with the increase in productivity, meant that those peasants who bought farms in this first wave of reform were very well served, for their debts soon became negligible. Those peasants who bought before the war-time inflation that occurred after 1799 began to drive land prices ahead of grain prices were particularly fortunate. This first wave of self-owners became the vanguard of the new peasant class and generally resisted quite well the hard times of 1807–27 which ruined so many urban merchants and great landowners.

In general, those peasants who had had the most before the reforms gained the most from them. Those who had had hereditary tenancy and who managed to commute their labor dues to cash payments were better off than those who had had a heavy burden of labor dues and who could not obtain a commutation. Similarly, those who had paid too high a price for their land during the period of combined high grain prices and wartime inflation sometimes found that they could not continue to meet their mortgage payments when grain prices fell after 1815. For the majority of the copyholder peasants, however, the reforms were a very dramatic gain, while for the others they held the hope, or even the implied promise, of future gains. Worst off, as always, were the cottager peasants, the landless laborers.

The poverty and dependence of the cottagers were naturally intensified when they lost their commons rights after reparcelling. Furthermore, their position at the bottom of the rural social structure had been made still worse in order to reconcile the great estate owners to the loss of their labor dues from their copyholders. Thus the labor dues expected from cottagers increased markedly, and they were unable to obtain cash commutation. The government had expected this to be the outcome of the liberation of the copyholders and did nothing to hinder it. The cottager group of the peasantry had to bear the costs of the rationalization which aided everyone above them. The reparcelling of copyholdings and the shift to self-ownership was an option which the better-off copyholders quickly seized, while those with less land or with less advantageous rent contracts often found it impossible to buy and were forced to join the ranks of the cottagers. The vacant tenancies left by such poorer copyholders were then bought up by the more prosperous peasants on the way to self-ownership, and the resultant larger parcels made for more viable middle-class peasant agriculture.

The reform movement thus reinforced and widened the gap already present within the structure of the peasant class, so that in the period from 1787 to 1805, a period of great population increase, the number of peasant farms (both copyhold and fee simple) actually decreased by about ten percent while the number of cottager families increased by a bit over twenty-five percent.[14] Shortly after the beginning of the nineteenth century, there were only 261,000 people in farmer families, while there were 323,000 people in cottager families;[15] at the beginning of the reforms in 1787 the size of the two groups had been equal, and around 1650 there had been about twice as many peasant farms as cottages,[16] so the reforms seem to have greatly accelerated what was already a secular trend. By the end of the reform period, the cottagers, who now constituted a majority of the peasantry, had only three to four percent of the arable land.[17]

About half of the cottager families had absolutely no land at all, forming a wretched rural proletariat whose labor obligations to the great landlords actually increased as more and more copyholders went free. The cottagers were a forgotten and almost totally unrepresented group in the politics of the first half of the nineteenth century, in spite of the fact that they were increasingly more numerous than the prosperous new farmer peasant class which was the proud result of the reforms.

Cottagers frequently held their houses (either with or without their pitifully small parcels of land) on very insecure leases, often subject to renewal or termination every three to six months. This meant that a landlord could threaten to displace a cottager family unless it was willing to pay rack rents, which often meant unbelievably heavy labor dues for very little land. In the Præstø area of southern Zealand around 1840, 1200 cottagers were collectively responsible for 29,000 days of labor per year for their houses (with, perhaps, a small plot)—almost 250 days' labor per year on the average! Furthermore, they were required to labor on additional days, as requested, for wages which were artificially low.[18] Another not uncommon practice was for a landlord to exhaust the energies of a cottager in rehabilitating a run-down house and overtaxed land during the most productive years of the tenant's life and then to expel him in order to rent the holding to a younger and more energetic man who could pay a higher rent for the now-improved property. Alternatively, a landlord could end a cottager's rent contract before the family had been in the parish long enough to qualify for public relief, and when this happened, often no one else, self-owner peasants included—taxpayers all—would rent to the dispossessed family in order to allow them to remain in the district long enough to qualify for help from the parish. Many cottagers thus became virtual migrants, and, ironically, conditions for cottagers were often hardest in districts where there were many new self-owner farmers. These latter, having little and wanting to get ahead, had to squeeze their impoverished fellow peasants the hardest. Most local parish councils looked upon these matters from an employer's point of view and were unwilling to destroy agriculture's basis of existence with better conditions. When the Advisory Assembly of Provincial Estates was established in the 1830's, the prevailing tone with respect to the cottagers and other rural poor (servants, etc.) was that they had life too easy, that they were treated too gently, were lazy, etc.

It was not until after 1848 that any relief was forthcoming for this large segment of the peasantry, and even then it was scarcely enough: the landlord's right to inflict corporal punishment and exert control over cottagers' dependents was ended, and labor dues could be commuted to cash. But the cottagers failed to get their key demand, namely, mandatory life tenure, and six-month leases were still common and were in fact on the increase in the latter nineteenth century.[19] The other key demand, the limitation of labor dues (or their commuted equivalent), was also unmet.

In the 1880's and after, the beginnings of mechanization made it possible for cereal agriculture to become less labor-intensive, while at the same time mechanization, credit unions, and cooperatives made possible the less land-intensive pork and dairy agriculture. Only then was it possible for the cottagers to work their way free of the grainfields, which no longer needed them, and achieve economic independence through self-help in producing the butter and bacon which modern steamships and refrigerated storage methods could carry quickly to the English market. Only when technology had changed so that they were no longer needed in their traditional captive labor market and there were new, compact, and efficient forms of agricultural production open to them—only then were the cottagers freed from their miserable servitude.

Thus, throughout the period we are examining, the cottagers constituted a very dark blot upon the brilliant accomplishments of the reform, a blot which was made all the darker by the very successes of the reform which divided the peasants against themselves and, to some degree, premised the success of the better-off peasants upon the immiseration of the unlucky. Until well after 1848 it was still fashionable to use the word "peasant" politically and mean the old, unified, pre-1787 peasant class which had not yet become fully aware of the inner divisions in its structure and which saw itself as united in the face of the ancient and common enemy, the great estate owners. Increasingly, however, as the nineteenth century wore on, this naive and inclusive use of the word peasant was political rhetoric only. It is true that the new self-owner farmers shared some common interests with the cottagers in wishing to see the liquidation of certain antique rights and practices that were still retained by the great landlords, and they shared with the cottagers a common glee in seeing their former masters humbled. But it became an open secret that the better-off peasants actually had much community of interest with the great estate owners in wishing to preserve the cottagers as a ready pool of cheap labor, so useful in harvest time. As we shall see, this division is reflected by the different audiences of Grundtvig and Kierkegaard. On the one hand, the religious and cultural awakener Grundtvig appealed primarily to the highly visible and self-confident portion of the peasantry who had managed to become self-owners. On the other hand, when Kierkegaard appealed to the "common man," he included in that term the *entire* rural population (as well as that part of the urban population that had escaped the taint of "high culture") and not merely the lucky children of the reform era.

Behind the great reforms and behind the literary brilliance of the Golden Age lurks the huge mass of the lower peasantry which constituted approximately one-third of the Danish population by the middle of the nineteenth century. These men, too, were given the vote in 1849. These men, too, were part of the common man whose age had just dawned. What would the ascendancy of the peasantry in general and the enfranchisement of this group in particular mean for the future of social, political, cultural, and religious life in Denmark after 1849? In the early 1850's no one knew, but many had their hopes and their fears.

C. ECONOMIC, POLITICAL, AND DIPLOMATIC DEVELOPMENTS, 1790–1830: THE DECLINE OF COPENHAGEN

The peasant reforms were accompanied by generally liberal tendencies in other spheres as well. Mercantile monopolies were abolished in the course of the 1780's and 1790's, and tariffs on imported goods, particularly raw materials but also foodstuffs and manufactured goods, were reduced after 1797. Trade policies combined with the decline of Danish shipping during the French Revolutionary and Napoleonic wars and with the increased importance of Danish agricultural exports to encourage the growth of provincial cities relative to Copenhagen.

At first, public opinion, particularly in Copenhagen, was free and liberal. There had been no press censorship since 1770, and the climate greatly favored the young Prince Frederick and his reforming government. In the late 1790's, however, Frederick's liberal and reforming zeal began to ebb, and the press was finally subjected to a strict censorship law and severe penalties. These developments were not the result of any real threat of sedition, but rather of Frederick's nervousness after Louis XVI's execution and were due particularly to increased pressure from Russia. A. P. Bernstorff, the leading libertarian in the reform clique, who was a wise and cautious diplomat as well, died in 1797, and power passed to the increasingly headstrong Frederick and to the more radically egalitarian of his reformers, who favored equality and a strong state but not libertarianism. The resulting censorship law, enacted in September 1799, quickly sent Denmark's most talented liberal political writer, the poet P. A. Heiberg, into exile in December of the same year. (The "radical" Heiberg, as we shall see later in this work, was the husband of Thomasine Buntzen Heiberg, later Fru Gyllembourg, who became a leading writer in the Golden Age and was the mother of P. A. Heiberg's child Johan Ludvig Heiberg, the great conservative and the greatest poet of the later Golden Age, whom we will later treat at some length.)

As late as 1794 and the Terror in France, P. A. Heiberg could still write and publish the crypto-republican song *Liberty, Equality, Fraternity*:

> Ring out, our song,
> In spite of every bond and link.
> Heavenly liberty! Gift of the Creator!
> Come! O come! Build thy throne among us!
>
> Nature formed us equal,
> And aristocracy is but a word.

> Indeed man ought only to yield
> To higher knowledge and to virtue.
>   Let us succeed! Let us succeed!
> When birth shall no longer oppress us,
>   Ring out, our song
> In spite of all pride and foolishness.
> Holy equality, jewel of humanity!
> Come and establish thy throne among us![20]

In the ensuing years, Frederick became increasingly fearful of this sort of rhetoric and even of the vast forces he had set in motion in the countryside with his peasant reforms. After 1800 a rigid conservatism set in, matching the increasingly gloomy and frightened mood of the Copenhagen patriciate which formed the original backbone of support for the absolute regime. The political climate resulting from this royal reaction and from the loss of self-confidence experienced by the Copenhagen *haute bourgeoisie* was transmitted to the Golden Age cultural movement which dominated the intellectual life of the city (and of the literate nation) in the first half of the nineteenth century. It is no accident that a king who had so lost his self-confidence and had become so opposed to public discussion—to "politics"— should have presided over the most golden years of the Golden Age, until 1839, setting the style for the cultivated public's "conservatism," i.e., its distaste for public life and politics in any form. Thus it was an ominous sign for the politics of the future when the following patriotic poem appeared in the window of a good Copenhagen burgher in the same year (1794) that P. A. Heiberg wrote his radical piece:

> No freedom!
> No liberty!
> The King's name
> Is my gain.
> Who loves not the person royal,
> May he be the devil's spoil![21]

The French Revolutionary wars of 1792 and 1793 were as profitable for Danish shipping as the earlier eighteenth-century wars had been. Denmark avoided attempts to coax her into various anti-French coalitions and enjoyed trading with all parties. Approximately 80 large Danish commercial houses divided up the world on an area-by-area basis so as to reduce competition among themselves and bound themselves together by agreements and family ties. These constituted the core of the Copenhagen patriciate. In the war years 1792–1800, Denmark succeeded in maintaining her neutrality, and the boom was enjoyed by all. The splendor of the period remains reflected in the grand palazzi which still dominate a stylish quarter of the old city; they were built in the period from 1795 to about 1807, after a devastating fire had destroyed much of the area in 1795.

But this fortuitous prosperity was about to come to an abrupt end, and the eighteenth century was the first and only century of Danish commercial brilliance. After 1793, when England entered the war against France, Danish neutral shipping became increasingly precarious. In 1797, after the death of A. P. Bernstorff, its greatest and most cautious statesman, Denmark began to lose its course in dangerous waters. In 1797–98 it began by refusing the right of belligerents to inspect neutral shipping, which alienated the English, who turned to harrying private shipping after Nelson's victory at Aboukir in 1799, leading to a number of Anglo-Danish incidents in the next two years. England was one of Denmark's most important customers, and Denmark should have sought a rapprochement with England in a war which seemed increasingly likely to force the choice of one side or the other. However, carelessness and pride seemed to lead Frederick to insist upon Danish neutrality, even though it had no real military basis upon which to assert that neutrality. Denmark's continuing insistence on the right to provide naval convoys to accompany its neutral shipping, and its refusal of the right of inspection led to Nelson's attempt to punish Copenhagen in April 1801, but the Danes resisted impressively, though they were militarily unprepared, and the English ultimately compromised and departed, leaving behind the stuff of great romantic poetry and delusions of Danish military-political grandeur. At this point the wisest course for Denmark still would have been an agreement with England, but this had become a psychological-political impossibility.

The period 1801–07 was actually the time of Copenhagen's greatest commercial success, for Napoleon had closed up most of the other continental ports. But neutrality was no longer the option it had been in the mid-eighteenth century, and England became increasingly nettled. Neither the Danish foreign ministry nor the business community wished to recognize the new situation after 1800, and they continued to reap enormous war profits while making no contingency plans for the inevitable future squeeze between France and England, both of whom coveted the Danish fleet. Frederick was becoming increasingly autocratic and attempted to make up in will for what he lacked in vision. His old circle of brilliant advisors was aging, dying, and falling out among themselves, and he fell under the influence of lesser men.

From 1805 onward, Frederick, his army, and his foreign secretary were in Holstein, a week's communication away from Copenhagen and foreign diplomats. Late in 1806 Napoleon blocked all trade between conquered areas and England, which in turn retaliated by banning all neutral trade with enemy ports. The Danes continued with no distinct policy and with protestations of neutrality. In March 1807 the bellicose Canning became British foreign minister, and in July 1807, at the Peace of Tilsit, the Russians switched from war against France to alliance with it. This terrified Canning, who believed incorrect rumors that Denmark was about to close its harbors to the English and turn its navy over to Napoleon. On August 8, 1807 the British fleet appeared in the Sound and demanded that the Danes turn over their fleet to the British. With foreign ambassadors, the navy, and the British at Copenhagen, and the King and the army a week away in Holstein, the situation was ludicrous. On August 16th the British bombardment started, and after burning much of the city, the British landed a large force which encircled and took the capital during the first days of September. On September 6th terms were signed, turning over the entire fleet to the British, who sailed much of it away the following month.

This was the abrupt end of the halcyon days of the Copenhagen merchant patriciate. War with England, continental blockade, military defeat, political dismemberment, and state bankruptcy followed in the next seven years. As late as September 1812, Denmark was offered the opportunity to desert Napoleon and ally with Sweden, Russia, and England, which probably would have averted the loss of Norway, but Frederick VI continued in his personal enmity to England and his blind faith in Napoleon's military abilities. Even as late as June 1813, Frederick, surrounded by England's allies, Sweden, Russia, and Prussia, still refused to change sides, remaining Napoleon's last ally, the only one to remain after the disastrous Russian campaign. In January 1814, at the Peace of Kiel, Denmark lost the whole of Norway. At Vienna in the following year, Holstein was restored to its former status as a merely personal possession of the Danish crown rather than an integral part of the monarchy, and was taken up into the German Confederation, an arrangement which was to cause trouble later in the century.

During the war, the common people, especially in the cities, had fared poorly because prices rose much more quickly than wages, but the merchant class often did rather well in these speculative boom-and-bust times. Inflation soon ruined many of the established fortunes, however. The gold value of paper currency was normally about fifteen to twenty percent less than its nominal face value, but by 1809 government notes were worth only one-third of their face value in gold; by 1810 only one-fifth; by 1811 one-seventh; and, by the end of 1812, one-fourteenth.[22] In January 1813 bankruptcy was declared by the state. All outstanding notes were to be replaced by new notes at about one-tenth of the original par, issued by a new bank which was to be financed by a heavy property tax (in silver). A six-year moratorium was proclaimed on the repayment of all debts, public and private. Par was not achieved on the new notes until 1838, and the twenty-five year period from 1813 to 1838 witnessed the gradually lifting specter of severe deflationary measures. These twenty-five years were somber for the Copenhagen bourgeoisie, but they were the heyday of the Golden Age of culture, coinciding almost exactly with the last quarter century of Frederick VI's reign and the first twenty-five years of Søren Kierkegaard's life. (Kierkegaard's family actually did rather well because his father had bought guaranteed gold-convertible bonds immediately before the crash, so that the family not only avoided losing its fortune, but, amid the spectacle of general ruin, actually improved its relative position.)

The period 1815–30 was thus a period of political timidity and economic difficulty for the Danish bourgeoisie, and only poetry and individual minds flourished. Frederick VI took on an increasingly reactionary coloration in this Metternichean era. His cabinet was now wholly dominated by dependent, pliable civil servants and bureaucrats chosen from the middle classes rather than by the noble, independent visionaries who had made the reforms of the 1780's and 1790's. Contrary to what many merchants had expected, overseas trade did not resume its former profitability after 1815. Renewed competition from formerly blockaded nations, the end of the captive Norwegian grain market as a capital source, the English Corn Laws, the increased relative importance of provincial towns, the slump in world grain prices—by 1824 Danish grain fetched only one-fourth of its earlier maximum[23]—and the world economic crisis after 1819 combined to all but ruin Copenhagen as a trade capital. The 1816–20 period saw 248 bankruptcies in Copenhagen, including ninety major failures.[24] Almost every firm of major importance was severely hit. As a center of international finance Copenhagen lost out to Hamburg, and as a trading city it lost ground, as mentioned, to the provincial towns, whose relative share of the Danish urban population increased greatly.

In the period from 1800 to 1840, the population of Denmark "proper" (Denmark minus Slesvig and Holstein) grew from 925,000 to 1,283,000, an increase of about 39 percent, while Copenhagen's population grew from 101,000 to 121,000, an increase of only 20 percent, or about one-half the national rate of increase.[25] (Another source uses slightly different figures but amply confirms this marked trend toward the diminution of Copenhagen's national importance. According to this source, in the period from 1801 to 1834, Copenhagen's population increased by 20 percent, while that of the provincial towns increased by 50 percent.)[26] Copenhagen was clearly losing its pre-eminence in relation to the rest of Denmark, while the countryside and the provincial market towns were gaining ground quickly. Between 1826 and 1837, Copenhagen's shipment of finished goods to the provinces diminished by 30 percent.[27] When England relaxed its Corn Laws, it was not Copenhagen, but the countryside with its provincial towns that reaped almost the entire benefit.

Copenhagen in the mid-1820's was a city of 115,000,[28] all crowded inside an antique set of confining walls. Much more than Denmark as a whole, Copenhagen was a society of extreme divisions between rich and poor. Copenhagen was squalid, crowded, torn between "culture" and barbarism. The countryside, ridden with inequities though it was, was a more democratic, prosperous, and healthy place to live. In the latter 1830's the life expectancy for a male in Copenhagen was 35 and for a female 39. In the countryside the life expectancy for both sexes was 50, among the highest in Europe at that time.[29] Even the persistent problem of the cottagers did not alter the fundamentally progressive and democratic aspect that the countryside presented when viewed in contrast to the capital.

Copenhagen in the 1820's was a city with a cowed press, a ludicrous adulation for royalty, a financial subjugation to Hamburg, and very little trade in the harbor. In the early 1830's the situation began to improve for the nation as a whole, but Copenhagen had to wait much longer to feel the improvement. Meanwhile, the city had its Golden Age in culture as consolation. This economically ruined patrician city sat astride a growing, reforming, healthy rural economy of middling farmers and small provincial cities, and yet, incongruously, Copenhagen remained the dictator of propriety in taste, "culture," and religion. Indeed, Copenhagen enjoyed its greatest cultural efflorescence in this economically bankrupt Golden Age of 1800–50, at the very time when the common man was about to burst the shell of the older Denmark.

There is an irony, then, in the fact that Copenhagen, which was characterized politically by its conservative, apolitical aristocratic temperament, and economically by bankruptcy and decline, was able to continue, through the instrumentality of its Golden Age, to serve as dictator and definer of "culture" for the provinces, which were characterized by successful agriculture and by a much more democratic temperament, by "the common man." There was an unresolved conflict between "culture" and agriculture, between the urbane aristocrat and "the common man." This is the fundamental cultural-political setting for the development of Kierkegaard's own views on society, and specifically on the relation between politics and religion. As we will note at the beginning of part two of the present work, Kierkegaard, half peasant, half urbane aristocrat, personally embodied this historical conflict and was thus perfectly situated to feel these historical forces working upon him and to attempt to re-define the relation of religion to politics and to "culture."

2. Religious Currents until 1820

O

Since the Reformation, Lutheran Christianity had been the official state religion of the Danish people. Official toleration was extended to several other "recognized religious societies," such as the small Calvinist and Jewish congregations and a limited number of Roman Catholics. In general, however, these deviating religious groups were considered to be foreigners or guests of the Danish state, e.g., the Calvinists were mostly Huguenot refugees, the Jews were mostly recent immigrants from Germany, etc. None of these non-Lutheran groups was considered "Danish," and their members existed in Danish society only under special dispensations and within certain restrictions.

Except for such few exceptions as the Crown might make, official Danish "citizenship" during the absolutist period (1660–1849) was extended only to baptized and confirmed members of the Lutheran State Church. For the peasant or artisan, this meant that marriage, the right to enter into contractual relationships, the right to enter a guild, to change one's place of residence, or to travel about the country all depended upon proving that one was legally adult, i.e., that one was a baptized and confirmed member of the Danish State Church. These restrictions held for the burgher also, and for him they meant, further, that access to the university, to the professions, and to the vast employment opportunities of the absolutist bureaucracy was similarly dependent upon the official espousal of State Lutheranism. While access to some of these areas was possible to those few who could prove that they were *bona fide* members of one of the other "recognized religious societies," for the vast majority—almost the entirety—of the Danish population, legal adulthood was conferred with the granting of the confirmation certificate by the pastor of the local parish of the official Lutheran State Church.

Every Dane was under a theoretical legal obligation to attend church on Sundays and feast days, though by the late-eighteenth and early nineteenth centuries this rule was only nominally enforced, and then only in the countryside, where peasants were assigned to the parish of their place of residence and thus lived under the watchful eye of the local pastor, who was usually the only local symbol of royal authority and of the culture of the capital. It was more difficult to enforce this sort of control in the towns, especially in Copenhagen, where any resident could legally attend any parish church he or she wished, which made it impossible for each clergyman to keep an eye on his flock.

It should also be noted that during the absolutist period the State Church was not a corporate body and had no constitution or self-government of its own. It was simply another arm of royal administration, wholly subservient to the upper levels of the royal bureaucracy.

B. THE OSCILLATION BETWEEN ORTHODOXY AND PIETISM: TRUE DOCTRINE AND GOOD WORKS

The Reformation doctrine of solafideism stressed faith and grace as anterior and superior to works and virtue, and this produced a historical oscillation between the orthodox stress upon right doctrine (the primacy of faith) and a pietistic emphasis upon right action (the importance of works). (In fact, Kierkegaard's own views on the relation of religion to politics and culture were a part of this swinging motion.)

Thus the original fervor of Luther, which had held together the two elements of faith and works, dissipated after his death into a rather rigid orthodoxy, characteristic of much of the official theology of the seventeenth century. This scholastic orthodoxy was in turn combatted by the works-conscious pietism of the later seventeenth and early eighteenth centuries, which was itself replaced by a cooler and more theoretical form of virtue religion, the various shadings of "rationalist" or "Enlightenment" Christianity, that predominated in the later eighteenth and early nineteenth centuries. This intellectualism tended, in turn, to generate its own antithesis in the neo-pietist mass revivals or "awakenings" of the early and mid-nineteenth century. It is these "awakenings" in particular which claim our attention, as they are a signal expression of the social and political transformation of the peasant class. These religious "awakenings" often developed quite directly into political movements, and they thus helped to put the question of the relation of religion to politics into the form in which it was presented to Golden Age writers and theologians in general, and to Søren Kierkegaard in particular. But these nineteenth-century awakenings are the result of the long and complex period of development and oscillation mentioned above, a period which we must examine in more detail in order to understand the tension between personal Christianity and official state Christianity that overshadowed all other religious questions in Kierkegaard's time and that was especially evident in the religious history of the Kierkegaard family itself.

The orthodox period of Lutheranism was characterized by a split between life and doctrine, between faith and works, with an emphasis upon faith and doctrine at the expense of life and works. The reaction against this one-sidedness began in Germany in the latter seventeenth century, in a pietist movement which stressed both passionate religious inwardness and serious striving toward becoming holy—sanctification—and not merely the justification which is dependent upon grace. This late seventeenth-, early eighteenth-century Protestant pietism was not rooted solely in the teachings of the Reformation, as was the orthodoxy against which it was directed, but rather had its roots in mediaeval mysticism and in counter-Reformation devotional literature and piety exercises, etc.[1] Pietism's subjectivism and anti-institutionalism placed it in alliance with toleration and the breaking down of confessional barriers, and it often contained a strain of anticlerical animosity to official religion as such.

The first great pietist writer was Philipp Jakob Spener (1635–1705), whose principal work was the *Pia Desideria*, published in 1675. In traditional Protestant fashion, Spener placed much emphasis upon Bible reading, but he stressed personal appropriation rather than critical exegesis. The purpose of the Bible reading and of sermons, which were likewise to be kept simple, was to call forth conversion and to produce visible effects in daily life. This increased importance of visible works was combined with a certain anti-intellectualism and was a reaction against the orthodox intellectualist tendency to equate faith with the intellectual assent to true doctrine. Even while implicitly de-emphasizing the solafideism of the Reformation's grace theology, Spener seized on other Reformation doctrines (notably such anti-institutional elements as the permissibility of lay preaching and the priesthood of all believers) and combined them with his anti-intellectualism and his re-emphasis on inner passion and on externally visible progress in sanctification. Yet, despite his implicit anti-institutional bias and his potentially un-Lutheran evaluation of human possibilities and works, Spener remained comparatively mild and cautious in his criticism of official Lutheranism, and he and his pietism were able to remain and prosper within the structure of official Lutheranism.

Spener's successor was August Hermann Francke (1663–1727), the second great leader of German pietism, whose period of greatest activity came about twenty years after that of Spener. Francke, a professor at Halle, was narrow-minded and fanatical in comparison with his predecessor. He was also a great organizer, and centered the movement around his activity in Halle. Great stress was laid upon the inwardness of the individual and rather less upon the importance of the sacraments or upon the common life of the congregation. The thousand-year empire of God was expected momentarily, and this led to the declaration that such things as card-playing, theatre, dancing, and other "adiaphora" were no longer of neutral significance as they had been for St. Paul, but were positively to be shunned and condemned as distractions from the need for radical conversion and preparation for the imminent kingdom.

Francke's pietism was extremely critical of old orthodox views and rituals and helped further to break down confidence in received traditions; thus, ironically, the more extreme sorts of pietism helped to prepare the way for the triumph, later in the eighteenth century, of Enlightenment Christianity's even more radical reinterpretation of the meaning of traditional doctrines.

Pietism placed great stress upon personal piety, conversion, and the conduct of life rather than upon doctrinal niceties. It viewed the Church not as the administrative responsibility of the clergy but as the collective responsibility of the entire congregation. Much emphasis was placed upon forcing the individual to an either-or decision for Christ, and there was often a great suspicion of the sincerity of the local pastor.[2] Pietists worried about the reality of repentance and saw the real Church as invisible. It could not follow the pragmatic Reformation practice of simply accepting as Christians those who were baptized. A Danish pietist saying of the early eighteenth century runs: "The country crawls with baptized souls, but where are faith's true glowing coals?"[3]

Pietist pastors and preaching reached Denmark as early as 1704; however, it remained more of a court movement than in Germany. Pietism generally involved a respectable portion of the upper class and was captained by various factions of the clergy (and opposed by others). This early eighteenth-century pietism was thus typically a top-down sort of movement, supported locally by priests trained and influenced in Copenhagen, and dying out with them.

There was another and more popular strain of pietism in Germany and Denmark, however, namely that of Count N. L. Zinzendorf (1700–60). Zinzendorf was the scion of a Franckian pietist family and organized his new sort of "populist" pietism in Saxony in the 1720's, concentrating first upon the peasants of his own estates and later broadening his interests to include larger areas of Germany and even international ties to Scandinavia and England. Even more than his predecessors, Zinzendorf avoided dwelling upon doctrinal points which could divide true believers and took all sorts of refugee and minority religious groups into his organization. He was accused, with some justice, of being anti-intellectualist. In the course of the 1730's, Zinzendorf's group—now called "Herrnhuters" because they had organized in the "shelter of the Lord" and had built a house of worship on Zinzendorf's estates—became officially separate from the Lutheran Church in Germany, but in Denmark the Herrnhuters always remained a parallel organization which was at least nominally within the official Church.[4] Zinzendorf was a masterful political organizer and had a good eye for the psychology and life of the congregation, but he was no theologian. He never came satisfactorily to terms with so fundamental a doctrine as the Holy Trinity, for example, and instead of doctrinal substance, his congregations were captivated by a highly emotional "blood theology," stressing the suffering Redeemer, Christ covered with blood, his wounds, death, etc. It was this primitive and emotional lay piety which took root among the popular classes in Denmark, and it was this Herrnhutism which formed much of the substance of Kierkegaard's religious upbringing.

Zinzendorf's pietism took hold in Denmark in the latter 1720's and the 1730's, and it seemed for a while as though it might become the officially sponsored strain, particularly after a successful visit of Zinzendorf to Copenhagen, which included an audience with the King. However, the emotional excesses and the dangerous latent strain of separatism which Herrnhutism contained caused the Crown to reject it, after much upheaval and intrigue, for the more moderate, if more superficial, Halle pietism. This official pietism flourished briefly during the early and mid-eighteenth century, and it did succeed in temporarily institutionalizing some of its zeal. (For example, all theatres were closed for a period, and there was an attempt to compel all Jews to attend church in order that they might be converted in time for the coming millennium.) However, the lasting influence of the official Halle pietism was restricted to such things as the introduction of much emotional religious literature into thousands of Danish homes, the promulgation of stricter Sabbath laws, and the introduction of confirmation as a compulsory rite for all Danish youth, so that confirmation became legally identical with adult citizenship. The only other lasting influence of this official pietism was, as mentioned, the subversion of the veneration and authority accorded to traditional Christian and Reformation doctrines. This subversion paved the way for the triumph of the radical reinterpretations espoused by Enlightenment Christianity, which was both the antithesis to and the child of pietism, and which was, in its turn, an irritant which helped to produce the neo-pietist awakening of the nineteenth century.

C. HERRNHUTISM IN DENMARK

While Halle pietism remained a rather localized phenomenon in Denmark, a religious attitude that was imported into the countryside by pastors who attempted to disseminate it in top-down fashion, it did help to set a certain emotional tone and to create an environment in which the more lay-oriented Herrnhut movement could take root and thrive as a critical pietism which paralleled, but did not replace, the Danish State Church. Thus, although many of its early excesses were curbed by royal and clerical authority, Herrnhutism grew and prospered privately, and Zinzendorf's pietism was the only strain which developed a genuinely popular lay religious following and which survived the glacial period of Enlightenment Christianity to set fruit in the great religious awakenings of the nineteenth century. The officially sponsored Danish variant of Halle pietism remained a movement of pastors and not of the people, and was unwilling to take seriously its original stress upon the priesthood of all believers. Herrnhutism, on the other hand, took its lay commitment far more seriously and was much more of a popular success.

Both Halle pietism and Herrnhutism stressed "awakening" and the importance of a clear break with sin, and both placed great emphasis upon Christ crucified, but Halle pietism paid far more attention to the crushing demands of the Law, while Herrnhutism taught the Gospel of grace and allowed the consciousness of sin to come slowly of itself. Especially in its early years, however, the overwhelmingly sentimental, emotional, and anti-intellectual character of Zinzendorf's pietism often led to an unhealthy stress upon conversion, which was seen as a precondition without which no amount of God-fearingness could suffice. Related to this was the notion of the perfectibility of the converted. Herrnhutism thus combined anti-intellectualism, covert anti-clericalism, and an emotional emphasis upon "blood and wonders," yet at the same time it insisted upon a religion of inwardness, saying that God was not interested in outward things, in rote, external exercises of piety, but only in a reborn heart.[5]

A typical testimony to this emotional lay piety can be found in the diary of a member of a Danish Herrnhut society from the mid-eighteenth century: "We have commemorated the Holy Trinity, whose feast it was today. We have been joyous about the Holy Family, bound together in blood, and have felt a blessed connection with our little Papa Heart and Mama and little Brother Lamb."[6] Jesus is depicted very sensually as "the man of pain" [Smertensmanden] who descends, bloody, from the cross and embraces the Herrnhut brotherhood.[7] He is referred to as "my bloody Man," and much is made of "the sweat of his bloody soul struggle," etc.[8] This enormously fantasy-laden sensual relation to Christ was accompanied by—and indeed seems to have occasioned—great physical modesty and sexual repression, often reminiscent of mediaeval asceticism. This repression in turn seems to have summoned up sensuality and sexual fears and thoughts even more—as was noted by the Herrnhut product, Søren Kierkegaard, who wrote in a discussion of Don Giovanni (in *Either/Or*) that "sensuality is first put forth as a principle, as a power, as a system in itself [when it is excluded] by Christianity."[9] The leading scholar of Danish Herrnhutism concludes that the Herrnhut education of children was quite overdrawn, in that it neglected every part of the life of the child, excepting religion, and was extremely one-sided, unnatural, and overwrought, e.g., in teaching children to burst into tears at the thought of the Savior's love for them as miserable sinners. Many Herrnhut children had a tendency to turn abruptly away from Herrnhutism as soon as they were adults, which is surely suspect:

> [T]he strings of religious emotion were all too tightly stretched. . . . There has been an over-nourishment of religion, and too large drafts have been written on religious fantasy. We could perhaps call the consequent condition a religiousness which has been worn out with watching [en religiøs Forvaagethed].[10]

Thus Herrnhutism was continually threatened by dissolution from within, by rejection from its own children, because of the very anticlerical and anti-intellectual emotionalism which lay at the root of its popular success.

Herrnhut pietism had a much greater appreciation of the importance of the congregation than did the more clerically oriented Halle pietism of Francke, and strong lay congregations were founded in Denmark as early as the 1730's. A lively and important society, the "Congregation of Brothers" [Brødremenighed], was founded in Copenhagen in 1739, and other societies of importance sprang up in Funen and especially in Jutland, where Herrnhut influence was strongest in a belt which ran along the west coast from the relatively impoverished district around Ringkøbing northward to the Limfjord. (This put the childhood home of Søren Kierkegaard's peasant-cum-business-man father, Michael Pedersen Kierkegaard, squarely in the center of the Jutland "Herrnhut belt," and he was apparently quite strongly influenced by the sect, for he enrolled in the Copenhagen Congregation shortly after arriving in the capital as a teenager.)

The number of Herrnhut families was not large—a scholarly estimate places the Herrnhut population of Jutland at 400 families in 1778; 700 in 1798; and 750 in 1803[11]—but the sect seems to have taken hold with considerable tenacity among a stubborn and vocal peasant minority. By the late eighteenth century, the only places in Jutland where there was any sort of religious awakening and lay piety remaining from the great wave of early eighteenth-century piety were precisely those districts which were dominated by the Herrnhuters.[12] There is no connection between the official Halle pietism of the early eighteenth century and the tumultuous neo-pietist awakenings of the nineteenth century, but there is a good deal of connection between Herrnhut pietism and the later movement. The wandering awakeners of the early nineteenth century were sympathetic to Herrnhutism, even though they were not themselves members, and by 1830 or so, many of the earlier Herrnhut districts in Funen and Jutland came to form much of the heartland of the new awakening movement.[13] As we shall see, in the decades after 1830, many of these same districts were again strongholds of the peasant movement and, after 1848, of the radically democratic Peasant Party.

In Copenhagen, after its founding in 1739 the Congregation of Brothers grew throughout the rest of the century, its membership comprising, in the words of one contemporary observer, "common citizens and artisans, occasionally a student."[14] Herrnhutism was "the middle term between remaining in the Church and separatism,"[15] and by the latter eighteenth century, when the pietist and separatist frenzy of the early and middle portions of the century had passed, the Copenhagen Herrnhut congregation inherited all the remaining anticlerical lay piety in the capital, and its membership swelled to around 450 families.[16]

In the late eighteenth century the only pastor in Copenhagen who was a member of the Congregation of Brothers was Peter Saxtorph, the curate at Nicholas Church from 1780–1803. It was during these years of commercial boom that Kierkegaard's father, Michael Pedersen Kierkegaard, made his extraordinary rise from a penniless peasant boy, the apprentice of his uncle, to a self-made man, a well-to-do merchant, and it is interesting to note that his association with the Herrnhut Congregation of Brothers seems to have been a way of preserving the rustic Jutland religiosity which he shared with his relatives. Herrnhutism appears to have eased the transition to urban life. Thus, M. P. Kierkegaard joined the Herrnhut Congregation almost immediately upon his arrival in Copenhagen (undoubtedly at the instance of his uncle and employer-protector, Niels Andersen Seding). Furthermore, when he joined a regular parish church within Copenhagen he joined the parish of Pastor Saxtorph, the only Herrnhuter and most confirmed pietist among the official clergy in Copenhagen and the next-door neighbor of M. P. Kierkegaard's uncle, N. A. Seding.[17] (This is revealing because, for residents of the capital—and for them alone—parish affiliation was a matter of personal choice and was thus was an important indicator of religious preference.) It is clear that the most powerful single personality in Søren Kierkegaard's life, his father, was profoundly immersed in the emotional and anticlerical lay pietism of Herrnhut, a sect which seems to have served as the vehicle for the urban acculturation of stubborn and vocal forms of peasant religious radicalism.

The disasters which war and bankruptcy visited upon urban, commercial Copenhagen greatly increased the membership of the Congregation of Brothers, especially after the terrible year 1813 (when, incidentally, Søren Kierkegaard was born). By 1816 the old meeting house was no longer sufficient for the Congregation, and it was decided to build a hall which could hold at least 600 members. Michael Pedersen Kierkegaard, now a wealthy businessman who had survived the crash of 1813, was chosen as chairman of the building committee.[18]

In these years after the turn of the century, the Congregation was one of the most powerful independent voices in the city's clerical affairs, and it was the principal stronghold of those who opposed the rational Enlightenment Christianity which predominated in the official State Church. True to its origins, the Copenhagen Congregation was thus a continuing source of a latent anticlericalism, a tendency which must undoubtedly have been bolstered by anti-urban and anticlerical rural attitudes of such peasant families as the Kierkegaards and the Sedings, who were among the leading members of the Copenhagen Congregation of Brothers.

Thus, when the brilliant young "anti-rationalist" preacher (and future Primate of Denmark) J. P. Mynster arrived in Copenhagen in 1812, the official State Church had for some time been faced with a serious threat to its legitimacy. By publicly placing himself on the anti-rationalist "left," Mynster came to enjoy great success with those who wished to oppose the regnant Enlightenment theology without incurring the stigma of being dangerously anticlerical in a climate which was becoming increasingly conformist and politically repressive. Little Søren Kierkegaard and his family thus attended Mynster's services at Copenhagen's principal church, the Church of Our Lady, on Sunday mornings, and then attended lay meetings at the Congregation of Brothers on Sunday evenings.

Later, when the peasant awakenings and the Grundtvigian Christianity of the 1820's, the 1830's, and thereafter began to challenge the official clerical establishment openly, the Herrnhut community appeared rather timid by contrast. In Copenhagen it was Grundtvig's movement particularly which seems to have taken many of the younger and more daring anticlerical people from the Herrnhut constituency. Typical of these was Søren Kierkegaard's elder brother, Peter Christian Kierkegaard, who deserted his father's Congregation of Brothers and became one of Grundtvig's earliest and most influential lieutenants. With many of its more vigorous members siphoned off into more openly defiant forms of religious activity, the membership of the Herrnhut movement dwindled steadily throughout the 1820's and 1830's, and, after 1840, when the national question became a burning issue, Herrnhutism's obviously "German" character ruined its remaining appeal and it disbanded.

D. RATIONALISM AND THE REACTION AGAINST IT

Pietism, being itself a form of subjectivist dependence upon the inner light, found it very hard to resist the intrusions of rational Enlightenment Christianity, which likewise depended not upon traditional dogmatic orthodoxy but upon the personal appropriation of an inner light, the light of Reason.[19] Rationalism, like pietism, placed much emphasis upon practical reforms which made a great difference in the lives of many people: schools, confirmation, and the spread of literacy. In its most general form, Enlightenment Christianity retained a belief in God, in good works, and in immortality and was thus practically indistinguishable from a Christian variant of natural religion in which there was no ultimate truth which was not accessible to Reason. The Bible was to be demystified, and the prevailing tone was one of optimism and moralism. Feelings of sin, guilt, and human insufficiency were absent, and Jesus Christ was looked up to as a moral exemplar but not as a redeemer. The historical and critical vision of the Enlightenment demonstrated that much traditional Christian doctrine which was not present in the Bible was merely an expression of a particular understanding of Christianity at some particular time in the past and was thus not to be viewed as binding upon the present which, having come further, was entitled to have another vision.

The first great pathbreaker for this position in Denmark was the playwright and essayist Ludvig Holberg (1684–1754), who favored a tolerant, moralistic Christianity and suggested that we ought to follow Reason as far as it leads us and accept mysteries which go beyond what we can know with our Reason. There can be no conflict between Reason and revelation, such a moderate rationalist position held, and were our Reason better we could see that it co-incides with the whole of Christianity. In any event, Holberg argued, honest searching is more pleasing to God than the blind orthodoxy which leaves us open to the attacks of freethinkers who claim that our faith cannot withstand examination.

In his brief but eventful ministry, J. F. Struensee (minister of state, 1770–72) gave the impetus to a much more radical sort of rationalism within the Church. Chief among the rational clerics who emerged in the last quarter of the century was Royal Confessor Christian Bastholm, who concluded that not merely traditional Christian dogmas but the Bible itself was "time-determined" and could be stripped of Hebraic and Oriental "symbolic expressions" to leave behind a religion of utility which would make people both good and happy. The doctrines of sin and grace were de-emphasized, and great stress was laid not upon Jesus' person, i.e., the Incarnation, but upon the content of Jesus' doctrines, that is, their moral worth. Such a moralistic and utilitarian Christianity was the only way in which the Church could be "saved" in Bastholm's view, and the existence of the clergy could thus be justified in an enlightened age by using them as an office for practical popular enlightenment. The urban pastors would continue to be trained in theology, but the vast majority, the rural pastors, would be trained in modern agriculture, economics, and medicine, in Bastholm's scheme, which coincided quite nicely with the long-range plans of the reformers who took control of the government in 1784 and enacted the peasant reforms.[20] In general, the 1784–1800 era of liberal reforms during the regency of Frederick VI was a period of the retreat of traditional Christian dogma in the face of the Enlightenment, and the leading Copenhagen intel-lectuals, such as the poets P. A. Heiberg and Jens Baggesen, tended to be freethinking and anticlerical.

When the repressive press law of 1799 brought a sudden end to this climate, one of its most notable features was the fact that it provided special sanctions against attacks on the Church or on clerical officials and that it also proscribed assaults upon the existence of God or the immortality of the soul. Not only did Christianity feel that it was under attack by freethinking Enlightenment radicals, but the fact that it had to pin its defense on the inviolability of the doctrines of the existence of God and the immortality of the soul is ironic testimony about the degree to which even the defenders of the faith had come to see the protection of a bare-bones moralistic deism as their first concern. Even the staunch defenders of traditional Christianity were not themselves immune to the enlightenment of the age and often gave a good deal of ground in order to defend what they saw as most valuable. Thus, the typical moderate theological position of the age was "neology," which held that the older, su-pernaturalist Enlightenment theology—such as Holberg's, which had insisted upon the harmony of Reason and revelation and upon the insufficiency of unaided Reason to reach the truth—had best be abandoned in order to move to a position which stressed Jesus' "mentality" rather than his redemptive acts.

An indication of the degree to which the times demanded rationality of Christianity can be seen in the case of Bishop N. E. Balle, Primate of the Danish State Church from 1783–1808. Balle was considered to be a stony conservative who adopted the most traditionalist position tenable in his campaign against the more radical rationalists such as Bastholm. Yet Balle's position itself was not really very traditional at all, but was a moderate or conservative supranaturalism which fifty years earlier had been quite innovative. However, regardless of whether his position was genuinely traditionalist or in fact semi-rationalistic, Balle's position was perceived by thousands of parishioners—who were bewildered by the cold, new intellectual religion of rational morality—as a heartening defense of old-time religion. Balle's vastly popular anti-Bastholm newsletter, *The Bible Defends Itself!*, had 3,000 subscribers in the 1790's.[21] Similarly, enlightened and progressive circles failed to find anything modern in Balle's supranaturalism, and his journal was seen as a vulgar laughingstock in many educated homes.

However watered down his allegiance to traditional Lutheran theology might have been, Bishop Balle demonstrated in 1805 that he could not only oppose the more extreme forms of Enlightenment rationalism which denied the necessity of revelation, but also the more modern forms of romantic anti-rationalism, which threatened to dissolve Christianity into an emotional pantheism and to portray Jesus' life as a "painting of the various changes of nature."[22] As we shall see later in the present work, Balle directed a frontal assault at Adam Oehlenschläger, Denmark's most gifted young poet and the real founder of its Golden Age in literature. The brilliantly successful Oehlenschläger had just written the daring and apparently pantheistic poem, "The Life of Jesus Christ Repeated in the Annual Cycle of Nature," and Bishop Balle issued a thundering rejection, in the name of traditional Christianity, of Oehlenschläger's romanticism. (We will later examine this incident in some detail, because it is a matter of extreme interest to see how the intervention of Oehlenschläger's young friend, the theologian J. P. Mynster, helped drape the cloak of Christian respectability upon Oehlenschläger's vague pantheism and thus make it possible to retain the poetry of the romantic Golden Age as a pillar of "Christian culture.")

Balle's successor as Bishop of Zealand and Primate of the Danish State Church was Frederik Münter (Bishop, 1808–30), a quiet and learned man, no enemy of rationalism, who began as a moderate neologist and moved closer to a liberal supranaturalist position. He was a middle-of-the-roader in theological questions, and at the Reformation Jubilee in 1817 he was able to assert, on the one hand, that although Christianity went beyond Reason, it did not contradict it. On the other hand, the only sure guide for the exegesis of the Bible was to be found in Reason. The moderate rationalist Münter opposed controversy, even when in the supposed defense of sacred truths, and favored clerical order, being unimpressed by the neo-pietism and the peasant awakenings which erupted in the last years of his life. It is in these areas of moderation, stability, and the resistance to untoward challenges to authority, rather than in the area of theology *per se*—which, ironically, turns out to be a matter of comparative indifference—that the continuity is to be sought between the "rationalist" Münter and his son-in-law J. P. Mynster. Mynster started his career as the warm foe of the "rationalist" Establishment, but ended it by marrying the Bishop's daughter and becoming Primate of the Church from 1834 to 1854. (Mynster's career and his place in the Christian cultural synthesis of the Golden Age will be dealt with in chapter 10.)

Meanwhile, the "rationalist" foe who had survived the collapse of liberal Copenhagen and who remained active into the 1820's and 1830's only to become the target of the troublesome Grundtvig and his followers, was a very different sort of creature than the shallow, optimistic Bastholm. The rationalist theology of the early decades of the nineteenth century was represented most nobly in the person of H. G. Clausen (1759–1840), who served first as curate, then as archdeacon of the Church of Our Lady in Copenhagen. With Clausen and the theologians who supported his position, Kant's influence made itself very evident in restraining the optimistic frivolity of earlier "rationalism." Clausen's "rationalism" rejected the shallow eudaimonistic talk of happiness and replaced it with sterner and more serious talk of duty. H. G. Clausen was a fearless and tough moralist who saw revelation in Christ as providing a truth which was also accessible to Reason, but he did not see in this fact any cause to indulge in light-hearted fantasies about overcoming the refractoriness of human nature and replacing it with a religion of happy utility. H. G. Clausen's example should serve to remind the reader that the "rationalist" enemy later attacked so mercilessly by Grundtvig and the peasant awakening movement was at least in part something of a straw man, and that behind these ostensible theological grievances there lay a deeper complaint, which was anticlerical and generally social and political in nature. H. G. Clausen also deserves note because he was the father and theological predecessor of the great theologian and liberal politician, H. N. Clausen, who was brutally libelled by Grundtvig in the 1820's but went on to become his *de facto* ally in the nationalist and peasant movements of the 1840's. (H. N. Clausen will be dealt with in chapter 14 as an archetypical representative of the urban liberalism which formed one of the counter-poles to the prevailing conservatism of the Golden Age.)

Whatever the richness of H. G. Clausen's Kantian rationalism of the 1810's and 1820's may have been, the calm and dryness of the prevailing Enlightenment religion of the late eighteenth and early nineteenth centuries was ended in the first decade of the nineteenth century by the separate and shattering conversions of Grundtvig and Mynster, who were soon to become the new century's leading exponents of two very different sorts of "anti-rational" or "traditional" Christianity. As we shall see, when the "anti-rational" reaction against Enlightenment religion came to Denmark in the nineteenth century, it divided itself, in its appeal and in its success, generally along class lines: The urbane and aristocratic Mynster found his reception in the upper bourgeoisie, and the nationalistic and populistic Grundtvig found his following in the new class of self-owner farmer peasants. The wretched cottagers were at first abandoned to the depredations of Baptists and Mormons and were only subsequently gathered up in the nets of the fundamentalist Inner Mission. These are the great social groupings and religious tendencies that came to shape the politics and religion of Golden Age Denmark, with its peasant "awakenings"; its notions of high and of national, or popular, "culture"; and its understanding of the meaning of Christianity and of its place in the life of the state. As we shall see, it was in response to these social and religious forces that Kierkegaard came to his own understanding of the relation between religion and politics.

3. The Peasant Awakenings of the 1820's and After

O

The leading historian of the "awakening movement" [Vækkelsesbevæg-else] rightly remarks that "awakening is a break with the old life, not only in a religious sense, but to the highest degree precisely in a *social* and *economic* sense, and thereby also in a *political* sense as well."[1]

Before the peasant reforms of the late eighteenth century, approximately three-quarters of the population were peasants who had lived in small, closely knit communities since the Viking age and who had been very dependent upon large estate owners since the sixteenth century. The "new" peasant of the post-reform era exchanged his visible dependence upon local forms of patriarchal authority for the invisible linkage to the diffuse and relatively anonymous credit and market forces of capitalist society. More and more, the peasant came to be liberated from the continual necessity to show deference to the time-honored local authority figures who had symbolized his status in the pre-reform era. The peasant who owned his own land, made his own agricultural decisions, and dealt daily with the impersonal forces of the cash economy came to feel a new measure of self-respect and a desire for personal "authority." This desire was quickly transformed, first, into defiance of the religious, social, and cultural authority of the local pastor, and later, into more overtly political forms of activity.

The local pastor functioned as the representative not only of heavenly but also of earthly authority. The parish pastor was usually the only local and visible representative of the Crown, and in addition to his ordinary pastoral and liturgical duties, he was also responsible for: collecting taxes; taking the census; helping to administer military levies; keeping the parish register of births, deaths, marriages, and confirmations; supervising and inspecting the local schools; encouraging agricultural innovation; supervising the poor relief system in the parish (a position in which the pastor could exercise great dis-cretionary power); and, after 1841, serving as chairman of the Local Councils under legislation which extended limited self-government to rural districts. In addition to all this, the parish pastor was also often the largest independent farmer in the parish. Unless a great estate owner happened to live in the district, the social ranking at all local functions invariably began with the parish pastor and proceeded downward to the schoolteachers, the independent farmers, the artisans, and the cottagers.[2] The local pastor was thus the most visible and often the most resented social superior of the peasant, particularly in the decades following the peasant reforms, when the peasantry came to feel that its period of tutelage was past and that its age of majority was at hand.

The rural "awakening" movement was a widespread religious revival which found expression in "divine assemblies" [gudelige Forsamlinger] which were led by young laymen, usually artisans and small-scale, independent farmers. In part because of the lay quality of their leadership, and in part because of the other social and economic circumstances in which they were embedded, these independent religious assemblies were bound to take on the social coloration of tacit or open defiance of the traditional sources of social and cultural as well as religious authority. As has been mentioned, the religious assemblies came into particular conflict with the local pastors, who symbolized the subservience of the peasant to the patrician, of countryside to city.

The awakenings of the early nineteenth century were the religious expression of the new individualism and self-assertiveness of the peasantry after the break-up of the ancient nucleated villages and the age-old traditions of collective agricultural decision making. The end of the traditional hierarchical and collective society meant not only new economic and social independence but also a new sense of loneliness and a desire to preserve part of the old communal identity, a desire which found expression in the establishment of lay religious societies where the recently scattered rural neighbors could come together in social and religious fellowship. Now that the nucleated village was dispersed, religion became the linchpin of rural life. Religion became more important than ever, but now it was increasingly not so much the parish pastor and his church around which rural religious life revolved but rather the lay meeting of the newly liberated, literate, and dispersed peasants, meetings which were thus "awakenings" in many senses of the term. The peculiarly dogged and vociferous quality of the awakening movement becomes understandable when one remembers that peasant liberation quickly came to mean both self-confidence and loneliness, and the social and religious character of the lay meetings served to assert the former and assuage the latter of these feelings.

Thus the awakenings embodied an apparent contradiction: viewed socially, they were community events, an attempt to re-establish collectivity and to banish the aloneness which accompanied the economic individualism of the peasant reforms; from the point of view of religious content, however, the awakenings preached a highly individualistic "personality religion," suitable to the independence and self-assertiveness which the reforms had likewise bequeathed the peasantry. Embodied as it was within this new sense of class consciousness, it was particularly this latter characteristic, this radically individualistic pietism, which confronted the local pastors with their greatest religious and social challenge. If the right to read and think for oneself in religious matters—if, indeed, religion itself—became a person's most important possession, then it was unavoidable that peasants would begin to become offended that they could not choose their own spiritual counselors, and it became less and less possible for the parish priest to combine spiritual counselor and civil servant in one person.

With the exception of Herrnhutism, the pietism of the eighteenth century had been an urban phenomenon; its individualism and its emphasis upon personality religion had rendered it unsuitable to the collective forms of rural life. But the new pietism of the nineteenth century was a rural phenomenon precisely because its individualism now answered to the changed needs of the post-reform countryside. Furthermore, the pietistic awakenings of the nineteenth century took hold of the peasantry precisely because this was not a top-down movement as eighteenth-century pietism had been. On the contrary, this was a grassroots movement and thus contained the added attraction of social protest, of class assertiveness, which had been lacking in the court pietism of the previous century.

The pietist revivals of the early nineteenth century were paralleled by similar awakenings, not only in Scandinavia and Germany, but also in England, and the Danish Bible Society (founded 1814) and the Danish Mission Society (founded 1821), for example, were both daughters of their English counterparts. All these movements shared a common evangelistic accent on conversion, sanctification (as opposed to justification), and Bible-reading—activities well-suited to lay implementation—and this placed adherents in an implicit adversary relationship to the official structures of the State Church. The pietistic awakenings of the early nineteenth century seem to have had no historical connection with the long-gone pietism of the early eighteenth century, with the exception of Herrnhutism, which had spread along routes almost identical to those followed by some of the leading revivalists of the later period.[3]

The beginnings of the nineteenth-century religious revolt can be found in the unruly "strong Jutlanders" [stærke Jyder] of the 1790's, when several rural parishes banded together in defiance of the law and refused to use the new officially mandated hymnals and doctrinal books, persisting instead in using older books which, the peasants claimed, contained the unsullied old-fashioned religion. The stubbornness of the Jutlanders seems to have been compounded from equal parts of peasant conservatism and the desire to defy clerical authority and "cultured," aristocratic norms.

The early nineteenth-century awakenings can be traced quite directly to the period of economic and agricultural depression from around 1818 to about 1828, which was the most difficult time for the newly liberated peasants, who made religious protest their primary mode of expression. The birthplace of these lay meetings or conventicles appears to have been the island of Funen, where one Kristen Madsen began evangelizing in 1819. His work was extremely popular among the peasantry, and disciples soon carried his lay religiosity to Jutland and Zealand. Madsen's work was quickly perceived as a threat by the local ecclesiastical authorities, and he was arrested in 1822 for unauthorized preaching of the Gospel. The general reaction of the clergy was not one of theological disapproval but of "class horror."[4]

On Zealand the awakeners came to be championed by a small group of young clerics who were radically populist and self-styled "orthodox" enemies of "rationalism" and followers of N. F. S. Grundtvig, the spectacular religious, cultural, and political awakener of the later 1820's and thereafter. By means of its supportive activities with the awakened peasants of Zealand, this group of young Grundtvigians—which included the brilliant theologian and organizer Jacob Christian Lindberg as well as Peter Christian Kierkegaard, Søren's older brother—came to form a sort of bridge between much of the early religious awakening movement and Grundtvig's later, broader movement, a movement which was regarded by many suspicious clerics as a sort of fifth column or as a church within the Church.

In the later 1820's and thereafter, the leading ecclesiastical opponent of the peasant awakenings was J. P. Mynster, who became Primate of Denmark in 1834. Mynster liked neither the peasants nor the predominantly Enlightenment-inspired "rationalist" pastors for whom the peasant awakeners reserved their sharpest attacks, but he supported the pastors for the sake of order. By 1836 Mynster was referring snidely to the portion of Zealand dominated by the Grundtvigians and the peasant awakeners as "the holy land," and he worked with the government to try to enforce a ban against the traveling lay preachers, whose work promised social as well as religious mischief. At a major national convocation in 1840 Mynster called upon God in prayer—in Latin, presumably to keep the message from reaching the common man—to "save us from these uproarious people, enflamed with false zeal."[5] Throughout the 1820's and 1830's Mynster and those of his opinion succeeded in committing the government to a policy of official repression, arrests, trials, fines, and imprisonment, but all these measures were unavailing, and the lay awakenings continued to spread in countless rural parishes. After the accession of Christian VIII in 1839, a more moderate policy was pursued, and unofficial religious toleration was extended to all but the Baptists, who, appealing as they did to the poorest of cottagers and artisans, were still beyond the pale of respectability and were thus fair game to the social sensibilities of Mynster, who embarked upon an (ill-fated) campaign of enforced infant baptism of Baptist children.

As will be shown in chapters 10 and 13 of the present work, Mynster and the official Church stood in an ambivalent relationship to Grundtvig and the majority wing of the peasant awakenings which his movement came eventually to represent. Mynster loathed the theatrical Grundtvig and his unruly followers, but he feared even more an open breach and a wholesale exodus from the

State Church, which might have led to the political collapse of established religion. Grundtvig, for his part, could use the peasant movement as a goad with which to compel the State Church to grant his wishes only so long as he hinted at the possibility of such an exodus, but he would of course lose all further bargaining strength if the breach ever took place.

By about 1840 the peasant awakening movement had split along what were essentially class lines. Those who could still be coaxed into remaining within the official framework of the State Church formed the majority Grundtvigian party of "Church-believers," drawing their support principally from the newly independent farmers. Those who remained obstinately anti-ecclesiastical and fundamentalist were the "Bible-believers," a smaller group which found its support primarily among the poorer cottagers. The Bible-believers continued to exist throughout the 1840's and thereafter as fragmented and rather apolitical groups, and they were the primary recruiting grounds for the Baptists, Mormons, and, later, the Inner Mission. The more well-organized and better-off Church-believers, on the other hand, became increasingly involved in broader social and political issues, with such religious revivalists as Rasmus Sørensen and the poor shoemaker J. A. Hansen becoming the first rural political leaders. Popular political and cultural awakening thus followed in the path of the religious revival which had contained the seeds of social protest from the very beginning. The historian Lindhardt stresses that the divine assemblies were the cradle of rural political awakening and democracy for the vast bulk of the people.[6] It was in these open lay meetings that the peasants learned to formulate in words their thoughts, their social resentments, and their religious ideas. These religious gatherings were Denmark's first popular assemblies, and it was here that the common man learned not to be embarrassed and overawed by the local notables.

4. The Rise of Liberalism in the 1830's

O

Under the terms of the Congress of Vienna of 1815, Holstein had been included in the German Confederation, and Frederick VI had been obligated to provide some sort of representative assembly for the duchy, a promise with which he was very loath to comply. During the 1820's, Frederick's delay in complying made the Holstein nobility angry and restive, and after the July Revolution of 1830 Metternich himself expressed his impatience and nervousness about Frederick's fifteen years of delay. After 1830 Frederick was thus finally compelled to fulfill his treaty obligations of 1815.

For political reasons it was seen as best to set up not merely one set of estates for Holstein, but four separate advisory assemblies, which together would cover the entire Danish-German state. In this way Holstein's special privileges would not create friction and jealousy, and it would also be possible in this way to provide separate estates for Slesvig and Holstein and thus, it was hoped, prevent the emergence of a pan-German "Slesvig-Holsteinism." Four parallel provincial Advisory Assemblies of Estates were thus established in four provincial towns: Itzehoe, for Holstein; the town of Slesvig, for Slesvig; Viborg, for Jutland; and Roskilde, for the islands. The two major cities of Kiel and Copenhagen were carefully avoided, in order to insulate the assemblies from popular pressure and render them royal instruments to the greatest extent possible.

Even more than the fragmentation of the monarchy into four assemblies and the placement of these assemblies in minor provincial towns, the manner in which the franchise was extended was designed to render the assemblies compliant and make them dependent upon the royal will. Thus Frederick expressed his distrust both of the urban middle and upper-middle classes and of the owners of the great estates, and weighted representation in favor of landed peasants of middling or more property, a social group which still felt itself indebted to Frederick because of the reforms of the 1780's and 1790's. Only landed subjects could vote or serve in the estates, but both independent farmers (if they possessed four Tønder Hartkorn of land) and copyholders (if they possessed five Tønder Hartkorn) were included in this group, and this effectively diluted the power of the owners of the great estates. Wealthy urban subjects were deprived of the franchise, however, if they did not possess sufficiently large amounts of taxable real property.

The most important of the assemblies was the Roskilde Estates, and the franchise rules and the composition of that body were typical. The Estates consisted of seventy members, including ten royally appointed members (two clergy, one university professor, four great landlords, two Icelanders, and one Faeroese); seventeen members elected by the 129 lords of major manors [Sædegårde]; twelve members elected by the city of Copenhagen (but this included only those with real property worth over 4,000 rigsdaler, which was 1692 electors, or 1½ percent of the city's population); eleven members chosen by the provincial towns, where the property qualification was only 1,000 rigsdaler; and twenty members chosen by the peasants, i.e., independent farmers and copyholders possessing, respectively, a minimum of four and five Tønder Hartkorn of land. This latter group included approximately 15,000 peasant families in the islands (or about 26,000 in the entire monarchy). In all, about 2½ percent of the population had some form of franchise, which was about equal to the franchise in Norway, Belgium, and England of the period, and much broader than that of the July Monarchy in France, where only one of 150 was enfranchised.[1] In order to be eligible for election to the Estates, the property qualifications were roughly double.

Thus, unlike Prussia, the great landlords were not given an overwhelming voice, and neither was the intangible property of the Copenhagen bourgeoisie given a major voice. Rather, it was the royal appointees, the provincial towns, and the better-off peasants who controlled well over half the seats. Both the extreme conservative and the liberal sentiments of the day had reason to feel offended, for the great landholders and the great towns were snubbed, and the advantage was given to middling property, to royal prerogative, and to cultured bureaucracy. Rentiers were often excluded from official participation in public life while prosperous peasants were not. It was thus expected that the creation of the Estates would actually enable the Crown to control and perhaps even to retard the development of public political life.

As was expressly noted in their official title, the four provincial Assemblies of Estates were *advisory* assemblies, empowered only to offer suggestions, and even then only in matters touching upon the personal and property rights, taxation, and the public duties of the king's subjects. The budget was not to be presented to these assemblies, and in any event their advice could be overlooked or ignored by the King and his council of state, and it often was. Finally, the Estates were not even to have much formative power over public opinion, for their deliberations were to be private, and they were deprived of the right to publish a *journal des débats*.

Even with so rigidly circumscribed a system of consulting the opinions of subjects, Frederick seems not to have been inclined to move precipitately, for the first draft law appeared in May 1831, while the system was not finally established until the law of May 15, 1834. Elections were held in the autumn of 1834, and the first Estates did not meet until September 1835, twenty years after the promise had been made at the Congress of Vienna.

B. THE ESTATES AND LIBERAL POLITICS IN THE 1830'S

Despite Frederick's wishes and careful plans, the tone set at the Roskilde Estates was quite liberal, and Copenhagen made its importance felt far beyond its numerical representation. The peasants tended to vote for their betters, though perhaps not as often as their betters might have wished; about one-half of the peasant representatives were themselves peasants,[2] but these men tended to be very reserved and exercised little influence on the tone or the outcome of the proceedings.

The promulgation of the 1834 law establishing the Estates set off a flurry of liberal political activity in Copenhagen. C. N. David, a moderate liberal and a university professor of political economy, founded the first liberal newspaper, The Fatherland [Fædrelandet], in September 1834. H. N. Clausen, the liberal theologian and coming political figure, and A. F. Tscherning, a left-liberal aristocrat, cooperated with more prosaic mercantile liberals to form an electoral organization which influenced public opinion far beyond the narrow Copenhagen electorate. (Tscherning later became Minister of War in the 1848 cabinet and eventually broke with the liberals to become a radical democratic leader of the peasant-based Left Party.)

When the Roskilde Estates finally convened, the moderate enlightened cabinet minister, A. S. Ørsted, served as the official spokesman for the King, while J. F. Schouw, a liberal and the official representative of the university, was quickly voted President of the Assembly, and L. N. Hvidt, a liberal Copenhagen businessman, was voted Vice President. The Roskilde Estates immediately came under the domination of three or four major landlords on Zealand and the Copenhagen liberals. Much to the dismay of Frederick, the peasants and the provincial towns were not capable of making effective exercise of the power they had been granted.

From their establishment in 1835 until the death of Frederick in 1839, the Estates pursued a rather moderate liberal policy of politely insisting upon frugality and more business-like methods in the royal management of the state. After a great deal of pressure, the Crown finally released a condensed form of the state budget for inspection by the Estates. It revealed that expenditures exceeded income by 6 percent, and worse, that over 40 percent of the state budget went for debt service and over 10 percent to cover the personal expenses of the royal court. These latter items, plus the apparent incompleteness of the budget and the apparently continuing imbalance between revenue and expenditures, awakened much discomfiture and criticism among the Copenhagen businessmen who set the tone for much of the debate, so the Estates petitioned the King to exercise fiscal restraint in his court expenses. Such was the limit of liberal politics in the Estates in the 1830's.

Even these timid attempts at criticism incensed the aging Frederick, however, and from the birth of liberal public life in 1834 to his death in 1839, Frederick was increasingly angered about what he considered to be the abuse of the press, even under his strict laws of 1799. It was inevitable that the rising tide of critical journalism, by means of which the liberal Copenhagen bourgeoisie was learning to express and define itself, would eventually come into conflict with royal authority and produce a major issue, a struggle around which the new liberal movement would coalesce. Frederick's irascibility quickly provided such an issue. In December 1834, C. N. David, the moderate liberal professor of economics who was editor of the fledgling newspaper *The Fatherland*, printed an unsigned article which urged the new Estates to make increasing use of the right to petition so as to pave the way for eventual popular government. Other articles which enraged Frederick called for the separation of governmental powers in order to check purported abuses. Frederick called for the suspension of David from his university post and for his prosecution for violation of the press laws, and he called further for an investigation to see if a genuinely reactionary press law—such as that in the German Confederation, which denied the possibility of judicial appeal—ought to be enacted in Denmark.[3] It was this latter proposal in particular which outraged not only A. S. Ørsted, Frederick's most moderate and intelligent advisor, but also the entire liberal intellectual community of Copenhagen, including Professors Schouw and Clausen, who in February 1835 brought a polite petition to Frederick, signed by nearly 600 of the nation's most eminent citizens, requesting that he desist from enacting the proposed new press law.

Frederick's reply to this petition for moderation was a famous imperious proclamation which began "We alone know" [Vi alene vide], a rejection so haughty and resounding and so infuriating to the liberal Copenhagen bourgeoisie that it sparked an immediate response in the founding of the first liberal movement to gain a broad following, "The Society for the Correct Use of the Freedom of the Press," founded in March 1835 by Clausen, Schouw, and a number of others. The "Free Press Society" [Trykkefrihedsselskabet], as it was popularly known, quickly gained over 2,000 members in Copenhagen. It soon established 30–40 chapters throughout the country and began to publish its own newspaper, the *Danish People's Paper* [Dansk Folkeblad].[4] Within two years the society had 5,000 members and sponsored political gatherings in Copenhagen that were attended by hundreds.[5] This was the real beginning of a liberal party, the core of which was composed of the upper-middle classes, much of the university student body, and others with academic training. There were close ties between the liberal academics and businessmen who supported the Free Press Society and the similar constituency which dominated the Roskilde Estates. Professor Schouw, for example, was both the chairman of the society and the first President of the Roskilde Estates, while Professor Clausen, who was also a co-founder of the society, was elected to the Estates in 1840 (when he had acquired sufficient real property) and was subsequently elected President of the Estates three times. The Free Press Society thus served as the first important liberal organization in Denmark and gave much oratorical, journalistic, and parliamentary exercise to budding liberal spokesmen. After the establishment of the Estates themselves, the rise of liberal journalism and the subsequent defense of press freedom was the most important political event of the 1830's.

C. LIBERALS AND CONSERVATIVES

The older generation of liberals who dominated Danish political life in the 1830's were by no means men of radical opinions. The great moderate political economist and journalist, C. N. David, who had been the *cause célèbre* of the Free Press Society, insisted, with a candor that angered the poorer peasants, that it would be deceitful to permit the rural lower classes to believe that the conditions of their lives could be bettered in this world. H. N. Clausen, another great liberal, was opposed on principle to allowing cottagers to have any voice in public affairs, while the liberal paper manufacturer J. C. Drewsen summed up the liberal position deftly in his slogan: *"Culture* [Dannelse], that is the rank and nobility of our age."[6] The typical liberal leadership of the 1830's was composed of middle-aged businessmen and academics such as Schouw, Clausen, Hvidt, and Drewsen. All of them favored a constitution with a broader franchise that would guarantee the sovereignty of representative institutions, but they saw this as a distant goal, not as a possibility in the near future.

The younger generation of liberals, typically university students, was led by the fiery Orla Lehmann (born 1810), and was considerably more outspoken. As early as 1832, i.e., before the free press fight, the young Lehmann had written that the middle classes had inherited the virtues of the previous ruling classes and that it was time for them to rule.[7] The unsigned article in *The Fatherland* that had gotten David in trouble with the government had in fact been written by Lehmann, who made himself prominent as early as 1835 and whose entire career (until 1848–49) consisted of goading the liberals into adopting increasingly more daring positions by pushing them further than they usually intended to go. As early as 1836 Lehmann urged the liberals to come to the aid of the Danish nationality in southern Jutland. This was the beginning of the powerful and fateful ideological combination of "National Liberalism," which became frozen into official liberal doctrine after another famous Lehmann speech, the so-called Skydebane address of 1842. In an address in 1845 Lehmann placed the seal of liberal legitimacy upon the *schwärmerisch* student "Scandinavianism" movement and helped commit the urban middle class to a policy of romantic and bellicose nationalism which eventually led to two civil wars and national disaster. In 1839 Lehmann was responsible for prompting the influential University Student Union to request a representative constitution from the new monarch, Christian VIII, which was again a step more brash than many other liberals dared to take. Lehmann's leadership provided Danish liberalism with dazzling pyrotechnics which served for a time to conceal some of the confusion and inconsistency which lay at the heart of the movement.

In the face of the liberal threat, a consciously conservative tendency also coalesced in the 1830's and 1840's. This group drew its principal strength from the owners of the great estates, the older and more powerful bureaucrats, the clergy, and most of the literary and poetic establishment of the Golden Age. The leaders of conservative opinion thus included in their front ranks such tastemakers as Bishop Mynster, who was for a long time Søren Kierkegaard's exemplar in religious matters, and the poet Johan Ludvig Heiberg, who was also for a time Kierkegaard's model of literary taste and elegance. The official literary and religious establishment was overwhelmingly on the side of the absolutist government, of hierarchy, public order, and good taste, and in this it reflected the views of much of the older and upper reaches of the urban elite, particularly those who were connected to the upper levels of the bureaucracy or who were not engaged in commerce.

Thus, it is not at all surprising that a budding young aesthete such as Søren Kierkegaard, who read Mynster for edification and was a fringe member of the Heiberg literary salon, should have made his first entry into public life in 1835 as a witty and incisive public opponent of Orla Lehmann's influence in student politics. Young Kierkegaard made his public debut in an address to the University Student Union in November 1835, in which he took issue with the speaker at the previous meeting, Orla Lehmann, who had given middle-class liberals credit for the rebirth of public life in Denmark.[8] Here, as later, Kierkegaard did not attack the liberals' position *per se* but rather their lack of genuine leadership and originality and their merely "aesthetic" posture. Over the next several months, this address was followed by a journalistic duel with Lehmann—Kierkegaard's first skirmish—in which he proved his wit and clearly won the day against his illustrious opponent.[9] Here, too, Kierkegaard never directly took issue with the substantive position of liberalism, but succeeded in exposing the Danish movement and mocking it for its lack of character.

It would be misleading to overdraw the differences between the liberals and the conservatives. Both groups alike drew most of their support from the wealthy and educated urban classes, a very closed and detached social world which was only tenuously connected with the broader changes taking place outside of it, particularly in the countryside. In the same *haute bourgeois* family, the older generation could easily be conservative, while the younger would be liberal. Orla Lehmann, for example, was considered a disappointment and a defector by his older protector and family friend, the scientist and Golden Age intellectual Hans Christian Ørsted. The educated public from which conservatives and liberals alike drew their adherents was small in size and narrow in social and geographical range. Both political groups were in fact opposed elites with no genuine mass following outside the capital and a few provincial towns. As mentioned, the split between liberal and conservative was often merely a split between the generations within this narrow elite, with certain occupational categories (e.g., commerce) leaning generally in a cautiously liberal direction, while certain others (e.g., the upper bureaucracy, artists, and writers) leaned in a conservative direction. Interestingly, two of the most important and most radical of the later liberals, Lehmann and the Scandinavianist Carl Ploug—both of whom were influential in making the "revolution" of 1848, in rendering inevitable the civil war over the national question, and in drafting the 1849 Constitution—tended to have the most tenuous social roots of all, living as perpetual students and charismatic journalists.

A look at the social make-up of this elite class and its relative share in the total population is quite revealing. The bearers of government and of public opinion were the bureaucrats who had key posts in the central administration, plus approximately twenty county administrators [Amtsmænd] and perhaps 200 judges, mayors, and city and county sheriffs [Byfogeder and Herredsfogeder]. The 1,300–1,400 priests of the Danish State Church constituted the largest class of public officials, and there were approximately 200 professors, teachers at various institutions of higher learning, librarians, and people affiliated with museums. There were approximately 500 physicians, of whom 100 served in an official capacity. Below them came around 100 pharmacists, and below them came the veterinarians, royal foresters, and army officers. This was the entire class of civil servants [Embedsmænd], about 3,000–4,000 men. In addition to this, the educated class could claim a fair number of academically educated men who lived in the free professions: private teachers and tutors, authors, journalists, artists, lawyers, engineers, etc.—about 2,000 in all.[10] These approximately 6,000 academically educated families were only the upper 25 percent of a large group of families with "non-material" professions—e.g., school teachers, policemen, non-commissioned officers, etc.—who looked to the academically educated for social and political leadership. Membership in the elite leadership of this group was limited to those who had completed an academic education. The University of Copenhagen was the only university in Denmark proper—there was also one in Kiel—and in the 1840's only around 150 students matriculated each year, and a considerably smaller number actually received their degrees. Furthermore, 60 percent of those who became students came from this same group of academically educated families, and the wealthy bourgeoisie supplied another 24 percent of the university student body, while the 75 percent of the population who tilled the soil supplied only .6 percent of the student population.[11] (Is it any wonder that the peasant nourished ill will toward urban culture?)

A social historian who has concerned himself with the period has concluded that "in the general consciousness, the approximately 6,000 families with an academic education were the real bearers of the period's intellectual life and its political stirrings, as well as of its new national movement".[12] As we shall see, in addition to being the principal recruiting grounds for both liberalism and conservatism, this numerically small and socially narrow elite group—or rather the upper crust of this group—also constituted nearly the entire audience for the remarkable body of intellectual and artistic creativity known as the Golden Age.

5. The Peasant Movement to the Late 1840's

O

A. CONDITIONS AND MATERIAL PROGRESS OF THE PEASANTRY

The period of the agricultural depression from 1818–28 saw no progress in the movement toward self-ownership among copyholder peasants, whereas the period from 1828 onward saw, first, gradual progress and then great strides in the 1830's. By 1835, 56 percent of all arable land, or 42,000 family farms, were in self-ownership, and by 1850 approximately two-thirds of the nation's agricultural land had passed into self-ownership.[1] Although grain prices after 1818 sank to one-third or one-fourth of their earlier high and were lower in the 1820–24 period than they had been in 1733, the situation eased greatly after England began to relax its tariffs in 1828, and by 1850 grain prices were double the low of 1824.[2] In addition to this steady improvement in prices after 1828 must be reckoned the great improvement in Danish grain production, which doubled between the 1830's and 1870's.[3] Taken together, these improvements in prices and productivity meant an improvement in the economic and political position of the self-owner and copyholder peasants as a group, an improvement which is reflected in the fact that agricultural indebtedness in the late 1840's was the lowest on record until that time.[4]

In 1835 there were around 67,000 landed peasant families (as opposed to cottagers), of whom approximately two-thirds were self-owners or guaranteed hereditary tenants with very advantageous terms. The remainder of these landed peasants had more tenuous forms of copyhold.[5] After 1848, the conditions of those landed peasants who were still copyholders improved greatly with respect to labor dues and other terms of copyhold arrangements, and those who remained in this group continued to push, in vain, for a rapid end to the copyhold status of the land—approximately one-third of the total acreage—which was still held in this form. This change took place gradually, with the government providing cash incentives to induce the great landlords to sell. The transition to self-ownership of the remaining copyhold land thus remained a burning issue for a considerable portion of the landed peasantry as late as the 1870's.

Conditions for the landless cottager peasants were quite different, however. Although, as we have seen in chapter 1, the cottager and landed peasant groups were roughly equal in size in 1800, with about 55,000–60,000 families in each group, by 1825–30 there were were about 70,000 cottagers who shared only 7 1/2 percent of the nation's arable land.[6] A rural underclass was growing in both absolute and relative size. It possessed little or no land and had neither rights nor protectors excepting the increasingly duplicitous rhetoric of the more prosperous landed peasants, who shared *sub rosa* with the traditional great landlords a continuing need for cheap cottager labor even while they publicly railed against the system. The year 1848 brought little improvement for the cottagers, for even though the cottagers' labor dues were now technically commuted to cash payments, the liberating effect of this reform was easily vitiated by linking the labor contract so closely to the rental contract that the cottager led the life of an indentured servant. As we have seen in chapter 1, the cottagers also remained extremely vulnerable, as the remaining copyholders were not, to the vicious practice of short-term lease arrangements and to diabolical parish poor laws concerning residency requirements. The cottager class experienced a further numerical increase of approximately fifty percent in the period from 1850 to the 1880's, while at the same time their political allies became fewer as the remaining copyholders gradually purchased their holdings. It was particularly in this latter period that the cottager group experienced a great wave of religious sectarianism and fundamentalism and a large-scale immigration to the New World. As has been mentioned earlier, conditions for the cottagers stabilized and improved only with the coming of the cooperative movement of the 1880's and after, which could make use of improved technology and open up pork and dairy production to the land-poor cottagers.

By 1850 the Danish countryside had witnessed the triumph of impersonal credit and market forces, as opposed to the personal relationships to landlords which had determined rural life for centuries. Governmental influence, the absence of long-term and well-organized speculative intervention in the land market, and the effects of the bankruptcy of 1813, which injured great landlords and potential speculators even more than copyholders, all improved the long-run position of the peasants and hindered either landlords or any other small group of creditors from achieving a new variant of the traditional stranglehold which the estate owners had exercised over the peasants. After 1813, the estate owners were too economically burdened themselves to profit very much from the peasants' difficulties, and they continued to want to sell land in order to help deal with their own cash shortages. Thus, many landlords promoted the formation of peasant credit unions to finance such purchases, in the knowledge that a continuing demand for land was the best way of keeping land prices high. As long as they held mortgages, though, the landlords still exercised much power over the peasants, and it was the growth in the 1830's, 1840's, and thereafter, of peasant-controlled credit unions and savings banks which finally curtailed landlord influence and gave the newly liberated self-owner peasants both economic power and economic and social independence. By the mid-nineteenth century, with respect to the new self-owner peasants, the darling children of the reform era, the great landlord could only make his power felt as the greatest landowner and farmer of the district, and no longer as a patriarch. The peasantry, or rather the more prosperous upper 40-45 percent of the peasantry, had come of age.[7]

B. PEASANT POLITICS

As we have seen in chapter 4, of the approximately 32,000 people enfranchised by the Provincial Estates of the 1830's and 1840's, over 26,000 were landed peasants, of whom about 85 percent actually voted, a much livelier electoral participation than that shown either by townsmen or landlords.[8] The peasants showed great solidarity and tenacity in pushing for their principal demands, but they had poor leadership in the Estates and little skill, as yet, in political oratory. (Given both their conservative royal purpose and their urban, liberal leadership, the Estates were scarcely the forum for peasant demands in any event.)

All the improvements in grain prices, in productivity, and in the progress of self-ownership among the landed peasants meant that, with the arrival of public political life and semi-representative institutions in the 1830's, local peasant politics would spring into being, and thus the peasant movement resumed its visible progress. It was in the mid-1830's that the first issues arose, particularly the questions of improved rural education, freedom from landlord discipline, and the insistence that the obligation for military service, which then fell only upon the sons of peasant families, be universally shared. Soon, the far more radical issues of the enforced transition from copyhold to self-ownership and the abolition of labor dues for cottagers began to be raised.

The principal vehicles for such political demands were usually wandering peasant (and artisan) agitators, many of whom had started as wandering preachers in the lay awakening movement of the 1820's and who continued to serve the peasants in a dual capacity. In the 1830's the peasants and their spokesmen typically remained aloof from the urban liberals and were suspicious of their overtures and their demands for constitutional government. In the countryside there was a stubborn, lingering loyalty to Frederick VI, who had granted the great land reforms fifty years earlier, even though Frederick was by this time a far different and more conservative monarch, indisposed toward any further reforms. This loyalist tendency toward absolutism was also reflected by Grundtvig, the pro-peasant cleric, who remained, socially, a staunch partisan of peasant egalitarianism, but who was, politically, a resolute supporter of the monarchy. He deeply mistrusted the urban liberal movement, one of whose principal leaders was his old theological opponent, the "rationalist" theologian H. N. Clausen.

Many older liberals, such as Clausen, had a very difficult time winning the peasants as allies in the drive toward constitutional, representative government in the late 1830's and 1840's. It was particularly the young firebrand Orla Lehmann who broke the ice in a June 1838 speech to a large peasant audience, where he reminded his listeners that he, too, as a liberal, felt that the peasant reforms were far from completed, and that all copyholders had a right to outright ownership of the land which they cultivated. Proposals to this effect, and proposals abolishing labor dues, were introduced in the Estates by peasant representatives in the late 1830's and early 1840's and were repeatedly rejected. What was significant in Lehmann's activity was that it marked the beginning of liberal support for such far-reaching proposals.

In another major peasant address to a large gathering on the island of Falster in 1841, Lehmann went further in attempting to wed the peasants to constitutionalism, proclaiming that the peasant advances achieved under absolutism would have had to come in any event and that absolutism and arbitrariness were enemies of the peasantry, and only a free constitution could help them. The right of a popularly elected parliament to vote taxes, Lehman continued, would prevent the government from skimming the cream off peasant industriousness. It is a great error, Lehmann insisted, to maintain, as many do, that "sovereign kings have done so much for the peasants and have protected them against the mighty."[9] Such talk bordered on *lèse majesté*, and won Lehman the popular martyrdom of a three-month jail sentence and the undying admiration of the peasantry, which now began to change its attitude toward liberalism.

In the 1840's, preachers of religious-social revival, such as Peder Hansen, Rasmus Sørensen, and J. A. Hansen wandered about Zealand, and their message became increasingly concerned with political themes and peasant reforms. Sørensen and his traveling companion, J. A. Hansen, were co-editors of a new peasant newspaper, *The Common People's Friend* [*Almuevennen*].[10] This endeavor was tied to the liberal movement by Lehmann, who secured J. A. Hansen's economic survival by obtaining for him a position on the staff of the leading liberal newspaper, *The Fatherland*, thus establishing both personal and journalistic ties between the urban and rural movements. J. A. Hansen was the first modern peasant politician, who started, typically, as a rural artisan and then became a preacher of religious awakening in the early 1830's. Soon, rebuffed by absolutist officialdom in his hopes of becoming a country schoolmaster, he became politicized, campaigned against "the aristocracy of royal bureaucrats" [Embedsaristokrati], and subsequently became co-editor of *The Common People's Friend*. Radical agitators who were more or less attached to Hansen's newspaper gave it an almost revolutionary character, and the government eyed it with great unease.

In the mid-1840's Hansen and his *Common People's Friend* set about championing the cause of the peasants in the Holbæk area of northern Zealand, where the great landowners were still unusually powerful and resisted the movement to self-ownership. Hansen and other agitators pushed for radical tax reform and a complete end to copyhold, and to this latter position they also appended pro-Lehmann and anti-absolutist, liberal sentiments. A series of mass meetings were held in the Holbæk area, and peasant feeling ran very high, while landlords were extremely distressed. This movement culminated in a massive meeting in June 1845, when seven to eight thousand peasants turned out to hear Rasmus Sørensen, Peder Hansen, and others. This sort of activity terrified both the local landowners and the uncertain government of Christian VIII, which at this time was increasingly beset with the monumental and apparently insoluble problems of the constitutional and cultural relationship between the kingdom proper and the duchies of Slesvig and Holstein.

The official government response was the "Bondecirkulær" [Peasant Ordinance] of November 1845, which required that all meetings to discuss peasant problems must secure prior police clearance and which forbade attendance at such meetings by any who came from outside the immediate parish. Further, the authorities were instructed to keep a sharp eye on those who traveled about and incited the peasants. This precipitated the final breach between the peasant movement and absolutism and pushed the peasants into the arms of the urban liberals. In *The Common People's Friend*, one peasant writer noted that the government had forgotten that the most trouble-creating peasant "meetings" of all were the enforced work parties in which labor dues were discharged.[11] Within two weeks of the promulgation of the Peasant Ordinance, a deputation of peasants presented Christian VIII a petition signed by 10,000 peasants, but the king refused to receive it, and on November 25, 1845, while they were in the capital, the peasant delegation proceeded to a gala reception and mass meeting prepared for them by a large number of liberals. Christian VIII had alienated the remaining reserves of peasant affection for absolute monarchy, and the liberals were quick to seize the opportunity presented them by this royal blunder.

By May 1846, the new peasant-liberal alliance took formal shape at a mass meeting in the same disputed Holbæk district of northern Zealand, and the "Bondevennernes Selskab" [Society of the Friends of the Peasant] was founded. The society was a mass movement whose program reflected both liberal and peasant demands, calling for the transition to self-ownership of all copyhold farms; the abolition of inequality of rights and duties between encumbered and unencumbered property; universal liability to military service; the establishment of a new commission on the peasant question; freedom of trade in both country and city; the abolition of landlord control over preferment in local parish churches; improved popular education; better conditions for cottagers; and, finally, and perhaps most significantly, a free, representative constitution, a demand which marked a major break with the old rural allegiance to absolute monarchy. The new alliance had been forged. The government now revoked the Peasant Ordinance of 1845, but this token gesture came too late to undo the effects of earlier royal neglect.

It should, however, be noted that it was only after the crown deliberately disappointed and ignored them that the peasants were finally induced to enter into a formal cooperation with the liberals, and even then not so much out of zeal for constitutional government as in the hope of winning full social equality for their class. They continued to distrust the fine, urbane, lady-bountiful type of liberal leader and preferred to choose their leaders from those who stood socially nearer—artisans and farmers. The battle slogan of the peasant movement reflects this populist outlook: "Up with the peasant for liberty, equality, and fraternity! Down with the power of the great lords, the priests, and the bureaucrats!" The priests and the bureaucrats, in any event, came from the same social stratum and represented the same urban culture as did the peasants' liberal allies, and, as we shall see, the cooperation between the rural peasant mass and the urban liberal elite was to be short-lived indeed.

6. The National Question in Southern Jutland

O

A. THE NATIONAL QUESTION AND LIBERALISM

Slesvig and Holstein, the two duchies of southern Jutland, were granted separate sets of Estates in the 1830's in order to underscore the point that their legal and political status set them apart not only from the kingdom of Denmark proper, but, more importantly, from one another as well. Holstein was additionally a member of the German Confederation, but Slesvig was not. What the Crown feared was the emergence of "Slesvig-Holsteinism," in which the German-speaking population of Slesvig, which was slightly less than half the population of that province, would combine political forces with the entirely German-speaking population of Holstein and push for a united, "German," southern Jutland, with strong ties to the rest of Germany. Such a development would contain the possibility, indeed the likelihood, that the combined Danish-German state [the "Helstat"], which was held together by the cosmopolitan institution of conservative absolutism, would dissolve into "German" and "Danish" fragments. Each of these fragments would be held together only by a militant nationalism that had a particular appeal, not for the aristocratic conservatives of the old order, but for younger, more liberal men. The success of German nationalism in Slesvig and Holstein, and the concomitant rise of Danish nationalism, particularly among the liberal middle class of Copenhagen, would destroy the traditional foundation of royal absolutism.

In the course of the 1830's, this fatal movement toward "Slesvig-Holsteinism" was indeed precisely the course chosen by the younger leaders of the German-speaking population of both duchies, who set about agitating for the legal and political union of Slesvig and Holstein and for the inclusion of the united province in the German Confederation. Simultaneously with this German agitation, a parallel movement began to develop among the Danish-speaking population of Slesvig, demanding, at first, better protection for the status of the Danish language in the duchy. (Even though Danish was the majority tongue in Slesvig, it had been relegated to second-class status as a peasant language, while German was the legal language of state and was used in most of the schools and churches.) Soon thereafter, the leaders of Danish-speaking

Slesvig demanded the full legal incorporation of the duchy into the Danish monarchy, into "Denmark proper." By the mid- and late 1830's, the Danish cause, at first only a local dispute in a faraway province, had captured the vocal and influential Copenhagen liberal movement, winning the support, first, of Orla Lehmann, *The Fatherland*, and the Free Press Society, and, a bit later, of the more respectable H. N. Clausen.

By the early 1840's the dispute had escalated into a choice between a clearly articulated Slesvig-Holsteinism on the one side, or the complete and forcible incorporation of Slesvig (including its sizable German population) into the Danish monarchy on the other. The former policy was of course favored by the German-speaking populations of the two duchies, but enjoyed virtually no support elsewhere in Denmark. The latter policy favored the total severance of Holstein from the state and drawing the national border at the Ejder River between Slesvig and Holstein, which was the traditional southern boundary of ancient Denmark. This was the "Ejder policy" [Ejderpolitikken] and was favored by the Danish-speaking population in southern Jutland and by the overwhelming majority of the Copenhagen liberal movement, for whom the Ejder policy became an article of faith which was scarcely separable from the demand for a constitution. The conservative supporters of the traditional, absolutist Danish-German "whole-state" [Helstat] could not, of course, side with either demand, and throughout the 1840's they sought desperately to promote local compromises in order to hold the compound state together. But the absolutist bi-national state seemed doomed in the face of this escalating and irreconcilable conflict, and Christian VIII, under whose reign the conflict ripened, followed an erratic course which ultimately alienated both sides.

A local settlement of the question finally became impossible, because the German cause was taken up by the German liberal movement beyond the borders of the Danish state, while the Danish cause became inextricably intertwined with Copenhagen liberalism. Events in Denmark quickly took on an accelerating pace of their own. In May 1842 Orla Lehmann addressed a large liberal meeting in Copenhagen and openly called for adding "Denmark to the Ejder" to the liberal creed. In November 1842 a Danish Slesviger spoke in Danish at a meeting of the Slesvig Estates and was ruled out of order, thus underscoring the fact that the Danish language had no legal standing in the province. Now even the conservative poet Heiberg was forced to come out in defense of the Danish tongue, and large delegations of liberals in Copenhagen protested to the Crown, as did official remonstrances of the Roskilde and Viborg Estates. The extremely respectable liberal Clausen now formed the "Committee for the Establishment of Danish Educational Institutions in Slesvig," and a broadly based mass meeting was planned for May 1843 to be held on Skamlingsbakken, the highest point in Slesvig. Six thousand people, including a large delegation of liberals, who had made the expensive and circuitous overland and boat trip from Copenhagen, gathered at Skamlingsbakken in 1843.

Still, Christian VIII refused to affirm the right of the Slesvig delegate to speak in Danish at the Estates because the delegate was an educated man who knew German, and hence must use it, even though a Dane. Thus, the mass meeting was repeated in 1844, when another large gathering which drew 12,000 people was held at Skamlingsbakken.[1] At this 1844 meeting, many influential men spoke, including the radical Jewish writer, M. A. Goldschmidt, the liberal Orla Lehmann, and, significantly, Grundtvig, who, though not a liberal, had become a firm supporter of the nationalist cause. Meanwhile, the German-speaking populations of Slesvig and Holstein held *sangfests* of their own.

Thus, in the course of the 1840's the national cause had at least neutralized the opposition of a portion of conservative opinion, while it strengthened its hold upon both the more respectable and the more extreme currents of liberalism and also captured the support of the Grundtvigian wing of the peasant awakening movement. (Grundtvig and his amazing career will be examined in chapter 13.) Here it will be illuminating to look briefly at the liberal Carl Ploug, who—as the leader of the literary-political student "Scandinavianism" movement, as a political poet, and as the incendiary editor of the liberal newspaper *The Fatherland*—was responsible, perhaps more than anyone else, for shaping urban middle-class sentiment on the national issue. Through his combined efforts as editor of *The Fatherland* and as the rather over-aged leader of the University Student Union, Ploug helped popularize the romantic political notion of Scandinavianism, in which Norway, Sweden, and Denmark would be united under a single crown, as in mediaeval times, governed by a pan-Scandinavian monarch—under a liberal representative constitution. Ploug's Scandinavianism was enormously popular among Danish university students, and it attracted some sympathy from Swedish and even a few Norwegian students. However, it was never a serious political possibility. Scandinavianism was a dangerous, heady pipe dream, concocted primarily to provide tiny Denmark with the shred of hope—namely of military assistance from the other Scandinavian states—that would permit liberal nationalist agitators to speak with bravado about defeating the German barbarians to the south and simply imposing the Danish will on southern Jutland by force of arms. Such delusions of grandeur would ultimately lead the National Liberal Party to disaster.

A typical Ploug poem from 1839 is "The Fatherland," excerpted below:

> A voice sounds in my breast,
> Which streams from the chamber of my heart.
> It fills my arm with strength
> And sets my will ablaze.
> It grasps my mind and captivates the senses,
> For the voice is—my fatherland's.
> . . . .
> Call only that state wretched and weak
> Which is lowliest among the low.

> But a good cause is mighty,
> A united people cannot be compelled.
> Just come, you eagles of the East! [Prussians, Russians]
> Come, I summon you to bloody doom![2]

Several years later the martial tone was even stronger, as can be seen in the following passage from "Call to Arms":

> My people! My people! Where are you?
> Do you not feel the voice of the times!
> Do you not sense life's power
> Streaming in your breast?
> You have built your future hopes
> Upon the grace of foreign despots,
> So loose your sword and solve the puzzle of fate
> And arise reborn from the baptism of battle![3]

The flavor of Ploug's writing seems to justify the harsh judgment passed upon him by Erik Henrichsen, a leading Danish historian of this period, who points out that Ploug exploited his position in the student movement and as editor of the nation's most influential paper in order, first, to widen the gap between urban "culture" and the countryside, and, second, to encourage the self-congratulating urban liberal middle class to adopt a far more uncompromising and bellicose stance than a sober view of reality would have dictated. Henrichsen concludes that "Ploug's nature had much to do with making the 'spirit of '48' what it was: tyrannical, dizzy, . . . self-satisfied, and, in the end, laughable and stupid."[4] When, in the course of the bitter and bloody first Slesvig war, from 1848 to 1851, a moderate liberal dared to make the reasonable suggestion that Slesvig be divided along linguistic boundaries, the suggestion was laughed out of court by the militant National Liberals who had been steeped in Ploug's poetry and in the brilliant oratory of men like Orla Lehmann.

B. CHRISTIAN VIII AND THE 1840'S

King Christian VIII was a solitary, well-meaning man caught in the middle of the impossible conflicts of the 1840's, particularly the interlocking questions of constitutional change and the status of southern Jutland. The liberal constitutionalists and the Danish-speaking population of Slesvig were wedded to the Ejder policy, while Denmark's traditional ally, Russia, feared constitutionalism (as did Denmark's powerful neighbor, Prussia), and Germans both in and out of the duchies favored a German "Slesvig-Holstein." Furthermore, shortly before his accession, Christian had privately assured Metternich that he harbored no constitutional dreams. Christian's attempts to mollify the various parties never succeeded and only made them all angrier, just as his foolish promulgation of the Peasant Ordinance of 1845 had lost him the support of the peasantry. He followed an erratic course and seemed determined to do as little as possible with respect to both the constitutional and the national questions, hoping that he could find a way to retain the integrity of the traditional Crown domains under the old arrangements of the bi-national state. But, at a time when nationalism seemed inescapably wedded to liberalism, Christian VIII's attempts to find a middle course were doomed.

Toward the end of his reign Christian seems to have favored some dramatic new constitutional initiative which he hoped would appease the liberals without worsening the situation in the duchies or offending the Great Powers, but he died in January 1848 before this could be effected. By the time of his death, Christian had alienated much of the respect that the peasantry had traditionally shown the Crown and had also lost the respect of almost all liberal opinion and of both sides in the dispute in southern Jutland. He left behind him an interlocking set of riddles of state which were more insoluble than those he had inherited, a dilemma which was only to be resolved by force. A month after Christian's death, revolution broke out in Paris, and the contagion of constitutionalism and conflicting nationalisms quickly spread northward.

7. 1848 and After

O

As we have seen, in the 1830's the provincial Estates were dominated for the most part by older, first-generation liberals, who did not provoke irreconcilable tensions with the government, but merely voiced continuing concern that absolutism get its financial house in order. However, starting immediately after the accession of Christian VIII in December 1839—when Orla Lehmann guided the Student Union in its demonstration and petition for a representative, constitutional government—the political climate changed dramatically. Now the younger, constitutionalist liberals took the front row, while the older, budget-minded businessman-liberals retired to the rear.

When in the course of the 1840's it became increasingly apparent that Christian's son, the heir apparent (later Frederick VII), was a far lesser man than his father, a majority in the Estates came to favor at least moderate constitutional reforms. A. S. Ørsted, the royal representative, now came into increasing conflict with the liberal Estates, and, after having been the revered moderate and voice of reason in Frederick VI's cabinets of the 1820's and 1830's, the aging Kantian became increasingly associated with reaction and blind support for absolutism. Constitutional issues, peasant issues, and the question of Slesvig and Holstein now dominated the Estates, and passions were greatly stirred. Although Grundtvig did not reassess his group's stance until 1848, in the early and mid-1840's the peasants were weakening in their support for absolutism. The government found its most abiding and loyal source of public support in the majority of writers and poets of the Golden Age; such men as Bishop Mynster, the theologian H. L. Martensen, Søren Kierkegaard, the poet Johan Ludvig Heiberg, and even the great populist troublemaker Grundtvig, all remained on absolutism's side throughout most of the 1840's and found the liberal spokesmen glib and superficial.

H. N. Clausen, the liberal theologian and political leader, emerged in the course of the 1840's as a great spokesman in the provincial Estates for the Danish cause in Slesvig, while Orla Lehmann and the rather more radical group for which he was spokesman presented the Estates with proposals for a parliament that would vote taxes and enact laws; for a broader franchise; for responsible ministers, etc. In the pre-1848 period, Lehmann's constitutional schemes were unable to gain a majority in the Roskilde Estates, which represented the islands but, significantly, did manage to do so in the Viborg Estates of central and northern Jutland. By 1847 it seemed certain that the prestigious Roskilde Estates would surely approve a similar demand for a liberal, representative constitution in the foreseeable future and that a majority of the nation's respectable, enlightened opinion would thus be marshaled into open conflict with the absolute authority of the Crown. By late 1847, Christian busied himself with drafts for a new constitution, but, as mentioned earlier, he died in January 1848 before any action could be taken.

In a pamphlet published to coincide with Christian's passing, the moderate liberals Clausen and Schouw stressed the absolute necessity of a free constitution, under which a parliament would be empowered to make laws, to consent to proposed taxes, and to hold ministers responsible for governmental policies. Significantly, however, the franchise proposed for this parliamentary government in Clausen and Schouw's widely circulated pamphlet was not much broader than that of the current Estates. At a meeting at Clausen's home on January 20, 1848, the evening of Christian VIII's death, Clausen and Schouw presented their scheme to a large gathering that included important Copenhagen civic leaders and the Copenhagen contingent of the Roskilde Estates.

Lehmann, the volatile leader of the younger liberals, was traveling in Italy at the time of Christian's death, and his talents were thus unavailable, so that a march to the royal palace to present petitions upon Frederik VII's accession could be turned away with the excuse that the King was extremely busy at the moment. Meanwhile, Frederik VII, who made no reference whatever to a constitution in his first address, prompted his council of state to come up with a very modest constitutional reform, which was proclaimed on January 28th. The royal proposal would have preserved the four existing provincial Estates and have set up, additionally, an overarching "Assembly Estates" that would exist in tandem with the local bodies and would have binding, decisive, and not merely advisory, authority. Absolutism would thus have been abolished by the terms of Frederik's proposal, but the liberals were not satisfied, because the scheme gave separate status and equal weight to the duchies, on one hand, and to the kingdom, on the other, and did not meet the liberal demand of incorporating Slesvig entirely while cutting Holstein loose. The Germans in the two duchies, on the other hand, feared that the King would use his power to appoint additional members to the overarching Assembly Estates in order to tip the balance in favor of the Danish Kingdom proper.

B. 1848: "REVOLUTION" AND CIVIL WAR

However, before much reaction and discussion could take place, the February Revolution in Paris overshadowed everything. On March 18, 1848 the liberal German nationalists in the duchies sent to Copenhagen a delegation which demanded, among other things: (1) that a constitutional assembly be called for the unified political entity of "Slesvig-Holstein"; (2) that Slesvig be included in the German Confederation; and (3) that the people be armed.

In Copenhagen, at the same time, Lehmann, who had returned from Italy, had assembled a broadly based committee (which, with typical braggadocio, he referred to as a "government") dedicated to the Ejder policy and a free constitution. Under pressure of the events unfolding in Denmark and all over Europe, older and more respectable liberals such as Schouw and Clausen now also joined Lehmann, and the National Liberal platform was sold to Copenhagen in a series of mass meetings. In one such meeting, which was attended by large numbers of craftsmen and artisans, the tone was far more "socialistic" or socially radical than liberal-nationalist, and spokesmen such as the journalist and writer Goldschmidt reminded the audience that the National Liberals were exploiting their enthusiasm while cheating them of universal (male) suffrage, of liberty, and of equality. Lehmann, a brilliant extemporaneous orator, rose to the occasion and won back his audience by declaring that universal (male) suffrage was his program as well. Thus, under threat of defection from the left, did the National Liberals almost accidentally and casually become committed to the explosive notion of universal (male) suffrage, which by enfranchising the artisan and peasant masses would soon come to pose a threat to the elitism upon which liberalism and conservatism alike were dependent.

Just as rumors of Copenhagen political activity had formed the basis upon which the Germans had formulated their rather drastic demands at their political meetings in the duchies, so did the rumors of these German meetings form the background which validated the radical Ejder policy advocated in the Copenhagen meetings organized by Lehmann. Thus, on March 20, 1848, a liberal caucus, meeting at the offices of *The Fatherland* under Lehmann's auspices, managed to get the older and more respectable liberals to agree to an address to the King that was to be presented the following day by the official corporate representatives of the city of Copenhagen. The address called for a free constitution for Denmark, including Slesvig, a constitution which was to be based upon "a truly popular [folkelig] election law." The address, which was to be formally presented by one of the older and most respected members of the *haute bourgeoisie* of the city, was in fact written by Lehmann, and it bluntly included a request that Frederick dismiss his ministers and save the nation, imploring Frederick "not to force the nation to the self-help of desperation."[1] The speech to the Crown thus openly posed the choice as one between royal consent or popular uprising, but even such cautious liberals as the director of the National Bank were willing to lend their support.

The proposed address to the Crown was presented to a mass meeting on the evening of March 20th and was enthusiastically received. The next morning, March 21, 1848, the civic representatives of Copenhagen marched to the royal palace at the head of a crowd of perhaps 15,000 and were received by the King. Presently they emerged from the royal residence and announced that the King had already dismissed his ministers (including the hapless A. S. Ørsted). This was greeted with a great hurrah and the crowd dispersed. Thus peacefully went the revolution of 1848 in Copenhagen. The triumph which brought liberalism, nationalism, and civil war was a triumph of city over country. The provincial towns and the peasant masses were never a part of the decision but were expected to follow along out of patriotism and the expectation of a broad, even universal (male) suffrage. After some hesitation this is exactly what the countryside did, and Copenhagen's victory eventually led to the triumph of the countryside.

On the evening of March 21st and all the following day, Frederick VII and a trusted friend attempted to piece together a satisfactory ministry and had almost come to the point of backing down and endorsing a predominantly conservative "whole-state" cabinet when the German emissaries, sent from the duchies four days earlier, finally arrived with their extreme demands. Angered at the radicality of the German demands, Frederick abruptly changed his mind and resolved to be true to his earlier commitment to support a liberal Ejder policy. He then appointed a cabinet in which prominent liberals had about half the portfolios (and most of the prestige and popular esteem). The German emissaries were sent back with a flat refusal which had been drafted by Lehmann and signed by the King: Holstein would receive a free constitution as an independent state within the German Confederation, but Slesvig would remain bound to Denmark by a common constitution, though with its own assembly and local administration. All suggestions from moderate circles for a division of Slesvig along linguistic lines were rejected in favor of the dogmatic liberal insistence upon the retention of the whole of Slesvig, all the way to the Ejder and the Dannevirke, which were the ancient fortifications marking the southern boundary of Viking Denmark and which had become a romantic symbol in the conflict over the duchies. When the news of Danish intransigence reached the duchies, the German liberals proclaimed a provisional revolutionary government and civil war began.

The war for southern Jutland raged on and off for three years and was only won for the Danes when the Prussians, who had come to the aid of the Germans in the duchies, signed a separate peace with Denmark. By the terms of the treaty, Prussia withdrew all support for the local German forces in the duchies, but the issue of right and wrong was left unresolved. The Slesvig-Holstein forces collapsed and surrendered in January 1851. Resentment remained strong in the German community, and henceforth it was clear that Slesvig could be retained only by relying upon the diplomatic support of the Great Powers, particularly Russia, a reactionary and mercurial ally with whom the Danish liberals, in particular, had difficulties in dealing.

Several times in the course of the conflict the Copenhagen liberals refused suggestions—some of them made by the Slesvig-Holstein provisional government itself—to partition Slesvig along linguistic lines, i.e., roughly the present-day boundary, which was settled upon, several wars later, by the plebiscite of 1920. The most positive and long-lasting result of the National Liberals' three-year war, perhaps, was the universalization of the conscription law, so that it was no longer peasant boys alone whom liberal politicians could send forth to die for liberal ideas.

C. 1848–49: SOCIAL DIVISIONS AND THE CONSTITUTION OF 1849

With the accession of the liberal-dominated "March Ministry" on March 24, 1848, a rather broad freedom of the press was immediately instituted, allowing the differences between the erstwhile allies in the fight against absolutism to make themselves immediately apparent. With the announcement that a Constitutional Assembly was to be convened in November 1848 and that its delegates were to be chosen by universal (male) suffrage, the rifts between rural peasant and urban liberal, concealed by the campaign against absolutism and against censorship restrictions, now came into the open. The liberal-peasant coalition dissolved into its original components of country versus city. There was much fear of unrest from the lowest classes of the rural poor. To meet the most pressing demands of the cottagers, the March ministry quickly commuted all their remaining labor dues to cash payments and abolished landlords' disciplinary rights. Shortly thereafter, the military obligation was made universal.

Many liberals who had endorsed the principle of universal (male) suffrage had done so only because they had expected that economic dependency and the fact that the voting would be held in the open would mean that the poorest classes of society—the cottagers and artisans—could hardly do otherwise than vote for their social betters, and not for their somewhat better-off neighbors or cousins, the self-owner or copyholder farmers. Further, the conservatives (and most of the liberals) in the March ministry hoped to be able to counterbalance the results of universal (male) suffrage by allowing the Crown (i.e., the ministry) to appoint 25 percent of the total delegates to the Constitutional Assembly. Liberals were divided on the issue, but most feared peasant tyranny and favored the "royal 25 percent." The issue of the "royal 25 percent" on which most liberals and conservatives were in agreement, bitterly divided the peasants against the liberals and forced a split in the liberal-peasant alliance, the Society of Friends of the Peasant, which was now captured by a peasant majority and refused to lend its support to any local candidate who would not disavow the "royal 25 percent."

Thus, on the question of using governmental influence to counterbalance the effects of the peasant vote, the liberals quickly found the conservative "enemy" far less threatening than the rural "friend"; the shared ties of elite urban culture [Dannelse] proved to be stronger than the mere ink and paper of the peasant-liberal alliance of 1846. The towns soon came to be similarly divided along class lines, and after the euphoria surrounding Lehmann's endorsement of universal (male) suffrage, the excitement of March 21st, and the fervor of the beginning of the civil war settled down, the craftsmen's movement supported peasant candidates and opposed the liberals and their "royal 25 percent." The social opposition between liberal and peasant was strongest on the islands, where the land was most valuable (and difficult to purchase), and the peasants were worst off. A particularly interesting and bitter fight was waged in a rural district of Zealand, where the great liberal leader Clausen, who a few months earlier would have been considered a sure winner, was forced to fight desperately for election against a poor weaver. (The social implications of this symbolic contest will be dealt with in chapter 14, where Clausen and Lehmann will be examined under the rubric of the liberal alternative to the conservative social-political mainstream of the Golden Age.)

When the results of the elections to the Constitutional Assembly were tallied, they showed that throughout the islands the candidates put forward by the Society of Friends of the Peasant, which was the best-organized political institution in the countryside, had won handily, while Jutland, with its poorer, cheaper soil and its higher proportion of self-owner, and hence less radical peasants, gave the society only one seat. The final composition of the Constitutional Assembly was thirty-three conservatives, thirty-two National Liberals, and forty-four "Friends of the Peasant."[2] Royal appointment (which had been approved) greatly swelled the ranks of the liberal and conservative delegations. In the end, the constitution produced by the Assembly reflected the dominant position of the liberals as the brokers between the peasants and the conservatives.

With the convocation of the Constitutional Assembly in November 1848, the March Ministry resigned, but two of its more prominent members, Lehmann and another young liberal, D. G. Monrad, continued to exercise a considerable influence upon the Constitutional Assembly. Lehmann and Monrad had written the draft of the constitution which the Assembly was to consider, and they played a key and continuing role as lobbyists for the document for the eight months during which the Constitutional Assembly remained in session.

By the winter of 1848–49, the tide of revolution had turned to reaction in many parts of Europe, and many people began to have doubts about universal (male) suffrage, particularly since (as we shall see in chapter 14) such able men as Clausen had been rejected in favor of common laborers. Lehmann, however, had become committed to the notion of universal (male) suffrage and defended it vigorously in the pages of *The Fatherland*.

To the left of the National Liberals, the peasants favored a unicameral legislature and universal (male) suffrage, while to the right the more moderate, older liberals favored a bicameral system with a property qualification for suffrage. The conservatives favored bicameralism and even greater restrictions on the franchise. In the end, a bicameral parliament, the *Rigsdag*, emerged, with a lower house, or *Folketing*, and an upper chamber, or *Landsting*, both of which were to be elected by all male householders. The lower house was to be directly elected on the basis of single-man constituencies, while the upper house was to be indirectly elected from much larger constituencies. The minimum age for election to the lower house was twenty-five; for the upper house it was forty, and eligibility for this house was further qualified by a minimum income provision. In special circumstances and when the Rigsdag was not in session, the King was permitted to pass "provisional laws," and in a lengthy "promise paragraph," details too complex to be spelled out with the haste the present national emergency demanded were guaranteed for the present in general terms, with a more specific formulation to be given in the future: civil freedom; freedom of press and religion; and, significantly, a constitution for the Danish Lutheran Church, which now had its name officially changed from the State Church to the "Danish People's Church" [den danske Folkekirke]. The King was recognized as head of state and was not responsible to the Rigsdag, while his ministers were.

In the Constitutional Assembly, the residual bitterness of the Peasant Party (the candidates put forth by the Society of Friends of the Peasant) was translated into a dogged attachment to unicameralism. For several months it appeared as though the peasant delegates would continue to remain intransigent on this issue and use their considerable strength to block any constitutional settlement which did not accord with their tastes. However, in the late spring of 1849, the peasant delegates backed down in the face of the reaction which was then sweeping Europe and agreed to vote for the liberal constitution as outlined above, which was essentially the constitution which Lehmann and Monrad had drafted several months earlier. The constitution passed overwhelmingly in May 1849 and was signed into law by Frederick VII on June 5, 1849, on which date Denmark became a constitutional monarchy with universal (male) suffrage, a revolutionary change from the bureaucratic absolutism which had immediately preceded it and a victory for the "common man" that was never undone in the years which followed.

D. 1849 AND AFTER: POLITICS AND SOCIETY

In the Rigsdag elections which followed the promulgation of the 1849 constitution, approximately one-half the members of the lower house were peasants, while no landlords could win seats there.[3] In the upper house, on the other hand, there were fewer Peasant Party delegates and fewer liberal professionals and civil servants but a number of great landlords.

In mid-1851, after its apparently successful conclusion of the civil war with the German-speaking duchies, the post-revolutionary liberal ministry was forced out, largely as a result of diplomatic problems attributable to pressure from Russia, which wanted assurances of a suitably conservative government in return for its continuing diplomatic support. A series of increasingly conservative but still pro-constitutional governments followed; all attempted to solve the problem of the duchies in a "whole-state" [Helstat] manner agreeable to Russia. There was no real swing to reaction until continuing liberal resistance and deadlock on the national question resulted in the recalling of the now-reactionary A. S. Ørsted in mid-1853. Ørsted really meant to sabotage constitutional government and to govern as autocratically as possible by circumventing and emasculating the Rigsdag, and he attempted to pass a conservative whole-state constitution entirely over the heads of the representative institutions. When his full intentions finally became clear to all, the liberals and peasants ended their electoral feuding for the time being and crushed Ørsted at the polls in December 1854. (Furthermore, by this time the Russian pressure had eased considerably, as Russia was embroiled in Crimea.) The victory for constitutional forces in the December 1854 elections—and no small amount of court intrigue—removed Ørsted and the threat of genuinely anti-constitutional reaction from the scene, and in December 1854 a new group of liberals came to power. These were not the dogmatic and bellicose nationalists of the March ministry, such as Lehmann, but men who were more pragmatic and innovative in dealing with the duchies.

These pragmatic liberals successfully amended the 1849 Constitution in 1855 by producing what amounted to a third chamber, which was to deal with matters common both to the kingdom and the duchies, and, to please conservatives both at home and abroad (as well as many increasingly dubious liberals), access to this third chamber, or Council of the Realm [Rigsraad], was to be extremely limited by income restrictions. One had to have an income roughly equivalent to what it took to serve in the upper house [Landsting] of the Rigsdag in order even to vote for members of the Rigsraad. This addition to the constitution was designed to bring the entire Danish-German state together by keeping the duchies under separate local assemblies, just as the kingdom proper was under the bicameral Rigsdag. However, the new scheme never really appeased German sentiment, and it was bitterly opposed by such fervently pro-peasant leaders as Grundtvig and the former preacher-agitator J. A. Hansen. Sensing the inevitable, former left-wing liberals such as Lehmann and Monrad captained the successful campaign for ratification of this moderate dilution of the 1849 Constitution. The tractable and constitutionally innovative group which came to power in December 1854 held power almost without interruption until 1864, when Bismarck ended the difficult problem of the duchies militarily, by seizing them for the Prussian-dominated Germany he was then assembling.

In the years following 1848, the positions of the peasants and the liberals with respect to constitutionalism, universal (male) suffrage, and the national question in southern Jutland can be summed up roughly as follows: With the exception of the nationalistic Grundtvigian group, the peasantry was much less concerned with the duchies or with anti-Germanism than were the liberals. They tended to emphasize democratic and social issues, e.g., land reform, unicameralism, and the preservation and extension of the principle of universal (male) suffrage. The liberals, on the other hand, were more concerned with the Danish cause in the duchies and tended to place nationalism ahead of the defense of constitutionalism and popular sovereignty. Of course these tendencies had their limits and tended to be self-correcting. The typical peasant position in the 1850's coincided with the conservative stance in favoring a whole-state policy and opposing the liberal nationalist position on the duchies. However, if the implications of their stand on the duchies threatened to force the peasants into accepting the entire conservative position, namely conservative anti-constitutionalism and continuing pressure to restrict the franchise— viz. Ørsted's position in 1853–54—then the peasants would eventually end their flirtation with conservatism and return to the liberal side, as they did in the electoral alliance of 1854. Similarly, the liberals might indeed soften a bit on their nationalism and constitutionalism if fear of peasant democracy made it expedient to compromise with conservatives—both at home and abroad—and adopt a modified version of the whole-state policy while also obtaining a reassuring property qualification on at least one of the realm's parliamentary chambers, as in the 1855 amendment to the Constitution. Just as a peasant triumph over the liberals would have meant a conservative ascendancy and the ultimate undoing of the peasantry, so could a liberal triumph over the conservatives have led to a peasant ascendancy and the undoing of the liberals. This was the general balance of political and social forces which prevailed in the fifteen or twenty years after 1848.

For their part, the urban and academic liberals in general would probably have preferred a suffrage limited to "cultured," i.e., propertied and/or educated, people, but in 1848 and the early part of 1849 the principle of universal (male) suffrage seemed to have conquered in France and Germany. Furthermore, in the national and military emergency which then prevailed, universal (male) suffrage was an expression of the necessary priority of Danishness over mere social class. As mentioned, the National Liberals had expected the peasants to choose their betters to watch over their interests, and when the peasants instead sent primarily their own kind (or the non-peasant nominees of the frighteningly well-organized Peasant Party) to the Rigsdag, the liberals felt bitter and disappointed. As demonstrated by the Clausen election (which was but a signal example which stood at the head of a list of countless other elections and incidents), the common people, in the liberal view, had not shown themselves to be mature.

Not only academically "cultured" people, but also the great and even the petite bourgeoisie, and even, to a considerable degree, the urban working class as well—in short, most who lived in cities—felt threatened by the peasant movement and generally closed ranks behind the National Liberals and the educated class. Many liberals openly regretted the age of the "common man" and sought means to turn back the clock or at least to stave off by any means available the day on which the rural masses would actually come to exercise decisive power. In the 1850's, the National Liberal press in Copenhagen, led by the nationalist poet Carl Ploug, became increasingly afraid of what it called "the common man's party" and waged a war of mockery and insult, ridiculing the simplicity, rude dress, boorish habits, narrow-mindedness, and lack of culture of the very peasantry which only a few years earlier liberalism had lionized in the pages of Ploug's newspaper and in the founding of the Society of Friends of the Peasant.

During the period until 1870—by which time the once-dominant liberals had become disunited and discredited in the wake of the military-diplomatic disaster which their nationalist policies had helped produce—the peasants stood in the shadow of the National Liberals, whose assistance had often been necessary in pressing for land reform and in defending the principle of popular sovereignty. Even though the Peasant Party enjoyed a majority in the lower house during this period, there was no talk of the peasantry actually forming their own government; that was reserved for finer folk. The Peasant Party was merely instrumental in making or breaking other governments. As has been noted, the peasants tended not to vote, as had been expected, for local notables or urban liberals, but made common cause against both the cities and the landlords.

In sum, as a leading Danish historian of the period has written, 1848 in Denmark can be best understood by considering what went before—absolutism, with political and social power in the hands of royal bureaucrats, aristocrats, bishops, etc.—and what came after, namely popular rule. The liberal generation of 1848 was neither the one nor the other, but representatives of intellect, ideality, and culture, who were pushed aside after the 1860's, when genuinely popular forces came to the fore, by which time the remaining survivors of the generation of 1848 had rejected the age of the common man, even though it was the logical consequence of their own achievment.[4]

E. THE CONSTITUTIONAL POSITION OF THE ESTABLISHED CHURCH AFTER 1849

After the Reformation, the Church had been simply absorbed into the state apparatus, without any thought given to a separate corporate existence or a Church constitution. Glædemark, the historian of this subject, writes that, indeed, this identification of Church and state was so natural and unconscious that in the first two hundred years after Luther's time, the word "church" occurs in documents only in the sense of "a church building" or of "the holy universal Church," and never in the sense of "the Danish Church" or "the state Church."[5] Conscious concern with the corporate structure of the Church and with its relation to the state was a preoccupation of the eighteenth and nineteenth centuries, when the established Church finally took on a name, first as the State Church and then, after 1849, as the People's Church. Thus, from a legal point of view, up to 1849, the Church had been completely engulfed within the state. As has been pointed out in an earlier connection, being an evangelical Lutheran was simply part of being a Dane. It is true that a limited legal recognition had been granted to the relative handful of Jews, Calvinists, and foreign Roman Catholics who found themselves in Denmark, but unbelief or neutrality in matters of religion had no legal existence whatever, excepting as a crime.

The Church had no constitution or legal corporate existence of its own, but was merely the religious arm of the absolutist administration, while for its part, that government had no definite policy of what its Church should be. The government merely valued tranquillity and order above all, allowing reasonable latitude to the clergy but none at all to the laity, who might disturb orderly procedures. In 1813, after considerable pressure from various (and conflicting) clerical factions, the government agreed to establish a commission to discuss a constitution for the Church. However, it soon became clear that opinions were so divided on the place and significance of the Church and the relations between Church and state that it was impossible to draft a new constitution without shattering the fragile, antique unity represented by the absolutist arrangements. It seemed wiser merely to patch up the old arrangement and muddle through. The Church Commission of 1813 worked for nearly twenty years without result, and J. P. Mynster, the last Primate of Denmark under the absolutist regime, made it clear that his attitude was one of *après moi le déluge*.

After the beginnings of the lay awakening movement and the Grundtvig-Clausen affair of 1825 (which will be examined in chapter 13), the official reins began to tighten, but the State Church, having no real views of its own, was powerless against those who did have plans, particularly Grundtvig, the awakeners, and such sectarians as the Baptists and Mormons. The liberal Clausen favored giving the Church a separate corporate existence under a synodal government, but seeing that any ecclesiastical reform was impossible under the absolutist regime, he turned to liberal politics in order first to change the state. Despite the fact that the Church was without a constitution, Denmark never developed a strenuous debate about the constitutional status of the Church, a situation which differs markedly from that of Prussia, similarly without a Church constitution, where, however, a burning debate upon the subject developed as a surrogate for politics.[6]

The clergy never met as a group between the "revolution" of 1848 and the promulgation of the Constitution of June 1849 and thus never had the opportunity to press for any particular constitutional arrangement. (Furthermore, given the nature of the divisions within the clergy—"orthodox," authoritarian, Grundtvigian, liberal, "rationalist," etc.—it is doubtful that any coherent position could have emerged from such a conclave.) The drafting of the portions of the 1849 Constitution dealing with the Church and with religion was thus left entirely to Orla Lehmann's co-worker, the liberal politician and theologian D. G. Monrad, who deliberately wrote in a vague and elliptical language which was designed to be read in various and conflicting ways and thus to please most of the various and conflicting factions within Danish Lutherdom.[7]

The Constitution of June 1849 guaranteed freedom of religion, stating categorically that "no one can be deprived of full use of his civil and political rights on the basis of religion," but it also contained the cryptic statement that "the Evangelical Lutheran Church is the Danish People's Church and as such is supported by the state."[8] The latter statement is deliberately vague. It is unclear whether it is intended to be a normative or a descriptive statement. That is, is it *because* the "Evangelical Lutheran Church" is "the Danish People's Church" (the Church adhered to by a majority of the Danish people) that it "is supported by the state"? Or is the reverse the case: Is the Church the "Danish People's Church" *because* it is the "Evangelical Lutheran Church," and is this why it enjoys "the support of the state," regardless of the actual spiritual and statistical status of the Danish people?

Finally, as if the fundamental vagueness of the above were not enough, the internal constitutional status of the Church and the form of its relation to the state—beyond the promise of state "support" for "the Danish People's Church"—were also left quite deliberately unclarified in the 1849 Constitution, which merely promises that "the constitution of the People's Church will be ordered by law."[9] At the time of its promulgation, this promise was generally interpreted as meaning that the Rigsdag would without delay promulgate an organic statute which would lay down the internal organization of the Church and specify the mode of its relationship to the state. However, this never came to pass, because the very same factors which made it impossible to arrive at any agreement prior to 1849 continued to hold true for the period after 1849 and were in fact exacerbated. The conservative Mynster-Martensen wing of the Church, for example, feared any form of lay democracy, while the Grundtvigians and other pietist groups feared that a legitimized clerical or episcopal dictatorship would enable the authorities to intrude more effectively into the lives of the various congregations and put an end to the *de facto* latitudinarianism which the Grundtvigians, in particular, had achieved in the course of the 1840's. Only the synodalist Clausen truly desired to see a Church constitution and to see the relationship between Church and state spelled out more clearly, and he was to be disappointed.

In the end, there was very little change from the absolutist period. Despite the 1849 Constitution and the triumph of liberalism, liberal secularism was never even attempted. The Church remained bound to the state administration more tightly than ever, and the cabinet portfolio of *Kultusminister* was established to oversee the Church, education, museums, the ballet and opera, and culture generally—which ought to give a fair idea of how, and in what categories, Christianity was construed by governing circles. Naturally, the Kultusminister, as with all other cabinet ministers, was responsible to the shifting majority in the Rigsdag. Under the liberal-democratic regime, the ministries and their Rigsdag majorities came to govern the Church just as firmly and just as politically as it had ever been governed under absolutism. The promise that "the constitution of the People's Church will be ordered by law" came to be interpreted as meaning that ecclesiastical affairs would be settled by laws or legislation, on a case-by-case basis, and that this—the direct rule of the Church by the government—was the "constitution of the People's Church."

Formally, nothing had in fact changed in the relation of Church to state after 1849, but there was in fact a great change, namely that the Church had become integrated into the political structure more firmly and legitimately than ever. For, under the old system, the Church had merely been a State Church of an absolute, royal regime, the property of the powerful bureaucrats and of a small educated elite in faraway Copenhagen. The legitimacy of the State Church in the lives of the common people was limited, and there was scarcely any danger that, if a choice had to be made, the established Church would have been seen as synonymous with Christianity. But, in the moral sense and (potentially, at least) in the actual political sense, the introduction of universal (male) suffrage in the post-1848 era had transformed the state into the people's state, and the State Church, too, had officially become the "People's Church." In the pre-1848 period, the common man could always dissociate himself morally and politically from the shortcomings of the state. It was not his government, it was their government, the government of the king and of those educated and wealthy people from Copenhagen. Similarly, the Church had no absolute moral legitimacy; it was their Church, and it sometimes impeded one's access to true religion. But now matters were truly different. In the age of the common man and popular sovereignty, the government was the common man's property, and the Church was his Church. Did not the new name, the People's Church, prove it? How, then, could the common man challenge the legitimacy of institutions which were, after all, his institutions?

The formal relationship of the Church to the state did not change at all after 1848–49, and the personnel, the procedures, and the socially supportive, cultural functions of the Church were likewise unchanged. But now, in the moral and political sense, the Church had been bound more tightly than ever to the state, and both of them had been made the inalienable moral and political property of the common man, whether he wanted this burden or not.

8. The Social Orientation and Intellectual Origins of the Golden Age

O

A. THE AUDIENCE OF THE GOLDEN AGE

Who constituted the audience, the principal appreciators, for the remarkable cultural outpouring between 1800 and 1850? For whom was this a Golden Age? First and foremost, it must be noted that it was not a literary Golden Age for the peasants. That portion of the population who were engaged in agriculture (approximately three-fourths of the total) generally had no real literature of their own excepting religious tracts, almanacs, the Bible, and a hymnal.[1]

As the historian of literature Svend Møller Kristensen has demonstrated in his analysis of the subscription lists for works by important Golden Age authors, it was the very narrow social group of academically educated men and, particularly, the upper levels of the absolutist bureaucracy, a group centered almost exclusively in Copenhagen, which was principally responsible for determining tastes, and which constituted the backbone of the public of the high culture of the Golden Age.[2] Within the range of production of any particular writer, of course, the appeal varied from one portion of the public to another. Thus, the great poet Oehlenschläger's collected poetry was particularly favored by the royal family and other members of the hereditary aristocracy, whereas his exotic novel, *An Island in the South Seas*, appealed in particular, as might be expected, to the non-academic mercantile bourgeoisie. These variations are only peripheral, however, for the vast bulk of the subscribers to both of these very different works was the academically educated upper-middle class: students, professors, priests, upper-level civil servants, etc.[3]

Møller Kristensen divides the literate class into three more or less distinct groups. At the apex of the social scale there was a small aristocracy of high nobility, the owners of great estates, and the very rich merchant families. Next came the much broader—and for determining literary taste much more important—academically educated portion of the upper bourgeoisie. And, finally, there was the less distinct and much larger uneducated portion of the bourgeoisie, extending from better-off shopkeepers to well-to-do craftsmen.[4] Of these three groups, which constituted virtually the entirety of the reading public for

Golden Age literature, it was generally the middle, academic-bourgeois group, which determined the taste and set the tone for the other two groups. As Møller Kristensen puts it, Denmark had "an apparently very homogeneous public of academically educated people who dominated and formed the taste of the other social groups."[5]

Thus, although this public was nominally bourgeois in social make-up, its orientation was predominantly academic and bureaucratic rather than commercial. It is thus no surprise that the literature of the Golden Age is for the most part anti-bourgeois, stressing poetry at the expense of prose, and is essentially aristocratic and conservative in its social and political outlook, appealing to the standards of the absolutist *ancien régime*. It seems likely that this conservative or anti-political orientation of the upper bourgeoisie and its Golden Age literature can be traced to the fact that the mercantile class, so liberal and enlightened in the eighteenth century, was largely arrested in its development (or economically ruined) after the beginning of the nineteenth century, while Frederick's absolute regime continued on its course with apparent imperturbability and remained the safest and the single most important source of employment for sons of the upper-middle class.

In summing up the social composition of the Golden Age audience, Møller Kristensen concludes that

> in comparison with countries such as France and England, the Danish public presents a unique picture in the first half of the nineteenth century, with an unusually strong and taste-making academic class with *one* center, Copenhagen; this is due first to the fact that Denmark was an agricultural country without any important industry and whose commerce had been destroyed, and second to the fact that an abnormally prolonged absolutism gave an advantage to the bureaucrat class.[6]

None (or scarcely any) of those who are now thought of as great Golden Age writers sold well at the time. Hans Christian Andersen's fame came mostly from abroad, while Møller Kristensen describes the readership of another Danish "classic," the superb and wittily elegant Paludan Müller, as "a nice little public . . . almost exclusively academic."[7] The work of the great poet, playwright, philosopher, and wit, Johan Ludvig Heiberg, who was by far the most important writer and tastemaker of the second half of the Golden Age (ca. 1825–50), also found a very narrow and numerically small audience. Heiberg's finest newspaper, the *Flyvende Post* [Flying Post] thus had virtually all of its subscribers in Copenhagen, and his most perfect book, *Nye Digte* [New Poems] took almost twenty years to sell out the first printing, and none of his other works did as well.[8]

In the Golden Age, a typical successful book by a "high culture" author[9] sold only 500–1,000 copies, and a poet of the period appropriately described the cultivated reading public as consisting of about 1,000 people! Møller Kristensen allows that this figure might be trebled or quadrupled to cover various areas of interest and different facets of the Golden Age public, but we are still left with a cultivated audience of a maximum of three to four thousand people for the *entire* output of the Golden Age.[10] This "primary public," Møller Kristensen concludes, was "in all likelihood as good as exclusively academic" and was centered in Copenhagen, with but a few rural representatives, primarily clergymen: "In the provinces, the pastors were about the only representatives of culture."[11] Thus, as a social phenomenon, the Golden Age was a culture of the capital and its conservative, apolitical, academically educated upper bourgeoisie, cut off both from the progressive influence of trade and from the social revolution taking place in the countryside, to which, on the contrary, literary Copenhagen was presumptuous enough to send its university-trained pastors as apostles of high culture.

B. CROSS-CONNECTIONS IN THE SOCIAL MATRIX OF GOLDEN AGE AUTHORS

The narrow social base of Golden Age authors is further illuminated by a brief look at the social and familial ties by which many of the leading writers of the Golden Age were related to one another and to the academic and bureaucratic upper class.

The doyen of Danish literary criticism in the latter eighteenth century was K. L. Rahbek, whose close friend, the fashionably "radical" poet P. A. Heiberg (cited in Chapter 1), was exiled in 1799. Heiberg's wife Thomasine, a daughter of a wealthy merchant family, was the mother of their son, the later poet, playwright, and tastemaker, Johan Ludvig Heiberg. Thomasine Heiberg divorced her husband after his exile and married a Swedish nobleman, from whom she took the name Thomasine Gyllembourg, under which she is known as one of the leading prose stylists of the Danish Golden Age.

K. L. Rahbek's wife, Kamma (*Karen Margarethe*) Rahbek, presided over Copenhagen's leading literary salon and was a very close friend and correspondent of J. P. Mynster, a brilliant and profound young cleric, who later married the daughter of the Primate of Denmark, subsequently becoming himself Primate of the Established Church. Furthermore, Kamma Rahbek was a very close friend of up-and-coming romantic poet Adam Oehlenschläger (whose father was the royal chamberlain in charge of the palace on the outskirts of Copenhagen, which dominated the suburban neighborhood in which the idyllic Rahbek home was situated). Oehlenschläger married Kamma Rahbek's sister, Christiane (Heger) Oehlenschläger, and thus for all his romantic rebelliousness against the eighteenth century, he became tied by marriage to the leading literary family of the previous generation.

Oehlenschläger's sister, Sophie Oehlenschläger, on the other hand, married A. S. Ørsted, the Kantian jurist who was to become the nation's leading statesman, one of the dominant members of the royal cabinet throughout the entire first half of the century. (As we have seen in chapter 7, A. S. Ørsted ended his career as the reactionary prime minister who attempted to dismantle constitutionalism in his final ministry in 1853–54. Thus, the coming of constitutionalism and of universal [male] suffrage, which brought the common man into the political arena, spelled the end of the elite society of the Golden Age, not only in a broad, social sense, but in a quite specific, personal sense as well.) A. S. Ørsted was also the greatest legal scholar of his time, perhaps the greatest Denmark has ever produced, and the brother of H. C. Ørsted, the discoverer of electromagnetism and Denmark's leading natural scientist and philosopher of science.

The catalyst of Oehlenschläger's poetic breakthrough, which is generally accepted as the beginning of the Golden Age, was the Danish-Norwegian philosopher and natural scientist Henrik Steffens, whose crucial 1802 lectures will be discussed below. Steffens was a close friend of Oehlenschläger and of several other members of Oehlenschläger's circle, including especially J. P. Mynster. Furthermore, Mynster's stepfather, the only parent he ever knew, was the head physician at the Royal Hospital and was also the brother both of Steffens' mother and of the mother of N. F. S. Grundtvig. Thus, Steffens and Grundtvig were first cousins, and Mynster was also a first "stepcousin" both to his good friend Steffens and to his future adversary Grundtvig, who for his part was to remain a vehement outsider in relation to the principal Oehlenschläger-Ørsted-Mynster group.

In the second generation of the Golden Age, literary and ecclesiastical leadership passed from Oehlenschläger and Mynster to two younger men, the above-mentioned Johan Ludvig Heiberg and his Hegelian ally, H. L. Martensen. The content of much of what the second generation had to say differed somewhat from that of the first generation—Oehlenschläger and Mynster could not abide the Hegelianism of Heiberg and Martensen, for example. However, the tone remained the same, that of a lofty and polished aristocracy of the spirit, which in turn presupposed the harmonious integration of civilized values—good taste and culture—with Christianity, which was seen as the guarantor of morality, culture, and social stability.

As a group the Golden Age writers thus constituted a very compact, interrelated, and remarkably homogeneous group, whose audience, as we have seen, was quite limited, and who wrote largely for one another's consumption. Every one of the above leaders of the Golden Age (with the exceptions of the elder Heiberg—who was exiled—and of the later Grundtvig) was politically conservative; that is, they had no politics and favored absolutism as a means of removing the nettlesome subject from public discussion and consciousness. Every one of the above was either from an academically educated or high civic official family or managed to enter that paper-thin social group. Every one of the above (with the exception of Grundtvig) looked to Copenhagen as the only focus worthy of real attention, despite the fact that, as we have seen, throughout this period, economic and social power in Denmark was quite perceptibly shifting to the countryside with its peasant farms and provincial towns, while Copenhagen, as we have also seen, was steadily losing its relative position on every front: population, shipping, finance, etc.

C. THE INTELLECTUAL ORIGINS OF THE DANISH GOLDEN AGE: HENRIK STEFFENS AND H. C. ØRSTED

As has been noted, Henrik Steffens (1773–1845), whose mother was the sister of Mynster's stepfather and of Grundtvig's mother, was thus a first cousin of these two (later mutually antagonistic) religious giants of the Golden Age. As a youth Steffens was an active member of Mynster's intellectual circle, and in 1794 wrote a prize essay on the "hidden spiritual unity in the manifold and interconnected processes of nature." Shortly after this Steffens left Copenhagen and Mynster's group to study at the University of Kiel, where the budding *Naturphilosoph* took a doctorate in mineralogy and was influenced by Fichte, Herder, the romantic nationalists Arnim and Brentano, and, particularly, by the romantic *Naturphilosophie* of Schelling, honoring the Schellingian motto: "Nature is visible spirit, and spirit is invisible nature." He became a Schellingian geologist and entered Schlegel's literary circle at Jena, where he met Tieck and Novalis.

In the summer of 1802 he returned from his travels in Germany and joined the circle of friends which included Oehlenschläger, Mynster, and both Ørsteds. Steffens and Oehlenschläger became inseparable, and it was decided that young Steffens should seek the vacant chair in philosophy at the University of Copenhagen, and that to this end he should hold a series of public lectures on the new philosophy. Steffens' philosophical lectures, which began in November 1802, were apparently an electrifying experience, particularly for the young. His audience included not only Oehlenschläger, Mynster, and the Ørsteds, but three to four hundred others, including both student enthusiasts and older, more skeptical academics. Virtually every major personality of the first generation of what was to be the Golden Age was present. Grundtvig, for example, came to hear his distinguished cousin speak, and, although the lectures seem to have made no immediate impression upon him, he soon had his own turbulent association with Schellingian romanticism, the effects of which he never escaped. Later, when Grundtvig made his "matchless discovery" in the 1820's, he drew his all-important doctrine of "the living word" from Steffens' lectures. The older academics and university officials in Steffens' audience were not impressed with the new romantic philosophy, however. Steffens' disdain for the Enlightenment and his reputation as a faddish enthusiast and seducer of youth kept him from the University chair, and he returned to Germany in 1804, after only two years in Denmark, during which time he had transmitted the intellectual and emotional spark which was to be the beginning of the Danish Golden Age.

In his lectures, Steffens presupposes in his listeners "the internal need to know the real essence of things, to solve the riddle of existence," and the capacity for "the internal view which composes each individual part into a whole, positing the absolutely whole, *the One*, as *the Real*."[12] Steffens promised his listeners that "I will open up a more significant vision of life and existence than that to which ordinary existence and daily life, confined as they are by finite needs, leads us."[13] Steffens' privileged mind, which is able to penetrate beyond the vulgar, the fragmentary, and the partial to the infinite and whole essence of things, thus leads the listener through a lengthy discussion of geology and zoology, of the animal kingdom, in which the blind instinct of food-gathering dominates at the bottom of the scale, and comes finally to human beings, who are governed by reason and morality. We are the crown of creation, but are part of a whole, a member of a continuity, and it is thus necessary to perceive the one spirit which unites the whole of nature with human history: "It is philosophy's task to recognize the freedom of reason in the necessity of nature, and to recognize the necessity of nature in history."[14] This is the general tenor of the romantic idealism and pantheism presented by Steffens in his lectures to the Copenhagen cultural elite.

At the time of his lectures Steffens was a romantic and pantheistic monist in religion, but after his return to Germany (Halle and Berlin) he subsequently converted to a very conservative Lutheran orthodoxy and implicitly labelled his youthful Schellingian period as pagan. Despite his own later preferences, however, the romantic idealism which Steffens had introduced into Denmark lived on after his departure, and his brief presence in Copenhagen served as the vital catalyst for a new phase in the intellectual life of the isolated northern capital. Thus, Steffens can be seen as a vitally important emissary of German intellectual life, bringing "high culture" to sensitive, culture-starved little Denmark from without, a situation precisely parallel to that of Heiberg, some twenty-five years later, who also awed "the cultured" [de Dannede] in Copenhagen with a German import, this time not Schelling, but Hegel. Because of Steffens' Schellingianism and his profound influence—particularly upon Oehlenschläger and H. C. Ørsted—one could with some justification call the first generation of the Golden Age a form of "Schellingian" romanticism, whereas the second generation—if one regards Heiberg and Martensen as the principals—is a cooler Hegelian variant. In both cases, one can see the cultivated Danish bourgeoisie dancing to the changing tune of German intellectual fashion, betraying their sense of Danish inferiority and isolation and their fear of being left out.

The principal Danish intellectual who remained behind to propound Steffens' Schellingianism in its theoretical form, and who can thus be seen as one of the chief theoretical spokesmen for the first generation of the Golden Age, was the *Naturphilosoph* H. C. Ørsted (1777–1851). H. C. Ørsted, as we have seen, was an important member of the innermost cultural circle, the brother of A. S. Ørsted, and a close friend both of Oehlenschläger and of the future bishop, J. P. Mynster. H. C. Ørsted's romantic philosophy finds its clearest and most popular expression in the composite volume *Aanden i Naturen* [The Spirit in Nature], which was published toward the end of his life and which contains his major public and programmatic statements of the philosophy which underlay the Golden Age, generally, and in particular, the first generation of that age. A brief examination of Ørsted's book and Steffens' lectures reveals several characteristic attitudes of the Golden Age: its yearning for the restoration of the lost unity of all things, its view of the relation between religion and culture, its identification of the purposes of religion and art, and its deification of the exceptional, gifted individual, the "genius."

"All history," Steffens had proclaimed, "begins with the gods. Behind all history lies mythology; this is a fact which no one can deny."[15]

> It is a *fact*: that in ancient times, which I call the epic period, the poetic and the religious coincided and were *one*; that this union of the two is the only remainder of that whole life of the past; [and] that these lingering echoes—those according to which we can judge the spirit of that age—point to a harmonic existence which gave even finite things an immediate relationship to the religious and the eternal.[16]

Although betraying his own natural-scientific point of view, Ørsted's view of the primal unity of religion and human nature seconds that of his friend Steffens: "In the uncorrupted years of its earliest development, science everywhere stood in such a close connection with religion, a connection which could be suspended for a time only by means of one or another sort of error."[17] Thus, if we view it properly, science shows us that "the whole of existence is a kingdom of reason," and we can perceive in the universe [Verdensalt] "the essential unity of knowledge" as well as the principles of beauty and morality.[18] When we thus realize the wholeness of existence, we will be able to restore to science and religion their ancient and essential unity, and to appreciate "the cultivation of science, viewed as the exercise of religion."[19]

Thus, the realization of the lost, essential unity of all things, and particularly the unity of human culture (science and poetry) with religion, is the desideratum which is essential to the early Steffens and to the Golden Age philosophy of his friend H. C. Ørsted. The problem, however, is that the present cultural landscape is flat and uninteresting; its concern for the finite and the everyday does not allow it to rise to the point where this essential unity can be perceived and vindicated. As Steffens put it,

> The special characteristics of our age are an irreligiosity and a predilection toward prose, such as has never before been seen in history. . . . What I call prose is what denigrates even that which bears the unmistakable stamp of the eternal into something which is merely finite. What I call poetry is that which finds the stamp of the eternal even in the finite.[20]

The only hope for the age to escape this prosaic existence is to recognize the superior, indeed the divine, rights and qualities of the exceptional, visionary individual, the genius.

> The genius is differentiated from mere talent, which is always one-sided, in that the genius is the most immediate revelation of the eternal, even in the finite, and therefore, even though he is the most individual of all, he is also the most universal. It is . . . generally known that the genius mocks the rules of prudence, breaks through all the regulations one wishes to set up for him, and paves his *own* way, and also that of an entire age . . . . Genius is divinity's own radiance which now and then breaks forth from the mass of things in splendor, gathering together in a clear harmony what one-sided talent has rent asunder. One can never apply the standards of the time in order to judge a genius. . . . [21]

Whatever spark of divinity ordinary men possess is present more perfectly and splendidly in the genius, to whom we owe homage:

> It is that in us which is divine; it is *that* which is *one* with *everything*, the image of the Deity, our real essence, which arises in an indistinct intimation, which reveals itself in every scientific effort, which unfolds itself in every talent, which reveals itself in its fullest splendor in the magnificent genius.[22]

Thus, for the Golden Age, the most perfect creations of culture are also manifestations of the special and magnificent presence of the Deity. The chosen, the exceptional, individual who is to be the vehicle of this divine revelation has the special, divine authority of genius. Culture and religion originally had—and, in the ideal sense, still have—the same task, which is to reveal the essential wholeness of everything in existence. As culture perfects itself, it will once again be capable of performing this task with its original profundity, and the vehicle of this perfection is the cultural genius. "Everything which bears the stamp of the eternal is poetry," it was proclaimed at the beginning of the Golden Age, and Oehlenschläger seconded this general, divinizing definition of poetry by proclaiming art to be "the organ of eternity." The artist's genius is a divine spark, and the artist is the high priest who mediates between the higher realms of the Deity and the finite world of ordinary mortals.

(As we shall see in part two of the present work, it is precisely this fundamental Golden Age notion of the artistic genius-cum-high priest with which Kierkegaard takes issue. His task is to make explicit the divorce between the finite world of culture and politics on the one hand, and the religious sphere on the other. Like the principal spokesmen of the Golden Age, Kierkegaard, too, is an individualist, and like the Golden Age, he recognizes the gift of genius. But Kierkegaard sees genius as something merely accidental, something which is far less important than—and trivial in comparison with—that which absolutely every individual possesses, namely the capacity for religious experience, for the individual relation to God, for *faith*. If culture, then, is taken to be that which constitutes the core and meaning of human existence, Kierkegaard will be seen to be a radical egalitarian who attacked the prevailing elitism of the Golden Age.)

The next chapters will examine the politics of the Golden Age, giving particular attention to the roles assigned to religion and culture by several representative figures, namely Oehlenschläger and Mynster on the one hand and Heiberg and Martensen on the other as the literary and religious representatives of the first and second generations, respectively, of the mainstream of the Golden Age. After having assessed the aristocratic, urban, and "conservative" (apolitical) mainstream represented by these four men, we will briefly examine the two principal alternatives to this dominant cultural synthesis, namely the peasant-oriented, populist, Christian nationalism of Grundtvig, and the urban, elitist liberalism of H. N. Clausen and Orla Lehmann. After some concluding remarks on politics and religion in the 1840's, the ground will have been prepared for an examination of Kierkegaard's views of politics and society. The reader will be better able to understand Kierkegaard's views after having seen the environment in which they developed and against which he reacted.

9. "The Rare Few": Adam Oehlenschläger and the First Generation of the Golden Age

O

A. BIOGRAPHICAL

Adam Oehlenschläger (1779–1850) came from a comfortable bureaucratic family in Copenhagen and was an early associate of Steffens, Mynster, and the Ørsted brothers. These latter encouraged Oehlenschläger in 1800 to attend the university in order to become a more suitable social match for his beloved— but social superior—Christiane Heger, whose sister Kamma Rahbek presided over much of Copenhagen's intellectual life in her famous salon at Hill House [Bakkehuset]. In the summer of 1802, Oehlenschläger met Henrik Steffens, fresh from Jena and full of the poetic-scientific romanticism of Schelling, and was electrified. The meeting immediately bore fruit in the form of Oehlenschläger's remarkable and epoch-making *Poems* [*Digte*], published on Christmas Day 1802. This volume contained the first Danish poetry in the new romantic style, and it was Oehlenschläger's first mature work, including some of the best poetry he was ever to write. Among the remarkable poems it contained were "The Golden Horns" [Guldhornene] and "The Death of Hakon Jarl" [Hakon Jarls Død] (which will be examined in the next sections of this chapter). Oehlenschläger's radically new poetry was received with some admiration and much wonder, but also with a bit of disapproval by the old school headed by K. L. Rahbek. Here, however, Oehlenschläger's good connections helped him, and he was protected against outright rejection by the fact that he was a close friend of Rahbek's wife, Kamma, to whose sister, Christiane, he was by this time engaged.

In 1805 he published his second collection of romantic poetry, *Poetical Writings* [*Poetiske Skrifter*], which enjoyed immediate acclaim and solidified his reputation. Oehlenschläger came to see an analogy between the sudden and wonderful development of his own capacities and that of Aladdin's genius, and he celebrated the triumph of genius in a drama of the same name which he published as a part of the *Poetical Writings* of 1805. The success of the *Poetical Writings* and of "Aladdin" in particular was so resounding that it won Oehlenschläger a four-year government stipend for a grand tour of Germany,

France, and Italy, during which he met the great German romantics and began the gradual process of moderating his own romanticism and of accommodating with a more settled, Goethean view of things.

Upon his return from the grand tour, Oehlenschläger married Christiane and proceeded to solidify his reputation with a decade or so of major poetry, principally dramas, soon winning a permanent place on the civil list and recognition as Denmark's leading poet, and in fact, as one of the greatest poets Denmark had ever produced. In the last twenty or thirty years of his life, however (from around 1818), Oehlenschläger's poetry went steadily downhill as he rested on his laurels and turned out reams of turgid dramas, the poor quality of which is particularly remarkable when contrasted with the extraordinary quality of his earlier work. Beginning in 1825, Johan Ludvig Heiberg began the task of demolishing Oehlenschläger's newer poetry and his preeminence as Denmark's leading arbiter of taste, a position which Heiberg quickly seized for himself. By the time of his death in 1850, Oehlenschläger's presence had long since become that of a divine and revolutionary poet of the preceding generation.

B. "THE RARE FEW": THE INTUITIVE GENIUS IN "THE GOLDEN HORNS"

The greatest lyric poem of Oehlenschläger's first collection of romantic poetry (*Poems*, 1802) was "The Golden Horns" [Guldhornene], which stands as the first truly splendid achievement in the new style of poetry. "The Golden Horns"[1] marks the entrance to the Golden Age; it was composed by Oehlenschläger in the summer of 1802 when he was under the spell of his friend Steffens. Two finely wrought golden horns, which were archaeological treasures from the Viking period, had been stolen from the museum shortly before, in May 1802, and Oehlenschläger poetically fantasized that they had been gifts of the gods who have now taken them back from the insensitive and unappreciative people of prosaic, present-day Denmark. (The priceless artifacts had in fact been stolen and melted down by a goldsmith who lived several doors away from Oehlenschläger, but this was not known at the time that the romantic piece was written.) In ancient times, Oehlenschläger imagined, people lived in the immediate presence of the gods and in living and immediate contact with nature; the world of nature and of human culture was impregnated with the divine. In the contourless present, however, these bonds have been broken, and we now seek to rediscover these lost secrets by means of slavish efforts and chilling intellectual reflection.

> They search and look
> In ancient books,
> In barrows high

> With prying eyes,
> Upon swords and shields
> In wall-girt fields,
> On rune-covered stones,
> In moldy bones.
>
> Deeds of old
> Suggest enchantment;
> But the ancient parchments
> Are concealed in darkness.
> The eye stares;
> The mind is confused
> And fumbles in the fog.
> "In the ancient, ancient, bygone days!
> When Scandinavia gleamed,
> When Heaven was on earth,
> *Let us see it one more time!*"[2]

Yet no amount of rational drudgery and mere labor can reveal the secrets of natural and immediate existence in contact with the divine. Thus, the discovery of the first of the golden horns was made, some centuries ago, by a young and innocent maid:

> Her cheeks are burnished;
> Her hands are lily-white.
> Light as a deer,
> With a spirit of cheer,
> She hurries and hovers.
> And, thinking of love,
> She stumbles!
> And stares and sees
> Golden light [a golden horn].[3]

This discovery is not one to be shared with the common herd of humanity, however, for, when they hear about it,

> [T]he great crowd
> Throngs to the place.
> They dig and seek
> To add to the treasure,
> But no gold!
> Their hopes have deceived them.
> They see only the mud
> From which they were taken.[4]

Thus was the first golden horn discovered, the prize of a simple girl who saw deeper than the mere crowd. A century later there appeared another soulful, simple, and unpretentious youth,

> Nature's son,
> Unknown, in private,
> But, like his fathers,
> Powerful and large,
> Working his land—
> We will honor him,
> He will find [treasure] *again!*[5]

Thus was the second of the precious golden horns discovered by another immediate and unreflective child of nature. Subsequently, both horns ended up in the museum, placed before the eyes of the merely curious:

> Mystical divinity hovers about
> Their ancient signs and marks.
> The glory of deity quivers about
> The wondrous works of eternity.
>
> Honor them, for this is ordained by fate!
> Perhaps they will soon disappear.
> Fill them with the blood of Jesus, on the Lord's
>   altar,
> Just as they were filled with blood in the groves
>   [i.e., the sacrificial groves of the ancient
>   Norse gods].[6]

(Note Oehlenschläger's casual equation of the Norse and Christian religions as apparently equally authentic. Later in this chapter, in the analysis of two other poems, we will note this rather loose assimilation of Christianity to Norse religion and to pantheistic Nature religion.)

The gods are displeased with the irreverent and prying attitude of ordinary people and so seize the divine treasures back into the heavens:

> But you see only the glow,
> And not what is honorable and the sublime!
> You exhibit them as splendid display
> For the jaded and curious eye.
>
> The heavens darken, the storm breaks!
> Thou art come, thou certain hour.
> What was given is taken back—
> The sacred objects disappear forever![7]

The moral of the poem is stated quite simply: The secrets of the universe are not available to everyone but only to "the rare few," that is, to the intuitive genius who understands how to recreate the ancient, integral culture in which we lived in immediate unity with nature and the gods:

> "For the rare few
> Who understand our gift,
> Who are not bound by earthly chains,
> But whose souls lift themselves
> To the pinnacle of eternity;
> Who perceive the High
> In nature's eye;
> Who worshipfully tremble
> Before rays of the deity,
> In the sun, in violets,
> In the least things and the greatest;
> Who burningly thirst
> After the life of life;
> Who—o great Spirit
> Of times gone by!—
> Who see thy divine brilliance
> Upon the sides of the sacred objects—
> For *them* our command sounds again."[8]

Steffens, who in 1802 was himself something of the intuitive genius, the intercessor with divinity, whom this poem celebrates, greatly approved of "The Golden Horns." The Golden Age was to be the age of "the rare few."

C. OEHLENSCHLÄGER'S CHRISTIANITY: NORSE RELIGION AND JESUS IN NATURE

In the examination of "The Golden Horns" we noted Oehlenschläger's casual unification of Norse and Christian religiosity. In "The Death of Hakon Jarl"[9] [Hakon Jarls Død], another poem from the same revolutionary collection of 1802, we note a deep ambivalence about the historical conquest of Scandinavia by Christianity and the consequent eradication of Norse religion.

The poem depicts the moment of the victorious introduction of Christianity by Olaf Trygvasson and the extermination of the ancient religion which is defended by Hakon Jarl. Oehlenschläger is quite equivocal in his portrayal of the goodness of Christianity and the badness of heathenism. Hakon Jarl is depicted as a betrayed man fighting honorably for a doomed cause, while the Christians seem vain and overconfident.

> [Before the final battle, in the new Christian church,]
> The moonlight rushes through the leaded window
> To the crucifix upon the altar, and smiles:
> 'Thou wilt surely win,
> Thou white Christ!
> Soon the northern latitudes

Will kneel before thy crown of thorns.'

Olaf Trygvasson lands in Norway
And boldly sings the mass upon the white strand.
From gloomy southern castles he brings monks
To the land of cliffs.
The Christian faith spreads more and more.
But mighty Hakon leads the peasants.
For the ancient faith,
In the land of their fathers,
They meet Olaf with brave honor;
But the king divides their gathered armies.
· · · · · · · · · · · · · · · ·
[Things go from bad to worse, but Hakon vows:]
'If every man in Norway became a cowardly slave
I still would not bring shame upon my ancient race. . . .'[10]

Hakon Jarl is murdered by his servant who fears the Christians and toadies to them, and the battle for Christianity is over, the Norse gods vanquished forever. The universe trembles:

Faint thunder rolls on the horizon
And softly shakes the sea and earth.
The varied throng of ancient gods
Disappears and will never again come to the North.
Instead of the august memorials of sacrificial groves,
One finds but churches and cloisters.
Only here and there
And near and far
Does one see a barrow and a giant stone
Which recalls the extinguished flames of antiquity.[11]

Which side does the nominally Christian Oehlenschläger take? We know that he greatly venerated "religiosity," but it seems clear that the ancient Norse religion, inasmuch as it was a hoary and integrated part of its culture and contributed to the sanctification of the life of the people—and was closely connected with "nature"—is seen as more "religious" than the overconfident, alien ("southern") religion of Christ. Christianity can only be admitted as a religion to the extent that it occupies the place in culture from which the Norse pantheon was forcibly ejected.

But there was soon to be a more striking illumination of the dubious nature of Oehlenschläger's Christianity. The long poem *The Life of Jesus Christ Repeated in the Annual Cycle of Nature* appeared in 1805 as a part of the highly successful collection published that year.[12] It was published in 1807 in a German translation under the title of *The Gospel of the Year*, which perhaps gives a better picture of the sort of nature-religion-cum-Christianity contained in the poem. As Oehlenschläger notes in his memoirs, it was written under the influence of

Novalis, who could be called "a beautiful soul" in the purest sense of the word
. . . I was inspired to write the poem *Jesus in Nature* [sic] by the piety in his
glorious hymns, which connected me with the religious feelings I had preserved
from childhood.[13]

Shortly after the poem first appeared in 1805, it was denounced as pantheistic by Bishop Balle, Primate of Denmark. Oehlenschläger himself was about
to leave on his government-sponsored grand tour and was thus prevented from
answering Bishop Balle in direct fashion, which would have been improper in
any case. It was soon decided among Oehlenschläger's circle—Kamma Rahbek,
H. C. Ørsted, and Oehlenschläger's fiancée Christiane Heger—that their promising young clerical friend, J. P. Mynster, then in southern Zealand with his
first parish, should write a review of the poem and defend it against the assaults
of obscurantism. (Mynster's defense and the circumstances surrounding it will
be dealt with in the chapter on Mynster, however, for the incident tells us
more about Mynster than about Oehlenschläger.)

The Life of Jesus Christ Repeated in the Annual Cycle of Nature, as we shall
see below, does indeed admit of a pantheistic reading, and in fact compels it.
Oehlenschläger was to some extent sensible of this fact, and made a number
of changes in later editions. Although these alterations cannot change one's
fundamental impression of the poem, we will examine a few of them, as well
as the general religious message of the poem, in order to gain a clear idea both
of Oehlenschläger's understanding of Christianity (which he shared with much
of the Golden Age) and of his notions about the demands of the regnant
Christian culture, and how they could be met.

The poem transfers the birth of Christ from the onset of winter to that of
spring, the better to coincide with a naturalistic and pantheistic understanding
of religion:

> Every spring, when the fogs disappear
> The little child Jesus is born again
> · · · · · · · · · · · · · ·
> God's angels then come into the field
> And hover and tremble in the moonlight,
> Singing: "Today a savior is born
> Of the womb of spring, of the chaste Mary."[14]

This apparent identification of the Virgin Mary with the spring is reinforced
in "Mary," the second poem of the composite work, where, in the original
version, it is written:

> Mild and warm
> With the sweet child in her arms,
> Young, innocent, chaste, and beautiful,
> She smiles to her beloved son![15]

This was probably found offensive to more orthodox official Christian taste, and in a later edition, apparently to make it clear that springtime and the Virgin Mary are not identical after all, Oehlenschläger changed the final line to: "Springtime smiles to her son. . . ."[16]

Oehlenschläger's romantic-aesthetic Nature religion (in respectable Christian dress) can also be seen in the section entitled "Christ's Manhood" which, in the original version, begins:

> Where wert thou, o chaste spirit?
> Where wert thou, o Jesus sweet?[17]

In a later version of the work, this was changed, first by re-titling the section, "The Flight to the Forest" (again, apparently to emphasize the difference rather than the identity of Jesus and Nature), and then by changing its opening lines to:

> Where wert thou, o spirit of beauty?
> Where wert thou, o boy so sweet?[18]

Many similar changes could be cited, in which Oehlenschläger, eager to please his Christian culture, tinkered with the work in order to make it more acceptable and less intrusive on orthodox precincts. Thus the original section, "Christ's Baptism" (which deals with rain!), is retitled more appropriately as "Heavenly Baptism," allowing Oehlenschläger to make use of the multiple meanings of "heavens," while "Jesus' Miracles" becomes the less offensive "The Miracles."[19] The section entitled "Holy Communion," which is sung in praise of harvest and wine, was concluded in the original version with the remark that, when one drinks wine,

> The sunken faith flames up again,
> It takes root deep in your breast.
> Drink, while you look to heaven,
> For it is the true blood of Jesus.[20]

A later version of this Bacchic Christianity is careful to rely on *double-entendre* and not invoke the name of Jesus:

> The sunken hope flames up again,
> It takes root deep in your breast.
> Drink, while you look to heaven,
> The heavenly-spiritual blood.[21]

In the section entitled "Gethsemane and Golgotha," which deals with the late autumn and the cold and darkness of winter, Oehlenschläger subsequently attempted to modify his poem by changing its referent from the Gospel ("the great and bloody tragedy") to the safer subject of nature ("the great winter pageant"), and the crime of Golgotha is now avenged, not by the apparently supernatural "unknown powers" of the original version, but by mere natural forces ("the powerful storm, the heavens").[22] Similarly, in the section entitled "The Jubilation Hymn of the Disciples," the biblical foe Satan is subsequently softened to the merely natural enemy "darkness."[23]

However, given the very design of the poem, and given Oehlenschläger's essentially formless and pantheistic understanding of Christianity, all these modifications are fruitless. The poet's insistence that "God is everywhere"[24] is quite clearly to be understood romantically and pantheistically and not merely as an expression of the omnipresence of God. Oehlenschläger is apparently nervous about incurring the disapproval of his officially Christian culture, and in "Pentecost," a new section which he added as the concluding poem of the (revised) cycle, he pleads with his readers that the Spirit has filled each of us with the power to speak divinely in our own tongue, i.e., after our own fashion:

> O, you who have just heard the bard sing,
> Do not mistake this pious fantasy!
> For does not every disciple speak in his own tongue?
> And did not he receive his own language, just as you?
> He felt the flame burning upon his temple,
> And enthusiasm loosed the bonds upon his tongue.
> The weary lips of the world speak differently—
> The Holy Spirit reveals itself in many ways.
> · · · · · · · · · · · · · · · · · ·
> And willingly, Jesus, thou united thy holy saga
> With holy nature.[25]

Thus the pentecostal pluralism of the Holy Spirit is invoked to gain acceptance for the very sort of nature religion from which Christianity (and Judaism) has painstakingly sought to distinguish itself since antiquity.

The essence of Oehlenschläger's pantheistic Christianity is thus enshrined in the concluding stanzas of "Simon Peter," which no amount of subsequent "orthodox" tinkering could materially change:

> Does not the eye which once was blind see its Creator?
> Has it finally learned, then, to decipher the mute
> speech?
> Does it find in the splendor of the flowers, in the
> bird's merry song,
> In the voice of the spring waters, in the lively
> swallow of the woods, in the journey of the sun,
> In the great legends of time, in the high sounds of the
> harp,
> In the song of the skald, in the ponderings of the wise,

in the deeds of the hero and the virtue of woman—
Does it find not merely a splendor which is extinguished,
   not merely a life which is suddenly killed,
But an eternal day, which breaks forth from the grave
   of night?
An army of rays of light which sparkle from pole to
   pole,
Which with sure direction are gathered in the splendid
   union of the sun?
Do you not see your Creator's finger pointing
   forward in everything,
Which guides every upward-striving spirit to its proper
   home?
When the thick fog was dispelled from your brave eyes,
   did you see
That in itself everything is nothing, but in all
   everything is all?[26]

Oehlenschläger's enthusiasm for an ill-defined "religiousness," his apparent doubts about the superiority of Christianity to the ancient Norse religion, and the all-engulfing pantheistic flavor of the Christianity that he did embrace ("in itself everything is nothing, but in all everything is all") made N. F. S. Grundtvig dubious about the authenticity of the specifically Christian character of Oehlenschläger's religiosity. Grundtvig himself had had a Schellingian period, but in a terrible period of crisis in 1810 he broke—completely, he felt—with romantic philosophy and promptly set about declaring war upon all that he found Christianly suspect, thereby embroiling himself with a large portion of the Copenhagen intelligentsia, particularly H. C. Ørsted, who saw Grundtvig as self-righteous, intellectually reactionary, and personally pugnacious.

In June 1812, in the midst of these fulminations, Grundtvig wrote Oehlenschläger—who was by then the unquestioned poet-king of the nation—saying: "I know Herr Professor [Oehlenschläger had been appointed titular professor] that you, like so many, regard me as an enthusiast and a fanatic, and it does not surprise me at all; but you can believe me that I am not."[27] Grundtvig explains that he has never dreamed of being Oehlenschläger's equal as a poet, for, as he writes, "I strive every day to use my talents only as a means in the service of Christianity."[28] Grundtvig freely admits that this religious purpose has harmed the aesthetic proportions of his work, that "being placed at the service of Christianity has damaged its poetic wholeness and that it is not a beautiful work of art."[29] Knowing that he, or his work, has won Oehlenschläger's firm disapproval, Grundtvig asks: "Is it perhaps my Christianity which offends you?"[30] Grundtvig then turns to what worries him in Oehlenschläger's work. He is not blind to the great beauty of Oehlenschläger's poetry, but, he writes, the fact that

religious seriousness is increasingly absent from your poems and that it is replaced in your most recent poems by a certain playing with spiritual things,
causes me an inner sadness. It hurts me most of all because such a change must
have its cause in the innermost being of the poet; it must be a consequence of
the fact that the poet abandons serious consideration of his own spiritual relation
to God, as His servant on earth—that he [the poet] places more stress upon his
own splendor, upon winning honor and approval, than upon elevating his brothers to the worship of God in spirit and in truth.[31]

Oehlenschläger's reply shows us a great deal about his conception of Christianity, and about the extent to which Grundtvig's accusations, tactlessly
phrased though they might have been, were justified. Oehlenschläger writes:

Instead of merely adhering to the sensory image of Christ, the poet seeks to
communicate the *spirit* of Christianity in a series of sensory images. This is his
calling, and no poetic art can exist without it. Eternal love has revealed itself all
ages, both before and after Christ. He himself stands as the most beautiful and
holy example of the union of the divine and the human. . . . In my view, the
true Christian is the person who reveals his faith in his works and who walks
openly, kindly, and cheerfully upon the industrious path to the truth, attentively
observing upon his wanderings the least straw in nature, as well as the great
sea in the heavens in which Omnipotence, All-Goodness, and Absolute Beauty
[Almagten, Algodheden, og Alskiønhed] reflect themselves.[32]

Oehlenschläger's religion thus reveals itself as a sentimental blending of
humanity and pantheism, dressed in the historical costume of Christianity. As
a close friend of Oehlenschläger's put it, Oehlenschläger "viewed Christ and
his doctrines from a naturalistic-poetic point of view."[33] Although he modified
his expression of this "Christianity" a bit (as in the later version of the Jesus-
Nature poem) in order to meet the more obvious objections of his more orthodox critics, Oehlenschläger never really understood that there was any fundamental difference between his Christianity and that of his critics and attributed their dissatisfaction to their own misunderstandings.[34]

Oehlenschläger's romantic disciple, the poet and playwright (and occasional natural scientist) Carsten Hauch, shared his master's "naturalistic-poetic
point of view" in religion and gave classical expression to the Golden Age
aesthetic understanding of religion in a statement from 1815, where he writes
that:

An eye for divinity is indispensable for deeper poetry. Therefore all true poets
have felt themselves involuntarily carried away by a deep religiosity; *poetry must
be the poet's innermost religion, just as, conversely, his religion must appear as
poetry*. Religion is the fundamental support of all art; it is art itself—*only with
the eye of the genius do we comprehend the idea of God*—and the most natural
thing of all.[35]

This Christianity was Schellingian "religiousness," a monism in which the crucial gap between reality and appearances, between noumena and phenomena, a distinction inherited by orthodox Christianity, has been blurred over or even bridged. The resulting sentimental piety saw "the True, the Good, and the Beautiful" as interchangeable and omnipresent—though of course they found their most perfect expression in Jesus, whom, as we have seen, Oehlenschläger calls "the most beautiful and holy example of the union of the divine and the human." This was the standard literary Christianity of the Golden Age. As we shall see, the leading clerics of the cultural elite either accepted this Christianity or, when they could not, attempted to compromise with it and lead it into somewhat more orthodox paths. Only rarely would a man such as Bishop Mynster, pressed as he was on other fronts by uproarious peasants and hyperorthodox Grundtvigians, ever attempt publicly to correct his life-long friends and allies, the literary "Christians" of Golden Age Copenhagen. The heart-felt acceptance by these Golden Age Christians of the religiosity that they called Christianity, and the status of this elite group as the creators of culture, made them valuable allies of men such as Mynster. He needed their support in the defense of urbane, conservative Christian culture or Christendom (which was a composite of worldly and religious elements) against the depredations of secular liberalism and enthusiastic populism.

D. OEHLENSCHLÄGER'S POLITICAL VIEWS

In politics Oehlenschläger typified what might be called the slightly more "progressive" wing of the apolitical conservatism of the Golden Age elite. He had retained a bourgeois distaste for hereditary nobility from his young manhood in the 1790's, and in his memoirs he writes that:

> All my life I have had strong feelings about human rights. . . . I soon came to the conviction that nobility is a remnant from the Middle Ages which really no longer has any significance. It did not seem to me to stand like a venerable old cathedral in a lovely flowering landscape, but as an old chest of drawers which took up too much space in a room with more practical furnishings.[36]

On the other hand, Oehlenschläger's dislike of this sort of nobility must not be interpreted as allied to any liberal or populist tendencies, for as a romantic artist, he preached the doctrine of a new sort of aristocracy, that of his own Aladdin, of the cult of genius, of "the rare few." This new type of aristocracy quickly won acclaim and recognition from the older, traditional social elites, and soon the more rebellious features of romanticism had been domesticated by this acceptance, even to the point of Oehlenschläger's attempt—unsuccessful, as we have seen—to tone down his pantheistic version of Christianity.

Thus, in his memoirs the bourgeois Oehlenschläger relates the great joy he took from the reception accorded him by nobility.

It is therefore not surprising that, immediately following the passage in his memoirs cited above, in which he recounted his distaste for nobility, Oehlenschläger launches into a defense of monarchy as the guarantor of the proper working atmosphere for the man of talent, the artist-genius. Politics and public life could only disturb the impartial recognition of talent, and monarchy is thus to be preferred, not as a form of politics, but as a *preventative* of politics. Oehlenschläger writes that

> The king was always holy to me; I early came to feel what was lordly, beautiful, and beneficial in that form, as in nature itself. . . . A poet, an artist, cannot do other than love monarchy. It is the right of the heart over the cold, slow sophistry which pays homage to mere external form and makes absolutely no exceptions, even those required by nature. According to its nature, monarchy is non-partisan and devoid of jealousy, and allows every merit to have its right, because it stands over them all. The poet and the artist must love monarchy, because the [royal] splendor can be ennobled unto beauty and has need of the beautiful. But the genius is envied and easily crushed by the cold, ambitious reasonableness of the crowd, who only look out for their daily domestic needs. The artist must indeed love noble and reasonable freedom, for everything great and beautiful and good must move freely. But he must hate the worship of *equality*. The excellent is found only in the exception, and where everything is equally good, then everything is equally bad, and the trivial reigns.[37]

Thus, even while he remained personally opposed to the snobbish pretentions of hereditary nobility, Oehlenschläger shared with the majority of his Golden Age intellectual colleagues a distaste for and a fear of the liberalism of the 1830's and 1840's, perhaps because of the gradual alliance of that movement with the more frightening and egalitarian demands of the peasantry.

In late March 1848, after the revolution which brought a liberal-dominated ministry to power and which held out the expectation of liberal constitutionalism, Oehlenschläger again expressed his belief in the elitism which was so typical of Golden Age intellectuals:

> There is something good and beautiful about the power of the king and of the royal court in certain areas, with respect to the favor and reward which may be preferred by excellent men, by the talented. Republican egalitarianism goes too far, so that in the end there is no difference between merit and lack of merit, because envy has been allowed too much free play.[38]

A year later, in the Spring of 1849, when the constitution was being debated, Oehlenschläger's remarks were blunter: "God grant that they might be able to limit the suffrage somewhat; otherwise we will all end up in the mud."[39] In the end, Oehlenschläger could live with a regime which extended the franchise to the liberal bourgeoisie, but he was greatly alarmed, as were most Golden Age intellectuals and a great many liberals as well, at the prospect of a universal (male) suffrage which would truly make the life of the state a *res publica* and would give a decisive voice to the vast rural mass, to the common man.

The fairest summary of Oehlenschläger's politics is perhaps to be found in a poem first published in 1846, entitled "The Progress of the Present Age" [Nutidens Fremskridt],[40] a monitory piece which is skeptically addressed to the present age, with all its purported excellences:

> You will mightily protect freedom and equality,
> And have put your greatest pride in this effort.
> But what is the landscape of the spirit without
> mountains?
> And what is everything, when everything is equally
> flat?[41]

Oehlenschläger's friend and colleague, the progress-oriented H. C. Ørsted, sums up the most generous position which the Golden Age could muster on political questions, namely the hope that tutelage by the elite would gradually lead to the progress of the other classes: "Genuine liberality seems to me to consist in trying to clear the way for the uncultivated to achieve the same intellectual heights, but not in giving them, without preparation, all the power which is naturally and properly possessed by enlightened opinion."[42] This is a typical and recurrent view of the conservative Golden Age mainstream, a view which we will encounter again in Heiberg, who also felt that the masses are to be taken into the tutelage of the cultivated. There is no irony or self-consciousness present in this position. It is the straightforward transmission of "culture" [Dannelse] from the greater to the lesser. Power, on the other hand, is not to be shared, and the responsibility for the exercise of power, when it is shared (as in universal suffrage), is not in itself cultivating. Power, in this view, can be legitimated only by culture, of which the urban elite is the sole creator and arbiter, whereas culture, for its part, could never stem from anything so vulgar as power.

10. Piety and Good Taste: J. P. Mynster's Religion and Politics

O

A. BACKGROUND AND THE SPJELLERUP "BREAKTHROUGH"

Jakob Peter Mynster was born in 1775 and was soon orphaned. His father died a bit over a year after his birth, and his mother, who had meanwhile married F. L. Bang, the Head Physician at the Royal Hospital, died about two years later, leaving little Jakob and his older brother Ole Heironymos to be raised by Dr. Bang, who, according to Jakob's later account, was a stern parent, a narrow and stuffy pietist. As a child, Jakob seems to have been quite shy and burdened with feelings of inferiority, and he rankled at being outshone by his more extroverted older brother, who soon followed in the footsteps of their stepfather and became a brilliant physician. In his early years as a university student, Jakob was a minor member of a radical student group dominated by his older brother and by Carl Heger, the brother of Christiane Heger (later Oehlenschläger's wife) and of Kamma Heger Rahbek, whose salon dominated the Copenhagen literary scene. Mynster was thus affiliated with the leading cultural circles and also had the youthful flirtation with radicalism in politics and religion which seems to have been obligatory for so many young men of the late eighteenth century, who later became nineteenth-century conservatives.

Radical politics and fringe membership in a fast literary set did not deter Mynster from taking his degree in theology in 1794, at the rather early age of nineteen. Mynster seems to have been an uncertain and insecure youth who was not wholly satisfied by the politics or religion of the radical Enlightenment, but who was also haunted by a feeling that he was unable to give himself wholly to Christianity. One of the reasons young Mynster had studied theology in first place was his stepfather's harsh judgment that Jakob was not clever enough to follow a career in medicine or natural science as his older brother had done,[1] and this sense of being second-best and an outsider, both in his brother's circle of friends and in his own relation to Christianity, seems to have weighed heavily upon the young Mynster. After passing his university examinations in 1794, the young theological graduate followed the not unusual course of seeking a position as a private tutor to a wealthy family, while he delayed seeking a call to a local parish, a delay which, in Mynster's case, was probably dictated as much by his own doubts as by his extreme youth. Mynster spent the next eight years as tutor to an enlightened aristocratic family and immersed himself in German romantic poetry and the philosophy of Kant and Schelling, while he also maintained correspondence and close friendship with the friends of his student days, including the young Henrik Steffens.[2]

Although the inner ferment and uncertainty in his personal life had not reached any clarification, and although he had not come into any profound and affirmative relation to Christianity, Mynster finally sought a parish. In 1802 he became pastor in the country village of Spjellerup in southern Zealand, where he remained until 1811. Mynster took up his pastorate with a troubled conscience, he notes in his remarkable and candid memoirs, for even though he was now to shepherd these humble souls, he still experienced within himself "the same lack and unrest which had embittered me for so many years ... Christ's Gospel was far from being clear to me;" Schelling, Steffens, and Novalis had brought him closer to Christian ideas, but "the Gospel story had almost exclusively poetic value for me."[3] The religiosity of the common people whom Mynster served was bound up with the historical truth of the Gospels, however, and Mynster therefore saw it as his duty to combat "the rationalists" who denied the historicity of the Gospel story. Therefore, Mynster presented the Gospel as historical truth, even though he "did not speak out of [my] own conviction," and even though he paused many times in his enthusiasm to ask himself: "But is this true and actual?"[4] In his memoirs, Mynster frankly reports that in his first year at Spjellerup he not only suffered from the self-torment of hypocrisy but that he "really suffered from" the feelings which had plagued him since his youth in Copenhagen: "the deep wants of a love-thirsty soul," "unsatisfied ambition," and "vanity."[5]

The unresolved problems of his adolescence compounded the self-doubt and hypocrisy engendered by his new career until, after a year at Spjellerup, in the summer of 1803, the air was finally cleared when—as Mynster reports—there "took place in my inner life a 'breakthrough' which was as definite and sudden as has ever taken place in any man's soul."[6] Mynster's account of his breakthrough is of great importance in assessing the content of his religion, and he summarizes the experience as follows:

> If conscience is not a meaningless figment of the imagination—and I had no doubts that it was not—then, if you must obey it in one thing, you must obey it in everything, without exception; you must act and speak in accordance with your duty, as fully as you know and are capable of, entirely unconcerned about the world's judgment, its praise or blame. And if there is a God—and there was likewise no doubt in my heart about this—and you do not refuse to bow before him and devote yourself to his will in *some things*, then you must do so in *everything*, without reservations, and entirely, quite entirely, entrust yourself and

all your concerns to his fatherly hand, being satisfied with the abilities which he apportions you and enduring the wants he assigns you. I had often made similar observations, but now the weight fell with full force upon the words "entirely, without reservations." . . . [A]t that instant my whole being focussed upon this knowledge, and commitment fused together with this knowledge. Then a peace such as I had never known dawned, or rather descended, into my soul, "the peace of God, which passes all understanding" . . . [and Mynster then came to realize that there is] an inexpressible Good . . . not of flesh and blood . . . but which belongs to a higher order of things which always comes close to man.

But I would scarcely have come to Christ that way if I had not already approached him, or him me, via another path [i.e., Bible study, etc.]. . . . [As for the truth of the Gospels, which had long been a source of trouble, Mynster now came to realize that] the acceptance of the truth of the Gospel accounts really depends upon the need to do so. Where that has awakened, all the doubts and uncertainties which remain disappear easily. . . .

I had had to feel myself utterly and painfully abandoned in the world in order to find what is the highest and most blessed of all. And nothing can compare with the delight, the internal jubilation, with which I said to myself: "I have a God and a Savior!"[7]

It was with this sudden sense of self-assurance that Mynster's successful career and steady ascent to the Primacy of Denmark began. He himself noted gladly that his self-confidence convinced not only himself, but others, of his sincerity and orthodoxy. Mynster was pleased to learn that his friend Steffens, after having visited him at Spjellerup and heard him preach, wrote home approvingly to his wife: "You should see that—a person can be a preacher and still be religious."[8]

B. THE RELIGION OF THE BREAKTHROUGH: STOICAL ENLIGHTENMENT DEISM IN ORTHODOX CHRISTIAN DRESS

The most thorough and judicious examination of Mynster's theology is undoubtedly the critical work of Kristoffer Olesen Larsen, who contends that for all Mynster's criticism of Enlightenment "rationalism," the religion of the "breakthrough" and afterwards was merely a lofty stoicism, a personally appropriated ethical religiousness, or what Kierkegaard would call "religiousness A." Mynster's religion, Olesen Larsen contends, was not a specifically Christian form of religiousness, which involves a radical break with our ordinary ethical understanding of world and self. Olesen Larsen writes:

Duty and Providence, conscience and the grace of Providence, these are the expressions around which Mynster's preaching concentrates itself. And indeed, this content is nothing new, Mynster says, but as old as the world; nor is it foreign to man, but is in agreement with his conscience and heart.[9]

Olesen Larsen concludes that, when one examines the content and the rhetoric of Mynster's religion, one sees that all his tribulations and insecurities had merely brought Mynster to "the Enlightenment's understanding of Christianity, plus the demand for personal appropriation of this."[10] It is Olesen Larsen's contention that for Mynster "Christianity is the 'historical costume' of Enlightenment religion, just as Enlightenment religion is the 'generalization' of Christianity,"[11] and that "in Mynster we do not encounter anything, from beginning to end, other than bourgeois humanism which has been united with a faith in Providence and dressed in orthodox expressions."[12]

Is Olesen Larsen's interpretation correct? Let us examine a few of Mynster's important sermons and his *Observations upon the Doctrines of the Christian Faith* [*Betragtninger over de christelige Troeslærdomme*], Mynster's popular, mature presentation of Christianity, in order to sample his religion and evaluate it for ourselves.

Although it is presumably the duty of a Christian preacher to make the specifically Christian gospel the principal message of every sermon, quite a number of Mynster's sermons seem to come no further than the general message of Providence, duty, and conscience which was the content of the Spjellerup breakthrough, and which Olesen Larsen has labelled mere "Enlightenment religion." In one such early sermon, which the young Mynster published in his popular collection of "Spjellerup sermons," Mynster's religion seems to be the melancholy resignation of the book of Ecclesiastes: "The more we observe the transitoriness of things, the more we are convinced that they do not have their beginning or their being in themselves."[13] This fleetingness of things leads one to a sense of God: "[M]an is like the flowers of the field, resplendent as they are in their brief beauty, and soon withered again, as they are; throughout all this the praise of God must always be heard, and this must strengthen our hearts."[14] But in the midst of this beauty and decay God has "ignited in us a spark of his life, elevated over the mutability of things, as he is elevated; immortal, as he is eternal."[15] "[D]eep within our breasts, our hearts give witness; from deep within us our conscience unites its holy voice with his [God's] word, to give witness that he is righteous. . . ."[16] Thus the melancholy face of the world directs us to the existence of the unchanging Deity, who has implanted within us a divine spark, a conscience, which witnesses to his unchanging righteousness.

This religion of conscience and duty is developed more explicitly in "The Value of Good Intentions," another of Mynster's Spjellerup sermons.

> We recognize conscience as the voice of God, as the stamp of our higher destiny, as the connection between earthly and heavenly life. . . . We must first of all allow it to speak to us as clearly as possible, for what often causes our unrest

and pain is that the demands of conscience are obscure to us. . . . [W]e must make duty clear to ourselves.[17]

But we must not expect too much of ourselves, for Mynster's religion is one, above all, of moderation, not of asceticism: "It is low and unworthy to will too little, but it can also be harmful to will too much. . . . [W]e will soon find that we can only come to peace by means of a serious and honest intention of perfect obedience."[18] Thus the religion put forth is one of conscience, of interiority, of the *intention* of obedience, and yet also one of moderation and of a "peace" which is attainable through human resignation. The individual must come firmly to the conclusion that

> I will follow the promptings of my conscience; I will do my duty however difficult it seems to me . . . for the demands of conscience do not admit of being refused; they are not conquered by the dishonest understanding, however many excuses it invents; the demands of conscience continue to punish the disobedient will and are only reconciled by your honest intention no longer to refuse, your intention to submit to what conscience requires; then it will reward you with the priceless peace which it alone can bestow.[19]

Thus peace is to be attained through the intention of absolute obedience to conscience; that is, it is not absolute obedience—the unattainable—which is required, but the intention of doing so, and this intention is attainable by us. In these sermons Mynster's religion does indeed appear as a lofty, personalized stoicism, clad in the rhetoric of Christianity, just as was the breakthrough which preceded these eloquent sermons and made them possible.

This same sermon on "good intentions" repeats the account of the Spjellerup breakthrough almost word for word:

> It profits us but little if we submit in one thing or another, but not in everything. . . . We must ultimately, with a truthful and honest intention, decide in our innermost being that we will obey it [conscience] without exception; that we will submit to it without reservations; and that, whatever it is which is required of us—easy or difficult, whether we have a desire to do it or not, whether it will go well or ill for us in the world—that we still will not refuse, but will do our duty according to what God requires by means of our conscience.[20]

"Therefore," as Mynster concludes his eloquent call to duty and intention, "I will do my duty as fully as I am capable, willingly and without concern, leaving everything else to him, who alone is able to rule. Whoever says this seriously has thereby become a new man."[21] This concluding sentence gives us the surest indication of how far Mynster's religion of duty and conscience is from Pauline Christianity. For Mynster the "new man" is born out of the stoical submission to the demands of conscience, while no mention is made of such categories as sin, grace, or rebirth in Christ. Stoical obedience and resignation give peace, and it is this peace which is labelled the "new man," a man who is certainly not identical with the "new being" of St. Paul. Mynster preaches merely the peace attendant upon the sincere *intention* of absolute obedience, and assures his listener that "this intention gives him the courage to face every fate," and that, having humbled himself in the intention of obedience, "he is sure of the approval of the Most High; he is reconciled with God, and therefore God lets his peace descend into his heart."[22] Clearly the "peace" promised by these two sermons of the Spjellerup period seems to be the peace of a profound and stoical Enlightenment deism, a peace of resignation, of duty, of submission to the demands of conscience, of the intention of absolute obedience. One looks in vain for the specifically Christian joy which is founded upon grace and rebirth in Christ.

In order to assess the extent of the Christian element in Mynster's religion (when Mynster chose particularly to emphasize that element), let us look at a later, more specifically Christian sermon which Mynster preached in 1817 on the occasion of the 500th anniversary of the Reformation. The Reformation jubilee sermon was entitled "The Importance of Faith in Jesus Christ as the Son of God and the Savior of Man," a title which seems to promise that here we will finally penetrate to the heart of Mynster's Christology. In assessing the special function of Jesus Christ, Mynster states that

> we need a *divine teacher*, whose words have a higher authority than merely human speech. Our reason is indeed capable of reasoning its way to knowledge about God and his Providence, yet man's ideas would not have been awakened without a higher reminder. . . . [W]e need a reminder which can speak to us with a higher authority and tell each of us: "Look here and know what is God's will and your duty!"[23]

Thus, Christ's divinity is conceded, but only as a *psychological* necessity which makes the Enlightenment religion of duty more real and pressing to us, for whom reason is weak and clouded and who thus need a "reminder."

Mynster's sermon continues in this vein:

> We need a *revelation by means of which God comes nearer to us*. For God is of course never far from us, and in blessed hours we often feel that we live, move, and have our being in God. But often we also feel that God dwells in a light to which no one can come; our thought cannot comprehend him, no more than our words can describe his being.[24]

Thus, Christ's being does not change anything. God exists in our midst, and we have unassisted certainty of this in some few "blessed hours." We cannot sustain this certainty unaided, however, and as "revelation" Christ serves to meet our psychological need to remain continuously assured of what is already the case. "We need a *redeemer*, who . . . can give us the full assurance that there is forgiveness for the repentant."[25] Again, in Mynster's Christology Christ has a primarily psychological function: even before Christ's revelation, the sins of the repentant are forgiven, but we need Christ in order to obtain "full assurance" of this fact.

Peace with God is thus seen as a psychic, rather than an ontological state; a psychological, rather than a soteriological event. Thus, "it is true that, guided by God's revelation, reason does indeed conclude securely that the better part of our being is immortal . . . [but] we need *a conqueror of death* to confirm to us that life is eternal."[26] Thus, just as God is always in our midst, just as the sins of the repentant are forgiven, so too is "the better part of our being immortal." All these facts are accessible to us prior to and extraneous of the revelation, incarnation, and redemptive acts of Jesus Christ; all these facts are accessible to us within a stoical Enlightenment Christianity, a religion within the limits of reason alone. But they are not vivid or reliable enough in this state, and the reality of Jesus Christ gives the individual a necessary psychological assist: In order truly to be made sensible of all these fundamentals of Enlightenment religion, we need Christ, not so much as the radical transformer of the nature of being but as guarantor of the truthfulness of what we already grasp by our earthly lights.

This sense of Christ as the psychologically necessary guarantor of the vividness of the truths of natural Enlightenment religion can also be seen to inform the Christology of Mynster's important collection of sermons from 1823, by which time he had become well established in Copenhagen as an extemely popular and "anti-rationalist" pastor and preacher at the important Church of Our Lady. The 1823 collection was to be the last important group of sermons Mynster published prior to his elevation to the Primacy of Denmark eleven years later. One of the sermons in the 1823 collection which focusses most consciously upon the specifically Christian element of Mynster's general religious message was "On the Great Good of Being a Christian," in which Mynster asks his audience: "Don't you need some assurance which can tell you that God is gracious?"[27] Christ, Mynster tells us, brings us "the firm word of divinity," "the sure claim upon the grace of the Almighty."[28] "God dwells in a light which no one can approach; the earthly eye is blinded by his majesty,"[29] and we mortals therefore have need of Christ to communicate God's message to us. Man needs "a friend from Heaven, on whose breast he can lean his weary head."[30] Thus, again, we have a psychological or pedagogical rather than an ontological or soteriological need for Christ in order to attain peace and "rest our weary heads." This merely psychological, subjective understanding of Christianity is the direct consequence of the content of the 1803 Spjellerup "breakthrough," which flowed from the realization that "the acceptance of the truth of the Gospel account depends upon one's *need* to do so." Mynster very revealingly concludes this 1823 sermon with the exclamation: "Lord! Show us the Father, and that is enough for us!"[31] The purpose of Jesus Christ in Mynster's

Christology is to serve as a personal reinforcement of the truth of Enlightenment religion and not to change that religion or the human *being* itself.

We will conclude this examination of the content of Mynster's Christianity by referring briefly to his *Observations* from 1833, which were the enormously popular capstone of Mynster's reputation and which were published just prior to his elevation to the Bishopric of Zealand and the Primacy of Denmark. In the remaining twenty years of his busy career, Mynster had little time for further scholarly and theological labors, as his time was completely given to the disputes of ecclesiastical and secular politics and to an attempt to impose order upon the chaotic situation of official Danish Christendom. Thus, for all practical purposes, the *Observations* of 1833 formed the conclusion of Mynster's mature understanding of Christianity and can also serve as the final exhibit, both in our investigation of Mynster's Christology and in our evaluation of Olesen Larsen's characterization of Mynster's religion as a mere "bourgeois humanism which has been united with a faith in Providence and dressed in orthodox expressions."

In the *Observations* Christ is once again presented to us as the psychological guarantor of God's gracious Providence. The fundamental truth about existence, Mynster tells us, is "the truth that divine governance embraces everything which happens on earth, the least as well as the greatest, [and this truth] is of course no more sublime than that it can be grasped by every human understanding and felt by every human heart."[32] Thus, the fundamental truth is nothing specifically Christian, but is the truth of Providence, the truth of natural religion, which can be grasped by every person prior to, and independent of, the revelation in Jesus Christ. Why, then, do we need Christianity? The answer is psychological: Although the reality of an all-powerful and gracious Providence is easy to grasp in good times, one doubts this reality in the more crushing of "life's movements," Mynster explains.[33] Therefore, we "need such an external Word of faith [Christ's Word] which can assure us of God's grace and bring us to hold still our tongues in the face of the salvation of the Lord."[34]

Olesen Larsen's assertions seem to be well-grounded. Mynster's Christ is "a divine teacher," "a reminder," "an external Word" which "assures" us of the validity of the pre-existent and occasionally accessible truths of Enlightenment religion, and the proper attitude in the face of this Deity is resignation, submission, the intention of following one's conscience and of doing one's duty absolutely. Christ does not transform us in our attempts at ethical religion but assures us and strengthens us in our endeavor by vouching for the fact that God is indeed what natural religion, however fleetingly or imperfectly, perceives him as being. If rationalism means a cold and impersonal religion of ethical universals and utility, then Mynster is surely the enemy of rationalism. But, for all his willingness to employ Christian terminology, it scarcely appears that he has abandoned the stoicism and natural religion so characteristic of the Enlightenment. If orthodoxy means adherence to ecclesiastical discipline and a willingness to use Christian terminology, Mynster was certainly orthodox. But if orthodoxy means adherence to Pauline notions of the radical transformation which takes place in the Christian person, then Mynster appears to be situated in the same camp as the "rationalists" whose eloquent opponent he was. Mynster was far more "orthodox" in appearance than most in his age, and he built his reputation and his career upon his steady and determined opposition to what he saw as the impersonality and emotional flatness of eighteenth-century religion. The historian must recognize the sources of Mynster's claim to orthodoxy and must view as sincere his sense of having broken with his past and his surroundings. However, an investigator living in the century of Karl Barth and neo-orthodoxy is not bound to accept uncritically Mynster's self-evaluation and the evaluation accorded him by the Golden Age as its most "profound" and "orthodox" interpreter of Christianity.

C. OEHLENSCHLÄGER DEFENDED

The first time that Mynster appeared in print under his own name was in the autumn of 1805 in a poetic defense of his good friend Adam Oehlenschläger's Jesus-Nature poem (which was examined in the previous chapter). Oehlenschläger was understandably nervous about the reception that official Christianity would accord his poem. As it turned out, the poem was soon publicly attacked by Bishop Balle, the conservative Primate of Denmark, who had acquired a reputation as a staunch defender and definer of Christian orthodoxy. As noted in the previous chapter, Oehlenschläger was about to leave on his grand tour and was unable to defend himself, which would have been unseemly in any event. Thus, Oehlenschläger and his friends, including the powerful Rahbek, decided to ask their brilliant young theologian-colleague Mynster, who was now the zealous and unimpeachably orthodox pastor of Spjellerup, to write a review of Oehlenschläger's poems.

Mynster's own retrospective account of how he came to write the review of Oehlenschläger's work is rather brief and vague—particularly with respect to the apparent agony of conscience which was associated with it—but he recalls having been "pressured" by Oehlenschläger, Rahbek, and others to provide a review of the censured and putatively pantheistic poem.[35] Mynster also recalls that "I myself also very much wanted to contribute to gaining them the appreciation they deserved;" however, he did not feel himself capable of analyzing each of Oehlenschläger's poems in detail, and "in order to rescue myself in this matter, I decided to express myself in verse, so that I could avoid these difficulties."[36] This is pretty much the whole of Mynster's recollection in his memoirs of his literary debut, in which he did a favor for a well-connected literary friend at the risk of betraying his own newly won sense of orthodoxy. However, if we examine the correspondence that passed among these friends at the time, we can gain a more precise sense of what was at stake and of the degree to which Mynster was willing to sacrifice his sense of piety in order to come to terms with what was clearly becoming the good literary taste of the new Golden Age.

Mynster's closest epistolary friend and confidante was Kamma Rahbek, the powerful salon hostess and literary wife who was soon to become Oehlenschläger's sister-in-law. In an undated letter of the early summer of 1805, Mynster writes to Kamma that he is generally pleased with Oehlenschläger's new poems but would like to escape, if possible, the difficult task of reviewing them:

> I have certainly wanted to review him, but I also see that it would both be difficult for me to find time for it now, if I am also to work on my sermons [which he was preparing for publication], and, more importantly, that *I can scarcely review him in such a way that both of us and the matter are well-served by it.* . . . . [S]ay to him [Oehlenschläger] that if I do not review him—and I have not yet given up the will to do so—he must by no means think that it is out of indifference toward him, toward poetry, or toward his poems. If I do not write a review, it will only be because I have been denied clarity of internal light.[37]

Mynster is clearly being evasive, for he finds it hard to say something politic, something that will see "both of us and the matter well-served," something that will free his fashionable literary friend from the charge of pantheistic impiety while still protecting his own sense of—and perhaps his reputation for—orthodoxy. Mynster is clearly afraid of being put into a position in which he will be forced publicly to choose between his orthodoxy—which we have seen to be at most rather diluted—and his ties with the literary circle which stood at the center of Danish cultural life.

On July 8, 1805 Kamma Rahbek replied to Mynster, reporting that Oehlenschläger had not been entirely pleased with Mynster's reluctance: "He has asked me repeatedly if I really couldn't get you to review him—but I dare not plague you further."[38]

Two days later (July 10, 1805) Oehlenschläger himself wrote to his reluctant clerical friend and noted that he has now received Mynster's greetings and messages via Kamma, continuing:

> as far as I could make out, you have half given up your decision to review me, which hurts me a great deal, for I must confess that I think you are the only person in the Kingdom of Denmark (including Norway) capable of doing this. If my entreaty is capable of anything with you, do not give this up. It doesn't have to be so lengthy, you know. A couple of strong words by a reasonable man can keep a good deal of gossip and slander off the streets. . . . It always has a good effect and it impresses the crowd when they hear that there are *many* who share the same opinion. It is generally the *duty* of the few who live together

in this befogged age to join together into a league and act with united strength, each according to his conviction and his character.[39]

Oehlenschläger is clearly becoming quite nervous about the effect that criticism of the Jesus-Nature poem might have upon respectable opinion, and he appeals to Mynster's perennially low self-esteem by offering him what amounts to a charter membership in "the rare few" if he will but overcome his reluctance and, with "a couple of strong words," lend his orthodox reputation to the cause of good poetry. The Jesus-Nature poem itself is still the unspoken bone of contention, and neither has yet dared mention that this poem is at the root of Mynster's reluctance.

On July 19, 1805, Mynster finally broached the problem in a forthright reply to Oehlenschläger in which he neither promises to review the poem nor withdraws his original offer to do so.

> Thanks especially for your poems which have particularly brought me joy. It will not surprise you that part of what is in the poetry is not entirely according to my lights, but you will learn *how much* it is in accordance with them if, God willing, I write about them. . . . It will be particularly difficult for me to say anything profitable and reasonable about the Jesus poem, for I do not possess a philosophy of Christianity, not even fragments of one, that I would need for such a purpose. As soon as I can I will tear myself away from what I am now doing and try what I can.[40]

Given the fact that we know from Mynster's memoirs that he had made a significant "breakthrough" in his understanding of Christianity in the summer of 1803, his protestations of being unfit to review the Jesus-Nature poem because he did not have even the "fragments" of a "philosophy of Christianity" is not entirely truthful, and is in fact a polite excuse. The truth is that Mynster's new orthodoxy, even such as it was, was totally incapable of lending support to the sentimentality and romantic pantheism of Oehlenschläger's disputed poem. Mynster comes much nearer the truth when he says that "the Jesus poem" is "particularly difficult" precisely because it is hard to say anything about it which is both "profitable and reasonable": If Mynster is to say anything "reasonable" (i.e., truthful) about his understanding of the Jesus-Nature poem, it will be "profitable" neither to Oehlenschläger nor to himself, while if he says something which is "profitable" to Oehlenschläger and himself, it will not be "reasonable" (i.e., truthful). Such was Mynster's dilemma.

On the same day that he wrote the above letter to Oehlenschläger (July 19th), Mynster also wrote to Kamma Rahbek, assuring her that he had not given up the intention of reviewing Oehlenschläger and asking her to inquire of her review editor husband, K. L. Rahbek, which particular journal would carry his review.[41] Shortly thereafter, on August 5, 1805, Oehlenschläger departed for Germany on the first leg of his grand tour, and the correspondence ceases for a time. Finally, on August 27, 1805, a senior member of the literary circle, the prestigious H. C. Ørsted, wrote to Mynster in Spjellerup, informing him that he has been "asked to request that you provide a review of Oehlenschläger's *Poetical Writings* as soon as time permits," and he adds a personal note, stating that

> I hope you follow through on your intention [to review Oehlenschläger] for the sake of the good cause. I am already happy about it, in the expectation that your review will lead to others, and that the Good thus will gain one more friend who *loudly* defends its cause.[42]

Once again, a powerful friend is reminding the vacillating Mynster of his membership in the cultural elite and of his obligation to defend the good taste of the romantic movement, "the good cause," against the vulgar obscurantists.

The literary elite showered even more attention upon the hapless Mynster, and two times in the course of their vacation in the late summer of 1805 the Rahbeks visited Mynster at his rural parsonage in Spjellerup. Oehlenschläger's poem and Mynster's obligation to review it cannot have failed to be an important item on the agenda of conversation, for we still have a letter of Kamma to Oehlenschläger from early October 1805, in which Kamma conveys Mynster's greetings to the poet and mentions their vacation visits to Spjellerup. She informs Oehlenschläger that she had suggested to Mynster that he focus only upon the Jesus-Nature poem in his review. (Since he was not an aesthetician but a cleric, Mynster's support was only needed or valuable at this point in any event.) She also notes that she appreciates Mynster's difficulty, but has confidence that Mynster will produce something suitable, even though, as she notes, "I cannot stand the fact that it is taking so long."[43]

Finally, in October 1805, Mynster finished his review of Oehlenschläger, a lengthy encomium in verse, and sent it to the journal editors for publication. A representative excerpt from Mynster's poem will make it clear that Mynster capitulated to the pressures which the Copenhagen literary elite had brought to bear upon him. He distorted his newfound sense of orthodox Christianity—feeble though it might be when viewed in Barthian categories—in order to affirm his membership in the inner circle, the "rare few" of the Golden Age and to pledge his allegiance to good taste and high culture by giving the new poetry his stamp of Christian approval.

To Adam Oehlenschläger

Whoever, free from the slavery of life,
Knows how to look undisturbedly within himself
Will also see the flame in nature
Which burns everywhere with holy splendor.
. . . .
Therefore—o friend!—I gladly and with festive joy

Have felt the sublime sound of your harp.
I have heard the powerful refrain, long silent,
Resound in your song.

Tell, who has revealed to your eye
The visions which the eye of the crowd has never seen?
. . . .
Who has shown you the life which deeply
Conceals itself in the thickets of the wood and the caves of
the mountain?

Indeed, the poet! His wealthy heart conceals
A world which is always born anew.
. . . .
The power to create heaven within our breast
Was laid down in the bard's pious voice.

Willingly, the wise man gives him honor;
He reawakens the courage and joy of life.
. . . .
Indeed, in days of old the singer was accorded his honor;
Then he was the pride and joy of his people.
He was supposed to interpret the noble customs
And the wisdom of bygone times with his voice.
Religion entrusted its pure joys
And its sublime consolation to his song.
Why else has power and grace been entrusted to the poet,
If not to proclaim the holy?

Good fortune to the one who lets the song sound forth again,
That it might comfort the soul within its prison.
The song which commands the heavy fogs of despondency to flee,
And orders thought to strive above the earthly prison!
When the lark arises early in the dawn,
Then the spirit rises up with holy longing:
Then the songs meet us sweetly
As harbingers of eternal daybreak.

It was to this task that your heart called you!
Good fortune to you, friend, that you did not fail it!
. . . .
Though above all there is one legend [Christ's life] upon
earth
Which draws all hearts toward it.
. . . .
You knew that it was not empty play,
Not a deception, woven of stealth and cunning.
. . . .
It is a wonderful and holy story
Well worth being honored among men.
To awaken them from their lazy torpor

It must continually be recalled, from generation to
　generation.
　. . . . . .
That was your message, singer, when you raised your eye
Gladly to the splendor of spring!
　. . . . .
Therefore you allowed everything to remind us of Him,
You let His blessed memory warm us.[44]

Thus did Mynster completely swallow his early misgivings about reviewing the Jesus-Nature poem and decided for the sake of his friend Oehlenschläger's reputation—and perhaps for the sake of his own continuing membership
in the highest cultural circles—to place a completely positive and laudatory
construction upon Oehlenschläger's pantheistic Nature-Christianity. Mynster's
difficulties with "the Jesus poem" are completely forgotten, and he unhesitatingly celebrates Oehlenschläger as the modern counterpart of "the singer" who
"in days of old was accorded honor," and whose primary task, far from refusing
to trespass into the fields of religion, is "to proclaim the holy." This, Mynster
now maintains, is what Oehlenschläger has done, and instead of being charged
with pantheistic impiety, the poet should be praised and honored for having
"raised [his] eye gladly to the splendor of the spring" and for having allowed
everything in Nature "to remind us of Him."

As Mynster had admitted to Oehlenschläger in his letter of July 19, 1805,
he had particular difficulties with the Jesus-Nature poem. Oehlenschläger's
1805 collection, which Mynster had been asked to review, contained a great
many other (and better) poems than this, and in his review Mynster could
have avoided his "difficulty" by concentrating upon them. But that would not
have been the best service to his friend Oehlenschläger, who needed the support of the brilliant and "profound" young cleric precisely at this point, and
Mynster was aware of this. Thus Mynster's opportunism—or his valuing of
loyalty to well-placed friends above loyalty to his own religious experience—
can be seen in the fact that it was precisely this poem which Mynster singled
out for praise and defense in his poetic review. Mynster concentrated on Oehlenschläger's poem, not because he agreed with the implications of that particular poem, but because that was where his friend was most vulnerable, where
he had in fact already been attacked by the Primate of Denmark and therefore
where he most needed defending, whether or not the position was defensible
from Mynster's own Christian point of view. By exchanging his initial reluctance for an enthusiasm about the Jesus-Nature poem, Mynster overrode his
own scruples and was able to praise the poem and say something which seemed
to him both "profitable and reasonable." This is a form of compromise which
one sees repeatedly in the Golden Age cultural synthesis of Christianity and
worldly concerns; again and again, substance, content, and principle are
deemed less important than good form, good taste, and decent order.

Having swallowed his principles, Mynster now basked in the approval, thanks, and congratulations that were due him. Upon receipt of Mynster's poetic review of Oehlenschläger, K. L. Rahbek quickly thanked Mynster for his contribution and for permitting him to say "a couple of words to the Bishop [Balle]," who was in a position to cause "personal harm to Oehlenschläger" by preventing "the favorable attitude that people have towards him at the present moment [from being] to his advantage." Rahbek continues by noting that he would have preferred that Mynster had found it possible to write an ordinary review in prose and that one is still needed. Although not himself an aesthetic ally of Oehlenschläger, Rahbek has finally decided to write the prose review himself, "in the absence of others and in fear of worse" reviewers. Besides, Rahbek continues, "a favorable review by a man who does not share Oehlenschläger's creed in other respects might perhaps not serve Oehlenschläger poorly at the present moment."[45]

At about this same time (October 24, 1805) Kamma Rahbek wrote to Oehlenschläger informing him that Mynster's review had finally arrived. She included the piece with her letter and noted to Oehlenschläger that she was certain that "it will please you."[46] Shortly thereafter, on November 2, 1805, Oehlenschläger wrote to Christiane Heger, who was Kamma's sister and his fiancée, and remarked how delighted he was to receive Kamma's letter, which contained "the glorious poem from Job." (Partly because it is a comical contraction of "Jakob" and partly, perhaps, because of his "deep" and long-suffering nature, "Job" had become Mynster's nickname among the inner circle of Golden Age intellectuals.) Oehlenschläger writes warmly of "the joy of having delighted so noble and so unusually deep a nature as Job Mynster's," and he asks Christiane to have her sister Kamma thank Mynster and say to him "that I regard the revelation of this poem to my soul as one of the greatest joys I have encountered in the world."[47] A bit later in the same month (November 15, 1805) Oehlenschläger wrote to Kamma directly and repeated his request that she "thank Job Mynster fervently for his beautiful poem,"[48] and shortly after this Kamma wrote to Mynster, conveying these exact lines to him.[49] On December 8, 1805, Kamma wrote back to Oehlenschläger and informed him that his thanks had been conveyed to Mynster, who in turn asked Kamma to give his regards to Oehlenschläger. Kamma remarks further to Oehlenschläger that "it pleased him [Mynster] unspeakably much that *you* were satisfied with what he has done. . . ."[50]

Finally, two years later (1807) Oehlenschläger wrote Mynster from Paris and discussed the matter directly: "Thank you now, personally, for your beautiful poem to me! It has caused me profound joy. One of the greatest rewards an artist has is that the noble, rare individuals in his time know and treasure him."[51] Thus, as he had hoped and expected, in exchange for compromising his scruples, the young, insecure, and ambitious Mynster was granted a secure patent of admission to the small group of "noble, rare individuals" who constituted the inner circle of the Golden Age. Mynster was one of "the rare few."[52]

Yet Mynster could not wholly conquer his scruples. He did not truly believe that Oehlenschläger was genuinely Christian, and doubts continued to plague him. In March, 1806, Mynster wrote to Kamma Rahbek concerning Oehlenschläger's ambiguously religious poem "Hakon Jarl" (which was examined in the previous chapter). Mynster notes that it is hard to make out "whether the piece is heathen or Christian,"[53] to which Kamma replies: "*I dare not decide* whether it is Christian or heathen."[54] Yet the question is not pursued further, and the matter was deliberately allowed to hover in indefiniteness. The upper ranks of the Golden Age literary intellectuals avoided breaches over such matters as religion and kept up the appearance of a polite Christian-cultural front—piety *and* good taste. At the same time, this Golden Age elite made common cause against the peasants and especially against N. F. S. Grundtvig, who may have been more orthodox (he certainly claimed to be), but who was self-righteous, boisterous, and rude, and who made no bones about egging on the peasants in their self-assertiveness.

Even though he avoided passing unambiguous public judgment on his Golden Age colleague, Mynster was surely not a pantheist. He saw Oehlenschläger's shortcomings clearly, but overlooked them for the sake of collegiality and cultural solidarity. By the time he wrote his *Observations* in 1833, when the reputations of both men—who, as has been stated, formed the literary and religious leadership of the first generation of the Golden Age—were secure and invulnerable, Mynster permitted himself to assail the pantheism of the Jesus-Nature poem, without, of course, mentioning it or Oehlenschläger by name:

> We continually experience in these times how easily, particularly for shrewd thinking, the living God is transformed into a nature, a universe [Alverden], an infinite force, a certain divine something, that penetrates the whole; or whatever other notions these people make for themselves, they take the shadow for the being, the ray of light which shines upon what is created for the eternal source of light.[55]

This was, of course, precisely Bishop Balle's criticism of Oehlenschläger in 1805, but at that time Mynster had found it impossible and impolitic to voice the sentiments which had given him difficulty with "the Jesus poem." Mynster consistently suppressed the profound differences in principle that he felt with leading Golden Age luminaries. For example, just as with his criticism of Oehlenschläger, he reserved his polite critique of H. C. Ørsted's Schellingian pantheism until after Ørsted published *The Spirit in Nature* [*Aanden i Naturen*]—the collected edition of his popular writings on *Naturphilosophie*—in 1850, by which time both the physicist and the bishop were grand and revered old men, secure from the adverse effects of criticism, and Ørsted himself only a year

away from the grave. Only when the religious views of such men as Oehlenschläger and Ørsted had had their major impact and when criticism no
longer entailed any risk—risk to their careers, to Mynster's career, to the close
web of personal associations that bound together the cultural elite, to social
peace, or to the synthetic religious-cultural edifice of "Christendom"—only then
would Mynster speak his mind, and even then only very cautiously.

At moments of high pathos, the criticism faded away altogether, and Mynster returned to the position of his review of 1805, in which the "idealism" and
"loftiness" of the romantic philosophy and poetry is portrayed as supportive
of and indeed as synonymous with the task of Christianity. This comes forward
most clearly in Mynster's January 1850 eulogy of Oehlenschläger. The great
departed poet, "who so often enchanted us away from the toils and the plagues
of life into lighter regions . . . [has made a beautiful] departure to the better
places, whose glory often filled his breast with holy intimations here [on
earth]."[56] Thus, the romantic poet is our messenger, if not exactly from the
biblical Paradise, then at any rate from the "better place" of romance, and
"what the artist presents with his works, what exists for the eye of the poet
when he reaches for his harp, is not borrowed by them from this reality below;
they are revelations from a higher world, intimations of what the morning of
resurrection will bring."[57]

However, even more important than his role as the genius-ambassador
from "a higher world," Mynster's Oehlenschläger was a pillar of religion and
civilization, and for Mynster, as for the Golden Age generally, religion and
civilization were inseparable and almost interchangeable and could not be
imagined in fundamental conflict with one another. Thus Mynster eulogizes
Oehlenschläger not only as a man of "the Spirit," but also as a defender of
civil and social order. Oehlenschläger, Mynster reminds his hearers,

> acted upon the entire people to awaken life, to call forth, nourish, and strengthen
> the respect for everything noble and beautiful, for all the feelings which unite
> people in honorable and joyous society. In a country in which the singer [of
> poetry] is silent, thought and effort fasten themselves more and more to merely
> temporal advantages and pleasures; the longing of the spirit is extinguished, its
> wings are paralyzed; and then the consuming passions come forth untamed;
> then the flame of discord burns; then rebellion howls; then the mockers of God
> break the bonds of modesty. But if, in our country, in the midst of moved and
> and troubled times, so many noble strivings of the Spirit are to be seen every-
> where; if there is courage in danger; if, in spite of many different conflicts, the
> people yet stands united around its king; if there is love and joy in life remaining;
> if so many ears still are open to the serious voice of the Law, so many hearts
> open to the soothing voice of the Gospel; this is due in large measure to you
> [Adam Oehlenschläger], you who for so many years occupied the elevated place
> among the influential men of this people![58]

From his early sermons, from his remarkable reputation from the years in Spjellerup, and from the brilliant anti-rationalist oratory of his Copenhagen career in the Church of Our Lady, the young Mynster had acquired a reputation for impeccable orthodoxy and profound piety and had even been given the nicknames "John the Baptist" and "Hans Hauge" (a fierce Norwegian revivalist)[59] by educated circles in the capital, whose fashionable preacher he was. No one could fault Mynster on his piety, but as we have seen from his defense of Oehlenschläger, Mynster learned early how he could both eat his cake and have it too: He was able both to gain renown for uncompromising piety and yet to maintain his connections with fashionable taste and culture, however dubious its religious credentials. For Mynster the difference between "profound" and "lofty" soulfulness and the vulgar everyday world of peasants and politics was perhaps more important than the difference between Romantic philosophy and Christian orthodoxy. High culture [Dannelse] erected a common front in which putative Christian orthodoxy and semi-pagan Romantic philosophy could come to terms in support of a vague notion of an otherworldly life—a "higher reality." This formed the core of the antipolitical ideology with which the urban cultured elite confronted the rise of the common man of the countryside. This was the religion of the man who was the family pastor for the Kierkegaards, as for so many other fashionable and well-to-do families of the capital. This was the religion of the Bishop against whom Søren Kierkegaard finally revolted, when the events of 1848 and 1849 convinced him that Mynster's message was more social and political than religious and that continuing acquiescence in it would entail irreparable harm to Christianity.

D. MYNSTER'S CAREER AFTER SPJELLERUP

In December 1811 Mynster came to Copenhagen as the curate of the Church of Our Lady, the principal church of the capital. He explains in memoirs that "this is the only office I have sought. . . everything else that I have become has sought me."[60] This disclaimer is only true in a technical sense, for Mynster had carefully prepared his appearance in Copenhagen with a series of articles, including a fashionable attack upon a "rationalistic" liturgical proposal, and with his brilliant sermons, on which he had labored long. It was common knowledge that a good post, preferably in the capital, was the indispensable prerequisite for upward mobility in the clerical establishment. When, additionally, one cultivates and retains the proper friends and literary connections, as Mynster did, and marries the daughter of the Primate of Denmark, as Mynster did, it is only to be expected that one will be asked to move up, that higher posts will "seek one." In a society as closed as that of Golden Age Copenhagen, this was simply the way that careers were made, and Mynster's protestations of modesty must be taken with a grain of salt.

In 1815, at age forty, Mynster took his doctoral degree from the university, and the same year married Fanny Münter, the nineteen-year-old daughter of Balthasar Münter, the Primate of Denmark. Two years later he was appointed to the Directorate of Higher Education, and in 1819 was elected a member of the Royal Scientific Society. In 1823 Mynster's third and very successful collection of sermons was published. In 1826, immediately following his prudent and vocal neutrality in the fight between the rude Grundtvig and the "rationalist" H. N. Clausen (which will be discussed in chapter 13), Mynster began to harvest the highest ecclesiastical honors, which prepared him for his elevation to the episcopacy of Zealand and the primacy of Denmark. Mynster's neutrality in the scandalous Grundtvig-Clausen dispute of 1825 was managed in such a way that Mynster accomplished what might at first have seemed impossible: While remaining outside and above the dispute, Mynster managed to tilt toward Clausen in such a way as to make it unmistakably clear that, whatever Grundtvig's message might be, his conduct had placed him beyond the pale. Yet, at the same time, Mynster remained untainted by Clausen's "rationalism," which he was well-known to oppose. (Mynster's neutrality in the Grundtvig-Clausen affair will be discussed in more detail later in the present chapter.) Thus, in the spring of 1826, Mynster was appointed Preacher to the Royal Court [Hofprædikant] "against my wishes,"[61] and shortly thereafter he was called to be Royal Confessor as well as Court and Palace Priest, posts that he accepted in order to be "less dependent upon popular approval."[62]

In 1830 Mynster's father-in-law, Bishop Münter, died, and Mynster reports in his memoirs that he had "for quite some time already been seen as chosen to be Münter's successor,"[63] but was happy to escape from this for the time being when Professor P. E. Müller was appointed Bishop of Zealand and Primate of Denmark. Müller, however, had had tuberculosis for years and was old and ailing even when he accepted the post. Müller's primacy can thus be regarded as a reign which had been expected by the government to be brief, perhaps in order to spare Mynster, who had risen very rapidly in the previous few years, from the charge of nepotism which might have arisen if he had inherited the post directly from his father-in-law. In any event, Müller's primacy was brief (1830–34), and Mynster acceded to the post four years after his father-in-law's death, just after the publication of his extraordinarily popular *Observations*. During Müller's lengthy terminal illness, which lasted a good portion of his reign, Mynster was aware that "according to the situation of the time, there was no one who could be thought of as his successor but me,"[64] and when he was offered the post in 1834, Mynster decided to accept, while also retaining his posts as Court and Palace Priest and as Royal Confessor.

Thus, in 1834, Mynster's brilliant rise from insecure orphan to Primate of Denmark had been completed. He had long since become the spokesman of educated, urban upper middle-class religious sensibilities: devout, yet tasteful and not excessive. The remaining twenty years of his life were given in untiring service as Bishop of Zealand and Primate of the Danish State Church (later the Danish People's Church), where he continually defended the Golden Age mainstream's conservative and apolitical vision of a hierarchical society married to Christianity—"Christendom"—the stable, serviceable synthesis of religion and society that had characterized the absolutist regime. In an era of enormous social change, when this conservative synthesis was attacked both by democratic political forces and by "orthodox" religious critics, Mynster remained the steadfast opponent of change and the defender of the idealistic Golden Age notion of Christendom as the institutional union of the invisible world of the sublime and the visible world of social utility. This was not an easy course to hold, for even within the Church the social forces which attempted to twist the helm of Golden Age Christendom were great indeed. As Mynster himself remarks, the task of being head of the Church was made extremely difficult "when so many clerics, even of the better and more reasonable group, give their voice to the Opposition, either by permitting themselves to be carried away by the spirit of the times, or merely out of pliability and cowardice."[65] When Mynster uses the term "opposition," he means both the political and the ecclesiastical opposition; he was characteristically and quite rightly unable to discriminate between the two sorts of opposition to his Church, which was, after all, a synthesis of this-worldly and other-worldly elements. In the 1840's, under the uncertain and rather pro-Grundtvig regime of Christian VIII, Mynster complains that "what is most difficult is the unclarity, the halfway nature, and the vacillation of the government, upon which no one can depend."[66]

As the influence which the old, elitist, urban veneer of Golden Age Copenhagen exercised over the changing agrarian society of "the common man" became weaker and weaker, a major portion of Mynster's career consisted of fighting rear-guard actions in order to defend the religious-political *status quo* which during the later 1830's and 1840's increasingly came under attack, often by those within the Church itself. Excepting for the gratification derived from the tightly knit society of his urban admirers, Mynster's twenty-year primacy was a tempest-ridden and thankless task for him.

E. THE CONFLICT WITH GRUNDTVIG

We have already seen how in 1812 the troublesome Grundtvig wrote imprudent letters to Oehlenschläger, the literary paladin of the first generation of the Golden Age, inquiring dubiously after the state of Oehlenschläger's spiritual health. In this same year—the year following Mynster's arrival in Copenhagen as a fashionable new preacher—Grundtvig also wrote similarly prying, concerned letters to Mynster, who was soon to exercise an influence on the Golden Age comparable only to the literary influence exercised by his friend Oehlenschläger.

Grundtvig notes in one letter that he has on occasion found Mynster "more meditating than believing [mere grundende end troende]," and has heard sermons by Mynster which were "like schoolish moral essays."[67] Grundtvig says that he has even heard it remarked that "Mynster only had a certain poetic reverence for the truths of the Christian faith."[68] Finally, Grundtvig continues, he himself went to hear Mynster preach at first hand, and Grundtvig notes that he must confess that "I was not all edified; indeed, I did not even find the sermon Christian, for you wished to speak about 'The Necessity of Faith,' and spoke only of a faith which has existed and which can exist without scriptural revelation."[69] Grundtvig insists that he must know whether he and Mynster "are in agreement about the highest things," about "the Holy Scripture," and he feels that as a Christian earnestly inquiring about the spiritual health of another, he has a right to ask.[70] Therefore, Grundtvig asks Mynster, as one concerned Christian to another: "What is your heart-felt opinion about the Bible and about faith in Christ?"[71] For the second time in a year, Grundtvig fears he has scented a mere aesthete in the Christian garb of the Golden Age.

Mynster's reply is as indignant as might be expected, beginning with a list of his published material which bears witness to his Christian understanding of the Bible and of life. Significantly, already in 1812—only seven years after his troubles in writing the Oehlenschläger review (1805)—Mynster seems to have forgotten his struggles of conscience over the Jesus-Nature poem, for he heads the list of his published work with the paean to Oehlenschläger, calling it "a happy greeting to a poet who had struck a note which I recognized as Christian."[72] Further, Mynster continues, his orthodoxy has been attested to by the attacks upon him by "the opposite party" (the rationalists).[73] As for the supposedly merely moral character of his sermons, Mynster replies that indeed they are moral; what else would Grundtvig have them be?[74] Mynster attempts to rebut directly Grundtvig's charge that Mynster's religion does not require divine revelation, noting that "without external revelation, man would likely only be an animal; man needs revelation both for truths which he could not otherwise know . . . and even in order to acknowledge the truths which are nevertheless engraved in his being."[75] This would seem to put Mynster safely beyond the murky romantic religion of the Golden Age, but his major statement on the question vitiates this stand and is indeed a sort of classic justification of Golden Age religiosity against the likes of such "orthodox" critics as Grundtvig:

Where a man, even without Scriptural and external revelation, clings closely to the Invisible Being, as if he saw him, the true faith is present. . . . You know that from very ancient times there have been *two* opinions about Christianity, of which the one would acknowledge nothing good or true except in that which genuinely and immediately adhered to Christianity, seeing everything else as profanity, vain pleasures, splendid vices; the other view, on the contrary, acknowledged God's spirit as active in every nation and in all ages, and saw the fruits of that spirit everywhere, even if imperfect. . . . I do not hesitate to embrace the latter view.[76]

Mynster's "catholic" view of religion was capable of mediating happily between the piously garbed, semi-pagan religiosity of Oehlenschläger and the Golden Age, on the one hand and the official requirements of conventional Christianity on the other. The clash of his religion with that of Grundtvig was not a superficial or accidental misunderstanding which could be cleared up by means of correspondence. Both correspondents remained quite properly and quite irreconcilably offended with respect to one another.

By the mid-1820's the Church was beginning to be racked by the battle between the Grundtvigian "orthodox" and the academic "rationalists." Mynster, who was well-connected and sublimely aloof from both parties, was in a perfect position to profit from the bloodletting on both sides. Thus, thirteen years after the epistolary exchange with Grundtvig outlined above, in the midst of the scandal caused by Grundtvig's tactless and merciless 1825 attack upon young H. N. Clausen as a "rationalist," Mynster delivered and immediately thereafter published a sermon entitled *On Christian Wisdom*[77] (to which, characteristically, Grundtvig replied with a published sermon entitled *On Christian Struggle*). Mynster's sermon revels in the conspicuous luxury of disinterestedness, and without espousing Clausen's "rationalist" theology, Mynster strongly takes his side as that of one injured by the impudent and tasteless Grundtvig. Looking back on this episode in his memoirs, Mynster notes that

> everywhere, the more earnestly I worked for the cause of Christianity and the more willingly I was heard, the more I sought in every way to renounce every share and part in that zealous party [i.e., Grundtvig's] which was extravagant in every respect, yet still eschewing all personal polemics.[78]

Mynster's apparently middle-of-the-road sermon *On Christian Wisdom* took neither Grundtvig's nor Clausen's side, but managed, in its neutrality, to be much more anti-Grundtvig than anti-Clausen. It is filled with phrases from the New Testament and with Solomonic evenhandedness, lauding "wisdom" at the outset, while decrying "vain honor" and "spiritual arrogance," and is obviously directed at Grundtvig. Mynster goes on to insist that "Christian wisdom" must reveal itself in three qualities: "reasonableness," "spirit," and "humility"; it is clear that the hot-headed Grundtvig is found lacking in the first of these qualities, Clausen in the second, and both in the third. However, it is particularly at the lack of "reasonableness" (Grundtvig's failing) that Mynster directs his fire:

> Even in the world of spiritual things, there is nothing that can be put in order or chosen or used without the clear light of the understanding . . . [and, like the

light of the understanding, so, too, is] the wonderful spark of fire, a great gift of God. If you entrust it to the hand of a reasonable man, he will use it to light the lamp which shines in the darkness; he will put it in a safe place, where it will warm, but not consume. But, place this fire in the hand of the rash, the furious, or the evil person, and soon the destructive flames will swirl toward heaven, if you cannot stop them. Then he will perhaps view the abominable destruction with insane joy. . . .[79]

But, of course, even while directing most of his condemnation at Grundt-vig's uncontrolled "fire" and lack of reasonableness, Mynster reserves criticism for Clausen as well, and points out that understanding alone does not constitute wisdom, even though there are people who think that this "fine gossamer, the light threads of thought, which they artificially place together, . . . this airy weave, is a garment which can beautify and warm one! They forget that the understanding cannot create anything. . . ."[80] Finally, of course, both parties are lacking in humility, Mynster concludes, for they are unwilling to remove the beam in their own eyes before they attempt to remove the splinter in their neighbor's.[81]

Mynster was well-satisfied with his sermon *On Christian Wisdom*, and in a letter of October 1825 to his good friend Laub, he makes it clear that the sermon's neutrality is only apparent. Mynster feels that putting his sermon in print was "a word at the right time," although it will probably not "make an impression upon those of the party which is over-eager to judge others," and is written "for the sake of those decent people who nowadays lean toward pietism," in order that they do not fall victim to the tactics of the judgmental "screechers."[82] (In his popular and influential *Observations*, published eight years later, Mynster was to make the same point, again directed clearly at the Grundtvigian party: "There is nothing so repulsive as pride and hatred and megalomania and the judgmental spirit, but we meet it in the world, and it does not surprise us, for the world is like that; in the Church of Christ, on the other hand, we should expect things to be different. . . .")[83]

However, even while admitting, in his letter to Laub, that the burden of his apparently even-handed "Christian Wisdom" was in fact directed at Grundtvig, Mynster also points out that on the other hand he has "little desire to cast [himself] into the ice-cold arms of the opposite theology, or to rest upon its hollow breast."[84] Thus, Mynster's deepest animus was directed toward the unseemly Grundtvig, but his own position was the Golden Mean. This elevated and neutral position enabled Mynster to profit from the feud between these two factions by delivering and, immediately thereafter, publishing—this im-mediate publication of an occasional piece was quite unusual for Mynster—his sermon, which was warmer than the cold Clausen, yet cooler than the fiery and choleric Grundtvig. (As was pointed out in the preceding section of this chapter, the rapid and final ascent of Mynster's career began several months after he took this very politic stand.)

In his memoirs, Mynster affirms again that it was with the fiery, intemperate Grundtvigians rather than with the cooler philosophical opponents that his most profound disagreement lay: "[T]he real, significant, and long-lasting conflict was with the party to which I can give no other name than the Grundtvigian."[85] As Bishop of Zealand, Mynster was obligated to make inspection tours of his parishes, a good number of which were led by Grundtvigian pastors, and in visiting one such pastor Mynster grudgingly states that although "the church was full of people," and "although the congregation seemed glad to hear him, it can hardly have profited from a sermon such as this," which was nothing but "unclear screeching."[86]

Behind this distaste for the Grundtvigian sort of pietism, we can glimpse a more profound criticism which, in turn, sheds light upon Mynster's own theory of the Church, with its unwavering formalism and its rigid insistence upon uniformity. The fundamental problem with the Grundtvigians, Mynster points out in one article, is that they wish to set up an aristocracy of the supposedly orthodox alongside the already-existing aristocracies, even while touting themselves as democratic.[87] Mynster, on the other hand, viewed his own formalism and conservatism as an institutional protection for the individual believer, however menial, which would guarantee him spiritual peace and provide a bulwark against noisy and intrusive zealots. An iron uniformity in official Christendom was the only shelter against the waves of fashionable hysteria which from time to time attempted to sweep over the State Church. Mynster argues in his memoirs that the spiritual despotism of the self-righteous Grundtvigian minority was closely related to the fashionable waves of liberalism and democracy, which similarly attempted to erode state power and institutional guarantees in order to impose a new and demagogic despotism:

> [I]n spite of the fact that there have been times in which there has been too much government, there can indeed also be too little government, and it is to this end that the demagogues of these times seek to influence those who have power, in order to pave the way for their own despotism.[88]

For Mynster, an open elitism that supported a strong and unyielding State Church was the only alternative to the covert elitism of the political and religious reformers—whom he almost always lumped together—which would lead to the rule of demagogues and self-proclaimed saints.

Once this is understood, the importance for Mynster of style and social appeal rather than content in theological matters can also be understood. Given Mynster's early and abiding distaste for the "rationalists," either the early Grundtvig or some of the followers of the divine assemblies might have been his natural theological allies. However, we must remember that social tone, institutional calm and stability, and reliance upon the authority of traditional elites provided Mynster with his only shelter against the "screeching" of the "demagogues." This is why Mynster came to terms with men whose theological position was quite far from what he—rightly or wrongly—understood his own to be, but whose social attitudes and behavior were far more acceptable than those of the Grundtvigians and the awakened.

To give a specific illustration of this, we have merely to examine Mynster's promotion of the university career of the Hegelian Martensen and his collaboration with the rationalist H. N. Clausen in doing so. Mynster could never stand Clausen personally, and felt Clausen's theology to be "ice-cold" and foreign to himself, but in his role as Primate of Denmark Mynster allied himself with Clausen, who was the brightest light on the university theological faculty, in advancing the fortunes of H. L. Martensen. Martensen, as a Hegelian, was theologically acceptable to neither Mynster nor Clausen, but was culturally well-connected and seemly in his social comportment. Most important, the only real alternatives to appointing Martensen to the theological faculty were several extremely capable scholars, the most notable of whom were Jacob Christian Lindberg and Peter Christian Kierkegaard (Søren Kierkegaard's brother), who many contemporary observers, and almost all subsequent observers, felt were the most brilliant and promising academic theologians of the 1840's. These men, however, were dedicated and public followers of Grundtvig, and thus, whatever the actual content of their theology or the depth of their learning, were disqualified from academic positions for reasons that were not ultimately theological but were matters of style and social appeal—that is, political reasons.[89] A certain political and social style was, finally, more determinative of Mynster's Golden Age religiosity than any particular content.

F. MYNSTER'S RELATIONSHIP TO HEGELIANISM, PARTICULARLY TO MARTENSEN

As an unsystematic and intuitive individualist, it is not surprising that Mynster conceived an instant distaste for Hegel's systematic philosophy as soon as he first became acquainted with it. In a letter of 1830 to his friend Engelbreth, Mynster writes that "scarcely any philosopher has formed a worse school than Hegel,"[90] and in his memoirs Mynster recounts his philosophical convictions during the 1820's and 1830's:

> Since Hegel's appointment in Berlin, his philosophy had become the only path to salvation, and the haughtiness of his adherents knew no bounds. I was well convinced that it would not last long but was disappointed in my expectation that it would be over with Hegel's death, because, on the contrary, it only began to dominate after that point.[91]

However, although Mynster disagreed with them, the Hegelians had a system and an intellectual base of operations, and he had none. Therefore he was obliged to try to make peace with them and compromise, a process that was rendered much easier by the geniality of Martensen, the modishness of Heiberg, and, above all, by the terrifying enthusiasm of the Grundtvigians, who, in the 1830's and the 1840's, were the principal alternative. Thus, in an 1839 letter to his son, Mynster writes that he had an

> interesting battle with Heiberg and Martensen about Hegelian principles, but it was carried on with all possible gallantry on the part of the opponents, and if I had the time I would certainly like to carry the dispute further. However, yesterday I had a long philosophical conversation with Martensen. Naturally, in spite of this dispute, we are the best of friends, and he is of course not nearly so strict an Hegelian as Heiberg.[92]

Mynster's public battle with Denmark's leading Hegelians was thus limited in scope and intensity and was in fact restricted to portions of three philosophical articles: *On Religious Conviction* (1833), *Rationalism, Supranaturalism* (1839), and *On Logical Principles* (1842).[93] Hegelianism, Mynster points out in one of these articles, claims a synoptic view of the whole of being, but for himself, Mynster must adopt a more modest point of departure:

> For my part, I must indeed give up the hope of managing to "see down from above" [à la Hegel]; but to those who, like myself, feel this same lack of ability, I wish the same consolation which soothes me, that one can also see that which is highest from below, and, when one continually fastens one's eyes upon it, one can ascend to it.[94]

While not masking his substantive disagreement with his Hegelian opponents, Mynster did not wish to make a major issue of it. As he points out in his memoirs, he had "neither the inclination nor the ability" to combat Hegelian philosophy in Denmark, and he participated only in a few "vanguard skirmishes."[95] After the third of his three articles on the subject, there "came an end to a dispute which did not occasion the least breach in the respect I had for the talents of both of my opponents or for the love I cherished toward the latter [Martensen], which has since grown with every passing year."[96] (The implied coolness towards Heiberg is perhaps due in part to Heiberg's brusque acerbity, his rather thoroughgoing paganism, his condescension toward and disrespect for traditional Christianity, and, not least, for his attack upon Mynster's friend Oehlenschläger.) In any event, Mynster's relationship with Heiberg and Martensen, with whom he had far more profound substantive differences than with Grundtvig, was marked by polite, even humble, disagreement: In *On Logical Principles*, Mynster refers to his Hegelian opponents as "the honored men, bound to me by friendship, whom I have had to call my opponents."[97] At the same time, his relationship to Grundtvig and to other pietist opponents such as the lay awakeners was marked by the deepest loathing and the most personal sort of pettiness and narrowness. The explanation must surely be sought in the fact that Martensen and Heiberg, whatever their religious views, represented good taste; they were socially safe. Pietists and lay awakeners, on the other hand, might be more traditional in their religion, but they were disorderly and socially dangerous. Thus Martensen became Mynster's protégé and eventual successor, while the various sorts of pietists were the bane of his episcopal existence.

G. MYNSTER'S POLITICAL VIEWS

Mynster was even more conservative, even more anti-political, than his beloved King Frederick VI. When Frederick moved to establish the Advisory Assembly of Estates in the mid-1830's, Mynster was deeply concerned with what he saw as the monarch's error in establishing even this tentative platform of debate. In Mynster's view, the Advisory Assembly could only lead to increased "political ferment."[98] Yet as the Primate of Denmark and as leader of the ecclesiastical delegation, it was Mynster's task to open the first meeting of the Roskilde Estates in October 1835 with a religious service and an address in which he humbly thanked the King for having graciously convened them. Mynster's perhaps excessive humility and thankfulness served to anger the liberal delegation, and prompted H. N. Clausen to publish a highly critical reply, entitled *On the Art of Thanking*. Mynster's sermon at the opening of the Roskilde Estates gives us a glimpse of his anti-liberal, wholistic or corporatist understanding of society:

> [W]e are all one body; for even if we—like the various limbs of the body—divide ourselves according to our offices and estates, yet we are still but one society, and everyone must strive faithfully to promote what is best for the whole. . . . [Great things can be accomplished] when the prince faithfully holds the scepter which God entrusted to his hand, and when the people gather faithfully around their prince. . . . [But we have also learned] how disunited social estates are capable of ripping up the bowels of the country.[99]

Order and paternalism were fundamental to Mynster's political vision; everyone must remain orderly and in his place according to his "office and estate."

With the death of Frederick VI in 1839, when Mynster had been Bishop for only five years, his time was already over even though he had many years left to serve. Mynster himself seems to have sensed that his time was past with the accession of Christian VIII, and his great eulogy of his late king, which begins "You men of Frederick VI!"[100] seems addressed most of all to himself. Mynster notes in his memoirs that "my feelings were not so changeable as those of the mob," and that he was struck with a severe sympathetic illness on hearing of the death of Frederick, so that it was only with great physical suffering that he was able to compose and deliver his eulogy.[101] It seemed to Mynster in 1839 as though an era had suddenly and disastrously come to an end, and indeed it had: The age in which a great father-king had ruled the nation without politics for over fifty years had ended; from now on, social life would become increasingly noisier, more turbulent, more polluted with the intrusion of "the common man," more "political." As Mynster remarks on the loss of Frederick VI: "None of us were abandoned on earth as long as we had him. Now it was over."[102]

Mynster did not at all like Christian VIII as a king. First of all, Christian's wife, the Queen, harbored an undisguised partiality for Grundtvig. But quite apart from this, Christian had shown himself to be a vacillating man and had earlier had well-known sentiments in favor of constitutionalism and reform. This made Christian an uncertain monarch who, on the one hand, "was not to the liking of the conservative mind," but who, on the other hand, "did not satisfy the party of movement," either.[103] Thus, in his opening sermon at the sitting of the 1842 Estates under Christian VIII, Mynster offered many prayers of thanks to God for the late great king, Frederick VI, whom He had given to Denmark: "[F]rom the lights on high the memory of him still descends to the people whose father he was called and was." Mention of the present King Christian, on the other hand, was noticeably cool and perfunctory, his name appearing only in the formulaic supplicatory prayers.[104]

In the course of the 1840's Mynster became increasingly distraught with the inroads that liberalism was making in educated society, noting in 1847 that "the times are sick with reform."[105] Liberals and democrats were generally lumped together pejoratively in Mynster's writing as "the modern genius," "the friends of light," or those imbued with "the principle of movement" and "the spirit of the times."[106] Mynster also seems to imply that, however objectionable its philosophical and theological content might be from a doctrinal point of view, the Hegelianism that loomed so large on the Danish intellectual scene in the 1830's and early 1840's was at least preferable to the recurrence of shallow Enlightenment liberalism that was tending to replace it:

> [A]ll the distorted and exaggerated ideas of freedom, all the platitudes and triviality, all the philistinism that had cursed the eighteenth century, and out of which reasonable men had gradually worked themselves, now returned in strengthened form, and dearly won experience was completely lost on the new generation. If Hegelian philosophy has had to yield its primacy in recent years [1847], it has happened in part because its subtleties and sophisms could not maintain themselves in the deluge of insipid Enlightenment which had now broken forth with unstoppable force.[107]

More disturbing even than liberalism, however, was the new sense of independence and personal importance that was making itself felt among the peasant masses, about whom and about whose political spokesmen Mynster could only speak with a scorn that was unseemly in a man called to lead the State Church in a predominantly agrarian society. In a typical slur on the peasant class, Mynster notes that among the representatives in the Estates were not "only the peasants and those who share the peasants' intellectual privileges, but also many who ought to have better sense."[108]

The "political" sermons that have been preserved (the sermons Mynster delivered before the Estates and which touch expressly on political matters) give us a rare and unequivocal insight into Mynster's general view of society. First of all, Mynster shares the Golden Age romantic view of a continuity between the two worlds of heaven and earth, between things visible and invisible:

> [T]he two worlds to which man belongs are not separated in the way that loose thinking feels, so that the one world begins where the other one ends. Where does the eternal, the all-encompassing, begin and end? Are there boundaries in time, from back of which eternity takes its beginning? Are there boundaries in space, so that the starry canopy separates the heavenly from the earthly? What is it, then, that fills the earth with beauty and glory, other than the heavenly, which submerges itself in the earth, as it were? Where does the earth repose, but in the embrace of the eternal? What are visible things other than a revelation of things unseen? What is the temporal but a revelation—incomplete and imperfect, it is true—of the eternal?[109]

It is the task of the absolute monarch, who holds his office by the grace of God, to mediate between the realms of the eternal and the temporal. Frederick VI

> strove to be His [God's] servant on earth, an enforcer of the eternal law, which no man gave, and no man can abolish, and which must be obeyed by high and low, without which no true and lasting fortune can blossom upon the earth, without which the Kingdom of God cannot come.[110]

The monarch is the enforcer not merely of civil, prudential law of the instrumental sort, but also of "the eternal law." Hence, disobedience to the monarch—civil disorder—is not merely a crime against the temporal, but also against the eternal, the divine order of things. Furthermore, here, as elsewhere, Mynster's syntax seems very strongly to imply that the temporal and the eternal realms are so related to one another that "the Kingdom of God" is unequivocally expressed by "true and lasting fortune blossoming upon the earth." Political disorder is religious disorder; political and social good fortune is a sign of divine approval.

Alas, however, our times are not times of such social harmony and divine approval, Mynster notes, for the spirit of dissent, of social disorder, of *politics*, is abroad in the land.

[For] when, as now, the bonds which formerly held men together are loosened more and more, when marriages lose their sacred character, when morals lose their purity, when one hears complaints from every quarter that rape and pillage, violence and murder, are increasing, then it is indeed a call to consider seriously what civic arrangements should be made in order that peaceful citizens can live in safety in this country, and that the sword of the law does not threaten the guilty in vain. . . . [In order to enact the measures necessary to restore order, the nation's leaders must be] unconcerned about the shouts of the crowd and the approval of the non-experts. . . . For a people's welfare can never be separated from its worth, and the Kingdom of God can never come in the external sense when it is not present within men's hearts.[111]

Here, again, what is most noteworthy in Mynster's political assumptions is not merely the insistence that rulers must disregard popular sentiment in restoring order nor the fact that the society about which Mynster was writing (Denmark, 1842) was not, even by European standards, particularly disorderly. Rather, the most striking feature of Mynster's politics is his simple assertion that "a people's welfare"—in the sense of orderly social conditions (the absence of crime, etc.)—is quite naturally assumed to constitute a portion of "the Kingdom of God in the external sense." In Mynster's Golden Age view of society, there seems to be no strict boundary between politics and social conditions ("a people's welfare") on the one hand and inner, spiritual conditions ("a people's worth") on the other. Rather, the visible and invisible realms are connected causally in a direct (if somewhat imperfect) correspondence. This is the real reason why we must be orderly and avoid politics. "Politics" is disorderly and hence is bad for our religious condition; "politics" prevents the coming of the Kingdom of God.

H. MYNSTER AGAINST THE "SCREECHERS": RELIGION AND POLITICS

In his memoirs, Mynster portrays himself as a lonely and embattled campaigner for good order and discipline within the State Church and sees as his principal opponent the peasant-based awakening movement:

The struggles that I have had to endure to defend the Danish Church and prevent its dissolution may well be forgotten. . . . But the Church is still threatened by many dangers, including the threats from the so-called divine assemblies . . . [which can] undermine the life force of the Church and the truth of the religious life.[112]

What Mynster found particularly offensive and dangerous was the religious and social insubordination of the mere laymen who have taken it upon themselves to preach the Gospel without state authorization and according to their own lights. "[T]he office of the teacher should be held in honor, and it should not be permitted for self-appointed preachers—often the most unworthy persons—to go about the country as the people's teachers."[113] Mynster points out that there are ordinances on the books against this sort of thing, "and where it is needed [they must be] enforced with strictness."[114] If nothing else works, force—arrests, criminal prosecution, and fines—must be employed against these "unworthy persons," these "wandering preachers."[115] Mynster is referring to the Conventicle Ordinance of 1741, which nearly everyone regarded as tyrannical and outdated. Mynster, however, although he sometimes declared himself to be opposed in principle to the use of force in spiritual matters, favored the retention of the ordinance for use in extreme cases, when the "screeching" of the lowly disturbed the orderly existence of the official religious monopoly.

The most notorious instance of Mynster's proclivity to use legal force and official state sanctions against the efforts of the lower classes to lead an independent religious life was his campaign against the Baptists in the 1840's, when he attempted to have the children of Baptists forcibly seized and baptized against their parents' will. In this attempt Mynster was ultimately defeated, and his memoirs contain much bitterness and self-justification about the controversial matter:

> For my part I cannot abandon my conviction that the State is justified in requiring every child to be immediately assigned to one of the religious societies recognized by the State, and that therefore, because the Baptists expressly declare that their children do not belong to their society until they declare themselves members as adults, our Church must thus take care of them as it does other abandoned children.[116]

The unfortunate Baptists were drawn almost exclusively from the lowest social classes, and particularly from among the cottagers, from whom everything else had been taken and who were now to lose their children as well. In addition to a brutal contempt for these poor people, Mynster's coolly reasoned statement also expresses quite neatly his matter-of-fact understanding of the complete dovetailing of the interests and spheres of the state and those of the official Church, where the necessity of good order was the one overriding concern.

Thus, when the Baptist affair ended first in stalemate and then in defeat (Christian VIII would not give Mynster the support that would have come immediately from Frederick VI), Mynster felt that the most lamentable of the results was not the loss of the unbaptized souls for which he had expressed such solicitude, but rather the resulting chaos and disorder in religious affairs, "for the matter thus remained undecided, so that everyone can do what he pleases."[117]

It was disorder—the notion that everyone is free to "do what he pleases"—which was most disturbing to Mynster, because underlying the issue of religious freedom was the issue of authority, and more particularly, of authority over

the vast rural mass of common people who were increasingly showing themselves to be "ungovernable": "[T]he ungovernable [Baptists, other peasant
awakeners, and various opposition political groups] . . . permit themselves to
do whatever they wish . . . [and this is in large measure because of] lax judges,
who expend their juridical art upon finding ingenious escapes for bad subjects."[118] Thus the real danger underlying religious disorder was that it was a
part of a larger social, *political* disorder. Mynster is quite explicit about this;
he favors the retention of the 1741 Conventicle Ordinance banning unauthorized
meetings not merely because of his fear of religious chaos, but because these
meetings often draw "up to 500 people," and "these assemblies in the present
times could easily take on a political character."[119] Everyday observation and
common sense forced Mynster to admit that it was true that many of the
members of the peasant awakening movement were in fact the most fervently
loyal of the king's subjects, but, he was quick to add, "on the other hand, it
cannot be denied that the religious movements of recent years are related in
many ways to the political movements, and that a desire to defy authority
often uses pretexts of religion and conscience."[120] The maintenance of authority
and order in religious matters was thus not merely the ultimate spiritual purpose
of the State; in more practical and everyday matters, such ecclesiastical authority was also the temporal order's first line of defense.

Because the religious and social-political movements of his times were far
too massive for him to control, Mynster's typical posture as bishop was one
of righteous paralysis. His memoirs thus contain passages which display a lively
bitterness which is extraordinary in a veteran and "profound" cleric writing at
the twilight of his life, but the bitterness is more comprehensible when one
considers the catalogue of accomplishments, or rather non-accomplishments,
which constitutes his career as Primate of Denmark. Mynster was defeated on
virtually every major issue which confronted the Church in his times. This
defeat included not only the overwhelming eclipse of his entire cultural view,
which was occasioned by the official entry of the common people into political
life after 1848, but also the defeat he suffered in connection with the Grundtvigian movement; the defeat in the campaigns against the Baptists and the
divine assemblies; and defeat in his various attempts to introduce a new liturgy,
a new altar ritual, and a new hymnal. Mynster was further embittered by the
fact that, in his paralysis, the vast bulk of the Copenhagen clergy set itself up
as a *de facto* legislative and deliberative body and was joined in this usurpation
by the theological faculty of the university—all of which reflected the leadership
vacuum which Mynster's rigid primacy had produced. Mynster comments
merely that "even though I might see the Church undermined by its unreasonable servants in union with its enemies, I must still seek to rescue what
can be rescued."[121] He goes on to decry both the fact that

> in recent years a disagreement between the views of a large portion of the clergy
> and my own has come to the fore, and that I do not dare to hope for support

from the clergy, but rather must expect opposition at every step; I cannot view this otherwise than sorrowfully, but I can do nothing about it.[122]

In the face of so much opposition from within the ranks of his own establishment, Mynster remained stoic and unmoved, and continued in his insistence "that our Church does not need any thoroughgoing reform."[123] Indeed, Mynster interprets both the opposition he met and his own intransigence as signs of his own rectitude:

> I could certainly have had it much easier if I could have seen it as defensible to bend with the fashion of the day and let everything go as it wanted . . . but I take comfort in the fact that I did not in any way cause myself to be called to the office which I now hold, and that I have carried out this office, and, God willing, will always carry it out, not according to the views of the moment, but according to a conviction which is serious, honest, and—so far as I am capable— drawn from all sides, a conviction which I cannot surrender to the impulses of the moment.[124]

Particularly after 1848, Mynster was proud of having stuck to unpopular principles rather than having "followed the current and won a popularity that . . . afterwards could not be preserved."[125] Thus Mynster (who seems to have acquired the nickname "Job" with good reason) in 1847 summed up his position as bishop by sighing: "I have remained here entirely alone."[126]

Yet he was not in fact *entirely* alone, as he himself noted with considerable pride, for he gives thanks that, though constantly beleaguered, "[I] have not been abandoned by my listeners, among whom I count many of the noblest people of the capital."[127] Indeed, Mynster writes, there are churches in Copenhagen, which "on ordinary Sundays, when the weather is tolerably fine, are almost overfilled. And if we look around among the audience, it is at least possible that even a majority of them belong to the more cultivated [dannede] classes."[128] Thus, although beset from virtually every side, Mynster took comfort in the fact that his understanding of Christianity still appealed to "the noblest people in the capital," "the more cultivated classes." In the cities, the poor and the working class seem not to have attended church very regularly— the total seating capacity of all Copenhagen's churches could not accommodate more than about four to five percent of the city's population, in any event. In the countryside, on the other hand, where the common people were fervently religious, this earnestness was dismissed by Mynster as mere "screeching," to be suppressed in favor of the good taste and orderliness preferred by the relative handful of "noble" and "cultivated" urban people who still believed in the disintegrating synthesis that was Christendom.

I. THE CHRISTIAN CHURCH AND ITS PLACE IN A "CHRISTIAN STATE"

Mynster's most coherent theoretical account of his understanding of the Church and of its place in the state is to be found in his unpublished *Outline of Christian Dogmatics.*[129] Mynster traces the genesis of an organized Church to the fact that "doctrine would be confused and all sorts of disorder would arise if everyone could come forth to teach publicly," and in support of this he cites I Corinthians 14, verses 33 and 40: "For God is not a God of confusion, but of peace . . . all things should be done decently and in good order."[130] (What Mynster does not point out is that the Pauline passage cited dealt with the thorny problem of speaking in tongues. Paul quite expressly differentiates speaking in tongues from teaching and prophecy, which he regarded as more important.) For Mynster the primary concern is order at any cost, even if he must turn to worldly authority to obtain it. The resulting dependence of the spiritual upon the temporal is not a problem for him. Mynster notes that "the right to call and appoint teachers [clergy]" does belong to the Church, technically, but care must be taken to see that this right is not exercised by "the crowd" within the Church, for then there is disorder, and the leaders will become dependent upon those whom they are supposed to lead. Therefore, Mynster concludes, the Church's "teachers are undoubtedly best appointed by those who govern [the state], if they are members of the Church."[131]

However, although the Church is thus delivered up defenseless into the hands of the state, its task ultimately is to remake and permeate the state:

> Because the state is by no means simply a society for the acquisition and protection of property, but ought to strive for the full development and ennoblement of humanity, the purpose of the Church is by no means foreign to the state, and one could say that the highest purpose of the state is to enable the Church to come to perfection within it. . . . [The duty of the ruler of the state is] to further the activity of the Church, so that the Church develops itself more and more, and increasingly penetrates the state.[132]

The Church and the state may coexist in this way because in Mynster's view their interests are not incompatible. This, in turn, is true because, as we have seen earlier in this chapter, Mynster shares the dominant Golden Age assumption that there is a continuity between the visible and invisible realms: The "Kingdom of God" is related to "true and lasting fortune blossoming upon the earth." That is, a people's "welfare" is ultimately related to its "worth."

Concretely, Mynster defines three general areas of competence for the state in relation to the Church. Firstly, the state must provide for the "direction" of Church affairs by establishing proper ecclesiastical authorities for deciding questions. Secondly, the state must provide for the "defense" of the Church, not only against "external enemies," but "also against those who would hinder the freedom of teaching [such 'freedom' being of course subject to the limitations imposed upon all state-appointed teachers], which is completely necessary to the Church's development and also against those who would let this freedom result in the impudence which works for the dissolution of the Church."[133] Finally, the state must provide for "the inspection of the Church (*inspectio secularis*), so that the Church, which in its proper course of development never comes into conflict with a well-ordered state, is not led astray into undertakings that could be dangerous to civic order and safety."[134] This final point is particularly telling: Not only is the Church to be given an opportunity to "penetrate" the state, but there is a *quid pro quo*, namely that the state has the task of policing the Church in order to suppress any tendencies which might threaten "civic order and safety."

In a sermon from an episcopal consecration on Easter Monday 1849, Mynster clearly summarizes his view of the supportive, sanctifying relation in which spiritual authority stands to the temporal world:

> Let the others cultivate their fields and attend to commerce, taking care of the other positions of life. All this must be done; all this is good and pleasing to God. But our calling is to contribute to sanctifying all this by God's Word and by prayer, so that—we might say—the scent of eternal life might be spread out over it.[135]

Thus, Christianity is not the proclamation of a new being which is other than, and indeed radically different from, the earthly life, but is the imprimatur of the eternal upon it. Official Christianity is the perfume of the Spirit upon the body of flesh.

In this same sermon, written while the new 1849 Constitution was still being formulated, Mynster goes even further and implies that an obligatory state religion is one of the indispensable bonds which constitutes a people as a people:

> We know ... how the ungodly fume and rage and the peoples give out vain counsels against the Lord and His Anointed. "Let us break their bonds and cast off their compulsion".... We know that there are many who would like to break the bonds that have hitherto so beautifully bound together all the people in the country into a Christian people.[136]

The sentiment implicit in this is spelled out explicitly in a sermon from Pentecost 1848, in which Mynster argues quite baldly for the social and national constitutive function of official Christianity: "*As long as our people is to be called a Christian people, there must also be ecclesiastical bonds, and whoever wishes to cast these off entirely thereby cuts himself off from the rest of the people and lives as a foreigner in the land.*"[137] Thus, one's participation in official Christianity was inextricably bound up with one's Danishness, and it is from this point of view, rooted as we have seen in his Golden Age understanding of the relationship between the visible and invisible worlds, that Mynster is able to make his peace with the constitutional consequences of 1848–49.

As mentioned in chapter 7, the triumphant liberals of 1848 did not attempt to carry out a secularizing policy of separation between Church and state, which would have been in keeping with the principles behind their political views. Many of these liberals (e.g., Monrad, the key figure in this regard) shared Mynster's fundamental Golden Age cultural assumptions. Instead, the men of '48 continued with the old synthetic notion of "Christendom," while giving it a democratic gloss by re-naming the State Church as "The People's Church." This was precisely the common ground on which Mynster could come to terms with the new order of things, for he also believed that the Church was an indispensable component of a people's nationhood, its social solidarity. Mynster's clearest statement of his understanding of the social and national function of official Christianity—and his clearest statement of the grounds upon which he was willing to come to terms with the new order—is contained in an eloquent sermon from the spring of 1852, entitled "Our Evangelical People's Church." Mynster decries the divisiveness which sectarianism brings and glories in the new name which official Christianity has received in Denmark, noting that

> there are other countries in which the different religious confessions are all at large, possessing thousands upon thousands of adherents, so that one can scarcely say which is the general religion of the people; but with us—thank God!—we still can tell which it is. . . . [L]et us cling fast to the beautiful, living phrase "People's Church"; it signifies that this is the Church to which the people cling, the Church whose confession is rooted in the people, the Church which is one of the strong bonds which holds the people together, and which is to connect the generations which follow with those that have gone before. Praise and thank God that we still have such a People's Church that holds together the vast preponderance of the people, so that those who deviate from it can quickly be added up. There are indeed people who live among us who confess another faith . . . but everyone feels, however, that these people are in many respects guests and foreigners, and that in essential ways they are not a part of our people.[138]

Thus, despite all the disappointments and defeats of his career as Bishop of Zealand and Primate of Denmark, Mynster could console himself that the greatest battle of all had not been lost: The new liberal and democratic age had found it impossible not to enshrine in its constitution an understanding of the Christian State—of "Christendom"—which expressed continuity with Mynster's assumptions and with those of the Golden Age.

11. Johan Ludvig Heiberg

○

The second generation of Golden Age leadership—whose leading figures were clearly Heiberg, in the literary sphere, and Martensen, in the religious—shows striking parallels with the first. Here, as with Oehlenschläger and Mynster, personal friendship and loyalty bound together the two leading figures. Here, as with the two earlier leaders, both unhesitatingly confessed a lofty Christianity as their religion, and both instinctively supported an urbane, elitist conservatism in their social attitudes and in their politics, which, as in the earlier case, can best be described as the fear of and the absence of politics. Again, as with the earlier pair of men, the professed Christianity of the poet was far more daring and unorthodox than that which society generally considered to be proper Christianity. And further, here, as earlier, it was the poet's theologian ally who stood as guarantor of the religious acceptability, of the "piety," of his more daring poet friend, while the poet, in turn, held open for the theologian access to the most advanced literary circles, to the realm of "good taste." The remarkable parallel continues even into specifics, for here, as in the earlier case, the unusual "Christianity" of the leading poet of the generation found expression in didactic poetry about Christianity and nature. Here, as earlier, that poetry was in danger of being misunderstood (or perhaps of being understood) as pantheism. And, finally, here, as earlier, a leading and extremely fashionable young theologian who was very well-connected (and a future Primate of Denmark) wrote a critical review that came to shape the success and acceptance with which society greeted those poems.

Yet despite all these parallels between the two generations of mainstream literary and ecclesiastical leadership in the Golden Age, there were also, of course, divergences or new developments. Heiberg established his position precisely by attacking and to some extent discrediting Oehlenschläger and Oehlenschläger's aesthetics—or rather, Oehlenschläger's lack of a conscious and coherent aesthetic theory. Heiberg demanded that literature, and drama in particular, be understood in relation to a consciously articulated, rigorous, and defensible aesthetic theory. Immediate, natural genius and sublime content were no longer enough for the generation Heiberg represented. Demands were now made for intellectual apprehensibility, for transparency and beauty of form rather than ponderous and chaotic content. Where Oehlenschläger had created his poetic triumphs upon the basis of a quickly imbibed and unclearly understood Schellingianism, a philosophy which seemed murky to many, Heiberg's intellectualism and formalism were based upon adherence to a clearly articulated version of Hegelian philosophy.

However, even though Oehlenschläger's cult of immediacy and the intellectualism and formalism of Heiberg inevitably led to a battle of the generations over aesthetics, both shared underlying assumptions about art, politics, and religion, and about the mutual relationship of all three in culture [Dannelse]. Heiberg represents more a continuation than a definitive break in the self-understanding of the Golden Age.

Martensen's relationship to Mynster shows similar sorts of differences in the face of underlying continuity. Mynster, as we have seen, was disquieted by Martensen's Hegelianism, but he took comfort in the fact that Martensen's version of Hegel was far less dogmatic than that of his literary friend Heiberg. When questions arose concerning Martensen's acceptability for the higher posts of Danish Christendom, what reassured Mynster most was perhaps the younger man's "gallantry," their personal and "honorable" friendship, and the knowledge that Martensen was firmly on the side of good taste and of ecclesiastical and social order in a world that contained increasing numbers of dangerous religious and political "screechers." Regardless of his theology, Martensen was a safe and in fact a splendid successor to Mynster. Indeed, in the turbulent 1840's and 1850's theological content could no longer be a major concern for Mynster and for conservative Christendom—if it ever had been—because what was of overriding importance was not content, but the question of style, of taste, of social tone; it was in these matters, no less than in speculative theology, that Martensen's sure touch prevailed.

Heiberg and Martensen, then, can be said to be the second pair of arbiters of the Christian culture of the Golden Age, and their mutual relationship was in many respects strikingly similar to that of Oehlenschläger and Mynster, whom they succeeded. The accession of the second generation took place, if not with the enthusiastic approval, then at least with the polite acquiescence of the first. In their shift of emphasis from the "immediacy" and "personal profundity" of Oehlenschläger and Mynster to formalism and intellectual apprehensibility, Heiberg and Martensen did not represent a revolution in any sense. They still stood upon the old ground of the synthetic Christian culture, and they still shared the old elitist horror of politics, an attitude which passed for conservatism. Let us examine the religion and politics of each of these Dioscuri whom we have chosen as representative of the second generation of the Golden Age's conservative mainstream.

B. HEIBERG, A BIOGRAPHICAL OVERVIEW

Johan Ludvig Heiberg was born in 1791, the son of the radical poet P. A. Heiberg and his vivacious *haute bourgeois* wife, Thomasine Buntzen Heiberg. Heiberg's mother divorced her husband in 1800, a year after he had been exiled for his political activity, and shortly thereafter married Count Gyllembourg, a wealthy Swedish political exile who died several years later, leaving Thomasine Gyllembourg to raise her only child, Johan Ludvig, in comfortable circumstances. For a while, the wrath of the boy's father, P. A. Heiberg, exiled in Paris, led to the child being made the unofficial ward, first of Kamma and K. L. Rahbek (whom we have met in earlier chapters), and later of a family relative. But the father's hurt feelings were eventually mollified, and Johan Ludvig returned to live with his mother, a brilliant, beautiful, shrewd, and wealthy widow. Johan Ludvig and his mother moved in the highest cultural circle of the capital, and frequent house guests included Oehlenschläger and H. C. Ørsted.

Johan Ludvig was a precocious boy and an unusually bright student, a polymath who studied entomology at the University of Copenhagen and took a doctorate in Spanish literature in 1817. Heiberg spent the years 1819–22 in Paris acquainting himself with French theatre and re-acquainting himself with his father. From 1822 to 1824 he taught Danish literature at the University of Kiel in Holstein, then Denmark's "other" university. In 1824 he traveled to Berlin, heard Hegel lecture, and afterwards visited him at his home. However, the German philosopher made no clear and immediate impression upon him, and Heiberg's conversion to Hegelianism was reserved for a sort of delayed-reaction epiphany which he experienced on shipboard on the way home to Copenhagen.

On the basis of his new philosophical creed, Heiberg wrote his brilliant essay *On Vaudeville*[1] in 1826 and propounded a theory of light and witty theatre as the Hegelian middle term between tragedy and comedy. In this and subsequent works Heiberg founded "scientific," i.e., systematic, literary criticism in Denmark.[2] The period 1826–30 saw Heiberg's most popular theatrical work[3] and his popular, dramatic, and aesthetic rout of the aging Oehlenschläger, who, as Heiberg suggested, was suited to the lyric, but not the tragic medium, where his style was too heavy and lacking in form. Heiberg carried on his aesthetic and philosophical campaign in his own journal, *Copenhagen's Flying Post* [*Kjøbenhavns flyvende Post*], which flourished on and off throughout the latter 1820's and the 1830's, sometimes supplemented by, sometimes replaced by, various weightier theoretical journals edited by Heiberg.[4]

By 1830 Heiberg was the most prestigious younger poet in the country and had an influential post at the Royal Theatre, where many of his works were performed. In 1831, at the age of forty, he married the leading lady of the Danish stage, the brilliant, gifted Johanne Luise Pätges, a nineteen-year-old girl up from the bottom of society, already long sought after by many aspiring young men of culture, leaving behind her a number of broken hearts and serving as the occasion for at least one well-known suicide.[5] Johan Ludvig and his namesake Johanne Luise Heiberg became the reigning cultural family of the nation and lived in a curious, lively, and childless *ménage à trois* with Heiberg's mother, Fru Gyllembourg, who herself, despite her relatively advanced age, was just embarking upon a highly successful (and at first anonymous) career as a writer of prose fiction. The Heiberg circle was the leading Copenhagen salon of its time and came to include the gifted young theologian Hans L. Martensen as one of its prominent members. Many other leading younger writers, such as Hans Christian Andersen and Søren Kierkegaard, were on close terms with the Heibergs.

The peak of Heiberg's popular esteem came in the late 1820's and the early 1830's, when he had brought the treasure of Hegelian philosophy up from Germany. Danish urban culture, perhaps feeling, as often, a bit inferior and isolated, grasped at the new philosophy almost as eagerly as it had grasped at Henrik Steffens' German cultural import a generation earlier. But by the late 1830's the social situation was changing; it was liberal politics, not aesthetics and philosophy, that increasingly claimed the attention of the younger cultured generation in Copenhagen, and Heiberg was unsuccessful in his attempt to woo this public away from its liberal political preoccupations and over to the "higher view" of speculative philosophy. Perhaps Heiberg's own cool, aristocratic, magisterial nature had something to do with this failure. Perhaps, too, we ought to remember that the Hegelian philosophy requires a great deal of effort to be understood, much more than that demanded by the brilliant aphorisms and picturesque metaphors of Steffens' Schellingianism. At any rate, a prolonged reprise of the sort of success which had greeted Steffens could not be sustained. Heiberg's major programmatic philosophical declaration, *On the Significance of Philosophy to the Present Age* (1833) (which will be discussed below) contained an invitation to a series of public lectures on the Hegelian philosophy. This programmatic declaration attracted a great deal of attention and retained an academic vogue for a decade or so, but it served more as the capstone of the aesthetic theory that had preceded it than as the beginning of any large-scale Hegelianization of the Danish public. The announced lectures were undersubscribed and had to be cancelled.[6]

The deeper reason for Heiberg's failure, however, does not lie in his own personality or in the difficulty of his subject so much as in the real and irreversible changes that were taking place around him: The relentless forward motion of the peasant mass and the pervasive consequences of the July Revolution of 1830 combined with Frederick VI's establishment of the Provincial Estates to make politics, and particularly liberal politics (and, later, liberal nationalism), the principal concern of the urban, cultured, younger generation. Heiberg, disappointed, found himself increasingly at odds with the audience he had hoped to win, and from around 1840 onward, when he published his most important political pieces, he can be seen as one of the last defenders of the anti-political conservative mainstream of the Golden Age. He became increasingly isolated and withdrew to lofty pessimism and his private observatory, where he enjoyed cultivating astronomy or, as he called it, "mathematics made concrete." He died in 1860, having spent the last decade of his life as the controversial and embattled director of the Royal Theatre, which he ruled with an iron hand, and where he is remembered for having excluded Ibsen and Ibsen's friends.

We will first look at Heiberg's Hegelianism and the place it accords to religion, and then turn to Heiberg's view of society and politics.

C. HEIBERG'S HEGELIANISM: *ON THE SIGNIFICANCE OF PHILOSOPHY TO THE PRESENT AGE* [7]

In his major Hegelian declaration of 1833, Heiberg sets forth a sketch that he hopes will demonstrate the supreme importance of the new philosophy, while at the same time he invites his readers to attend a series of lectures in which the philosophy will be explained in more detail. Heiberg's lectures will be "an 'Introduction to Philosophy' comprehensible to all people of culture [Dannede]," he explains, gallantly adding that this includes "cultured ladies" as well as men.[8]

The present age, Heiberg declares, is a transitional period, "a crisis."[9] It is still in the process of coming into being, and only that which is past and finished can be known, for then it is dead; then it is "material" [Stof] upon which the intellect may work.[10] This is Heiberg's version of the familiar Hegelian notion that the owl of Minerva flies only at dusk. This sense of crisis and transition is particularly true for "us as Christians," Heiberg adds, for the founder of our own religion did not bring forth something new by himself, but came "in the fullness of time," when the old culture, the Roman Empire, was "dead," a "formless substance," which could now be reformed.[11] The Romans had radically separated the divine from the human, and man, abandoned by the divine, lived entirely in finitude. This situation

> contained in itself the necessity of the return of the divine to humanity, so that in this way the finite might be reconciled with the infinite. . . . Therefore one can rightly say that the Christian religion was a work not of Christ, but of the human race; it is precisely because of all this that the Son was sent forth, not by himself, but by the Father, for what is a work of the human race is a work of God.[12]

Thus we can see that Heiberg's version of the Hegelian theodicy contains an implied equation of "the human race" and God, which, when stated baldly, could not help but offend traditional Christian opinion. To say that God is sovereign is but another way of saying that the human race is sovereign.

Still, Heiberg explains, humanity does not exist merely as "the human race," but has representative individuals—artists, poets, teachers of religion, philosophers—"in whom consciousness has awakened to a higher clarity, while it is more or less asleep in the mass."[13] These highest representatives of humanity form a sort of "upper house," while "the mass" can be divided into two groups: "cultured" [dannede] and "uncultured" [udannede]. Like the highest representatives, the cultured members of the mass could also

> be viewed as the representatives of the human race, but as a sort of more numerous and popular chamber, a sort of lower house, in contrast to the aristocratic, less numerous chamber which is constituted of those to whom we really give the name of "representatives"; the uncultured, on the other hand, are limited to the merely individual life and are excluded from representing other than their own persons.[14]

There is no question as to which "house" Heiberg imagines himself and his immediate circle as inhabiting. What is more interesting, however, is Heiberg's appeal to the egoism of "the better portion" [den finere Portion] of the bourgeoisie, which imagines itself "cultured" and is thus entitled to sit in the "lower house," as well as the casual assignment of the approximately ninety-five percent of the population who are "uncultured" to a merely blind and selfish existence with no higher prospect.

Religion and politics—at least what is understood by the vulgar who indulge in these activities—are assigned an unenviable position in Heiberg's scheme.

> If we look at the present, we see, first of all, that certain endeavors, which possess the life of the present and the interest of the moment for the uncultured, are viewed by the cultured as concluded material that belongs to the past. The most striking example of this is our frequent theological disputes, which are carried out exclusively for the edification of the uncultured, while the cultured, who have come beyond that standpoint, are almost entirely unaffected by this, but have their heaven and hell in political ferment. . . . The cultured know very well that literal faith and heresy-hunting are ghosts of a by-gone era, without flesh and blood. . . . It is politics which in our times forms the presence in which the cultured world lives; but precisely because it is something present, its material is not yet completed, at least not for those who live in this presence. Whether those who constitute what was above called humanity's "upper house" have come so far that they can regard the political question as answered, and whether they can regard the uncritical notions of the cultured mass about freedom as the completed material for a new and higher form—all this is another question.[15]

Thus, the uncultured are caught up in theological disputes; that is, the peasant masses are attracted to awakeners and to Grundtvig. Many of the cultured, on the other hand, chase after politics; that is, liberalism is gaining ground among the urban upper-middle class. Heiberg had hoped to recruit his audience from this class and had hoped he could woo it away from immersing itself in the blind and foolish finitudes of politics so that it could come to clarity via his "higher viewpoint."

In the present crisis, or transitional stage, when the mass is still involved in religion and much of the better portion of society seems about to leap into politics feet first, philosophy has a crucial, clarifying role to play, Heiberg insists. A critical or transitional state such as our own also necessarily contains the seeds of its own abolition and replacement by a new, stable synthesis. "Critical ferment has no other purpose than to bring forth its own opposite: the calm clarity that can serve as a mirror for the Idea."[16] This is the task of philosophy:

> What is it then which will bring order out of the present chaos? . . .It is *philosophy* that will make an end to the confusion. . . .For *truth* is at once philosophy's content and its form; further, it is its only content and only form. Philosophy is the truth itself and nothing else. . . . It is in this sense that one can say that philosophy stands above art, poetry, and religion, despite the fact that philosophy, just as these others, has the infinite as its object; thus, because the form in which it [philosophy] presents this object [the infinite] is the truth, all other forms of the infinite have their own justification in philosophy.[17]

Thus "[p]hilosophy is nothing other than the cognition of the eternal or the speculative idea, reason, the truth; the different expressions all refer to the same truth."[18] Philosophy is the queen of the sciences in which all the others will find themselves explained as relative or partial expressions of "the Truth." Yet philosophy's ascendancy will not be at the expense of these others:

> So far is it from being the case that philosophy will render art, poetry, and religion superfluous, that it is on the contrary the case that it will gain recognition for them in the actual world. . . . If, for the present, they lack this recognition, it is not because people have doubts about the truth as a substance, but only because they have doubts as to whether it is contained in the accidental forms in which it is presented by these activities [i.e., art, poetry, and religion]. Thus it is a matter of grasping these three spiritual spheres as actual relationships of substance, that is, of *conceiving* them, or of grasping them in their *concept*. . . . [T]he truth is the common substantial content that unites them [the "spiritual spheres"], while what separates them is only their accidental form—and one acknowledges this by *conceiving* them, that is, by grasping the common substance as *concept*, in which the accidental form with its differences is taken up and suspended [ophæves]; and this is philosophy—then they [art, poetry, and religion] will all exist peacefully side by side.[19]

Thus, although religion's absolute primacy (as well as that of art and poetry) is denied by Heiberg's philosophy, religion is assured a comfortable and continued existence once it has permitted itself to be "conceived" and "clarified" as part of a unified "concept."

But this is precisely the problem with religion in the present age, according to Heiberg. It has refused to accept the assistance and clarification available to it from philosophy and has remained mired in an antiquated and superstitious universe of thought, which is of interest only to the ignorant multitude. "[T]he cultured world has abolished religion," Heiberg informs us.[20] "It does no good for us to conceal or gloss over the truth. We must admit to ourselves that in our times religion is primarily a matter only for the uncultured, while for the cultured world it belongs to the past."[21] Cultured people (at any rate, those who have not yet turned wholly to politics) seek themselves in poetry rather than religion, Heiberg continues, in his imperious tone which states controversial propositions as though they were indisputable matters of fact:

> One will also undoubtedly admit that in the present cultured world poetry has taken the place of religion in part, because true edification is sought more in the former than in the latter; and this is no wonder, because a stern and somber view of human nature's infinite distance from divinity, and an unconsoling view of unattainable eternity, are by no means edifying. On the contrary, only that edification is genuine which brings about a cheerful, encouraging enjoyment of the divine *in its presence*, and thus really reconciles divinity and man.[22]

Thus Heiberg, tentatively at least, embraces the earlier Golden Age notion of the divine and reconciling function of poetry, even though he reserves the right to insist that, like religion, so also must its sister and successor, poetry, be "conceived," "clarified," and "taken up into" philosophy, which, however, will not abolish religion, poetry, etc., but will "preserve" them in all their relative validity. For now, however, one thing is absolutely certain: Religion has lost its appeal and its meaning for cultivated people. If the *"honest* believers of our times—that is, those who lie only to themselves and not to others"— were offered a certain proof of the existence of God and the immortality of the soul, Heiberg queries, would they not grasp it greedily and with thanks? Would not such a person admit that "only now does he have certainty, while that which he previously had called firm belief was nothing other than a hope, and, consequently, a doubt?"[23] Thus does Heiberg denigrate faith, for his system is incapable of recognizing it as a qualitatively different mode from intellectual apprehension. Heiberg recognizes only one qualitative mode, just as there is only one "substance" or "truth," which is displayed in its varying "accidental" forms in art, poetry, religion, etc. but which appears absolutely and "according to its concept" only in philosophy. Consequently, faith must be quantitatively inferior, less "certain," than intellectual apprehension. Like art and poetry, religion differs from philosophy in that it "presents the infinite from the point of view of *finitude.*"[24] "Religion makes the accidental into the essential,"[25] hence its relativity and intellectual inadequacy. Philosophy, on the other hand, "sees the *concept* in the *substantial*,"[26] hence its higher perfection.

Furthermore, just as philosophy is the only thing that can both supplant and redeem religion, so, too, can philosophy redeem politics from the trivialities of the finite: "Only philosophy is capable of penetrating into the many details of our finite—especially our political—purposes; only philosophy is capable of seeing their tendencies toward the Infinite, and, by means of this knowledge, of clarifying what is obscure in them."[27] Thus, in philosophy lies the possibility of making good on the Golden Age's promise that the finite and visible world is related to the invisible and infinite world by multifarious subterranean connections which the genius or the man of "spirit" can search out. For Heiberg, as for his predecessors, worldly concerns are still capable of being sanctified by the Spirit, and the resulting sanctified synthesis of the visible and invisible is "culture," a composite formation that is in itself the articulation of the harmonious wholeness of being. Ultimately there are not two kingdoms but one. Under the apparent duality of things lies a unity.

It is philosophy's task to find that unity, which is present in all things that truly are, that are truly *human*, a unity that was before all things were, a unity that is also the goal to which all things tend:

> Philosophy could not be the final thing in which all finite activity loses itself if it were not the first, from which they all sprang forth, as from their substantial fundament. Only with this insight can one understand that art, poetry, and religion contain the same substance as philosophy, for from where can they have received their substance if not from it? From philosophy they have received it and to philosophy they return it. . . . [Philosophy is both produced by the human race and produces it.] The product is here what produces, and the sought is the found. It is *found* because two of the human race's highest representatives [Hegel and Goethe] have already presented it in humanity's name; it is *sought* because the majority of the cultured have not yet appropriated it and are not yet conscious of it.[28]

Thus, for Heiberg, in its concern with the Alpha and Omega of all being, philosophy occupies the place usually reserved for religion. The first unity to be understood is that of God and humanity. Religion's assertion of God's absolute transcendence is groundless and alienating. "The spirit of God is the spirit of humanity; we would be bad Christians if we were to separate what Christ has joined."[29] Heiberg calls himself a "Christian," but he is careful to interpret Christ not as a personal redeemer but as the principle of the unity of the human and the divine.

Finally, the purpose of every pursuit in the "spiritual sphere" is not to introduce us to anything absolutely new but to return us to our own deepest being:

Art, poetry, religion, philosophy—these forms of humankind's thought are incapable of giving anything really new . . . ; on the contrary, that which they give us is our own and what is most anciently ours; they do not increase our property, but they open our eyes to that which we already possess.[30]

Heiberg's understanding of truth is precisely what Kierkegaard will later call "Socratic recollection," which he contrasted with the radically new and external truth brought to humanity by the consciousness of sin and the reality of redemption. Heiberg's view could, however, perhaps be assimilated to Mynster's psychological Christianity, in which, it will be remembered, it was Christ's task to "remind" us and "assure" us about the way things already are, without in fact introducing any radical change in the nature of things: "Show us the Father, that is enough."

According to Heiberg, then, for cultured people religion has largely been superseded by poetry, and in any event, religion, poetry, art, politics, etc. will all find their ultimate "clarification" in philosophy. Humanity's "two highest representatives" are the poet Goethe and the philosopher Hegel, and it is the task of modern philosophy to merge into poetry, Heiberg concludes, adding that "this can be done in *the didactic poem.*"[31] Let us turn from Heiberg's principal philosophical declaration to a few of his most important didactic poems in order to see how Heiberg the poet fulfills the pledge of Heiberg the philosopher.

D. HEIBERG'S DIDACTIC POETRY

The first of Heiberg's major didactic poems in which he attempted to cast his understanding of religion and philosophy into poetic form was his *Reformation Cantata,*[32] composed in 1839 in honor, characteristically, both of a university festival and of the three hundredth anniversary of the introduction of the Reformation into Denmark. The version which we now possess is a revised one, the first having been rejected by the university theological faculty as too abstract and philosophical. (H. N. Clausen had remarked that "Heiberg has not sung of the Reformation, but of Hegelian philosophy."[33]) It is difficult to see how even the present, revised version could have met most of these objections.

God is hailed as a reflexive, self-revealing, and self-discovering God, who by revealing himself to "thought"—i.e., human thought, specifically the "thought" of Hegelian philosophy—has truly become himself:

> Hail, o light from the source of truth,
> Which has shined for three centuries,
> Which shall never be darkened,
> But will, rather, shed clarity, life, and fortune!

> You streamed into the eye of the world,
> And thought became clear to itself;
> And God became manifest for Thought. . . .
> For thought ascended on high
> When it descended into Itself.[34]

Having completed its task of guaranteeing the dignity and independence of "Thought," the specific significance of the Reformation has been exhausted, and religion may retire in favor of the free intellectual existence it has made possible: ". . . Freedom's noble cedars / Were planted deep within the Church's ground, / In which they grew into a grove / That now protects the school."[35] The intellectual freedom that the Reformation is credited with having created is thus praised as the precondition of philosophy's present supersession of religion.

Later the next year (1840), Heiberg produced what was perhaps his most perfect and enduring volume, *New Poems* [*Nye Digte*].[36] Heiberg's *New Poems* contained not only the witty social and philosophical comedy *A Soul After Death* (which will be discussed in the next section, which deals with Heiberg's view of society and politics) but also two ingenious religio-philosophical nature poems, *Divine Services: A Spring Fantasy* and *Protestantism in Nature: A Mystery*, both of which we will examine here as Hegelian counterparts to Oehlenschläger's Schellingian "Jesus-Nature" poem.

The great Danish historian of literature, Hans Brix, writes that *Divine Services* came out of intimate conversations between Heiberg and his theologian friend Martensen, and that "in this work Heiberg has given poetic expression to Martensen's theology, to the extent that he was willing to follow Martensen. His *Divine Services* does not *exclude* a personal God, but it is rather difficult to see Him."[37] Upon its publication, Martensen served as the ideal interpreter and reviewer of the work which had in large measure grown out of his own influence, and, in typical unabashed Golden Age fashion, Martensen wrote one of the principal reviews of Heiberg's *New Poems* when it appeared, receiving it very favorably, and singling out *Divine Services* for a lengthy discussion and high praise. Martensen praised Heiberg's work as "a poetic breakthrough," which has "the peculiar charm and freshness of something new." Heiberg's religious poetry shows "that just as poetry only receives its true transfiguration in religion, so, in many cases, a more profound aesthetic contemplation can reflect fruitfully upon theology." "With this work," Martensen writes, Heiberg "has raised himself and our literature to new heights that we have never known before."[38] Thus again, as in the case of Mynster's review of Oehlenschläger's "Jesus-Nature" poem, a bright and respected young theologian helped secure a welcome and favorable reception by official Christian culture for poetry which many might have found suspect, or even pagan, from a traditional Christian point of view.

In *Divine Services,* a solitary, soulful individual, "the poet," is walking in a forest on a beautiful Pentecost morning. This particular Church festival, as we will shortly see, is of enormous importance to understanding the underlying Hegelian theme in the poem. The poet is delighted to be in the forest, and proclaims the place to be "the temple for my God . . . nature's Pentecost," where "better priests preach than in those gloomy halls," i.e., the churches of orthodox Christendom. Here in the woods, nature performs her "pentecostal miracles," whereas in the church there are only "words."

Then the poet is suddenly bid welcome by Pan, who proclaims himself, to the poet's surprise, to be the poet's God. Pan admonishes the solitary poet to remain solitary, "for I can and will only hear your prayers in solitary fashion." The poet gladly agrees:

> If I want to unite with my God
> I will seek a lonely spot,
> Where I am all alone with God.
> There my devotion will not be hindered
> By a foolish and sleepy crowd;
> There I will find society enough
> With the thoughts of my own interior.[39]

In parting, Pan informs the poet that although perhaps he is most sought in nature, he is also accessible in church, provided one is entirely alone. There is a Christian as well as a merely natural variant of pantheism. The important thing is that one be solitary. Pan disappears.

Next, our poet hears another voice in the forest, saying:

> Turn your thoughts away from loneliness!
> For where two or three
> Are gathered together in my name,
> There I myself am present among them.[40]

The poet is upbraided for his solitary preferences:

> You are calling upon your *own*
> Savior in prayer,
> Not upon Him Who descended
> To the *entire* fallen race
> . . . .
> Do as He did, practice here below
> The first commandment of love;
> Join a congregation,
> And through it come to God.[41]

And the poet confesses his weakness as a Christian and his tendency toward pantheism:

> You elevate me unto truth,
> But you require a difficult sacrifice.
> Alas! I shamefully confess
> That the poet easily turns toward heathenism,
> Even when he kneels before God . . .
> . . . .
> Alas! I ought not deny that
> My Christianity is far from genuine,
> For the life which nature announces to me
> Prefers intercourse with the ancient gods. . . .[42]

The poet admits that he is especially drawn toward "Pan, the god of gods, who never fails," who remains "as the Infinite" when all the other gods flee before thought.[43] "I more and more come to grasp that if one wishes to be philosophic about one's God, one comes to Pan."[44] We see this, Heiberg tells us, in the fact that Socrates' abolition of the gods led to Plato's "panic" elevation of the idea, while even Judaism resulted in "Spinoza's pantheism."[45] Yet, the poet continues, he realizes that only Christianity is capable of an intellectually adequate religion:

> I know that only Christ's teaching
> Can be a sure home for the explorations of thought.
> Only there are there forests and caves and grottoes
> In which Pan does not hide.[46]

So, the poet resolves, let us Christianize nature with visible symbols; let us place

> [God's] Grace's precious signs
> Among the unconscious works of nature.
> Let the cross be planted amid the wild beeches. . . .
> Make every hill to a Golgotha;
> Let cloisters rise amid the groves. . . . [47]

But, alas, the poet realizes, such tangible, "Catholic" Christianity is not possible in Scandinavia, where "a poor poet cannot avoid pantheism"; whereupon the voice in the forest, which has proven to be that of an angel, replies, "No, we are Protestants."[48] The angel then turns Hegelian and explains that it is not nature which is to save us, but we who are to "save" nature by using our mind to bring to consciousness the unconscious longing that is present in nature, its need to be understood, to be "conceived" according to its concept. We need to perform an act of intellectual salvation for the entire universe:

> Why plant a cross in the forest?
> Isn't the cross everywhere,
> Here on earth and on high,

In every living form?
. . . .
You, who have the power of speech,
Don't you know the message
That Nature unconsciously knows
In its silent striving?
. . . .
Don't you believe that nature is obscurely longing
For the hour of its deliverance. . . . [49]

Heiberg is here sounding the Pauline note of nature crying out in tribulation and placing upon it a Hegelian-intellectualist interpretation:

Nature wishes to confess
Its half-understood thoughts,
Its obscure pains and pleasures,
To a breast in which a heart beats.
. . . .
If humanity could but comprehend!
If humanity could understand!
. . . .
Hear it, poet! Listen to it!
It is you to whom it speaks,
So that you might clarify
The dark forces with your harp.[50]

It is the poet's task to express brotherly love for his fellows and solidarity with the natural universe by performing an act of cognition and interpretation. A "chorus from the forest" concludes the poem:

All of nature has need of union,
It strives toward humanity, before it strives toward God;
The poet comprehends its secret meaning,
And sings of its longings with his lyre.
Everything in nature wishes to be looked upon and heard
By an understanding, loving breast;
It wants to be comprehended with love,
And to be led toward salvation, to the joy of freedom.[51]

This is our commission, not to worship nature, but to penetrate and explain it, thus leading it to freedom and salvation. It is for this purpose that we have been filled with the Spirit, and it is for this purpose that the poet has been given the gift of speaking in tongues. This explains Heiberg's choice of Pentecost, the day of inspiration and of linguistic miracles, as the setting for this poetic exposition of his Hegelian version of "Protestant Christianity."

The concluding work of the *New Poems* of 1840 is *Protestantism in Nature: A Mystery*. The title could easily have been applied to *Divine Services*, which we have just examined, but the theme of this poem is somewhat different, more personal, more reflective and pessimistic. *Protestantism in Nature* forms a sort of counterpart to the demythologized, post-Catholic world of the *Reformation Cantata*.[52] The campaign against the mere externality of things was "a battle of life and death" in which "the inner armed itself against the outer" and won.[53] The inner—i.e., "thought"—"has begun to sparkle"; it can no longer be stopped. "It wants to conquer the world, nothing less."[54] That is Heiberg's understanding of the victory of "Protestantism." This victory is all well and good, and even more important, it is necessary. But it has drained the visible world of its divinity and its excitement. "Faith no longer elevates itself to the vision of God," Heiberg complains. God

> Only hovers behind his work
> Invisibly, as a thought.
> Alas! And nature no longer smiles
> Benignly as the cloak in which his essence was;
> Sundered from God, it reposes
> Spiritless and empty.[55]

However, the cure for this is not the return to the immediacy of Catholicism but rather the rediscovery within ourselves of that which we thought we had seen in nature:

> Turn your gaze upon your own interior!
> You will find in your thought
> What was lost in your world.
> Everything that has disappeared takes on
> Life and existence within.
>
> The God you seek is your own God.
> What more do you want?
> He does not appear as an object out there
> Amid the others, amid the many.
> . . . .
> Nature bedecked in all her glory
> Is all too lowly
> To produce, with all her quiet industry,
> A worthy cloak for Him.
> But it is not therefore empty and spiritless,
> And not abandoned.[56]

Thus we are back to the point of view of *Divine Services*, though in a chastened and somber mood. Now, however, in *Protestantism in Nature*, the subjectivity berated in *Divine Services*, where the angel chided the poet for "calling upon your *own* savior in prayer," has been restored to its rights, and it is proudly announced that "the God you seek is your own God, what more do you want?" The principle of subjectivity, of seeking one's *own* God by reflecting into one's own interior, is vindicated, though not in the sense of the selfishness which romantically eschews "the crowd"—Heiberg's Hegelianism, no less than Feuerbach's, sees our true life as the life of our "species-being." Rather, Heiberg's Christianity vindicates subjectivity against the the the claims of orthodox Christianity, where God and "the truth" are revealed dogma which are made accessible to man objectively, from without. The liberation of thought, so praised in the *Reformation Cantata* as the essence of Protestantism, must not be allowed merely to be loosed upon the external world as a conqueror, but must first and foremost give us occasion to turn inward, to re-create internally the wonder that Protestantism has drained from the mythic, immediate world of Catholicism. Then we will be able to meet the challenge of *Divine Services* and win the world of nature, not as conqueror, but as liberator:

> The light of the spirit glows with intensity
> In the chamber of the soul.
> It views both God and itself by the same flames,
> In the same vision.
> And with this light,
> Which arose in humanity's breast like a star,
> Nature, even unto her utmost distances,
> Will become clear and lift up her voice
> And will answer the questions which lately
> Humanity has vainly put.
> And nature will reveal its life
> As a striving toward the light of freedom.[57]

In Heiberg's philosophic-religious vision, the Hegelian element seems to tend very strongly in the mystical or pantheistic direction in spite of its better knowledge. The absence of divine evidence, the absence of mystery in the visible world of nature, and the terrible emptiness in the Protestant world of the hidden God seem to speak to Heiberg with a voice that all his intellectualist bravado could not drown out. The call of the visible Universe, even in its most abstract form, namely the motion of the stars as geometrical points, seems to have been irresistible for Heiberg, and after 1840 he turned increasingly toward a sort of neo-Platonic astronomy, a study of spheric harmony, which allowed him to vent his hatred of empiricism and his disdain for the wretchedness and foibles of the human race.

Heiberg's Hegelian "religiousness" was a lofty, personal intellectualism. It is hard to explain his preference for calling himself a Christian and a Protestant as other than the result of social convention in an officially Christian society where Christianity was very loosely defined in any event and often seemed to have more to do with good taste, social order, "morality," and "the great values" than with any specific doctrinal content. (As we have seen, from a point of view such as Mynster's, the disruptive Grundtvig and the divine assemblies were greater threats to Christianity than was Heiberg.) Heiberg's biographer, Morton Borup, seems to have summed up Heiberg's version of Golden Age religiosity best in saying that "his relationship to Christianity was respectful, but deep inside he was cool to it. . . . [H]e wished to ally with theology as an intellectual power that was related to philosophy and that was usable in building a bulwark against the materialism of the age."[58] Heiberg's view of religion, then, was ultimately at the service of his view of society, his loathing for the contagion of liberalism and materialism that was stealing his own middle-class constituency and channelling it into mere politics and finitude. Let us now turn to an examination of Heiberg's view of society and politics.

E. HEIBERG'S SOCIAL VIEWS: *A SOUL AFTER DEATH*

Heiberg's liveliest and most readable social criticism is contained in the "apocalyptic comedy" *A Soul After Death* which, as has been mentioned, was the principal work in his *New Poems* of 1840, which also contained the two didactic poems we have just examined. *A Soul After Death* was Heiberg's revenge upon the "philistine" Copenhagen which had begun to turn its back upon him, and the philistines, like all philistines, loved being roasted by the poet. The play was an enormous success.

The plot was a simple one. "A worthy man is dead!," it begins, "a faithful husband, a dear father, an honest friend, a citizen, one of the few."[59] As we shall soon see, our worthy soul turns out to be a shallow and rather silly philistine, a typical member of that part of the Copenhagen public which reckoned itself as "cultured" but which did not wish to subscribe to Heiberg's philosophical lectures. When our "worthy man," or "the Soul" as he is called, presents himself to St. Peter at the gate of Paradise, the Christian heaven, he insists upon his right to admission:

> I am, so far as I can see
> Indeed worthy of being rewarded by the Lord.
> I have honestly earned my living;
> I have never coveted my neighbor's property;
> I gave every man his due, worked ceaselessly,
> Left no debts behind when I died,
> But, on the contrary, a fortune,
> So that my wife, if she will live modestly as a widow
> —And I know that she is capable of that—
> Will have no need of help.[60]

The poor "Soul" is concerned only with material considerations, and soon reveals himself ignorant of Christian teachings: "It is so long since I was confirmed," he whines.[61]

Condemned by his ignorance of things Christian, he is excluded by St. Peter from Paradise and is transported further to Elysium, the happy afterlife of the classicists, whose gate is guarded by Aristophanes. Our poor philistine soul again reveals his ignorance of Latin and Greek and his boorish bad taste. He has not studied languages, he admits, but was determined at an early age to be suited for "the business world."[62] When asked about "classic" art and "classic" wisdom, the poor philistine brightly replies: "Classic? Yes, I went to business class."[63] Old things do not interest him anyway, he continues, but he must have news and newspapers constantly. Nor has he really participated in the revival of art and literature in Golden Age Copenhagen, though he has given six dollars to the museum and is a member of the Society for Freedom of the Press. Finally disgusted, Aristophanes tells the Soul to "Go to Hell!," which he does.

Hell, of course, is just the place for the philistine. There is no restrictive watchman at the gate. There is plenty to eat and drink, and lots of newspapers. Mediocre theatre and mediocre books abound. Hell has its clubs, a stock exchange, and a university and learned societies. Work here is meaningless and repetitive, and the soul finds just the kind of people and politics he is used to: "Here we are liberal!"[64]

Mephistopheles, his hospitable guide, explains the liberal principle of the establishment:

> Here we reject everything which has a fundament.[65]
> Here there are flat places, but never a bottom.
> Here everything is independent and free,
> No difference between coal and chalk.
> Here freedom and equality are ready;
> Here the state is in its beginning,
> And it never, no matter how much it hurries,
> Ever comes away from its beginning.[66]

This has its philosophical explanation, Mephistopheles continues:

> If you understood philosophy
> I could easily explain the matter to you:
> Our kingdom is the immediate,
> Which no amount of Eternity can liberate,
> Because it contains no fundament within itself. . . . [67]

Thus, Mephistopheles concludes, you will see

> That you will have about the same life here

As that which you knew on earth.
Since I hate to lie or boast,
You have learned from my discourse
That you will have things no better than there,
But no worse either. And that is always something,
Isn't it my good fellow?[68]

The only problem with the place, Mephistopheles admits, is that it is "the Kingdom of Boredom, we do a lot of yawning in this country."[69] "Well," sighs the philistine soul, "I'm used to being bored." "So," Mephistopheles counters,

It is as if you were made for this place.
In general, everything you learned down there
Will come in very handy here.[70]

Next, however, the soul insists upon knowing the name of this wonderful land he has entered, and is shocked to learn it is "Hell":

But good God, how can that be?
I don't want to be in Hell.
I must have come here by mistake.
I have always been a correct man
And respected as a citizen in my country.[71]

To which Mephistopheles gives the perfect Golden Age, anti-philistine, aristocratic reply:

That is exactly why you are here, my friend!
. . . .
. . . Most of the people here are respectable fellows,
And they are treated respectably and honestly.
And this is the way it will go for you and your friends.
No torture is being prepared for you.
As I have said, you will find the same life,
The same busyness, the same pastimes,
As before were in the earthly kingdom.
This is due, I must tell you, to the fact that
You, my friend, and those like you,
When you lived, you were in Hell.[72]

"I was in Hell?!," the soul interrupts. "As almost everyone," Mephistopheles replies, adhering to the continuing Golden Age faith in the rare few:

Except people do not often *call* it that,
That fat, phlegmatic life on earth
In which they believe in the real
And never get to see the least glimpse

Of that meager skeleton they call the idea.[73]

The conditions for admission into anything other than Hell, then, include not only proper education, good taste, and seemly social comportment, but, as an integral part of these, a participation in the intellectual vision of speculative idealism. The poor philistine soul quickly comes to terms with his infernal location, however, when he learns, happily, that nothing has really changed. In the final scene he is taken to his assigned task, the meaningless and endlessly repeated task of working with many others to fill an enormous and bottomless vessel. While the workers labor, a chorus chants:

> No fundament!
> No bottom!
> Bring your bucket, bring your scoop!
> Busyness, busyness is our watchword
> Until the final hour of the world.[74]

The vision of busyness and shared activity gladdens the soul, and he congratulates himself: "How lucky I finally found my place!"[75] Whereupon his (similarly philistine, of course) mourning survivors on earth are heard to console themselves with a hope the irony of which they do not suspect: "We will all be together by and by."[76]

A Soul After Death strikes the basic and continuing chord of Heiberg's social views. Only the truly cultured can be saved in any sense, and bitter experience has taught him that they are always a handful. Oehlenschläger's notion of the rare few remained valid for the second generation of the Golden Age. The possibility of salvation was held out to the cultivated mass who constitute humanity's "lower house," but they have spurned it, preferring business ventures and liberal politics instead. They have rejected salvation.

Yet it must be noted that salvation does not depend upon specific religious belief or moral character, but, as indicated, upon proper education, proper social attitudes, and proper intellectual orientation. It was not any particular sin or failing of character that excluded the Soul from Paradise and Elysium—and the implied parity of these destinations puts Heiberg's putative Christianity in a suspicious light once again—but a lack of specific knowledge about Biblical facts and a lack of classical education. Worse, of course, is that the Soul reveals himself as having been destined for the business world and defines himself socially by his material endeavors and his liberal newspapers. Let us turn from this to Heiberg's more direct political and social statements, which generally emerge as digressions in his massive output of literary criticism.

F. HEIBERG'S POLITICS

Two years after he published A Soul After Death, Heiberg began publishing a joint venture entitled Denmark, A Painter's Atlas.[77] It contained illustrations of Danish scenes by a well-known artist of the time, accompanied by poetic texts of Heiberg. The subscription sold very poorly, and the work was never really completed. The public again rejected Heiberg, even though it had flocked to see *A Soul After Death*, and the reason was perhaps that people were coming to resent Heiberg's persistent and increasing bitterness in relation to "the public." In the *Atlas* the humor is largely gone from the satire, and only the bitterness remains.

In one long and notorious *Atlas* piece, "The Playhouse," we hear Thalia, the muse of comic theatre, berating a typical middle-class, philistine pseudo-intellectual named "The Public," who wishes for a larger theatre, suitable for shows with horses and tiger hunts, and who never speaks his mind or utters an opinion until he has asked others or until he

> Reads in the papers, in black and white,
> A well-grounded, reasoned judgment
> Which tells me what I ought to like.[78]

Thalia tells him that he defiles her temple:

> You sit lazily upon the temple benches.
> You do not hear, nor think.
> For you the spirit is nothing but a stink.
> · · · · · · · · · · · · · · ·
> It is your money they want to take,
> And they coquette a bit with your praise;
> For such a person as you now are
> No longer claims the least respect.
> And no wonder, for you yourself
> Have lost respect for beauty
> And have no faith in ideas,
> And respect art as much as if it were a bean.[79]

Artists no longer produce great dramatic works, in order for "fools to judge them."[80] And soon Denmark will lose her illustrious stage, one of the few areas in which the little nation was great in Europe:

> You will soon stand in the nations' ring
> As gray in art as in other things.[81]

Thalia dwells in particular upon one of the major socio-political and cultural tenets of the Golden Age, namely that the arts and culture are a school for society. The theatre, Thalia says,

> Is a temple and a school
> In which you enter not merely with your Sunday clothes

But also with a Sunday attitude . . .
. . . .
Don't think that they look down from the stage
With trembling when they see your lazy body.
No, *you* must look *up* to the stage
As to a higher, better level
Than the street-level from which you come.
. . . .
Remember, you are to be brought up by us . . .
And listen to our songs like a child.[82]

Let us investigate Heiberg's aesthetic and socio-political conception of "the public," for it is central to understanding his politics.

In *On the Theater*,[83] a series of articles Heiberg published in *The Fatherland* in 1840, he finds the theatre analogous to the state. It has three elements: the poet, who is the legislator; the performer, who is the executive; and the public, who is the judge. Above all of them stand the directors of the theatre, who attempt to keep order between the three constituent elements by "representing the Idea itself of the entire institution,"[84] and by making sure that each element acts according to the requirements of "true, objective Reason."[85]

It is the public which is most interesting to us in the present context. "A good public" learns from itself and not from external authorities. It is an organic whole in which the less advanced learn from the more advanced. The public represents the principle of "subjectivity," Heiberg explains, and its judgments are "infallible" to the extent that it does not abandon its real feelings and become corrupted by dishonesty to itself by leaning upon some form of external tradition or authority, particularly the false authority of mediocre reviewers. When the public awaits the judgment of the reviewers before passing its own judgment, as happens all too often, it "surrenders its character as a *public*." It becomes an incoherent mass of nervous and mutually envious, insecure individuals, in which the rule is every person for himself, some remaining silent, embarrassed to have any opinion, while others "prostitute" their subjectivity to sources wholly external to the public itself. Then the public has lost its spontaneity, its true and healthy subjectivity and its organic character, and has instead been transformed into a mere nervous group of atomistic individuals.

> [I]n a good public it is the best who set the tone and represent the whole as if by tacit agreement. The good public is not, as the bad, an atomistic juxtaposition of the most different sorts of individuals who are all, nevertheless, equal in rights, . . . but is an aristocracy of those who do have rights, whose tutelage is accepted by those who do not have rights, who have not attained the age of majority, and who then cultivate themselves until they achieve the same sort of mastery, instead of instantly and immediately asserting their atom of opinion.[86]

One could scarcely find a more compact and coherent articulation of the typical social views of the mainstream of the Golden Age. Heiberg's viewpoint is diametrically opposed to the principles of equality of rights and atomistic individualism that classical liberalism enshrines. There is a Lockean epistemological modesty which underlies the classical liberal and empiricist assumption that it is impossible to penetrate to the "real" worth of each personality, to decide who are the bearers of "culture" and who are not, or to determine who are the "real" personalities and who are the drones. Unlike the classical liberals, Heiberg (along with the aristocratic and idealist mainstream of the Golden Age) rejected this modesty and believed in the existence of an objective standard of measure which made it possible to discriminate in this way. Thus Heiberg, like the Golden Age mainstream generally, was opposed to the principles of equality of rights and atomistic individualism. He called for a society that was hierarchically organized and intentionally inegalitarian. His inegalitarianism was not simply a matter of inequality of property and of representation in matters of state—even liberals could not embrace economic equality, and many liberals also rejected equality of representation. Heiberg's inegalitarianism went further; he believed that society should extend differential recognition to different groups of people—that is, that there should be unequal social recognition of people's rights as human beings, in accordance with society's official perception of their worth as members of their culture. Because of its *a priori* assumption regarding the coherence of the whole of existence, the Golden Age insisted that the scale of aesthetic cultivation was necessarily linked to moral worth and to political importance and was the important visible indicator of these.

For the Golden Age mainstream, the universe was whole; the outer was not irremediably sundered from the inner reality, but when properly interpreted could be understood in its connection to it. Liberalism's epistemological "agnosticism," which admits ignorance of the inner and concentrates only on the outer, on the empirical, was foreign, ice-cold, and even immoral to the Golden Age. Christianity was a delicate issue and had to be handled gingerly: on the one hand, it was a guarantor of "values" and of social order, and various understandings of the God-Man Jesus Christ were employed as means of maintaining communication between the human and the divine, the visible and the invisible realities. But, on the other hand, Protestantism's hidden God could make the universe terribly cold and could lend support to the uncomfortable notion that the visible, fallen world stood in no discernable and predictable relation to invisible reality, a notion that could have "liberal" consequences—it is no accident that one of liberalism's most prominent politicians, Professor H. N. Clausen, was a devout Christian and a brilliant theologian.

The Golden Age rejected liberalism (and, of course, democracy), but did not embrace a static military-agrarian hierarchy of hereditary nobility and landlords—the social origins of the Golden Age were much too bourgeois and absolutist for that. Rather, the Golden Age preferred a hierarchy of taste and cultivation, in which the lesser stood in an attitude of attentive deference to the greater. Thus, the Golden Age model of society was not the manor farm or the free marketplace—both of which are rooted in some form of economic activity and vulgar material concerns—but rather the school, which hovers in the realm of the "Spirit," the ethereal world of *haute bourgeois* imaginings, and was ultimately connected to no social or economic base other than the upper reaches of the absolutist bureaucracy. It was therefore destined to be a social view which would begin to dissipate with the rise of middle-class liberalism and materialism in the 1830's and 1840's and which would be shattered entirely after 1848, with the political enfranchisement that ratified the rise of the common man to economic and cultural independence.

Liberals, of course, were also capable of the same "schoolish" sentiments, the same condescension towards the "uncultivated," as the Golden Age mainstream (as for example in the speech of Orla Lehmann that will be examined in chapter 14). But this only shows that the Copenhagen liberal bourgeoisie shared much of the same social and academic background as the Golden Age poets, whose recalcitrant audience it was. The liberals generally shared Golden Age elitism and often subscribed to large portions of the idealist aesthetics and philosophy they had imbibed from the Golden Age writers. Yet they were moving away from that conservative, apolitical cultural synthesis. Powerful social and economic forces made it impossible for the liberals to accept the view of society and politics that Golden Age aesthetics entailed. Therefore, just as it is important to note that a leading liberal such as Lehmann can seem as elitist and schoolish as Heiberg, it is equally important—indeed more important—to note that some of Lehmann's most elitist-sounding remarks are contained in a speech in which he inveighed against any limitation of universal (male) suffrage.

Let us turn from Heiberg's theatrical to his specifically political investigation of the public. After 1840, he came to distinguish, not between a "good" and a "bad" public but between "people" and "public" respectively. In his review of the play *Svend Grathe*[87] from 1842, Heiberg once again picks up his argument that the public needs to be reformed, for it is being led astray by its abuse of its "subjective rights."

> In political matters the error is to be clearly seen in the many who wish to dissolve the state into an atomistic mass of subjects all of whom possess equal rights, all of whose particular opinions must be taken into account. . . . It is really an effort to transform *the people* [Folket] into a *public* [Publikum], for a *people* is an organism in which the individual atom does not matter by itself, but only in relation to the whole, while a *public* is a soggy mass in which all organic differences disappear. It consequently lies in the nature of a public that, in order to become respectable (which the mere mass can never become) it must acquire some organization—at least enough so that reasonable differences can show themselves—as a precondition for a reasonable general will. (It is perhaps necessary to remark, with reference to the uncultivated standpoint at which many

of our liberals find themselves, that the *general will* is not the sum of the individual wills, but is the will of reason, revealed in the best of people).[88]

Heiberg resoundingly repudiates liberalism's atomism and embraces the perennially ambiguous Rousseauian general will, drawing the elitist rather than
the democratic conclusion. Until the public reforms itself so that "within the
public a spiritual aristocracy can take shape, which will dominate and gradually
lead the unformed mass," the public will remain "a *mass* [and] therefore the
object of contempt for all competent people."[89]

The ideas touched upon in the review of *Svend Grathe* received fuller
treatment in two long articles published shortly thereafter, *People and Public*[90]
and *On Authority*.[91] Here Heiberg completes the transition from theatre criticism
to politics and gives us his Hegelian theory of the state and of the individual's
place in it. The practical significance of the theory, as well as Heiberg's concrete
sense of what the present time requires, were further illuminated by a series
of comments and asides contained in a lengthy review of Lope de Vega's *The
King and the Peasant*,[92] published in 1843.

In the old days, Heiberg argues in *People and Public*, the public was viewed
as identical with the people, and authors addressed a theatrical public as "the
Danish people." There was a time when it was "true that the public was the
representative of the people, because in those days only the most intelligent
people, those really in possession of the right to do so, appropriated to themselves the right to speak."[93] Now, however, all cultured people know that
people and public have become utterly divergent. This is so because

> on the whole, the political tendencies cannot be separated from the literary,
> religious, etc., since the same forces are at work in all the different movements
> of the age. . . . [U]pon closer inspection poetry can be seen to be connected to
> politics in ways that are much more profound than the simple use of political
> material.[94]

In its political and its cultural ascendancy, the public has "converted the ringing
silver of the idea into the coarse copper coin of realism."[95] As in art, so in
politics. We are cursed with the mere atomistic individual, and we must recognize "the atomistic individual's nothingness and lack of any rights."[96]

This split between an organic order, in which the individual has a place,
and a mere atomistic collection of particulars was further developed in Heiberg's *Lyric Poetry*[97] from 1843, where the dichotomy is made very clear.

> What is individual in a person is the eternal; it is the guarantee of his immortality.
> The particular, on the other hand, is much more that which is destined to be
> abolished [ophævet] in him. To the extent that a person possesses only partic-
> ularism instead of individuality, he will be annihilated instead of being made
> immortal.

Now, since very few people are "real individuals," this would put the doctrine of immortality in danger if we did not dare to assume that individuality is present in everyone like a germ that in the life to come can receive the development it lacked in this life.[98]

Even in *A Soul After Death*, Heiberg had hinted that there was perhaps a way out of Hell, which perhaps served only a purgatory function. But this was not stressed in the play, for it would have diluted its polemical function. In this life, at any rate, *"the real, the true personalities*, those whose individuality has already been developed here on earth, stand before us as *the visible representatives of Eternity*, as *living proofs of immortality."*[99] Thus the "beautiful individual" is not a mere accidental genius but a witness of eternity. This is very much in keeping with the general Golden Age doctrine that "the rare few" can act as messengers of a higher reality, as living links with the divine, as creators of "culture," which all must imbibe upon pain of being "annihilated" as significant human beings, or, at the very least, of being sent to purgatory.

Against this background, we can return to the articles *People and Public* and *On Authority* and examine Heiberg's treatment of the state as such. "The state is an organism," Heiberg writes, and "in an organism only what is organic has validity and rights. . . . [I]n the organism of the state nothing has political rights except the things that are themselves organized, thus estates and corporations. . . ."[100] For example, any representation according to geographical districts, or any other system that tends to give the impression that it is individuals who are being represented, is invalid, for any system which sees "individuals as possessing rights vis-à-vis the state" will eventually "destroy all political organisms, dissolve the authority of the state, and transform the people into a public."[101]

> [P]resent-day constitutions, which have all more or less adopted the erroneous, atomistic principle that representation is to be the representation of masses instead of organisms, of individuals instead of estates and corporations . . . have therefore established election according to districts. . . . This is the dissolution of the state; it is atomism.[102]

This error can also be seen in the common and erroneous notion of popular sovereignty, Heiberg continues, for a sovereign can never be a people but only a state or its representative, the monarch.[103]

The relationship between the individual and the state is one of authority, or of an education or an "upbringing," which may be strict and disciplinarian or mutual and cooperative, all according to the age and development of the individual. Authority, first of all, has a naked existence as power: "All authority is a *power* which acts as a power, that is, by its mere existence, and not by means of reasons. . . . Its right [is] nothing other than the fact that it exists."[104] It is of the essence of authority, in every institution in which it is present, that the whole is superior to its parts: "[E]very essential institution cannot dispense with authority, and must necessarily stand in a relationship of superiority to the individuals, who are subordinated."[105] This is because "every idea has its authority from itself and not from the individuals who labor in its service. . . . Therefore the state has its authority from itself, and not from its citizens, who, on the contrary, must bow before its power."[106] Thus, "under every form of government the state must assert its *authority*, and by this means place itself in a relationship of *superiority* to all its individual citizens. . . ."[107] We could not ask for a clearer antithesis to the liberal state, in which the interest of the whole can never exceed the interest of the sum of its parts. This is the Hegelian state, which has its being and its justification not in any individual concerns— much less any material concerns—but in its Idea, which it is the task of history to realize.

But, Heiberg assures us, authority is not only exercised blindly. It is true that

> authority, insofar as it is a power, acts *blindly* and exercises a *despotic* mastery. . . . Only when it is *acknowledged* in its rational necessity does any other "because" reveal itself than that which reposes in its mere existence. . . . But as long as it is not taken up in recognition, that is, in *free* recognition, the condition which it establishes is that of *slavery*. . . . [108]

Analogous to this condition of "slavery," Heiberg continues, is the Jewish religion, in which Jehovah was a wholly alien authority related to in fear, whereas the development of Christianity, in coming to knowledge and free recognition of God, made the relationship to his authority one of love. Thus, whether one is slave or free does not depend upon the objective properties of authority but upon one's subjective relation to authority. When one properly acquiesces in authority, one understands one's own tutelage in relation to it. In such a situation, "[a]uthority becomes the object of cognition and recognition [Erkjendelse], and this is its own natural development by which it is elevated to a higher existence."[109] Both the authority (the known) and the individual subject (the knower) are then raised to a higher existence. This is true both of divine authority—God and humanity are raised to a higher level by our knowledge of God—and of political authority, where "the way in which the state is taken up into the consciousness of the citizens, and the varying degrees of this consciousness, exercises an essential influence upon the existence of the state itself."[110] Thus, in Hegelian politics, as in Hegelian epistemology, the Knower affects the Known. In classical Hegelian language, the Idea is not only Substance—an objectively other, alien entity—but also Subject—it is potentially related to the Knower, whose task it is to realize that potential. But it is important that the Known be known in the right way, and this problem, as we will see, is precisely where the failure of liberalism is to be found, in Heiberg's view.

Depending upon the development of the people in relation to the authority of the state, there can be periods of equilibrium or of disequilibrium, the latter of which are periods of development, of transition. There can be an antithesis between Power and Right (as humanly understood) at certain times, and the present historical situation is such a time. Just as we have sundered people from public, so also has Power been sundered from the common understanding of Right. Heiberg sees a "necessity of reason" in the development of the present schism, but he also sees that there is an equally strong "necessity of reason for its being taken up into unity."[111]

What is most lamentable, in Heiberg's view, is that in this particular period of development neither the party of movement nor the party of order makes intelligent statements of its position, but both speak of benefits to citizens and not of the idea of the state. Both the liberals, who work for a constitution, and the conservatives, who defend the present order, do so, almost without exception, with "a complete failure to appreciate the Idea," for they attack or justify upon "the basis of simple utility," on the basis of "the benefits provided for the citizens."[112] However,

> what matters here is something completely other than what can guarantee the largest number of benefits to citizens. The only benefit which matters is not the one-sided development of the people, but the development of the state to a higher standpoint, in which its idea is realized more perfectly than at the preceding level. Whether or not the citizens come into the possession of more benefits is a matter of complete indifference, for the state does not exist for the sake of its citizens, but the citizens for the sake of the state.[113]

Thus, Heiberg continues, although the battles of our society have been fought primarily on the political front in recent years, neither the defenders of the old order nor the new liberals have a full or profound understanding of the differences between them. What is needed is "a *genius*, who really *understands* the movements of his times,"[114] who will raise the entire debate above the wretched level of mere utility, of gossip and sniping. Change for the better seems unlikely in present-day Denmark, however, for both sides have stubbornly refused to see the light of the Idea which Heiberg has attempted to reveal. And "when our politicians dissolve the state into separate individuals, then the so-called general human rights become the basis of the state, and because it is right which is to justify power, then it is the authority of individuals which constitutes that of the state."[115] Heiberg, who had been unable to sell his Hegelianism very successfully even to the conservative elite of the capital, came in the 1840's to espouse a variant of the Golden Age understanding of society so elitist that he was led to call down a plague upon both parties, to retire into conversation with only a very few associates and into communion with the cold and lofty stars.

There is much talk of a "freer" constitution, Heiberg admits, but it is important to realize that where there are freer constitutions, these are the result and not the precondition of the people's development, which was most certainly a gradual development. Freer constitutions—as in England, where such a development is best displayed—have their justification in the fact that what has come to pass gradually, and in stages, is that "the state itself, as an idea, gains and grows in intensity by living in the cognition and recognition of its citizens, but *not* that the citizens themselves come to exert greater influence."[116] If this latter comes to pass, as in England, it is a consequence, indifferent in itself, of a freer constitution, but by no means the justification or purpose of that constitution.

We may grant that the notion of greater civic freedom is compatible with a higher development of the Idea of the state, Heiberg argues, but only as a "result" and not as a *"precondition"* for such a development of the state. "In other words, when the state has really been taken up into the consciousness of the citizens and lives within it, then that consciousness will have a retroactive effect upon the state,"[117] and any new constitution will merely reflect the new state of affairs brought about by the reciprocal development that has already taken place. Constitutions, like owls of Minerva, fly only at close of day.

Yet we do not sit on our hands waiting for the constitutional owl to take flight, as Heiberg reminds us:

> This does not contain any political fatalism or quietism . . . [Heiberg, like other Hegelians, seems nervous about this charge]. One must remember that the Idea only acts when it is taken up into human consciousness. . . . Consequently, so far is it from being the case that individuals are to adopt a passive attitude, that it is, on the contrary, to them and them alone that the Idea announces its call to enter into its service and do its work. But the work does not consist in acting *immediately* for the introduction of a new constitution for the state; rather, it consists in bringing forth the higher consciousness, the organic civic sense, which already in itself does in fact contain a changed constitution.[118]

Heiberg thus rebuts the charge that his philosophy is apolitical, but when one examines the meaning of his position, it is that we must do without political activity as that term is commonly understood. Rather, we must work on ourselves (our "consciousness"), so that we are entirely saturated with the state and are comfortable within it. When we recognize, with our freedom, the necessity of the state's existence, we will no longer be in an oppositional relationship to the state, but neither will it be in such a relationship to us. The Idea, having already been seen to be "substance," will now also come to be seen as "subject," and the state, having been taken up into ourselves, is now in a position to grant us greater liberty.

As a corollary of the notion that politics means working upon one's own consciousness, Heiberg propounds the optimistic Hegelian notion of theodicy that denies, as do all theodicies, that any amount of apparently negative evidence or any number of apparent setbacks for the development of the Idea can be of any ultimate significance. Negative appearances are merely a sign that the Good is on its way, and where there is degeneration, regeneration must follow. Thus, on the one hand, the transition—which in one sense Heiberg finds so lamentable—of the public from "an organic representation" into "an atomistic mass representing nothing" is a regression. But on the other hand this transition can be seen as a "necessary" step on the way to "a new and more perfect organization."[119] For the time being, however, the outlook is admittedly bleak:

> [I]t is undoubtedly the *political* regeneration which must precede all others, because the state, as the outward and empirical existence of the Spirit, is the sphere in which absolutely all have their dwelling, and where they must first become comfortable before they can orient themselves in the higher and more ideal regions. But the prospects of political regeneration seem to be quite dark everywhere in the world. . . .[120]

Therefore, in Heiberg's view, *until* regeneration comes what is required is *discipline* (indeed repression) for the unruly public, and order for the personal development of the people. There is always a mass of individuals "who stand outside the recognition of this"; that is, there is always, in addition to a people, a public, which is "a mass of individuals upon whom authority ought to act and has to act as a blind power. . . . The politicizing public must be held in awe of the state's fundamental law in the same way that the *canaille* must be in awe of the civil and criminal law. . . ."[121] This is but another way of saying that politics, as the term is ordinarily understood, must be suppressed, in order that people may work on themselves. The "politicizing public" must in effect be forced to be free. In case his apparently even-handed condemnation of the errors of both the liberal and conservative parties had created any doubts about where he stands, Heiberg is here declaring his allegiance to the fundamental Golden Age rejection of politics and his dedication to absolutism as a surrogate for political life. Heiberg's elaborate Hegelian justification of his claim that his Golden Age anti-politics are ultimately political is an attempt to cloud the issue somewhat by allowing his patent loathing for politics to deck itself out as "politics" in some "profound" sense. However, Heiberg makes his true position on politics clear in a typical Golden Age paean to absolutism, which we will examine below.

In his 1843 review of Lope de Vega's *The King and the Peasant*, Heiberg presents his classic and most articulate Golden Age defense of absolutism, which is presented as the most desirable political form precisely because it is the absence of politics. Absolutism is the constitutional form perfectly suited to the present, and the social bulwark of absolutism, Heiberg contends, is the uncorrupted peasant who, in the romantic Golden Age understanding, formed—or ought to have formed—a barrier against the precipitate changes, or politics, sought by "the politicizing public." The "peasant's point of view," Heiberg argues, concurs completely with the evaluations assigned to personal and political freedom by absolute monarchy. The (idealized) peasant eschews politics because participation in the chores of government would be for him "a burden without any enjoyment."[122] "Participation in public affairs, not to mention the supreme control of such matters, cannot in any way be united with the even, tranquil spirit which is best situated when it remains within the boundaries of narrowly circumscribed activity,"[123] i.e., rural agrarian existence. "Had the poet depicted the peasant as a member of an Assembly of Estates or even of a communal council [both of which had recently admitted peasants in Denmark], then he [the peasant] could not have basked in the innocent, patriarchal happiness which is precisely what makes him so appealing."[124]

Elsewhere, in Heiberg's socially critical *Atlas*, a "peasant minstrel" reflects the author's romantic view of the proper, "immediate" nature of this social class and of how that class is being misled into politics:

> I play only for the present hour,
> And if I am asked about the future's riddle,
> The only answer that I speak
> Is: "I rely upon my fiddle."
>
> See, that's my politics, as true
> As sun and moon above the earth do hover.
> And if I play a little false sometimes,
> Well, I'm doing as the others.[125]

In his review of *The King and the Peasant*, after he presents his never-never Golden Age understanding of the peasant, Heiberg puts forth the quintessential Golden Age defense of absolutism, which, for the purposes of the present work, will stand as the supreme example of the political (or anti-political) view of the "conservative" Golden Age mainstream:

> In despotism, there is one person who is master, and all others are slaves. In absolute monarchy there is also one person who is master, but the others are not slaves. On the contrary, absolute monarchy, just as much as constitutional monarchy, is founded upon the idea of freedom. . . . The freedom which absolute monarchy guarantees its citizens is indeed not political, but individual, and in this, this form of government differs essentially from despotism, where it is precisely individual freedom which is restrained or even strangled. What is restrained in the absolute monarchy, on the other hand, is political freedom, but along with this limitation individual freedom is given a degree of development it cannot receive under a constitutional monarchy, much less a republic.[126]

This is because in the democratic forms of government very few will have "the independence and insight which is required in order to choose true freedom,"[127] and most will therefore be swept up in a "swift current" which deprives them of their individual freedom. In an absolute monarchy, on the other hand, there is no such swift current because there is no political freedom to be abused, and the individual thus reposes securely in individual freedom.

Absolute monarchy is thus political atomism—the absence of politics—in that one only relates oneself, in matters of politics, directly to the king and not to other individuals. But this political atomism is a means of putting politics into abeyance so that a rich, organic life of the individual might be lived, and true mutuality might have a chance to develop, prior to politics: "Reciprocal sympathies, benevolent efforts, and jovial assemblies thus assert themselves much more here than where political party spirit strews the seed of discord in familial and fraternal relationships."[128]

Here Heiberg openly reveals his own preference regarding what is appropriate for the present age of immaturity during which we "work on ourselves," namely, the continuation of an enlightened, absolute monarchy and the absence of "political freedom"—that is, the absence of politics. As I have attempted to show, this distaste for politics was a general tenet of the Golden Age cultural mainstream. Heiberg's rhapsodic sketch of the peasant, in which he serves as spokesman for the Golden Age, reflects a hopeless misunderstanding of the realities of Danish social and economic life of the 1840's, particularly with respect to the peasant movement. It is no wonder that, for the Golden Age, the real world continued to disappoint "the Idea."

As far as he personally was concerned, by the mid-1840's Heiberg was weary and cynical about the possibilities of elevating his faithless age to a level that would enable it to devote itself to the service of the Idea, and he took refuge in lofty detachment. Heiberg sums up his attitude in the bitter poem "Charlottenlund,"[129] which forms part of his *Atlas*. "The poet" takes a distant, weary look at the whole scene of human activity:

> I think you become dizzy in the head
> If you do not stand above the whole thing.
> The observer ought to stand at a distance,
> At a point outside the throng.[130]

"The Starry Heaven," another poem in the *Atlas*, allows the celestial sphere, serenely above the wretched earth, to give the final, resigned advice which the astronomer Heiberg himself follows:

> The mass crawls about, blind,
> Amongst its low and narrow business.
> My ceaseless motion is the judgment of time
> Upon everyone who mucks about and fusses.

> But you who wish to dwell in peace,
> Undisturbed by planless dither,
> Lift yourself to me and sample the calm
> Provided by my tranquil rhythm.[131]

This was Heiberg's ultimate, despairing resignation in the face of the unruly and politicizing public, who in the waning decade of the Golden Age, would no longer attend the school of "culture."

12. H. L. Martensen

O

Hans Lassen Martensen was born in 1808 in the town of Flensborg in the mixed German-Danish district of central Slesvig. His mother was of German extraction, and his father, of North Slesvig Danish peasant stock, was a ship's captain in Flensborg and, after 1817, when the family moved to Copenhagen, an author on maritime subjects. Martensen was thus from a half-German provincial family of moderate means, but he was a bright child and an excellent student and succeeded in winning a full scholarship to the Metropolitan School, one of Copenhagen's finest preparatory schools. In due time he matriculated into the theological course at the University of Copenhagen, where he again excelled, and after taking his degree he was granted a government travel stipend which, in the years 1834–36, made possible the completion of his education in Germany.

Martensen's initial theological sympathies had been with Schleiermacher, but his stay in Berlin soon caused him to shift his allegiance to Hegel, in whom the young theologian completely immersed himself. Hegel's philosophy caught him up "in a magical net,"[1] Martensen recounts in his memoirs, but the heady effects of the powerful speculative system soon caused Martensen to undergo a profound "crisis" of conscience that was followed by a severe physical and then a psychic sickness, or despair, characterized by "doubts" in which "all reality, both in the world of things and of ideas was dissolved into shadows for me."[2] Concretely, Martensen recounts in his memoirs (written some fifty years afterward), the crisis meant that he had to choose between "theism and pantheism," between "the living God, the God of revelation" and "the god of heathendom"—God as mere "logical idea, logical process, logical spirit . . . an impersonal relationship," such as was found in the "one-sided intellectualism" characteristic of dogmatic Hegelianism.[3] Although "much that was in pantheism attracted [Martensen] mightily," he recounts in his memoirs that he recovered by moving more in the direction of personal faith, and he remembered that "it is faith that carries all our cognition of the personal God and his revelations. It is faith from which cognition draws its life in the deepest sense."[4]

Martensen thus moved towards a modified Hegelianism that subordinated cognition to faith and made room for a personal relationship to a God of revelation.

This did not happen all at once in Berlin in 1835, but, on the contrary, "it was only at a later time that this dawned on me fully and clearly, and it took longer before my inner self could come into proper order."[5] It is unclear exactly when Martensen's conversion away from a more radical Hegelianism took place, but it cannot in any event have been complete before he met Johan Ludvig and Fru Johanne Luise Heiberg for the first time in Paris in the summer of 1836. Martensen was utterly captivated by them and they by him, and they became fast friends without there being any insurmountable barriers in the area of religion and dogmatics. Furthermore, as we shall see, Martensen's reception in Copenhagen in the late 1830's and 1840's was quite markedly the reception of a Hegelian, and he won quite a following as a stylish university teacher, sufficiently modish and Hegelian to earn him the suspicious attention of Mynster, who promptly set out to disarm and convert him. It therefore seems most appropriate to date the completion of Martensen's recovery to the period of Mynster's dawning influence over him, namely the early and mid-1840's, when Martensen's dazzling ecclesiastical career began its ascent under Mynster's guidance.

In 1837, after his return to Copenhagen, Martensen became a docent at the university, and when Poul Martin Møller, a popular and leading professor of philosophy, died in the spring of 1838, young Martensen filled his place as a lecturer for two years and became Extraordinary Professor in 1840, at age thirty-two. In 1845 Martensen, still retaining his academic appointment, was appointed with Mynster's influence to Mynster's old post of Court Preacher [Hofprædikant], a very prestigious position and a sure stepping stone for an ecclesiastic on the way up. In 1850, one year after the publication of his *magnum opus*, the *Christian Dogmatics*, he was made Ordinary Professor, and in 1854, upon the death of Mynster, Martensen became Bishop of Zealand and Primate of Denmark, a position which he retained until his death in 1884.

Martensen's theological and philosophical position can be described as Hegelian in method and in much of the architecture of its overall vision, with the significant alteration that it is far more Christocentric than, for example, the position of his good friend Heiberg. Consequently, Martensen views religion as the apex of all human activity and not merely as philosophy's handmaiden (as, again, in Heiberg). These divergences from Heiberg's Hegelianism, while of great importance from the purely theological point of view, had little impact on Martensen's view of politics and of the role of the state. Martensen viewed the state both as the expression of the religious, moral, and intellectual development of a hierarchic and organic Christian society and as the means of that society's further development.

Although in the early and mid-1840's, Martensen's all-reconciling, modified Hegelian Christian speculation was just what educated Copenhagen thought it wanted,[6] by 1850 or so he was already seen as intellectually passé. It was rather as Mynster's pupil and successor, both in conservative Church politics and in classical sermonizing, that Martensen entered the Danish cultural and ecclesiastical pantheon. The brief reactionary ministry of A. S. Ørsted, which coincided with Mynster's timely death, made it possible for the old conservative statesman of Golden Age Christendom, in his final hour of political influence, to install Martensen at the head of the Danish People's Church. Martensen would hold this position for thirty years, long after all the other cultural luminaries of the Golden Age absolutist period had passed from the scene and Denmark had long since become a liberal constitutional state. Despite his theological differences with Mynster, Martensen's fundamental views on religion, politics, and culture coincided with those of his protector and with the Golden Age mainstream, so that, differences in theological content notwithstanding, Martensen's episcopacy represented the most important sort of continuity, that of form and style.

B. MARTENSEN'S *MORAL PHILOSOPHY:* THE HUMAN RACE, "THE IDEAL," AND THE STATE

Martensen's university lectures of the late 1830's and the 1840's were the great academic success of his life, and they made his career. Speculative thought now stormed—briefly—through the university. (It ought to be noted, however, that excepting Martensen, almost everyone who was smitten with Hegelianism in the 1830's and 1840's soon came to reject it emphatically; this was the case for Poul Møller and Frederick Sibbern, Kierkegaard's philosophy teachers at the university, and for Rasmus Nielsen, another philosophy professor at the university, who later became the spokesman for what he believed to be a systematic exposition of Kierkegaard's point of view and who became Martensen's principal academic opponent.)

Unfortunately, Martensen's brilliant lectures on speculative dogmatics which captivated theological students in the later 1830's and the 1840's have not survived, and we have only the drier and somewhat transformed distillate of these, the *Christian Dogmatics*, published in 1849 when Martensen's academic popularity (and the popularity of speculative theology generally) had already waned considerably, and his university career was nearing its end. Coming as it did at the end, rather than at the outset of his academic career, the *Dogmatics* will be dealt with later in this chapter. Martensen's ethics, which constituted the other half of his speculative edifice, did not receive full exposition until the three-volume *Christian Ethics* of the 1870's, which is far beyond the time-span of the Golden Age which here interests us. For an understanding of Martensen's presentation of ethical theory during his most influential period we must turn instead to his highly compressed and rather Hegelian *Outline of the System of Moral Philosophy* from 1841, which is the only surviving work of importance from Martensen's early period at the university.

Skat Arildsen, Martensen's biographer, finds that the *Moral Philosophy* is particularly dependent upon Hegel and upon the Hegelian Karl Rosenkranz.[7] This seems to be quite clearly the case, even though in his later memoirs Martensen downplays the significance of the Hegelianism of the late 1830's and early 1840's,[8] which had made him so popular with university students and with Heiberg. Thus, in the Foreword to the original edition of the *Moral Philosophy*, Martensen hailed Hegel as "the living beginning-point of a new development" and noted that the Hegelian system has "freedom as its principle" and "will show itself to be all the more rich in great ethical views, pointing all the more definitely toward the idea of personality as the gravitational point of thought."[9] When Martensen, as Bishop of Zealand and Primate of Denmark, published a second edition of his youthful *Moral Philosophy* in 1864, he noted in the new Foreword that, although the original work was being reprinted in its entirety, he was omitting the original (Hegelian) Foreword as "not necessary."[10]

The *Moral Philosophy* begins in good Hegelian style, dwelling upon its "concept" as a science, and therefore, as a system which can only understand itself reflexively or retrospectively: "Because the concept of a science is not different from the completely developed science itself, it cannot be known at the beginning of the system, but only in the conclusion."[11] Martensen's Minervan owl, like those of Hegel and Heiberg, flies only at close of day.

The fundament upon which the *Moral Philosophy* rests is a rather Hegelian understanding of the Christian God as an evolving self-knower.

> In the Christian view of life God is not merely the creational beginning of life, but also its result, its all-encompassing final purpose. As such, or as the *highest* Good, he will be realized by human freedom. The divine purpose is in no way different from God himself, and the meaning of all of God's requirements to humanity [Mennesket] is that he himself wants to be All in All, that he wants to win personal form in the human individual. God himself is what he commands; with every commandment he means only himself.[12]

Thus, in good Hegelian fashion, the human race is the means by which God returns into himself, having become himself more fully and at a higher level of consciousness.

There is a division of labor between moral philosophy and religion, the latter concerning itself with faith, the former with action. The "object" of moral philosophy is "the idea of the Good," which is also religion's "object," though religion and moral philosophy each view the Good from a different standpoint. "Religion and moral consciousness are related to one another as life's peace and rest are related to its struggle and labor."[13] Religion perceives the need for reconciliation, a need that is quickened by the "ideal requirements" of ethics and that in turn spurs ethics further on in its task, which is "to give the religious principle its development and its actual implementation in the world."[14] Thus, moral philosophy, while a profane science, is the active, worldly arm of religion. There is indeed a close working relationship between common-sense everyday mores [Sædelighed] and religion, and morality forms the bridge between these two: "Moral philosophy presupposes the actual everyday morality [den virkelige Sædelighed] that in all nations is closely connected with religion, in which it has its final fundament."[15] It is through the medium of moral philosophy that the highest, invisible realm of religion is intimately connected with the tangible workaday world.

Ethics views humanity as "a link in the total organization that the Spirit has constructed for itself, a world which in its various moments expresses freedom's own system (the family, the state, the Church)."[16] Thus social life is the necessary tool for developing the ideal in the human race, for although "the Good becomes humanity's ideal, . . . this subjective unity with the Good is insufficient if it has not developed itself through the objective forms of social life."[17] There are no private roads to the highest realms, for humanity is a species-being. The highest task of the human race is thus embodied in the task of real human history, for the "definite content of the ideal must be developed by the *historical view of the world*."[18] Further, the historical development of the ideal is worked out concretely in the life of the state, and "the form of the state has been determined by the moral and religious principle with which the nations were saturated" at any given time in their development.[19]

The state is the true developmental medium of the self:

> The state is the kingdom of the personality in its formal universality and necessity. The general right of freedom and equality that individuals have is realized through their necessary inequality, through the *systematic* limitation of their freedom. Therefore, the life of the state organizes itself into different estates and into the relationship between government and subjects.[20]

Thus, the state is an organic, corporative, moral whole through which each individual receives his or her moral development in the direction of the ideal, and

> the coherence of the state with the idea of the Good reveals itself in the fact that external justice finds its deeper justification in internal justice and in the fact that the system of rights is guaranteed by a system of inner obligations, by moral consciousness, and by mutual confidence and recognition.[21]

Martensen's notion of the corporate state as the historical organ of morality and the only medium through which the individual can live in the highest sense is diametrically opposed to the classical liberal notion of the state as a material association, dedicated to the protection of the property interests of its various members, who are free to develop their moral existence within their separate, individual lives. In Martensen's view,

> in order for civic virtue to be capable of being developed, the individual must belong to a definite *estate* and make himself the organ for one of the universal purposes of the state. . . . The activity of the individual estate is only a collaborative effort as part of the whole, and civic virtue therefore contains developed social consciousness.[22]

A "people" is a linguistic and ethnic entity, a quasi-natural substance or material which can only approach the ideal insofar as the higher reality of the state acts upon it.

> The concept of the state is inseparable from the concept of the people. The spirits of those peoples, whose natural boundaries are language, take on their external legal existence in the states. Only when a people comes into a genuine condition of law does it really come into possession of its spiritual property, does it come to feel and know itself as a people.[23]

The active moral force which binds a people together is civic virtue, whose "essential elements" are "justice and a spiritual love of one's fatherland."[24] Furthermore,

> [p]iety and admiration for the great individuals of the nation are inseparable from love of one's country. In admiration we feel our own lowliness, our distance from the spiritual greatness to which we look up, but admiration also lifts us above ourselves and makes us certain of the reality of our ideal.[25]

Martensen's emphasis upon "the great individuals of the nation" echoes what was expressed in the other Golden Age examples of genius cultivation we have examined, e.g., Oehlenschläger's cultivation of "the rare few" and, even more apposite here, Heiberg's elevation of the great heroes of culture as "living proofs of our immortality." Through the veneration of the great men of one's society, the ordinary, fleshly eye can perceive "spiritual greatness," and one can even rise "above oneself." For Martensen, as for the Golden Age generally, the "great men" of one's society form the links between the invisible and the visible realms, and culture is a composite in which spiritual realities are made tangible.

Yet for Martensen, love of one's country, like the function of the state generally, is not an absolute in itself but is a specific means to a general end or goal outside itself: "Love of one's fatherland is . . . only the *spiritual, natural form* of [a] higher, universal love. Nationality is holy because it is a means through which that which is holy in and for itself—the eternal and the universal—are to be taken up and appropriated."[26] Thus, the individual is ultimately related through the state but not to it:

> The category of the individual is not simply absorbed into that of the state, for it is by means of the state that the individual is related to the Kingdom of the Absolute Idea, the kingdom in which the individuals are actual in their pure ideality. Inasmuch as they are the spheres in which the Spirit of the people comes to consciousness of the infinite, art, science, and religion are purposes of the state. But in positing these purposes, the state also *presupposes* the internal independence and integrity of these spheres, and the state thereby points beyond itself.[27]

Therefore, important as it is, the state remains a means and not an end. Martensen's Christocentricity and his commitment to the independence and ultimate primacy of religion make his notion of the state less absolute than Heiberg's. The state remains the necessary means for the individual's highest self-realization, however, and Martensen's view is but a variant of the Golden Age view of a hierarchical society in which an aristocracy of the Spirit presides over a well-ordered Christendom, where the practical or utilitarian advantages of the community are seen as accidental and its moral and spiritual worth are of primary significance. Thus, despite certain theoretical differences, in matters of social views and practical politics Martensen shared in the underlying vision of the Golden Age mainstream and the intensely conservative, apolitical, and aristocratic stance adopted by such men as Mynster and Heiberg. Their common stance was characterized negatively by a loathing for the mere instrumentalism of middle-class liberalism as well as by a fear of the "uncultured" rural mass—and by a certain blindness concerning the rapidity with which that rural mass was coming into its majority.

C. *CHRISTIAN DOGMATICS*: SPECULATIVE MODERATION AND RETREAT FROM HEGEL

Martensen's greatest work was his *Christian Dogmatics* of 1849, in which he completed the task of moderating his earlier Hegelian position. It is interesting to note that Martensen's original title for the book was to have been *Speculative Dogmatics*, but he thought better of it and decided upon the less controversial *Christian Dogmatics*.[28] The *Dogmatics* is less philosophical and dialectical than Martensen's earlier work, and his relationship to Christianity is quite noticeably less speculative than that which he displayed in, for example, his 1841 review of Heiberg's *New Poems*. By 1849, Martensen had been influenced by Mynster's more disciplined and traditional understanding of dogma. To cite a couple of examples, Martensen's 1837 doctoral dissertation had claimed that philosophy was the universal science of which theology was the crown, while by 1849 theology and philosophy were seen as forms of knowledge which were different in principle, though they both shared the speculative method; again, the 1837 dissertation had claimed that sin, though it darkened other areas of human life, did not obscure our cognitive capacities, while by 1849 sin was portrayed as obscuring the cognitive capacities also, making rebirth necessary in this area as well.[29] The point of view adopted in the *Dogmatics* has been aptly labelled a "religion of *Christian idealism* and humanity" that sets no sharp boundary between the concept of God held by philosophical idealism and that held by theology and Christianity. The latter conception is the completion of the former, and Martensen firmly rejects any dualism between reason and nature on the one hand, and revelation on the other.[30] The best term for Martensen's position in 1849 is eclecticism.

In the Foreword to the *Dogmatics*, Martensen stresses that it is Christianity's task and right to select what is serviceable from speculative thought, without being swallowed by it. A Christian dogmatics must, Martensen says, cleave to the golden middle way and avoid the extremes of excessive speculation and of anti-rational rejection of speculation. Thus, although Martensen sees the importance of "speculative thought," he wishes to stress that it must serve religion, and not the reverse. In this connection, he finds lamentable the influence of thought that has been liberated from such religious purposes. He does not wish to concern himself with the matter in the *Dogmatics*, but he points out that "the theoretical self-legislation" of "modern free-thinking" could fruitfully be compared with the unfortunate "self-legislation in practical matters that has revealed itself in the recent events of the times . . . , [i.e., in the revolutions of 1848]."[31] Therefore, while Martensen is still able to describe himself as a speculative thinker, he wants very much to disassociate himself at the outset from the autonomous and irreligious variants of speculative thought—particularly left-wing Hegelianism—which he sees as not unconnected to the woes of Europe in 1849 and especially to the recent ascendancy of the detestable, unruly, "self-legislating" elements. This point is made more forcefully later in the *Dogmatics*, where Martensen is willing to grant that, although they are pantheists, "there is a religious, an ethical, mysticism in Schelling, Fichte, and Hegel that contains the germ of a personal relationship to God."[32] All too often, however, these thinkers have been boiled down into a simple pantheistic formula which has recently been "preached from the rooftops. . . . This 'universally understandable' pantheism has, like leavening, fermented in the masses, and has become one of the most active forces in the movements of recent times."[33] Thus the troubles of 1848 originated in the abuse and vulgarization of speculative thought, but Martensen insists that this is no reason to abandon speculative thought altogether. (It is interesting to note that Kierkegaard makes the same curious claim in *The Sickness Unto Death*, where he holds Hegelianism responsible for mob rule. Yet—ultimately—Kierkegaard was prepared to make his peace with the age of democracy and to reject entirely the intrusion of speculation in Christianity, which is precisely the opposite of Martensen's position.)

In keeping with the eclectic balance in the Foreword to his *Dogmatics*, Martensen insists that despite the abuses of speculation, he will not give up the hope of an intellectually satisfying and coherent theological system: "I hope to be able to maintain the conviction that theological thinking—indeed, theological speculation—which is coherent in itself, is both possible and necessary. . . ." Furthermore, Martensen insists, he maintains this position in spite of assaults on speculative theology in the name of faith and religious individualism, which have been put forth unsystematically in "stray thoughts and aphorisms, sudden discoveries and hints" and in "ingenious paradox."[34] Continuing, Martensen insists that it is wrong for such a critic of theological speculation to address himself to "*the* believer," for the only one who corresponds to that category is "the entire universal Church," and we must therefore "guard carefully against making our own individual, perhaps one-sided, perhaps even rather sickly, faith-life into a rule for all believers."[35] In other words, just as the first half of Martensen's Foreword was directed against revolutionary and free-thinking, left-wing Hegelians, the second half serves notice that Martensen does not intend to let the ill-repute gained by some speculation bully him into accepting the anti-intellectual and sickly individualism of *Søren Kierkegaard*. Martensen insists that instead of accepting either Kierkegaard or the revolutionary speculators, we must persevere in the attempt to make "continuing progress toward the unity of faith and knowledge."[36]

In the body of the *Dogmatics* itself, Martensen goes on to point out that speculation is only an aid to Christianity, an aid that can be dispensed with, for "the absolute truth of Christianity is given for dogmatics in advance of and independently of all speculation."[37] Dogmatics is a summary of faith, and is neither mere "subjective human opinion" nor "a pure truth of reason whose universal validity is obvious with mathematical or logical necessity; it is a truth of *faith*."[38] Thus Martensen clearly distances himself from Heiberg's heretical sentiment that all reasonable people would gladly exchange faith for a mathematically necessary certainty, and Martensen continually points out that, although he values speculation, he places it in Christianity's service. The *Dogmatics* is Martensen's declaration of intellectual independence from his friend Heiberg. Dogmatics, Martensen continues, is therefore not only a science about faith, but is a knowledge in faith and from faith.[39] Faith does not have to have dogmatics, and dogmatics is "not an emergency help for faith, but is to the glory of faith"; furthermore, "dogmatics has its own independent principle and does not have to take its kingdom as a fief of any externally given philosophy."[40] Thus Christianity is doubly insulated against being swallowed by philosophy: it does not *have* to have dogmatics, and dogmatics, in turn, is not enfeoffed to any "external" philosophy.

Yet, speculation is not uncongenial to Christianity. They do not conflict, provided that the dogmatist bears in mind the priority and sublimity of religion's claims, remembering that "divine revelation relates itself to [the dogmatist's] researches as the answer given in advance relates to a mathematical problem."[41]

> It is thus the task of dogmatics to present the Christian view [Anskuelse] as a *doctrinal concept* [Begreb] which is coherent in itself. Dogmatic conceiving [Begriben] is most nearly an *explicative* conceiving. . . . [And] yet it is not possible to separate explicative and speculative conceiving with a firm and immovable boundary . . . [because speculative conceiving is] a very mobile and dialectical concept.[42]

Both religion and philosophy, therefore, involve the same thing; both are forms of "the consciousness of God," but religion is also "society with God" and "union with God." Thus, philosophy, or "the speculative and aesthetic relationship to God, is only a relationship at one remove, a relationship via the Idea, via thought and image, while the religious relationship to God is an existential relationship."[43] The religious consciousness of God does not conflict with that of philosophy or art, but is "higher."[44]

The compatibility of faith and philosophy is rooted in the fact that the "first and second creations"—"Creation" and "Grace," respectively—are all one system of creation that is knowable by one reason which has two different "intensities," i.e., two different quantitative forms, namely, philosophy and theology. Thus the single system of creation has two principal levels, Creation and Grace (or Incarnation). And, "just as there is only one system of Creation, in spite of the fact that it has two principal levels, so is there only one system of reason, in spite of the fact that it contains two intensities of reason's revelation."[45] Arildsen explains that "the first Creation is the expression of the fact that natural man, as created in God's image, possesses essential humanity. The second Creation expresses subjectively that the reborn man makes his *essential* humanity into his *actual* humanity."[46] Therefore, no true philosophy can be incompatible with divine revelation, for revelation is reasonable in the profoundest sense and is susceptible of assimilation to the "one system of Reason."

Philosophy, Martensen continues, can teach us "mediately" about the Kingdom of God, because "every real philosophy sheds new light upon the Kingdom of Nature, which is the precondition for the Kingdom of Grace,"[47] and the latter presupposes the former. Therefore, Martensen concludes, we must speak in ambiguous terms, as does Scripture: "We know everything," and yet "our knowledge is but partial."[48] On the basis of philosophy alone "we could certainly have a true, but not an adequate knowledge of God's being";[49] that is, our philosophical knowledge is incomplete but is true in itself as far as it goes. Martensen grants that Kant says that divine things are "inconceivable" for reason, but Martensen points out that Kant must be thinking only of "the reason which has fallen away from God and which is abandoned to itself, but not of the reason enlightened with God's Word and Spirit."[50]

Thus, while modifying considerably the more immoderate claims of philosophy, Martensen is still able to preserve the right of philosophy to enter everywhere and embrace the whole of existence, for philosophy is "knowledge of the Universe," whereas theology is "knowledge of God. . . . Philosophy presents what is universal, theology what is central in Christian knowledge. Philosophy is at home everywhere [i.e., including the Church]; theology has its home in the Church."[51] Even while breaking with a more radical Hegelianism, Martensen is able to preserve the fundamental Golden Age unity of the invisible and visible realms, the unity of culture, because philosophy is the principal gem in the diadem of human culture, and culture [Dannelse] thus has a Christian significance as the preparatory stage for religion. This world and its life of philosophy and culture is neither hostile nor indifferent to the world of religion but is its active ally.

Although everything that is, both Nature and History (or Spirit), contains revelations of God's will, it is history and, specifically, "history within history," that is the highest intensity of revelation, and hence theology is ultimately superior to philosophy. "[T]he inner categories of reason within nature and history must be viewed according to their innermost significance as revealed categories of the will of the God of Creation and of Providence, who proclaims his eternal might and divinity through the world."[52] Both Nature and Spirit are saturated by the same "Creator's Spirit," but the revelation available to us through nature (and the natural religion of philosophy) is obscure and indirect, whereas "the direct, unambiguous revelation can only be found in the Spirit's own world, in the world of the Word, of conscience, of freedom, or in *History*," that is, in "a history within history," in a "*holy history*, in which God reveals himself as God, a history in which *the holy purpose of the world* reveals itself as such."[53] To be specific, God's Word and deeds "find their end and their fulfillment in *Christ's holy history*, from which point the history of the Christian *Church* streams throughout world history as a new history within history."[54]

We have now reached the specifically Christian content of Martensen's theology. There is the deepest imaginable opposition between Creator and creature, between holy God and sinful man, and "this problem is solved only by Christianity with its Gospel of *God's becoming man* in Christ. The antithesis is not solved with images or myths, for it is an antithesis in existence and must be solved in existence. The Word became *flesh* and dwelt among us."[55] Martensen inveighs against a Kantian, merely moral interpretation, which takes the message but ignores the miracle, for in Christianity the miracle is the message.

> The founder of the religion is the content of the religion itself. He is not simply an historic founder of a religion, whose personality can be separated from the doctrine he preaches, but Christ's personality has an eternal, a continuously present significance for the human race. As he is the mediator and the reconciler,

the holy point of unity between God and the sinful world, so does he remain
as the *Redeemer* of the human race.[56]

Christ was not a "religious or moral genius" but was "a new *Adam*," whose
existence has a deeper than moral significance. Christ is the "world-saving
mediator, who must necessarily be thought of in an *eternal* relationship to both
the Father and the human race,"[57] for "all eons move about him as their all-
determining mid-point which gives each eon its own true significance."[58] The
Son appears in a dual role, both as Reason (Logos) and as the unification of
the divine and human natures, who elevates mankind to divinity: "In the revelation of Logos, the Son proceeded from the Father as God (ἐν μορφῇ θεοῦ);
but in the revelation of Christ, he returns to the Father as the God-Man, and
his return is richer than his departure because he returns with a whole Kingdom
of God's children."[59]

Here, when God evolves into his true, "richer" self by means of his saving
association with the human race, we can still glimpse what remains of the
Hegelian Christology of the *Moral Philosophy*, under the orthodox and traditional dress. (In the *Moral Philosophy*, it had been stated that God "wants to
be All in All [and wants to] win personal form in the human individual. . . .
He will be realized by human freedom.") Yet Hegel has been pretty well purged
from Martensen's *Dogmatics*, and Martensen deliberately provokes his Hegelian
friend Heiberg on such questions as the immortality of the soul *versus* the
resurrection of the body, which Heiberg had expressly denied. Martensen notes
that "Christian hope not only expects immortality, which is a negative concept,
but eternal life, not only for the mind [which was the most that Heiberg was
willing to grant] and the spirit, but also the resurrection of the body."[60] The
Dogmatics thus stands as Martensen's certificate of acceptability, if any were
still needed, of his complete rehabilitation after his initial entrapment in "the
magical net" of Hegelian "pantheism." And now Martensen, who had retained
the friendship of Heiberg while gaining the admiration of Mynster—no mean
feat—was ideally situated for further upward movement within the ecclesiastical
establishment.

Before leaving this discussion of the content of Martensen's Christianity
as it is put forth in the *Dogmatics* and turning to an examination of his relation
to culture, to politics, and to various Golden Age luminaries, we should emphasize one further important aspect of Martensen's Christianity, namely, its
stress upon the importance of the Christian community, the congregation. Religion is a communal activity, a common undertaking, not a private, individualistic relation to God, because "theism only gains life-strength and fulness
in the concept of the God of a congregation."[61] "The purpose of Christian
dogmatics is to search out [ransage] God as the Spirit Who is not only the God
of all Creation, but Who has also been revealed in Christ as the God of his
congregation."[62] Therefore, Martensen concludes, "what is important is not the

universal, merely essential omnipresence [of God]—which equally embraces all creatures and in which there is nothing redeeming—but God's special presence in the congregation."[63] (As Martensen explains in the sermon he delivered upon his consecration as Bishop in 1854, "Must we not say that it is through Christ's Church that Christ's Gospel has come to us?—that it is through Christ's Church that God's Spirit made its way to our hearts? . . . Do you not thank him [God] because his Church taught you, guided you, handed down to you the Holy Scripture . . . ?"[64]) Religious consciousness may be present in "the individual" [den Enkelte], but it requires a community to reach its highest development:

> Only in a *Kingdom* of God, only in a kingdom of individuals who have their souls from God, who relate to one another in a reciprocity of productivity and receptivity, of communication and reception—only there can religion develop its richness. History is filled with testimony to the society-forming power of religion. . . . Where religion remains a merely private matter, remains *only* the matter of individuals, it is a sign that a condition of dissolution, a break between the subjective and the objective, is present.[65]

Martensen insists that "the human individual is the real object of divine foresight (*providentia specialissima*), not in atomistic separation from the race but as a member of the great spiritual body."[66] Therefore, "in hope, the Church views itself as liberated unto its true reality [as a great spiritual body], or as triumphant."[67] Martensen's insistence upon the congregation and "the great spiritual body" of the Church, apart from which there is no religious life in the deeper sense, and his insistence upon "the society-forming power of religion" is directed at the fragmentation threatened by the awakeners, the sects, and the Grundtvigians. And in particular, Martensen's stress on the congregation is directed against the dangers of the religious individualism implicit in liberalism and explicitly proposed by Søren Kierkegaard, whose emphasis upon "the individual" [den Enkelte] represented the precise reverse of Martensen's priorities. The communal emphasis in Martensen's *Dogmatics* is the self-defense of the religious-political synthesis of Golden Age culture against those forces that threatened to destroy it.

D. MARTENSEN'S RELATION TO HEIBERG AND GOLDEN AGE CULTURE

The ghost of Martensen's youthful infatuation with Hegel continued to haunt him throughout his life. It was a matter that required very delicate treatment: On the one hand, Martensen could not alienate his early protector and lifelong friend, Heiberg, who was his principal avenue of access to high and refined literary culture. On the other hand, Martensen's solicitude for Heiberg had to be kept from interfering with his relationship to the clerical establishment generally and, specifically, to Bishop Mynster, his second protector. In his memoirs Martensen admits that he was often regarded as "Hegelianism's representative" in his early years at the university,[68] but he adds that the people who accused him of Hegelianism "did not see that, even if I made use of Hegelian formulae, it was nevertheless a very different viewpoint from Hegel's that worked its way to the fore in me."[69]

> I had to lead my listeners *through* Hegel; we could not remain with him, but had to go beyond him, as it was called. I had to excite them about Hegel, if it were possible, and yet I had to combat him and bring them to oppose him. Whether I always succeeded in this will have to remain undecided, but I can claim with certainty that I maintained my theonomous standpoint throughout in opposition to Hegel's autonomous standpoint; I have maintained throughout that the viewpoints of faith and revelation were crucial to me, in contrast to the autonomous view of Hegel. I could not agree with thinking that wished to produce its own content.[70]

At any rate, Martensen concludes, soon a Hegelian Left appeared at the university and opposed him from "a pantheistic point of view. The spirits of philosophy had been loosed, and it was a matter of exorcising them."[71] Martensen elsewhere admits that Hegel himself—and thus by implication his friend Heiberg as well—shared this pantheism. However, theologically heterodox though he was, Heiberg was not dangerous and did not need to be exorcised, because he was not socially dangerous. As with the case of Mynster and Oehlenschläger, so with the case of Martensen and Heiberg: Pantheism and other forms of unorthodoxy or heresy were incapable by themselves of arousing the ire and condemnation of the reigning Christian culture, but unseemly social comportment, whatever its theological or philosophical complexion, was quickly declared anathema.

Thus Martensen is able, on the one hand, to express with equanimity his mild disapproval of Heiberg, when he recalls his "many conversations with him about theological and philosophical problems. And here I must emphasize that he held firmly and faithfully to his Hegelianism, in which he continued until the end of his life."[72] And, at the same time, Martensen can also note that he enjoyed many years of "both joy and culture" at Heiberg's house, for Heiberg was "a true representative of humanity. What was human lived in him in its most various and most noble forms, and he possessed a rare union of genius and thoughtfulness, moderation, equilibrium. . . ."[73]

Martensen's appreciation of Heiberg did not go unacknowledged. We have already noted Martensen's glowing 1841 review of Heiberg's *New Poems* in which Heiberg was credited with having "raised himself and our literature to new heights." It is noteworthy that Martensen let pass an opportunity to criticize the Christianity contained in "Divine Services" and "Protestantism in Nature." Following yet another positive review by Martensen, Heiberg wrote a very grateful letter to the young theologian, remarking that

Your presentation of my own poetic work has lifted me up in my own eyes, as it were, and truly seems to be pretty near the most precious reward I have yet received for it. However numerous those who now and then reckon themselves as one's public, fundamentally one really writes for only a very small number of readers. You are the first of these few from whom I have received recognition of which I can truly be proud and happy, and I predict that from now on when I write something new, you will—even more than in the past—be for me the representative of the few whom I especially seek to please.[74]

Thus, in thanks for his much-valued public appreciation of Heiberg, Martensen has been assured by the poet that he is one of "the few" for whom he "really writes." The theologian's public praise of the heterodox poet has been rewarded with a passport admitting him to the innermost literary circle of the Golden Age. The parallel to Mynster and Oehlenschläger is complete, even to the letter of thanks, which comes close to echoing word for word Oehlenschläger's grateful letter to Mynster, cited in chapter 10.

Thus, Martensen was able to tread a middle path between Mynster and Heiberg, miraculously satisfying both and maintaining—as Mynster in *his* time had done—official Christianity as the socially correct synthesis of refined literary culture and a vaguely defined "Christianity." In *On the Significance of Philosophy for the Present Age* Heiberg had held that Christianity and philosophy taught the same essential truth, but that philosophy should be the world view of cultured people, whereas Christianity was the lingering outlook of the uncultured. Martensen, though a member of Heiberg's circle, changed that a bit, so that Christianity and culture were still united but in such a way as to place Christianity at the center of culture and, indeed, of all life. Martensen's Christianity became increasingly "orthodox" and less "speculative" over the years, but he always saw the unification of Christianity and philosophy as a desirable and a possible goal. It may safely be concluded that, although Martensen was never the Hegelian enthusiast Heiberg was, in his memoirs he surely underemphasized and minimized his allegiance to Hegel and Heiberg in the late 1830's and early 1840's. After Mynster's influence upon him increased, beginning in the early 1840's, Martensen began to move in a direction more acceptable to the clerical establishment. Fortunately for Martensen, the demands of philosophical and religious categories were not as inflexible as the demands of social comportment, and as he advanced toward his episcopacy it was possible for him to become increasingly biblical in his religious outlook while still retaining his ties with Heiberg, the nation's leading poet, in much the same way as Mynster had managed to establish himself as impeccably orthodox without having to break with Oehlenschläger.

In his (1883) memoirs, with the distance provided by the passage of several decades, Martensen was able to pass balanced judgments upon Oehlenschläger and Heiberg, the two great poets of the Golden Age. Oehlenschläger, Martensen reveals, at one point proposed to him a romantic-poetic version of the doctrine of the Trinity, in which the "the True, the Good, and the Beautiful" represented the Father, the Son, and the Holy Spirit, respectively; however, Martensen remarks in polite denigration, "[I] could not use it."[75] Similarly, Martensen feels that Oehlenschläger's early poetry was undeniably his best because, "in many of the poems (excepting *The Life of Jesus Christ Repeated in the Annual Cycle of Nature*) the influence of the universal within the individual reveals itself in an elevation and enrichment of the poems' meaning."[76] Unlike Mynster, Martensen was not bound by any special personal tie to defend Oehlenschläger's Jesus-Nature poem, and here he takes Oehlenschläger—and implicitly Mynster—very gently to task. However, on balance, Martensen's final judgment on Oehlenschläger is quite positive, and it is interesting to note that the aging Bishop Martensen phrased his concluding praise of Oehlenschläger in such a way as to dissociate his own views from those of his Hegelian-intellectualist friend Heiberg:

> It must be said, to Oehlenschläger's praise and honor, . . . that the highest thing for him is the Good; it is the central thing to which we must always look. . . . I stand on Oehlenschläger's side when he posits the Good as the highest thing, and I cannot agree with Heiberg who, with Hegel, puts not the ethical, but the *logical*—that is, cognition—in the highest place.[77]

Thus, too, Martensen's eloquent and interesting eulogy to Heiberg is also very revealing: It is a eulogy to taste and culture, which is then very casually and weakly related to Christianity. "Wasn't it the Danish spirit [not the *Holy* Spirit!] which was upon him [Heiberg]" when he used his wonderful gift for portraying human foolishness in a witty and liberating fashion? Martensen asks at graveside in 1860.[78] Heiberg was a "songbird in the forest" as well as "an arrow and a shield, a defense against crudity and barbarism,"[79] Martensen continues. Now that darkness seems to have come upon the Golden Age with the extinction of its final great star, what is to be feared, Martensen warns, is "that when the poets fall silent, a spirit easily develops itself within the people, a spirit for which sensual well-being and temporal utility and tangible goods and earthly gain are the highest, indeed the only, reality."[80] Thus Heiberg, who is quite expressly not alluded to as a *Christian*, is nevertheless hailed as being tantamount to the same thing for the officially Christian culture of the Golden Age: He was an apostle of "the Danish spirit" who fought against mere utility and materialism, against "crudity and barbarism."

The similarity to Mynster's eulogy of Oehlenschläger is striking. In such eulogies, which formed a part of the official service of Christian burial, the religious faith of the deceased is usually the focal point; here, Heiberg's faith is alluded to only tangentially. Turning to Heiberg's lofty *Reformation Cantata*, Martensen cites a didactic passage which ends "Morning began, the day is long." Martensen builds on the Heiberg passage, making a plea that "the day be long for our country";[81] Martensen pleads, in other words, that the sun of the Golden Age might not set so finally upon Denmark. Thus, in his eulogy of Heiberg, Martensen seems quite deliberately to confuse the purportedly Christian "sun" of the Reformation with the merely cultural "sun" of the Golden Age, a typical enough confusion for an official Christian culture, in which anything "high" or "deep" or "spiritual" was *ipso facto* also Christian.

An even better example of Martensen's sense of loss at the end of the Golden Age can be seen in his 1860 eulogy over A. S. Ørsted, the old Kantian jurist and former prime minister, who, in his last, reactionary ministry had succeeded in installing Martensen as Bishop of Zealand and Primate of the People's Church.[82] A. S. Ørsted is dead, and his death is portrayed by Martensen as one of a series which marks the final extinguishing of the Golden Age. Let us hark back, Martensen says, to an earlier time, "a time of dawn for our nation, when the call of the Spirit moved mightily among us" and gave us one who was called by the Spirit "to call forth memories of the past in immortal songs, in order to awaken the patriotic spirit of the people" [Oehlenschläger, died 1850]; one who was called by the Spirit "to search out nature, to search out the secrets of the visible world" [H. C. Ørsted, died 1851]; one who was called by the Spirit "to proclaim Christ's Gospel again in its purity and glory" [Mynster, died 1854]; and finally, one who was called "to search out the laws of the moral world, to search out the wonderful laws in humanity's interior, which lift us above Nature and Nature's laws with the consciousness of duty and accountability and responsibility [A. S. Ørsted, died 1860]."[83] The great heroes of poetry, science, religion, and moral philosophy were gone, and only Heiberg (who died shortly thereafter) and Martensen himself (who survived until 1884) were left. Martensen sees that the day of the Golden Age, his own day, is coming to a close, and he ends his eulogy over A. S. Ørsted with a prayer to God, to the God who gave Denmark the gifts of Oehlenschläger, Mynster, and the Ørsteds, asking that He might again "give times of dawn with children of dawn!"[84] The present hour, of course, was the hour of liberal constitutional government, of the beginnings of mass participation in political and cultural life, and was, compared to the bright day of the Golden Age, an hour of great darkness for Martensen and the hierarchical, officially Christian society he represented.

E. MARTENSEN AND MYNSTER

Martensen and Mynster at first represented opposed styles and principles in the Church, Mynster being more confessional and semi-pietist in his religion, while Martensen was more intellectual and speculative. However, they eventually found one another as allies working in the same direction and were impelled—perhaps more by social than by theological reasons—to work together out of common fear of Grundtvig, the awakeners, and the liberals.

Martensen admits that when he began his university career, his Hegelianism put Mynster off:

> [I] was seen as the representative of a tendency in which Mynster did not have full confidence, even when that tendency strove for unity with Christianity. . . . Mynster had never had full confidence in Hegelianism, and, because he assumed that I was more taken with Hegelianism than I really was, neither could he have full confidence in me.[85]

"Mynster did not have full confidence in Hegelianism," Martensen repeats, "not even in its best form,"[86] that is, not even in the form represented by Heiberg and himself.

But Mynster set out to disarm and convert Martensen, and he succeeded. The two theologians had a series of conversations, Martensen recalls, in which Mynster "peered into my interior; the consequence was that he gained confidence in me and came to the conviction that that which I most profoundly wanted was the same as what he wanted, even if I trod a different path from his in scholarly respects."[87] Martensen was profoundly changed, indeed, "confirmed anew by Mynster's sermons. . . . I owe Mynster a confirmation of the inner person, something which I have not acquired like this from anyone else. Every time I heard him it was a fresh drink from the pure spring of the Gospel."[88]

Mynster was "not a speculative genius," Martensen grants, but he was "a religious-ethical genius" whose greatness was to communicate not a "doctrine" but his own "personality." It was in this latter capacity that Mynster (and Mynster's son-in-law, Martensen's close friend Paulli) came to be Martensen's principal "spiritual counselors."[89] Martensen recounts, again from the safe distance of several decades, that for his part he could not endorse Mynster's insistence upon the use of police to secure the forcible baptism of Baptist children, though he "sympathized" with Mynster's principles and "understood" Mynster's point of view.[90] (Thus Martensen makes a double gain: he disassociates himself from Mynster's understandably unpopular position, yet expresses his tolerant friendship with a great man.) Shortly after the Baptist episode, Martensen notes, events proved that Mynster's fears were not altogether exaggerated, for "we received an overabundance of freedom in this country, where the rights of society have been entirely repressed out of regard for mere naked individualism,"[91] (which presumably included the naked individualism of preferring adult baptism). The real reason, Martensen explains, for Mynster's occasional lack of popularity, was due "in an essential degree to his high culture and intellectual superiority."[92] Thus, as Martensen would have it, common people disliked Mynster not because Mynster imprisoned lay preachers and tried to seize the children of Baptists but because they resented his culture and intelligence.

In his memorial to Mynster, published at the end of 1855, about eighteen months after Mynster's death and shortly after the death of Kierkegaard (who had spent his last year attacking official Danish Christianity, generally, and the reputation of Mynster, in particular) Martensen sums up the broadly cultural and social cast of Mynster's religion: "He was never able to sympathize with any current of piety that wanted to isolate Christianity from the great context of human life, from scholarship and art, from fatherland and people, and which would not acknowledge the revelation of the same God in the Kingdom of Nature and the Kingdom of Grace, in reason and in the Gospel. . . ."[93] Martensen's summary of Mynster's all-encompassing notion of religion is in perfect harmony with Mynster's reply of 1812 to Grundtvig's offensively personal query. Martensen and Mynster understood one another perfectly, and Martensen, like his great protector and predecessor, also adopted the broad cultural definition of Christianity, which stressed not the radical separation between the worldly and religious spheres but rather their cooperation and compatibility. Martensen therefore writes that "a Christian ethics ought to strive for the union of the Christian and the human. . . . [T]his was the need of the times. . . . [N]ot only the rationalistic one-sidedness, but also the pietistic, ought to be guarded against."[94] As a good Golden Age Christian, Martensen states that he has always conceived of his task as "the proper union of the Christian and the humane,"[95] because "the Gospel is in a fine harmony with that which is human and, in the truest sense, natural."[96]

Martensen's harmony with Mynster's views formed the common ground upon which they had been able to meet when Martensen's brilliant success in the late 1830's had threatened to sweep Mynster aside. Mynster won Martensen over in a series of tête-à-têtes, as we have seen, and Martensen subsequently moderated his position. Soon thereafter, Martensen became the principal recipient of Mynster's patronage, and it was with Mynster's assistance that Martensen was promoted to professor in 1840 and elected to the Royal Scientific Society soon after. Martensen relates in his memoirs that in the course of the 1840's Mynster "came to the view that I ought to unite a position in the Church with my University position, and he caused me to be named as Court Preacher" in 1845.[97] "Mynster never said to me that I should be his successor. [That would of course have been very gauche.] But he did indeed say that if I should ever desire an episcopal post in the future, it was important that the preaching of the Word not be foreign to me."[98] Mynster thus sponsored Martensen's elevation to the high ecclesiastical post, and three years later helped secure Martensen's election as a Knight of the Dannebrog, the highest order of the kingdom. In the 1840's Martensen became a regular member of Mynster's inner circle, and, having received all this favor, it is not surprising that Martensen cites Mynster again and again in his Christian Dogmatics (1849) as an important authority in a number of weighty theological matters. Yet, in spite of all this grooming and protection, which was quite apparent to other observers, Martensen insists that he never "desired" the post of Bishop of Zealand nor "suspected" at the time that he was being prepared for it.[99] (As we have already seen, Mynster, in statements regarding his preparation for elevation to the episcopacy, made similarly implausible claims of modesty and putative naiveté.)

F. BECOMING BISHOP: RESISTING THE TEMPTATIONS OF SLESVIG AND OVERCOMING THE OPPOSITION OF FREDERICK VII

In September 1850 Martensen was offered the vacant bishopric in Slesvig, and it was hoped that he would accept it because, as a half-German native of Slesvig and a man with strong intellectual ties to Germany, he seemed the ideal candidate to restore ecclesiastical peace and unity to the strife-ridden duchy. Martensen turned down the offer, however, because he was repelled by the civil war and anarchy that prevailed there at the time, and quite understandably had no desire to be "viewed as someone whose authority resides in the bayonets of our army. I therefore do not think that I have acted in conflict with my duty by avoiding these entanglements that seem, for the present time at least, to be insoluble,"[100] he wrote to his close ecclesiastical friend, L. Gude.

In February 1852 peace had finally been restored to the duchies of southern Jutland, and Martensen was again offered the post. On this occasion he wrote to Gude:

> At times it seems to me as if a debt weighed upon me from my birth, which Slesvig continues to require of me, and sometimes I feel that it is as if this land of my birth continues to present me with an unpaid bill, and that they will eventually accuse me of cowardice and of a tendency toward seeking my own comfort, and in a way make me responsible for the fact that, year after year, the Church in Slesvig becomes more and more barren and dissolute, without any attempt being made at improvement.[101]

On considering the matter, Martensen does not think he could do anything great with the Church in Slesvig, "but with God's help I could perhaps bring about *some* solidarity in the Church, *some* leavening, *some* salt."[102] Therefore, Martensen concludes, "it is truly an ethical collision, for I seem to violate a duty whatever I do."[103] It is illuminating to note Martensen's remark, uttered half in jest, that he could, at any rate, count "as a reason *to go* to Slesvig, that I would thereby be liberated from every dependence upon the Danish Parliament and, at least in the beginning, be under an *absolute* monarchy."[104] (Because of the civil war and the possibility of diplomatic repercussions, Slesvig had not been included in the liberal constitution of 1849.)

Martensen points out to Gude that he has refused this offer at various times in the past and that Bishop Mynster has strongly advised him against accepting.[105] Despite Martensen's disclaimer in his memoirs that he never "suspected" that he was being groomed for Mynster's post, this bit of friendly advice from the aging Bishop prompted Martensen to remark to Gude that, with respect to the question of accepting the call to Slesvig, "I ought not take into account in my reasoning my future prospects in Denmark, which of course lie beyond our calculation."[106] The statements in his memoirs to the contrary notwithstanding, Martensen, as any reasonable man, seems to have had a pretty clear idea whither his personal fortunes were tending. The problem of the Slesvig episcopacy deeply troubled Martensen, who was forced to admit to himself—and to his friend Gude—that "the Slesvig Church is ... more *needy* than the Danish."[107] Nevertheless, Martensen decided not to accept, because he felt he was also needed at the theological faculty of the university which, if he were to leave it, would "go into a state of dissolution."[108] Furthermore, if he were to accept the post in Slesvig, Martensen insists he would lose "the intellectual freedom and inner tranquility that are necessary to me for my productivity."[109] Thus, at the end of February 1852, Martensen definitely decided to reject the offer. The whole matter has been "a battle of conscience" for him, he writes to his friend: "The Slesvig Church's cry for help and its suffering condition and my own childhood memories ... again blossomed forth in me."[110] But in the end he decided that the task was too hopeless, that he was unequal to it, and that he was needed at the university. The bishop's chair in Slesvig remained unfilled.

Less than two years later, however, Martensen's qualms about leaving the university had disappeared. In January 1854, Mynster died, and Martensen noted that, while the dominant liberal political mood favored H. N. Clausen for the vacant post of Primate, the majority of the clergy favored himself.[111] Fortunately for Martensen, A. S. Ørsted's ministry, the only genuinely reactionary post-1848 government, was then in power, and after considerable difficulties with the boorish and liberal-leaning King Frederick VII, who had no great liking for Martensen's cool, aristocratic personality, he was finally called to head the Church at the end of March 1854. Martensen's letters show that he waited very tensely and impatiently during A. S. Ørsted's uncertain struggle to get him the bishop's chair. The King became furious in his opposition, even feigning an abdication in a vain attempt to block Martensen's appointment. It was only after Ørsted made Martensen's case a cabinet question that the King finally gave way and agreed to appoint Martensen, who was extremely relieved. Thus, in defiance of the royal will, was Denmark's last genuinely absolutist Primate appointed, and this irony is compounded by the fact that Martensen was an opponent of "the worldly ministerial regime" and a supporter of absolute monarchy "where only one rules"—except, apparently, in his own case.

Martensen claims in his memoirs that he had no knowledge of why the King and his wife were so passionately opposed to his appointment, but in this he is not being truthful, for in the summer of 1852 he had delivered a notorious sermon criticizing the enormous popular receptions accorded the King and his commoner wife on their tours. Furthermore, Martensen had participated in the remarkable social boycott by all "respectable" people, of the King and his wife, who had sinned against educated taste and public morality. The King had been twice married before, for reasons of state, to royal women who had made him miserable; now he was finally married to a woman of his own choosing, a commoner with a seamy past, and was blissfully happy with her. But for the Copenhagen elite happiness was a poor second to decorum, and a complete social boycott, led by the Heibergs and Martensen, was arranged. Martensen's insulting sermon was a part of this organized humiliation of the royal family. The sermon, which Martensen delivered in his capacity as Court Preacher in the summer of 1852, was entitled "What Is It to Love the Lord Jesus?"[112] The answer, apparently, was that to marry a fallen woman is *not* to love the Lord Jesus. In the sermon, Martensen told his palace congregation that it must remember

> that sin is sin, that what is unworthy is unworthy, that disgrace is disgrace. We must hold firmly to this testimony about sin and righteousness and judgement, even if a lying and hypocritical climate of the times wishes to stamp what is low and unworthy as something good and honorable. . . . [An example of this can be found] in those who should be shepherds of the people, who sit in the high places, who should be examples to the people in everything that is honorable and praiseworthy and good, but who consider but little their responsibility, their accountability. . . . [113]

It is perfectly clear in Martensen's letters from this period that he was aware that his insulting sermon was the cause of royal ill-feeling. In a letter to Gude of July 1852, when the King and his wife were being given heroes' welcomes on their tour of Jutland, Martensen writes that "the scandal in Jutland [the heroic reception accorded the royal couple] is of course frightful." It shows we are "demoralized," and "the national honor" is "shattered by these dishonorable scenes" in which "not only the people, but especially the [local Jutland] clergy" have extended an unnecessarily warm welcome to the royal pair and have thus demonstrated their "corruption." "A new rottenness has been revealed in the People's Church," and the entire sad spectacle is a "defeat that is much worse than our defeat at Eckenförde" (a serious military defeat in the civil war).[114] All this because the people of Jutland and, especially, the clergy—who, being clerics and cultural emissaries of Copenhagen where they were trained, should presumably have known better—did not participate in the boycott of the royal family organized by the cultural elite of Copenhagen! In March 1854 Martensen wrote his friend Gude again, pointing out that the fact that he now faces royal opposition and "real hatred is undoubtedly a consequence of a sermon I held during the Jutland journey."[115]

Martensen fails to mention any of this in his memoirs, where his insistence that the source of the royal opposition to his appointment was "inexplicable to me" is less than truthful and unworthy of a bishop. The fact is that here, as in so many cases, considerations of decorum and the requirements of "culture" took precedence over common human decency, and a would-be bishop (and self-proclaimed absolutist!) had been indulging in the nastiest sort of backbiting and prudishness directed at his own monarch, whose resentment was thus entirely understandable.

Frederick VII was indeed something of a buffoon. But there had been earlier absolute kings who had been buffoons and who had had domestic lives far seamier, from the purely moral point of view, than Frederick's. These earlier monarchs had not been singled out for the sort of social abuse heaped upon Frederick VII by the cultured elite of the capital, but then *they* had not signed a constitution which granted the meanest peasant a vote equal to that of the wealthiest gentleman. One senses a good deal of political bitterness behind all the bourgeois-philistine prudishness and all the paeans to Christian morality.

When Frederick VII died in 1863, Martensen pronounced a rather decent and antiseptic eulogy over him, for he was, after all, a king. Yet, in his memoirs of some twenty years later, Martensen still feels a need to apologize to decent folk for having spoken well of Frederick in his eulogy, and in his excuses for having eulogized that monarch, Martensen finally touches the real social-political nerve which lay at the root of all the cultured, moralistic horror of the man. In extenuation for having eulogized Frederick, Martensen pleads, first of all, that one does not "say the *whole* truth" in eulogies, and that "in Frederick VII there was a great deal about which one ought not to speak."[116] One ought not speak ill of the dead, and this is Martensen's excuse to his cultured admirers for having been so crass as to eulogize the King who appointed him but who could never satisfy his cultured taste and sense of decency. He was a king who was not royal enough for the monarchists. What was specifically objectionable, Martensen tells us, was "Frederick VII's marriage and court life, in which one could not help but find something unworthy and demoralizing."[117] Finally, with respect to all the monuments raised to the late Frederick VII by the common people, Martensen asks whether "our people" are "really still so delighted with the Constitution and the universal suffrage which Frederick VII gave us? Or is this movement only called forth by a single political party which uses Frederick VII as a *symbol* for its own policy . . . ?"[118] Thus, at the writing of his memoirs in 1883, almost forty years after the introduction of universal (male) suffrage, Martensen still cannot accept the victory of popular sovereignty as anything other than a merely partisan position, and in saying this he reveals a great deal about his own political presuppositions and about the real underpinnings of the detestation that the urban cultural elite had felt for Frederick VII. Let us look more specifically at Martensen's politics.

G. RELIGION AND POLITICS, OR CULTURE AND BARBARISM

Martensen recalls fondly in his memoirs that when he was Court Preacher, his church was always full, and his listeners included those who were among "the noblest and most cultivated in the capital," including Mynster and Mynster's son-in-law Paulli.[119] (Martensen's satisfaction at preaching for the noble and cultivated repeats almost word for word the similar satisfactions we have noted in Mynster's writings.) It is very sad, Martensen continues, to observe a person from "the so-called lower social classes" who has begun the process of Christian rebirth and still "to see in him the old person in all its ignorance and barbarism, and often—as is usual with us—a rude and wretched 'popular' character [Folkelighed]."[120] Martensen writes that he has been accused of preaching principally for the cultured, but he insists that this is not so. And in any event,

> [i]t must be noted that it is of great importance that the cultivated people are preached to, and it would be one of the saddest things if the cultivated remained outside the Church, alien and indifferent in relation to the Gospel. Culture is the highest power in society, and the preacher who can seize hold of the cultivated seizes hold of the most important part of society, which can influence the rest.[121]

Martensen's politics had been markedly conservative well before the drastic lessons of 1848, he notes. He found himself unable to agree with "the bitter and reckless political opposition" which had arisen during Christian VIII's reign in the 1840's, because, after his initial excitement over the July Revolution of 1830 and an infatuation with liberalism, "my political ideas had already taken on another direction in my study of Hegel, and because of my personal association with men of conservative tendency," particularly A. S. Ørsted.[122] 1848 itself was a mixture of light and darkness, Martensen notes, and did involve, at least in France, "the bringing forth of suppressed truths and the judging and punishing of abuses and neglect which had taken place."[123] On the other hand, the 1848 revolution revealed that it contained within itself "demonic powers, a falling-away from God and from Christ, not merely the absence of religion but hatred of religion, hatred of Christianity."[124] Martensen was incapable of interpreting an attack on the social order—which claimed to be, after all, an officially "Christian" order of things—as other than an attack upon Christianity itself. In the Golden Age view, social and religious order were inseparable, and *Christianity* was inconceivable apart from *Christendom*.

1848 was thus, in several senses, "a year of awakening," for "that year contributed much to awakening the religious sense," and it gave many a chance to see "the unbelievable corruption that revealed itself in the revolutionary masses."[125] The lack of religious fundament in many people's lives was made painfully clear to anyone who looked: "Who can fail to perceive that the tumult which is now going throughout the world also has meaning for a completely other kingdom than the political-popular, which at present seems to be the only kingdom that most people have *within* them?"[126] (No one would have agreed with this statement of the relationship between religion and politics more than Kierkegaard. But Kierkegaard would go on to draw the opposite conclusion, namely, that the times do *not* need a more sophisticated system of theology to bolster the old synthetic political-religious culture of Christendom, but, on the contrary, what is needed is a courageous acceptance of the triumph of "the common man" [den menige Mand], of "politics" and a plunge into the icy but invigorating waters of post-Christendom culture.)

1848 was also a year of "political awakening" in which the world saw the fulfillment of liberalism's "agitations and demonstrations . . . [demanding] self-government and self-rule, . . . a throne surrounded by republican institutions . . . a Parliament that possessed power and that had the power to compel the King to choose his ministers according to its will."[127] Martensen—writing in 1883, after several decades of parliamentary rule—goes on to speak denigratingly of "the freedoms with which they wanted to make the world happy, religious freedom for all sects, freedom of press, freedom of occupation, juries, etc."[128] Martensen is willing to grant that the liberal opposition was often right in its negative criticisms, but it was devoid of any positive content or ideas:

> The one idea was freedom. But its lack of intellectual substance consisted in the fact that this freedom was without content and was essentially only conceived of as freedom for the individual who, freed of all bonds which were stamped as oppressive, could move freely in the most various directions. . . .[129]

Liberalism has led to "popular self-government" in which "all authority must certainly disappear."[130] "Authority has more and more disappeared in human society. . . . [A] wild, democratic freedom had made its appearance instead. . . . God and obedience to God and his commands were abolished, and human self-government and self-rule became dominant. . . ."[131] The implication here is that God's commands were always those of an absolutist king and his circle of loyal officials and that any broader form of sovereignty within the state is ungodly. Martensen summarizes his friend Heiberg's political position with approval:

> I could well sympathize with him [Heiberg] in politics. He had an organic view of the state, in which he agreed with Hegel, whose philosophy of right also attracted me. His heart was set against the liberal-democratic tendency which, in its fanaticism for mere individual freedom and its putting aside of society and social institutions, must necessarily lead to the dissolution of society, which the course of time has shown to be the case. He was grieved to see authority disappear more and more, and to see our situation characterized by the predominance of a freedom that is without authority. One time, not long before his

death, he once said to me: "It has come to the point that individuals now only adhere to the highest, unshakable authority, to God. All intermediate authorities (earthly, human authorities) have lost their power and respect."[132]

(Kierkegaard would have agreed entirely with the latter portion of Heiberg's statement, as well as with the statement by Martensen at the beginning of the present paragraph. In fact, in his book *A Literary Review*, Kierkegaard says something almost identical to the lines here cited from Heiberg. The difference, again, is that Kierkegaard ultimately drew a conclusion which is precisely the opposite of the one drawn by Heiberg and Martensen: Instead of enlisting the authority of Christianity and culture in a vain attempt to hold back this tide—an attempt that can only fail, leaving Christianity open to charges of bankruptcy and social relativity—the challenge, according to Kierkegaard, is to welcome a secular, liberal democracy, to embrace the future, and to find a saving possibility within its freedom.)

The politics of Martensen, as of Heiberg and the Golden Age mainstream generally, were to have no politics—to venerate the bygone era of absolutism and to curse the irremediable perdition of the present. A typical example of this loathing for politics may be seen in a letter Martensen wrote in May 1854. The situation is that the cleric and liberal politician, D. G. Monrad, who had been made a bishop under a previous liberal government, has now been removed from office by the Ørsted government for having supported a petition of no confidence directed at that government's attempt to change the constitution without consulting Parliament. Martensen writes:

> Do you know of anyone to suggest for the vacant episcopacy of Lolland? It is truly of great importance how it is filled. One must have something of the opposite tendency of the previous bishop, for that area is of course entirely infected with politics.[133]

Thus the detestable thing about liberals is not merely the content of their political convictions but the fact that they are political—that they insist upon the importance of public life—at all. Thus, again, the conservatism of the Golden Age mainstream is not really a political conservatism in the strict sense but a loathing for politics and a preference for absolutism, whose single important distinguishing political characteristic was the absence of politics. The liberals, on the other hand, have foolishly hated absolutism, Martensen argues:

> They overlooked the fact that absolutism can cloak itself in the most various forms. . . . [F]rom royal absolutism we came under an absolutism of the lowest, democratic character, a mass regimentation which is much more burdensome and in general far more harmful to the country than the old absolutism, when only a single individual ruled.[134]

Thus, as for Heiberg, so also for Martensen: The absence of politics—rule by "only a single individual"—is far preferable to too much politics, i.e., democracy.

When Martensen turns to drawing up the balance sheet for the Church on the results of 1848, he finds a qualified victory for Christian culture and its elite. When the revolution came in the spring of 1848 and a constitution was to be drawn up, the great question with respect to religion was

> whether Church and state should continue to be united; whether, thus, there should continue to be a State Church, even if it was called a People's Church [the window-dressing of a name change certainly did not fool Martensen]; or whether state and Church . . . should be entirely separated and all religious societies be placed on an equal footing.[135]

Martensen is very happy that liberalism's secularizing principles did not triumph in Denmark, but he is distressed that more orderly internal regulation of the Church and a measure of ecclesiastical autonomy have not accompanied this. He resents having the Church at the mercy of the merely "worldly" ministries and Parliament, i.e., the liberal-democratic state, which is a "purely worldly ministerial regime . . . [characterized by] an arbitrariness [that is] much greater than under absolutism."[136] Yet, Martensen wants official Christianity to be accorded the special protection and social solidarity which are the consequences of being a "State Church." He appears to want things both ways: a Christian society which is guaranteed by a State Church, but in which that Church is not, in turn, accountable to the state, to that society's government. The problem with the present situation, in Martensen's view, is that "under liberalism the Danish People's Church has certainly gotten an overabundance of individual freedoms [i.e., freedom of religion] which to some extent dissolve the Church, but as an institution in society, the Church has been held in the most unworthy sort of unfreedom"; that is, it has been held accountable to the state.[137] Thus, Martensen could not fail to feel dissatisfied despite the fundamental victory of having preserved the State Church more or less intact in a liberal era.

Martensen's remarks on the need for a dissenter law in order to regulate religious activity serve to illuminate his own view of the Church's role as a social institution and his distaste for liberalism's freedom of religion. Denmark, in Martensen's view, has not received one of the things it most needs in religious matters, namely "a dissenter law."

> Freedom of religion without a dissenter law, and thus without control by the state, is a disorder. The people of the country are thereby placed at the mercy of all sorts of seductions, errors, and fanaticism. The usual rule, that nothing ought to be taught which conflicts with decency and public order, is all too loose and indistinct. . . . In well-organized states, care is taken to see that the religious

societies which deviate from the People's Church have a regular teacher class,
that no one is appointed as a teacher or a leader without those who possess the
necessary knowledge and cultivation for their offices being authorized for their
offices by the government. It is also proper that their freedom of religion and
their freedom to worship God is only granted under certain limitations. . . .
[There is a question with respect to Catholics and the sects, for example] whether
their freedom can be so extensive that they can be permitted to hold public
processions in the streets; whether they should be permitted to send missionaries
out into the countryside in order to broadcast their teachings and proselytize. . . .
The Catholics and the other parties have themselves answered many of these
and related questions according to their own convenience. This is what we
disapprove of, because the state itself ought to answer and decide these questions
and uphold the decisions it makes in these matters.[138]

Instead of state authority in religious matters, we now have "*laissez aller* and
laissez faire."[139]

In Martensen's view, the problem is that the state has not been intervening
in matters that liberalism regards as private, and he feels that religious questions
ought to be subject to state regulation, because they are social matters, matters
of public concern. Lurking behind the whole of his position is his merely
grudging acceptance of freedom of religion in the first place, because for Martensen, as for Mynster, religion is ultimately bound up with nationality. Dis-
senters are "foreigners," not real citizens, and ought to be subject to such
reasonable regulation as are resident aliens. A Danish Roman Catholic is not
seen as a fully equal citizen but as an exotic nuisance. "Freedom of religion"
can never mean for Martensen a free forum for all religion (and unreligion).
Rather, for Martensen, religious freedom merely designates a situation in which
there is a State Church which is not simply *primus inter pares*, but is the specially
privileged institution of the nation as such, which mercifully grants minority
positions the right to exist as tolerated aliens. The citizenry of the state cannot
be trusted to sort the wheat from the chaff by themselves; this must be done
for them by a special group of "knowledgeable and cultured men." Unfortunately for Martensen, after 1848 Denmark moved more and more into an era
of representative, popular government which, though not fully embracing the
secularism that liberalism implied, could at any rate not go to the opposite,
absolutist extreme which was the Church-State ideal of Mynster and Martensen.

H. CONCLUSION: THE CONSERVATIVE MAINSTREAM OF THE GOLDEN AGE

In examining these two generations of the literary and religious leadership
of the dominant conservative mainstream of the Golden Age, we see a remarkable continuity and stability underneath all lesser changes. In both gen-

erations the principal literary figures (Oehlenschläger and Heiberg) were officially perceived as Christian poets and presented themselves as pillars, not of the Church, but of the Christian social and cultural synthesis, i.e., *Christendom*. They espoused a conservative, apolitical, urban, and hierarchic ("organic") view of society, in which the institutions of absolute monarchy settled all vulgar political matters, allowing matters of social worth to devolve upon an aristocracy, not necessarily of money or birth, but of "culture" [Dannelse].

But in fact these officially Christian poets were very far from anything resembling an orthodox and traditional understanding of Christianity. This is something which was noticeable at the time by those who took the pains to inquire more deeply into it. It was not only Bishop Balle and the troubled (and troublesome) Grundtvig who had doubts about the authenticity of the poetic Christianity of Oehlenschläger; as we have seen, Mynster, too, had grave doubts and scruples about Oehlenschläger's religion (as did Mynster's friend and correspondent, Kamma Rahbek, who was Oehlenschläger's sister-in-law). In like fashion, given the increasing divergence in their versions of Hegelian Christianity, it seems impossible for Martensen not to have entertained similar doubts about Heiberg. (Witness the remarkable silence on the matter of religion in Martensen's eulogy of Heiberg.)

But even more noteworthy than the doubts which the clerics entertained about their poetic comrades is their silence about these doubts, and indeed— as in Mynster's 1805 review of Oehlenschläger's Jesus-Nature poem and Martensen's 1841 review of Heiberg's *New Poems*—the clerics vouched for the Christianity of the poets. It seems clear that the need for a common social and cultural front—Golden Age "Christendom"—blinded the clerical leaders to what they saw in their literary allies or even convinced them that they were seeing what they did not see. The fear of politics, of cold middle-class liberalism, of the unknown terrors held in store by the peasant mass, made it seem necessary to place the preservation of "culture" or "civilization" ahead of religious scruples and ahead of doubts about whether the faith of the literati was in fact Christianity at all. Christianity could be argued about—politely—among gentlefolk at a later date and in private, but if the social order were overthrown, if politics came to stay, religion would be lost forever in the ensuing deluge. It did not matter that under other and calmer circumstances Mynster and Martensen might perhaps have been more convinced of the authenticity of the Christianity espoused by the peasant "divine assemblies" or by Grundtvig than of that espoused by Oehlenschläger or Heiberg. The former remained the enemies of Danish Christendom, not primarily because of their religious positions but because of the unseemly social conduct that they appeared to advocate and represent. On the other hand, Oehlenschläger and Heiberg, regardless of their actual religious positions, were allies of Danish Christendom because they rejected such unseemly conduct.

13. N. F. S. Grundtvig and History's Flock: National Popular Culture in the Service of Religion

○

A. GRUNDTVIG'S BACKGROUND AND DEVELOPMENT: AN OVERVIEW

N. F. S. Grundtvig (1783–1872) was surely the most gigantic and protean figure of the Danish Golden Age. Poet and pastor; politician and prophet; theologian and philologist; historian and popular educator—this titan broke all normal boundaries in his restless and almost unlimited productivity. This chapter will focus on only one series of developments in Grundtvig's exceedingly ramified career, namely the changing significance which Grundtvig attributed to the divine realm of religion and to the human realm of culture and history. Ultimately these developments led to Grundtvig's emergence as the prophet of a new understanding of Christianity, as an awakener of national popular [folkelig] culture, and, finally, as a democratic political spokesman.

What is of particular importance in relation to our investigation of the Golden Age is that, in opposition to the Christian culture espoused by the conservative mainstream of that period, Grundtvig came to propose a secularism that no longer saw the worldly and religious realms as merged in the synthesis of the Christian state. Rather, Grundtvig proposed a separate existence for each. Yet, as we shall see, Grundtvig, no less than his Golden Age opponents, saw "history" as the medium through which the Divine Will is continually being realized in humanity, and he held out the hope that the workings of "history" might once again bring about the union of what hard times and faithlessness had rent asunder. Specifically, the religious and the cultural-political lives of the Danish people, which were now lived separately, as the lives of the congregation and the nation respectively, could once again be united in a flourishing whole if only the nation could develop and awaken its *Folkelighed* [i.e., its popular character or its character as a people] in such a way as to allow itself to become permeated and leavened by the congregation. Thus, in opposition to the Golden Age mainstream, Grundtvig proposed secularism and liberal democracy, but unlike genuine secular liberalism, Grundtvig's secularism was not intended as an absolute and final divorce of the visible and invisible worlds. Rather, Grundtvig's secularism was a solution that was suited to the present age, an age in transition from absolutism to popular sovereignty. With respect to the future, however, Grundtvig maintained that if Denmark (or, alternatively, "Scandinavia" [Norden]) remains faithful to her historic mission, the necessary parturient breach which secularism entails will be healed over in a new, higher unity, which would be a culture that is at the same time truly popular [folkelig] and Christian.

All this is to anticipate what will follow in this chapter and to provide some preliminary orientation. Grundtvig underwent a three-stage development in his view of the relation of the cultural-political and the religious spheres to one another; let us briefly recapitulate these three stages before turning to examine each of them in detail.

Grundtvig was born in 1783 into an old ecclesiastical family in Udby in southern Zealand, where his father was a parish priest. Through his mother, Grundtvig was related to one of the most ancient and legendary families in Scandinavia, and he was, as has been noted, first cousin to Henrik Steffens and first stepcousin to Jakob Mynster. Grundtvig matriculated in the University of Copenhagen in 1800 and enrolled in the theological faculty, for he, like his three brothers, was destined to become a priest in the State Church. He took his degree in 1803 and not long afterwards took a position as a tutor to a wealthy family on the island of Langeland, where he fell into a profound but forbidden— and hence repressed—passion for the beautiful mistress of the estate. Sublimated erotic impulses no doubt lent urgency to a poetic and religious awakening that was already present in the young Grundtvig, and in 1808 he tore himself away from Langeland and went back to the capital where he was determined to set out on a course of prophetic thundering in the romantic style which Oehlenschläger had popularized, calling for the rebirth both of religion (Christian or Norse) and of a poetic national culture.

In late 1810-early 1811, Grundtvig's overconfident trumpeting came to a sudden and painful end with a profound crisis of self-doubt, so typical for figures of the period. Soon, Grundtvig recovered from his paralysis and launched again into a crusade. In this post-crisis period of activism (1811 to about 1815), however, Grundtvig's notion of culture and its relation to religion was profoundly transformed, and he came to view the agitation of his precrisis period as having been based upon a confused, pagan-romantic hybridization of Christianity with Norse religion and other merely worldly elements. Thus, in the post-crisis period, Grundtvig became a fierce enemy of merely human culture and, unlike his earlier period, asserted Christianity against culture.

This second period (around 1811–30), which we will label the period of "Christianity against culture," had two phases. The first phase, mentioned above, was the time of intense activity from 1811 to about 1815, when Grundtvig, though clearly aware of what he did not like, had not yet arrived at a new and wholly satisfying understanding of the Christianity he was seeking. The second phase of this period, from 1824 to around 1828 or 1830—which came after several relatively quiescent years (about 1817–24)—was still characterized by the opposition between culture and Christianity, but Grundtvig had now made his "matchless discovery" and had come to a positive understanding of Christianity. As we shall see later in this chapter, Grundtvig's new understanding resulted in his disastrous and libelous attack on the liberal theologian H. N. Clausen, and the disgrace and sanctions that were heaped upon Grundtvig had a share in forcing him to remold his antagonistic stance and to rethink his basic understanding of the opposition between culture and Christianity.

The third period, which began after 1830 was the final stage in the development of Grundtvig's understanding of the relationship between religion and culture. In this final stage, Grundtvig shows the influence of the liberal social order and broad church which so interested him on the lengthy visits he made to England in the years following the Clausen debacle. This is the period of the mature Grundtvig, who emphasized both religion—the newly understood Christianity of the "matchless discovery"—and culture. For the time being, religion and culture were to be kept separate, even though, as mentioned above, their eventual assimilation was hoped for and intended.

In the view of the mature Grundtvig, the future would hold still another phase of the development of the relationship between culture and religion. In that fourth phase, the synthesis of Christianity and culture that Grundtvig had espoused in his naive and foolish, pagan-romantic, pre-crisis days would be regained at a higher level of both Christian and cultural existence. For the present, however, the mature Grundtvig of 1830 and after saw culture as something wholly secular and separate from religion. Yet culture was related to religion as a preparatory stage, because, just as Creation precedes Incarnation, so must one first be a human before one can become a Christian. This, in capsule form, is the development of Grundtvig's view of Christianity and culture, a development which we will examine more closely in this chapter.

B. GRUNDTVIG'S DEVELOPMENT TO 1810: THE ROMANTIC ALLIANCE OF CHRISTIANITY AND SCANDINAVIAN CULTURE

Let us first look briefly at the romantic Grundtvig of the period prior to his 1810 crisis and sample his Oehlenschlägerian jumble of "deep soulfulness": Christianity, Norse religion, and Danish historical culture, all mixed in equal parts and associating with one another on equal terms. The remarkable poem "Gunderslev Wood"[1] of 1808 recalls the mood and content of Oehlenschläger's "Golden Horns" and "Hakon Jarl's Death":

> Leave this beaten path!
> It does not lead to the altar.

> For where the mob rushes forth
> The gods do not dwell.
> Here I see a path concealed
> Under the grass, a faint track. . . .
>
> . . . Holy devotion fills my breast.
> I rush, I rush with winged feet
> To cast myself before the altar of the Ases
> And praise the gods who have passed away.[2]

Here, as in Oehlenschläger's "Golden Horns," the romantic poet celebrates the cult of the rare few, the ancient religiosity which is not accessible to the crowd. The ancient Norse pagan religion of the Ases is clearly placed on a par with Christianity, and the important thing is not the proclamation of the Gospel of redemption but the self-congratulatory indulgence in one's own soulfulness and profundity, the ability to see and follow "a faint track under the grass," which is not seen by "the mob." The fact that the faint track thus seen leads to the ancient pagan altar of the Norse sacrificial groves is of no importance; what matters to the early Grundtvig is the ability to discern what the vulgar multitude do not see, and in this he is quite in harmony with the Golden Age mainstream.

A similar message can be seen in Grundtvig's pointed *Masquerade Ball in Denmark*,[3] also from 1808, in which a vision appears to merry revellers who have forgotten their country in the hour of its need and suffering. (Denmark had just been attacked by England, Copenhagen burned, and the fleet stolen.) Grundtvig passes harsh judgment upon those who have abandoned the faith and the land of their fathers, and here, as elsewhere, the romantic in Grundtvig sees religion and politics wedded to one another, historical fate and religious faith intimately entwined. At the end of this judgmental vision, it is made clear that judgment is not being passed by Christianity alone, but by religion in general and by the historical culture to which religion is wedded. In the vision of judgment, Denmark's mighty ancestors, heathen and Christian alike, are summoned up and dance as brothers around a bonfire which they consecrate both with the sign of the cross and the sign of Thor's hammer. Profundity of feeling and purity of motive seem to be the common ground into which both religions dissolve and unite. The mood is not unlike that of Oehlenschläger, and Grundtvig had his united Danish chorus of Christians and Norse pagans chant in unison:

> High Odin! White Christ!
> Our dispute is ended.
> Both are sons of the Father of All.
> With our cross and with our sword
> We consecrate this fire to you,
> Both of you, who loved our Father.[4]

The important thing, of course, is that both Christ and Odin have served as unifying and vivifying influences in Danish culture, and both of them can be worshipped in parity as opponents of all those whose selfishness and philistine shallowness have marked them as enemies of that culture in its present hour of need. No such trivial niceties as doctrinal orthodoxy are allowed to disturb the happy romantic union.

In this pre-crisis phase, Grundtvig felt himself to be called as judge and prophet to the people of his times and as their chastiser for having embraced shallow Enlightenment and mere rationalism while neglecting "deeper" religious truth. The most definitive expression of this early, judgmental self-confidence is Grundtvig's probational sermon from the spring of 1810 (only about ten months prior to his crisis and breakdown), *Why Has the Lord's Word Disappeared from His House?*[5] in which the merely prosaic, de-mystifying, "enlightened" religion of the times is condemned from the "higher viewpoint" that romanticism had afforded him. Grundtvig condemns "our age's contempt for and blindness to the heavenly light."[6] "Our churches," Grundtvig complains, "are no longer Christ's," for they are dedicated to "vain chatter about all sorts of earthly, petty things, . . . shrewd discourses . . . [and] teachings which are merely the commands of men."[7] We have lost our sense of the divine, and Christianity has lost its hold upon us sophisticated people and is even coming to lose its hold upon "the simple person."[8] The harshness with which the young romantic rebuked rationalist preachers for their "vain chatter" and inattention to the "heavenly light" quickly brought an outcry from the clergy in the capital, led by the senior Clausen, and Grundtvig was officially reprimanded for the unauthorized publication of a probational sermon. Yet Grundtvig's self-confident, romantic-prophetic posture was not to continue much longer; in December 1810 he suffered a profound personal crisis of faith.

C. GRUNDTVIG'S CRISIS OF 1810–11 AND CHRISTIANITY *AGAINST* CULTURE, PHASE I (1811–15): THE PROPHET *WITHOUT* A REVELATION

The crisis of December 1810-January 1811, which is so crucial for the understanding of Grundtvig, was characterized by heavy Oedipal overtones. Grundtvig's aged father had for a number of months been asking the young firebrand to come back to his boyhood home and assist him in ministering to the parish of Udby in southern Zealand. The romantic Grundtvig, who already fancied himself a leading prophet and poet, felt that he was more urgently needed in the capital and was loath to work for his father in an obscure rural district. The struggle with his father and the conflict between what he saw as his mission and what he understood to be his filial duty had put young Grundtvig in a state of unresolved tension for some time. However, even more than a father-son conflict, Grundtvig's crisis was above all a crisis of hubris and humiliation. The self-confident judge of others now asked himself: "Are you yourself a Christian? And have you the forgiveness of your sins?"[9] The answer, he discovered to his profound despair, was No.

In order to fight his way out of this dead-end, the young Grundtvig forced himself to break with the nature-worshipping, harmonizing, all-embracing Schellingian monism which had characterized his early period, just as it continued to characterize the Golden Age giant Oehlenschläger. It was now no longer possible for Grundtvig to follow the Golden Age in praising the rare profundity of "spirit" and to embrace simultaneously both the Norse and Christian gods. In a later autobiographical piece, Grundtvig writes that prior to his crisis he was interested in both ancient Scandinavian religion and Christianity but that "it was, however, only the lives of the Norse gods which *inspired* me.... All my writings before 1811 were characterized by this dream-life of mine."[10] After the crisis, however, he broke with the romantic paganism and philosophical monism of the earlier period and insisted upon radical dualism and, correspondingly, upon the superiority of Christianity over paganism and of scriptural revelation over the "revelations" of Nature. This new understanding is best expressed in the poem "The Strand Hill at Egelokke,"[11] in which Grundtvig states that he has finally broken with his past and has come to learn that:

> The fragrance of flowers is poisonous;
> There is death in the spicy air.[12]

Grundtvig thanks God for this discovery, which has de-sacralized Nature and put a radical separation between the worlds of Nature and Spirit, even though this discovery has been an extremely painful one:

> Thank you for wounding my heart!
> Thank you for sending me pain!
> Thanks, for you made me certain.
> The Holy Book was shrouded
> In a heavy veil for me,
> And, bewitched by sirens,
> I dreamed that I, fool, was wise.[13]

But now:

> The Spirit opened its eye
> And looked into the edge of the abyss
> And looked so hard and so carefully
> For a Savior—and found,
> Found where it looked, God everywhere.
> Found him in the song of the poets.
> Found him in the words of the wise.

> Found him in the myths of the Norsemen.
> Found him in the course of time.
> But surest and clearest,
> It found him in the Book of Books.[14]

Thus, although the old pantheistic romanticism which put Christianity on a par with nature and Norsemen was broken, these things—particularly history and Norse myths—were not utterly rejected but were granted the status of supplemental revelations. Grundtvig continued to feel that the study of the past can be very revealing for an understanding of the spiritual status and religious tasks of the present, and despite the break with romanticism, the lines of communication between the sacred and the profane were still kept open. Properly interpreted, profane history can be seen to have sacred importance, and this is a viewpoint which Grundtvig continued to share with the various shadings—both Schellingian and Hegelian—of the poetic mainstream of the Golden Age. Grundtvig did not adopt an Enlightenment or "agnostic" attitude about the ultimate significance of historical events, but persisted, even if in chastened form, in seeing links between the spiritual health and status of a nation and its political well-being. This vision would ultimately make it possible for Grundtvig to weld together the great causes of Danish nationality and Christianity into one movement. As will be seen later in this chapter, Grundtvig's perception of the spiritual significance of history, "Scandinavia," and the Danish cause in southern Jutland in the 1830's and 40's also made it imperative for him to shift his politics from a naive and starry-eyed, albeit pro-peasant, absolutist position to that of a "folkelig" democratic liberal.[15]

But this brings us a bit ahead of ourselves. Before Grundtvig could find his way to such a new synergy of the divine and the human, he felt called upon to break violently with the high culture that (according to Grundtvig) had subordinated Christian orthodoxy to mere Enlightenment humanism or to romantic aesthetics and Schelling's philosophy. In 1812, as the beginning of his settling of accounts with the reigning culture, Grundtvig wrote the searching—if perhaps arrogant or self-righteous—letters to Oehlenschläger and Mynster which we have already discussed. Quite understandably, they rebuffed Grundtvig as impudent, prying, and narrow. The same year (1812), Grundtvig further excluded himself from polite culture by publishing his *Chronicle of World History*,[16] which passed resoundingly negative judgment both upon the utilitarian moralism and rational theology of the eighteenth century and upon the romantic synthesis of the nineteenth. All of modern civilization was subjected to a stern "biblical" standard and much was found wanting. Grundtvig earned the reputation of an obscurantist barbarian, and his exile from the polite society of the Golden Age was sealed in this period, when he engaged in a lengthy and bitter polemic with H. C. Ørsted, who stood as the defender both of Schellingian romanticism and of natural science and progress.[17]

Typical of Grundtvig's holy war against worldly culture and against the primacy of both Enlightenment and romantic philosophy is his *On the Human Condition*[18] (1813 et seq.), where he posits an absolute disjunction between true, traditional Christianity and the high culture which is built upon mere philosophy. "Everything that our age called enlightenment was the destruction of the spiritual dwellings of our fathers," Grundtvig writes.[19]

> [I]t is not a lack of knowledge of which I here or anywhere accuse the 18th century, but its furious, presumptuous, and disastrous fancy that it was enlightened and scientific, that it possessed within itself a light which made all other enlightenment not merely unnecessary, but unthinkable. . . . [20]
> [T]he conceited men of our times have confused the mind with false and empty thoughts. . . . [T]hey have covered up man's innermost being. . . . [T]hey have mixed lie and truth together. . . . [T]hey have made us imagine that truths, which only now have become clear, contradict the Holy Scriptures. . . . [T]hey have confused and distorted the clear meaning of the Scriptures.[21]

Grundtvig decries the elevation of reason over Scripture and faith and declares his intention of finding a way of restoring faith to its proper primacy, yet without abolishing reason, which he does not want to "belittle,"[22] for "reason itself, when it is not blinded by pride and other sinful lusts, leads us to the boundaries of revelation."[23]

But it is not only eighteenth-century philosophy and the "rationalists" whom Grundtvig now opposes, but also nineteenth-century romantic philosophy and its adepts such as Oehlenschläger and H. C. Ørsted. The tool with which Grundtvig claims he will dismantle the false philosophy of the present (i.e., monistic Schellingianism) is "the principle of contradiction,"[24] which is the foundation of all "disjunction" [Skilsmisse] and the fundamental law of all thinking.[25] "Disjunction" came to be the basic characteristic of Grundtvig's prophetic mode of thinking and expressing himself, insisting as it did upon the impossibility of mediation between such absolute opposites as light and darkness, truth and lie, life and death, etc. Much of Grundtvig's later theology is based upon his disjunctive "principle of contradiction," which, ironically enough, he borrowed from the eighteenth-century philosophy of Wolff—the better to combat the nineteenth-century romantic philosophy. Grundtvig's Wolffian "principle of contradiction" asserts that if anything is unthinkable, because thinking it would involve one in a contradiction then its opposite must be true. In the present case, the principle of contradiction enables Grundtvig to demonstrate our ultimate dependence, and, therefore, "the necessity of placing the foundation of human life outside of the human race,"[26] that is, in an absolute and transcendent (i.e., "living") God.[27] Thus, on Grundtvig's terms, romantic pantheism is impossible. The truth of this is not only clear by demonstration to the reasonable man, Grundtvig concludes, but is also accessible, immediately and intuitively, to the tiny child. Alas, for too long the "mother" has "concealed the Holy Name from her little one," but Grundtvig feels that there is now cause to take heart, for it looks as though "our Mother Denmark has found her God again."[28] The times have begun to re-awaken the nation to its religious roots and to complete the destruction of all forms of shallow, self-confident philosophy.

It is important to remember that Grundtvig's crisis of 1810–11 immediately preceded a grave period of political and military-diplomatic crisis for Denmark, which had for too long supported the losing side in the Napoleonic wars and which in the years 1812–15 was successively invaded, bankrupted, humiliated, and dismembered. Grundtvig could not fail to see an analogy between his own life and the life of the Danish nation. Grundtvig's former perdition and his subsequent crisis had brought him close to death, but had ultimately given him a newfound understanding of life. Denmark's perdition and present crisis, Grundtvig hoped, might ultimately propel the nation into a renewed spiritual selfhood and a sense of life. Political fate ultimately reflects spiritual health, in Grundtvig's view. The overriding question was whether the nation would make the same good use of its crisis that Grundtvig had made of his own and take extremity as a signal to recover what was essential. Political failure ought to result in a new relationship, in which worldly culture and political concerns were obedient to religion.

An illustration, from the years immediately following his crisis, of Grundtvig's new conception of the relation of religion to worldly culture and politics can be found in his medieval romance *Bishop William and King Sven*.[29] In this narrative poem, the crown—and by implication everything worldly—humbles itself before the miter, yet King and Bishop remain the best of friends, "like David and his Jonathan,"[30] ultimately dying almost simultaneously (the one out of grief over the other) and are buried side by side. In *Ole Vind*,[31] a closely related historical poem, we see another fearless cleric, Ole Vind, who castigates the failings of the worldly regime and who insists upon religion's independence and honesty, its right to criticize everything according to "what stands in my Bible"—because "God's Word can never teach *politeness*" of the sort that allows religion to acquiesce in the sins of the state.[32] Yet the rude and trouble-making Ole Vind (who is clearly a model for the impolite yet loyal absolutist Grundtvig) is protected and warmly appreciated by his king, who tells him to continue to hammer away at the sins of the regime and its polite ruling class. The message is similar to that of *Bishop William and King Sven*: The church owes the worldly realm fearless criticism and steadfast loyalty, and the worldly realm must accept and appreciate both equally. But alas, Grundtvig continues, Denmark has become corrupted in its religious and political life since those days, and *Bishop William* concludes:

> I can certainly add
> That the castle stands near the church,

> But only rarely does one see
> King and Bishop hand in hand.[33]

Religion has become shallow and has fallen into disuse, and in Grundtvig's view the political results of this spiritual anemia were all too evident, for the poem was published in 1814, when Norway had been lost and Denmark's humiliation was complete.

In another important poem of this period, entitled "Peace"[34] (written 1813, published 1816), Grundtvig expands upon this theme of perdition, political extremity, and the necessity of spiritual rebirth. In these sad times of war and tribulation, Grundtvig writes, everyone longs for peace, for the peace of the good old days of the turn of the century. But was that peace after all?

> What was your peace in the tranquil days
> Which you now sorely wish you had back again?
> Did you have the *peace of God* in your heart?
> Did you struggle in spirit to win laurels?
> Did you thank the Lord in meadow and in church
> Gladly and deeply for his splendid gifts?[35]

No, Grundtvig concludes, the peace of the recent past was but a time of selfish enjoyment, sensual delights, a love of "carnality," of mindless prosperity based upon the plunderings of trade.[36] Denmark was a people who forsook God and "sang praises to human cleverness, forgetting the Lord Who alone is certain."[37] But, after all,

> What is our peace when we forget
> The House in which peace dwells?
> What is our peace when we are afraid,
> When we tremble before our old churchyard?[38]

In the fashion of an Old Testament prophet, Grundtvig does not hesitate to traverse from the spiritual realm to the worldly and back again: Denmark's present suffering in the world of politics and war is the consequence of an inner faithlessness during the peace of its recent past. The only way forward and out of present difficulties is to realize that the peace of the past is not to be envied—and then move on to acquire the inner peace that only comes as a consequence of faithfulness and fear of God. The visible realities of the present political situation are seen to be both the consequence of a previous invisible, spiritual condition and an admonition to rise to a new, higher spiritual state. There is a definite dialectical interplay between the visible and the invisible— between politics and history on the one hand, and religious faith on the other. And the collective, communal aspect of the process is clear: A nation, a people, sins together, suffers together, and is reborn together.

The message of peace is spelled out in all its consequences in an essay written in the same year (1813), entitled *To the Fatherland, Concerning its Interests and Dangers.*[39] Denmark had been forced into bankruptcy and defeat and was about to be deprived of Norway by Sweden in a disastrous and humiliating end of the dual monarchy. In this context Grundtvig writes that

> Danes and Norwegians are at the point where it may be decided for centuries, indeed, perhaps for all time, whether they must be wiped out as a people in the spiritual sense, and, corporeally, sink into wretchedness and slavery, *or* whether, reborn to a new life, they will raise themselves up and shine like a light amid the unbelieving and degenerate race.[40]

We have come to this frightful point, Grundtvig says, because we have been ruled by "self-interest and lust for gain that knows no bounds."[41] We exploit one another viciously and particularly victimize the poor. "Our age is the most corrupt upon which the sun has shone in a long time . . . [and thus, we have need of] a serious *conversion* to God and a humbling under his mighty hand."[42] All this is so because *"in the life of a people its internal state is made visible."*[43] Outward fate is a sign of inward faith. Thus, Grundtvig asks rhetorically: "Was there ever a God-fearing people that was annihilated by its enemies?" He replies in the negative.[44] Political and historical events contain judgements upon the moral and religious conduct of peoples, and "this is of course as plain as day to every simple eye."[45]

The age is characterized by the selfish individualism which has produced the present state of ruin, Grundtvig complains; every person seeks private advantage, and "what do they care about the dangers facing the state as long as they have money enough?"[46] We have made *"self-interest* our God,"[47] Grundtvig notes. Money has become "the soul in the life of the state," while in fact "a state should be a great body of which the government is the soul and of which all the individuals are members."[48] Here we can see most clearly that in his post-crisis prophetic stage, even while his intemperate criticism alienated such Golden Age leaders as Oehlenschläger and H. C. Ørsted, Grundtvig still shared the general Golden Age political orientation, with its loathing of individualism and self-interest and its love of absolutism and the corporate, moral state. (As we will see, it is only in the period after this that Grundtvig comes to see that his new understanding of Christianity can best coexist with a liberal secular state in which self-interest has its legitimate rights within its firmly demarcated sphere.)

In 1813 the Golden Age prophet and troublemaker was still sufficiently anti-liberal to conclude that Denmark need not fear any external enemies: "No, it is ourselves, it is our unbelief, we must fear; it is that which will destroy us. . . . *Self interest will destroy us."*[49] If, on the other hand, Denmark puts self-interest aside and we place ourselves in the hands of "the God of the Lord of Hosts, of the Lord Sabaoth," then "whatever happens, the men of the dual monarchy will continue to constitute one people and be members of one body. . . ."[50] Thus, it is clear that the inner is reflected in the outer in the negative sense: Religious apostasy leads to moral decline and bourgeois self-interest, which in turn leads to political and military disaster. It is equally clear that this is true in a positive sense: Religious rebirth is the precondition of national survival. Grundtvig's religious message in these post-crisis years is very much that of an Old Testament prophet. He speaks of apostasy, perdition, disaster, and repentance, but only rarely of the redeeming grace of Jesus Christ. (In the period 1824–26, the second phase of his role as a prophet of religion *against* culture, Grundtvig will have made his "matchless discovery"; he will then be a prophet with a revelation. His critique will take on a more specifically Christian flavor and will result, in the post-1830 period, in an entirely new interpretation of the relation of religion to culture.)

And yet, even in this bleak period of Denmark's defeat and Grundtvig's thundering prophecy, there are intimations of the light to come, just as, to the Christian eye, the Old Testament is pregnant with the New. Thus, in January 1814 Grundtvig was proud to serve as chaplain and advisor to a group of university students who proposed to form an irregular military force to fight the Swedish troops occupying Jutland and thereby do their bit for preventing the separation of Norway from the dual monarchy. In *The Epiphany Light*,[51] a prose pamphlet which Grundtvig wrote in connection with this quixotic venture, he finds much reason for hope in the fact that so many (forty-four, in fact) students of the present generation are willing to risk their lives in a national crusade which builds upon specifically Christian assumptions about atonement and rebirth. Three years later, in 1817, this qualified hope in the future was given poetic expression in *The Easter Lily*,[52] a mystery play about the resurrection of Christ. The play is framed by passages on the easter lily, which is a "winter flower [that] announces spring"[53] and whose message is symbolic of the Christian message of rebirth and resurrection. The easter lily proclaims near the beginning of the play that "if the dead cannot rise up, we have no meaning,"[54] and the play itself makes it clear that the dead do indeed arise and that there is thus hope for the dead nation of Denmark. Grundtvig's hope for the nation's future has begun to take on an increasingly populist tinge, which is reflected poetically in the fact that the mystery play depicts hope as arising from the soil in the humblest form. He notes repeatedly that the lily, like the hope of Denmark, is "a peasant flower."[55] The lily is a peasant flower which holds out the possibility of national regeneration:

> Winter storms and hail and rain
> Blow and dash upon the earth,
> But I stand as a sign
> Of a blossom time in the North.[56]

With this glimmer of hope, let us leave Grundtvig's post-crisis prophetic state and turn to the mid-1820's, when he was the prophet with a revelation, the discoverer of the "matchless discovery."

D. THE "MATCHLESS DISCOVERY" AND THE CLAUSEN AFFAIR. CHRISTIANITY *AGAINST* CULTURE, PHASE II (1824–26): THE PROPHET *WITH* A REVELATION

After the disasters of war and defeat were sealed by the Congress of Vienna in 1815, Grundtvig's furious and prophetic authorship abated, and he turned to his study, where he worked on the translation of ancient Scandinavian and Anglo-Saxon classics into popular Danish. In 1821 he received a call to serve as pastor in the provincial parish of Præstø in southern Zealand, and he accepted, continuing his period of relative quiescence and obscurity there until, shortly thereafter (1822), he was offered a pastorate at the Church of Our Saviour on Amager in Copenhagen. Upon leaving his rural parish to accept this more prestigious post in the capital, Grundtvig revealed the ambivalence contained in his pro-peasant, anti-urban views. Copenhagen, he noted, is "the city from which unbelief spread over the land," yet one must go there and seek a position if one is to counter the capital's influence; one must fight fire with fire urbanely, for Copenhagen is also the place "from which everything which is to spread over the land must stream forth."⁵⁷

At the Church of Our Saviour, in the autumn of 1823, while preparing a sermon for the first Sunday in Advent, which was to be based upon the assigned text of Romans 13:12 ("night is far gone and day is at hand"), Grundtvig felt a new wave of hope for rebirth and regeneration for his country. In his foreword to the remarkable *New Year's Morn* of 1824, he reiterates that this hope, as all Christian hope, is "an unreasonable hope."⁵⁸ It is the hope of "a blessed New Year's morn in mid-summer."⁵⁹ It is a hope of spiritual and cultural rebirth, a hope that "will be realized [if we] depend upon the Lord and keep our eye continually upon *the great goal* which he surely wills: *the revival of the heroic spirit of Scandinavia unto Christian deeds in a manner which befits the needs and conditions of the times!!*" [emphasis here, as in other Grundtvig citations, in the original].⁶⁰ Grundtvig is aware that "*this,* [just as] *everything which makes us spiritually alive, will be called fanaticism,*"⁶¹ yet he is sure that "despite all visible signs, *the dead of Denmark are only slumbering and will now suddenly arise.*"⁶² Denmark's resurrection will take place because Denmark has a chosen place in God's development of history.

> [T]he observation of the present shows me that if God's Word will endure, a miraculous awakening must occur, and it is not merely my ancestry which has nourished my hope of seeing this happen in Scandinavia—it is all of human history that points to it like the finger of God. . . . *Denmark is history's Palestine.*⁶³

In practice this talk of rebirth and resurrection meant that after nearly ten years of relative quiet, Grundtvig would have a second burst of furious public activity in the years 1824–26, an eruption of which *New Year's Morn* signals the beginning. First and foremost, Grundtvig's renewed activism resulted in the formulation of his "churchly view" [kirkelig Anskuelse] or, as he also called it, "the matchless discovery" [den mageløse Opdagelse]—which was a principle of church organization utterly at odds with accepted doctrine in Denmark or, for that matter, anywhere else. Secondly, Grundtvig's renewed activism and his new "discovery" led to his disastrous attack on the "rationalist" theologian (and coming liberal politician) H. N. Clausen in the summer of 1825.

Ever since his crisis of 1810–11, Grundtvig had felt himself converted away from Romantic pantheism to *"biblical* Christianity." He wished to wrest the Church away from the literate unbelievers of the city and return it to the common peasant. The only problem with taking a stand on the Bible, as Grundtvig was well aware, was that the Bible is very unclear on many points, contains many contradictions, and does not contain any unambiguous statement of what most Christian Churches consider indispensable dogma, such as the Trinity, the means of grace, etc. In short, the Bible cries out for interpretation. Yet who did its interpreters invariably turn out to be?—the professors of theology at the university. Thus for Grundtvig it was no solace to rescue Christianity from the hands of pantheistic poets and shallow philosophers only to put it into the possession of the theology professors, particularly the cold and "rationalistic" sort which Clausen was—rather unfairly—accused of being.

The immediate occasion for Grundtvig's attack was Clausen's publication in the summer of 1825 of *Catholicism and Protestantism: Their Church Constitutions, Doctrines, and Rites.*[64] In this treatise Clausen took the rather unremarkable position that the primary difference between Catholicism and Protestantism is that the former relies upon "the principle of the Church," while the latter relies upon "the principle of Scripture." Scripture, furthermore, is necessarily subject to rational interpretation, for "it is only by means of reason that revelation becomes accessible to man."[65] We must guard ourselves against attributing any authority to the Church as such, Clausen concludes, because *"every real belief in the Church is unbelief in Scripture."*[66] The most reliable instruments of reason are of course professors of Biblical theology, experts in these matters.

All this, of course, infuriated Grundtvig, first of all because it delivered Christianity into the hands of the experts but also because it contained an implicit rationalist individualism and an explicit denigration of the Church as a body of believers. Grundtvig wanted to maintain the religious validity of the believing community *qua* community, and he wanted to assert a Christianity that was indisputably "orthodox" but that derived its orthodoxy from a source that could not be wrested from the believing community by the university professors and the experts in biblical exegesis. As long as Grundtvig insisted upon building everything—Luther-style—upon the Bible, there was no way out of his dilemma, and it is here that his "matchless discovery" enters in.

The Church's Reply[67] is the somewhat sanctimonious title of Grundtvig's polemical response to Clausen's book, and it is an extremely coarse and abusive assault on Clausen, which misrepresents a great deal of his argument. Clausen's insistence upon Scripture as the only norm for Protestantism and his view that it must necessarily be interpreted, professionally, by the light of reason prompted Grundtvig to denounce him for prolonging the "*exegetical popery under which the entire Christian congregation now suffers.*"[68] Grundtvig vilifies Clausen as "*a false teacher*"[69] whose "*Christianity* is completely *false*, his Protestant *Church a temple of a false god*,"[70] and who "has with this book placed himself at the head of all the enemies of the Christian Church and all the despisers of God's Word in this country."[71] Therefore, Grundtvig concludes, "as an honest man he must *either* make a solemn apology to the Christian Church for his unchristian and offensive teachings *or* lay down his office and renounce his name as a Christian."[72]

The actual polemic against Clausen is of no interest to us except insofar as its gross and libelous character caused Clausen to sue Grundtvig. Clausen won the suit, and as a result, life-long prior police censorship (which in fact lasted only until 1838) was imposed on all Grundtvig's publications, and Grundtvig's pastorate was ended (although it was restored thirteen years later). During this interruption he formulated his position more clearly and recast his entire theory of the relationship of religion to civil society.

What is of greater interest in The Church's Reply, however, is not the polemic against Clausen (which, Grundtvig admits, might just as easily have been levelled at any of a large number of academic theologians), but rather the positive position—the "matchless discovery"—on the basis of which Grundtvig felt able to make his attack on traditional Protestant scripturalism. Grundtvig explains that he had not taken this step earlier, "in a time that teems with false teachers," because "I have only recently come to a clear knowledge of the unshakable and unchangeable foundation of the Christian Church."[73] Clausen's Protestantism, Grundtvig continues, makes "the written Word everything," so that "even the spoken Word of Jesus" could not prevail against it.[74] What Grundtvig now understands, however, is that the Christian Church is not a group of people who have gathered around a book, but rather "*a society of faith* with a *Creed*."[75]

Therefore, it is not the New Testament that created the Church, but the Church, which pre-existed the New Testament, which has vouched for and witnessed to the New Testament: "[T]he *authenticity* of the New Testament does not prove itself, but is proven only by the Church's clear testimony."[76] What has bound the Church together from the very beginning, even before the New Testament, is "the means of Grace, with the Creed that goes along with them, which is *the only thing which all Christians, in all positions, in all congregations, at all times*, have had in common."[77] "*The Apostles' Creed* [is] the exclusive condition for incorporation into the society [that] attributes a redemptive power to the means of Grace—*baptism and Holy Communion*."[78] Thus it is "the Creed that forms the narrow portal of the Church,"[79] and "our Creed is really what was orally present in the Christian Church from the first time it spoke."[80]

This is Grundtvig's "matchless discovery": that an oral tradition, carried in the congregation, precedes and validates Scripture instead of being validated by it; that this oral tradition is particularly to be found in the Lord's Prayer, the words of institution of baptism and Holy Communion, and in the Apostles' Creed, all of which are direct sayings "from the mouth of the Lord;"[81] and that, therefore, the Christian Church is a cultic community built around these divine words and these acts of sacramental intercourse with the divine. It is this cultic community, bound together by these identical oral testimonies from the very beginning, which makes use of Scripture and which thus must not be tyrannized over by learned experts. Grundtvig's "matchless discovery" or "churchly view" combatted the traditional Protestant tendency toward individualism and placed in its stead the continuing witness of a cultic community in which each generation was bound to all preceding generations by the uniformity of the oral formulae by which it defined itself and its relation to God.

This "matchless discovery" was elaborated in detail over the next decade or two, and it received what was perhaps its most coherent statement as late as the *Churchly Information*[82] of the early 1840's, while the full view of Grundtvig's "dogmatics" came in the *Elementary Christian Teachings*[83] of the late 1850's. In *Churchly Information* it becomes clear that the "matchless discovery" was made upon the basis of the "principle of contradiction" that Grundtvig had hammered out in the post-crisis years when he was settling accounts with romanticism. The application of "the principle of contradiction" in "the matchless discovery" runs as follows:

> If *Jesus Christ* was God's only son, *the truth* and *the Word* itself, and if he founded a society of faith upon the earth, then it must certainly be unchangeable and imperishable, but above all it must be *recognizable* by a "Word of Truth," common to *all* the society's members, that is, an *oral* creed, pronounced at one's *incorporation* into the society, which is *the only thing* which *all* members necessarily have in common.[84]

Thus, Grundtvig maintains that everyone who believes in the truth and divinity of Jesus Christ; in the claim that Jesus Christ founded an earthly religious community; and who also believes in "the principle of contradiction" is clearly compelled to accept the fact that Jesus Christ himself instituted the Apostles' Creed. If Christ did found such a community, it would have been self-contradictory for him not to have given it such an oral Creed, and therefore (since the principle of contradiction commands us to espouse any proposition whose negation would be a self-contradiction) Christ did institute the Creed. The oral words of the Lord's Prayer, the sacraments, and the Creed are thus the only Christian "sources of life" [Livskilde],[85] while the Bible remains merely a "source of light" [Lyskilde] but not of life. At other times, Grundtvig could be pushed so far as to call the Bible "the dead Word" as opposed to "the living Word" of the Creed, the Lord's Prayer, and the sacraments—a formulation that lost him the fundamentalist right wing of the lay awakening movement.

E. 1830 AND AFTER: CULTURE AND CHRISTIANITY IN A NEW RELATIONSHIP AND THE RISE OF GRUNDTVIGIANISM AS A MASS RELIGIOUS MOVEMENT

As has been noted above, in 1826 Grundtvig lost his legal battle with Clausen, was humiliated, placed under lifelong censorship, and he felt compelled to resign his pastorate at Our Saviour's Church and to retire once again into his study—into an apparent dormancy which is part of a familiar rhythm in Grundtvig's volcanic life. In official disgrace, he turned to philological studies once again and spent much of the years 1830–32 in England, where he did research on Anglo-Saxon documents (laying the groundwork for much modern study in that field). While he was in England, his views of the relationship between Church and society began to change under the influence of that tolerant, broad-Church, industrious, and "progressive" nation. Although Grundtvig's religious ideas themselves, his "matchless discovery," did not change fundamentally, his conception of the place of the Christian in society, of the relation between Church and state, certainly did, and this change was part of a much broader change in his understanding of the relation between that which is natural and that which is specifically Christian in a person.

Society and its institutions are no longer to be seen as Christian in themselves, nor are they to be polemicized against as anti-Christian. Rather, in Grundtvig's post-1830 view, the this-worldly and the other-worldly communities are to be seen as complementary. A broad Church and a tolerant civil society are the homes within which the Christian community can grow and prosper but are themselves civil and not religious institutions. This is the form in which Grundtvig's views became "Grundtvigianism" and went on to become extremely formative influences in the Danish Church and in Danish politics from the 1830's until the twentieth century.

Grundtvig felt that although his discovery was new, it only summarized the de facto faith of the great mass of simple, orthodox, "old-fashioned" believers. The problem of protecting the religious integrity of the "true" believers or "old-fashioned" Christians still remained for Grundtvig, but after the fiasco of the Clausen affair and after his experience of the mild and reasonable climate of England, he felt that he had proceeded wrongly in the 1820's. Henceforth, the method of protecting the "old-fashioned" believers in the Church would not be to thunder against the "rationalists" (much less libel them), nor to demand their expulsion from the Church apparatus, nor to insist upon legally enforced institutional uniformity and doctrinal orthodoxy, which Grundtvig now saw to be a chimera. Instead, Grundtvig saw that the interests of the old-fashioned Christianity of his matchless discovery were best served by restricting, rather than increasing, the capacity of the state to compel uniformity in matters of doctrine and conscience.

In effect, Grundtvig wished to employ the liberal English principles of the free market in the sphere of religion and to remove government regulation from "producer" and "consumer," from priest and parishioner, alike. Thus, in the course of the 1830's Grundtvig evolved a program with two rather simple fundamental principles. First, there was "priest freedom" [Præstefrihed], which would greatly broaden and legalize the already rather broad freedoms of conscience that the priest enjoyed in his proclamation of Scripture and his administration of the sacraments. This proposal would eliminate the interminable wrangling and accusations and counter-accusations about orthodoxy with which the Church had been plagued for some time. As a practical matter, priest freedom was not overly radical because it would only grant to a limited number of educated and cultivated men a freedom that many took for themselves in any event, dealing with Scripture, sacrament, and dogma as they best saw fit. This was freedom for the producer. Much more radical, however, was freedom for the consumer, or "the loosening of parish bonds" [Sognebaandsløsning], which would enable every individual to worship and to participate in sacramental and official clerical acts (e.g., confirmation, marriage, burial) in the parish of his or her choice. At this time, all Christians were officially permitted to participate in sacramental and clerical acts only in the parish in which they resided. True, in Copenhagen anyone could become a member of any of the several parishes in the city, but in the countryside, where these things mattered most, an "old-fashioned" peasant who was saddled with a "rationalist" priest was forced to endure that version of the Gospel and sacraments, even if a more "orthodox" priest might preside over the parish immediately adjacent. (And distances were no obstacle, for the ongoing awakening movement of this period demonstrated all too clearly to the clergy that great numbers of peasants were willing to travel considerable distances in order to hear their preferred version of Christianity propounded, most likely illegally, by a wandering lay preacher.)

The loosening of "parish bonds" would clearly have a revolutionary effect upon the religious self-consciousness of the already-restive peasants, and it was fiercely resisted by ecclesiastical and civil authorities out of the fear that it would make the Church, and perhaps the peasant class, ungovernable. Grundtvig first hinted at the loosening of parish bonds in 1827, but the proposal only received its classic formulation in 1831 in *Shall the Lutheran Reformation Really Be Continued?*[86] where it formed a part of Grundtvig's exposition of the "free-market" view of the Church which had come to him during his English travels. (It would be, however, almost a quarter-century later—1855—before the peasants would be free to conduct their religious affairs in a parish other than that of their residence. By then Denmark was no longer an absolute monarchy and had had for six years a franchise which included an overwhelming peasant majority. It was not until after the death of the autocratic Bishop Mynster and the shocks of rampant sectarianism—especially Mormonism—and, particularly, the shock of Kierkegaard's assault on official "Christendom" that it seemed necessary to put Grundtvig's free market into effect in an effort to protect the reputation of the Church against charges of corrupt and monopolistic practices.)

In 1834, in *The Danish State Church, an Unpartisan View*,[87] Grundtvig drew an even broader conclusion from his new understanding of Christianity and of the relation between Church and state. Grundtvig now maintained that the old mediaeval unity of Church and state in the Christian state was long since outmoded and that the state ought to recognize itself as a "civil state" [Borgerstat],[88] as in England, and treat the Church as an "arrangement of state" [Stats-Indretning][89] or "civil arrangement." The state ought to protect the Church as an institution, but such a civic arrangement would be a broad umbrella in which the community of orthodox believers (as well as a number of other tendencies, perhaps) would find the shelter and physical sustenance necessary to maintain their spiritual existence. In this manner, with freedom of conscience guaranteed for all, internecine squabbles would be at an end, and peace would be established both within the broad, "civil" Church and between the "orthodox" believers and the secular state.

The final presentation of Grundtvig's view of the Church as a "civil arrangement" is in the 1851 essay *The People, the People's Church, and Popular Belief in Denmark*.[90] Adapting the biblical statement that the Sabbath was made for man and not man for the Sabbath, Grundtvig writes: "[T]he Church exists *for the sake of the people*, and not the people for the sake of the Church. . . ."[91] Therefore, Grundtvig concludes, we must remove all civic compulsion in religious matters, just as the 1849 Constitution promises, and this not only in relation to those outside the People's Church but also in granting religious freedom (the loosening of parish bonds, the right to civil marriage, etc.) to those *within* the People's Church. The clergy, however, is continuing to behave "as if the so-called *People's Church* had inherited from the old State Church a certain *right of compulsion* over the Danish people,"[92] and priests continue to report those who refuse to allow their children to be baptized, who do not get confirmed by age eighteen, etc. to the legal, civil authorities. If we wish to have a genuine "People's Church," Grundtvig continues, we must make the situation within that Church "a matter of freedom," because "even the most divine words of institution [of the sacraments] must lose all their augustness and all their blessedness in the eyes of those upon whom they are forced or pressed in worldly or civil fashion."[93]

Therefore, it seems to Grundtvig that we must either

"turn everyone loose" and make civil arrangements completely independent of the ecclesiastical relationships of the inhabitants, thus making these relationships individual matters as they are in *North America, or* we must make it our business to come up with a new ecclesiastical arrangement. Such an arrangement would give the individual man's faith and ideas of divinity, and in general his ideas about the relationship between heaven and earth, time and eternity, the visible and the invisible—give them so *free* an area for movement that one could hope that pretty much the entire people would thereby feel itself satisfied.[94]

Grundtvig thus sees the options very clearly; if compulsion is to be completely removed from religious matters, society must choose between total disestablishment on the American model, or an extremely broad "People's Church," broad enough, he tells us, to include not only that which usually passes for religion but also many widely held popular beliefs which are commonly called superstition. Grundtvig unhesitatingly opts for the latter alternative, clearly because it is the only way of maintaining a living connection between his cherished "popular culture" and the "orthodox" Christianity into which he believes that culture is capable of growing. We must therefore not be alarmed by those who say that such religious freedom would result in a relapse into "heathenism," Grundtvig concludes, and we must recognize the heathen for what he is, namely, "the old, natural, *pre-Christian* self" who has always been prevalent among us, even in the most "Christian" of times but who is capable of slow and steady growth and transformation.[95] We must not foolishly imagine the transformation into the new being, the Christian, as a sudden and miraculous process accomplished at birth, Grundtvig adds, but, rather, we must recognize that "the transformation of the *old* into the *new* human life [is] a *progressive* renewal and transfiguration of Christ's human nature in his believers, and [is] carried out by the Spirit through love."[96]

Barring such a broad Church arrangement, however—and the immediate prospects for such changes were not at all encouraging—Grundtvig hinted that a walk-out, a separatist movement, might be needed in order to protect the freedom of the faithful. Grundtvig's notoriety as a champion of the "old-fashioned" or "orthodox" believers and as a warrior against official clerical "unbelief" had been greatly enhanced as a result of the Clausen affair. At the same time, the lay awakening movement of the 1820's continued into the 1830's and indeed gathered strength as it progressed through a series of well-publicized clashes with royal ecclesiastical and judicial authority, so that by the early 1830's a number of key lay religious leaders had begun to look to Grundtvig to provide support and leadership at the highest levels. Several of the earliest adherents of Grundtvig, including the brilliant theologian J. C. Lindberg, possessed a talent that Grundtvig notably lacked, namely an ability for lively and sympathetic personal contact with the common man, particularly the newly independent and increasingly self-confident "self-owner" peasants, those who had benefitted most tangibly from the land reforms of the late eighteenth and early nineteenth centuries and who wished now to determine the forms of their worship.

During the 1830's, then, bridges began to be built and personal ties forged between Grundtvig—along with the handful of radical clerics who clustered around him, including Søren Kierkegaard's elder brother, Peter Christian, who was among the very first loyal "Grundtvigians"—and the peasant awakening movement, which was beginning to assume proportions that put it beyond the effective legal control of the government. By the mid-1830's it was possible to speak of a "Grundtvigian party" and mean not only Grundtvig and a limited number of like-minded priests but also a large and indistinct lay movement that had ties to an even larger pietist awakening movement beyond itself, and then to a still larger body of peasants beyond that. The threat to established royal authority—both civil and ecclesiastical—seemed real enough, and Grundtvig repeatedly used the threat of secession from the Established Church, and the chaos which that seemed to imply, in order to extort concessions.

After 1826, when he lost his parish and was subjected to censorship, Grundtvig felt that he was continually being subjected to petty harassment by the authorities, particularly by Mynster, whom Grundtvig had at one time hoped to win over to his sort of vigorous, communitarian Christianity. For example, although he was an ordained priest, Grundtvig was forbidden by Mynster to administer the sacraments or even to confirm his own sons. In the spring of 1832, Grundtvig hinted at retaliation by forming the beginnings of a connection with a "divine assembly" not far from Copenhagen, and shortly thereafter royal permission was suddenly granted—when before it had not seemed to be possible—for Grundtvig to hold authorized evensong meetings for his flock in a Copenhagen church one night a week. Grundtvig, ever the skillful tactician, recognized this *quid pro quo* and broke off his nascent affiliation with the divine assembly. He was still forbidden to administer the sacraments and even forbidden—in spite of the fact that he was certainly the most prolific and quite possibly the most remarkably gifted writer of hymns the Danish Church had ever seen—to sing any hymns other than those in the official hymnal, which of course included none of Grundtvig's creations. Yet even with these limitations and prohibitions, and despite the fact that some of his more extreme supporters thought that the permission for evensong services was a very poor compromise, a cooptation, Grundtvig and the majority of his followers regarded it as a qualified victory, and his unofficial "parish" grew considerably in size and influence, absorbing, for example, a portion of the Herrnhut Brotherhood congregation to which the Kierkegaard family had belonged. (This seems to have been one of Peter Christian Kierkegaard's avenues of access to Grundtvig. Peter's younger brother, Søren, however, was sceptical of Grundtvig's "matchless discovery" and regarded Grundtvig's series of compromises with the established Church as self-serving treachery and a betrayal of the divine assemblies, which Grundtvig had only used as a threat by means of which to obtain his own ends.)[97]

A further series of compromises completed the 1830's. In 1838 the lifelong prior censorship was lifted, and in 1839 Grundtvig was finally awarded a parish, albeit an unusual one, in "Vartov," a home for aged women in Copenhagen, around which the faithful could now flock and enjoy the full range of churchly activities. The Vartov congregation remained the focal point and center of leadership for the Grundtvigian movement for the rest of Grundtvig's career. As Mynster notes in his memoirs, he advised the King repeatedly to give Grundtvig the Vartov congregation on the theory that he would create more unrest without a parish than with one.[98] It is impossible to know whether Mynster was correct, of course, but Grundtvig, even having been "coopted" by the government, still managed to create a good deal of unrest. Yet it is true that the compromise with Grundtvig probably kept the larger and more important portion of the pietist movement within the State (or People's) Church and prevented a "Methodist" situation from arising in Denmark as it did in England and other Scandinavian countries. Grundtvig was never forced to carry out any of his threats of secession, and he continued to obtain his reforms one at a time.

The 1840's saw great gains in Grundtvig's popularity, in part because increased movement on the peasant political scene gave Grundtvig increasing credibility, and in part because Queen Caroline Amalie, wife of the new King Christian VIII, was personally quite devoted to Grundtvig and helped to create a more favorable climate for him at court. However, real, tangible gains were obtained only after 1848, in piecemeal fashion, with Grundtvig employing the familiar vague threats and deploying his considerable strength to extract them from the Rigsdag. As we have seen in chapter 7, the 1849 Constitution stated that "the constitution of the People's Church will be ordered by law," and this was generally interpreted as a promise that the Rigsdag would pass a constitution, an organic act, for the Church, which would thus obtain a large measure of self-government in internal matters. The Grundtvigians, however, were certain, on the one hand, that under any sort of "democratic" church constitution the "orthodox" would always be swamped by the combined forces of the various sorts of "unbelievers," while on the other hand, any "hierarchical" church constitution, particularly in a Church presided over by Mynster or Martensen, would permit the higher clergy to persecute the orthodox common man. Because any church constitution would have to lean either in the democratic direction of majoritarian lay rule or in the hierarchical direction of elitist rule by the clergy, the Grundtvigians preferred to dispense altogether with a church constitution and to interpret the 1849 Constitution as meaning that the Church would be regulated by "laws," i.e., by individual pieces of legislation passed by the Rigsdag on a case-by-case basis. This placed the real power in

the Church in the hands of the worldly Rigsdag, much to the discomfiture of
Martensen and many others.

This solution ratified the Grundtvigian vision of a broad Church as a merely
civil arrangement and at the same time had the practical effect of giving the
Grundtvigians a great deal of control, for their predominantly peasant constituency was always a very large contingent in the Rigsdag. Thus, Grundtvig's
matchless discovery or his churchly view came to be tolerated within the shelter
of the established Church without it ever becoming necessary for the movement
to secede. It has always been a question whether the religious fervor and moral
validity of the original movement were undermined by remaining within the
Establishment and by trading political favors in the Rigsdag for religious advantages and freedom of conscience.

F. GRUNDTVIGIANISM AS A CULTURAL MOVEMENT: THE MATCHLESS
DISCOVERY MAKES DENMARK THE LIGHT OF THE WORLD

In addition to being a religious movement, Grundtvigianism came increasingly in the course of the 1830's to be a "popular" movement, which came in
practice to mean a political movement, first for cultural self-determination and
national rebirth and then, after 1848, for liberal democracy as well. Here again,
in the evolution of Grundtvig from a romantic absolutist to a vigorous spokesman for democracy, the influence of England is to be seen. As a corollary to
his "free-market" understanding of the Church, Grundtvig also came to see
that a free and vigorous popular life, in economic, cultural, and finally in
political matters, is a valuable preparatory stage for the national rebirth of
which the ultimate flower would be religion. Liberal secularism, an English
import, came to replace Grundtvig's earlier view of the absolutist Christian
state.

Yet Grundtvig's liberalism was pressed into the service of his continuing
romantic and historical vision, in which he held that human beings live their
spiritual lives collectively, as nations, as peoples, and that each people reaches
the pinnacle of its development when it realizes the special spiritual task for
which God has singled it out. Historical existence is the unambiguous vehicle
of spiritual existence, and political fate is the clear result of previous spiritual
conduct.

For Grundtvig, in the final analysis, the political and the religious spheres,
the outer and the inner, remain related—just as the goal of politics, of "human"
life, is the "Christian" life to which healthy human life leads. The fission of
the older notion of the Christian state into liberal secularism and the small,
"orthodox" spiritual community which confesses the Christianity of the
"matchless discovery" is thus temporary and instrumental, for it is the goal of

politics to ripen souls for religion, just as it is the task of the "orthodox" to help leaven the lump of the nation.

Politics ("the human") remains related to religion ("the Christian") as its anteroom, its preparation. Therefore, even when Grundtvig shifts his political ideal from the absolutist ("Christian") state to the liberal ("civil arrangement") state, Denmark *qua* Denmark—or, alternatively, as part of Scandinavia [Norden]—remains a specific vehicle of God's plan for the world. This view is most pronouncedly expressed in *The Pleiades of Christendom*,[99] a series of seven long songs published in 1854–55, in which the apocalyptic talk of "seven churches" in the book of Revelations is interpreted as referring to the world-historical progress of Christianity through seven historical national congregations, each of which brought (or will bring) Christianity to a higher degree of development. Of these seven congregations, the congregation of Denmark—or the "triple kingdom" [Trillingriget] of Scandinavia as Grundtvig often called it—was the penultimate, and was indeed the place at which the historical development of Christendom now rested.[100] Grundtvig writes:

> Only with us in the *Scandinavian* [høinordiske] *Congregation*, can Christian life gradually regain *human* form and human growth as the *new person*, in faith and hope and love, as the work of the Word and of the Holy Spirit. This is so, because in *God's Word to us*, we have found the *living concept* of faith and hope and love. Further, we see the living connection between the *Word* and *faith*, between *faith* and *baptism*, between *baptism* and *Holy Communion*, and thus, in turn, between *baptism* and *hope*, and between *Holy Communion* and *love*—because the entire Christian course of life, from the first living contact with God's Word to the full, hearty fellowship with Our Lord in his Love, lies illuminated for us, so that whoever wishes to begin *spiritually* in the womb with *Christ* can also be born and grow with him into a divine-human organism [gud-menneskelige Vært].[101]

Thus, in brief, it is Grundtvig's "matchless discovery" (the discovery of the "living Word," the "living concept" of Christianity) which makes Denmark (or Scandinavia) the locus of the present world-historical congregation. The task of this "Scandinavian Congregation" is to give "*human* form" to religion and make it possible for a person to join Christ and become "a divine-human organism." The matchless discovery is therefore quite explicitly summarized in the song of the Scandinavian Congregation:

> It is plain as day that *the mouth of God*
> Alone has the key *to the Word of God*
> . . . Thus Our Lord
> Has left his mouth [sic!] behind on earth [i.e., as
>   enshrined in the "living" oral traditions of the
>   Apostles' Creed, etc.].
>   . . . .

> *The Spirit* is drawn nigh *by word of mouth*,
> As our Lord's [mouth] is, after all,
> Enshrined in his *congregation!*[102]
> . . . .
> If the Lord has not deceived us,
> There is nothing which has borne his house
> But the *living Word of God!*[103]

Politics and religion—or our "human" and "Christian" selves—will ultimately be reunited, and Denmark is the place where this will take place. For the immediate present, however, the Grundtvigian movement was to consist not of one organism but of two parallel strands, a religious-churchly movement, which we have discussed, and a more short-term, practical political movement, which we will now examine. Precisely because the matchless discovery is a Danish discovery, the responsibility of appropriating it for all of humanity is also Danish (or Scandinavian), and therefore the Scandinavians have been chosen as one of the handful of "principal peoples"[104] of the world. Furthermore, the specific possession that constitutes the Danish (or Scandinavian) people as such is their "mother tongue," which is the property of all the people, and which they must learn to cherish as a cultural gift, as the entrée into the divine:

> The people's language, the *mother tongue* [Moders-Maalet],
> Mirror of the Spirit and speech of the heart,
> Neither borrowed nor stolen,
> Love it! Embrace it! Even kiss it!
> Only in it, as in the womb [Moders-Livet],
> Is the *Word* given to us by God. . . . [105]

Just as the Danish people possess in common the language which makes them capable of performing their historic role for Christianity, so must Denmark come to itself *as a people*, as a popular culture, in order truly to approach its spiritual destiny. The "popular" is the necessary predecessor of the religious:

> If our own *people* and *the land of our fathers*
> Are empty words and sounds to us—
> If we do not know what they signify
> Other than masses, earth, and shoreline—
> Then every word we speak
> About the mountains and the valleys of *God's Kingdom*,
> About *God's People* and his congregation,
> Is *vanity*.[106]

Thus, a Danish popular culture must come into its own as a precondition for Denmark's performance of her historic religious task, and Grundtvig's English experience has made it clear to him that the only mode by which popular

culture can be realized is "freedom." Not only must there be freedom of conscience in the Church—the broad-church solution or "civil arrangement"—but
even the success of the Christian cause itself is ultimately linked to the human
cause of culture, which in turn has need of the same freedom and diversity
which Grundtvig had called for in the Church. The classic expression of Grundtvig's call for a general cultural freedom in all areas of human life is contained
in the poetic foreword to his *Scandinavian Mythology*,[107] written and published
in 1832, just after his English experience. We Scandinavians are the sons of a
great race of giants, Grundtvig argues, and our future greatness depends upon
the courage with which we can embrace an exhilarating, dangerous, and unconditional freedom:

> Yes, you sons of the giant race!
> Let us understand our advantages properly!
> We are each made according to our last,
> And *freedom* is what serves us best . . .

> Let freedom be our watchword in the North:
> Freedom for Loki [the troublemaker and killer of Balder]
>   as well as for *Thor*.

Grundtvig imagines:

> The sea of *thought*, of *faith*, and of *knowledge*
> Is the grave of the gods unless there is freedom.
> But when the forces compete for primacy
> It [the "sea"] resembles a blossoming, billowing meadow.
> . . . .
> *Freedom* for everything which comes of the *spirit* . . .
> [C]hallenge intangible things
> Only with words and with spirit![108]

In practice, this "freedom" was the market-place of ideas of *On Liberty*.
This freedom was a secular liberalism which entailed, for example, getting
religious instruction out of the schools, as Grundtvig advocated in *Is Faith
Really a Matter for the Schools?* (1836).[109] The religious sphere can hold its own
very well, and the secular sphere has good reason and every right to look after
itself, so it is wrong and unworkable to mix them together, to demand that
schoolmasters—who certainly ought to have knowledge and expertise—hold
orthodox religious views. "*Faith*, thank God, is *not a matter for schools at all!*
. . . [A]ll the religious instruction with which we have tormented ourselves and
our children in schools for centuries is one great *error*. . . ."[110] Grundtvig hopes
that "all reasonable people will quickly come to agree on disavowing religious
instruction in the public schools," which cannot fail to offend the "orthodox,"
the unbeliever, the Christian, the Jew, and the heathen.[111] It does not work. It

is one great confusion. Similarly, Grundtvig adds for good measure, another glaring example of religion's meaningless intrusion into civil society ought to be removed, namely *confirmation*, which was the precondition of all civil rights and of legal adulthood. It should be replaced by a sort of civil confirmation, "as a matter concerning only *education and knowledge*, [which] could well be carried out on a parish-by-parish basis without the least attention paid to the faith of the person involved, and [which] would thereby be set in connection with a nice national ceremony of incorporation into civil society."[112] Thus, just as Denmark's capacity to live up to her religious mission depended upon the introduction of a free popular culture, so, in turn, did this freedom depend upon the eradication of all forms of religious compulsion and the transformation of the absolutist State Church into a highly tolerant umbrella or "civil arrangement" within which many different tendencies could thrive unmolested.

G. GRUNDTVIG'S POLITICS UNDER FREDERICK VI: POPULIST ABSOLUTISM

Grundtvig's conversion to liberalism in the sphere of culture and religion did not propel him in the direction of liberalism in politics during the 1830's, nor, in fact, until the Revolution of 1848 was an accomplished fact and it was simply a question of embracing the notion of representative government or springing into the arms of the reaction. Frederick VI, the absolute king who introduced peasant reforms in his youth and the Provincial Estates in his old age, remained the poetic and political ideal for Grundtvig, as for so many other Golden Age figures such as H. C. Andersen, Mynster, etc., if for different reasons. Grundtvig remained a curious sort of "absolutist populist" during the 1830's and 40's, supporting the poetic notion of a happy union of "free king" and "free people," which existed over the heads of all elitist intermediate bodies.

An essay from 1836 entitled "King and People" (part of *The Danish Four-Leaf Clover)*[113] illustrates Grundtvig's poetic political notions as well as his rather down-to-earth cultural liberalism. In ancient times, Grundtvig recounts, Denmark was a free and happy kingdom characterized by *"the absolute rule of the king"* and *"the audible, free voice of the people,"*[114] which, together, were the fundamental laws of the land. However, the foreign inventions of aristocracy and clergy clouded this idyll for many centuries, for "when the clergy and aristocracy are as good as everything, then the king and people are as good as nothing. . . . When *the people* are *silenced* and *the king* stands with *bound hands*, then *the free kingdom* no longer has a history. . . ."[115] Luckily, however, two "giant steps" have been taken in order to restore the primal bliss of the Danish kingdom. The first step was the restoration of the king's "freedom" with the introduction of absolutism in 1660, which was the "people's gift" to the king. The second and final step was the re-establishment in 1835 of the people's "free voice" through the "people's council of state" (the Provincial Estates), a gesture which was, in turn, "the king's gift" to the people.[116] With these two giant steps taken, "the people and civil society in Denmark [may] resume their natural position, . . . [and then] the rest follows of itself; then it is only a matter of living old-fashioned in a new way. . . . "[117] Absolutism and a popular advisory "voice" are thus a restoration, not a new departure, and the ancient harmony of Denmark will "resume"; people will learn to "live old-fashioned in a new way."

For good measure, Grundtvig points out that among the first and most important tasks facing this renewed order is the removal of all compulsion from religious matters, taking religion out of the schools and transforming the schools, in turn, from "scholastic rehabilitation houses" into "school[s] for life," into "high schools for civic youth, which will carefully foster the cultivation and enlightenment we must wish present both in the council of state and in its electors."[118] This is the foundation for the later Grundtvigian movement's remarkable activity in establishing secular and free "people's high schools" [Folkehøjskoler], which were designed to lay the groundwork both for civic well-being and for subsequent religious growth. (Many of these extraordinary schools still flourish today.)

This same poetic and populist adulation of enlightened absolutism in general, and that of Frederick VI in particular, is visible in numerous poems from the later 1830's, when the fiftieth anniversary of the peasant reforms was celebrated. The aged (and increasingly crotchety) Frederick was honored, first as a legend in his own lifetime and then (1839) as a departed hero, often praised—as in Grundtvig's appreciation of Frederick's establishment of the Provincial Estates—for having had motives that he never possessed. In "The Welfare of the Free Danish Peasant,"[119] written in 1838 to celebrate the fiftieth anniversary of the peasant reforms, the message of the earlier essay "King and People" and of the "two giant steps" is repeated:

> The King's word and the people's voice,
> Freedom home among us!

Let the birds sing:

> Of the *bonds* that freedom *knits,*
> Of the *council* that *helps* the realm,
> Of how gracefully the King's hand
> beckons to the people's spirit!

Let us give honor:

> . . . to the King whose heart bled
> For the condition of the lowly!
> · · · · · · · · · · · ·

> Now the people's voice is lifted
> Freely as the council of the King . . .
>
> The peasant who moves about freely
>   speaks his case with strength.
> He is the kingdom's freedom monument,
>   standing under royal flag.
>   . . . .
> The King's word as the spirit of the people,
> The people's strength in the hand of the King,
> Let the people's voice be the King's honor—
> All this is freedom's token.
>   . . . .
> Long live the hater of slavery,
> The friend of truth, and the nation's father!
> *He* as absolute monarch will establish
> Everything for the common good![120]

In another similar poem, from 1839, Grundtvig plays upon the same themes again:

> King's hand and people's voice,
> Both strong and both free.[121]

This was the happy condition of Denmark in centuries past, and it is Denmark's good fortune to have regained it in the present decade, with the reciprocal accommodation of people and king. The nation is particularly fortunate to have a king who is willing to take the risks that freedom entails and to put up with the attendant difficulties:

> Therefore, Denmark! You are not like
> Other kingdoms on the earth!
> Heaven cannot bless them
> As this little spot in Scandinavia,
> Where power and gentleness
> Walk together as youthful friends,
> Where we believe what everyone knows:
> Love is the life of omnipotence.[122]

At Frederick's death later the same year, Grundtvig, no less than Mynster, broke into deep mourning:

> O mother tongue! O peasantry!
> O folk songs and voices!
> If you can forget Frederick
> You no longer have a fatherland.[123]

H. FROM DEMOCRATIC CULTURE TO DEMOCRATIC POLITICS (1839–1848)

Frederick VI was the last monarch who could automatically command the respect of Mynster and Grundtvig, of burgher and peasant, of German and Dane, and who could thus postpone serious political discussion and dampen national and social divisions. The 1840's, as we have seen, were a time of increasing urgency in matters of the Church, of politics, and of nationality. By the end of that decade, Grundtvig was ripe for the push into democratic politics *per se*, just as the nation, in its own political development, had become ready to administer that shove.

The preparations for Grundtvig's final break with the poetic, pre-political world of populist absolutism can best be seen in his increasing preoccupation, during the latter 1830's and the 1840's, with the purely secular themes of popular enlightenment and cultural growth. In a wonderful poem from 1839, entitled "Enlightenment," he queries:

> Is light only for the learned
> To learn how to spell properly?
> No, heaven grants good things to many
> And light is the gift of heaven.
> And the sun gets up with the peasant,
> Not with the learned,
> Enlightening best, from head to toe,
> Those who are most out and about.[124]

A more complete humanist-Christian manifesto can be found in Grundtvig's famous "Person [or Human] First" [Menneske Først],[125] which was written in 1837, though only posthumously published.

> *Person first and then Christian,*
> Only that is life's order.
> . . . .
> Person first, and then Christian,
> That is the main thing.
> We receive Christianity free, for nothing:
> It is pure blessing
> But it is the blessing that only befalls those
> Who are in all fundamentals the friends of God
> And the sons of the noble race of *truth*.
>
> Therefore, every person upon this earth
> Should strive to be a true person,
> Opening his ear to the word of truth,
> And granting God his honor!
> Then, since Christianity is the cause of truth,
> If he is not a Christian today,

He will become one tomorrow.[126]

The essay *Popular Culture and Christianity*,[127] written in 1847, is a sort of detailed commentary on "Person First, and Then Christian." Grundtvig had been accused of mixing together the national and popular sphere of "Danishness" [Danskhed] with the sphere of Christianity in an inadmissible fashion, and he seeks to clarify his position in this essay. Grundtvig freely admits what we have already observed in this chapter, namely that "it is true that in my youth I often mentioned Danishness and Christianity in one breath and in so obscure a connection that one could easily have thought that I was mixing them together in one way or another."[128] But, he adds, he has long since come to the conclusion that true Christianity has always "related itself to the *popular culture* as a heavenly guest to an earthly home."[129] Consequently, "neither *violence* nor *falsity* is in the *spirit of Christianity*," but rather "*love* and *truth* are in the spirit of Christianity," which therefore can never use "cunning or force to annihilate or repress *popular culture* . . . and [Christianity] is very ill-served when this is done in its name, as the *papists* undeniably did."[130] Protestant Christianity, Grundtvig continues, is nowadays willing to acknowledge the wrongness of the spread of Christianity by force and by the conquest of popular life from the top down. However, in living as it does with official and compulsory Christian culture, Protestantism is continuing to profit from past wrongs rather than seeking to rectify the situation by removing all forms of official compulsion and "placing Christianity and the people in a *free* relationship to one another."[131] This would be a gain both for the people and (especially) for Christianity, because Christianity is not a "new *Law of God* that wishes to *dominate the world*," but "a heavenly *Gospel*."[132] Any other relationship than a free relationship is "a *fundamentally false relationship of faith*, and thus *abominable* to the *true* God and *intolerable* for the *truthful* person."[133]

> In matters of salvation, *spiritual slavery* is under every possible circumstance just as *unchristian* and *ungodly* as it is *inhuman*, for only when Christians everywhere make common cause with the *natural* person [Natur-Menneskene] in this respect, only then will *Christianity* and *popular culture* [Folkelighed] generally, and especially in Denmark, come into their original, free, and only proper and natural relationship.[134]

Thus the natural person has rights and an existence of its own, independently of and prior to Christianity, just as, historically, people lived decently and freely in Denmark prior to the introduction of Christianity.

> Far from seeking any sort of spiritual slavery, *Christianity* passionately loathes it and struggles against it with all its might. And, far from wishing to repress *popular culture*, Christianity has itself awakened it and nurtured it . . . , because, in order to act according to its spirit, Christianity either must find spiritual freedom and popular culture present, or, if they are lacking, must create them.[135]

The Reformation began the return to this proper, free, and supportive relationship of Christianity and popular culture by introducing *"the people's mother
tongue"* into the Church.[136]

> I know very well that many orthodox upholders of the State Church [i.e., Myns-
> ter, Martensen] regard spiritual freedom as something which *Christianity* must
> necessarily combat, and many of the so-called holy [i.e., pietist awakeners] regard
> human nature the same way . . . ; [but] whoever does not *naturally* have faith
> in God and a desire for the eternal life does not have an eye for the Gospel
> about *God's Son* and the Word of *Eternal Life*. So, whenever Christianity is to
> work in a beneficial fashion, it must, as has been mentioned, either discover
> spiritual freedom and popular culture, or it must call them forth.[137]

What this means concretely for Denmark in the present situation is that
the primary necessity is the awakening of a free national life and popular
culture, a pride in a Danish national culture which is the full property of all
the people. This is a precondition for the growth of true Christianity. Those
who would awaken Christianity must start by awakening the natural person
in all its freedom and cultural equality; Christianity presupposes a sort of democratic ethos and not an elitist, hierarchical notion of culture such as that which
characterized the Golden Age mainstream.

> Under these circumstances [i.e., the stultifying circumstances of elitist Golden
> Age culture] it is naturally of no use to speak to the *Danish People* about *life* in
> *Christ*, which necessarily is the only *living Christianity* . . . , because wherever
> the *temporal* life *is lacking* or is only a sort of burden that greatly pains the heart,
> all talk of the *eternal* life, when it is not a sort of mockery, is still necessarily
> fruitless. . . . [T]he death of the *Danish* popular culture is the spiritual death of
> the people, which must be healed by the resurrection of popular culture before
> the people can be talked to about *living Christianity* in any other sense than
> mere shouting into the wind. . . . The reason that a people must have a living
> consciousness of *itself* before it does any good for any spirit other than their
> own to speak with them is of course the same reason that it is necessary for a
> *person* to become aware of *himself* before it does any good to speak to him about
> what he, *as a person*, has or lacks. . . .
> 　　[Thus] it is necessarily so in *Denmark*, and everywhere else, just as in *Judea*,
> that if the *Word of God* is to find a *well-prepared people*, then a *popular* [folkeligt]
> word in *the mother tongue* must first have turned the *children's* hearts to their
> *forefathers*, and the *parents'* hearts to their *children*, so that they feel that *death*,
> in all its forms, is their arch-enemy and the arch-enemy of humanity, and that
> *he* who can and will grant us *eternal life* is the only true Saviour. . . . *First* we
> must be *Danish*, just as all people must *first* be *living*, before it does any good
> to speak to them either about the *temporal* or about the *eternal* life.[138]

A "popular," supportive, free society, democratic in spirit, is the first step
toward the victory of true Christianity. This is Grundtvig's message in 1847,

and in both time and doctrine, it was only a very short step from this position to his 1848 position which embraced a democratic polity as part of the necessary fundament of a democratic culture and society, which, in turn, was the fundament of true Christianity. Society and politics—the sphere of the human community as such—are certainly viewed as "worldly" and "secular," but their sphere is not a wholly separate, parallel domain which is indifferent (or even hostile) to the spiritual sphere. In this, Grundtvig's position differs from secular liberalism generally, and, as we shall see, from Kierkegaard's position in particular. For Grundtvig, the visible, secular, political world is (or ought to be) related to the invisible, spiritual world of Christianity in a hospitable, complementary, and indeed necessarily preparatory fashion: "Person first, and then Christian." In classical secular liberalism, the visible world of politics keeps out of the invisible world of religion and relates itself to it only "agnostically," because—in the truly secular liberal scheme of things—the visible "knows nothing" of the invisible, politics "knows nothing" of religion. Grundtvig's secularism bears only a superficial resemblance to this position. Thus, it required no intellectual or moral acrobatics for Grundtvig, as it would for a dogmatic secular liberal, to justify the continuing existence of a State Church and his own continuing utilization of it. For Grundtvig, the task of worldly society is ultimately religious, and his secularism is therefore only a conditional secularism. Thus, it is possible in this qualified, attenuated sense of "secular" for Grundtvig to admit a broad State Church as a secular institution, a civil arrangement, in which the true Church can "dwell" and grow—just as Christianity in general may grow to maturity within the framework of a free secular society. Grundtvig's secularism, therefore, is not a liberal, dogmatic secularism, and his views of politics and worldly community, as well as his broad "civil" notion of the State Church, reflect this fact.

If Grundtvig's "secularism" in culture and his ideas of Church government cannot properly be called liberal, his *politics* certainly can be, though of course his liberalism is marked by much distrust of paper documents and foreign-sounding slogans and by a fiercely populist spirit. All this is perhaps most clear in his essay *On Constitution and Arrangements of State in Denmark*,[139] written in 1848 as the nation was preparing to draft a new constitution. First of all, Grundtvig points out, "constitution" is a foreign word that is indifferent as to its object and contains no inner determination of its own character. Every nation has some sort of constitution, good or ill, written or unwritten, so we cannot define what we fervently desire as a "constitution" but rather as a "fundamental law" [Grundlov] which binds both citizen and authority alike and which is "honest, popular [folkelig], gainful, lenient, equal, and clear."[140]

Grundtvig shies away from the phrase "democratic arrangements of state," though he finds that he can agree with the "many well-thinking and reflective men" who favor this phrase.[141] Indeed, in this transitional essay Grundtvig admits that he himself can even favor democracy, insofar as those who speak of it

> mean, by *democratic* arrangements of state, a *popular government* [*folkelig Styr-else*]; for it follows of itself that the government which is to be profitable to a people must be calculated not according to what is best for a *single individual,* or for certain *individuals,* but for the whole *people.*[142]

But Grundtvig is no formalist, and prefers the spirit of what the best democrats mean to the letter of what many democratic prattlers write. The goal is a genuinely *"popular government"* that really is "in accordance with the people's head and heart" rather than the "democratic arrangement of state" that is merely "formal," that merely arranges things so that "it *seems* as though *all the people* in the country *governed themselves.*"[143] As "the old friend and spokesman of *the people* and of *freedom,*" Grundtvig inveighs against "a bu-reaucratic . . . arrangement of state with the *appearance* of democracy," and pronounces himself the champion of "a *good fundamental law* and a *popular government* for the *common good,* under a blossoming royal sceptre."[144]

Under all this rhetoric, one discerns Grundtvig creating the necessary jus-tification for his transition from a poetic and apolitical absolutism to a tren-chantly liberal-democratic politics which was in harmony with his social and cultural views and in keeping with the new times. Thus, the democracy Grundt-vig favored was not the sham of republican dogmatists or liberal bureaucrats but the true union of "popular rule" and "royal sceptre," i.e., a form of mon-archy that was constitutional and democratic (despite Grundtvig's distaste for both words as foreign), in which "the king's hand and the people's voice" were "both strong and both free." Grundtvig's populist cultural vision enabled him to make the transition from apolitical absolutism to liberal-democratic politics with a minimum amount of pain, while, as we have seen, the main-stream of the Golden Age was never really able to acquiesce in politics at all and continued to pursue the elusive hope of returning to a *status quo ante* in which all would be spared the woes of public life, of politics.

The specifically liberal cast to Grundtvig's political views can be seen in the content of the "freedom" that he insists must be the essential element in any constitutional solution. Most of all, Grundtvig stresses in his 1848 essay on the constitution, the desideratum of a fundamental law is that it express what will serve the people at all times and not merely in one or another specific historical situation, and this is *"freedom"*:

> *Freedom* to let what one *believes* be known, when one has belief; or one's *unbelief,* if one has no belief; *freedom* to use both *hand* and *foot* as one will [i.e., freedom of occupation and of movement], in seemly fashion; *equal access* to every position and occupation when one can show, in any way, that one is fit for it. . . . [145]

But such a "fundamental law" must not enshrine principles that might seem useful at one time but harmful at another. This means, in practice, that it must guarantee only legal equality and equality of access but not any form of economic equality or even guaranteed assistance:

> One must not make it the *civil duty* of the *state* to feed and clothe the *poor*, for all experience indicates that in so doing one heads in the direction of turning the *entire people* into *paupers*, who neither feed nor clothe themselves or each other; one severs the *bond of love* which is the only thing that profitably binds the rich and poor together; one *fosters laziness*, so that *industriousness* might *starve*; and one undermines all *property rights* by which wealth stands and falls.[146]

Though fiercely populist in his understanding of culture and, after 1848, radically democratic in his determination to secure the broadest franchise, it is clear from the above passage that Grundtvig was only a political and not a social democrat. His politics were geared to the defense of middling peasant property, and this made him a liberal individualist in political and economic questions—in short, in all secular affairs—whereas his communitarianism was confined to the religious sphere, to the cultic community of the matchless discovery.

Culture and politics must be understood in their proper role. It is not the task of culture or politics to foster a specific religion (as was the case in the old unified Christian culture of absolutism) but, rather, to provide the fertile basis for personal growth which can result in the eventual maturation into Christianity, "true" Christianity, the Christianity of the matchless discovery. The treasure of culture is of utmost importance; it is secular; and it is not the guarded property of the rare few, as in the Golden Age mainstream, but, rather, it is the property of absolutely everyone, which in Denmark meant the peasant *par excellence*. Grundtvig's entire program, religious and cultural-political, was indeed perfectly suited to the advancing and successful portion of the peasantry, the new class of self-owners.

In the religious sphere, as we have seen, Grundtvig's emphasis upon "old-fashioned" orthodoxy was united with a new and exciting understanding of the Christian life as a communal life, a congregation of the faithful bound by supposedly unshakable oral traditions to the earliest Christian community and indeed to Christ himself. The emphasis on Christian community and on the primacy of the congregation was vital to these early generations of liberated peasants, who were experiencing a social earthquake in the destruction of the age-old nucleated village in the name of private property and of rationalized, compact agricultural holdings. The liberated peasants now lived strewn all over the landscape, and traditions of neighborliness and agricultural fellowship suffered greatly as the common lands disappeared and every man decided for himself how best to farm his land. The Church, therefore, became increasingly important as the focal point of rural society.

Grundtvig's accentuation of the importance of the role of the congregation, as well as his anti-clerical jibes, came at an extremely opportune moment for peasants, who were experiencing both personal isolation and increasing animosity toward the priest as the symbol of distant authority and of a foreign, urban culture, which seemed to denigrate rural life and the life of the congregation. Of further importance in this area were the recently established parish councils, which gave every rural neighborhood a measure of self-government and which were the only possibility of political expression open to most rural people. The parish councils, like the parish congregation itself, revolved around the ecclesiastical and administrative unit of the parish, the physical presence of the church building, and the human actors (often antagonists) of priest and peasantry. Grundtvigianism was a vital weapon in the rural arsenal.

On the cultural front, Grundtvig's optimism and Christian humanism suited the rising self-owner peasant class very well. And after 1848, on the openly political front, Grundtvig's anti-elitist populism translated into a thoroughgoing democratic opposition that likewise suited the needs of these advancing peasants: His program was trenchantly in favor of the common man but was still a form of liberalism, which insisted upon the inviolability of private property, the importance of individualism and initiative, the outmodedness of old guild restrictions, and the desirability of the "right to work" [Næringsfrihed], etc.

Thus Grundtvig's movement was communitarian in religious matters; optimistic and populist in cultural matters; and staunchly democratic, liberal, and individualistic in political and economic matters. All this made it the natural vehicle for the land-owning peasants. On the other hand, cultural optimism and economic individualism did not correspond to the needs of the landless rural poor, the cottagers, who tended to be Biblical fundamentalists and were greatly offended by Grundtvig's labelling the Bible as a mere "book of instruction" or even as "the dead word" in contrast to "the living word" of the Creed, etc. This latter group, a wretched and often mute class, comprised, as we have seen, perhaps half the rural population in our period, but they had no real political spokesmen and were often covertly victimized by the better-off peasants, just as they were openly preyed upon by the great landlords. The cottager group constituted the right wing of the pietist awakening movement and, just as it felt itself out of place in Mynster's and Martensen's Church, so did it refuse the Grundtvigian alternative. They were at first the recruiting ground for sects (Baptists, Mormons, and Irvingians) and later formed the basis of the conservative and fundamentalist (but *official*) Inner Mission movement, which espoused just such a bleak and gloomy view of earthly existence as in fact corresponded to the real experience of the landless poor.[147]

I. THE EMERGENCE OF THE DEMOCRAT (1848 AND AFTER)

Grundtvig's actual entry into politics was made in the Præstø area of southern Zealand, where he had been a parish priest in 1821–22 and where his old opponent, the leading liberal theologian and politician H. N. Clausen, had been defeated by the poor weaver Hans Hansen, who himself had been so badly smeared and tarnished that he found it best to withdraw. It was Grundtvig who stepped into the breach: he was an urbanite, academically educated yet not urbane or elitist. He was, rather, rural and popular in his preferences, a supporter of the common man, the peasant, yet not a common man himself and certainly not a rabble-rouser from the poorest levels of society. Thus, not a liberal elitist nor yet a dangerous man from the bottom, Grundtvig was the obvious alternative to Clausen and Hansen. (The Præstø election will be discussed further in the Clausen section of the next chapter.) Grundtvig's successful candidacy was not merely politically obvious, but was also a symbol, both of the social character of the peasant revolution that was sealed in the events of 1848–49 and of Grundtvig's own movement itself: neither urban elitist nor ultimately socially dangerous, but the relatively peaceful advance of a broadly based, propertied agrarian class, respectful both of property and of "the people."

Grundtvig's campaign address in Præstø is remarkable for its popular tone, its simplicity, its general poverty of ideas, its rampant nationalism, and, most of all, its appeal to the self-esteem of the common peasant. *What Will N. F. S. Grundtvig Do in the Rigsdag?*[148] is the title of his address, and the answer, first and foremost, is that he will "put in a *Danish* word" and combat "the learned gentlemen" who "are tempted to speak *gibberish*, so they lard their poor Danish speech with *German* and *French, Latin* and *Greek.* . . ."[149] Grundtvig will be able to use his "beak and claws" to "bite those learned gentlemen who, with all their fineness, still often have skin on their ears that is as thick as that which the peasants have on their fists. . . ."[150] Grundtvig is a learned man, but he is the peasants' learned man, and thus

> . . . he not only can chatter gibberish with the learned, but he also can and dares to make fun of their gibberish and of all the wisdom which it contains; and he [Grundtvig] can speak Danish, so that all the Danish people, from Zealand and Jutland and even from Slesvig, can understand him, and he is not afraid to say right to the face of the learned what he has often written to them and said in print: that it is from the *peasants*, who know no other language than their *mother tongue*, it is from them that the learned must learn to speak Danish. . . .[151]

Grundtvig promises to press for vigorous prosecution of the war in Slesvig and Holstein not only in order to keep the German language out of the Rigsdag but even "to teach the Germans Danish."[152]

Finally, concerning the drafting of the constitution, which was, after all, the actual purpose of this first Constitutional [grundlovgivende] Assembly, Grundtvig has remarkably little of substance to say. He will, again, keep "the Germans" out and, again, combat "the learned gentlemen" who are trying to install "many wildly foreign things" in the constitution.[153] But none of this is further defined, nor did it have to be for Grundtvig's audience, whom he promises that he will not fail with respect to the most important thing, namely, "that if I come into the Rigsdag, then all Danes, and especially *the peasants of Zealand*, can be sure that there will never have been heard so friendly and daring a word spoken *for them* in at least five hundred years . . . !"[154]

Grundtvig was of course elected and served in the constitutional convention, and although, because of various objections, he voted against the constitution itself, he served in the lower house of the Rigsdag it created until 1858. Several years thereafter, unable to remain inactive for long, Grundtvig came out of retirement (at age eighty-three). He resumed his parliamentary service, this time in the upper house, as the defender of the 1849 Constitution against the wave of reaction and the various proposed restrictions on univeral (male) suffrage that were advanced in the wake of the disaster which descended upon liberal constitutionalism after Denmark's defeat in the German war of 1864.

In 1850, two years after his election to the Constitutional Assembly, Grundtvig authored an essay entitled *The People's Gain in Denmark in the Revolution of 1848*[155] in which he reflected upon the transformation of Denmark since 1848. He noted that the greatest gain from "the revolution" [Omsvinget] was surely the war with Germany, which was still continuing. Grundtvig insisted that it was not from any blood lust that he felt the war to be a blessing, but he felt that without it Denmark would never have pulled itself together as a nation and that "German and Germanness would . . . soon have swallowed up Danish and Danishness in the whole of Jutland," while the rest of Denmark would never have had the courage to "wrest ourselves from the intellectual guardianship of the German professors."[156] It was national self-consciousness and popular culture, then, rather than any political arrangements as such which for Grundtvig were the primary fruits of 1848.

The second great gain of 1848 was likewise not an institutional arrangement but an enormous increase in the *"publicness"* [Offentlighed] of things, which has in turn forced the government, whatever its form, to act more in accordance with "the Danish way of thinking," particularly in matters "concerning the *people's* life and blood and the *existence* of the *nation*."[157] The most important avenue of this openness, Grundtvig continues, is of course the free press, without which all the forms and guarantees of government, e.g., ministerial responsibility, have nothing more than *"nominal value*."[158] In fact, Grundtvig goes so far as to agree with Jefferson in preferring a free press to any particular form of government or even, perhaps, to government itself:

All the information which a *government*, by its own volition, supplies to a *people's council* is indeed similar to *gas lights*, which can be blindingly bright one moment, but at the next moment, if it pleases those who stand at the gas-cock, can completely disappear. *Freedom of speech* creates a *watch guard*, whose street illumination is not the best, and which usually smacks more of whale than of oil, but which is much steadier than the gas lights of the Rigsdag hall, and does not hinder, but rather guarantees them.[159]

As for the result of 1848, namely the constitution itself, Grundtvig reminds his readers that one must not have too great expectations of such a document, and then one will not be disappointed. It will not create "a *condition of bliss*" but is merely a tool, "the *means* to procure a free-born people all the *openness, freedom,* and *equality* which are the preconditions for an *active* and *happy* life."[160] But we must not become so fixed upon the constitution that we regard its completion as the signal for lapsing into inaction, for "the law of the *life of a people,* as of every *life,* is *ceaseless movement*."[161] Movement, to a libertarian such as Grundtvig, always contains within itself the possibilities of positive change, and Grundtvig is proud to place himself on the side of "the party of movement," regardless of the risks entailed: "We will fear *standstill* far more than *movement,* however disorderly and wild it might be."[162] Political ferment is the precondition of free cultural activity, which, as we have seen, is in turn the precondition of Grundtvig's ultimate religious goal.

Therefore, Grundtvig concludes, "all we can require of a *constitution* and a *parliament* is that they give us the *permission* and the *opportunity* to use and enjoy popular life [Folke-Livet] as *best* we can. . . ."[163] What this means, in other words, is that the constitution is to create forms and opportunities which must be filled by free human activity. A constitution removes hindrances, but it does not attempt to provide positive substance itself. That must come, unforced, from the people, if there is to be a free popular life. For Grundtvig, then, the virtue of the constitution is that it is a liberal one, in the classic sense in which that term is used in the present book: Its purpose is "to *guarantee,* insofar as it is possible, to all those who have the life and the desire for it, a *free movement* in all *human* directions, and an *equal* access to all the positions and areas of activity for which they are suited. . . ."[164] It is, on the other hand, not the purpose of a constitution or a parliament to "procure us 'guaranteed livelihood' "—Grundtvig is surely thinking of the June Days in Paris—or "to situate us in a *condition of bliss* in which we may remain sitting or lying as it suits us. . . ."[165]

In sum, Grundtvig's assessment of the positive accomplishment of 1848 is, first of all, the awakening of popular self-consciousness; second, the enormous strengthening of the organs of publicity, press, and popular cultural freedom; and third—and least in importance—the development of constitutional guarantees of political freedom, a freedom which Grundtvig defines in wholly liberal terms as the negative freedom for individuals to act and move without obstruction as they see fit. Grundtvig, of course, hoped and expected that the people would use this new freedom of action to move in the direction of the communitarian Christianity of the matchless discovery. That is, Grundtvig hoped to use secular liberalism as the means by which to bridge the painful but necessary—and hopefully temporary—gap between Christianity and culture.

14. H. N. Clausen and Orla Lehmann: The Liberal Alternative to the Golden Age Mainstream

O

The second major alternative to the conservative social vision of the Golden Age mainstream (after Grundtvigianism) was liberalism, which has been discussed earlier, but which will here be examined further. Although the liberals were supporters of constitutionalism, which the peasants and Grundtvigians came to espouse in the later 1840's, and although the liberals were leading exponents of the national cause in southern Jutland, which Grundtvig also supported, they differed profoundly with the Grundtvigian position on almost every other point of substance and on every point of style. The Grundtvigians were thoroughgoing democrats and populists, who believed that power should always emanate from the bottom up. Whereas Grundtvig favored retaining and extending the principle of popular sovereignty, the liberal politician Clausen favored the restriction of universal (male) suffrage.

The root of the split between the Grundtvigian movement and such liberals as Clausen (or Lehmann) can best be summed up in their respective attitudes toward culture [Dannelse]. The Grundtvigians believed that true culture—that is, what was most valuable about human experience—was the property of every living soul. Furthermore, the Grundtvigian position maintained that if culture had any special or particular locus, it was surely with the "common man" (among what was "popular" [folkelig]), whereas, if it were absent anywhere, it could only be absent among those elitists who denigrated the common man and what was popular. Such liberals as Clausen held precisely the opposite view and shared essentially the same elitist or "mandarin" view of culture that the conservative Golden Age mainstream celebrated: Culture was a treasure to be guarded by the rare few. In a society composed largely of rural bumpkins, culture was the possession of the academically educated urban minority.

Thus, Clausen and other liberals were opposed to the conservative mainstream in that they espoused constitutional schemes and opposed the romantic—particularly the Schellingian or Hegelian—philosophical and historical views of the conservative Golden Age. On the other hand, the liberals also opposed the romanticism, and more importantly, the populism of the Grundt-vigian alternative to the Golden Age mainstream.

Nowhere is the nature and depth of the elitism which separated liberalism from the real affection of the rural masses more clearly and concisely illumi-nated than in the famous Præstø election of 1848, which has been alluded to several times. In the summer and fall of 1848, it will be remembered, every district of Denmark was engaged in electing delegates to the coming Consti-tutional Assembly on the basis of universal (male) suffrage. The liberals had expected peasant support at the polls, but, fearing the possible consequences of the suffrage, they had included the proviso of a government-appointed "royal 25 percent" to counterbalance any possible peasant ascendancy. This stipulation completely alienated the peasant movement and led to a break between the Society of Friends of the Peasant (later the Peasant Party) and their erstwhile liberal allies. No one who did not publicly repudiate the royal 25 percent could be given the support of the well-organized Society of Friends of the Peasant. Virtually all liberals refused to repudiate the royal 25 percent, and they were thus doomed to run opposed by candidates who had the backing of the formidable Society.

One such liberal candidate was the theologian and politician H. N. Clau-sen, ironically one of the early supporters of the Society. It was decided that the great Clausen should seek election to the Constitutional Assembly from the district of Præstø in southern Zealand, the same district he had represented as a deputy to the Roskilde Estates since 1840, but now, of course, the electorate was incomparably broader than that for the provincial Estates, which was to be the liberal Clausen's undoing. Clausen points out in his memoirs that he had been elected from Præstø several times before and "had not neglected to participate according to my abilities in rural matters, and especially to speak out for arrangements which would better the lot of cottagers."[1] What Clausen does not point out is that he had spoken out on numerous occasions against granting any form of suffrage to cottagers and other poor, rural people. Clau-sen's opponent was the poor, simple weaver Hans Hansen, who, Clausen noted, was a man of dubious honor and reputation because he had once been arrested under suspicion of theft. Although nothing had been proven against Hansen, who was later released, Clausen notes with bourgeois horror that the poor artisan remained "under the special surveillance of the police."[2] Clausen's local allies seized upon Hans Hansen's "criminal record" and initiated a cam-paign of character assassination against the poor weaver. Indeed, Hansen was even preached against from the pulpits of parish churches, but to no avail, for the poor, ignorant artisan defeated the great liberal churchman by about 570 votes to 330.[3]

Clausen and most liberals were shocked and alarmed at this defeat and at what it portended for liberalism generally. Despite the fact that he shortly thereafter received a letter signed by a number of faithful peasant supporters in which they "denied having any share in 'the blindness which had seized so many as a result of a party's efforts to entrap them,' "⁴ Clausen's feelings and fears were not mollified. He writes in his memoirs that the election "revealed to me a serious picture of the danger of a suffrage which is so broad, in which the decisive element is merely the number of votes, quite aside from all other elements."⁵ Electoral defeat ratified Clausen's liberal and elitist bias in the direction of special privilege for property and culture.

On the occasion of this famous and bitterly symbolic confrontation, the poet Emil Aarestrup, one of the finest lyricists of the Golden Age and one of the few with democratic sympathies, penned the following stinging poem, which sums up the significance of the Clausen-Hansen election:

Professor Clausen and Weaver Hansen

In shrewdness and eloquence a learned master,
Freedom's abstract friend, who fearlessly
Did lead the fight with Christian decency
Against absolutism and orthodox pastors.

A poor devil, not even a copyholder,
A cotton weaver in a hut behind a fence,
Degraded and hardened by dirty work,
Recently released from the lockup.

Choose, Danish people! Choose one of these two!
You chose the latter. I must admit that it is true,
He is the natural defender of your cause.

You gather yourselves stoutly before the polling place
                              in person,
In the choice is a revenge, a mockery in thought,
A bitterness, whose rightness I do not deny.⁶

The smear campaign that Clausen's supporters had waged against Hansen continued to have its effects, however, and Hansen was eventually so weakened and damaged by insinuations that he was forced to withdraw his name and cause a new election to be held.

But the bitter symbolism of the Præstø election was not ended with Clausen's defeat and the forced withdrawal of Hansen. Indeed, the circumstances and the outcome of the new election were a climax of irony that says much, not only about the elitist and anti-rural sensibilities of Danish liberalism but also about the *sub rosa* respectability of Clausen's erstwhile enemy, Grundtvig. If the schema adumbrated at the beginning of this chapter were correct without amendment, then it would be respectability and urbane elitism that separated Clausen from the peasant masses, whereas the opposite would hold for Grundtvig. In fact, however, the difference between Grundtvig and Clausen was not nearly so absolute as it might appear. In the poignant and symbolic by-election that was held after the forced withdrawal of Hans Hansen, Grundtvig was chosen by acclamation as a compromise between the genuinely "populist" Hans Hansen and the "mandarin" Clausen. Clausen was Grundtvig's old opponent from the theological battle of 1825, which had first gained Grundtvig much of his popularity and notoriety among the peasant awakeners. Now, in 1848, Grundtvig was a man of compromise, a popular enough candidate to please many peasants, yet, for all his populist rhetoric and wild gestures, an educated, an urban, indeed even—by the new standards of the age of the common man—a respectable man. For all his threats, he had remained a priest in the official Danish Church, a product of the finest academic training that Denmark could offer, bearing the seal of official approval. For all his rural sympathies, Grundtvig had remained a resident of Copenhagen where he enjoyed a virtual sinecure as a well-paid pastor at a home for the elderly.

What is perhaps even more revealing than Grundtvig's respectability in the eyes of the liberals was the apparent acceptability of the liberals to the Grundtvigian movement when Grundtvigianism was confronted with a clear-cut choice between a genuinely popular character, such as the weaver Hansen, and a liberal mandarin, even so notorious an enemy of Grundtvigianism as Clausen himself. For the fact is, that when faced with the candidacy of Hans Hansen in the first Præstø election, the Grundtvigian movement, which was particularly strong in that district of southern Zealand, actively supported Clausen's campaign, and the Grundtvigians led the attempt to smear Hansen and to destroy his reputation. It was the popular and influential Grundtvigian clergyman, Peter Rørdam, the pastor of a local parish in the Præstø district, who most viciously attacked Hansen from the pulpit, comparing him to the thief Barabbas, on whom the Jews of Jerusalem had wasted their "universal suffrage"![7] Pastor Rørdam's Grundtvigian notion of the popular thus apparently did not extend to elections, for he did his best to support the interests of Clausen, who was Rørdam's putative theological enemy but his equal in gentility. The example of Clausen's electoral contest in Præstø helps to clarify the fact that there was no absolute conflict between liberal elitism and the Grundtvigian version of populism. We can therefore see how Grundtvig could apparently regard his candidacy in the Præstø by-election as his civic duty and at the same time as an opportunity to exploit his reputation for being both pro-peasant and an academically educated man, a pastor in the Established Church, cultured, safe. Grundtvig saw himself uniquely fitted to mediate the difference between country and city, between common man and gentleman. Clausen, the defeated mandarin, was forced to settle for a government-appointed seat: he became part of the hotly contested royal 25 percent.

The example of the Præstø election is very helpful in clarifying the lay of the Danish cultural-political landscape at mid-century. Despite genuine political differences, the disagreement between the social vision of the liberals and that held by their Golden Age mainstream opponents was only relative and not absolute. Again, the disagreement between the populist Grundtvigians and their "respectable" opponents, liberal and conservative mainstream alike, was similarly only a relative one. Neither of the alternatives to the conservative social vision of the Golden Age mainstream—that is, neither liberalism nor Grundtvigianism—represented an absolute disjunction with that culture. Part two of the present work will argue that Søren Kierkegaard's vision did present such a radical alternative to the Golden Age.

B. ORLA LEHMANN: THE RADICAL LIBERAL BEGINS TO COOL

Orla Lehmann, like his more moderate colleague Clausen, also came personally to experience the electoral consequences of being an urban liberal in the age of the rural common man. In a subsequent election, when Lehmann ran in an apparently safe district on the out-of-the-way island of Bornholm, he was also rejected in favor of a local peasant.

However, unlike Clausen, who never shared Lehmann's faith in a broad franchise, Lehmann never gave up his belief in the principle of universal (male) suffrage after he first espoused it publicly and indeed almost by accident, in the heady days of March 1848. Yet like all liberals, even the fiery Lehmann believed that universal (male) suffrage had to be used "properly," and when he witnessed its "abuses"—the election of unlettered peasants to the Rigsdag—his doubts about the broad franchise manifested themselves in an 1861 speech in which he revealed his family resemblance to the other mandarins who constituted his party and indeed, his kinship to the Golden Age conservatives as well.

In his 1861 address, Lehmann's fears and disappointments as well as his liberal faith in meritocracy are shown very clearly. By this time, other liberals had become quite lukewarm in their support for universal (male) suffrage and were even ready to abandon their beloved June Constitution in order to get rid of its franchise provisions. Lehmann, on the other hand, points out that he will not disown the June Constitution,

> ... which has elevated us to the great dignity of being citizens of a free state. . . . Let us love liberty with all its dangers. . . . In Denmark not only are all equal before the law, but all have equal access to the goods of society and to participation in the governance of the state. I say "equal access," and I add, "everyone according to his ability". . . . The task of equality is not to drag down that which stands higher, but to lift up that which is low. . . . Therefore there is nothing more contrary to the spirit of the constitution than when liberty's bastard children among us seek to whip up class egoism in order that they might build up an unjustifiable power on this basis. This situation is no more "popular" [folkelig] simply because it is now the peasants, just as in the old days it was the nobles, who claim to be the whole people. . . . When in 1848 Denmark performed the daring feat of transferring power to the whole people, it was not in

order to place the guidance of the state in the hands of the unenlightened common peasants [Almuen], even less to turn it over to self-serving and devious demagogues. It is the talented, the cultured, and the well-to-do who in every civilized society have the dominant voice in the guidance of public affairs, and all that equality can require and can do is to make it as easy as possible for every talented person to acquire culture [Dannelse] and wealth, and thereby, respect and influence.[8]

Yet, Lehmann was a noble and principled soul, and his speech, condescending though it was, was essentially a defense of the universal (male) suffrage of the June 1849 Constitution. Therefore, Lehmann concludes that the desired predominance of the talented, cultured, and wealthy must not be secured by limiting the franchise but rather by showing solicitude toward, and gaining the respect of, the lower classes. When "the constitution left it to the whole people, and thus essentially to the common peasant [Almuen] to decide to whom it would entrust itself," it created a "political necessity for the enlightened and possessing middle class to win the devotion and confidence of the common peasant by showing a respectful and loving concern for his well-being." By this means "intellect and insight and wealth can preserve their *justifiable dominance,* even under a democratic constitution," a dominance that the people's good sense will surely acknowledge if "upper-class pride and desire for domination" does not encourage the growth of "the suspicion and envy that the common man has inherited from the past." The constitution will not make the rich, the educated, and the talented into slaves of the commons, but will set for them "new conditions by which to preserve their old influence," a situation which, Lehmann was convinced, "is essentially only an expression for the noblest teachings of humanity and *Christianity.*"[9]

Thus, the ultimate mental and spiritual possession of the liberals—even such doctrinaire and left-wing liberals as Orla Lehmann—was a Christian cultural synthesis that justified, albeit in the most high-minded and idealistic fashion, the continuation of the rule of the urban upper classes. The liberal view was that the universal (male) suffrage provisions of the June Constitution should not change the real distribution of social power but should give new vitality and legitimacy to the existing order, in which a cultivated urbane elite governed the common peasants [Almuen] *in loco parentis.* Representative government, thus understood, was the expression of a lofty, liberal Christian-humanitarian synthesis. The urban, elitist, Christian-humane notion of society put forth by the Golden Age liberals was not really so very different from the Christian-humane "conservative" vision espoused by the mainstream of the Golden Age.

On the other hand, the grounds on which the peasantry supported the liberal-democratic regime after 1848 were much more hard-headed and less metaphysical. It was in fact the common peasants, rather than the upper mid-

dle-class liberals, who had the "classical liberal"—secular, instrumentalist, prudential—notion of politics. In this position the peasants were joined by Søren
Kierkegaard, who, as we will see, ultimately came to champion the "common
man" and to embrace the verdict of 1848–49 as a breath of "fresh air" that
would once and for all divest politics of the religious and metaphysical trap-
pings with which the bankrupt traditional culture had attempted to support
and justify itself.

15. The Golden Age and Its Alternatives

O

We have now examined three different religious and cultural-political positions in early and mid-nineteenth-century Denmark. First, we examined the conservative Golden Age "mainstream," represented in its first generation by Oehlenschläger and Mynster and in its second generation by Heiberg and Martensen. Then we examined two alternatives to that mainstream, namely Grundtvig and his movement, on the one hand, and liberalism, which we have represented with H. N. Clausen and Orla Lehmann, on the other. Each of these three positions differs sharply from the other two on certain key questions yet agrees with its opponents on other questions. In order to make sense of this complex intellectual, cultural-political, and theological terrain in as brief and compressed a manner as possible, and in order to make clear where Kierkegaard will fit into this picture, let us single out two key questions from the many we have touched upon.

Let us first look at how each of these positions deals with the question: What is the importance of "History" as the key to understanding the meaning and significance of one's present-day life?

What we will label a "romantic" position finds in historical development the key to grasping the meaning of the present, and what we will label an "Enlightenment" or "agnostic" position either denies this or is uncertain what role history plays in determining the significance of an individual's situation. Clearly, the Golden Age mainstream—one thinks of Oehlenschläger's historical dramas and philo-Norse verse and of Heiberg's Hegelianism—stressed the importance of history and deserves the "romantic" label, and Grundtvigianism likewise shares this "romantic" emphasis upon history's significance to the present. Liberalism, however, generally found its philosophical roots in the eighteenth century and was far less inclined to posit general theses on the significance of history. We will therefore place the liberals in the agnostic camp with respect to the ultimate significance of history.

The second question we will pose is that of "culture": What is the significant kernel of human experience which we call "Culture," and who are its bearers or guardians?

Here we will term the alternative positions "mandarin" and "populist." The mandarins would maintain that the significant core of human experience is a high literary tradition that is studied, guarded, and passed on by a relatively narrow elite, through whom all genuine cultural enlightenment is mediated. The populists, on the other hand, would claim that that which is most valuable and significant in human life is the property of the entire people and that the greatest treasures are—potentially, at least—within the grasp of the lowliest citizen, regardless of his or her literary or formal education. With respect to the question of culture, the Golden Age mainstream and the urban liberals were clearly "mandarins," whereas Grundtvig and his followers were "populists."

Thus, each of the two major alternatives to the Golden Age mainstream opposes that mainstream on one point but agrees with it on the other: The Grundtvigians, like the mainstream, were romantics with respect to History but differed with the mainstream on the question of Culture; the liberals, on the other hand, shared the mandarin cultural orientation of the Golden Age mainstream but differed on the question of History. The situation can most easily be expressed in the following chart:

HISTORY

	ROMANTIC	AGNOSTIC
MANDARIN	Golden Age Mainstream	Liberalism
POPULIST	Grundtvig	

CULTURE

Thus, the Golden Age mainstream was "mandarin romantic," whereas the Grundtvigians were "populist romantics," and the liberals were "mandarin agnostics." Insofar as it coincides with the Golden Age mainstream on neither of the two important questions I have asked, the lower right-hand square represents the diametrical opposite of the Golden Age mainstream position and is empty. Part two of the present work will argue that Søren Kierkegaard fills the empty square and completes our diagram. Kierkegaard made no compromises with the mandarin romanticism of the Golden Age mainstream. He was not a mandarin agnostic like the liberal Clausen, because he could not share, as Clausen and liberals could, the Golden Age elitist notion of culture. He was not a populist romantic like Grundtvig, because he could not share, as Grundtvig and his followers could, the Golden Age faith in history. Kierkegaard was thoroughly his own person, an original—an agnostic on the significance of History, a populist on the locus of Culture, and a genuinely modern, post-1848 alternative to the *ancien régime* world-view of the Golden Age.

View of the Jægerspris district, by Jens Juel, 1782. This is a fine representation of rural Zealand prior to the reparcelling brought about by the land reforms. Note the tightly clustered farmhouses of the peasant village. (Courtesy of the Statens Museum for Kunst.)

View of the Østerbro neighborhood (Copenhagen), by Christian Købke, 1836. This is the way the fringes of the city looked when Kierkegaard took his long walks. (Courtesy of the Statens Museum for Kunst.)

View of Højbroplads (Copenhagen), by Sally Henriques, 1844. Højbroplads
[Highbridge Place] was a busy neighborhood in the heart of the city. (Courtesy
of the Statens Museum for Kunst.)

Adam Oehlenschläger (1779–1850), by J. L. Lund, 1809. (Courtesy of Det Nationalhistoriske Museum på Frederiksborg.)

Adam Oehlenschläger, by J. V. Gertner, 1846. (Courtesy of Det Nationalhistoriske Museum på Frederiksborg.)

Jacob P. Mynster (1775–1854), by J. L. Lund, ca. 1820's. (Courtesy of Det Kongelige Bibliotek.)

Jacob P. Mynster, by J. V. Gernter, 1842. (Courtesy of Det Nationalhistoriske Museum på Frederiksborg.)

Johan Ludvig Heiberg (1791–1860), by D. Monies, 1844. (Courtesy of Det Kongelige Bibliotek.)

Hans Lassen Martensen (1808–84) at the time he was elected Bishop of Zealand and Primate of Denmark, by J. V. Gertner, 1854. (Courtesy of Det Nationalhistoriske Museum på Frederiksborg.)

N. F. S. Grundtvig (1783–1872), by C. F. Christensen, 1830. (Courtesy of Det Nationalhistoriske Museum på Frederiksborg.)

N. F. S. Grundtvig, by P. C. Skovgaard, 1847. (Courtesy of Det Nationalhistoriske Museum på Frederiksborg.)

Henrik Nikolai Clausen (1793–1877), by C. A. Jensen, 1836. (Courtesy of Det Kongelige Bibliotek.)

Orla Lehmann (1810–70), by Elisabeth Jerichau Baumann, 1848. (Courtesy of Det Nationalhistoriske Museum på Frederiksborg.)

Nytorv [New Market] and Part of Gammeltorv [Old Market] (Copenhagen), by C. E. Balsgaard, 1839. The Kierkegaard family lived in the second house from the corner (to the right of the Town Hall). (Courtesy of The Royal Danish Embassy, Washington, D.C.)

Søren Kierkegaard, ca. 1853–55, by H. P. Hansen. Despite their caricature-like quality, the sketches by Hansen and Wilhelm Marstrand are generally thought to be accurate representations of Kierkegaard. (Courtesy of Det Nationalhistoriske Museum på Frederiksborg.)

Søren Kierkegaard, by Wilhelm Marstrand, drawn from memory, 1870. (Courtesy of Det Nationalhistoriske Museum på Frederiksborg.)

PART TWO

DENMARK'S KIERKEGAARD

16. Søren Kierkegaard: Life and Literary Career to February 1846

O

Any account of the life of Søren Kierkegaard[1] (hereafter, "SK") must begin with his father, Michael Pedersen Kierkegaard (1756–1838), whose powerful influence loomed over the lives of all his children. Michael Pedersen was born into a poor family in Sædding, in Ringkøbing Amt, Jutland, one of the bleakest and most impoverished districts in Denmark. He spent his early youth as a cold and ill-fed shepherd boy on his native heath. His family were very likely Herrnhuters, but in any event, when eleven-year-old Michael Pedersen was sent to Copenhagen in 1768 to live as an apprentice with the family of fairly well-to-do relatives who had recently left the Sædding area themselves, he was quickly put under the spiritual tutelage of a Herrnhut-pietist pastor in Copenhagen. This deep rural-based pietism, with its anticlerical undercurrent, never abandoned Michael Pedersen and exercised a profound influence upon his children, who were first-generation urbanites.

Coming to Copenhagen turned out to be the decisive event in the life of young Michael Pedersen. He was a clever apprentice and an enterprising spirit, and the economic situation in Copenhagen in the 1770's, '80's, and '90's was extremely favorable. Thus the young man soon acquired his own dry goods business, expanded it several times, bought a good deal of real estate and began investing in stocks and bonds. The former shepherd boy was a successful independent businessman in his twenties and a quite wealthy man in his thirties.

As was noted in passing in chapter 2, Michael Pedersen became an important financial supporter and social pillar of the Copenhagen Herrnhut group known as the Congregation of Brothers. At the same time, however, the former peasant kept his fences mended with official, urban Christianity, and when Mynster came to Copenhagen in the early nineteenth century, Michael Pedersen became one of the future bishop's prominent parishioners and devout supporters. Thus there was a tension in the religious life—and certainly in the social self-understanding as well—of the Kierkegaard family, a tension between rural and urban religion, between peasant pietism and Golden Age oratory. This tension, never resolved by the father, was resolved in different ways by the two sons who survived him: Peter Christian, the Grundtvigian, and Søren, who became an enemy of the officially Christian society of the Golden Age.

Michael Pedersen Kierkegaard was by all accounts a brilliant and self-taught man who could hold his own in intellectual discourse with those who came to visit. Among those who visited the wealthy and devout businessman and auto-didact in his large, prominent house at the corner of Copenhagen's New Market Square [Nytorv] were Mynster, Mynster's opponent Grundtvig, and various leading Grundtvigians—these latter were often brought home by Søren's older brother Peter Christian, who was an enthusiastic early Grundt-vigian. Michael Pedersen is also generally reputed to have been a dark, gloomy, and profoundly melancholy man, whose somber temper made itself deeply felt in the family, especially in the lives of Søren and Peter Christian. This is undoubtedly so, though despite the ingenious speculation of various Kierke-gaard biographers, we shall never know the ultimate source of the Kierkegaard family melancholia. Some biographers root Michael Pedersen's melancholia in a possible childhood blasphemy, the consequence of which always brooded over the man's life, so that he interpreted his worldly success as a form of mockery visited upon him by God in ironic retaliation for his youthful impiety. Others, more plausibly in my estimation, find the father's melancholia rooted in lingering guilt about the sexual infraction of having impregnated his cousin and housekeeper, Ane Sørensdatter Lund, less than a year after the death of his first wife, an imprudence which compelled Michael Pedersen quickly to marry the peasant woman who was to be the mother of all his seven children. In any event, the source (and even the fact) of Michael Pedersen's melancholia is not of great importance to the present study, whereas the family's social origins and circumstances and the latent social tensions present within the family's situation are.

At about the time of his second, enforced, marriage in 1797, the widowed and childless Michael Pedersen put his business in the hands of trustees and lived the second half of his life in retirement, amid his growing family and his books, in the house on New Market Square. The middle-aged rentier and father of seven did not wholly lose interest in his financial affairs, however, for just prior to the disastrous state bankruptcy in 1813, which ruined so many wealthy Copenhagen families, he transferred a large portion of his capital into guar-anteed gold-convertible bonds and thus emerged relatively unscathed from the catastrophe, having in fact enhanced his relative position vis-a-vis many older, wealthier families in the city.[2] He lived another twenty-five years after the crash, dying in 1838 at the age of eighty-two.

Søren Kierkegaard was the seventh and last child of the aging father and was born in 1813, the year of the inflation and bankruptcy in which, as SK so wryly notes in his journal, "so many other crazy notes were also put in circulation."[3] Søren was a somewhat frail and sheltered child who was quite smothered by his father's strictness and concern. At home he was under a heavy pietistic influence, and at school—the successful peasant's son went, of course, to the capital's finest preparatory school—he was noted as a bright student with a rather sharp tongue and an acerbic wit. Søren, like the rest of the family, was subjected to a large dose of religion—Mynster in the morning and the Herrnhut Congregation in the evening. As has been mentioned, Søren's religious upbringing reflected the urban-rural tension which the first-generation *nouveau riche* must have felt in every area of his life. The family was wealthy, but the father forced petty peasant economies on his son, which made him stand out unenviably among his aristocratic fellow pupils. Ought the son be proud of his peasant and pietist roots, his father's odd dress and rural accent? Or ought he seek to assimilate as quickly as possible into the upper crust of Golden Age literary society which became open to him when he matriculated into the university at age seventeen and showed himself to be a brilliant, though fitful and perhaps fashionably frivolous young man? Søren enrolled in the theological course of study in 1830, as was his father's wish and as his brother Peter Christian had done before him, but for several years he did not take his studies seriously, dabbling instead in the literary fashions of the time. He became a hanger-on of the Heiberg circle and made his public debut with a student address in 1835[4] and some newspaper articles in 1836 and 1837,[5] where he made his mark as a witty spokesman for the aristocratic-conservative Golden Age point of view and as an opponent of shallow liberalism.

In 1838, with the deaths of his father and of his teacher and moral mentor, philosophy professor Poul Martin Møller, SK got down to serious business, producing his first work of substance and making rapid progress in his studies for his theological examinations. Thus, in late 1838 appeared SK's *From the Papers of One Still Living*,[6] a devastating attack on his young colleague Hans Christian Andersen, in which SK charged that Andersen's work was marred by mawkish self-pity and sentimentality and was lacking in the notion of an ethical, autonomous, and responsible human personality. Shortly thereafter, SK finally signed up to take his theological examinations, which he passed in July 1840. SK then began work on his second book, his doctoral dissertation *On the Concept of Irony*,[7] in which modern romantic irony is invidiously contrasted with the irony of SK's hero Socrates. The dissertation was completed and published in July 1841, when SK's formal education ended and he began the life of a writer of independent means. For various reasons, several attempts, or half-way attempts, to obtain a rural parish never succeeded, and SK remained a writer, living on a gradually diminishing capital, for the rest of his life. Although he was for a time engaged (September 1840-October 1841) to Regine Olsen, the young and pretty daughter of a wealthy bourgeois family, SK broke off the engagement for profound personal reasons which have never been satisfactorily clarified—and which are immaterial to the present study—and he never married, living the rest of his life alone in various Copenhagen apartments, generally attended by a manservant.

After the broken engagement in October 1841, SK traveled to Germany to hear Schelling lecture and to begin work on his forthcoming authorship. (SK traveled to Germany three times in all, and with the exception of a brief trip across the Sound to Sweden and a pilgrimage to his father's birthplace in Jutland, his other travels were confined to rambles in the capital and carriage tours to the woods and fields of the immediately surrounding countryside.) Schelling disappointed SK, but he returned home in March 1842 with a great bulk of manuscript, and in February 1843 the enormous authorship got under way with the publication of the two large volumes of the popular *Either/Or*.[8] SK's authorship, as he explains in a later autobiographical work, has from this time onward a curious and deliberate bifurcation, so that each of the "aesthetic" works, generally pseudonymous, was "accompanied" by a parallel "edifying" work in sermon form, always published in SK's own name.

In the three years from February 1843 to February 1846 SK published seven major works and many "edifying" discourses. *Either/Or*, as has been noted, appeared in February 1843 and was a curious collection of supposedly "found" documents which highlight the difference between a merely aesthetic life, which is lived within the categories of sensuality and intellectual interestingness, and the ethical life, in which one lives in the universally valid ethical forms of the family and community and even participates in a sort of Kantian Christianity. In October 1843, two more pseudonymous books, *Repetition*[9] and *Fear and Trembling*,[10] appeared, and they dealt specifically with the religious sphere of existence and its difference from lesser spheres. *Fear and Trembling*, in particular, deals with the relationship between the absolute imperatives of faith and the universal ethical norms of society. SK points out that the religious person may be compelled by religious reasons to transgress ethical universals yet nonetheless return to live life as an individual in society, having realized the relativity of even the ethical universals and having thus become capable of relating "absolutely to what is absolute and relatively to what is relative." *The Concept of Anxiety*,[11] published in June 1844, is a difficult and rather obscure work on psychology and was complemented—and, it can be argued, to a considerable extent superseded[12]—by a later psychological work. (That work, *The Sickness Unto Death*,[13] published in 1849, is an enormously important work which will be dealt with in detail in chapter 23 of the present work.) *Philosophical Fragments*[14] was also published in June 1844, and it is the opening round of a decisive settling of accounts with all philosophy and philosophical Christianity (particularly the Hegelian variety). In the *Fragments* SK puts forward Socrates as the greatest of philosophers and shows how far short he falls of the categories of genuine and "paradoxical" Christianity. *Stages on Life's Way*[15] appeared in April 1845 and was an updated recapitulation of the theory of stages put forth in *Either/Or*; many of the characters from the earlier work reappear in the *Stages*, where their positions are given fuller treatment. The final major work of the period prior to that which most concerns us is the massive *Concluding Unscientific Postscript*,[16] published in February 1846. This was SK's last "aesthetic" pseudonymous work, and he conceived of it as completing the architecture of his literary plan and thus ending his authorship. With typical Kierkegaardian humor, the enormous *Postscript* was technically an addendum to the tiny *Philosophical Fragments*, and it does indeed continue and complete the task of outlining an existential or "paradoxical" Christianity which defies assimilation to any systematic philosophical categories, particularly the Hegelian. SK takes this opportunity to fire what he hoped were parting shots at a number of his opponents, especially Martensen, but Grundtvig also receives a sound drubbing.

SK closes the *Postscript* with a "First and Last Declaration" to his reader, in which he acknowledges his previous pseudonymous work; it is plain that the writer now hoped to lay aside his masks forever and cease writing. This was not to be, however, and it is precisely the predominantly non-pseudonymous authorship written after the *Postscript* that is of interest in the present work. Because of its straightforwardness—it poses few of the hermeneutical problems that abound in the earlier works—this post-aesthetic (or "post-*Postscript*") authorship is relatively easy to deal with, and it is of particular interest because of its increasingly social-political character.

The seven major pseudonymous works from February 1843 to February 1846 mentioned above have generally attracted most of the attention which scholars have given to SK, and from a philosophical and literary point of view their importance is indisputable. In contrast, the works from the period after the *Postscript* have usually not been accorded the same quantity or quality of attention, and indeed the final few years (after 1850), which culminated in the "attack on Christendom," have usually been dealt with either not at all or in order to discredit SK's attack or explain it away. However, for the purpose of understanding SK's view of society and of the relationship between religion on the one hand and politics and culture on the other, it is this second half of SK's literary career which is more important. This is the period that began with the publication of *A Literary Review* in March 1846, that was punctuated by the revolutionary events of 1848–49, and that ended in the "attack" of 1854–55.

We will now examine this later period, bearing in mind that SK was deeply torn. He was torn between city and country; between Mynster and Herrnhut. He was torn between the gravitational pull of the elegant and conservative—but perhaps only nominally Christian—Golden Age, with its literary paragon, the Hegelian Heiberg, and finding his own way to assert his "peasant" understanding of culture, politics, and Christianity. SK also resisted the two generally available alternatives to the Golden Age position: the Grundtvigian movement, which SK saw as a vulgar mixture of worldly motives and superstitious "pact religion" and the shallow elitism of the liberals. It should also

be borne in mind that many of the most important themes of the later Kierkegaard were present in the earlier; the focus here on the period after the
Postscript is not intended to deny this thread of development. For example,
although as we will see, the events of 1848 and after gave SK the decisive push
in moving to a new understanding of politics and of the relation of politics to
religion, he was fiercely egalitarian long before then, as shown by the following
passages from the *Postscript*: "[T]he wise person ought first to understand the
same as what the simple person understands, and feel himself obligated by
the same things which obligate the simple person—and only then ought he go
on to world-historical matters."[17] Again, "when one is rooted most deeply in
one's individual uniqueness, and then grasps equality most powerfully—this
is the noble piety of the simple wise man."[18] But just as the "highest things"
are available to the most lowly, they can become less accessible to those whose
"cultivated" self-esteem makes them incapable of simplicity: "The more culture
and knowledge, the more difficult it is to become a Christian."[19] Again, "if it
admits of being grasped and maintained by the simplest person, then it is only
the more difficult for the 'cultured' person to reach. O wonderful, inspiring
Christian humanity—the highest is common to everyone. . . ."[20]

Let us examine the "politics" of the author of these lines in the years after
he wrote the *Postscript*. Let us examine Søren Kierkegaard's view of society
and of the relation between politics, culture, and religion in the second half of
his career. Let us examine the views of this wonderfully prodigal son of the
Golden Age, who has been consistently misinterpreted as a reactionary supporter of the conservative, hierarchical *ancien régime*.

17. *A Literary Review*

O

A Literary Review [*En literair Anmeldelse*][1] was published by SK on March 30, 1846, in the middle of his quarrel with the satirical journal *The Corsair* [*Corsaren*] and just one month after the publication of the *Concluding Unscientific Postscript*. *A Literary Review* deserves our special attention because it is SK's most specifically political work and because it was, with the exception of the earlier *Edifying Discourses* and his university dissertation (*The Concept of Irony*), the first work SK published under his own name, without the dialectical distance provided by a pseudonym. The *Review* is thus a direct political statement in which SK spoke for the first time about secular things without the help of his persona, and it must be understood as such. The fact that the work was written during the most painful portion of his collision with *The Corsair* certainly explains some of the personal bitterness in the tone, but the *Review* is not a mere occasional piece or a passing fancy. It was begun in mid-December 1845 [cf. Pap. VII 1 B 71, p. 259],[2] i.e., before the *Corsair* fight (which SK then had no notion would take the tragic and painful course it did) and immediately after the completion of the manuscript of the *Postscript*. Furthermore, near the beginning and the conclusion of the *Review* there are direct references [pp. 22 and 103n.] to SK's very first book, *From the Papers of One Still Living*, a pseudonymous work, the one work which SK had not acknowledged in his afterword to the just-completed *Postscript* and which he finally acknowledges here in the *Review*. There are several ostensible reasons for the mention of this early review of a novel by Hans Christian Andersen in the present *Review*. One is that, in that early work, SK had also discussed the work of Fru Gyllembourg, who is the author of the novel which now serves as the occasion for *A Literary Review*. Secondly, SK wishes to call attention to the fact that the early pseudonymous review, like the present *Review*, concerns itself with the problem of the whole, ethically integrated personality. However, the most important reason that the first book review is brought up in this present *Review* is that SK is mentioning it "in conclusion" [p. 22]; that is, SK sees *A Literary Review* as the concluding work of his literary production. Thus, his literary work began with a lengthy and pseudonymous book review that concerned itself with ethical questions, and it concludes—with the symbolic symmetry that SK loved so well—with another lengthy ethical-political book review which this time is, significantly, not pseudonymous but in SK's own name. By pointedly alluding to *From the Papers of One Still Living* in *A Literary Review*, SK calls attention to the symmetry of the authorship he hoped he was concluding, an authorship that had allowed for the repetition and deepening of the same themes over and over again but that had also seen the essential movement from pseudonymity to direct communication. *A Literary Review* was thus intended as a closing statement, as SK's first and final treatment, in his own name, of a secular problem, namely the political and ethical condition of "the present age" as compared with that of "the Revolutionary Age" of the previous generation.

B. THE MESSAGE OF THE *TWO AGES*

As mentioned above, the formal vehicle for *A Literary Review* is a book review of the novel *Two Ages*, which was published anonymously in 1845 by Fru Gyllembourg, the mother of Johan Ludvig Heiberg. She had (anonymously) been one of Denmark's most popular writers of prose fiction since her debut in her son's *Flying Post* [*Flyvende Post*] in 1827. As we have seen earlier, Fru Gyllembourg (*née* Thomasine Buntzen), born 1773, was the daughter of a wealthy Copenhagen merchant family and as an extraordinarily beautiful and intellectually gifted young woman had moved in very progressive political circles in the 1790's. She was married for a time to P. A. Heiberg, who fathered their famous son, the author Johan Ludvig. P. A. Heiberg was himself a witty political writer, who was involved in a famous censorship case in 1799 and was exiled for his daring. Young Thomasine, who in the course of their marriage had had a series of admirers, including the dashing diplomatic representative of revolutionary France, seized upon the hardship of exile in order to importune the Crown, successfully, for a divorce from her radical husband. She kept custody of young Johan Ludvig and soon married her lover, the Swedish nobleman Carl Gustav Gyllembourg, who had been exiled from Sweden for his political views and alleged complicity in a conspiracy. Fru Gyllembourg was thus well versed in the passions and politics of the salon culture of the Revolutionary period and was ideally suited to write a novel in which that period was contrasted with the prosaic present of the 1840's, to the obvious disparagement of the latter—hence the title and the principal theme of her novel *Two Ages*, around which SK constructed his political *Review*.

In SK's *Review*, as in Fru Gyllembourg's novel, the negative picture of "the present age" is only comprehensible when understood in the uncomplimentary light cast upon it by "the Revolutionary age." In *A Literary Review*, as in the novel it uses as its vehicle, the present age is a specific historical period, namely the 1840's. This was the decade in which bourgeois liberalism and aristocratic Hegelian conservatism were in fashion. The critical mirror held up to that age is an equally specifiable historical period, namely "the Revolutionary age," the radical years of the 1790's and the turn of the century. *A Literary Review* is a political book which is subtle and dialectical, and it can only be understood by preserving the tension between the "present" and "Revolutionary" ages.

At the beginning of his *Review*, SK states that just as he has been freed from military service, so also does he feel himself freed from service in defense of the younger generation of writers who owe allegiance to "the times," which is a concept that does not concern itself with "the individual" [den Enkelte]. Rather than speak for the times, SK declares, he will defend the older generation of writers and the notion of "being human," a notion that is always on guard, Socratically, against deception, especially "presumptuous self-deception" [p. 10]. Thus, here at the outset of his review of *Two Ages*, SK, in the same manner as the author of the novel herself, clearly takes the part of the former of the two ages, the older generation to which the author belongs. SK proclaims the point of view represented by the author and the older generation to be the ethical standpoint, "the universally paradigmatic" [p. 12]. The "extreme religious enthusiast" might wish to take exception to *Two Ages*, SK writes, but it is the work of an author whose realism is a sign of commitment to the ethical standpoint; the novel thus helps to develop the notion of "the individual," which is the fundamental unit for ethics and religion alike.

In categorizing writers according to the three stages developed by his pseudonyms, SK thus consigns the aesthete or poet to the realm of "the fantastic," the religious writer to "the religious," and the ethical writer to the transitional middle ground, "actuality" [Virkelighed]. While he does not commit himself to this middle, ethical standpoint in any permanent sense, in reviewing *Two Ages* SK is glad to embrace and second its author's viewpoint as a serviceable one, which, though it may not appear in the final accounting of the religious stage, can nevertheless be invaluable to the development of the individual. In welcoming the ethical realism of the author of *Two Ages*, SK shuns both the frivolous unconcern with the world of politics and actuality that characterizes the merely aesthetic stage as well as the simple contempt for the world and its politics that is characteristic of a narrow-minded and pietistic religious posture. In reviewing *Two Ages* SK contents himself, tentatively at least, with the ethical worldliness represented by that book's author and by the older generation and the "Revolutionary age" for which she stands.

"The Revolutionary Age is essentially passionate" [p. 58], and this revolutionary passion is the sort of "education" [Dannelse] [ibid.] that forms character. The present age, on the other hand, is "in the romantic and inward sense essentially passionless. This is precisely why there occasionally appears a sudden utterance of despair in a desperate action or decision, which is the lawless law of the extremes in such an existence" [p. 50]. Typical of the present age is one of the novel's characters, who lacks passionate inwardness, who is merely the sum of her external characteristics, and who does not have the concentration of character required to understand that "purity of heart is in willing one thing" [ibid.].[3]

SK then goes on to describe the proper basis for "real" politics, which the Revolutionary age has taught us.

> When individuals, each one separately, relate themselves to an idea, essentially and with passion, and thereby, in union, relate their essential selves to the same idea, then the relationship is completed and normal. The relationship differentiates individually (each has himself for himself) and unites ideally. In this essential inward directedness there is a chaste bashfulness [blufærdige Undseelse] between man and man which hinders barbarous impertinence; . . . Thus the individuals never come too close to one another in the bestial sense, precisely because they are united in ideal distance. The unity of differentiation [Udsondringens Samdrægtighed] is complete and well-instrumented music. [p. 59]

Thus passion is required, but mediate passion, which is the consequence of a prior inwardness and is governed by "the chastity of inwardness" [Inderlighedens Blufærdighed] [p. 60]. Mediate passion prevents excesses and intolerable demands upon the individual and frees one to participate in "the unity of differentiation." The present, on the other hand, has lost both true inwardness and character-forming passion and is mired in a swamp of reflection, with neither ideals nor character, in which "town gossip and rumors" [ibid.] are the substitute for genuine passion and solidarity.

The Revolutionary age was essentially passionate, but it had the self-discipline and decorum of its passion, just as poetry is both passionate and "bound speech." The present, on the other hand, is not passionate or poetic but is formlessly prosaic. This lack of form is really lack of content [p. 62]. Despite its push toward uniformity, when the Revolutionary age espoused equality, that concept was not formless but had content and passion. The Revolutionary age had not abolished the principle of contradiction and knew that it could and would choose between good and evil. (SK's critique of the middle-class liberalism and the egalitarianism which were fashionable in the 1840's here takes an unexpected turn, in that he here finds the weaknesses of the present age to be grounded in the suspension of "the principle of contradiction." Disregard for the absoluteness of this principle was of course one of the philosophical foundations of speculative idealism, and in particular Hegelianism, which, as we have seen, had found vogue in Denmark in the conservative, aristocratic work of Heiberg and his followers.)

In the modern age, however, the espousal of equality is an empty abstraction, devoid of passion and of the will to decision. The present age has forgotten that reason, by itself, will never come to a decision, to ethical action in the world, and that those who live by reason alone will always be unable to understand their lives in the present moment and will be tempted to make up for it by providing *ex post* explanations for everything. This reference to the modern penchant for explanation after the fact is another clear allusion to the pernicious influence of Hegelianism, as is the subsequent mention of the present age's preference for the glib theoretician over the courageous ethical actor: "Instead of the quiet and laconic divine child of decision, the generation gives birth to a changeling of the understanding, who knows everything on his fingertips" [p. 64].

"The present age is essentially *reasoning, reflective, passionless, fickly flaring up in enthusiasm and shrewdly resting in indolence*" [ibid.]. This is SK's indictment of philistinism and unseriousness, echoing Heiberg's *A Soul After Death*, but it finds fault not only with the unthinking liberals and pompous old-fashioned conservatives whom Heiberg lampoons but also with the shrewd, cool, reflective, and passionless type of the present age, e.g., the elegant Heiberg and his circle. In this same vein, SK further maintains that the present age delights in swimming in the shallows and prefers "light-armored Encyclopedia" which "settle accounts with all knowledge and the whole of existence *en passant*" [p. 67], instead of the hard work and seriousness of the eighteenth-century Encyclopedists. SK is here emphasizing an invidious distinction by praising the Encyclopedists of the eighteenth century, upon whose efforts the previous generation had built its revolutionary politics, while making casual and deadly reference to the flimsy and know-it-all "light-armored Encyclopedia" of the present (i.e., Hegel and his followers). Thus, far from attacking liberalism *per se*, SK is placing himself upon the same eighteenth-century, sceptical-empirical epistemological terrain on which liberalism operated, and is thereby emphasizing the chasm between his own position and the speculative idealism espoused by the aristocratic conservatism of the present.

Our age, SK continues, thinks of itself as satirical but fails to see that satire must be grounded in self-sacrificing, ethical selflessness. Our age wishes to be witty without the riches of inwardness; it wishes "to sell its trousers in order to buy a wig" [p. 70]. Great deeds are past; participants are now spectators; everything is represented rather than experienced, and money becomes representative of everything, the ultimate abstraction. In the dispassionate and reflective era of the present, "struggles" are transformed into "problems." King and citizen no longer struggle, but the citizen becomes spectator to the solution of the problem called "the relationship between king and subject" [p. 74]. The whole generation has renounced lesser but real problems in order to participate in "the Highest," a relationship of thinking about relationships. Thus it has become a representation, but it can no longer remember what it represents or for whose sake. Everything is replaced by a theoretical consideration of the problem it represents.

SK here continues his attack on the bourgeois liberal wave of the 1840's, even while tracing the origin of that liberalism to the intellectualism and abstractionism of the (conservative) speculative idealists. While the general approach SK here takes seems based upon what is perhaps a dubious interpretation,[4] the underlying view of politics that SK sets forth in *A Literary Review* transcends any such weakness and demands and deserves interpretation. *A Literary Review* is usually seen as SK's scathing critique of the liberalism of the 1840's and the mob rule which liberalism seemed to imply. This is only a partial truth. *A Literary Review* is certainly a political piece, and its principal force is indeed directed against the bourgeois liberals of SK's Copenhagen. But liberalism's individualism and the principles of constitutional and popular government that had been an important part of the European intellectual and political landscape since the French Revolution are by no means attacked. In fact, SK makes his major point precisely by drawing the unflattering comparison between the liberals of his day—whom he considered a shallow and reflexive lot—and the revolutionaries from the turn of the previous century, whom SK approvingly characterizes as profound and passionate figures who knew how to combine the integral and autonomous individual self with the group associations that political endeavor requires. In connection with this, we have already cited SK's definition of "genuine" politics (which he approvingly attributes to the Revolutionary age) as "essential inward directedness" in which all relate themselves as individuals passionately to an idea, and then, with "chaste bashfulness," to one another in the "unity of differentiation." This constitutes the healthy principle of association, the "complete and well-instrumented music."

The Revolutionary age thus engaged in politics properly, because it proceeded from the fully formed and passionately understood self to the idea which, held in common with other such individuals, formed the basis of the political activity of the group. In the modern liberalism which had become so fashionable among the younger members of Copenhagen's middle class, however, SK saw the tendency to flock together in groups as a sign of foolish self-certainty and an unexamined belief in "progress" and "the requirements of the times." Neither in the case of the revolutionary generation nor in the case of its pale and optimistic successor does SK really examine the political principle nominally espoused. In fact, the theoretical principles of the generation of the French Revolution—SK is clearly not thinking of the Robespierrean or Babeuvist radicals, but of the trend-setting liberal constitutionalists—and those espoused by the middle-class liberals of SK's time were the same: constitutional government based upon a significant (but probably not universal) franchise. To the limited degree to which SK takes a position on constitutional representative government *per se*, one cannot say that he was negatively disposed. However, it is not so much the principle of government espoused by one or another generation or group which here concerns SK but rather the way in which the

principle is appropriated. Any honestly and passionately held idea which respects the individual as an integral unit and as the starting point for all further
association would meet SK's criteria, and one can thus easily imagine quite a
range of political systems—conservative, liberal, democratic, etc.—to which SK
could assent.

Thus, rather than being seen as an attack on liberal*ism*—or as an attack
on, or an espousal of, any political idea *per se*—*A Literary Review* must be seen
as an attack on the liberals of SK's Copenhagen, who, not because of the ideas
they embraced but because of the way they embraced them, were held to be
sorely lacking in the passion and individual integration that politics, like all
ethical action, requires.

Further evidence that *A Literary Review* is an attack on ways of being
political rather than on liberalism as such can be found in the fact, noted above,
that SK also sends some very penetrating shafts in the direction of Hegelianism.
As we have seen, Hegelianism was, in Denmark, the ideology of the self-
satisfied and aristocratic form of conservatism that glorified the status quo. (The
radical and socially critical form of Hegelianism personified by Marx *et al.* does
not seem to have found its way to Denmark in SK's time.) J. L. Heiberg was
Copenhagen's leading Hegelian, conservative snob, and tastemaker, and it is
clear that SK's anti-Hegelian remarks cannot be seen as other than an attack
on him. SK was almost certainly aware that Fru Gyllembourg was the "anonymous" author under review. His review praises the revolutionary virtue of
the older generation represented by that author and finds the following generation a dismal let-down. J. L. Heiberg was, in the most literal sense, the
"younger generation" in relation to the Revolutionary age represented by his
mother.

SK's scorn for the shallow liberals who constituted the vocal majority of
middle-class political opinion is matched by his scorn for the snobbish and
conservative Hegelianism that claimed to have all the answers "on its fingertips" in advance. An attack upon the way in which his generation went about
being political, *A Literary Review* puts just as much distance between SK and
the conservative good taste of the Hegelians, represented most of all by Heiberg
and Martensen, as it does between SK and the facile (and almost equally elitist)
liberalism of Orla Lehmann and H. N. Clausen.

Let us complete our examination of SK's diagnosis and proposed cure of
"the present age" with all this in mind, remembering particularly that for SK
it is precisely in the mirror of the revolutionary age of the 1790's that the faults
of the present become most visible. This should help avoid any simplistic
interpretation of SK's theory of politics as just another Golden Age endorsement
of anti-liberalism, authoritarianism, and absolutism.

The present age erodes from within the meaning of things—Christian terminology, the power of the King, the excellence of the great—while allowing
everything to remain apparently unchanged. It does not have the revolutionary

courage of its convictions to attack openly the things which it wishes to change but imagines itself "ironic" in relation to the present—"as if the true ironist were not the hidden enthusiast in a negative time (just as the hero is the manifest enthusiast in a positive time) . . ." [p.76]. History is thus seen by SK as characterized by the alternation of positive and negative periods, with the Revolutionary age representing the former and "the present age" the latter. Furthermore, the serious individual, who has appropriated himself in passion and inwardness, is seen in a "positive age" as an "enthusiast" who manifests himself as a "hero" (e.g., the revolutionary-romantic genius) and, in a "negative age," as a "true ironist" (e.g., Socrates—or presumably, SK himself). The passion for an idea, or manifest enthusiasm [Begeistring], is the unifying principle of positive times, such as the Revolutionary age. The "envy" [Misundelse] produced by reflection is the unifying principle of the present. Reflective envy is an abstraction that finds expression in the silent, mathematical, and abstract call for levelling [Nivellering] and is related to the revolutionary cry for equality only as shadow is related to substance. Unlike the positive expression of "the principle of association," which has been stressed above, levelling is mere "mathematical equality," the "negative unity of the negative reciprocity of individuals" [p. 79].

> Reflection's envy holds one's will and power imprisoned, as it were. The individual must first break out of the prison in which his own reflection holds him, and when this has succeeded he is still not free, but is in the huge prison which is formed by the reflection of his surroundings . . . from which only religious inwardness can free him. [p. 76]

One must thus not only break the hold reflective envy has upon one's soul, but one must also break out of the prison created by the reigning society which is one's surroundings. And this liberation is only possible with "religious inwardness," the first mention SK gives of a possible cure for his age. The religious inwardness of individuation thus becomes an essential moment in making politics possible. Politics requires free and passionate individuals, who have "acquired themselves" in religious inwardness. Politics and religion have, therefore, much to do with one another.

"Genuine" politics has to do with associations of people who have been through the individuating process of religious inwardness, and such politics will not transgress upon the religious sphere, because it will safeguard the integrity of the individual, which is its most basic unit, its presupposition, its starting and finishing point. In attempting to paralyze the individual and imprison his will in reflective envy, "modern" politics has usurped religion's place. This is why "the inwardness of religion" is needed to make one free, so that religion can once again stand in the proper relation of priority to politics. Thus, "genuine" politics can again become possible.

"The separation of the religious individual before God in the responsibility of eternity is being ignored" by the present age because one is not seen first as an individual but primarily as a member of an abstraction [p. 80]. The resultant levelling is not the deed of any individual but of an abstract power [p. 81] and cannot be stopped once unleashed, even if the present time wished it: "[I]t can only be stopped if the individual, in individual differentiation, wins the fearlessness of the religious" [ibid.]. Or again, this levelling comes upon us like a judgement when "the inwardness of the individual in his differentiation in religion is lacking" [p. 82]. It is a sort of "spontaneous combustion of the human race" that marches forward in the name of "sheer humanity" [den rene Menneskehed, ibid.]. This abstract levelling cannot be stopped by a group because it is precisely groups that are now in the service of reflection and levelling. Nor can it be stopped by an individual because, as we have seen, "the age of heroes is past" [ibid.].

Still, the firestorm of the present age may, in a way, burn itself out. In its very all-consuming terribleness it may serve as an *"examen rigorosum"* to help individuals "win the essentiality of the religious in themselves" [ibid.]. "[F]or the individual, each one separately, [levelling] can become the point of departure to the highest life, if one wills it in honesty before God—for that person it will be truly educating [dannende] to live in the time of levelling" [ibid.]. Thus, for such a person the trials of the present time will be a true form of *the education which forms character* [Dannelse], just as the passion and inwardness of the Revolutionary age was a form of genuine *Dannelse* in that time [p. 58]; both sorts of Dannelse stand in sharp contrast to the pseudo-cultured Dannelse which characterizes most of the conservatives and liberals of "the present age." Such a truly educated person will understand the comic, and with the penetration of comic insight will evaporate all the abstractions, organizations, and other "middle terms" under which "humanity" parades; such a person will understand the real "sheer humanity" and will lead that notion home to its proper dwelling place in "the essentiality of the religious in the single individual" [p. 82]. The comic insight that religion gives in matters of politics and society is a sceptical nominalism that dissolves the pomposities and abstractions of the present time.

In this way, the very lostness of the present age opens the way to its refinding itself; its forlorn touting of "sheer humanity" may in fact lead individuals to discover humanity, not in the ridiculous abstractions of the present age but in the individuality that is grounded in the God-relation. The individual who learns to find himself in the hard climate of levelling will not be the outstanding individual or hero: "No, he will be merely an essential human being in the completely egalitarian sense. This is the idea of the religious" [p. 83]. Here we have the roots of SK's "populism" or egalitarianism: Only religion can redeem the genuine meaning of the battle words of the day, "equality," "sheer humanity," etc.

In antiquity, individuality was celebrated "in its immediate and beautiful form," and the individual served as the representative figure around whom the generation grouped itself. Abstract reflection, or levelling, which at present seems to threaten individuality so much, is actually just as powerless against genuine religious individualism in its eternally true and essential form as it is capable of sweeping away all intermediate forms of organization and understanding. Thus, the modern period will actually burn away all that is temporary or based upon appearance, and

> thereby develop the individual, with his own cooperation, religiously, into an essential human being. . . . Reflection is a sling, in which one is caught, but with the enthusiastic leap of the religious the situation changes; then the sling becomes that which catapults one into the embrace of the Eternal. [ibid.]

SK asserts that the eternal truth—the individual in his relation to God—and nothing temporary or intermediate can stop or survive the present levelling process (which thus seems a sort of theodicy or liberating necessity). SK appears to say that any political or social formations built upon the naive appearance-world of past positive ages will be burned away by the critical negativity of the present. Therefore, new social and political forms can be built only upon the basis of a quite conscious respect for the integrity of the individual in relation to God.

The meaning of SK's interpretation of the "two ages" seems to be that, despite the utility of the positiveness of the Revolutionary age in criticizing the present, we can no more return to it than we can return to any other positive age of the past. The trials of the present make possible the conscious development of the essentially religious core of the individual, and the acid quality of reflection in the present age makes this sort of individuality the only possible future for "real politics." Naiveté is past. The future holds either monstrosities—deifications of the state, social class, etc.—which make infinite claims about the finite and attempt to bar transcendence, or a sober and modest politics, which is fully conscious of its presuppositions and limitations in the individual personality. In the well-known words of a Kierkegaardian pseudonym, the proper situation for the individual would be one in which the individual relates absolutely only to that which is absolute and relatively to that which is relative.

The levelling process of the present age requires a phantom, a monstrous abstraction, "the Public," which is at once everything and nothing, more numerous than all the people taken together, yet without a single representative. It lives through the press. It has no court of responsibility; it can act in opposite, contradictory ways and remain the same. The public does not know the value of silence and inwardness but must chatter, and in its chatter it denies the distinction between public and private, prying where it ought not, trying to appropriate all to itself; in its chatter the public betrays its lack of real education [Udannethed] [pp. 86–91]. Still, it is exactly this omnipresence and facelessness which denies the individual, that refers the individual back to himself [p. 85]. "[T]he public is also the terrible abstraction by which individuals must be religiously educated—or perish" [p. 87].

> But it is precisely by means of this abstraction and this abstract discipline that the individual—if he does not perish—is educated [dannes] (to the extent that he has not been educated already by his own inwardness) to be satisfied, in the highest religious sense, with himself and his God-relation; to put unity with himself in place of unity with the public, which consumes all the relative concretions of individuality; to find rest in himself and in God instead of counting and counting. And this will be modernity's absolute difference from antiquity: that the whole is not the concretion which supports and educates the individual [as, for example, in Greece] (without, however, developing him absolutely [i.e., as an indissoluble individual before God]), but is an abstraction, which in its abstract quality, repels him and helps him to be educated in the absolute sense [i.e., as an individual in relation to God]—if he does not perish. The hopelessness of antiquity was that the great were what the others *could not* be; the exciting thing [in the present age] will be that he who wins himself religiously will be only what *everyone can* be. [p. 86]

This is SK's most concise statement of the saving and educating, or refining, value of the badness of the present age, which will help to realize a new era in which all have the opportunity for greatness. In antiquity the possibility of greatness was an option reserved for the outstanding few. The greatness which now comes within reach of all is an "absolute," a greater form of greatness than that which had been available to the few; it is the absolute integrity of the individual personality before God.

SK's critique, which finds a sort of saving chastisement in the present age, is a polemic against the liberalism and democratic currents which characterized much of the political climate of the 1840's, but there is also a deeper polemic against the cultured elitism of the "rare few" for whom real excellence, Dannelse, was supposedly reserved. This elitism, as we have seen, was characteristic of conservative and liberal alike in Golden Age Copenhagen, and SK seems here to be throwing down the gauntlet to all "educated" political and cultural opinion, by espousing a sort of divine egalitarianism in which existing notions of Dannelse are worthless and in which only the simple integrity of the individual before God—which is available to everyone—has any worth.

Furthermore, SK's "populist" individualism also seems indebted to the middle-class liberalism whose present excrescences he rejects. SK's inextinguishable faith in the absolute validity of every individual parallels the political individualism of the Enlightenment. His notion of the freedom of every individual to achieve the absolute in the relation to God or to "perish," reflects the same notion of the self, with its responsibility and self-reliance, that can be seen everywhere in the liberalism of the middle classes but nowhere more clearly than in the doctrines of meritocracy and economic laissez-faire. SK did not consider himself a liberal—and indeed *A Literary Review* seems to expend even more energy attacking liberals than conservatives—but it is very instructive to see the degree to which he is dependent upon liberal and Enlightenment notions and the degree to which he borrows words from the liberal and democratic vocabulary of his day (e.g., "equality") and transforms their content. SK is a "populist" in his view of culture and Dannelse, a pragmatic "agnostic" in his view of political arrangements, and a "liberal" with respect to his sink-or-swim individualistic notion of salvation.

Politics will not be excluded forever but will become possible only after the present age has managed to turn its back on "the principle of association" and has won itself in the privacy of individuality.

> In our time, the principle of association (which at most is valid with respect to material interests) is not affirmative, but negative—an escape, a diversion, a sensory deception, whose dialectic consists in ennervating individuals as it strengthens them numerically and in solidarity; but it is, ethically understood, a weakening. Only when the individual has won an ethical posture in himself despite the whole world, only then can there be talk of truly uniting in groups. . . . [p. 99]

We return to the fact that in "the present age" (unlike the "positive" age of the Revolution) the idea of association is an avoidance of the necessity of individual development, and it is this individual development that will form the only possible basis for a future and positive development of association and politics [see similar remarks p. 59]. We have passed from a positive, but naive, age in which political association was gainful to a negative, reflective age in which the principle of association must be avoided—rife and tempting though it is—in order to develop the individual and prepare for a new positive age in which we will once again be able to have politics "in truth" [i Sandhed]. (In rejecting, for the present, the principle of association, SK groups it interchangeably with "the idea of sociality, of the congregation [Menighed]" [p. 99]. This casual use of "congregation" in this connection seems a clear and negative reference to Grundtvig, for whom the congregation, rather than the individual, was the nexus of God with humanity and the focal point of all real life.)

Although he holds out the hope of a new, modest, chastened politics, SK stresses that what is needed now is not any form of association but individuals who understand that they are to remain unrecognizable and without "authority"—because recognized authority is for prophets and judges who have received special, private instructions from God. No, we need individuals who have "understood the universal in equality before God" [p. 100], and who understand that the task is to make it clear that "individuals must help themselves, each one by himself" [ibid.]. Such an individual understands that, unlike the chosen individuals of "an older formation" (presumably the visible heroes of the positive, Revolutionary age), it is his task not to show himself, not to claim authority, even if those he is trying to help should beg him for it [pp. 101–102].[5]

> . . . [I]t must not be as in the past, when individuals, as soon as things began to become dizzying to them, could look to the nearest great man in order to orient themselves. This is past; they must either become lost in the dizziness of abstract infinity, or be saved infinitely in the essentiality of the religious. . . . This development is, however, progress, because all the individuals who are saved win the specific gravity of the religious, win its essentiality first-hand from God. Then the word will be: "See, everything is ready; see the terribleness of abstraction which makes finitude reveal itself, disappointingly, as itself; see the chasm of the infinite open up; see the sharp scythe of levelling forcing everyone to jump over the blade—see, the God waits! So leap, then, into the embrace of divinity!" [pp. 100–101]

Only after this "leap" into the individual God-relationship will politics ("truly uniting in groups") become possible, and this requires that we have passed out of our naiveté and into and through reflection and shrewdness [Klogskab] to emerge in new simplicity. There is nothing wrong with reflection *per se*: "Reflection is not itself or in itself corrupting . . . on the contrary, working one's way through it is the condition for being able to act more intensively . . ." [p. 103]. Shrewdness is something we must learn to deal with and become familiar with, so that it no longer has any power of attraction over us and we can ultimately put it aside. Then politics, or unions of simple, integral individuals, would become possible. But

> the question is whether it [the "new simplicity" of individualism in the God-relation] can ever become so popular—i.e., whether shrewdness will ever become so presupposed among the average of humanity that it will lose its seductive witchery in their eyes, so that people thus not only have power over shrewdness, but can squander it, as it were, in the highest enthusiasm. . . . [ibid.]

Thus, it is only after we have worked our way through the apparent power that reflective shrewdness confers that we can really be free to renounce it. However, it is an unanswered question whether most people will ever be able to make such a renunciation of shrewdness, whether they will ever acquire the inner wealth which would allow them to squander their resources imprudently, to "let go." Although SK provides a definition of "real" politics, the question of whether we are actually likely to make such a new world in which real politics could be carried on remains unanswered. At any rate, "the present age" is a sort of holocaust from which only those who have won themselves in religious struggle will emerge, and there is in this a hopeful element of theodicy: To learn our limits is a way to greater self-knowledge; it is salvation's way.

This is the first work of SK's that we will examine in detail, and it is especially useful for pointing out the reciprocal interpenetration in which SK's religious notions were influenced by the social history and political vocabulary of the middle class of which he was a part—and in which his political notions were saturated by the religious interpretation he placed upon key political terms. Very much a hybrid and his own person, SK, in his most political work, *A Literary Review*, cannot be called a liberal, a democrat, or a conservative in the usual senses of the terms, although it can be seen how dependent upon liberalism in its origins and how egalitarian and anti-elitist in its expression his "conservatism" was. "Radical," in the deepest, original, sense seems to fit him best. *A Literary Review* stands as a programmatic statement of SK's politics at the beginning of his later, preponderantly non-pseudonymous, authorship, and it is an ideal point of departure for viewing the development of his conception of politics and social responsibility in the years which followed.

18. *Edifying Discourses in Various Spirits*

○

A. INTRODUCTION

Kierkegaard's next work was the *Edifying Discourses in Various Spirits* [*Op-byggelige Taler i forskjellige Aand*] [SV VIII, pp. 107–416], written between May and November 1846 and published in March 1847. The three sections of this rather voluminous work can easily be read separately. (In fact, the largest of the three sections has been published—in English translation—as an independent volume, *Purity of Heart is to Will One Thing*.) But there is much to be gained from reading the work in its entirety. It will be seen that the three sections constitute a single whole, which concentrates on the problem of ethics, first within the categories of human reason and natural religion, or "Religiousness A" (to use the term employed by Johannes Climacus in the *Concluding Unscientific Postscript*). Thereafter the focus shifts to the threshold of a religious ethics which is not based on universal categories and is not accessible to the natural man but is a specifically revealed, Christian ethics. The *Edifying Discourses in Various Spirits* form the preface or presupposition to SK's Christian ethics, which in turn await full development in SK's next work, *Works of Love*.

Examination of the book in its historical context makes it clear that the unity of the *Edifying Discourses in Various Spirits* is not only to be found in the work's preoccupation with ethics but also and especially in the fact that the book is a coordinated attack on the leading political and clerical tendencies of Golden Age Denmark. The structure, content, and emphases of the arguments that are made in many of the book's discourses, especially the key discourses, have been shaped by SK as critiques of: (1) the growing political liberalism of the Danish middle classes; (2) the smug, culture-conscious conservatism of the upper bourgeoisie, Romanticism's second generation; (3) the (to SK) superficial and polished "profundity" and worldly opportunism of Bishop J. P. Mynster and the intellectualized Christianity of H. L. Martensen—who together were the principal spiritual advisors of the cultured bourgeoisie; and finally, (4) the (to SK) shallow, optimistic Christianity of N. F. S. Grundtvig, who expressed the fervent hopes and ambitions of the rising peasant class.

Historical investigation also makes it plain that SK was deeply engaged in the particulars of the political and church-political climate not only in his criticism but also in his positive solution. SK consciously borrowed from the current political language, especially that of liberalism, in putting forth a position in which both individualism and egalitarianism are developed so radically that liberalism, as the classic ideology of individualism, must take umbrage. On the other hand, the snobbish and refined conservatism of the Heiberg circle, with its good taste and self-restraint, could hardly fail to take offense either.

B. "PURITY OF HEART IS TO WILL ONE THING"

"Purity of Heart" [Hjertets Reenhed], as this major discourse has come to be known, is technically entitled "An Occasional Discourse" [En Leiligheds-Tale] and is the first and principal of the three sections that make up the *Edifying Discourses in Various Spirits*. It was completed by SK in May 1846, during which time (from May 4th to May 14th) he was in Berlin for his third stay, having gone there in part to escape the insults of the *Corsair*, which greatly upset him during the winter and spring of 1846. It was the first piece that he finished after publication of *A Literary Review*, on March 30, 1846. The monumental *Concluding Unscientific Postscript*, completed the previous fall, had also recently been published (February 27, 1846). As has been mentioned, along with the rest of the *Edifying Discourses in Various Spirits*, "Purity of Heart" would not be published until 1847, the year which also saw publication of SK's next, and closely related book, *Works of Love*.

"Purity of Heart," which is surely one of SK's most beautifully written and compactly argued pieces, is written on the occasion of confession. It begins with an Opening Prayer, which is repeated, verbatim, at the end of the work. At the beginning of the work, when it is read for the first time, the prayer is not entirely comprehensible to the reader. God is asked to help the reader's understanding, heart, and will to comprehend, receive, and will "one thing," but what this one thing is, or why it should be just one thing, is not immediately clear. It is only by reading the work through to the end, where the prayer is repeated, that the prayer can make sense to the reader. Thus we, too, will delay consideration of this important part of the work until the end. But in addition to introducing the as yet unexplained notion of "willing one thing," we must note another point in the Opening Prayer. SK talks of the chasm of sinfulness which intervenes in life, separating the willing of the young person from that of the old, as a "pause" [Standsning] and an "interruption" [Afbrydelse], and he uses exactly the same words (pause, interruption) to describe the act of repentance which is involved in confession [pp. 119–20]. Thus we are told in advance that the discourse has to do with pauses, interruptions, in fact with an interruption (repentance) within an interruption (sinfulness), thus, in what SK would call the eternal sense, a continuation in the midst of worldly "busyness" [Travlhed]. We shall return to this point later.

The discourse begins by quoting Solomon's observation that there are times and seasons for all things. SK uses this as the occasion for setting forth, by implication, an anthropology in capsule form. For humans as changeable beings, as nature, yes, there is indeed a time and a season appropriate for every activity, but we are composite beings who partake of eternity as well as of time [pp.120–22]. For a person as related to the eternal, it is always the season, always the right time. Repentance is such a relation to the eternal, and it is always the appropriate time, always "the eleventh hour," for repentance because eternity is always present [pp. 124–27]. The other principle SK puts forth in the introductory pages is "unity with oneself" [Enighed med sig selv] [p. 130], which is the key to confession, for one confesses not to apprise God of any new facts—God knows all—but to learn about oneself, change oneself, and eliminate self-deception, which is a form of being *dis*united with oneself, or as SK calls it, "doublemindedness" [Tvesindethed] [pp. 133–34].

It is these two considerations—the perennial appropriateness of repentance as something relating to the eternal and the question of the unity (as opposed to the disunity) of self necessary to such repentance—that have led SK to base his confessional discourse on the text of James 4:8: "Purify your hearts, ye double-minded!"

From here on the discourse assumes a very firm and systematic form. First, "purity of heart" is derived negatively from *"double*-mindedness" and is defined as willing one thing. Then double-mindedness, which prevents one from willing one thing "in truth," is dealt with in four variant forms, in increasing order of subtlety and difficulty of extirpation. Next, willing one thing, viewed as the product of a unitary, whole person, is dealt with under two categories: the "active" person who wills to do all for the Good, and the "suffering" person who wills to suffer all for the Good. Finally, SK returns to the confessional occasion of the discourse in order to make the message personally edifying and to charge the reader with the responsibility of living as an individual[1] before God. The Closing Prayer, the same as the Opening, repeats the same plea for help in willing one thing and the same language about pauses and interruptions, but this time it is comprehensible to the reader.

Double-mindedness is the evil alternative to willing *one* thing. Only the Good admits of being willed exclusively, as one thing; all else has ulterior motivations, cross purposes, is grounded in falsity, material or self-interest, fear, etc. All worldly, temporal reality is subject to vicissitude, change, even reversal. Only the Good is in its essence one and unchangeable, and only that which is in essence one—the Good—can be willed as one thing [pp. 135–38]. Evil is essentially riven and split, as are evil people. Thus, everyone who wishes to follow James' call to purify his heart and put away double-mindedness must will one thing, must will the Good [pp. 142–43].

In order truly to will one thing, SK continues, one must will one thing "in truth," which means renouncing all forms of double-mindedness. Double-mindedness is divided into four categories—the first three "strong" and relatively uncommon, the latter "weak" and very common.

The first form of double-mindedness is doing the Good in hope of reward. No ulterior motive could be more obvious. The Good must be willed in itself, and as for rewards, nothing is more certain than that "eternally" the Good is a reward in itself, while temporally it is likely that the reward will be poverty, the mockery of the world, etc. [pp. 144–47]. (Since SK's entire argument in "Purity of Heart" seems deliberately to circle around the Kantian notion of the Good Will, the "eternal" should be construed both in the philosophical sense of the timeless ethical realm and in the traditional religious sense of "the kingdom of heaven," which is both that which is to come and that which is already eschatologically present at hand to the eternal dimension of our compound anthropology.)

Fear of punishment is the second form of double-mindedness which must be renounced. It is obviously wrong to fear the punishment of the world, SK writes, as this is unworthy of being feared. We ourselves often proclaim the falsity and vanity of the world's judgments, but we are usually untrue to that observation at other moments and fall prey to the prestige and blandishments of the world. If, on the other hand, we fear the punishments of God, and will the Good out of such fear, this is also an error, because, far from being feared, the chastisement of God should be welcomed as something which guides us to the Good, helps us to be free. In any event, God's discipline cannot *force* us to will the Good because the essence of willing the Good is freedom [pp. 151–57].

The third form of willing the Good double-mindedly is willing the Good out of "self-centered willfulness" [Selv-Raadighed], out of a desire to see the triumph of the Good, to participate in it, to feel oneself as necessary to it. Such a person does not see the Good and its triumph as one thing, but as two separate things. He has neither the patience to see the Good slowed and humbled in time, nor the humility to see that the Good can do without him, to see that it is he who needs the Good and not vice versa [pp. 164–66].

The fourth and final form of double-mindedness in willing the Good is willing the Good "to a certain degree" [til en vis Grad]. As the most prevalent form of error—and as we shall see, the form most appropriate to the age—SK gives this "weak" form the most careful attention, as will we, for an understanding of it is vital to understanding the discourse "Purity of Heart" as a historical product, which cast its general message in the particular form suited to its time.

In his discussion of willing the Good to a certain degree, SK stresses the "busyness" which is characteristic of the world. The world cannot bear to be stopped or interrupted, and the whole purpose of repentance and of this discourse is to encourage the individual to pause, to interrupt the world's busyness. Eternity is not busy; it can be exacting, and it cares to look and see if the Good is being willed entirely or only "to a certain degree." In busyness there is neither time nor peace to win the "transparency" [Gjennemsigtighed, an important concept in this work, as also in *Works of Love* and *The Sickness Unto Death*] which is necessary to self-understanding in willing one thing. We need the simplicity of "clarity," SK writes, but the world's busyness surrounds us instead with a maze of "excuses" [pp. 168–70].

After thus setting up the busyness of the world and its excuses as the temptations that continually try to disturb the clarity and transparency necessary to will the Good entirely, SK goes on to examine us as feeling, knowing, and willing beings in order to pinpoint exactly how one comes to will the Good "to a certain degree."

Immediate feeling is a barrier to our understanding of others and their suffering; it is self-involved, double-minded, and divisive; it cannot understand others. In order to reach others one must go beyond immediacy of feeling, because "only in the well-understood equality of honesty can there be unity" [kun i Oprigtighedens vel forstaaede Ligelighed kan der være Eenhed] [p. 173]. The error in immediate feeling is thus a failure to abstract oneself from the immediate and accidental into the "well-understood equality of honesty," which seems to mean the realm of the ethical universal in which one is freed from the selfish partiality of immediacy and can will the Good wholly.

Our failure, as knowing beings, to will the Good entirely seems more important to SK and is in fact one of the most important points in the discourse. As a knowing being, one is tempted to make "observations" [Betragtninger] [pp. 173–77] about the Good which, while in themselves true, are shallow, ineffectual, and ultimately pernicious, since they do not lead one to expect the difficulties and resistance that the Good will meet in empirical reality, in time. The danger of such observations is that the truth they contain lends itself to enjoyment in the quiet, devotional "moments" [Øieblikke] in which one is able to imbibe them and hold them seriously before one's attention.

SK calls such moments or quiet hours "falsified eternity" [den forfalskede Evighed] [p. 174], which is always rudely broken off by the harsh facts of time, and the danger is that one who cultivates "observations" will spend his life shuttling back and forth between the enticing quietness of such moments of falsified eternity and the rude bustle of the world, unable to renounce either. For good measure, the "observational" method promises the likelihood, at least, of earthly recognition for willing the Good. So the observational way contains a double danger. First, although it correctly praises the superiority of the Good, it does so on the basis of insufficient experience of temporal reality, leading one by a shortcut into a falsified eternity that is bound to be disappointing. Second, it also holds out the likelihood of worldly reward and recognition for those who will the Good. The "observing" individual is thus trapped into a very dangerous double-mindedness, clinging both to the piquancy of quiet moments of falsified eternity and to the hope of worldly reward. He can only

will the Good "to a certain degree." The truths enshrined in such an observational method are, SK noted, true enough in themselves, but in order to
apprehend them correctly and eliminate the danger of double-mindedness, they
must be appropriated slowly and in full knowledge of the resistance of the
world. Only thus can the Good be willed entirely [pp. 174–75].

This section clearly foreshadows SK's increasing preoccupation with asceticism and with the notion that persecution and martyrdom are the likely,
or even the necessary, lot of the individual who holds up to the world the
claims of the Good, of Eternity. More importantly, however, this section constitutes a clear and very devastating attack on the religion of Bishop Mynster,
with whom SK was still, officially, on very good terms. As we have seen,
Mynster's most important and most widely read book was entitled *Observations
Upon the Doctrines of the Christian Faith* [*Betragtninger over de christelige
Troeslærdomme*], often referred to, simply, as *Observations* [*Betragtninger*]. To
what could the observational style of expressing the truth in the form of savory
moments of falsified eternity refer other than to Mynster's highly personalizing,
idealizing Christianity of the *Observations* and his fashionable Sunday morning
devotions to which cultured Christendom flocked? The merely personal side
of the relationship of SK to Mynster is not of interest here and will not be
pursued. However, for understanding the view of the individual and society
that underlies "Purity of Heart" and the whole latter half of SK's authorship,
and for understanding the historical realities which conditioned and shaped
this view, it is of great importance to see that this scarcely veiled public rejection
of Mynster was no mere personal rejection of the Bishop—whatever the psychological forces and biographical details may have been. Rather, it is a sign
of SK's break with the reigning view of life—of humanity, God, religion, the
world, eternity—shared by the cultured bourgeoisie ("den bedre Portion," the
better portion, as it was called) of Golden Age Copenhagen.

This "observational" religion, which wills the Good "to a certain degree,"
was not disappointed in its hope that it might in addition achieve recognition
and worldly reward. As has been noted in Part One of the present work, this
was the case not merely for the ambitious, be-ribboned Mynster but also for
his closest circle and many of his followers. SK had already made some dis-
paraging remarks about "observations" in *A Literary Review*, but they are not
so clear and stinging as the criticisms in "Purity of Heart," and only with the
help of hindsight can those remarks be connected with the specifically Mynsterian element of the Danish bourgeois world-view. In the much more strident
Training in Christianity, SK carries this attack on "observations" much further,
but *Training* was published, with much trepidation, three eventful years after
"Purity of Heart" and preceded a four-year period during which SK published
very little while he waited for an opportunity to settle accounts with "Christendom." Thus quite aside from its other merits, the attack on the religion and
world view of Mynster and the cultured bourgeoisie which "Purity of Heart"

contains makes the piece a landmark in the development of SK's critical view of his society.

The third and final way in which we are characterized as willing the Good "to a certain degree" is as willing beings who keep looking for ways to motivate our will into willing the Good. One searches for reasons, rules, sound advice, etc. on the basis of which one can will the Good, not realizing that it is the will itself which motivates all else, that it is the elementary component. Repeating Kant, we could say that there is nothing absolutely Good besides a good will. A will which seeks a motive for willing the Good has completely misunderstood the nature of the problem; it is, as SK says, "immature" [umoden].

In short, one falls into the "weak" form of double-mindedness—willing the Good "to a certain degree"—by being partially right, by being clouded by the busyness of the world so that one lacks the clarity or "transparency" necessary to will the Good "in truth" as one thing. Such a person's faculties are characterized not by resoluteness, defiance, passion, or any obvious evil, but by a certain confusion: His feeling is selfish and immediate; his knowledge is mere "observations," glimpses of "false eternity"; his will seeks motivation and is immature [p. 177]. Such a person, SK writes, is easy prey for double-mindedness, because he has not realized that it is only in eternity that the Good is sure to triumph. In time, willing the Good is likely to meet with every kind of resistance and difficulty, and we had best strengthen ourselves by becoming aware of this.

The first three forms of double-mindedness—willing the Good with hope of reward, with fear of punishment, or with self-centered willfulness—are, as has been mentioned above, the "strong" forms, which means that they involve great passions of defiance, fear, pride, etc., and as such they are rarities. The fourth and final form of double-mindedness—willing the Good to a certain degree—is the "weak" form which stems from prosaic confusion and is an everyday occurrence. The strong forms might be called the conscious forms, as they are principally characterized by attempts at deception, whereas the weak form is unconscious, principally characterized by self-deception.

I believe it is permissible and illuminating in connection with this dichotomy between the strong-passionate and the weak-prosaic forms of double-mindedness to bear in mind the view of recent history which SK had just set forth in his latest work, *A Literary Review*. In that work the revolutionary-passionate era of a few decades past is juxtaposed with the bourgeois-prosaic era of the present, which appears muddled and cowardly by comparison. It seems clear that the social and historical analogue to the "strong" forms of double-mindedness is the passionate, defiant revolutionary-romantic hero, whereas the "weak" form corresponds to the modern "Christian gentleman" of Golden Age culture. Furthermore, if SK's reasoning is followed through to its logical conclusion, it is clear that the usual dialectical irony prevails: Despite the fact that his defiance makes him a more lost character than the well-bred and well-intentioned bourgeois gentleman, the passionate hero is actually closer to reform and conversion. Reform and conversion are closer for the strong-minded person because he is consciously deceptive and can see the flagrancy of his errors and repent of them more easily than the unconscious, self-deceptive, cultured salon-Christian can break out of his round of quiet hours and "observations," which, precisely because they contain a germ of truth, have an innoculating or anesthetizing effect, and never lead to a decisive step, to repentance, to willing the Good "in truth." Though seriously in error, the revolutionary-romantic of yesteryear is not as pathetically entrapped in perdition as today's bourgeois philistine admirer of Mynster's Christianity. (This split between "weak" and "strong" forms of error will be seen again in *The Sickness Unto Death*, where unconsciousness or "spiritlessness" is seen as the form of despair distressingly characteristic of modern "Christendom," while the more conscious and defiant forms are both rarer and, paradoxically, nearer to salvation.)

Having dealt with the varieties of error—namely the forms of double-mindedness that prevent one from truly willing the Good—the discourse goes on to investigate the two forms of truth: "doing" all for the Good and "suffering" all for the Good. Doing all is the active, ethical form, whereas suffering all is the quiet, and in a temporal sense, "useless" form. Yet both forms are ways in which one does one's all for the Good. Every all—like the widow's mite—is all; thus those who do all and those who suffer all for the Good are absolutely equal, SK stresses [pp. 178–79]. Furthermore, it is not with anything tangible or visible, not with the success of doing or suffering all, that we are concerned but with an inner, eternal reality, namely "to will to be and to remain with the Good in *decision* [Afgørelsen]" [p. 180, emphasis added]. Both the active and the suffering individuals are equally capable of remaining with the Good in decision, so here again is an assertion of the equality of all those who will the Good and an argument against invidious distinctions.

Both those who would do all and those who would suffer all for the Good are tempted to use shrewdness [Klogskab] to escape the decision of being in and remaining with the Good [p. 182]. For the person who would do all, shrewdness tempts one internally to forsake decision by proposing evasions and externally by proposing deceptions that will increase the world's meager pay for the Good by surrounding one with admirers of the Good who will give one honor. But what does this mean, this desire for worldly honor, this desire, in doing the Good, "to do something in the world" [pp. 182–88]? Here SK goes on to supplement the concise anthropology given at the beginning of the discourse with a brief, clear account of the relation between the eternal and the temporal. We must distinguish between "doing something" in the temporal and the eternal senses because time is not merely a transparent medium of the eternal, such that that which is Good in the temporal is a direct image of that which is Good in eternity. No, the temporal is always a *refraction* [Brydning][2] of the eternal, such that the more of the Eternal the individual has in him, the greater the refraction (or struggle). The supreme example is that of Jesus Christ, who was, in the eternal sense, the embodiment of the Good, yet was crucified in time. The temporal and the eternal views of "doing something" are in fact opposite [pp. 188–90].

If the relation of time to eternity is one of refraction and opposition, how is it possible for one to be ethically integrated in one's time, a good Lutheran and a responsible citizen? Indeed, SK's theory of refraction and opposition here leads sharply away from the Lutheran doctrine of the calling and in the direction of the notions of asceticism and martyrdom advanced later in his authorship. (We shall deal increasingly with the tension between "the citizen" and "the saint" in SK's view of the relation of the individual to the world. Here, apparently in order to avoid being trapped in this corner at this time, SK—inconsistently, in my view—raises the possibility of a rare and chance coincidence of the eternal and temporal views of the Good.)

One who would do all for the Good uses shrewdness internally to avoid evasions and to persist in the decision for the Good. Success in the worldly sense may or may not come [pp. 191–93]. (Here SK seems back in a Lutheran, dialectical relation to the world rather than a simple undialectical relation of opposition between eternity and time.) Externally, such a person uses shrewdness by refusing to play up to the crowd [Mængden] or to respect it. Instead, such a person uses shrewdness to break it up into individuals, who, as separate units, are incapable of the same bestialities they would commit in the secure anonymity of the mass. But one ought not seek the support of the crowd even in order to break it up. How one ought to act in this regard will vary according to the needs of the times: John the Baptist went to the desert and the people came to him; Socrates used a joke in order to keep his generation from taking the seriousness of the Good in vain. These men did not judge their age, but their age, in judging them, judged itself [pp. 193–95].

> He always has the task, not with words, nor with intent, but with the introspection of honesty, to use his life to expose a hostile environment to the maximum degree—not that he thus judges with words, but that his life serves the Good unconditionally in action. The task is his own obligation in the service of the Good; the judgment is not his own action, not his doing, but a consequence of the way in which the surrounding world relates itself to him. [p. 195]

Thus one is a mirror to one's times; one judges incidentally, as a by-product of one's integrity, of "the introspection of honesty."

Just as the active person does all so that the Good might triumph in the world, so does the suffering person suffer all that the Good might triumph in himself [p. 197]. The nature of action—of doing the Good—was such that the principal temptation of shrewdness was in the external direction of deception, crowd-pleasing, worldly approbation. The nature of suffering, on the other hand, leaves it open only to the internal sort of shrewdness, i.e., the evasion of the steadfastness required to remain in the decision for the Good. Concretely, such evasion takes the form of refusing to accept the finality of one's suffering, of clinging to a false earthly hope of succor, instead of accepting the inevitability of suffering and opening oneself to the eternal. Instead, one ought to use shrewdness to uncover evasions, in order to push oneself to the decision for the Good. One must not try to forget one's suffering and let go of the eternal. However separated one feels from one's fellow beings, one is never separated from the eternal; however trapped one feels, one is always free to be with the Good in decision; however useless one's sufferings seem, they have helped one to that which is "the highest" [pp. 197–200]. Those who are busy [travl] imagine that they have avoided suffering, but they have merely slipped into meaninglessness. Though one feels abandoned by the whole human race, there is human fellowship to be had in the work of edification, which, though it is humanity's common project, must be done by each person individually. One is never alone, but always in the presence of God [pp. 201–203].

SK spends a good deal of time developing the category of the hopeless sufferer, the born sufferer, who almost makes a mockery of the notion of Providence. SK wishes to develop the sufferer as an ideal type, the type to whom the least has been given but who is equally capable of attaining "the highest." "By observing suffering one learns most reliably what is the highest" [p. 214]. Not only is such a luckless person, as we shall see, the best illustration of humanity's essential equality in relation to the Good but also the best indictment of our "busy" times. Posit such a person, SK writes, as unlucky as possible; our age would like to get him out of the way, out of sight, even out of the Church, so *busy* is our age. Yet, "the Bible almost always seems to prefer the blind, the lame, and the leprous"; and Christ, when his disciples were becoming too busy, put a child in their midst to recall them to essential things [p. 206]. Our age needs a sufferer, SK concludes, in order to cure it of its busyness as the child did for the disciples [ibid.]. Thus the sufferer, in much the same way as the active person, is an incidental mirror to his or her age.

Though the sufferer is cut off from social reciprocity, or society's "measure for measure" [Lige for Lige] [ibid.], though he can do nothing for others and is the object of sympathy and compassion, often a burden to others, yet he participates in a *"blessed equality"* [salige Ligelighed] [p. 207], in that the sufferer, like everyone, can do his all for the highest.

Just as the active person who does all for the Good must first have been inwardly conquered by the Good, so, too, the sufferer who suffers all for the Good can serve outwardly as a sort of example, encouragement, or challenge to others, showing how much has been accomplished with so little. Even those who suffer in total isolation partake of humanity's common concern [p. 211]. All good people, SK writes, hope for a resurrection [Opstandelse] after death, when all inequality will be removed, but there is also a sort of resurrection of equality in this life, in which every person, even sufferers, can "stand up" [staa op] for the Good [p. 207]. All are equally capable of equal victory. "O, praised be the Eternal's blessed equality" [p. 212]. SK clearly sets up a dichotomy between ordinary worldly "social reciprocity" or "measure for measure" and the "blessed equality," which is available to all in their relation to the Good. While SK's equality has to do with the eternal, this does not mean that it is principally concerned with the afterlife. (SK devotes little or no attention to the eternal in the sense of an afterlife.) Rather, because the eternal is everywhere present in this life, its "blessed equality" makes its consequences felt every-where, even to those who cannot share in social reciprocity. There is an es-chatological equality, fully relevant for our earthly life, which is more important than, and prior to, social reciprocity.

The final point of importance about the sufferer is that not only does he serve as an exemplar to a busy world and not only is he, to whom the least possible has been given, fully equal, in the eternal sense, with his fellows, but he is likewise, in the eternal sense, free, even in his bondage to suffering. Those who voluntarily take on suffering show courage by making themselves pris-oners when they could be free. But we were dealing with an extreme example, an individual who suffers of necessity. Such an individual can voluntarily take up his suffering and make it his own, and in so doing he shows patience and does something even greater than the person of courage: He makes himself free in his captivity. Not in the sense of sour grapes but in the eternal and ideal sense, "he makes of necessity a virtue, he brings a category of freedom (virtue) out of what has been determined as necessity" [p. 213]. Such is the perfect marriage of freedom and necessity, of willing that which one is.

Having now dealt with the proposition that willing one thing is willing the Good and that truly willing the Good is willing the Good "in truth"— without any of the four forms of double-mindedness but under the heading of doing all or suffering all for the Good—SK inserts a beautiful intermezzo in the discourse. Purity of heart is lyrically compared to the sea's purity, its depth and transparency: "[I]ts purity is its continuity in being deep and being trans-parent" [p.215], reflecting in its depth the loftiness of heaven.

After this short intermezzo SK now turns to the third and concluding subdivision of "Purity of Heart." This third section is untitled in the published version, but SK's drafts show that it was originally to have been entitled "It Was on the Occasion of Confession" [Pap. VII 1 B 174]. In this section, therefore, SK tries especially to personalize the message of the discourse, to confront the reader with the obligation to live always as "the individual" [den Enkelte]. The confessional discourse itself, SK stresses, is not the important thing; it is but the whispering from the prompter's box that should encourage the reader to make the text one's own in confessing as an individual before God. All those who are not cut off by madness or self-disdain share in common humanity as their starting point. It is taken as a given that one wills the Good; the question is whether one wills it "in truth," and this question, in turn, can only be answered if one has already chosen the invisible, the internal in life, if one thus has time for such questions and is not busy with the noisy crowd.

In short, one cannot will the Good in truth unless one lives as an individual and does not try to hide by membership in some group or other, seeking security in numbers. In eternity there is no "common shipwreck" [fælles Skibbrud] [p. 237]. In confession, as in eternity, responsibility is entirely individual: "[T]hose who confess are not together in a society; each is an individual before God" [p. 239]. It would be contradictory if the aloneness required for confession were not also required in what is most important for daily life. God sees only individuals responsible for their actions and their failures, and despite the noise and busyness of the world, in eternity the voice of conscience is the only sound heard by every individual. Nor will eternity ignore the silence dictated by worldly shrewdness but commands that every individual speak the truth when he or she knows it [pp. 238–39].

SK's theory of the relation between the individual and society as it is developed in this discourse is, in brief, that we are, as individuals, all equal, all common sharers in that which is universally human, because we are all equal before the eternal claims of the Good, before God. Our individuality before God is what separates us from one another, but it is also the source of our common humanity, which unites us.

As a responsible individual, one must be slow to judge others. One is not required to have an opinion about what one does not understand, even though the media and the crowds of the city are constantly trying to compel one to judge. The fact that one's right to judge is limited frees one from the distraction of needless judging, in order that one can will one thing [pp. 223–26]. One must judge especially slowly in unusual cases, remembering that the crowd is usually on the wrong side, remembering "eternity's true thought, that everything in life appears reversed" [p. 226]. It may perhaps be impossible for any individual to split up the crowd and compel each to bear responsibility, but eternity, which leaves every individual ultimately with the voice of his conscience, will succeed. Earthly disrespect and resistance is all that SK can promise the person who follows this path and lives always as an individual. He insists that one must fear God and not the crowd. The disapproval of the crowd is merely a sign that one is on the right path [p. 227].

But, SK continues, it is not required that one put away worldly vocation, civic responsibilities, and a happy domestic life in order to ponder eternal questions—one then only acquires an additional debt on one's reckoning—but merely that, in one's ordinary life, one remain conscious of the requirement of eternity. This requirement, by keeping one out of busyness and time wasting, will actually help one and give one more time for one's worldly responsibilities [p. 228]. This is reminiscent of SK's earlier discussion of time's refraction [Brydning] of eternity's notion of the Good. Here again, the notion of the necessary resistance of the world and of the world's reversal of eternity's values leads SK to the brink of a rejection of the Lutheran ideas of worldly vocation and ethical integration in society. However, SK again steps back and refuses to draw any conclusions about the necessity of asceticism and martyrdom and, on the contrary, expressly emphasizes the opposite possibility of the individual who has become a better husband, father, and employee by following the claim of the Good. What is required is thus that one give eternity its due, that one respect its *priority*; then, far from being removed from one's worldly social responsibilities, one is better able to shoulder them. In a subsequent chapter, when it intrudes more insistently into SK's writings, we will examine the latent conflict in his social vision between such a "prioritarian" view of the relation to the world and the notion of straightforward martyrdom.

The discourse continues in this Lutheran vein, stressing that one's work must be something of which one can be proud, a calling or vocation to which one feels responsible, regardless of worldly success or failure. In one's vocation one must always consider oneself a "useless servant" [unyttig Tjener, cf. Luke 17:10], serving the Good, which is not a mercurial master but which always requires the same thing, *honesty* [Oprigtighed] [pp. 230–31]. The notion of honesty or integrity is an important leitmotif in this discourse, where the Kantian key is ever-present—see, for example, the notion of "the well-understood equality of honesty" [Oprigtighedens vel forstaaede Ligelighed] [p. 173], which is the necessary condition of any interpersonal unity that can transcend selfish immediacy of feeling. Continuing in a Kantian tenor, the discourse stresses that one must regard the means one employs in one's work as of equal importance to the end in view. It is no disgrace, eternally, if one does not reach the end, but one will be held eternally responsible for the means one uses. And, combining both Kantian and Christian-eschatological language, SK emphasizes that when one uses only means which are good, one is already at the end, in the eternal sense [p. 231].

Continuing in the same spirit, the discourse asks about one's "attitude" [Sind] toward others. Are you in "unity" [Samdrægtighed] with all by willing one thing, or is "your hand raised against all and all against you" [p. 233]?[3] Do you wish for all what you wish for yourself; do you do unto others what you would have them do unto you—by willing one thing? (Both Kant and the Golden Rule are woven into the argument.) In willing one thing you enter into "unity with all people," even those long dead or far away, who together with you enter "into family with divinity" [i Slægt med Guddommen] by so willing [ibid.]. Do you submit yourself to the same rules which hold for all others?

Thus the discourse posits an ethic that is both religious and philosophical, proposing that willing one thing (the Good "in truth") puts one both "in family with divinity" and in conformity with the categorical imperative which insists upon the universality of law and upon the necessity of willing in unity with that which can be willed by all. Both the religious and the philosophical language could be subsumed under the general term "the eternal"—or under "religiousness A" which SK developed earlier in his (chiefly pseudonymous) authorship.

Any other form of human fellowship than that which can be willed by all (i.e., "one thing") is merely "solidarity" [Sammenhold], which, because it falls short of the absolutely universal, is actually a form of exclusiveness and is the enemy of genuine human "unity" [Samdrægtighed]. "All solidarity is divisiveness against that which is the universally human. But willing one thing, willing the Good in truth, holding oneself as an individual together with God, which absolutely everyone can do—that is unity" [p. 234]. The dichotomy developed between "unity" and "solidarity" is parallel to the dichotomy developed earlier in the discourse [p. 206] between ordinary "social reciprocity" [Lige for Lige] and "blessed equality" [salige Ligelighed]. SK thus stresses the absolute universality and the genuine humanity of willing the Good "in truth" with God. Only that which is absolutely universal can be genuinely human.

If this is not intended to be Kant's ethic, it is certainly a religious ethic deliberately dressed in Kantian language in order to show the philosophically minded that this religious ethic is the only ethic that truly fulfills Kant's criteria. Like Kant's, this ethic of universals is the ethic of "the Law"; positing the Law is as far as any ordinary human ethics, or "religiousness A" can come, and, as we shall see in *Works of Love*, this is only far enough to humble one and make one realize that one cannot fulfill the Law. To go further requires a Christian ethics which presupposes not only the Law but the Grace that transcends the Law. However, this is not the task of "Purity of Heart," where we are merely led to formulate the highest ethics available to humanity (and to natural religion) short of revelation.

In closing the discourse, SK refers back to the Solomonic text cited in the beginning, namely that there are times and seasons for everything "under Heaven"—for temporal things—and he reiterates his implicit extension of the text, namely that for eternal things, on the other hand, it is always the opportune moment, always the eleventh hour. And if one has not felt oneself visited by eternal opportunity under any other form, one ought to meet it under the form of repentance, for which it is always the right time. It is always the right time to purify one's heart by willing one thing, the Good "in truth," and this, Kierkegaard now stresses, is precisely the task for every person as an individual, avoiding all evasions and distracting comparisons with others—for it is precisely as an individual that every person is "incomparable" [p. 240]. The consciousness that one is an individual whose task is to will the Good "in truth" is the strait gate and the narrow way through which each must pass, because "only the individual can will the Good in truth" [ibid.]. And though the way is difficult, the path is the correct one, because one has placed oneself in relation to the demand that requires purity of heart in willing one thing.

Before moving on to the Closing Prayer, SK issues a warning, almost as an aside, against those who impatiently skip over the "pause" [Standsning] and the introspective concentration required by confession and by willing one thing. Those whom SK takes to task are the optimistic and eager souls who already "know" what "comes after" confession and who "cannot be stopped" with the "pause" and the concentration required to teach "a single individual" something which is, after all, elementary doctrine, obvious to all in a Christian country. Such bright and impatient souls want to "go further" and "know" Christianity, SK notes; yet, he continues, it is exactly in these busy times that there is need to "stop," to stress the individual, and to concentrate upon confession, repentance, and the fact that purity of heart consists in willing one thing.

> Because to pause is not lazy calm; to pause is also movement: It is the heart's inward movement, it is the deepening of the self in inwardness [Inderlighed]. But merely going further is a way of going forward superficially. One will never come to will one thing that way. Only when one who has been stopped in the decisive sense goes further, and again stops before he goes further—only then can he will one thing. But purity of heart was to will one thing. [p. 241]

Just as the earlier criticism of "observational" religion was aimed at Mynster, so is this parting criticism in "Purity of Heart" aimed at the intellectual Christianity of H. L. Martensen, who claimed that it was time to "go further" than Hegel in producing a theology which fulfilled the program of philosophy. The ethics that SK adumbrates in "Purity of Heart" is, as has been pointed out, an ethics of the Law; it stresses obedience and repentance, but nowhere states the factual impossibility of fulfilling such a self-contained philosophical-religious ethics. This is the function of the Law: to provide an ideal guide for the individual—a program drawn up within the highest categories available to the natural person, the categories of disinterested Reason and philosophical religion (religiousness A)—a guide that ultimately crushes and humbles one, forces one to "pause" in repentance, and leaves one open to the proper reception of grace and of the religion of grace, Christianity (religiousness B). But in his intellectualism—his desire to "go further" and "know" rather than to "pause" and repent—Martensen has ignored the limitations of the natural self and of human reason. He has ignored the radicality of sin, and in so doing he has cheapened grace by robbing it of the "pause," the repentance, the fear and trembling, which must accompany it.

Thus, in "Purity of Heart" SK attacks the two major, fashionable currents of the Christianity of Golden Age establishment Copenhagen, both Mynster's calm, introspective, "observational" religion and Martensen's intellectualism, which was anxious to "go further" and comprehend Christianity, converting it into knowledge.

Finally, the discourse repeats the prayer with which it began. At the outset, the language of the prayer may have seemed strange and not readily understandable. It requested God's help—wisdom [Viisdommen] for the understanding; honesty [Oprigtighed] for the heart; and purity [Reenhed] for the will—in willing one thing. It interpreted the chasm of sin as an interruption [Afbrydelse] and a pause, or a stop [Standsning], in the life of the individual. Likewise it designated repentance in the midst of these "busy" times as another form of pause and interruption, which makes one alone in God's presence, a different sort of interruption, which leads back to the beginning and joins together what has been separated [pp. 241–42]. In short, this interruption is, as mentioned earlier, an interruption within the interruption of eternity caused by the sinfulness of the busy temporal world. SK's proposed interruption is thus, in the eternal sense, a continuation.

By the end of the discourse, all of this language about "stopping" in the midst of these "busy" times in order to "will one thing" should have become clear. The discourse aims itself at the distractions and evasions of SK's Denmark, its cultured and occasionally reflective Christian bourgeoisie, its "double-mindedness" in unreligion and religion alike, and particularly in the Christianities of Mynster and Martensen, which SK found lacking in seriousness. Instead of the Christendom of the Golden Age, the discourse proposes—not without occasional deviations in the direction of asceticism, martyrdom, and straightforward rejection of the world—an intensely individualistic but egalitarian religious ethic, Lutheran in character and in places quite reminiscent of Kant, an ethic whose purpose is to be sought in the context of repentance, where SK has placed it. "Purity of Heart" is not the final formulation of SK's ethical position any more than repentance is the ultimate posture of the Christian, but both correspond to the stage at which one takes leave of that which is universally human (and the Law) and enters into the realm of Christianity proper (the Gospel), in which one lives in grace and in "fear and trembling." "Purity of Heart" thus sets forth a repentant ethics that formulates the universal demands of the Good, or the Law, which is the highest a person can go without entering the specific precincts of Christianity. A repentant ethics is not the last word; rather, it is a construction that will situate us or place us in relation to the Law in such a way that our own inadequacy—and the Law's impossibility of fulfillment—dawns upon us. Only then, after confession and repentance, are we really ready for the specifically Christian ethics that builds upon grace.

C. "WHAT WE LEARN FROM THE LILIES OF THE FIELD AND THE BIRDS OF THE AIR"

The second of the three subdivisions of SK's *Edifying Discourses in Various Spirits* is a collection of three discourses, collectively entitled "What We Learn From the Lilies of the Field and the Birds of the Air." They are all in sermon form, based on the text of Matthew 6:24–34, a portion of the Sermon on the

Mount, in which we, who are worried and concerned about social and material well-being, are adjured to forsake the primacy of worldly things: No one can serve two masters, for he must love the one and hate the other, or vice versa; choose God rather than Mammon and do not fear worldly troubles; consider the lilies of the field and the birds of the air—God cares for them, will he not care for you? Seek first the Kingdom of God and his righteousness, and all these things will be added unto you.

This is SK's first important use of Matthew 6:24–34, which over the next several years becomes the *locus classicus* of his "prioritarian" interpretation of the relation of the individual to the social and political responsibilities of the world: Concern with the affairs of the world is not in itself wrong, but it must be seen as subordinate to the individual's relation to God. If one remembers always to order priorities correctly, and to "seek *first* the Kingdom of God and his righteousness," then one can attend to the needs and affairs of the world—"all these things will be added unto you." This "prioritarian" possibility is the role of the Christian "citizen," a role which coexists (with increasing tension) with another possibility, namely the Christian as "exceptional," as the martyr-Apostle or "saint," who is unequivocally opposed to any form of social integration.

The three discourses in this set are increasingly intense and stark in their message. They place progressively greater emphasis on the eternal moment in the human synthesis of the temporal and the eternal, and, correspondingly, the temporal nature of the lilies and the birds is placed in an increasingly baleful light. As SK himself remarks in his journals [Pap. VIII 1 A 1], these discourses shift character from the aesthetic to the ethical and finally, to the religious, so that the third discourse is the most important of the three and represents, in miniature, the final message which SK wishes to communicate, just as the three discourses themselves are, in their three-stage architecture, a miniature of the authorship as a whole.

In the first discourse the tone is light. Nature is bright and cheerful. The lilies and the birds are clearly our superiors and our teachers, who will teach us "to be satisfied with being human" [p. 251]. The lilies in their simple splendor, which they all share by virtue of the fact that God made them lilies, teach us to eschew worldly comparison and differences and to find joy in our common humanity, our essential equality. They teach us, in short, to avoid socially generated worry [pp. 255–60]. On the other hand, the birds, whom God feeds, teach us, by their carefree attitude toward life, to avoid physically generated worry. The message is firmly egalitarian. No one, rich or poor, ultimately feeds oneself; we are equally dependent upon Providence, and we must learn to let Providence take care. We realize our essential equality when we realize that, with respect to our subsistence, all must let God be God and not presume to possess a false independence [pp. 261–69].

In the second discourse nature's standing has become more equivocal. The lilies and birds are indeed our teachers, but we are their superiors. They distract us from our worries and direct our attention instead to "how glorious it is to be human" [p. 274]. The lily once again serves as a reminder of our essential equality and as a corrective to our social worries, our tendency to concentrate on comparisons and on human differences, but in a somewhat different way. The visible glory and uniformity of the lilies directs our attention to something even greater, namely our invisible glory in having been created in God's image [pp. 278–79]. The "uniformity" of humankind, surpassing that of the lilies, has the wonderful characteristic that our *common* humanity is expressed precisely in our capacity to exist as individuals. As in the first discourse of this group, the birds again teach us to avoid worries about material subsistence, but, like the lilies in this discourse, the birds stand inferior to us, their pupils. The birds have no worries about their material life, but this is because, living as they do exclusively in the moment, they are unable to have such worries. The glory of humankind, however, is that we, as conscious beings who live both in time and in eternity, are capable of having such worries, but we are also capable, by coming into conscious relation with God, of choosing not to have such worries [pp. 280–81]. Similarly, it is the bird's luck not to work, because it is not able to work, whereas it is our glory to be able to work, to be able, in SK's use of St. Paul's phrase, to be "God's co-worker[s]" [p. 284]. And the egalitarian element is again stressed by emphasizing that this is a glory which is open unconditionally to all, whether they work for bread or for millions.

In the third discourse we have moved decisively into the religious sphere, and nature has become a darkened landscape whose death, decay, and transitoriness are to teach us the vanity of the kingdom of this world and induce us to choose another kingdom instead. We no longer deal with the portion of the text which talks of lilies and birds, as these teachers have exhausted their usefulness for us. Now we concentrate upon the portions of Matthew 6:24–34 in which we are compelled to choose between God and Mammon and are adjured to "seek first the Kingdom of God and his righteousness." In this final lesson, the vanity of nature stands as a negative example, teaching us, this time, "what blessedness our humanity is promised" [p. 288]. Choose God not Mammon, is the message; our greatness is precisely that we can *choose* [pp. 290–91]. This elevates us over all the transience and decay of the natural world. And, again, SK emphasizes that with respect to this essential attribute, we are all equally situated; God is available to all, while "mammon," the world, which can just as easily be a farthing as a fortune, can also be chosen by all.

"Seek ye *first* the Kingdom of God and his righteousness," the Gospel reads, "and all these things will be added unto you." The visible world of social and material relations, about which the lilies and the birds, respectively, have taught us so much, must be renounced and set aside, SK writes, and the invisible world of the Kingdom of God must be chosen first. Only after one has recognized the primacy of the relation to God and the hope of blessedness which is our essential humanity can one busy oneself with visible reality in a way that is worthy of humankind. Social responsibility, politics, ethics, will all follow of themselves, afterwards, but they will come. (This is what I have called SK's "prioritarian" vision of social and political obligation.) SK merely says that if we follow the words of the Gospel and seek the Kingdom of God first, we will be incapable of unrighteousness toward other people [p. 293]. The text simply says that all these things—material and social concerns—will be "added unto" us; it does not bother itself with details, and therefore, neither does SK. He is satisfied with stating the Pauline and Lutheran position on works as important, but secondary, a natural consequence of the God-relation. It is in this sense that SK's emphasis upon "equality" (a concept with both political and extra-political overtones) must be understood, and it is this which stands at the heart of SK's political vision and which is the principal message and conclusion of the entire "Lilies and Birds" section.

It is, in short, a question of getting priorities right, of "life's order." SK writes: "Seek *first* God's Kingdom. That is the order . . ." [Søger *først* Guds Rige. Dette er Ordenen . . .] [ibid.]. These words—as, indeed, the entire cumulative message (God-relation first, world afterwards) of the "Lilies and Birds" progression—almost sound like a direct assault on the lighter worldview of Grundtvig, who, as we have seen, expressed precisely the reverse of SK's priorities in his famous 1837 hymn "Person First and Christian Afterwards, That Alone is Life's Order." SK comes to social-political reality *via* the God-relation, whereas for Grundtvig we come to the God-relation via social-political reality. The visible world of lilies and birds, of nature, with its social and material worries, teaches us to be satisfied with our common humanity in which all participate equally, to find glory in it, and finally to appreciate the expectation of blessedness which it entails. Our common humanity consists precisely in the fact that we can and ought to relate ourselves to invisible reality, "the Kingdom of God," before we concern ourselves with visible reality, "the world." This is the message of the "Lilies and Birds," and it may also be construed as a direct attack upon Grundtvig's optimistic view of an uncomplicated and direct relationship to the social-political sphere.

D. "THE GOSPEL OF SUFFERINGS"

The third and concluding section of the *Edifying Discourses in Various Spirits* is a series of seven discourses which—delighting as the Kierkegaardian literature always does in apparent contradiction—concern themselves with why suffering can be a special and particular cause for joy in the sufferer. For our purposes the "Gospel of Sufferings" is important, first of all, in its entirety, because it develops SK's notion of suffering and of the two opposed characters—the individuated self and the world—which suffering entails. Secondly, the "Gospel of Sufferings" is important to this inquiry because its seventh and final discourse—which thus concludes both the "Gospel" and the entire volume of *Edifying Discourses in Various Spirits*—is a specifically political piece. First, we will deal with several of the more important points in the first six discourses, and then we will turn to deal with the seventh in some detail.

In the first and third discourses the notion of equality is the special cause for joy in the sufferer, in that the sufferer becomes aware that his or her suffering serves as an occasion for realizing the principles of equality and universality, namely in the individual relation to God. Thus, in the first discourse, the sufferer who wishes to follow after Christ in all the humiliation, mockery, suffering, and even death which the world has to offer, can find joy first and foremost in the fact that this "following after" [Efterfølgelse, which can also be translated "imitation" in the sense of *Imitation of Christ*] is something that is available to everyone, no matter how humble or poor. In a pun, SK sets "the envious [misundelige] differences of earthly life" against "heaven's merciful [miskundelige] thought that this [following Christ] is something which *everyone* can do" [p. 313, emphasis added]. Thus, chief among the joys of following Christ is that it enables one to realize perfectly the goals of equality and universality, which temporal life (whose very essence is "differences") defeats. In the third discourse we are told that suffering schools us for the eternal, i.e., for the most important truth, namely that we must learn through obedience that God rules and that we must let him rule [p. 342]. This is the only thing which in principle, all can learn, as opposed to worldly knowledge, which we learn according to our aptitudes, our differences [p. 338]. This egalitarianism recalls important parts of "Purity of Heart" and the "Lilies and Birds" earlier in the book.

The fourth discourse of the "Gospel of Sufferings" is not vital to the present inquiry, while in the second discourse we will limit ourselves to directing attention briefly to an aside which SK makes concerning slavery but which could as easily have been made in connection with any other political institution or situation. Following St. Paul, SK writes that Christ did not come into this world to abolish slavery, though he insists that this follows from what He did [p. 328]. SK is here taking the Lutheran (and Pauline) position with respect to good works, which bear no necessary generative relation to faith but are its natural fruits. This position is the same as that espoused earlier, in the "Lilies and Birds" section, where it is stressed that if we seek the kingdom of God first, we will be incapable of acting unrighteously toward our fellows [p. 293].

The fifth discourse merits a somewhat longer look, as it portrays Christianity as a posture of suffering, and, by resurrecting some of the barbed language from "Purity of Heart," it focuses quite specifically on the incompatibility of this Christianity with the cautious, moderate Christianity of Mynster and the cultured bourgeoisie. Life is a *way*, SK asserts, and this way is not a *what*, not one or another topological or rulebook alternative, but a *how* one walks [p. 370]. There is joy for the sufferer in the thought that it isn't the way that is "narrow" [trang]—for that would be a characteristic of one or another alternative external to ourselves—but "afflictions" [Trængsler] that *are* the way [p. 373]. That is, the way is a posture that is personally appropriated, and "walking" on it consists specifically in accepting the fact that the afflictions one suffers are the way. There is thus no chance connection between afflictions and the way; there is no possibility for doubt to insinuate itself between the individual and his immediate application to his task, his burden of affliction. SK is again pitting eschatological language—which, finding victory in the here and now, stretches normal language to its limits—against the cunning logical language of doubt, which wishes to search everywhere for ways and solutions. In embracing one's affliction, in understanding the way as a posture rather than as a quest outside oneself, the end—the way—is present at the outset.

Remember also, SK continues, that affliction is the way *all the way* and not just at the start. Then you will be protected from the disappointments and impatience which come from "willing the Good to a certain degree" or from thinking that "the Good will be rewarded in this world, to a certain degree" [p. 377]. Beware of "a certain shrewdness which is very reluctant to break entirely with the Good but which is also terribly reluctant to give up worldly advantage and easy times" [p. 378]. This applies perfectly to the Christian bourgeoisie of Golden Age Copenhagen, who were polite, "cultured" [dannede] folk, lacking the courage either to be demonic (and break with the Good) or to be Christian (and break with the priority of "the world"). This is a clear reference, in content, tone, and specific language, to "Purity of Heart" and its attack on the bourgeois Christianity of worldly compromise and mediocrity, an attack that I have argued was specifically directed at Mynster and the bourgeoisie who idolized him. The repetition of language here ("willing the Good *to a certain degree*," etc.), near the end of this large and somewhat diffuse book, is a reminder from SK that the work has a definite inner coherence and a central concern, namely, it is the beginning of an attack on bourgeois Christendom and its cultured adherents. Thus, in this "Gospel of Sufferings," the importance of suffering is that, by highlighting that which is most extremely and painfully Christian, it separates the bourgeois philistine [Spidsborger] "Christian" from the Christianity of "individuals." The difference between the two ways of being Christian becomes clear when we remember, as SK points out here, that it is not *where* the path is (i.e., *what* one calls oneself—for example, "Christian," "Primate of Denmark," etc.) but *how* one walks (i.e., in suffering and individuation such as no philistine could be troubled with), which determines whether one is "on" the way.

The sixth discourse also merits attention, as it, too, is formed in negative contrast to the prevailing Golden Age culture. Here SK stresses the absolute and essential difference between eternal and temporal qualities, in which the excellence of the eternal makes it clear that the two sorts of qualities defy comparison. Thus he who suffers under a burden of temporal afflictions is told to find joy in the fact that, just as the least quantity of eternity outweighs the greatest quantity of temporality, so will his temporal afflictions be outweighed by the eternal blessedness which lies in store (II Corinthians 4:17) [pp. 386–87]. There are two dangers standing in the way of this simple joy. First of all, one might come to feel that eternal blessedness is a merited reward for having undergone suffering. This is countered with a simple reference to the Lutheran emphasis upon grace, in which the greatness of one's joy is seen as consisting precisely in the fact that eternal blessedness is a "universal receipt" [General-Qvittering] and does not bother with accounts and merits [p. 397]. The second and more important danger threatening the proper reception of this simple joy is that the so-called Christianity with which one is surrounded continually gives such empty-headed and thoughtless homage to the greatness of eternal blessedness that it becomes saccharine and insipid. "The greatest fault of the age is that it does not respect eternity's blessedness" [ibid.]. In the "Gospel of Sufferings," SK charges that the habitual Christianity of bourgeois-philistine Copenhagen is rooted in mediocrity, in the safety of moderation, and is unwilling to experience extremes. By refusing to undergo the bitterness and individuation of suffering, it is likewise excluded from the blessedness of the eternal. Its talk of eternity is cheap talk.

The seventh and concluding discourse of the "Gospel of Sufferings" is one of SK's principal cultural-political assessments prior to the "attack on Christendom," and during the March days of 1848, SK refers in his journals to the importance of this discourse in this connection [Pap. VIII 1 A 598]. Our consideration of it will be rather extended because (particularly for our purposes) it is, after "Purity of Heart," the high point of the *Edifying Discourses in Various Spirits*, and its choice as the conclusion of this massive work was no coincidence.

It is most shameful to hide what one believes for fear of worldly disapproval or in hope of worldly gain, SK begins [p. 398]. In the old days—in early Christianity—to proclaim Christianity was to confess it in a hostile environment which wanted one to deny it. What about the present? To confess Christianity from within Christendom, SK continues, would be by implication to judge one's fellow Christians, to call them, at best, unconscious and thoughtless, and at worst, hypocrites [pp. 399–400]. But who can know whether or not people in Christendom are truly Christians; who can see that reality, which is an invisible, spiritual reality? Only "the Knower of Hearts" [Hjertekjenderen] [p. 401], SK replies to his own question. Thus, the question of whether one is required to confess Christianity in Christendom can only be answered with caution: One must beware of such judgmental confessing of the faith, as it can lead to "sectarian self-importance and presumption" [p. 402]; at the same time, however, one cannot rule out the possibility that one might be called to confess Christianity among the "Christians." This, however, we must "consign to the individual's serious self-examination" [Selvprøvelse] [ibid.].[4] What this discourse concerns itself with, continues SK, is not the question of confessing Christ but the more general notion of what it means to "struggle for a conviction" rather than hide what one believes. SK raises this very thorny and explosive issue here and then hesitates and puts it aside again, having made a rhetorical feint against "Christendom" without having committed himself.

Having raised very serious doubts about the genuineness of his contemporary Christian culture (without committing himself to discussing it at this point), SK switches rather abruptly to a discussion of present political and cultural conditions, in which he finds a conspiracy against the "open-hearted courage" [Frimodighed] that an individual needs if he is to suffer for and defend his convictions. SK writes that "gradually, as a certain superficial culture [en vis overfladisk Dannelse] spreads" [ibid.], we become increasingly fearful of other people, who become our anonymous oppressors via what SK elsewhere calls "the tyranny of the fear of people" [Menneske-Frygtens Tyrannie]. This tyranny is far more dangerous than the one-man tyrannies of old, for at least they were identifiable and could be overthrown. Nowadays, all become the anonymous oppressors of all, SK writes, because each person has lost the individual relation to God, which is the only thing that enables one to resist dissolution and quantification into one or another negotiable form of social power [pp. 403–404]. The relation to God is the only real refuge of the individual human personality. If the political and social conditions in which one exists—the bourgeois Christendom of Golden Age Copenhagen—can succeed in their relentless attempts to break down the integrity and earnestness of the God-relation, that many more souls are added to "the public" and transformed from individuals into units of weight in the anonymous political calculus.

This half-begun attack on Christendom which opens the discourse is intimately connected with SK's notion of the politics and culture of his Copenhagen. The two topics that SK has raised thus far in the discourse—the problem of judging in confessing Christianity in Christendom and the tendency of modern culture to deny the privacy and integrity of the individual—may seem at first to be only distantly related to one another. However, they can be seen to be closely connected in SK's thought, and he here uses the notion of "open-hearted courage" [Frimodighed] to mediate between them. It is in this connection that SK now shifts to the text, Acts 5:41 ("And they departed from the presence of the council, rejoicing that they were counted worthy to suffer shame for His name"). SK writes that this passage should cause us to consider the joy that can be felt by the person who suffers for his convictions, the joy that arises from the fact that "open-hearted courage succeeds sufferingly in taking power from the world, and has the power to transform mockery into honor, defeat into victory" [p. 404].[5] The world has reversed eternal values: The truth is not honored, but the lie is given great respect, etc. The "reversedness of open-hearted courage" [Frimodighedens Omvendthed] is required in order to reverse the world's reversal of values and set things right. When one has this open-hearted courage one is able, sufferingly, to transform defeat into victory, to welcome the world's mockery as honor, etc. [pp. 406–407]. This was the case, SK argues, with the Apostles, and he shifts the discourse once again to the lofty level of apostolic courage and suffering, supposedly in order to emphasize the principle behind "suffering for a conviction" in general, but more importantly, for the rhetorical purpose of holding an uncomplimentary mirror up to the present.

SK argues that when an Apostle welcomed mockery and torment as an honor, and when he welcomed the loss of worldly advantage not merely as a small loss or as nothing, but as a positive *gain*, his words seemed like mockery to his tormentors and seem close to madness to us. However, it was neither mockery nor madness but a sincerity so simple that, upon reflection, it can indeed terrify us. For the Apostle, the opposition of the world is welcomed, in suffering and with open-hearted courage, as a blessing, because this opposition is the occasion for the Apostle to enter more intensely into the individuation of the God-relation. This can be terrifying to us others because, far from mocking his tormentors (by calling their torments blessings), the Apostle has really nothing to do with them; he does not oppose them or try to prove that he is right; he simply suffers and is related to God. "What people do to them [the Apostles] really does not concern them, and at most only [serves] as an occasion to take refuge in the God-relation, in which alone, quite abandoned, they have their life" [pp. 410–11]. The aloneness of the Apostle in his suffering is terrible to us, and therefore we find it more comfortable to interpret his utterings of joy as ironic mockery or madness. The suffering, courageous Apostle is the paradigmatic individual, and it is no wonder that he seems threatening. Whether or not *we* are called upon to be "Apostles" is not dealt with here, but the chance of being so called remains an explosive possibility in SK's interpretation of the Christian's relationship to political and social life. The issue is dealt with again—inconclusively—in *Two Minor Ethico-Religious Essays* and is touched upon after that without being finally decided. (In this connection see below, the closing pages of chapter 23 on *The Sickness Unto Death*.) For now, the Apostle is more an example of seriousness (with which to criticize what SK saw as the frivolousness of Danish Christendom) than a challenge for the individual actually to enter into such a total isolation from the world.

In a further non-committal, rhetorical feint at contemporary Christendom, SK makes polemical application of the mediaeval terms *ecclesia militans* and *ecclesia triumphans*. Originally these were terms for the Christians still on earth and those in heaven, respectively, but they are used here to make an implicitly invidious comparison between the Christianity of the Apostles and that of modern times. The Apostles, SK claims, acted as they did because they embraced the "struggling view" [den stridende Anskuelse] and expected the faith to be persecuted, the Good to be defeated in the world, its servants hunted, mocked, treated as madmen [pp. 412–13]. What would these Apostles have thought, SK muses aloud, of those who embrace "the triumphant view" [den sejrende Anskuelse] in which people are paid and honored for preaching the Gospel, in which preachers welcome the world's power and honor and are convinced "that the mass of people, on the average, are possessed of the truth" [at Menneskenes Mængden i Gjennemsnit er af Sandheden] [p. 413].[6] This is a clear assault upon the clerical situation which prevailed in Denmark (among other places), where the clergy was an honored part of state power and the bureaucracy. SK now closes his attack by carefully covering his flank and adding an escape clause in which he maintains that, "of course, in its time, it could be the case that the age, on the average, is good" [p. 414] and that, if this were so, it would be "the unhealthy exaggeration of vehemence" [ibid.] to refuse to accept such power and honor.

In closing, SK goes through this same attack and retreat one more time, asserting once again, on the one hand, that the great danger, in peaceful times, is that one "takes the spirit in vain" and that in such spiritually slack times the torment of the world would indeed make "an Apostle glad," because such suffering restores to existence its pith and salty savor [ibid.].[7] However, on the other hand, we must remember that this joyful thought about open-hearted courage turning the world's mockery into honor is "strong medicine," and must be used very sparingly. "It will probably be the case very rarely in our times that a person dare truthfully say that he suffers for the sake of Christ; we recommend repeatedly the sobriety that bears in mind that one really does not dare to appeal straightforwardly to the Apostle's relation to a heathen world" [p. 415].[8]

Thus the discourse ends by reminding us once again that, in considering the Apostles, we have been dealing with an exceptional, limiting case and that it has been the intent of this discourse only to draw strength from their example so that we might, when we "suffer for a conviction," learn how to use such open-hearted courage to turn the world's defeat into victory, mockery into honor, etc. Note that "suffering for a conviction" is not a specifically Christian category and that SK is not willing, in this discourse, to stand quite entirely behind his attack. These sallies are directed, first and foremost, at the politics and culture of mid-nineteenth-century bourgeois Denmark. The particular target of these maneuvers is the Danish religious-political situation, which SK was able to characterize deftly by means of negative comparison with the early Christianity of the Apostles. Still, SK was unwilling, in this discourse at any rate, to "sign the portrait," to call upon the authority of the Apostolic Church and insist that his readers see a perfect fit between current reality and the negative view of Christendom here sketched. Here, as elsewhere, SK circles around the problems of "authority" [Myndighed] and of the special character of "Apostles." SK deals elsewhere with both sides of the question. In *Philosophical Fragments* SK argues that chronological contemporaneity with Christ is no essential advantage and that every individual in every age has the same possibility of standing in a contemporaneous, apostolic relation to the truth. In "The Difference Between a Genius and an Apostle,"[9] on the other hand, SK puts considerable distance between his own position and the authoritative stance of the Apostle and indeed leaves it an open question as to whether one can be an Apostle in Christendom.

In this discourse SK has provided himself shelter against direct political-clerical application by leaving carefully placed phrases that warn against "sectarian self-importance and presumption" and "the unhealthy exaggeration of vehemence." Even so, we cannot escape the sharply critical tendency of the piece with which SK chose to conclude this large and rambling book, *Edifying Discourses in Various Spirits*. Nor ought we overlook the very important connection between SK's criticism of modernity's unseriousness in religious matters and the dangerous political and social climate of the coming bourgeois liberal culture. For example, although Mynster and Martensen (to name names) were by no means liberals, SK could not criticize bourgeois culture and the liberalism of the 1840's without also attacking those who had helped sanitize Christianity for general consumption. Even though SK refused to draw these conclusions in this final discourse and did not explicitly label his own age as corresponding to the one whose evils he here conjures forth, the reader is forced toward this conclusion. Such a conclusion draws upon what SK had already written elsewhere (for example, in *A Literary Review*) as well as what he had written in this very book, in particular "Purity of Heart" and several of the other discourses included in the "Gospel of Sufferings."

The message of this final discourse also serves as the message of the entire "Gospel of Sufferings," which we have been considering, and is a very important component in SK's politics: We should take joy in our sufferings in this world because suffering is the occasion of the individuation which the God-relation entails. Suffering does not necessarily lead to the God-relation, but the individual's relation to God (in this context, "the eternal") is impossible without suffering. Becoming an individual, then, requires suffering as well as the relation to God. All true social and political life must build upon individuals. Modern society, however, with its notions of politics, culture, and domesticated Christendom, wishes to sabotage the individual personality, and it begins by trying to break down the God-relation, to which the individual, in suffering, must cling fast. As individuals we must learn to see in our suffering the signs of our continuing steadfastness in the God-relation, of our resistance, our continuing refusal to be dissolved. Therefore, in this suffering, we must see our continuing reasons for joy.

E. CONCLUSION

Thus the movement of the *Edifying Discourses in Various Spirits* as a whole is from: (1) "Purity of Heart"; to (2) "The Lilies and Birds"; and finally to (3)

"The Gospel of Sufferings." "Purity of Heart" puts forth the command to set aside all "double-mindedness" and to will one thing, the Good, "in Truth" and thereby posits the highest human ethic, an ethic of repentance and confession, which is the preparatory stage for a Christian ethics of grace. "The Lilies and the Birds," based on Matthew 6:24–34, puts forth the "prioritarian" vision of the Christian's relation to the world. "The Gospel of Sufferings" stresses individuation most strongly and sketches the possibility of an alternative social posture for the Christian, namely that of "Apostle." Finally, the work as a whole is strongly critical both of contemporary ecclesiastical and of political tendencies. The ecclesiastical criticism can be seen in the barbs SK directs at the Christianities of Mynster, Martensen, and Grundtvig, and the political criticism can be seen in SK's emphasis upon individualism *contra* the group, and in his continuing religious application of such liberal and democratic political catchwords as "universality," "equality," and "unity."

19. *Works of Love*

○

SK's next book was *Works of Love* [Kjerlighedens Gjerninger] [SV IX, pp. 1–365], written between late January and August 1847 and published September 29, 1847. A demanding and in some respects a quite difficult book, it is SK's clearest and starkest formulation of a Christian ethics, a continuation and a companion piece to the ethics he had developed in "Purity of Heart." There are in fact a number of references to "purity of heart" and "willing the Good in truth" which make it clear that SK himself saw *Works of Love* as a sequel to the ethics adumbrated in *Edifying Discourses in Various Spirits*. *Works of Love* is SK's major ethical work and one of the most important works in his entire authorship.

A. THE WORLDLY FORMS OF LOVE VS. CHRISTIAN LOVE

The distinction that underlies the whole of *Works of Love* is that between friendship and "romantic love" [Elskov] on the one hand and "Christian love" [Kjerlighed] on the other.[1] All forms of worldly, poetic, and romantic love can be reduced to self-love, in which one loves the other as "the second I," the alter ego. The other is loved for his or her differences, either for the differences that the other has in relation to oneself or for a shared difference that unites both lover and beloved over against other people. Thus, romantic love searches for "the only one," an other who is defined by his or her differences from all others [p. 53]. Classical civilization, which so abhorred self-love, elevated and venerated admiration and friendship, which were thought to be the opposite of self-love. But, as SK demonstrates, these classical virtues are also forms of devotion to "the second I" and thus are merely hidden forms of self-love [pp. 56–60].

In Christian love, on the other hand, one learns in self-denial to love one's "Neighbor," every person, the first person one sees, "the first Thou" rather than the "second I." Just as predilection is the middle term [Mellembestemmelse] in all worldly love and friendship, so is God or the love of God the middle term in all Christian love [pp. 58–60]. When God, as the third party, is excluded, and love is simply a relation between two, it becomes mere "reciprocity" [p. 117] or "solidarity in self-love" [Sammenhold i Selvkjerlighed], which are simply forms of inclination in which human differences are decisive. To demonstrate that the predilection expressed in classical friendship is merely a form of self-love for the "second I," all one must do is interpose anyone, "a Neighbor," between the two friends, and jealousy and exclusiveness will develop immediately. Thus friendship, like all the forms of worldly love, is ruled by the laws governing predilection, namely "self-centered willfulness" [Selvraadighed] and "arbitrariness" [Vilkaarlighed] and cannot be the expression of anything eternal, for nothing eternal can depend upon arbitrariness. It is therefore clear that not only romantic-poetic love and eroticism but also the classical virtues of love and friendship fall short of the eternal validity required of genuine Christian love.

The basic content of the Christian message is our real kinship with God, and we resemble God, in whom there is no predilection, when we love our "Neighbor." The Neighbor is the key term and the original discovery of Christian love. As opposed to "the only one" of poetry, the Neighbor is "the first person one sees." To see one's Neighbor one must look away from all differences and toward "the equality of eternity" [det Eviges Ligelighed], in which we all stand before God. "Predilection's passionate boundlessness in making exclusions is only to love one single one; self-denial's boundlessness of devotion is not to exclude one single one" [p. 54]. We must, SK says, love "the people we see."

Your Neighbor is not your Neighbor in virtue of any likeness you both share vis-à-vis others who are different from you: "[H]e is your Neighbor in his equality with you before God, but this equality is something which unconditionally every person has, and has it unconditionally" [p. 62].

> *Love of your Neighbor is therefore the eternal equality in loving,* but this eternal equality is the opposite of predilection.... Indeed, equality is precisely not making differences, and eternal equality is, unconditionally not to make the least difference, boundlessly not to make the least difference; predilection, on the other hand, [is] to make differences, passionate predilection, boundlessly to make differences. [p. 60]

The Neighbor is "the pure category of spirit" [den ren Aandsbestemmelse] [p. 69], which one sees with the spiritual eye when one looks away from worldly differences, whereas in worldly love one sees with the fleshly eye, which looks *toward* differences [p. 70]. Here we are again faced with the dualism of spiritual equality versus worldly differences, which, we have seen in earlier works, lies at the heart of SK's ethics. The new departure in *Works of Love* will be the radicality with which SK takes the notion of equality and ethics up into a sphere that is distinctively Christian and that stands in an extraordinarily pain-ful relation to the temporal world with its ordinary ethics and its politics. Thus SK stresses the dualism already inherent in Christianity and, using the meta-phor of St. Paul, calls Christian love "sobriety," whereas worldly love, in all its selfish forms, is "drunkenness," intoxication with the world of appearances [pp. 58–60].

Unlike the immediacy of worldly liaisons, all love of one's Neighbor is mediated through love of God; such love has God as its "middle term." This means that we owe all our love to God, but that he commands us to express this in loving our Neighbor; one loves God by loving one's Neighbor. Thus every relation of Christian love is a three-party affair, and therefore, SK states, "love endures"; that is, such a three-party relationship cannot be terminated by the Neighbor's hostility, because, with the God Who is Love, one always has a two-thirds majority. Only when one ceases oneself to be loving can the relation be broken off. (This reflexive and self-revelatory character of Christian love will be dealt with shortly.) The reactions of one's Neighbor and of "the world" have no real significance or effect; they cannot release one from the obligation to remain loving. And Love is not an obligation or accomplishment for the specially endowed, the extraordinary; the spiritual equality which makes everyone one's Neighbor also makes it clear that absolutely and uncondition-ally everyone can be "the loving person" [den Kjerlige] [p. 340].

B. THE STRICT AND THE MILD "MEASURE-FOR-MEASURE": LAW AND GOSPEL

Now that we have clarified the underlying distinction between worldly, differentiating love and Christian, egalitarian love, let us turn to the two forms of Love's "measure-for-measure" [Lige for Lige], which can be understood as the Law and the Gospel. Immediate, or worldly, love is never certain that it is being reciprocated, knows no rest, has no certainty, lacks eternity within itself. On the other hand, the Love that is commanded, that has become ob-ligation, does not test the other, and never changes; it is eternal. Immediate love is always making comparisons, is always jealous. Love must undergo "the transformation of eternity by becoming duty" [p. 38], because that love which is dependent upon its object can never be independent, since it has "the law of its existence outside itself" [p. 41]. Genuine love, on the other hand, which relates itself to "the eternal," is truly independent, because

> the only thing upon which it is dependent is duty, and duty is the only thing that liberates. Immediate love makes a person free and in the next moment dependent. . . . Duty, on the other hand, makes a person dependent and in the same moment eternally independent. "Only the Law can give freedom.". . .

without the Law freedom absolutely does not exist, and it is the Law that gives freedom. [pp. 41–42]

This is the core of SK's exegesis of the passage he chooses: "Thou *shalt* love." The language is very Kantian and recalls the language about "willing one thing" in "Purity of Heart." SK makes it clear that "the Law" is to be understood in the broadest sense. Only when we realize that SK's dual sense of "the Law" is meant to summon up both its Enlightenment philosophical sense and its traditional New Testament dogmatic sense, can we see what SK means. The law is rational, universal standards of ethical conduct *and* it is the Mosaic Law or "the Law" in the Pauline sense. The ethical standpoint presented in "Purity of Heart" was intended by SK to develop the philosophical language about "the Good" and "willing one thing" in such a way that the reader was led into the religious sphere and a decisive relationship to "the eternal." Yet the religiousness to which "duty" and "the eternal" led one was not the highest and most absolute form of the religious, because, although it taught "the Law" and our obligation to it, it did not also teach that we are ultimately unequal to the Law's demands. We are lost beings, not merely in the sense that we are in ignorance, but in the deeper sense of being willfully self-lost, possessed always by the possibility of evil, of the demonic, within us. In short, we are not merely lost but fallen, and we have need for a religion more absolute, outreaching, and personal than the religion of rational, universal, ethical statements ("the Law") and "the eternal." The Law is in fact the death of the natural self, who thereby learns to know sin. One thus begins in infinite debt to God, becomes nothing before God, but only thus can one receive all from God [p. 101]. We must realize that the religion that speaks to one as one really is—and not as the abstract and rational being one cannot be—must be a religion of grace, in sum, Christianity. The Law is a preparatory stage whose function is to show us that it does not admit of human fulfillment. This is the case both with the New Testament, dogmatic-Pauline understanding of "the Law" and with the more recent development of the lofty and abstract "Law" of ethical universals. In effect and put very simply, SK indicates that what Moses was to St. Paul, Kant can be to us.

SK endorses and explains St. Paul's dictum that "love is the fulfillment of the Law" (Romans 13:10). Because we still live in the world, we must live under the Law, and yet, as Christians, we are no longer bound by it—that is, we realize that we cannot fulfill it and ought not to give up all hope over the fact that we cannot. "Love" is the fulfillment of the Law in two senses: *first*, in the sense that Jesus Christ, the Son of the God who *is* Love, kept the Law perfectly and died out of love for humanity, which can thus share in the merits of Christ, who has shattered the crippling power of the Law once and for all; and *second*, in the sense that we, who are now freed from the fear of the Law, can do "good works" in Love—"works of Love"—out of sheer joy over our release from bondage into grace and will attribute these works of Love, not to any merit of our own in any effort to keep the Law but to the power of the grace of God who is Love, working through us. Both Love and Law involve good works; both have their "measure-for-measure," but they are very different indeed.

Thus the chapter containing SK's exposition of "Thou *shalt* love" was a resumé, a working through of natural, philosophical religion with its rational ethical imperatives. It restates the fundamental position of "Purity of Heart" and stresses duty in relation to "the eternal." This is the highest one can reach without revelation. The next chapter, "Thou shalt love thy *Neighbor*," is where we encounter the specifically Christian love, which is love of one's Neighbor. As we have seen, Christianity goes beyond "the second I" of the generalized rational self (which is the abstract personality that forms the basis of philosophical religion); it discovers the first other, the "first Thou." Rational religion is a noble, but in fact impossible task, for it requires us to relate to others (and ourselves) as perfectible, rational abstractions of our best selves, whereas the Christian ethics of *Works of Love* accepts the other, as well as the self, with all the shortcomings and ineradicable sinfulness that they really have. These two chapters of *Works of Love* thus relate to one another, in miniature, in the same way that "Purity of Heart" as a whole relates to *Works of Love* as a whole; or as "religiousness A" relates to "religiousness B"; or as philosophical religion relates to revealed religion; or, most significantly, as Law relates to Gospel.

Love and Law speak the same language, as they must, because as we have already noted, the Christian still lives in the ordinary world of appearances. But what they speak is understood differently. The Christian understands figuratively and according to the spirit, but he who is still the thrall of the Law hears with the fleshly intellectual [sandselig-sjelelig] ear. He who has ears to hear, can hear [pp. 201–202].

The best way to understand how Love differs from the Law is not to examine external actions but to look at the "measure-for-measure" that Love and the Law contain internally. Stated most simply, Christianity has merely turned the external "measure-for-measure" of the Mosaic Law into an inward relationship to God.

> Christianity directs attention entirely away from the external [det Udvortes], turns it inward, makes every one of your relationships to other people into a God-relationship. . . . Christianly understood, a person has . . . only to do with God, even though he must remain in the world. . . . [p. 357]

God forgives us as we forgive others; the act of finding the splinter in another's eye is itself the beam in our own eye before God.

> Christianly understood, you have absolutely nothing to do with what the others do to you. . . . You have only to do with what you do to others, or with how

you take what others do to you. The direction is inward: Before God, you essentially have only to do with yourself. [p. 363]

"God himself is really this pure measure-for-measure, the pure repetition of how you *yourself* are" [ibid.].

Thus one has the choice of being either strict or mild, of applying the strict measure-for-measure of the Law to one's expectations of one's Neighbor or of living in grace and loving him or her unconditionally. Whichever one chooses, one receives the same from God. One can apply the Law and reap God's judgment according to the Law; this is the measure-for-measure of strictness. Or one can exercise Love, which shows that one accepts the grace of God in infinite indebtedness to him (and through him to one's Neighbor), and receive grace; this is the measure-for-measure of mildness. "[E]verything that you say and do to other people is merely repeated by God; He repeats it with the amplification of infinity" [p. 364]. In the face of this, one who accepts grace must have

> an unforgettable fear and trembling, even though he reposes in God's Love. Such a person will certainly avoid talking to God about the injustice of others toward himself, about the splinter in his brother's eye; because such a person will preferably talk to God only of grace, so that the fateful word "Right" [Ret, which also means "Law"] will not forfeit him everything, in accordance with the strict measure-for-measure that he himself has summoned up. [p. 365]

If we are forgiving, we rest in the mild measure-for-measure of grace. If we are accusing, we rest in the strict measure-for-measure of judgment. We are free to choose. Grace is to be chosen, yet not frivolously, always with "fear and trembling," remembering that the Law stands behind. The Law gives meaning and seriousness to grace. If we refuse grace, we stand condemned under the Law.

Though the position is quite simple, one does not come lightly to grace. It was this failure to take grace seriously that particularly appalled SK in his assessment of official Protestantism in Golden Age Denmark, and therefore, in demanding *works* of love, he can seem to come close to rejecting the Lutheran solafideist position with its emphasis upon grace. SK felt that the Lutheran position had been abused by a lazy tendency toward "cheap grace," which had not learned the lesson of the Law and which no longer accepted grace in "fear and trembling." The whole of *Works of Love* runs in this revisionistic direction.[2] Yet, as we have seen, "works of love" were understood by SK to be wholly without merit and were to be performed in acceptance of infinite indebtedness in grace, so the position here taken, although shifting the emphasis of Luther's position, is certainly well within the Pauline and Lutheran tradition. (We will later deal in more detail with the complaints voiced about contemporary Christendom in *Works of Love*.)

We have seen that the strict measure-for-measure of the Law is concentrated in "the fateful word 'Right.' " This strict measure-for-measure of the Law, in a Kantian or purely rational ethics of philosophical religion, places an insupportable burden upon people—upon one's fellow beings and upon oneself. In the mild measure-for-measure we acknowledge our indebtedness, accept grace and God's love, and love others without calculation of Right or considerations of justice. In ordinary predilection or romantic love, we love others for their differences. In the strict measure-for-measure of the Law, we love others for their impossible, abstract uniformity in (unattainable) conformity with the rational moral law. In the mild measure-for-measure of grace, we love others for their equality, with all their real and visible sins and weaknesses, because we forgive them and, seeing with the eye of faith, we cannot see their shortcomings. We "love the people we see."

The Christian lives as though bound by the Law—thus he or she appears to others—but knows he or she is liberated in grace. The Christian must, as we have noted, still speak human language, which is the medium of human reason, of ethical universals, of "the Law," but he or she means and hears something other than what the non-Christian means and hears. The Christian is bound to use speech—a metaphor for remaining within the world of human life, understanding, and action—but, because he or she means something different by it, the Christian is also outside the universals of human life and beyond comprehensibility. Thus, the Christian must suffer, and he or she suffers the special Christian self-denial in which his or her suffering is incomprehensible and absurd to others, who constantly misinterpret it. (We will later deal with these special problems of self-denial, exclusion from the universal, and incomprehensibility.)

Works of Love is divided by SK into two books or "sequences" [Følger] of discourses. The first book posits the notions of the Neighbor and of the Law's demand, and we are compelled to confront the radical absoluteness of Christian ethics and our inability to live accordingly. We are led to the threshold of grace. The second book deals with one who has been granted the grace of God and who is active as "the loving person" [den Kjerlige].[3] The two halves of *Works of Love* thus relate to one another as "theory" (the Law) and "practice" (the Gospel). The spark that connects them—and that carries one from the helplessness of legal obligation to the "sheer activity" of loving—is grace.

The division between Law and Gospel divides the two halves of *Works of Love* from one another thematically but not absolutely. That is, the two halves of the book, like Law and Gospel in general, are not at odds with one another; rather, the second half, the Gospel, presupposes that one has been through the crushing experience of the Law, which, taken alone, is a dead end. This division between Law and Gospel runs through the whole of SK's authorship like a fault line, separating, as has been noted, "Purity of Heart" from *Works of Love* as a whole. It is the division between the highest that humanity can achieve—which is to *posit* (but not to fulfill) the demand for rationality, Right [Ret], justice [Retfærdighed], and equality [Lighed]—*and* that which God can offer (and we can attain) namely, mercy [Barmhjertighed], Love, and "blessed equality" [salige Ligelighed].

The difference between justice and Love is the difference between human reason and divine paradox, or (to use again the language of Johannes Climacus) between religiousness A and B. The former is the world of rational demands for justice, whereas the latter is the world of those who realize that their "guilt" [Skyld], their inability to meet the demands of justice that the Law imposes, is actually "sin" [Synd], whose radical evil places it beyond human ability to eradicate it.[4] One who sees oneself as a sinner thus sees oneself related not merely as a rational being to "the eternal" but as a sinner to a gracious God, who alone can transcend the human categories of reciprocity and redeem the promises of justice, right, and equality—categories which ethics and natural religion can posit but on which they cannot deliver. The political implication of this is that any "real" politics must have the humility to acknowledge that these goals—justice, right, and equality—which had been political battle slogans ever since the Enlightenment, cannot ultimately be fulfilled in the merely human sphere, and any human attempt to do so leads to the "demonic." These political slogans have a lofty sound precisely because they have been borrowed from the language of the Law. Therefore, because the Law is only to be "fulfilled" (in the Pauline sense) in the Love which we have through grace in our individual relation to God, we must come to the realization that we ought not dare to set such transcendental and utopian projects for politics. The proper sphere of politics is much more modest indeed, namely the making, by the human community, of such arrangements for its material well-being as seem prudent.[5] To promise to deliver more is to spawn monsters that attempt to cut the individual off from his ground of being in God. I maintain that this is, in brief, the view of politics at which SK arrived in *Works of Love*, and the remainder of the present chapter will develop this interpretation.

C. THE SELF-REVELATORY CHARACTER OF LOVE

Perhaps the most important characteristic of Love, as it is exercised by "the loving person" described in the discourses which constitute the second half of *Works of Love*, is its *self-revelatory* or reflexive character. The Lover, in having to do with others, has essentially to do with him- or herself and learns thereby who he or she is. In the discourse "Love Endures" [pp. 286–99], we deal with the three-way nature of the love relationship, which we have already discussed. A love relationship depends, not upon the Neighbor's hostility or receptivity, but upon oneself (and God), and can only be terminated if one stops loving.

In the discourse "Love Believes All—and Yet is Never Deceived" [pp. 216–34], the self-revelatory quality of love is even clearer. The "loving person" *believes* [or trusts, or has faith in; Danish = "tror"] his Neighbor, and in so doing chooses who he himself is. Knowledge, based as it is upon the way things appear, is in itself neutral. It does not compel us to a position of either belief or mistrust in our Neighbor. When one chooses, in the manner of "worldly shrewdness," to act upon the basis of the possibility of the Bad in one's Neighbor, this choice passes itself off as "scientific" and as compelled by the state of appearances. Yet the information from the world of appearances upon which we base our knowledge is never finally collected and interpreted. The world of external appearances can never justify a final judgment about the internal reality of one's Neighbor. To pass off suspiciousness and mistrust as grounded in knowledge is an abuse of knowledge. "One does not *believe* by virtue of *knowledge*. . . . The secret and the falsity lie in the fact that it [mistrustfulness] now simply converts this *knowledge* into *belief* [in the possibility of the Bad] . . ." [p. 218, emphasis added]. Mistrustfulness deceives itself in claiming that it concludes something (namely, to be suspicious) on the basis of knowledge, for knowledge is neutral and ultimately cannot compel any conclusion. One could just as easily and with just as much (or as little) justification conclude the opposite, namely to be trusting, and this is precisely the choice made by "the loving person." Yet in choosing to "believe all," one is aware that one is *choosing*, i.e., that one is determining one's life-posture on the basis of something that is not simply the automatic consequence of knowledge. Mistrustfulness points out, quite correctly, that deception is always possible, that every reality can be perfectly mimicked in its appearances by deception. But when mistrustfulness comes to a conclusion on the basis of the possibility of deception, it is itself already deceived, first, in that no choice ever follows "naturally" out of knowledge and more profoundly in that it has thereby deceived itself out of Love. Mistrustfulness errs in forgetting that this is a life question, that it concerns oneself in making such a judgment.

Knowledge is indeed neutral: "Knowledge does not contaminate a person. It is mistrustfulness that contaminates a person, just as Love purifies one" [p. 223]. When you choose, on the basis of neutral knowledge, between whether *you* will be suspicious or trusting, when you choose between "the opposite possibilities poised in equilibrium . . . you *choose*, in judging, that that which dwells in you might become apparent. . . . In every instant you live, existence judges you, because to live is to judge oneself, to become apparent" [p. 218]. Therefore, one reveals, in one's posture toward others, whether one contains suspicion or Love. As for the relation between faith and knowledge, SK states that "in knowledge there is no decision [Afgørelse]. The decision, the determination and definiteness of the personality, exist first in *ergo*, in faith" [p. 221].

Of course, SK continues, it is possible to confuse categories and to claim to communicate decision in knowledge or vice versa, and "in these times" this dangerous nonsense has become "profound thought." This seems clearly a jibe at speculative idealism, in particular Hegelianism, which passed for "profound thought" in Denmark in the 1840's and which, in SK's view, made precisely this claim of being able to go from intellection to volition. Thus, a conservative Hegelian theologian like Martensen is tarred with the same brush that we have seen used on liberal politicians; both claim to be able to proceed from reason to something that is determinative for the individual. Both commit unconscionable confusions of categories, in SK's opinion. The neutrality of knowledge *per se* is paralleled by the neutrality of the sphere of politics *per se*, and it is just as wrong to invoke "the name of knowledge" when one chooses to be mistrustful as it is to invoke the lofty principles of the Law or "the name of Christianity" in opting for one or another political alternative. (This latter position, which is particularly important to the present work, will be developed at the conclusion of this chapter.)

Finally, though it "believes all," Love "is never deceived." One can of course be deceived many times in the ordinary sense, but one can never really be deceived—i.e., fall out of love, out of the God-relation—in the higher sense, unless one ceases to love, ceases to "believe all." The only real deception is *self*-deception. To stop loving is to be deceived. All other dangers to body and soul are only illusory, as the apparent motion of the sun [p. 226].

In its emphasis upon the reflexive and self-revelatory nature of Love, the discourse "Love *Hopes* All—But is Never Disappointed" [pp. 235–51] is a close parallel to "Love *Believes* All." In the apparently outward motion of "hoping all" for the best with respect to one's Neighbor, one must choose, thus breaking the neutral equilibrium of possibilities that reason suspends before us. There is no compelling rational ground for the choice, but, as in "believing all," "hoping all" reveals something about oneself, when one positions oneself in relation to others. The "loving person" lovingly hopes all and gives his Neighbor the benefit of the doubt. To give up hope for another is to be hopeless about oneself, as one cannot hope for oneself without being loving and hopeful for others.

In the discourse "The Work of Love in Remembering One Who is Dead" [pp. 327–39], SK demonstrates with wry simplicity how Love is entirely dependent upon "the loving person" rather than upon Love's object. When one lovingly remembers one who is dead, it is clear that Love must fulfill the requirements of unselfishness, freedom, and faithfulness, regardless of the response of the other person, who is in this case an unchangeable object, who cannot help or reward Love in any way, and "who is no real object; he is simply an occasion who always reveals what dwells within the living" [p. 329]. "In relation to a dead person you have a yardstick against which you can test yourself . . ." [p. 339].

Finally, the reflexive and self-revelatory nature of Love is especially clear in the discourse "Love Builds Up" [pp. 201–15]. By "Love builds up" SK means that in "building up" (the phrase is St. Paul's—I Cor. 8:1) Love in another, one must assume the presence of the ground of Love in that person from the start and then build upon it by putting the best interpretation upon one's Neighbor's actions and intentions. (A further reason that "the loving person" must assume the presence of Love's ground in the Neighbor is that the alternative would be to give one person the power to lay down—or destroy—the possibility of Love in another, and this is a power that no person can or ought to have over another.) "The loving person" begins by assuming Love's "ground" or fundament to be present in the Neighbor,[6] and proceeds by loving forth Love maieutically in the other; then, with loving humility and self-denial, "the loving person" disappears in the final result. One "builds up" Love in one's Neighbor by building up oneself, and one must be gracious enough not to take the credit for the accomplishment—one must remember Love's self-denial, which is characterized by necessary incognito and by maieutic modesty. We will now examine these incognito and maieutic features in more detail, as they are intermediate links in understanding the necessity of Love's conflict with the world and the consequently sorry state of "Christendom"; these latter factors, in turn, form the foundations of SK's view of politics and of the proper boundaries between the personal-religious and the social-political spheres.

D. THE FORMS OF LOVE'S SELF-DENIAL: THE INCOGNITO AND THE MAIEUTIC

The life of Love, like all lives, is hidden, and we can talk only of its fruits— "the works of Love." But even these are not to be known outwardly by any sure sign. Love must live its life incognito. Not every obvious "deed of charity" [Kjerlighedsgjerning] is a "work of Love" [Kjerlighedens Gjerning], and vice versa. This is because Love is not any particular thing but a *how* [*hvorledes*] something is done [p. 17]. SK reminds us, however, that although the Gospel commands us to bear fruits and says that trees will be known by their fruits, it does not tell us that it is *our* task to know which trees are which [pp. 18–19]. The only thing one knows for certain is one's own conscience [Samvittighed], and one knows it only with God, who knows all. We, who originally "knew with" [vidste sammen] God what was true and what was not, receive the world anew—restored by Christianity—so that now we again come to live transparently in the God-relation, in conscience. "The relation between the individual and God, the God-relation, is conscience" [p. 137]. However, the world is fallen, just as are our sinful, natural selves, and we must remember that the relation of conscience will be invisible to the world and will be misinterpreted by it. Hence, the necessary incognito of Love, which will last as long as the world is the world and not the perfection of eternity.

Therefore, SK asserts, Christianity maintains a strict separation between the outward [Udvortes] and the inward [Indvortes]. Christianity has learned to eschew "childish" attempts to express the inward outwardly (as in the cloister movement of the Middle Ages), but nowadays, when people should know better, "worldly Christendom" is still constantly pressing to confuse Christianity's categories of the internal and the external [p. 140]. This sally of SK's against the dangerous confusions of "worldly Christendom" is quite pointed and seems to refer to his pet clerical enemies, Martensen and the Hegelians on the one hand and Grundtvig and his followers on the other. The Hegelian principle with respect to the inward and the outward was in fact ridiculed in the very first lines of SK's first major book, *Either/Or*: "It has perhaps sometimes occurred to you, dear reader, to doubt a bit concerning the correctness of the well-known philosophical principle, that the outward is the inward, the inward the outward."[7] The Grundtvigians' campaign regarding the importance and sanctity of precise liturgical language and their exaggerated exactitude concerning the rituals of baptism and communion also made them clear targets for SK's criticism regarding the confusion of the inward and the outward.

For SK, the incognito of Love must be maintained—despite the fact that this leads to misunderstanding, incomprehensibility, and opposition in the world—or all would be lost for Christianity. In fact, if all could be seen outwardly in a fixed relation to the inward, Christianity would no longer be possible, SK asserts. The infinite difference between one individual and another, so that two people who are to all appearances identical can in fact be opposites, is the human race's *differentia specifica*, and it is what makes humanity great and the God-relation possible. Without this infinite variety, unpredictability, and freedom,

> the God-relation would essentially not exist, not in its deepest sense. If one could judge every person unconditionally correctly according to a general, given yardstick, the God-relation would be essentially abolished. Everything would be turned outward, consummating itself heathen-style in civic or social life, and living would become all too easy, but also terribly empty. [pp. 220–21]

Without the hiddenness and unpredictability that allows the individual personality to house itself in the inviolable privacy of conscience, of the God-relation, no Christianity—and for SK, no serious life—is possible. In such an all-public situation, everything would become politics "heathen-style." This possibility is an important negative determinant of SK's own politics.

A further sign of the self-denial or self-effacement that characterizes Love is to be seen in the maieutic properties of Love. The word "maieutic" is from the Greek adjective "μαιευτικoϛ" ["pertaining to midwifery"] and is most commonly associated with Socrates, who referred to himself as a midwife in the development of others, a catalyst, who withdrew and disappeared in the final result. SK, who often enjoyed comparing his role to that of Socrates, uses this word (which is even more unusual in Danish than it is in English) in an allied sense, denoting the unselfish catalytic role which "the loving person" takes on in relation to the Neighbor. In the discourse "Love Builds Up" [pp.

201–15], which has already been mentioned, we have seen how the Lover disappears maieutically in loving forth Love from another. A similar note is struck in the discourse "Love Seeks Not Its Own" [pp. 252–66], where "the loving person" is seen as seeking, self-denyingly, to disappear in the deed of helping others to stand on their own in their own Love or God-relation. The Lover vanishes, unselfishly, as a tool, a co-worker with God, "so that all the loving person's help infinitely disappears in the God-relation" [p. 264]. The Lover disappears quite in the manner of Socrates, yet without the ironic smile of Socrates, who protested that he had done nothing for his pupil yet secretly knew that he had. "The loving person" has no such smugness, and his or her maieutic self-effacement is genuine, for the "loving person" constantly bears in mind the fact that he or she rests in grace "with fear and trembling" and that any works of Love he or she might be able to perform are not to be reckoned to individual merit but to the spirit of the God who is Love working through him or her.

A final and most poignant example of maieutic self-denial is to be found in the final discourse, "The Work of Love in Praising Love" [pp. 340–54], in which SK discusses his own activity. If one is to be "a loving person," SK writes, one must not make any claim upon the momentary; one must agree to be scorned by the present, not taken seriously, made fun of. One must become nothing, a tool, for God, to help lead others to Love and thus a selfless servant to one's fellows. One must not, however, expect or desire to be understood as such and must disappear from the process maieutically, even while in the midst of the mockery that sees one as the opposite of what one is. Real Christian Love will not be recognized by the world as such. Alluding to himself as the author of *Works of Love* in which this very discourse is contained, SK writes that the person who praises Love, for example, *could* be vain and selfish, or *could* be performing a work of Love [p. 354]. So saying, SK himself disappears maieutically before the reader's eyes, and leaves one confronted with the problem of the book, which has nothing to do with whether or not *another person* (even the author of *Works of Love*) acts out of Love, but with whether one is *oneself*, at every moment, loving. SK's "real" intentions in writing *Works of Love* will never be fathomable, but as a demonstration of a self-disciplined act of maieutic disappearance it is unsurpassed. We must now pass over from the discussion of the particular forms of Love's self-denial to SK's explanation of the inescapability of opposition in the world and to the related question of the sorry state of "Christendom."

E. THE INESCAPABILITY OF OPPOSITION IN THE WORLD, AND THE CONDITION OF CHRISTENDOM

A work of Love must entail giving up all hope of dessert or reward, or it becomes a work of the Law, from which, as we have seen, it cannot be externally distinguished. For "the loving person" who truly gives himself or herself to his or her Neighbor, self-denial and letting go of the world and its esteem must be total or not at all. SK turns up the tension between the world and Christianity to the highest degree and shows that friendship, ordinary love, and worldly esteem are often the rewards of those who forget the God-relation, and are denied to those who remember it [pp. 122–25]. The "loving person" must always be prepared to see all forms of worldly love as forms of self-love, to do without them ("hate" them), to be branded as mad or self-loving in turn. The "loving person" must never forget that no love on earth between one person and another can ever be completely happy, as it will always hold the danger that the two-way relationship of worldly love will come to outweigh the three-way relationship of Love [pp. 124–25]. God can require us, like Abraham, to sacrifice all human relationships at any moment.

Human love is noble in its way, and SK does not mean to denigrate it, rare as it is. However, try as it might, it can never quite forsake the world but insists upon being loved in return, upon being understood: In human love "one wants to forsake everything, but one does not, however, intend thereby to be abandoned by language and human understanding" [p. 126]. Thus, as we have seen earlier, Christian Love runs the risk of incomprehensibility, of being regarded as madness and perversity. Placing itself outside the circle of human language is a symbolic expression of Love's willingness to abandon, if necessary, participation in the rational, ethical universals upon which social and political life is based.

One is ultimately driven back to the phrase, terrible as it sounds, that "Love of God is hatred of the world" [p. 351], though this statement must not be understood as perverse misanthropy but as an expression of priorities, bearing in mind the special senses of "the world" and of "God"—who requires all our Love, but demands that we make delivery to our Neighbor. The cruelest possibility which "the loving person" must face is that preaching self-denial will be seen by the world as self-love, for "the world" reverses values. So "hatred" of the world remains a possibility that "the loving person" must choose if forced, and "the world" is such that, sooner or later, this opposition will be his lot. The "loving person" is confronted with what SK calls the "double danger," first, of risking or giving up an advantage in order to help another, and second, the danger of being misunderstood, mocked, and perhaps persecuted for having taken the first risk. SK proposes the telling example of a rich person who abandons all propriety ["den gode Tone"] [p. 76] and breaks with the conspiracy of snobbery of his own class against the poor, trying to relate to the poor in Love. In addition to whatever wealth and advantage he loses, such a person will suffer misunderstanding and abandonment by his own class and will be clasped by the poor to its bosom, again in misunderstanding, and be expected to lead a revolt. He thus ends up scorned and rejected by both classes [pp. 75–76]. (Although he also gives a perfunctory example of the reverse situation—a person of the lower class who breaks ranks and relates to the wealthy in Love [pp. 80–81]—the verve and vividness in SK's language in the first example seem to point very clearly to the fact that SK understood this example autobiographically. He felt abandoned by his own "dannede" class, misunderstood by the lower classes, and the laughingstock of all.)

Christian Love is bound to be a dangerous and thankless business in this world. In a clear reference to "Purity of Heart"—and to the ethical argument begun there, which is led to its conclusion in *Works of Love*—SK points out that if one is "the person who, in order truly to will One Thing, chose to will the Good in truth," there is solace to be found in the fact that one suffers only once, but wins eternally [p. 88]. Collision with the world is inescapable because it is simply the case that, although the world and Christianity both claim to honor "love" and to disdain "self-love," they mean extremely different things by these terms. That which the world calls love in solidarity [Sammenhold] is seen by Christianity as an extended form of self-love in which the community replaces God in his rightful supremacy. Real Love requires sacrifice, but the sacrifice that the world praises in "civic love" is rewarded by social praise and is thus not sacrifice in the Christian sense, which receives no compensation and is rejected as madness. Love that genuinely sacrifices in the Stoic, but not yet Christian, sense is seen by the world as madness, and Christian Love is seen by the world as disgusting and is persecuted [pp. 115–16]. Any apparent agreement posited between the Christian and worldly forms of love is false and superficial.

The inescapability of suffering for "the loving person" can be seen in the deplorable state of official Christianity itself, which has been co-opted and has joined forces with the world of appearances instead of witnessing to the world's inadequacy, or at least to its own inadequacy. The surest sign that the Christian must face opposition in the world can be seen in the dismaying hybrid phenomenon that is both worldly and Christian, namely Christendom. Christianity has always made claims of being something higher than the world, and, SK writes, it is indeed "something higher," but not in such a way that it stands related to the world via a comfortable transition, as for example in all the loose theological and philosophical intellectualizing about "higher, highest, most high" [høiere, høieste, allerhøieste] [p. 61]. Rather, Christianity is "something higher" in an absolute way, which radically sunders itself from the world and unavoidably gives offense.[8] "The way to Christianity goes through offense" [ibid.]. The most frightful thing of all is to have a sort of indifferent fellowship with the Highest, to convert its gift to the individual into a gift to the race [Slægt], in which the individual is merely a participant; the God-relation is defined precisely by its claim upon and fulfillment of the individual human personality. "[A]nd this is precisely the greatest thing. You can have it in common with all" [p. 31]. In rejecting the intellectualizing which wishes to mediate between the world and Christianity, SK is clearly once again attacking the speculative theology of Martensen, *et al.* And in stressing the frightfulness of making the God-relation a collective transaction, SK seems to be aiming at the congregational-liturgical theology of Grundtvig and his followers.

In pursuing the theme of the inescapability of suffering in the world and the wretched condition of official Christianity in this respect, SK remarks that it is sad to hear sermons in Christendom in which the speaker fails to stress or is afraid to stress that "the Good is rewarded with hate, disdain, persecution" [p. 183]. These difficulties are absolutely certain, and if they come upon the ill-prepared youth unexpectedly, the youth may think it a unique fault or believe that something highly unusual has happened and leave the faith. Many a well-spoken sermonizer, SK continues, has been afraid of stressing that the way of Christian Love is also the way of worldly persecution, out of fear of scaring his listeners—or perhaps himself—away. Here SK is picking up the same criticism of the shallowly optimistic and popular preachers of official Christianity which we have seen in portions of the *Edifying Discourses in Various Spirits*, particularly in the "Gospel of Sufferings," criticism which seemed specifically directed at Bishop Mynster. It is true that many good and moral actions will not bring persecution, but perhaps honor. Still, specifically Christian Love consists precisely in selflessness and in willingness to be rejected by universal, rational human norms, and it is in its silence about this that the official Church betrays its call. We must remember, SK continues, that the warning against the world's resistance to Christian Love is not merely good counsel to be used in the accidental case when difficulty arises. On the contrary, worldly persecution is related to Christianity not by chance, but essentially. "[C]hristianly understood, the opposition of the world stands in an *essential* relation to the inwardness of the Christian" [p. 184].

Christian Love, with its self-denial, thus involves the "double danger," in that one must: (1) give up all selfish desires and serve the Good (this can also be accomplished by ordinary human self-denial), and (2) give up hope of praise and acceptance by the human community and abandon oneself to God [pp. 185–87]. Human self-denial ventures forth into a single peril that is called "danger," and is honored by the world, whereas Christian self-denial ventures into what is called "foolishness" and is found laughable by the world. If the world were so good that Christian self-denial were impossible, it would have reached the perfection of Eternity, and Christianity, which has to do with witnessing to the perfection of the eternal within the imperfection of time, would be rendered impossible.

We should thus also be on guard against flattering talk about Christianity, because Christianity is like an enormously sharp and dangerous instrument, and we must not deceive ourselves into thinking that it is a flower, even the rarest of flowers, which we hold in our hands. No, SK concludes (referring to a favorite passage, I Cor. 1:23), divinely understood, Christianity is the highest Good, but humanly understood it is the most dangerous thing, not a rare flower but "... offense and foolishness, now as in the beginning and as long as the world exists" [pp. 188–89].

Thus, in these times, it may be necessary in Christian sermons to preach against Christianity, "because we know full well where the distress of these times rubs: that with foolish and flattering Sunday talk they have deceived Christianity into a sensory illusion, and us people into the imagination that we thus are Christians" [p. 188]. Originally, when Christianity came into the world, its offense was plain to all, and it proclaimed it itself. "But now, now that the world has become Christian, now Christianity must watch out for offense for all it is worth" [p. 189]. When Christianity first came into the world it was clear to all that it was at odds with human reason, but now that it

> has married itself to human reason, now that Christianity and reason have become on familiar terms, now Christianity must watch out for the stumbling block for all it is worth. . . . Only the possibility of offense (antidote against the sleeping potion of apologetics) is capable of waking him who has been put to sleep, capable of calling the bewitched person back again, so that Christianity is itself again.
>
> If the Holy Scripture says "Woe to him by whom offense comes" (Matthew 18:7), we take comfort in saying woe to him who first thought of preaching Christianity without the possibility of offense. Woe to him who flatteringly, triflingly, commendingly, convincingly foisted off some unmanly something which was supposed to be Christianity! Woe to him who could make the miracle comprehensible, or who at any rate opens for us the bright prospect that this will soon be possible! . . . Woe to him who could conceive of the possibility of atonement without taking some notice of the possibility of offense . . . . O sadly wasted learning and acumen, o sadly wasted time on this enormous task of defending Christianity! [p. 190]

This is because, as SK continues, Christianity needs no defense and becomes more shrunken and distorted the better the defense! Rather, it is *we* who should defend ourselves and our choice when Christianity frightfully forces us to choose between Christianity and offense.

> Therefore, take away the possibility of offense from Christianity, or take away the struggle of the anguished conscience from the forgiveness of sins (to which, however, according to Luther's excellent explanation, the whole of that doctrine leads), and you had best close the churches the sooner the better, or turn them into places of amusement which are open around the clock. [p. 191]

SK's strong attack upon "apologists" who "make the miracle comprehensible" is directly tailored for Martensen, just as his attack upon soothing sermons seems unmistakably aimed at Mynster, both of them the twin paladins of the official clerical establishment. These modern "Christians" are seen by SK as abusing the Lutheran doctrines, and are dispensing cheap grace, forgetting that if one leaves out the possibility of offense or "takes away the struggle of the anguished conscience from the forgiveness of sins," all is lost. Thus, in a time when *grace* is taken vainly, SK speaks of the *works* of Love, yet without abandoning the Lutheran doctrine that insists that these "works" have nothing to do with externality or merit but are signs of the seriousness ("fear and trembling") with which one accepts the gifts of grace. With this explanation of how SK believed he could emphasize works and still remain within the pale of Lutheran orthodoxy, we will end our discussion of SK's indictment of "Christendom" and his notion of the unavoidability of opposition in the world. Next, based upon what we have learned thus far of *Works of Love*, we will conclude our discussion of the book by directing our attention to the problem of priorities and distinctions—of the boundaries between religion and politics, Gospel and Law.

F. PRIORITIES, DISTINCTIONS, BOUNDARIES: RELIGION AND POLITICS, GOSPEL AND LAW

The most general, basic rule SK lays down for ordering the religious-private and the political-social spheres in their proper relation is that one must relate infinitely only to the eternal. One must not relate oneself infinitely to anything finite, as this is despair [Fortvivlelse]. Despair is that state of spiritual unhealth in which one lacks the eternal component of the composite that is the human personality [pp. 43–44].[9] But, precisely because the personality *is* a composite, it contains both an eternal and a temporal component. Although in the properly ordered individual the eternal element certainly must occupy the higher place, the temporal element also has its rightful domain, and SK's prescription is far from being an unrealistic or inhuman puritanism.

Christian love does not banish worldly love and friendship; it "dethrones" them [p. 47]. The command to love one's Neighbor, SK asserts, does not begin with an order to cease loving those for whom one has a predilection but rather to understand the priorities within which one relates oneself to them [pp. 63–64]. Christianity, in SK's view, does not forbid ordinary love or even advocate that one diminish the exercise of one's passions, but it insists only that one love in such a way that the loss of the loved one would not reveal that one has been in despair all along, namely by having been related infinitely to something finite. There is no enmity in Christianity between spirit and flesh, SK insists, and Christianity does not reject sensuality *per se* any more than it rejects trees, stones, etc. SK cites St. Paul's "it is better to marry than to burn" [I. Cor. 7:9] and concludes that Christianity only rejects the flesh insofar as the flesh is understood selfishly.[10]

SK's specific understanding of the task of politics in *Works of Love* is to be sought within these general priorities. First of all, SK stresses, Christianity, with its concern for the absolute equality of every individual before God, does not concern itself with ordinary and ineradicable, relative differences [pp. 70–71]. We must guard against "those false prophets of worldliness in Christianity's name" who claim that, because the rich have offended with respect to differences, the poor are thereby justified in doing absolutely anything in order to obtain worldly equality [p. 72]. On the contrary, "Christianity will not abolish differences, neither those of the exalted nor those of the lowly, but on the other hand, there is no temporal difference, not even that which is the most reasonable and acceptable in the eyes of the world, to which Christianity will cling partisanly" [ibid.]. With respect to the abolition of worldly differences, SK continues, "for one thing, it is impossible, and for another, the equality [Lighed] of all in sharing the same temporal difference is, however, in no way Christian equality [Ligelighed]; worldly equality [Lighed], if it were possible, is not Christian equality [Ligelighed]" [p. 73]. Here, again, we have the same contrast between two forms of equality—"Lighed" and "Ligelighed"—which we saw in "Purity of Heart" as the world's "measure-for-measure" [Lige for Lige] versus Christianity's "blessed equality" [salige Ligelighed].

In understanding these passages it is of crucial importance that the reader note that—with the exception of SK's own personal judgment that, as a practical matter, worldly equality is unattainable—SK's stance is completely open and "agnostic" on the question of politics *per se*, be they conservative, egalitarian, etc. The political implications of SK's stance here are neither egalitarian nor inegalitarian, and here as elsewhere, it can be seen that the traditional arch-conservative version of his politics is an interpretive fiction.

What SK does say is that Christianity will not abolish differences; that it is unjustifiable for "false prophets of worldliness" to excite the social ambitions of the poor "*in Christianity's name*"; that Christian equality is not the same as worldly equality. But all that these remarks establish is that Christianity's concerns must not be confused with political concerns. SK is concerned with boundaries and distinctions, but the content of politics itself is a matter of complete freedom, so long as there is respect for the priority of the "eternal" over the "temporal"—the inviolability of the individual in his or her right to rest securely in the God-relation, to ground the self transparently in it, and to seek transcendence only there. Far from prescribing any content for politics, SK stresses that Christianity will not "cling partisanly" to any "temporal difference," i.e., any social or political position.

Christianity is thus the only representative of "the universally human" [det Almene-Menneskelige], whereas every group formation within society represents something less, namely mere "solidarity" [Sammenhold] which, precisely because it lacks unconditional universality, cannot participate in "the Good" [pp. 73–74]. And although, in their proper place, formations of social solidarity are in order, there is always the danger that the members of one or another such group, class, party, or point of view will conceive of themselves and their political notions as coterminous with "humanity": "[T]hat which is inhuman and un-Christian consists . . . in wishing to deny one's kinship to all people, to every person unconditionally" [p. 75].

As has been noted earlier in conjunction with the examination of *A Literary Review*, however much SK might have protested that his specifically personal opinions on the issues of the day were generally not those of the "liberals," his notion of politics, while in itself neutral and "agnostic," is a variation on classical liberalism. And, like John Stuart Mill (another and contemporaneous thinker who was willy-nilly related to liberalism), SK was forced to confront the problem that created so much trouble for second-generation liberalism, namely the problem of finding, amid the welter of conflicting interests that were supposed to order themselves in accordance with the "invisible hand," a steady and unwavering locus of the truly human interest, which stood above the fray and was itself *dis*interested in all the lesser battles. For the troubled Mill, this spiritual anchor for society was to be a particular group of individuals, the intellectual "clerisy," the rightful successor to the mediaeval clergy which, in theory, had in its day represented the common, non-material interests of society. For SK, however, the haven in the liberal wilderness of competing interests was the inviolability and priority of the God-relation in every individual. Everyone was a member of a universal clerisy; every individual was the representative of "the universally human."

There is a very revealing aside in the discourse "Love Hides a Multitude of Sins" [pp. 267–85], in which SK off-handedly shows how the boundary is to be drawn between the realms of religion and politics or, within the self, between the "loving person" and the citizen. The topic of the discourse, that Love hides a multitude of sins, leads SK into a discussion of how, by giving an "extenuating explanation" [formildende Forklaring] of his Neighbor's behavior, the "loving person" chooses between the opposed possibilities of interpretation and always puts the best construction upon appearances, regardless of how unlikely this appears to the eye of worldly shrewdness. (The argument is thus quite similar to those we have touched upon in the discourses "Love Believes All" and "Love Hopes All.") SK writes,

> Let the judges appointed by the government, let the servants of righteousness [Retfærdighed], labor to discover guilt or crime. We others are indeed neither called to be judges nor to be servants of righteousness, but are, on the contrary, called by God to Love—thus, called, with the help of an extenuating explanation, to hide the multitude of sins. [p. 279]

Only insofar as we are citizens and servants of the state and participants in public life are we called to evenhandedness, to justice in all its sternness, to accurate, rational, human judgment within the ethical universals of society. But prior to and superior to one's call to serve in this capacity—and here it is a matter of indifference whether one is a citizen of a democracy where all are so called and all must serve as judges, or one is in an absolutist state where only servants of the king are called, for SK would be the last person to deny that royal servants can also be "loving persons"—is the duty of every person to be a "loving person," to exercise generosity, to choose the kindest interpretation. How these two duties, when they conflict, can coexist, SK does not explain in this particular passage, but the answer, based upon *Works of Love* as a whole, is obvious: They can coexist only in the suffering and self-denial that allows the duty to be loving to assert its priority, regardless of the cost to the individual.

At another point SK makes it even clearer that his relationship to politics is not one of content but of priorities. Referring approvingly to the beginning of the recent movement of political liberation, in which the peasant reforms of recent decades have seen the end of "the disgusting period of serfdom," SK remarks that now, however, this movement has transgressed its proper bounds and is attempting "to abolish a person's serfdom in relation to God" [p. 111]. Thus, people "are seeking to liberate the emotional ties between one person and another from the bonds which bind one to God, and bind one in everything, in every utterance of life. . . . [T]hey are trying to teach people the freedom that 'is without God in the world' [Eph. 2:12]" [ibid.]. In confusing political liberation with liberation from God, we are committing a corruption of categories that has the effect of placing humanity not "in *humanity's* rights . . . no, that isn't necessary, that God has already done—but thus, in *God's* rights; the position does indeed become vacant when God is dismissed" [p. 112].

Some movements toward political liberation, SK says here, are gainful, but other "liberation" movements are pernicious, when, for example, under the device of *vox populi, vox Dei*, they attempt to usurp the proper sphere of religion and, making absolute claims for the finite world of politics, effect a violation of priorities within the individual. Though this passage does reflect SK's personal judgment about some of the liberal tendencies of his time, it is in itself of neutral political coloration and is a simple assertion of the necessity of the distinction between religion and politics.

SK's incidental treatment of the question of women's rights is another typical treatment of a political issue that shows his concern for distinctions or boundaries rather than for the concrete contents of politics *per se*. Women, SK freely admits, are treated as second-rate by society, but Christianity, in elevating the validity of conscience and in insisting on the absolute and equal worth of every soul, has destroyed this discrimination in the most important, inward, sense. But it is not Christianity's business to fight for equal rights for women in this world. Christianity's kingdom is not of this world, and only "foolish people" will push for equal rights for women in this world "in the name of Christianity" [p. 133]. Read strictly, and apart from his own personal prejudices, SK's statement is neutral regarding the issue of civic equality for women. SK is only polemical with respect to the question of pressing for such equality "in the name of Christianity," which confuses the worldly with the religious sphere. Here, as elsewhere, SK seems quite the classical liberal, non-dogmatic and agnostic with respect to political solutions, as long as they respect individual rights, which in SK's case means that they do not deify anything finite so that the individual's access to the "common property" of the infinite is blocked. SK's insistence upon boundaries and priorities within an otherwise free political field is his version of the classical liberal problem of the sedition law: how to protect society, which guarantees maximum freedom to all, against those who wish to abolish freedom and to use their own freedom only to compel or deny the freedom of others? Aside from these necessary ground rules, there is no specifically "Christian" politics. In SK's view, these problems are left to ordinary human ethical-political rules, the "Law."

In one final example we will examine how SK, with obvious relish and with (only apparent) perversity, turns the tension between the humanitarianism of this world and the "true humanism" of Love up to its excruciating limit, in order to illustrate as starkly as possible the difference between spiritual and political virtues. In his journals, SK tells us that the discourse entitled "Mercy, a Work of Love, Even If It Can Give Nothing and Cannot Manage to Do Anything" [pp. 300–14], was written specifically against "communism" (which was an exceedingly hazy concept in SK's Denmark, at any rate for SK) [cf. Pap. VIII 1 A 299]. Against this target, presumably chosen because it was the ultimate political expression of organized "generosity," SK sets the spiritual act of "mercy" in the most deliciously annoying way. The mode of argumentation is simple. "Generosity" is possible only with money and is very much in fashion these days, SK says. However, we must remember that "mercy" is a spiritual category which can be exercised even when it has nothing at its disposal to give (though, of course, if it has anything material to give, mercy does so gladly). The world thinks it is so serious and important and humane with its shouts of money and generosity, and yet, if SK had to choose between the generosity of the rich and the mercy of the poor, he would choose the latter without hesitation. SK means that at best generosity must be understood as a quantifiable, socially gainful program of rational "politics," whereas mercy is a qualitative category of spirit and need not occur in conjunction with any sure, external sign. SK sharpens the disjunction still further with a deliberately maddening injunction to the poor: Do not be merciless to the rich because they are ungenerous to you. SK continues in his exhortation to the poor: Think of all the people whom money has made merciless; how terrible it would be now if money, by its absence, could also succeed in robbing mercy from you as well! The unhappy poor person who refrains from disturbing the happiness of those better off is actually more capable of mercy than the wealthy person.

SK then continues in specific opposition to those who say that the need is so great and crushing among the poor that the most important thing is to minister to that need, whatever the means or motives. No, he replies, there is only one danger, that is that mercy should fail to be exercised. Even if all need were alleviated, it is not, however, thereby decided that it happened with mercy, and if this were not the case, then the misery, that mercy was simply not exercised, would be greater than all temporal need. [pp. 310–11]

This must not be understood as a reactionary or anti-human tirade but as a mode of stressing a qualitative difference and an assertion of a priority.

If mercy possesses means for generosity, it will surely exercise them [p. 301], in accordance with the Lutheran doctrine that once the inward relation of faith has been affirmed as the superior element over the outward, then works, generosity, will flow of themselves, not as attempts at righteousness but out of sheer joy. For illustrative purposes this second movement has here been relatively de-emphasized by SK, but the position he takes is not that of a reactionary Scrooge. "Is it mercy to give a hundred thousand to the poor? No. Is it mercy to give half a shilling to the poor? No. Mercy is *how* [*hvorledes*] it is given" [p. 312]. SK explains specifically that he has chosen the extraordinary case of the extremely poor person for heuristic purposes; it rids the picture, SK says, of all "dazzling externality" [glimrende Udvorteshed] [ibid.].

SK has been deliberately irritating to the social sensibilities of his reader in order to guarantee that the message, by its very abrasiveness, gets through, and the message is quite simply one of *priorities*, namely the priority of the personal and spiritual sphere of Love (which is accessible to everyone without exception) over the realm of political action and social concern (in which, whether we like it or not, we act according to our differences). In a remark elsewhere in *Works of Love*, SK notes that "a pure heart" is "free" in having been bound to God by immortal bonds; over such a heart God always has "first priority" [første Prioritet] [p. 142]. This remark can serve to tie together our understanding of this book and the previous book (to which the remark alludes).

In *Works of Love* the ethic of the Law is placed in relation to the Christian ethic of Love, and politics is seen as a free field, provided that the priorities of the God-relation, of "Love," are respected. In practice, the exercise of Love will always call forth worldly opposition and suffering, but the extremity of such suffering—and thus the question of whether one can integrate oneself socially as a citizen and still remain a Christian, or whether one *must* choose the isolated, oppositional role of the "saint"—is not clearly determined in *Works of Love*. The "citizen" position still seems quite open, but, in relation to SK's preceding work, the dark possibilities of the saint have again been amplified. The problem has not yet been resolved for SK.

20. *The Crisis and a Crisis in the Life of an Actress*

O

At the same time that SK was beginning *Works of Love,* in the first two months of 1847, he also wrote a series of articles entitled *The Crisis and a Crisis in the Life of an Actress* [*Krisen og en Krise i en Skuespillerindes Liv*] [SV X, pp. 319–44], which he published under the pseudonym "Inter et Inter" in the summer of 1848. The articles constitute a short dissertation on the realization of the aesthetic ideal in the individual, in this case (though she is not mentioned by name), Fru Johanne Luise Heiberg, the leading lady of the Danish stage and a figure very much at the center of the circle which created taste for the educated classes in Copenhagen. *The Crisis* focuses its attention upon the metamorphosis of a young, gifted, "immediate" actress of seventeen into a mature woman in her thirties who has really come into possession of herself and has redeemed her talent as her own. Such an actress undergoes a transformation which is the aesthetic analogue to ethical self-appropriation.

At the beginning of her career, she has "luck," youthfulness, and a certain "roguishness," but is also, even in her very "exuberance," perfectly reliable— her unreflected passion is perfectly attuned to her aesthetic "Idea," and she is in perfect "rapport with the tension of the theater" [p. 331], so that anxiety, instead of depressing her, propels her to a fantastic, euphoric lightness as an actress. Still, a true aesthetician examining her performance would say "No, her time has not yet really come" [p. 333].

Fourteen years later she is still praised and adored by the public, but her youthful charm is fading, and for the mass of people who have really only loved her for her obvious graces, the repeated praise has now become hollow, having been cheated of deeper meaning by time and the force of habit. Of course, SK writes, she could have kept up the pitch of popular enthusiasm by being secretive, by making rare and carefully planned appearances, like the Most Elevated Court Preacher [Oberhofprædikant], the German Theremin, who acquired fame by preaching rarely and with great ado [p. 336]. (Here SK is taking careful aim at Martensen, who had recently been appointed Court Preacher in Denmark and who was a very close friend of Fru Heiberg. We shall return to these remarks presently.) But no, SK writes, our actress has refused to shore up her reputation with deception. She has been a part of her people, has been among them and exposed to them every day. The people find it hard to accustom themselves to her aging, yet true aesthetics knows that her time has really only just begun. Now that she is no longer merely a very talented girl, she can relate to her Idea "at a distance," purely ideally, for time has stripped her personality and talent of all merely accidental attributes. Now she can "serve" her Idea in humility. "Only when one is in an absolutely serving relationship to the Idea is chance made absolutely impossible" [p. 342]. Only now can the actress regain her talent on a higher level and make it truly her own.

It is this latter point, that there is an aesthetic analogue to the ethical acquisition of the self, which is the real content of *The Crisis*, but for our purposes it is the occasion of this little book which is more important. Apart from various biographical and personal considerations which are not of concern here, *The Crisis* was occasioned by SK's desire to show that even when one becomes an almost exclusively religious writer, one can still appreciate and write on aesthetic matters. As the aesthetic realm of life was accessible in its full validity to the ethicist, Judge William in *Either/Or*, so is it also fully accessible to one who has devoted himself to the religious sphere, SK himself. This is in line with the views we have seen adumbrated in *Edifying Discourses in Various Spirits* and in *Works of Love*. The common theme is that if one orders one's *priorities* correctly and "seeks *first* the Kingdom of God and His righteousness," if one grants the religious sphere its superiority, then all lesser spheres—as we have seen earlier, political and social responsibility, and as we see here, aesthetics as well—become one's own again, i.e., "all these things shall be added unto you." As SK writes in his journals [Pap. IX A 175, p. 85] concerning the publication of *The Crisis*: "The world is indeed so weak that, when it believes that a person who proclaims the religious is incapable of the aesthetic, it overlooks the religious"—*ergo* SK's publication of *The Crisis*.

A second reason that SK wrote *The Crisis* deserves mention as well, namely the slur on Martensen alluded to above [cf. Pap. IX A 229, p. 127, where SK straightforwardly calls it "a little allusion to Martensen"]. By attacking Martensen even while praising Martensen's good friend Fru Heiberg, SK was deliberately stirring up unrest in the leading circle of the "dannede." As SK writes in connection with *The Crisis*, "my tactic has always been to sow discord in the coteries. . . . The great coterie is: Mynster, Heiberg, Martensen and company" [Pap. IX A 206, p. 103; cf. also ibid., p. 104 and IX A 229, p. 127]. Even in a relatively minor series of articles on aesthetics, SK's war upon the self-appointed guardians of "culture" continued. Both SK's acid irony and the actual lay of the cultural landscape prompted him to devote *A Literary Review* and *The Crisis*—both of which were critical of the Heiberg-Martensen cultural axis—to the work of the mother and the wife, respectively, of the great Johan Ludvig Heiberg.

21. *Two Minor Ethico-Religious Essays*

O

A. INTRODUCTION

In the period from late August/September 1847 until December 1847 (i.e., the months immediately following the completion of *Works of Love*), SK put his *Two Minor Ethico-Religious Essays* [*Tvende ethisk-religieuse Smaa-Afhandling-er*] [SV XI, pp. 47–109] into their final form. Both of these essays dealt with the difficult and potentially dangerous problem of divine authority [guddommelig Myndighed], which was an unavoidable component of any critique of Christian culture and a question which had interested SK for some time, especially since 1846, when his own cultural critique had begun in earnest. The year 1846 also saw the publication of controversial works by the eccentric Pastor Adler, in which the cleric claimed to have received divine revelations. In the problem he created for the Danish Church (which ultimately defrocked him, with pension), Adler made current the question of authority, giving SK an opportunity to deal with the question and its ramifications in a way which went far beyond the case of the unfortunate pastor. But the problem of authority (and the attendant problem of hubris or self-righteousness) was so dangerous and potentially explosive that SK chose to write on it pseudonymously, under the name "H. H." Furthermore, in the course of 1846–47 (the period during which he wrote the non-pseudonymous "Christian" works we have so far discussed in detail) SK had written an entire book on the Adler case. However, he decided to publish only a small section, which constitutes one of the *Two Essays*, "On the Difference Between a Genius and an Apostle" [Om Forskjellen mellem et Genie og en Apostel].[1] Though SK cast the essay into its final shape in the fall of 1847, it was not until May 1849 that he decided to publish it along with a companion piece, "Has a Human Being the Right to Allow Himself to Be Put to Death for the Truth?" [Har et Menneske Lov til at lade sig ihjelslaae for Sandheden?], even then under an assumed name. (This second essay was not taken from the draft of the Adler book, though it was similar in theme.)

It is very clear that SK saw these two pieces as valuable but dangerous weapons in criticism: "It is gold," he writes in his journals, "but it must be used with great caution" [Pap. X 1 A 79, p. 67]; a bit later he writes that the two essays are to serve as "skirmishes," but that "they must be given in as small doses as possible" [Pap. X 1 A 263]. Let us look a bit closer at this dangerous medicine in order to understand how these essays, with their peculiar and apparently obscure titles, served as part of the cultural critique which was claiming more and more of SK's attention.

B. "HAS A HUMAN BEING THE RIGHT TO ALLOW HIMSELF TO BE PUT TO DEATH FOR THE TRUTH?"

"Has a *Human Being* the *Right* to Allow Himself to Be Put to Death for the Truth?" (emphasis mine), asks SK's pseudonym "H. H." H. H. is a very earnest Christian who has received a strict pietistic upbringing—not unlike SK's own Herrnhut-style experience—in which he was continually exposed to pictures of the suffering Christ and has thus become preoccupied with the question of imitating Christ, even unto martyrdom. The question is whether a human being [Menneske] has this right, and thus does not concern Christ, who was God, who was the Truth itself, and whose conflict with the world was absolute and was, in addition, an act of redemption which retroactively atoned even for the act of murder it involved. The question is whether a human being has the *right* to allow himself to be martyred for the truth, and thus to allow others to be burdened with the guilt for this; that is, the question is not whether one has the *courage* to do so but whether one stands in such an *absolute* relation to the truth that he can fairly allow others to become absolutely guilty [p. 75]. In brief, is the would-be martyr related to his would-be slayers absolutely or only relatively? Thus, if the martyr is related absolutely to his environment, this means that the others *sin* in killing him. As H. H. writes: "Do I thus, as a human being, myself a part of the evil world, dare I say that the world in relation to me is evil, is sinful—that is, that I am pure and holy? If not, then it is indeed . . . blasphemy to make such a great case of it: to let oneself be killed for the truth" [p. 78].

Now this appears to be a discussion of the rather specialized problem of martyrdom but that is only the vehicle for the exposition of the question of authority which, as has been mentioned, informs both of these essays. In brief, the only persons who can allow themselves to be killed are those who possess divine authority which sets them absolutely apart from their environment and makes the defiant and hate-filled relationship of the environment to the authority in them (and not to such persons themselves in their merely human capacity) one of *sin* rather than simple ignorance. Thus Christ and the Apostles could allow themselves to be killed by the Jews and the pagans, since, by virtue of their authority and the heterogeneity of their environment, there was an absolute difference between them and their slayers. H. H. writes,

Can a *human being* be justified in looking upon his times as evil, or is not a human being, as a human being, precisely so relative in relation to other people that there can at the most be talk of their weakness and mediocrity? . . . If it were possible for a human being to be in absolute possession of the truth, then it would be absolutely indefensible, an infinite guilt [to compromise the truth]; because He who is the Truth cannot yield the least bit. But there is indeed no human being who is in this situation, least of all in relation to other people. Every human being is himself a sinner. He thus relates not as a pure one to sinners, but as a sinner to sinners. [pp. 85–86]

Thus, H. H. concludes, ". . . a *human being* does not have the right to allow himself to be put to death for the truth" [p. 86].

Furthermore, though we have only discussed the relation between *one human being and another* (i.e., in heathendom), the relationship between Christian and Christian is similarly relative, for "in the relation between Christian and Christian, as in the relation between one human being and another, there can only be relative differences" [p. 89]. Thus, "only in the relationship between Christianity and non-Christianity can it occur that one is put to death for the truth" [p. 88]. We seem to have reached the definitive answer to the question, namely No, neither in heathendom nor in Christendom is it permissible to allow others to put one to death for the truth, for to do so would be to assert an impermissible degree of heterogeneity with the culture to which one is, after all, related. Thus H. H. seemingly ends his essay with an unequivocally negative answer and calls upon all those who have considered the question of martyrdom to submit to serious "self-examination,"[2] after which they will conclude that such an option is impermissible.

However, this comfortingly negative answer, which disposes of the bothersome question of martyrdom, is only the apparent conclusion of the essay, and H. H. has deliberately concealed within it a polemical interpretation of "the present age" which admits of an opposite conclusion. It remains true, in accordance with the argument that H. H. has developed, that such relative differences between a person and his environment as do occur in heathendom and Christendom do not justify him in involving others in the guilt of his death—a martyr must represent an absolute difference. However, it is also true that such an absolute relationship does exist in relation to a conflict between heathendom and the Christian. By virtue of his derived relation to Christ, the Christian does indeed stand, in relation to heathens [Hedninge], in absolute truth [ibid.]. One could dismiss this possibility as mooted by history and out of the question, at any rate in Christendom's Denmark, and indeed, this comforting notion is the primary note which H. H. intends to strike—in order to conceal all the better his real potential sting, namely that it is at least possible that Christendom itself has degenerated into a heathendom worse than that of ancient times. H. H. writes, "if, on the other hand, it is to be permissible to allow oneself to be put to death for the truth within Christendom, then it must first be a condition that the so-called Christendom is not Christian at all, that just like 'spiritlessness' [Aandløshed, SK's favorite term for characterizing the philistine bourgeoisie with its 'Christianity of habit'], it is much more heathen than heathendom was" [p. 89]. Thus, if one is willing to see Christendom as heathendom, the possibility of martyrdom is still open. When he had prematurely decided that human beings did not have the right to let themselves be put to death for the truth, H. H. found it distressing that humanity seemed to be abandoned to living on a level which did not correspond to the urgency of the inner conviction he felt. The race becomes more and more "indolent" he lamented, more and more "reasonable," more and more "busy," and more and more "worldly." "The Absolute is going more and more out of use," H. H. complains, "an awakening will become more and more necessary. But where will an awakening come from when one dare not use the only true means of awakening—allowing oneself to be put to death for the truth?" [p. 86]. Still, he concludes, one dare not be a martyr unless—as we have seen him state elsewhere in the argument—Christendom can be shown to be heathen.

H. H. gives the rudiments of an argument for the heathenism of his culture, and they are worthy of note as further documentation of SK's gravitation toward open warfare with Christendom. Near the outset of the essay H. H. declares in a sort of confession of faith that a Christian believes because a Christian must believe, rather than believing "as it is said, meaninglessly, *because he can comprehend*" [begribe] [p. 63]. This attack upon self-confident, intellectualizing, speculative theology, for which the problems of martyrdom, *et al.* do not exist, is continued a bit later in the piece, where the desire to "comprehend" the faith or to "comprehend" Christ is specifically labelled "blasphemy" [p. 69]. H. H. has here drawn a very clear line between his personally engaged Christianity and the respectable academic theology of Martensen and others.

In describing the political-nationalistic situation of the Jews at the time of Christ, which encouraged them to take Christ in vain, H. H. also seems to be drawing a parallel to the confusion and perdition of the present Danish national and political situation. Thus, by implication, H. H. appears to raise the possibility that the time may well be ripe for a martyr-critic in Denmark. H. H. writes of the Jews in the time of Christ:

> This nationally and religiously proud people, bound in a servitude they despised, sighed with an increasingly mad pride. For that pride is the maddest that oscillates between deifying and despising oneself. The country was in its downfall. All minds were taken up with the concerns of nationality. Everything was politics unto despair. [p. 65]

One does not need to look very hard to see behind this picture the nationalist Denmark of the late 1840's, with its peculiar blend of feelings of inferiority and superiority. Two very powerful groups, both within the Danish Church and without—the liberals, who counted H. N. Clausen in their front ranks, and the

Grundtvigian party—had made their causes inseparable from a very shrill nationalism. The only other major faction, which was not so vocally Germanophobic and which was the only group capable of mediating in such explosive questions as the South Slesvig issue, was the conservative-aristocratic group that included Martensen, Mynster, and Heiberg. But this group was disinclined to intervene.[3] In the view of H. H. there is a clear, implicit parallel between first-century Jewish culture and his contemporary Denmark with respect to the heterogeneity of the martyr-critic and the decadent and nationalistically self-involved environment. Once again, the disturbing possibility of martyrdom in nineteenth-century Denmark belies H. H.'s apparently comforting conclusion.

In one final example, we can see H. H. taunting Danish pietism by developing his notion of the "preacher of penitence" [Straffeprædikant] as a sort of Christian edition of the Socratic gadfly, whose task it is to let the times understand that the truth is not its own invention. H. H. writes that

> [t]o be the great preacher of penitance is to be put to death. The so-called preacher of penitence, on the other hand, strikes from the pulpit and fights with the air, which indeed does not give the times the passion to put him to death. In this way he achieves his ridiculous purpose, to be the most ridiculous of all freaks: a preacher of penitence who is respected and honored, greeted with acclamation. [p. 82]

This attack seems to be directed at both wings of Danish pietism, the respectable bourgeois side, represented by Mynster, and the more popular, fire-eating wing which had Grundtvig as its chief. Certainly the question of martyrdom was far from their own concerns, and this mode of formulating it could not fail to be embarrassing to them. Thus H. H. has laid the groundwork for a damningly critical interpretation of Christian culture, which opens the possibility of martyrdom "within Christendom" even while he is formally concluding the opposite. Furthermore, at the very time that he was writing the *Two Essays*, SK was also writing the *Christian Discourses*. As we will see, the *Christian Discourses* include a series of discourses on "The Worries of the Heathen," in which one of the principal points is that heathendom, in the purest sense of the term, occurs only *within* so-called Christendom.[4]

All this, however, raises the very difficult question of how one can *know* that Christendom is really heathendom. Is this not the province of God, "the knower of hearts" [Hjertekjenderen]? It seems to require "authority," at the very least, but what are authority's earmarks? How can one avoid being deceived by fanatics or devilish adventurers? One is on the horns of a dilemma: If the possibility of martyrdom is not open to people who live in a "Christian culture," their experience of Christianity, as H. H. lamented above, is fundamentally different from and diluted in comparison with that of the disciples, and one is in a sense a "disciple at second hand," which contradicts one of SK's most important points and the message of, e.g., the *Philosophical Frag-*

ments. If, on the other hand, one can be a martyr within Christendom, one must do so at the risk of calling Christendom heathendom and of viewing as heathens people who call themselves Christians. This seems to violate the principle of subjectivity, which is another of SK's basic precepts. SK is thus walking on very dangerous ground here, being unwilling either to claim absolute authority for himself (or "H. H.") or to renounce his use of the concept of authority (and the distinction "Christian/heathen") as a very devastating weapon in his criticism of Christian culture. The key concept here is *authority*, and it is treated further in the second of the *Two Essays*, "On the Difference Between a Genius and an Apostle."

C. "ON THE DIFFERENCE BETWEEN A GENIUS AND AN APOSTLE"

This second essay, as we have seen, was extracted from the book on Pastor Adler, who felt that he had been vouchsafed various revelations. The essay on the genius and the Apostle was not so much an attack upon the insignificant Adler as it was an attempt to use his case as a vehicle for the discussion of authority and thus further to develop SK's threat to the clerical and cultural establishment. Before one could evaluate Adler's claim to Apostolic revelations, one would have to know what an "Apostle" is and how the sphere in which such a person belongs differs from that of worldly, immanent exceptionality, which H. H. calls "genius."

Simply stated, a genius is a person who is highly talented relative to others and who imparts something new and undreamt of to humanity. However, the new element which the genius introduces is eventually understood and assimilated into the common property of the human race, if not in the genius' own lifetime, then at least in later centuries. Whatever the genius is, he is in himself, and similarly his task is what it is in itself; it is self-contained, or as H. H. says, it has its *telos* in itself. The genius exists in the sphere of "immanence" [p. 96]. In short, the genius differs from the common run of humanity quantitatively or relatively, but his heterogeneity is not absolute or beyond the pale of rational understanding.

The Apostle, on the other hand, in his capacity as Apostle, is what he is by virtue of something *outside* himself, by divine authority. "The Apostle's call is a paradoxical fact which, from the first to the last moment of his life, remains paradoxically outside his personal identity with himself as the distinct person he is" [p. 97]. "*Divine authority is the qualitatively decisive factor*" [p. 98]. His message, the essentially new thing that he imparts to humanity, is and remains radically "other" to humanity. The race can never assimilate it into its lawful possession by virtue of rational understanding. Even the very notion of the Apostolic relationship with God "does not admit of being thought, but only of being believed" [p. 102]. The Apostle's *telos* lies not in himself but outside himself in the task laid upon him by God, namely to impart his message. He is qualitatively different from the common run of humanity, and there is thus an absolute heterogeneity between him and others. He is the same person described in the previous essay as one who has the right to be a martyr for the truth.

Up to this point H. H.'s exposition is clear and unproblematic, but problems begin as soon as one asks how one may distinguish between a fanatical fool or a consciously wicked deceiver[5] and a genuine Apostle. (Or, for that matter, how would one know whether one was oneself constituted by divine authority?) Apostles, like martyrs, differ from others in that they have divine authority, certainly, but divine authority never allows itself to be recognized by straightforward and certain physical signs. It is, H. H. writes, "nonsense to have *physical* certainty that an Apostle is an Apostle, . . . just as it is nonsense to have *physical* certainty that God exists, for God is of course *spirit*" [p. 99]. Furthermore, "if one could prove it *physically*, he would thereby not be an Apostle. He has no other proof than his own assertion" [p. 106]. In a negative allusion to Adler, who remained undisturbed in his parsonage while publishing what SK called his "clever uncertainties" [cf. p. 108], SK adds rather weakly that an Apostle will certainly be an active and outgoing person, taken up with the work of God. However, such a physical sign is at best a very uncertain indication, since H. H. also says that even willingness to suffer is at best only a presumptive sign that someone is an Apostle: "An Apostle has no other proof than his own word, or at the most his willingness to suffer anything gladly for the sake of the message" [p. 106]. Nor, finally, has the Apostle's message itself any intrinsic properties that distinguish its divine authenticity [p. 99]. Indeed, H. H. says, the same message may be divinely authorized in one person's mouth and a merely ordinary utterance in someone else's.

Although this second of the *Two Essays* has further clarified the notion of divine authority by dwelling upon the difference between worldly, relative, or quantitative exceptionality in the genius and divine, qualitative, or absolute exceptionality in the Apostle, it has not really gotten H. H. out of the dilemma he was in in the article on martyrdom. There, it was a question of whether one possessed the authority to distinguish between so-called and genuine Christians, whereas here there is the nearly identical question of how one can distinguish between genuine and putative Apostles. Total scepticism in this regard excludes one from the possibility of receiving word of a divine revelation, and the only alternative seems to place one at the mercy of mad or consciously wicked individuals, or even of one's own fantasy.

In his mounting criticism of Christendom, SK could not set aside the notion of divine authority despite its highly problematic nature. However much one senses from SK's journals and from his discussion of the role of "divine Governance" in his authorship that he was mightily attracted to the notion of divine authority, he never claimed such authority for himself—he was always extremely scrupulous about disclaimers in this regard. However, SK did use authority as a paradigm whose absence was a severe judgment upon the state of "Christendom." SK remarks in his journals that his pseudonym H. H. was very careful to point out that the *Two Essays* would "probably be of interest only to theologians," which would thus show to whom the essays' real point was addressed; SK also notes that H. H. has most pointedly reminded his readers that "I am 'without authority'; I am a genius—not an Apostle. . . . But such a one [an Apostle] must be set forth" [Pap. X 1 A 328, p. 218]. Thus the Apostle and the notion of authority remain heuristic devices. But even this negative use of the notion of authority for the purposes of cultural criticism was an extremely dangerous activity, a form of playing with fire, for if one cannot prove the presence of divine authority, how dare one assert, or even imply, its absence?

Before we end this examination of these essays and the difficulties they contain, we should identify the enemy against whom the essay on the genius and the Apostle was directed. Certainly it was not directed principally against poor Pastor Adler. According to H. H., the enemy is "erroneous exegesis and speculation" which has confused that which is Christian [det Christelige] by pushing "the paradoxical-religious sphere" back into the aesthetic, whereby that which is specifically Christian has lost its qualitative difference, so that an Apostle simply becomes a very exceptional, very talented person, a genius [p. 95]. Further, this erroneous speculation also asserts the "blasphemy" that the difference between God and humanity is only transitory, a property of temporal existence, and that "God and humanity become equals in Eternity" [p. 102]. The erroneous speculation that H. H. is here attacking is clearly that of idealism in general and Hegelianism in particular. H. H. seems to indict both the Left and the Right Hegelians in saying that "the error is moreover not only that of heterodoxy [presumably Feuerbach, *et al.*], but also that of hyperorthodoxy [presumably Danish churchmen such as Martensen, *et al.*] and of thoughtlessness in general" [p. 95n.]. Christ, H. H. maintains, ought to be obeyed on the basis of his divine authority and not on the basis of his possession of specific attributes and excellences that properly belong under the rubric of genius. To praise Christ or any of the Apostles or to recommend Christianity on the basis of any immanent quality is blasphemy, H. H. continues, but one rarely hears a religious talk these days without hearing Christ or the Gospels praised for profundity, cleverness, etc. Here H. H. cites the example of a German bishop, Sailer, much in the same fashion that "Inter et Inter," the pseudonymous author of *The Crisis*, cited the example of the Most Elevated Court Preacher Theremin, and the point here, as there, seems to be a not-very-veiled attack upon Martensen. The identification of H. H.'s target seems to be even clearer when he specifies his charges further:

> What is corrupting is when the sermon's train of thought is affected, when its orthodoxy is attained by putting the accent upon the wrong thing, when it

basically calls for one to believe in Christ, and preaches faith in him on the basis of something which simply cannot be an object of faith. . . . And thus it is also affectation when there is so much talk of appropriating Christianity for oneself and of believing in Christ because of the profundity of the doctrine. One falsely appropriates orthodoxy by accenting the entirely wrong thing. All the modern speculation ["den moderne Spekulation," a common term for the Hegelian philosophy and its outliers] is therefore affected, in that it has abolished *obedience* on the one side and *authority* on the other side, and has at the same time wished, nevertheless, to be orthodox. [pp. 105–106]

It is clear that by speaking through the pseudonym of H. H. and by attacking the strawman Adler on the obscure issue of the difference between a genius and an Apostle, SK was in fact using the notion of authority to attack, among other things, his familiar enemy Martensen and to ridicule Martensen's attempt to create the basis of a Christian culture by assimilating Christianity to the categories of immanence and the rational understanding.

We have thus far seen SK develop two notions of how the Christians can relate themselves to worldly social and political obligations. The dominant point of view has been what I have called the "prioritarian" vision of the Christian who is also a "citizen." The "citizen" takes on responsibilities within the universal ethical norms available to the natural self, though these responsibilities are always ordered as secondary to the citizen's relationship to God and to the integrity of the individual personality in that relationship. The individuation of the God-relationship is the indestructible and non-negotiable fundament upon which all worldly politics must be built. One must (in the words of Matthew 6:33–34) "seek *first* God's kingdom and His righteousness," but *then*, "all these things will be added unto you." The actual forms of political and social association are a matter of prudence and convenience, provided only that the integrity of the individual personality and of the God-relationship are respected, and they can vary to suit the exigencies of the situation. We have also seen that in its individualism, its choice of vocabulary, and its "agnostic" attitude toward the concrete contents of political action, among other things, this prioritarian vision of the Christian who is also "citizen" has a good deal in common with the liberalism that so dominated SK's century.

But there has also been a second possible form for a Christian's relation to society, namely one of radical and absolute opposition, the martyr, the Apostle, or the Christian as "saint," as I have put it, to differentiate this figure from the Christian as "citizen." This possibility resounds with increasing frequency in the works we examine here, and it lives in an uneasy tension with the notion of the Christian citizen. At this point SK dares neither to reject the possibility of the saint nor to embrace it to the exclusion of the citizen. The *Two Essays* concentrate upon this problem, but do not resolve it.

22. Christian Discourses

○

A. INTRODUCTION

Christian Discourses [*Christelige Taler*] [SV X, pp. 1–317] was the last of the three large series of discourses that constitute the bulk of SK's "middle period," the period that begins after his attack on *The Corsair* (December 1845) and ends around the time of the revolutionary events of the spring of 1848. The *Christian Discourses* were begun immediately after SK completed *Works of Love* in August 1847 and were completed in the early part of February 1848, a few days before the revolution in Paris set in motion the train of events that led, in March, to the rising in Slesvig and Holstein and to the popular movement in Copenhagen that resulted in parliamentary government in Denmark. The book was published on April 26, 1848, three days after the first military engagement in Slesvig, where the Danish forces had been mustered by the quasi-revolutionary cabinet, which was a sort of liberal junta. In these turbulent circumstances SK was a bit hesitant to let his *Christian Discourses* be published, for he felt that their religious iconoclasm and their deflationary attitude toward social constellations might bring him into trouble—which, predictably, they did not, thus providing an illustration of SK's overestimate of his contemporary significance.[1] SK regarded these discourses as incendiary both to the conservative establishment that was passing away and to the liberal order that appeared to be replacing it. He finally decided in favor of publication on the grounds that, although they were written before the recent weeks of revolution and war, they were precisely what such unsettled times required.

The *Christian Discourses* are divided into four sections of seven discourses each: I. "The Worries of the Heathen"; II. "Moods in the Struggle of Sufferings"; III. "Thoughts Which Stab in the Back—for Edification"; and IV. "Discourses at the Communion on Fridays." The structure of the *Discourses* could perhaps be called musical, with an opening shock which consists in the assertion that it is precisely the participants in Christian culture who are the "heathens" *par excellence*. This section is followed by a series of exhortations—"dark sayings," SK called them, citing Psalm 49, where the psalmist, like SK himself, sings in evil days of the empty pomposity of the great. This second section stresses the unavoidability of suffering to the Christian, while discounting its significance to the believer. Next come the "Thoughts Which Stab in the Back" (literal translation: "Thoughts Which Wound from Behind"), in which SK's trouble-making sallies against the established culture reach new heights of polemical daring. Finally, the communion discourses form an abrupt transition to a peace-able emphasis upon inwardness and conclude on a note so tranquil that SK even entertained the idea of dedicating them to Bishop Mynster—but decided against it lest he be seen as making gestures to the establishment in expectation of official favor [Pap. VIII 1 A 438]!

It can quickly be seen that of the four sections, it is the first and the third—those which deal with the "heathen" and those which "stab in the back"—that have the greatest direct bearing upon SK's cultural critique, and they will claim most of our attention in what follows.

B. "THE WORRIES OF THE HEATHEN"

"The Worries of the Heathen" builds upon the familiar text of Matthew 6:24–34, which deals with lilies and birds, the impossibility of serving both God and Mammon, and the necessity of a choice, culminating in the verse: "Seek first the kingdom of God and his righteousness, and all these things [i.e., worldly concerns] will be added unto you." We have already seen how this verse reverberates through SK's authorship, where it was specifically used as the base line for a large portion of the *Edifying Discourses in Various Spirits*. This same passage from Matthew recurs again in the final phases of SK's work, where it appears as the decisive text not only here, but in the three "godly discourses" on the lilies and the birds from 1849 and in the second half of *Judge for Yourselves!* from 1851–52. It is also alluded to in many other places. The lesson of the lilies and the birds and the principle of seeking *first* God's kingdom and then having "all these things" stands in fact as the rubric under which can be placed one whole side of SK's view of human culture, in particular of society and political arrangements. I have termed this principle one of "prior-ities"—SK called it one of "de-throning" (but not abolishing) the worldly. The principle of priorities plays no major role in the earlier portion of the authorship, but assumes great importance in the preponderantly post-pseudonymous por-tion with which we are dealing. Matthew 6:24–34, with its emphasis upon single-mindedness (no man can serve two masters), security (do not worry like the "heathen"), and priority (seek *first* the kingdom of God, etc.), thus stresses faith. As one of the twin pillars of the entire edifice of SK's later work, Matthew thus stands alongside of SK's equally frequent use of the epistle of James, which stresses works. Matthew and James are the two paramount biblical loci for SK, and understanding the way in which SK manages to dovetail their two messages is of crucial importance for an understanding of SK's critical work in the last years.

The lilies and the birds, SK tells us, stand outside the opposition between Christian and heathen; they are our neutral teachers about worries. Birds do not worry, but this is because they cannot. Human beings, on the other hand, can worry—and the heathen do worry, whereas Christians do not. Thus, Christians stand higher and heathens lower than the birds. But who, specifically, are the heathen? SK carefully couches his answer as a rhetorical denial: We will not be "strict" and say that so-called Christians who worry are heathens, for only an angel could mock us thus strictly. But we must not forget that "the heathens who are in Christendom are those who have sunk the deepest" [p. 18]. This, then, is to be a series of discourses addressed to the putative "Christians" of SK's culture, exhorting them to abandon all worldly worries and not to live like the heathen.

In these discourses SK describes the various sorts of worries that can plague the heathen: the worries of poverty, wealth, lowliness, exaltedness, presumption, self-torture, doubt, fickleness, and disconsolateness. These are not abstract descriptions, but are carefully aimed at those in his society who are not what they seem.

In his discussion of the "worries of poverty," SK describes one such person who is not what he seems, namely, the typical respectable citizen: "a man who has learned what life's seriousness is . . . husband, citizen, and father," a "serious man" who finds the Bible lacking in seriousness, not at all helpful in finding the money to meet mortgage payments and taxes, a book suitable for women, etc. [pp. 24–25]. Such a man is actually a typical heathen, who "lives in the world without God" [p. 25]. As for the "worries of poverty," in the deepest sense the poorest Christian is richer than the bird whom God cares for and arrays in feathered finery, whereas the richest heathen, in his worries, is poorer than the poorest. SK does not overlook the necessity of earning a living: "All these things will be added unto you." He merely states that one may work [arbeide] but not slave [trælle] for one's daily bread, the difference being not one of outward actions but of inward posture and priorities [pp. 26–27]. In itself, "bread" is not sinful.

With respect to the "worries of wealth," SK states (in language reminiscent of St. Paul—I Cor. 7:30–31)[2] that the rich Christian learns to have things as though he has them not [p. 32]. The Christian is capable, by means of thought, of destroying "the idea of possession" [Besiddelsens Tanke] with "the idea of eternity" [Evighedens Tanke], which teaches us that we cannot really come to possess anything worldly, while, on the other hand, nothing which is *really* possessed can ever be lost [pp. 33–34]. This is a form of spiritual surgery that leaves "the wound which brings healing" [det helbredende Saar] in the mind of the well-to-do (or any) Christian, who remains in the deepest sense ignorant of his wealth; he is "a traveller" [en Reisende], always ready to depart, always surprised by his discovery that he has earthly wealth with which he can do good [pp. 35–36]. In this ethic, charity is not understood in serial fashion as an end—e.g., first one gathers wealth together, then one disburses it in socially useful projects—but rather as something that is a natural consequence of having all things as though one had them not, precisely in the manner of one who seeks first God's kingdom and then has "all these things" (philanthropy, social responsibility, etc.) "added unto one." The wealthy Christian, then, has things as though he did not have them, while the worried heathen, however rich he is, has things as though he had nothing else, and is poorer than the poorest animal [p. 40].

The worries of "lowliness," SK continues, can burden one only if one tries to exist primarily "for others." If one exists *first* for God and *then* for others, one will not be burdened by any such worldly worries. "When one is oneself in existing in Him who is in and for Himself [i.e., God], one can exist in or for others, but one cannot be oneself if one exists only for others" [p. 45]. This is the familiar prioritarian SK; first personal identity in the God-relation, then social identity. Social identity, like "working" for one's daily bread, like the charity of the rich Christian who is "ignorant" of his wealth, is permissible and commendable if the priorities are respected. The "heathen," on the other hand, has *only* a social identity and no personal identity; he allows "the enormous weight of comparisons" to burden him and make him *truly* lowly [p. 49].

The worries of "exaltedness" are similar. The socially exalted Christian knows that "no one can become or be a Christian except in the capacity of a lowly person" [p. 56]. He sees through his own exaltation. Christianity does not prompt or approve of "the revolting impudence of ungodly worldliness," which laughs in a worldly way at the highness of the high; however, exalted Christians, as Christians, laugh at it themselves. SK is here upholding the Lutheran and Pauline doctrine of the two kingdoms: In *Works of Love*[3] we have seen him castigate those who prophesy against the social order "in the name of Christianity," and here again he takes aim at the liberal anti-authoritarianism which calls itself Christian. At this point SK is still very concerned with avoiding the misunderstanding in which his critique might be construed as lending support to that of the liberals, and he very stringently insists upon recognizing the legitimacy of the world within its limits, of letting it have its due and rendering unto Caesar. The only point on which worldly authority is to be criticized *in the name of Christianity* is when it transgresses into the personal-religious sphere and commandeers Christianity as a stabilizing component in the social order. However, the misuse of worldly authority must not be criticized in the wrong way or for the wrong reasons. One must not attempt to make liberal political capital in attacking the established social order, and in this connection it is thus of decisive significance that SK delayed his principal attack until late 1854, when the new liberal-constitutionalist regime was firmly established and safely beyond the threat of dismantling by the reaction (as had happened in Germany and Austria after 1848).

SK's discussion of the worries of "presumption" differs from the preceding in that it does not deal with qualities like riches, poverty, or lowliness, which are indifferent in themselves. Instead, it uses the evil of "presumptuousness" as a vehicle for a psychological argument that echoes *The Concept of Anxiety* in outlining a developmental psychology of immediacy-distance-new immediacy. This discourse also prefigures SK's final psychological work, *The Sickness Unto Death*, in setting forth two major forms of despair: the spiritlessness [Aandløshed] of the philistine bourgeoisie and the defiance of the romantic rebel. These two forms of despair correspond, as we have seen in our discussion of *A Literary Review*, to the "present" and the "Revolutionary" ages respectively. The psychological development of the individual goes from ignorant consent in God's will (simple immediacy); to the possibility of "presumption" (distance); to mature consent in God's will, now understood as grace (new immediacy or faith). The opposite of the acceptance of grace in new immediacy is presumption, which in its various forms, is anxiety [Angest] (in *The Concept of Anxiety*) and despair [Fortvivlelse] (in *The Sickness Unto Death*).

"Presumption is thus either *to wish to have God's help* in a forbidden, a rebellious, an ungodly way, *or to wish to do without God's help* in a forbidden, a rebellious, an ungodly way" [p. 67]. The former of these two forms of presumption is superstition, which desires to accept God's grace, but on worldly terms. (This is perhaps directed at Grundtvigian Christianity.) The latter of these two forms of presumption, which wishes to do without God's help, is broken down by SK into two sub-forms. The higher, conscious form is called defiant unbelief, which seems to refer not only to the romantic rebel but also to the pantheistic tendencies of speculative idealism, since SK comments in this connection that as "these times have understood it . . . it [is] . . . God who needs humanity" [p. 71]. (This seems to refer to the Hegelian notion of God coming to know himself as reflected in the world, or perhaps to the more radical Feuerbachian, left-wing Hegelian notion that God is the dependent projection of human consciousness.) But SK's chief feud here is neither with superstition nor with defiance, and one senses that they are included only for the sake of taxonomical completeness. His real force is reserved for the castigation of the weaker form of willing to do without God, namely "spiritlessness," which is the desire "spiritlessly, to remain ignorant about how a person needs God's help every moment, about the fact that he is nothing without God" [p. 67]. Such a person dwells in willed ignorance and consciously seeks to extinguish the spark of spirit which constitutes the self. He seeks to lose himself in worldly concerns and sensual reality. He thinks he is without worry but is in fact embedded in what Anti-Climacus, the pseudonymous author of *The Sickness Unto Death*, would call unconscious despair. Worst of all, and most important for SK's critique of Christian culture, is the fact that "the presumptuousness of *spiritlessness* . . . really only occurs in Christendom" [p. 69]. We have already seen from SK's description of the manifestations of this spiritlessness that it occurs precisely among those whom the times cherish as the most serious and respected citizens. In the *Christian Discourses,* as in everything else we have examined thus far, SK continues to direct his special criticism not at those who might have been seen as trouble-makers or as enemies of the Established Order (though they do not slip lightly from his lash) but at the respectable bourgeoisie of Christendom.[4]

In discussing the worries of "self-torture," SK points out that the birds have no sense of time, no worries for the morrow, and, hence, "no self" [p. 75]. On the other hand, the human individual, who is a synthesis of the temporal and the eternal, can have such worries and needs to learn how to "take leave of the morrow" and learn how to become "contemporary with himself" [p. 78] rather than being far from himself in worry, never present to himself, i.e., self-abstracted as are the heathen.

The last of the "Worries of the Heathen" that SK discusses is the worry of doubt, fickleness, and disconsolateness. Doubt, SK points out, comes from *double*ness, from trying to serve two masters (against the injunction of Matthew 6:24). SK echoes "Purity of Heart," with its talk of "double-mindedness" and willing the Good, by pointing out here that only the choice of God is the choice of *one thing;* all else is doubt and doubleness. The bird cannot have any other will than God's, while the Christian can, but sacrifices his will to God and becomes free of the worries of doubt and fickleness. All beings praise God, but only man praises God in the full understanding that he does not understand. The Christian, SK continues, knows this simple, single-minded obedience, whereas the heathen wavers, wants time to consider things, wants reasons, has two wills, and ultimately seeks to forget the problem of God entirely by becoming "busy" with what he calls "life's seriousness" [p. 92]. Once again, SK emphasizes that this calculated attempt to avoid the God-relationship through busyness, this attempt to forget the self by being "serious," is far more dangerous than rebellion or defiance. It is

> [t]he most frightful sort of disobedience, more frightful than all defiance; hating God, cursing him is not so frightful as losing him like this, or what is the same thing, losing oneself. . . . For there is indeed not only an infinite difference between what one loses in one case and what one loses in another, but also between *how* one person and another loses. To lose God in such a way that repentance hurries after, in grief, to bring back that which was lost; to lose God such that one is offended by him, rebels against him, or murmurs against him; to lose God such that one despairs over it: but to lose God as though he were nothing, and as though it were nothing! [pp. 92–93]

The quiet despair of respectable people is the most terrifying and dangerous of all. This is the last and greatest of the worries of the heathen which concerns

SK, and there can be no doubt that these heathen are the same prosaic, respectable souls who populate "the present age" of *A Literary Review*; their lostness is once again seen as far more dangerous than that of the defiant rebel of "the Revolutionary age," whose energy and consciousness always contain the possibility of repentance.

C. "MOODS IN THE STRUGGLE OF SUFFERINGS"

The second of the four sections of the *Christian Discourses*, "Moods in the Struggle of Sufferings," is a parallel to the discourses on "The Gospel of Sufferings" in the *Edifying Discourses in Various Spirits*, in that these discourses, like their predecessors, dwell upon "the joy" contained in sufferings, and they delight in drawing their simple basic idea out of apparent contradictions. The basic thought underlying all of them is that there is an absolute difference between eternal and worldly things, that the relative values of the temporal and the eternal always appear reversed in the world of time, and that, consequently, the only evil to be feared is not worldly opposition or suffering, but "sin." "Only sin corrupts" is the refrain with which all these discourses end, and sin consists precisely in confusing the priorities between the worldly and the eternal. SK writes: "*Only the temporal can be lost temporally*; it is impossible for time as such to take anything other than temporal things from you; . . . If the frightful thing happened, that a person *temporally* lost *the eternal*, then there is no longer talk of a *loss* [Tab]—this is *perdition* [Fortabelse]" [p. 140]. Sin, thus, is not to be casuistically construed as extreme, individual actions, but as an entire life-posture: "Sin, properly, is: *to lose the eternal temporally*" [ibid.], by overvaluing temporal things and by refusing to allow our temporal losses and sufferings to teach us how to let go, to "die away," in order to let the eternal element in us grow all the more.

In this vein SK dwells upon a series of contradictions: "Suffering Makes Hope Available"; "The Poorer You Are, the Richer You Can Make Others"; etc. They all make the point that suffering helps show us what is non-essential and thus points our way to the essential, eternal element in us. This message is difficult, indeed radically disturbing to worldliness, but the worst is that in "these times" people are no longer capable either of wonder or of taking offense, and so no one even bothers to struggle against this message [p. 112]. One wins "everything" by "dying away," and the person who bears this message will be hated for it by the world and will be a difficult, disrespectful, "reckless" [hensynsløs] individual [p. 150].

In the final discourse of this section, "Opposition is Support" [Modgang er Medgang], the tension between time and eternity becomes most extreme. Time and eternity understand things in opposite ways, and one must consequently steer into the wind, for the world's opposition (and not merely its indifference) is a sign that one approaches the goal of eternity. Here SK seems headed toward resolving the tension between "saint" and "citizen" unequivocally in the direction of martyrdom. This is the point to which these seven discourses build, yet he draws back and softens his point and makes it into another case of priorities, referring to the ever-present Matthew 6:24–34: "When it says 'seek *first* the Kingdom of God,' the goal of eternity is hereby set up as that after which a person must seek. . . . [S]o what counts for everything is that a person does not *first* come to seek after anything else" [p. 157, emphasis in original]. By his emphasis on the word *"first,"* SK here implies that if, on the other hand, one seeks God's Kingdom first, then (and only then, it is true) one may occupy oneself with "all these things." SK—who, as we have seen, viewed himself as a genius but not as an Apostle—shied away from demanding that the tension in our temporal-eternal synthesis be undialectically resolved in favor of martyrdom. The only alternative, in the absence of the possession of such "authority," was a strong emphasis on the problem of priorities, an emphasis which, in order to maintain its bite and savor, had to stress the first, "offensive" part of the passage from Matthew, the part about seeking *first* the Kingdom of God. SK's emphasis had to border on a command to martyrdom in order to have the necessary awakening effect upon its intended audience of respectable "Christians." Still, here again SK backs away from a straightforward rejection of the world and permits one to be a "citizen" and to embrace both the religious and the social-political spheres, provided, that is, one embraces them *in that order.* The worst creatures are the bourgeois gentlefolk of Golden Age Christendom, who have achieved a spiritless or semi-conscious "synthesis" of the religious and the social-political, such that the former is an integrated and supportive element of the latter.

D. "THOUGHTS WHICH STAB IN THE BACK—FOR EDIFICATION"

The third, and for us the most important of the four subdivisions of the *Christian Discourses* is the "Thoughts Which Stab in the Back—for Edification." As we have already noted, SK felt that the criticism they contained was so severe and provocative that it might get him in trouble, but he saw "stabbing in the back" as fundamental to his authorship and could not bear to leave the discourses unpublished. Shortly after the publication of the *Christian Discourses,* SK writes in his journal that Christendom is in such unfortunate shape that it is necessary to start over, all the way from the beginning, with "Heathendom," and it is necessary to proceed from there with daring, for "all of my frightful authorship is one grand thought, that is: to stab in the back" [Pap. VIII 1 A 548]. SK thought of publishing the "Thoughts Which Stab in the Back" separately, as the first part of a trilogy, in which they would be "the polemical element, like the 'Worries of the Heathen,' but a bit stronger"; the trilogy was to have been continued with *The Sickness Unto Death* and finally concluded with an unwritten work, *Fundamental Recovery* [Pap. VIII 1 A 558]. But SK decided that the thought of suppressing this difficult third section of the *Christian Discourses* and holding it for possible later publication was a temptation to be "shrewd" and self-serving, and that "without the 3rd section the *Christian Discourses* are much too mild [and] untrue to my character" [Pap. VIII 1 A 560, p. 260]. In his journals SK concludes that he is happy to have taken the risk and is satisfied with the way the book stands, with "the strongest possible and most passionate" opposition between the third and fourth sections: "[f]irst . . . a temple-cleansing feast, and then the most serene and devout of all divine services: a communion on Friday" [Pap. VIII 1 A 590]. In considering SK's critique of his officially Christian society, the "Thoughts Which Stab in the Back" deserve careful attention.

SK obviously paid considerable attention to the structure of the "Thoughts Which Stab in the Back." This collection of discourses begins on a low and muted note with the peacefulness of the "house of the Lord," but the tone rises quickly as he points out the danger hidden in that calm, and builds to a climax as he approaches the question of the stance required of the Christian with regard to "the world." Is it enough, SK asks, to be *willing* to suffer, or are outward suffering and literal martyrdom *necessary* for the Christian? As SK works out his conclusions in the remainder of the collection, the tension created by this question diminishes, and the collection ends in the relative calm of his assertion that faith is subjective in nature.

The first of the discourses of the collection is thus entitled "Watch Your Step When You Enter the House of the Lord," and it sets the tone for the entire group. The church is serene and splendid, but "how much danger [there is] in this security!" [p. 168]. The priest preaches "in order to tranquilize," to satisfy human needs or "the demands of the times," and in order, with well-spoken-ness and vanity, to protect from terrifying reality those people who, "in world-liness and ungodliness, [want to] sit quite safely in God's House" [p. 169]. There is so much in church which "lulls to sleep" that even though the priest's "observations" [Betragtninger] might in themselves be of an awakening nature, they lose their significance through the effects of habit and repetition, just as a much-used spring loses its elasticity [ibid.]. This is SK's resounding rejection of the two major wings of Danish Christianity, each of which was in its own way descended from the pietist wave of the early nineteenth century: the Mynsterian "observations" of the respectable classes and the popular ritual theology of Grundtvig, with his "cozy and peaceful, God, is Thy House!"[5]

SK stresses that churchly reassurance is dangerous and that Christianity must not forget the pain of self-denial and the terrors of sin. Christianity is not a free gift, a safe, quiet hour of experiencing the divine, but is something that involves the whole person in utter seriousness, a risk: "[P]recisely because there is everything to gain, there is also everything to lose" [p. 177]. God understands only "one sort of honesty, that a person's life express what one says" [p. 171]. Be careful, SK warns, when you say that you thirst for the truth, for you may come to learn the truth, which is that

> it can be required of you that you must, in self-denial, give up everything in which the natural person has its life, its happiness, its pastimes. . . . The truth teaches that a person must die away from finitude. . . . [I]n the Lord's House, you come to know the truth: that you must die away from the world. [p. 175]

SK's message seems almost self-contradictory. In comparison to Mynster and Grundtvig it is sheer sternness; it is even sterner than his earlier message in "Opposition is Support": One must die away. Yet it is only in the conditional: "[I]t can be required of you" that you must give up everything. The solution seems to be that, in comparison to the Christianities of Mynster and Grundtvig, SK must indeed strike a note of sternness and risk, but at the same time, he does not take it upon himself to preach a religion of universal and unavoidable martyrdom. All must "die away" from the world in such a way that they are continually in readiness for whatever sacrifices eternity "can require" of them. In short, this is not an undialectical gospel of martyrdom but remains SK's familiar gospel of priorities: "Die away" internally, in possibility; give up all, literally, physically, if required. Have all things, in short, as though you had them not. SK concludes that one must walk a middle path: One ought neither scare people utterly away from Christianity (for what is fear and trembling in human terms is blessedness in Christian terms) nor ought one to invite people under falsely calm and comforting pretences. "Woe to you, if you win them in such a way that you omit what is frightful" [p. 178], SK concludes, echoing similar sentiments expressed in *Works of Love* about those who proclaim a saccharine Christianity and dare to leave out "the possibility of offense."[6]

The next of the "Thoughts Which Stab in the Back" is entitled "'See, We Have Left Everything and Followed You, What Shall We Have' (Matthew 11:28)—And What Shall *We* Have?" The tension builds here, as SK makes the critical edge of the preceding discourse even sharper. SK writes that Job had everything taken from him, but Christianity is something more: "*[v]oluntarily* to give up everything, that is Christianity" [p. 181], and this is "something which so-called Christendom would rather not mention" [p. 182]. The daily arrangement of our lives so that we never have to face any trials or dangers, but remain good Christians all the way through—this is worse than the Christian of old who broke down on the torture table. This is because the apostasy of old was simply wrong action and was not sinful in the strictest sense. The comfortable circumstances SK describes, on the other hand, are sin, properly understood, not casuistically, but as a condition, a state of being, "the continuing, daily sin—or a life which, with consciousness and with a view of the situation, has arranged itself in sin, and which has also provided itself with the hypocrisy necessary to preserve the appearance of goodness" [p. 183]. We will see this definition of sin developed further in *The Sickness Unto Death*. What can be seen here is that SK's theoretical definition of sin is clearly linked to the practical-polemical argument that underlies "the attack on the church," with its criticism of the established "Christianity of habit" which (as we have seen and will see again) is the special characteristic of the "spiritless" philistine bourgeoisie. "In God's eyes, therefore, there is no sin so disgusting as the sin of shrewdness" [ibid.]. What "the world" really condemns in the Christian who renounces Christ in the hour of trial is not his apostasy but his lack of shrewdness in getting involved in a dangerous situation in the first place. The Apostles, for example, left everything, left their "accustomed jobs, a quiet bourgeois life" [p. 184] and ventured into uncertainty and the double danger of suffering and of rejection by their fellows, loosing all ties in order to seek "God's Kingdom and his righteousness" [Matthew 6:33]. Here, in stressing a Christianity that involves suffering and the opposition of the world, SK again fails to cite the rest of the now-familiar scriptural passage, namely that then "all these things will be added unto you." Even so, while SK seems to take a tough, ascetic line, the prioritarian vision is implicitly present.

In going further with this problem, SK arrives at the critical question: Am *I* prepared to abandon all and follow Christ? Have I the right to lay this burden upon myself or expect it of others—is outward suffering and literal martyrdom necessary, or is it enough that one be willing to shoulder this burden if God requires it? Having asked the question, SK cannot find an easy answer; he demurs and begins to search for a resolution. It would be "dishonesty toward God" if one demanded literal and necessary sacrifice of others [p. 187], and then if they said that they would indeed gladly give up all should it be required—"yes, how dare I say that it was not true?" [p. 188]. Still, though, SK has nagging doubts. Look at the numbers, he says; just about everyone claims to be a Christian, but in biblical times very few actually met the test. Here SK borders on one of the major problems of the "attack on the Church": One suspects that the overwhelming majority are frauds, yet who are they? SK backs off, and instead of calling upon people to abandon all things, which perhaps God does not require of them, he calls on us to praise "honesty," which God does require of everyone [ibid.]. This call for honesty is the root of the later call for the established Church to make an "admission" of inadequacy, the theme that dominated the early phase of the "attack on the Church." SK concludes that he who would forsake all, if God required it, acts Christianly, just as he who, in humble self-awareness does not forsake all if God does not require it, also acts Christianly. Indeed, SK does not know whether there is anywhere in Christianity an unconditional demand for Christians literally to forsake all [p. 189]. But, what God will not tolerate is "dishonesty," which is the sin which makes grace impossible. Dishonesty begs for the cheap grace which avoids martyrdom but refuses to confess inadequacy and weakness. However much SK attempts to tighten the tension between Christianity and human society, he still cannot bring himself definitively to take leave of the prioritarian position of Matthew 6:33–34.

The third of this group of disturbing discourses is entitled "Everything Works for Our Good—*When* We Love God." SK here asserts a need for a personal engagement with faith, and polemicizes against speculative neo-Hegelian theology. He attacks the fashion of theorizing and constructing proofs for Christianity by those theory-minded Christians who wish to "go further" (SK cites Martensen's phrase), for every objective proof is deceptive in that it actually leads one *away* from what it pretends to prove [p. 200]. What is needed is to appropriate Christianity personally; only then is Christianity true *for you*; only then, when one understands that God is Love for you, does everything serve for one's good. God, in short, cannot be understood to be Providence as an objective attribute, but only from within a personal faith.

"The Resurrection of the Dead is at Hand, of the Just and of the Unjust" is the title of the discourse which follows, and, like the previous discourse, it is directed against the intellectualizing of Martensen and speculative theology and insists instead upon personal appropriation. At the risk of being "unscholarly and uncultured" [uvidenskabeligt og udannet], SK wants to "disturb security" [p. 204] by raising the issue of resurrection and immortality not as a theoretical problem, but as a personal concern. "They have made immortality into a question, have turned what is a task into a question, what is a task for action into a question for thought" [p. 206]. Rather, SK writes, one ought not to direct the "attention of cultured people" [Dannets Opmærksomhed] to the question of immortality. Instead we should acknowledge that "immortality is judgment," that it exists whether we will it or not; immortality is certain, and we must tremble for it [ibid.]. We must remember that immortality is our inescapable condition, that what is eternal is the separation between right and wrong, and we must abhor foolish security and live—in fear and trembling— in grace, which is equally removed from despair [Fortvivlelse] and mere safety [Sikkerhed] [p. 211].

Above all, we must not trivialize the importance of immortality by being drawn into endless theoretical speculation, which does not obligate *us* to anything. This is what "the [human] race" always does: It problematizes immortality and subtly abolishes God as ruler. It "abolishes God" and "makes the race into God" [p. 213]. The person who insists on referring to people as "individuals" [Enkelte] is a rebel in God's name against this usurpation. Here, as later in *The Sickness Unto Death*,[7] speculative philosophy, which was a fashionable ideology of a tiny cultured elite, is held responsible for unleashing a sort of spiritual rebellion that usurps God's place and ends in mob rule. The speculative sins of the elite lead to the triumph of the mob.

In the fifth of the "Thoughts Which Stab in the Back," entitled "We Are Now Nearer to Our Salvation Than When We Became Believers," SK again circles around the question of whether Christendom and so-called Christians are really heathens, and again he draws back. Referring to the scriptural citation that makes up the title of the discourse, SK asks: Have we, in fact, ever become believers? Where are we? Are we in Christendom? "He who must speak of Christianity in Christendom, is he a missionary who must broadcast Christianity, so that all this about Christendom is a fantasy? Or must he assume that we are all Christians? Or must he make distinctions, and if so, how shall he make distinctions—where are we?" [p. 214–15]. Again we see the beginning of the underlying problem of the attack on the Church, and it is significant that SK attempts no simple answers here, but only an assertion that we must not be "secure" [tryg] in "sensory illusion and fantasy" [p. 220]; we must remember that Christianity is not a "doctrine at a scholarly distance" but rather a personal task, a question of how one *relates* to doctrine [p. 215].

The sixth of the "Thoughts Which Stab in the Back," entitled "It is Blessed to Suffer Mockery for a Good Cause," is perhaps the most troubling of them all. Here one can most clearly see the tension in SK's position between, on the one hand, the desire to castigate Christian culture and preach the necessity of conflict with one's worldly surroundings and on the other hand, the fear of claiming the "authority" straightforwardly to preach martyrdom or political change. As can be seen from remarks in SK's journal, socially and politically understood, this discourse hangs suspended in the tension between rejection of the social snobbery and exclusivist notion of culture represented by Mynster and his coterie and an equally powerful rejection of what SK labels "communism" or "the tyranny of the fear of people" [Menneske-Frygtens Tyrannie], which was the anonymous, all-corrosive end-product of the development and deification of human equality [Pap. VII 1 A 598, p. 276; cf. also ibid., X 2 A 237]. In short, SK wished to destroy the official Christian culture of the Golden Age, but without substituting for it a triumphant and omnipotent "people" whose voice was the voice of God. He wanted neither the amalgamated Christian state, which was Denmark's (and Europe's) mediaeval inheritance, nor the modern version of the classical pagan state in which, according to the Rousseauian dictum, the general will, as anonymous as it is ubiquitous, is greater than the will of all. Let us look more closely at the discourse.

Mockery, SK writes, is an honor to one who serves a good cause. Next, however, SK goes a long step further and asserts that indeed, any other form of recognition, such as worldly honor, respect, power, etc., makes the good which one has done into something less! [p. 223]. This is a highly controversial formulation of the necessity of suffering for Christianity, a formulation which SK subsequently qualifies almost to the point of unrecognizability in order to preserve the dialectical and subjective nature of the God-relation. Christianity, SK continues, is at any rate "suspicious" of honor and respect, and, he says, Christianity claims that it is "among those who were mocked while they lived . . . [that] the true Christian is ordinarily found" [p. 226]. But again SK strengthens his claim of heterogeneity between Christianity and worldly power: "For this is the opinion of Christianity: It is impossible that the eternal, the true, can win the approval of the moment [Øieblikket]; [it] must necessarily win its disapproval" [ibid.]. Here SK seems to have again retreated into a simplistic requirement of opposition to the world. However, in the very next sentence he adds that when Christianity talks about those who are not witnesses to true Christianity and are

> among the honored and respected, Christianity does not mean simply high positions and offices. This is especially important to emphasize—and indefensible to conceal—in view of the claim of these times, which rebel against all government, that this very unruliness is supposed to be Christianity. It is also certain that such a life in highness and power is often lived in true sacrifice of real respect and honor. [pp. 226–27]

SK is here caught in a cleftstick and is trying to get out. On the one hand, by asserting the inescapability of suffering and self-denial in the personal appropriation of the God-relation, SK wants to oppose the respectable Golden Age clerical establishment, with its Mynsterian "observations" and neo-Hegelian theorizing, and he points to the opposition of the world and of Christendom as signs of such suffering. On the other hand, SK wants to avoid being caught in the trap of labelling as false Christians all those who enjoy power and respect, and he especially wants to avoid giving a blank check to the radical democratic critics of the establishment, who delighted in making just such criticisms and in calling their critique "Christian."

This is a theme that has been sounded earlier—in *Works of Love* and in the discourse on "the worries of exaltedness"—namely the rejection of those unruly members of the party of movement who have "the revolting impudence of ungodly worldliness" to laugh in a worldly way at the authority of the exalted and who justify such political laughter with an appeal to the transcendental categories of religion. SK insists that even though Christianity knows that all earthly power and respect is vanity, it condemns as a blasphemous misuse of religion any attempt to press this religious insight into the service of politics. In short, SK is condemning the confusion of categories which invokes the name of Christianity to cover what is really only liberal or democratic politics. However, as has been noted throughout the present work, in taking such a stand SK carefully avoids making any judgment about a liberal or a democratic rearrangement of the state *per se*. Thus, SK here attempts to escape from a tight spot and to kill several birds with one stone. He asserts a Christianity that is critical of the surrounding culture, yet protected by the shroud of subjectivity from simplistic demands that it be straightforwardly recognizable, demands for signs and wonders. And, at the same time, SK attacks liberal and democratic forces for having confused the categories of religion and politics.

SK thus seems to want to have it both ways, to assert that Christians never win the approval, but always the disapproval, of their times, and, at the same time to assert that while Christians "ordinarily" are among those mocked by the world, it is often the case that those who enjoy the world's honor and respect lead lives of "real" sacrifice. The problem for SK was to define a position that made it possible to criticize "Christendom" without giving support to (or being lumped together with) liberal or democratic political-religious views on power and authority. In terms of church politics, this meant to discredit the view of Christianity represented by Mynster and Martensen, but not in such a way that it could be construed as lending support to the positions represented by Clausen or Grundtvig.

SK's conclusion is that it is ungodly, that it is forgetful of the eternal, to seek worldly honor, to live for the moment, or, as he puts it (with clear reference to the familiar Matthew 6:33–34), to *"seek first* the moment" [p. 227, emphasis added]. But in his zeal to criticize the compromising mildness of his age's Christianity, SK does not spell out the full conclusion entailed by his statement; he omits the conclusion of the scriptural passage to which he alludes, namely that if one does have one's priorities correctly ordered, then "all these things will be added unto you." SK's position, which does indeed build upon the whole of Matthew 6:33–34, is presented in a truncated, abbreviated version, owing to the rhetorical needs of his immediate political position. But the only tenable construction to place on his argument is that positions of worldly honor and respect are acceptable as long as one does not "seek them *first."* SK does not develop this side of his position here, as it would make it difficult for him to criticize those within the Church of whom he disapproved. Indeed, SK goes rhetorically in the opposite direction and stresses that Christianity, in becoming bound up in the cultural concretion known as "Christendom," has failed; it has conquered in the world, but in a worldly fashion [p. 228]. The true conquest, however, is internal: "To conquer oneself is to become a Christian" [pp. 228–29]. Therefore, "in Christendom there are perhaps a good number of true Christians, but every one of them is also a struggling Christian" [p. 229]. SK has now again retreated to a more dialectical, less straightforwardly polemical position. Yet he seeks to sharpen his point all the same; he reminds his readers that all this about struggle is easy enough to approve of in the abstract, but problems arise in putting it into the context of "the present age," which always prides itself in being at last rid of the hypocrisies and shortcomings of the past. Think of the comedy, SK writes, of preaching suffering and struggle before the respected and powerful people who call themselves "Christians" but who are really "worshippers and cultivators of the fear of people [Menneskefrygten], that is, a gathering of the honored and respected" [p. 231]. But who, specifically, are these powerful and respected "Christians" who cultivate the fear of people? SK will, quite properly, not be pinned down; he wriggles away.

However, if we focus attention on some of SK's private notations in his journals, we can see very clearly at whom these remarks were aimed. In March 1848, when the *Christian Discourses* were finished in manuscript and had probably already gone to press, SK reflected on this particular discourse and saw it as aimed at the party of movement or "the communists" as he rather loosely called them.

> [T]o equality corresponds a form of tyranny: fear of people [Menneske-Frygt]. I have already drawn attention to this in the last discourse of the Gospel of Sufferings [in *Edifying Discourses in Various Spirits*]. It is to this I have again drawn attention in the 6th discourse of the 3rd section of *Christian Discourses*. It is the most dangerous of all tyrannies, in part because one needs to have one's attention drawn to it, because it cannot be seen straightforwardly. The communists here in Denmark and elsewhere fight for human rights. Good, so do I. Precisely therefore do I use all my strength to combat the tyranny of the fear of people. [Pap. VIII 1 A 598, p. 276]

So, those who are targeted in SK's attack on "the tyranny of the fear of people" are "the communists," i.e., the party of movement, the radical reformers and revolutionaries, the liberals and democrats. But is it *only* them? Is not SK's criticism directed even more at those who sit in church and call themselves Christians, while they secretly are "worshippers and cultivators of the fear of people"? To answer this, we must look a bit further in SK's journals, to the time shortly after the *Christian Discourses* were published, when the conservative old churchman Mynster proved himself to be a wily politician who could accept the terms of the new regime. Mynster was quite willing to bargain with the liberals in church politics by ordaining, without protest, the liberal politician Monrad as the bishop of Lolland-Falster in an overtly political bargain between the new and old orders. It becomes clear from SK's journals that it is not simply the "communists" who worship "the fear of people" and cling to power but also *Mynster*, who has demonstrated by ordaining Monrad without a murmur that his life is "a lie. The lie consists in the fact that in cowardly fashion he has avoided reality [and has] arranged a sort of privatissimum of important social circles—in which he knows, by the way, that Christianity is not exactly dominant—and has lived in it" [Pap. X 2 A 237, p. 177 from 1849; cf. also X 6 B 212 in connection with Mynster's ordination of Monrad]. This sixth discourse of the "Thoughts Which Stab in the Back," on which SK sacrificed an inordinate amount of time, reflection, and concern, is thus not only directed against the party of movement but with perhaps even greater vehemence against the party of order, the ruling circles of official Christendom, who combine a quiet thirst for power with their taste for "Dannelse" and exclusive social coteries. SK finds the cynical flexibility of the conservative elite even more offensive than the anonymous power represented by the newer forces.

In the seventh and last of the "Thoughts Which Stab in the Back," entitled "He is Believed in the World (I Timothy 3:16)," SK re-emphasizes the subjective nature of faith as a personal engagement and completes his retreat from pronouncing specific judgments on the religious postures of others. The important thing, SK tells us, is not the objective statement that "He is believed in the world," but the subjective fact that *you* believe. "One person cannot see into another's heart, where faith dwells, or better, where it can be seen whether faith is or is not there. It is only the individual himself, before God, who knows, concerning himself, whether or not he has faith" [p. 235]. The only one besides oneself who knows is God, who has "the omniscience of the Knower of Hearts" [Hjertekjenderens Alvidenhed] [p. 236]. The polemical, judgmental, "objective" tone is replaced by a subjective, personal one: "Faith relates itself to the personality; but personally understood, when *I* have believed, it is indifferent how many others have also believed; and when *I* have not believed, it is indifferent how many others have or have not believed" [p. 237].

SK then develops a "poetic-experimental" person who loves father, children, wife, native land, etc. but who would be willing to put them all aside—without being untrue to them, SK insists—were it religiously required of him. However, this person, who is taken up by religious concerns all the time, feels himself a stranger in Christendom, and Christendom in turn thinks it "strange and exaggerated" to find such a passionate interest in religion in someone who is not professionally connected with it [p. 242]. Yet, though tempted, this person will not judge his fellow "Christians" in Christendom, but will simply interpret the scriptural passage "He is believed in the world" as having been confirmed by his own personal faith.

> I conclude nothing from this concerning the extent to which all of those who live in Christendom really are believers; I know nothing at all about others concerning faith. But this I know, "He is believed in the world," and I know it quite simply from the fact that I have believed and believe in him. [Ibid.]

SK thereby reins in his (public) criticism of Christendom before it can come to concern specific personalities, or indeed others, at all. The important thing is to turn away from the objective—objective proofs of Christianity, objective criticism—to the subjective.

We are clear enough about the objective, doctrinal contents of Christianity, SK writes, and this ground does not need to be gone over yet another time. What is lacking in the midst of all this doctrinal theorizing is the personal element. It is possible that Christianity could disappear while the theoreticians are busy putting it in its final theoretical form. "Certainly it is required that in order for a person to be Christian he must believe something *definite*, but just as certainly it is also required that it is *quite definitely* 'he' who believes" [ibid.]. The government has seen to it that there is plenty, more than sufficient, enlightenment as to *what* Christianity is about, SK continues; what is needed, however, is not more expertise but for people to take the risks of faith, to achieve "the complete inward reformation of the spirit, whereby a person, in mortal danger for his spirit, in seriousness, in true inwardness, comes to believe at least something of the great deal of Christianity which he knows" [p. 243]. Otherwise, we merely have more "learned scholarly bother" [p. 244].

In this final discourse of the most important section of the *Christian Discourses*, SK's criticism has found an uneasy point of rest and balance. Here, the emotions and suspicions summoned up by the decadent state of Christian culture—with its intellectualizing theorists, its well-spoken sermonizers, and its invocation of the name of Christianity to support the politics of liberal, of democratic-demagogic, and of snobbish conservative circles—are channelled away from overt criticism and into an intensification of the private, subjective God-relation of faith. This last of the "Thoughts Which Stab in the Back" is muted in comparison to the others and prepares the transition to the quiet devotion of the "Discourses at the Communion on Fridays" which conclude the *Christian Discourses*.

E. "DISCOURSES AT THE COMMUNION ON FRIDAYS"

The seven concluding "Discourses at the Communion on Fridays" are remarkable only in their characteristically Lutheran combination of quiet optimism and a confession of man's abjection. All are guilty; all have crucified Christ and do so even now in their hearts; all labor with the burden of guilt, or more correctly, sin. The Gospel is preached to all, but not to humanity-in-general; one comes to the altar one at a time. One comes to the altar to receive God's blessing. "Blessing is everything. For what is blessing? Blessing is what God does; everything that God does is blessing" [p. 316]—though at the altar, where we come to receive God's blessing, we are incapable of anything, even of maintaining the thought of our own unworthiness which makes us capable of receiving the blessing, and even of holding ourselves on the pinnacle of the consciousness that one has need of blessing and grace. One must be supported by blessing even at the altar where one has come to receive it [ibid.]. God's transcendence is radical and absolute, our abjection total, yet there is ground for optimism, for God is greater than our own self-accusations in condemning ourselves. He will hold us fast even as we are unfaithful, for "God fundamentally holds onto us" [Gud i Grunden holder paa os] [p. 299]—an echo of the underlying optimism that we glimpse in *Works of Love*, where SK talks of "love's presence in the fundament of things" [Kjerligheden i Grunden] like "the sprout in the seed."[8] Despite the fact that we are freely situated with respect to choice, the respective claims upon us by good and evil are not *absolutely* equal. For all our freedom, we are not suspended in sheer equilibrium.

Despite our perdition, the good has a deeper presence in us; it is in the fundament of things, just as, in our freedom, God fundamentally holds onto us. SK concludes his otherwise so polemical *Christian Discourses* on this "inward," positive note.

Christian Discourses is the most polemical of the works we have examined. Its mood is very dark indeed, and it contains many passages that tend in the direction of recommending a purely oppositional martyr role as the only way for the Christian individual to relate to the social and political sphere. The "saint" is certainly in the ascendant. Yet, SK's fundamental view of social and political engagement still remains rooted in Matthew 6:33–34. Thus, although he seems to enjoy quoting or alluding to only the first half of the Matthew passage, in which one is adjured to choose God's kingdom first, he cannot escape from, and continually makes allowances for, the second half, which holds the promise that the Christian can also be a "citizen," i.e., can *then* partake of "all these things." *Christian Discourses*, for all its pessimism, still retains the prioritarian vision and defends it against "ungodly confusions"—both those of the conservative Golden Age cultural junta, with its speculative philosophy and eloquent sermonizing, and those of the ill-assorted party of movement, the "communists."

23. *The Sickness Unto Death*

○

A. INTRODUCTION

SK composed *The Sickness Unto Death* [*Sygdommen til Døden*] [SV XI, pp. 111–241], his most perfect book, in the first five months of 1848, the period from just before his completion of *Christian Discourses* until mid-May. These were the months which in Denmark saw both the successful and revolutionary change of regime from absolutism to liberal constitutionalism and the outbreak of the long and bitter civil war with the German-speaking provinces. Like the next major work, *Training in Christianity, The Sickness Unto Death* was released under the pseudonym "Anti-Climacus," though in both cases the Kierkegaardian authorship was made quite clear by the appearance of SK's name on the title page as "editor." "Anti-Climacus" was SK's only important use of pseudonymity during the entire period under study, and the name was chosen to designate someone "Christian to an extraordinary degree," in contradistinction to "Johannes Climacus," the pseudonymous author of *Philosophical Fragments* and the *Concluding Unscientific Postscript*. Johannes Climacus was a non-Christian who described Christianity from without and was therefore at the opposite remove from SK himself. *Sickness* thus ought to be read together with *Training* as SK's expression of the ideal or absolute demands which Christianity makes upon the individual, demands which SK did not dare to formulate under his own name but which he felt deserved expression nonetheless, by an ideal and hyper-Christian pseudonym. Even with the distance which a pseudonym provided, SK deliberated for thirteen months before deciding to commit *Sickness* to print, and it did not appear until July 13, 1849.

A full-scale investigation of this concentrated and difficult psychological study would be a book in itself and is not required here, where we are interested in SK's critique of his society and in the views of politics and social responsibility present in his work. Thus we will here confine ourselves to a brief look at the conceptual vocabulary developed in *Sickness*. Thereafter, we will turn our attention, first, to the social-historical correlatives of the varying sorts of "sickness" described, and then to the notions of politics and "health" that are also present in the book.

B. THE CONCEPTUAL VOCABULARY OF *THE SICKNESS UNTO DEATH*

On the title page, *The Sickness Unto Death* is further qualified as a "Christian psychological exposition for edification and awakening." SK[1] wishes by this description to differentiate the book from ordinary, profane scholarship, which is characterized by an "indifferent" scholarly detachment that claims to be humanistic "heroism" but that is actually "inhuman curiosity." Genuinely Christian knowledge, SK contends, is not at a distance; it is engaged, "concerned" [bekymret], and genuinely serious in that it relates to "the reality of the personality" and involves true heroism. True heroism is not the stoical neutrality of scholarship but a "daring entirely to be oneself, an individual person, this particular individual person, alone before God, alone in that enormous effort and that enormous responsibility" [p. 117]. As Christianity understands matters, SK insists, there is no neutral, scientific ground. Everything that is not "edifying"[2] is thereby un-Christian [ibid.]. This is SK's formulation of Romans 14:23, "Everything that is not of faith is of sin," a scriptural citation which appears numerous times in the book and which is a principal leitmotif.

The "sickness unto death," Christianly understood, is a sickness worse than any physical ailment, and it involves a death worse than any physical death. It is a sickness of the spirit, and it leads ultimately to the death of the spirit. The self, SK explains, is spirit, that is, a self-reflective or self-conscious relationship between necessity and possibility, finitude and infinity, body and mind. That is, the self is *that* this relationship between two elements of a synthesis can also reflect upon itself. In addition, since the human self is posited by God, the self is also *that* this relationship can relate itself to God [pp. 127–28].

The sickness unto death, which is a sickness of the spirit or of the self, is a misrelationship within the self and is known generically as despair, and within specifically Christian categories as sin. Because of the complex structure of the self-system, there are three fundamental forms of despair, which vary in intensity according to the level of complexity at which the misrelationship has fastened itself. The lowest form of despair is "spiritlessness" [Aandløshed], which is to be unconscious that one has a self, i.e., that one is a spiritual and not merely a physical or mental-physical being. This is to fail to realize that one is capable of reflection; to fail to reflect upon the fact that one is a synthesis; and to fail to realize that one can not only reflect upon this, but that reflection can reflect upon itself. The next form of despair involves awareness that one is a self, but this self wishes, despairingly, not to be itself. The self wishes to escape the self that it is aware it is. It wishes to abandon its humanity. This is the despair of weakness. The third and highest level of despair is that of the self that is aware of being a self and that wishes, despairingly, to affirm itself as the human self it is, but to affirm itself without at the same time recognizing the relatedness and ultimate dependence of that human self upon God. This is the despair of defiance.

Thus the three levels of intensification of despair correspond to the three levels of increasing complexity within one's consciousness of the structure of the self: (1) at the lowest level is spiritlessness, i.e., unconsciousness of being a self-reflective synthesis; (2) at the next level is weakness, i.e., consciousness of being such a human self, combined with the desire to escape from that condition; (3) and the highest level is defiance, in which the self proudly affirms its self-consciousness and its humanity but wishes to end its systematic understanding of itself while still on the purely human plane of self-sufficiency, without acknowledging any transcendent relationship to God. If, on the other hand, one is the (hypothetical) healthy individual, one "relates oneself to oneself, and in willing to be oneself, the self grounds itself transparently in the Power [God] which established it" [p. 128].

Thus far the forms of the sickness unto death have been sketched from the point of view of natural humanity and have been defined as forms of despair. However, if one examines the forms of the sickness from the specifically Christian point of view, the sickness itself can be seen to be the revealed, dogmatic state or condition known as sin, and the individual types of despair [Fortvivlelse] can be seen to be various intensifications of "offense" [Forargelse].[3]

Because the self is not a static essence but a relation that relates (or misrelates) itself to itself and that also relates (or misrelates) itself to God, sin is not an individual action or series of individual actions or "sins," but an ongoing misrelationship or posture. Likewise, SK continues, the opposite of sin is not, as the pagans thought, the individual right action or series of right actions called "virtue" but rather the ongoing relationship of health, which is faith. Thus the Socratic definition of sin, for example, corresponded to the static, heathen view of the self, and sin was seen as ignorance of the Good. This Socratic conception, SK contends, was too naive to grasp the situation as it really is. The categories of ordinary human thought, of which the Socratic philosophy was the best representative, "lack a dialectical category appropriate to the transition from having *understood* something [the Good] to *doing* it" [p. 204, emphasis added]. Here Christianity comes in with the notions of will, of defiance, and with the revealed dogma of original sin.

For modern philosophy the motto is *cogito ergo sum*, for in ideality, as in Socratic thought, thinking is identical with being, and there is no time between knowing the Good and doing it. For Socrates, as the greatest of all heathen philosophers, this error was excusable, but the crime of modern philosophy is that it repeats this error while passing itself off as "Christian" [ibid.]. Here *The Sickness Unto Death* develops the by-now-obligatory attack on "modern speculative Christianity," i.e., Martensen's speculative dogmatics, which in lecture form had been the wonder of the Danish theological world in the 1840's and which were published in their definitive book form as *Christian Dogmatics* in the summer of 1849, almost simultaneously with *Sickness*. Speculation, SK complains, claims to have an orthodox Christian understanding of sin, but at the same time it gives up the paradoxical quality of this Christian concept and makes Christianity "comprehensible" [begribelig] by "going further" than Socrates, by understanding "the highest," and rolling everything up into a synthesis called "the result" [p. 203]. No, SK insists, Christianity says that man is in sin and cannot understand the Good because *he does not want to*, and that he requires God's revelation to show that he is in sin [p. 206]. Sin itself is thus a revealed, dogmatic, Christian category, not accessible to natural humanity or to speculation, and in fact, SK daringly asserts, it is not the doctrine of atonement but the doctrine of sin which separates Christianity from heathenism [pp. 200–201]. SK's final, careful formulation is that "Sin is, after having been informed by a revelation from God about what sin is, before God, despairingly to will not to be oneself, *or* before God, despairingly to will to be oneself" [p. 207]. Thus the definition of the sickness unto death as sin is identical with the earlier definition of this sickness as despair, with the difference that the sickness is now observed from within definitively Christian categories—i.e., that the entire process is now seen as taking place "before God" and after having received divine revelation in the form of Christianity. After the advent of Christianity as a divine gift, the categories of natural humanity and natural illumination no longer suffice for describing the human condition and the human sickness.

"The Christian doctrine of sin is sheer impudence against humanity," SK writes [p. 206], and may be rejected as an "offense," which is the specifically Christian form of despair. All sinners are to a greater or lesser extent offended, SK writes, and those who try to defend Christianity by removing offense do it a disservice by minimizing or overlooking its radically heterogeneous demands. Rather, SK writes, continuing his running feud with speculative theology, we should call attention to offense and warn against it [p. 195]. "He who first discovered the idea of defending Christianity from within Christendom is *de facto* a second Judas; he, too, betrays with a kiss, only this treachery is that of stupidity. To defend something is always to disrecommend it" [p. 198]. Similarly, every individual exists in full individuality before God, and this also raises the possibility of offense, with which speculation attempts to compromise by avoiding the notion of the individual before God and substituting instead a universal concept, such as the human race.

Sin, thus, is not Socrates' lapsus, or a negation, but an existential state, a willed condition, a "position," as SK calls it. This is something upon which orthodoxy insists, and so-called orthodox dogmatics has also claimed that sin is a position, but it has at the same time claimed that it can "comprehend" [begribe] the fact that sin is a position. "The secret in all comprehension is that comprehending is itself higher than every position which it posits" [p. 207], and speculative dogmatics thus backhandedly, by a "queer misunderstanding," pulls the dogma down into the realm of logic and out of revelation. Speculation insists that its understanding of sin is orthodox, that sin is indeed a position, but, SK adds, what speculation really means is that sin is a position "only to a certain degree,"[4] i.e., only so much of a position that it can also be comprehended by thought. "The Christian [version is] that sin is a position, though not such that it can be comprehended, but as a paradox which must be believed" [p. 208]. When Christianity commands that we must either believe or be offended, it is "shamelessness" or "thoughtlessness" to want to comprehend it, and it takes "perhaps no little self-denial, in such speculative times, when all 'the others' are busy comprehending, to confess that one neither can nor will comprehend it" [p. 209]. We need a bit of the old Socratic ignorance to maintain the qualitative boundary line between God and humanity in order to keep them from running together in "the system"; we must hold fast to faith and paradox [p. 210]. This attack on speculative philosophy and theology, which is an integral part of SK's definition of the sickness unto death as sin, also has a very concrete function, as we shall see shortly, in SK's diagnosis of the political expression of that sickness.

Because of our peculiar anthropology, the capacity to despair is a sign of the eternal in us, the sign of our greatness. The *reality* of despair, however, is humanity's greatest misfortune. Despair is our never-ending, impotent attempt to be quit of our own spirit, of our connection with the eternal; it is "an impotent self-consumption" [p. 132]. Because we are established by God, despair is an objective condition that can exist without our being conscious of it, and to be unconscious of being in despair is a particular—and the lowest—form of despair, spiritlessness. The other forms of despair, in which one is in varying degrees conscious of one's condition, are higher and more intense, in one sense at a greater remove from health, while in another sense, that of potential energy or consciousness, closer to health. Everyone, SK writes, must have had some sense of being at least a bit ill, or one has not awakened. There is no immediate form of spiritual health [p. 139]. The immediacy of the child or animal, for example, is not a category of spirit, for spirit is precisely mediacy or consciousness. SK thus writes of a relatively intense form of despair that it is "precisely because this despair is more intense that [it is] in a certain sense nearer to salvation" [p. 174]. A person who without affectation admits to having this sickness is closer to being healed than those who do not believe they have it. It is the greatest misfortune never to have had this sickness, but at the same time it is the most dangerous sickness when one refuses to allow oneself to be healed from it [p. 140]. To win health, one must come to the highest level of consciousness, to the realization that one is spirit and that one exists, as the individual one is, for God, and this "prize of infinity is never won except through despair" [ibid.].

When trying to find one's way amid difficult concepts such as these concerning the dialectical relationship of sickness and health, one is often best served by taking one's cue from the metaphorical language one glimpses and in directing one's attempts at understanding accordingly. In discussing despair and its Christian correlative, offense, *The Sickness Unto Death* frequently employs metaphors borrowed from astronomy and physics, and one is thus directed to think in terms of points in space and of absolute and relative motion in relation to these points. Despair and offense are in themselves neutral ("dialectical," SK would call them) *points*, whereas sin and its opposite, faith, are *directions* or *movements*. Although the viewpoint generally adopted in the book is that the forms of despair are mileposts on the road of sin, which leads away from self-realization and the affirmation of the God-relationship,[5] when viewed from the other side, if one is moving in the opposite direction, the various forms of despair can be mileposts on the road of health. "In the life of the spirit everything is dialectical," SK writes in this connection [p. 226n.]. Thus, for example, despair over the fact that one is a sinner can be the first moment of faith, when one is moving in that direction, but when the movement is in the opposite direction, despair over one's sinful condition is merely new sin, a confirmation and consolidation of one's journey on the road of perdition [ibid.].

If one is self-aware and moving in the direction of faith, but is repelled by offense, that is a form of sin, but it is an even worse situation if one is so distant from oneself that one cannot even be offended by Christianity [ibid.]. Thus, too, one can believe oneself to be healthy and happy and to be in motion in the direction of self-fulfillment, but the motion that one perceives by virtue of one's limited consciousness of the self is, in effect, only relative motion, and in order for that motion to be the movement of faith it must be in the direction of realizing one's ultimate dependence upon God. One may believe oneself to be rising but in fact be sinking [p. 220]. Only when motion is measured in relation to an absolute, fixed grid or ground is it absolute motion; only when one's perceptions coincide with absolute and objective reality can they be trusted as indicators of the actual situation. Thus, as in Newtonian physics, where all motion is ultimately referred to the absolute gridwork of the Universe which Newton calls "God's sensorium," so also, in the Kierkegaardian "physics" of perceived and actual health, all motion is ultimately referred to God or to the fact that we all exist, not exactly in God's sensorium but "grounded in the Power which established us." Thus, too, a study of the sickness unto death becomes—in another of SK's deliberate allusions to the language of physics—the study of "the law of motion in the intensification [of despair]" [p. 218], where one's perception of one's position becomes increasingly correct in accordance with one's level of consciousness. Increasing intensity in despair does not itself heal, but the increased consciousness of one's position, which the higher levels of intensity involve, is a precondition of health. Again, we can see that "the prize of infinity is never won except through despair."

C. THE SOCIAL TYPOLOGY OF *THE SICKNESS UNTO DEATH*

Let us turn from the "law of motion" of this sickness to its particular phases, in order to see to what extent they contain a tacit or explicit analysis of particular social types. Because the self is a synthesis of finitude and infinity, necessity and possibility, etc., the human sickness can be described according to whether it excludes or overemphasizes one or the other of the moments of that synthesis, and SK does sketch the rudiments of such a logical analysis. But the human self, in addition to being a synthesis, is also, to one degree or another, a *conscious* being, and the sickness unto death therefore admits of examination under the rubric of the varying degrees of consciousness; it is this latter phenomenological approach that most engages SK's attention.[6] Both sorts of analysis, however, lead to essentially the same results, namely a tripartite description of the levels of intensity that the sickness can take, and in our examination of these levels, or forms, and their social correlatives, we will go through the three levels in ascending order of intensity of consciousness.

The lowest form of despair, viewed from the point of view of consciousness, is, as we have seen, "spiritlessness." (This is also the condition of those who, viewed under the rubric of self-as-synthesis, lack infinitude or possibility.) Further, as one might expect from the other works we have examined, spiritlessness is the most widespread form of despair and is precisely and specifically characteristic of the well-integrated and self-satisfied philistine bourgeoisie of Golden Age Christendom, of Christian gentlefolk. SK states quite explicitly that, when viewed as a person lacking the component of infinitude in his or her make-up, the sick person is the "bourgeois philistine" [Spidsborger],[7] a member of the crowd, characterized by ethical limitedness and narrowness [Begrændsethed og Bornerthed] [p. 146]. But this sort of despair is very little noticed in the world, where it is in fact these people who are most often admired as successful [pp. 147–48].

As a social group, the "philistine bourgeoisie" can be more precisely defined as members of the comfortable urban middle class, more likely to be of the world of business, perhaps, than their betters, the intellectuals and professionals who often held appointments as royal officials and who enjoyed greater social esteem. Because of their business connections, the philistines were also more likely to entertain, if rather timidly, liberal political notions than the more respected upper crust of intellectuals and office holders, which was generally quite conservative in outlook. As we have seen in part one of the present work, both segments of the bourgeoisie, regardless of political outlook, were in general quite elitist. The philistines constituted the bulk of the bourgeoisie and of the literate public, yet they were not themselves tastemakers. Rather, they were followers, consumers of the taste or ideology that had been prepared by their superiors in "Dannelse" or "Culture." Culture was the revered value of philistines and the cultured alike. The philistines sadly acknowledged their short-comings in this respect and took their lessons and corrections from their betters, who, in turn, delighted in serving as schoolmasters in matters of taste and culture. This is the relationship we have noted in Heiberg's *A Soul After Death*. The two portions of the bourgeoisie thus lived in mutual dependence, in a symbiosis of producer and consumer of ideology.

A more detailed examination of this social type can be made if one continues by examining this individual as a person whose synthesis lacks possibility, i.e., a person in whom necessity reigns at possibility's expense. If such a person follows this imbalance to its logical conclusion, he or she is a determinist or fatalist, a frightful state to be sure, but one which at least looks the absence of possibility squarely in the eye and which, precisely because of its radicality, contains the possibility of growth and change. More common, however, is the more stable and normal denial of possibility within the self, and this is the condition of the bourgeois philistine.

> Bourgeois philistinism is spiritlessness.... Bourgeois philistinism lacks every category of spirit and is taken up into the realm of probability, within which the possible has its little bit of room.... [I]n order to become aware of oneself and of God, fantasy must swing a person to something higher than the atmosphere of probability.... [p. 153]

Philistinism, then, operates within the boundaries of shrewdness, of probability, within which it attempts to accommodate "the possible." This is SK's description of bourgeois calculation and self-protection, where business-like methods presumably are transferred into the life of the spirit, with predictably deadly results. Unlike fatalism or determinism, which faces squarely a disquieting reality, bourgeois philistinism tranquilizes itself into spiritlessness with its apparently comforting compromise notion of "probability." "It leads Possibility around captive in the cage of Probability, exhibits it, imagines itself to be in charge, not noticing that it has thereby imprisoned itself to be the slave of spiritlessness and the most wretched thing of all" [p. 154].

Viewed specifically under the rubric of consciousness, the spiritless person is one who is ignorant of having a self, or of having an eternal self, and is in despair even though he or she is not aware of this despair. That this form of despair can exist at all is possible, as has already been noted, only because we have been established by God; because, consequently, our nature and the truth in us has an objective quality, independent of all consciousness about it; and because the truth insists on having its own, on having what is its right [Sanhedens Rethaveri] [p. 155]. All forms of despair are forms of negativity or negations of the God-relationship that is essential to the human self, and ignorance of one's own despair is but another negativity. "In order to reach the truth one must go through every negativity" [p. 156], so that the spiritless person, far from being freed from his or her despair by this ignorance of it, is actually more deeply mired in it and has another layer through which he or she must go if health is to be attained. In a reference to the dangers of this unconscious despair, SK points out that the person who *is* conscious of being in despair is only closer to salvation in one sense, but SK continues by saying that "so far is ignorance from abolishing despair or making it into non-despair that, on the contrary, it can be the most dangerous form of despair" [p. 157]. Spiritlessness or ignorance is by far the most common form of despair, and it is characteristic of "the heathen," both those of classical times and, especially, those of Christendom. (It was this latter group of "heathen" to whom the first section of the *Christian Discourses* had been addressed.) In a simple, direct sense, the classical heathens lacked self-consciousness of being spirit, while the latter-day heathens "lack spirit in the direction of being opposed to spirit, or by having fallen away from it, and are therefore spiritless in the strictest sense" [p. 159].[8]

In the second, and more specifically Christian half of *The Sickness Unto Death*, SK pursues his quarry of spiritlessness still further, and it becomes even more forcefully clear that not only is this type a bourgeois philistine but that this person is the specialized product of Christian culture: the cautious, respectable, unruffled, middle-class Christian gentleman, a consumer of the ideology of respectable Christianity dispensed by the Heiberg-Mynster-Martensen circle. Take, for example, the extraordinary claim that Jesus Christ can forgive sins. If one is not a self-conscious, healthy person (i.e., in faith), it takes "an unusually high degree of spiritlessness, that is, that which is ordinarily found in Christendom" to avoid being offended by this claim [p. 226]. But, of course, Golden Age Christendom has managed to produce just this degree of blandness. SK asserts that Christendom is in fact so spiritless that, for the most part, it is not even, in the strictly Christian sense, in *sin*. "Most people's lives are, Christianly understood, too spiritless even to be called sin in the strictly Christian sense" [p. 214]. Of course, SK points out,

> to be a sinner in the strictest sense is certainly very far from being advantageous. But on the other hand, how in all the world can one find an essential consciousness of sin (and note, that this is something Christianity indeed wants) in a life which is so sunken in triviality, in silly aspiring after "the others," that one almost cannot call it—that it is too spiritless to be called—sin, and is only worth, as the scripture says, "to be spit out." [p. 212]

Yet we also know, from what we have already learned in *The Sickness Unto Death*, that even this self-satisfied ignorance of spiritlessness is in fact a form of sin, for sin is an objective condition that exists independently of one's awareness of it—just as our synthetic composition and our God-relatedness are also objective conditions. One's ignorance of one's condition is a *"produced ignorance" [frembragt* Uvidenhed, p. 199, emphasis added], as SK puts it. The spiritlessness that makes spiritual concepts simply inapplicable—"like a jack-screw in a bog" [p. 212]—is brought upon the individual by himself or herself. "Is it [spiritlessness] something that happens to a person? No, it is the person's own fault. No person is born with spiritlessness" [ibid.]. Where, then, does it come from? Who helps the people lull themselves to sleep? Naturally, Chris-tendom, Christian culture itself, is the worst and most clever enemy of Chris-tianity and consciousness. It must be said, SK insists, "as unreservedly as possible" that

> this so-called Christendom—in which everyone by the millions is thus without further ado Christian, so that there are just as many, exactly as many, Christians as there are people—is not merely a poor edition of Christianity, full of typo-graphical errors that distort the meaning, and thoughtless omissions and ad-ditions, but that it is a misuse of it, that it has taken Christianity in vain. [Ibid.]

Christendom is a demonically stable compound, a self-affirming and symbiotic relationship of the tastemakers and the priests, on the one hand and the phil-istines, on the other.

In Christendom, SK writes, people typically are only occasionally, mo-mentarily conscious of being spirit, once a week for an hour (i.e., in church), which is a "bestial way of being spirit" [p. 215]. Yet this is the consequence of Christian culture, of "the priests," who have so abused the nearness of God in Christianity that people, when they do go to church, go there in conde-scension, to honor God with their presence [p. 225]. Thus, too, most people have become, have been permitted and encouraged to become, so spiritless that they can avoid the open, conscious forms of offense at Christianity and have instead tacitly decided to withhold judgment on Christ [p. 239]. Most people would indeed not find this to be a form of offense, but offense, like the other modes of describing the sickness unto death, is an objective fact, whether we wish to dignify such spiritlessness with the name "offense" or not, because Christianity requires us to take a position. The cautiousness of taking no po-sition is itself a position. In the mediocre Christianity that is proclaimed now-adays, SK writes, perhaps many may never have heard the word "must," which is an essential part of Christianity, and it is to deny Christ his divinity if one denies him the power to compel decision. Indifference is no more a permissible position with respect to God than it is with respect to the self [ibid.].

The critique of "spiritlessness" has broadened from a personality critique of a specific social group, the philistine bourgeoisie, to an indictment of Chris-tendom *per se*. As has been noted earlier in the present work, both the "spir-itless" philistine followers and the cultured leaders of Christendom—regardless of the fact that the former were likely to be associated with the respectable fringe of the party of movement, whereas the latter were likely to be solidly for the party of order—shared the same notions of elitism, of refinement, and of a hybrid Christian culture. Both are seen by SK as the interconnected components of Christendom when he rejects them and gives them the blame for the nation's decadent spiritual constitution. We will turn to the specifically political side of SK's attack later in this chapter. For now it is sufficient to have established that SK's description of the lowest and perhaps most dangerous form of the sickness unto death, spiritlessness, is specifically linked to the philistine bourgeoisie and that it is through the medium of "Christendom" that this group has been helped to consolidate itself in its ignorance and complacency. Later we will see that this "misuse" of Christianity has also led to the release of a dangerous virus which threatens to destroy all social, as well as all religious, order. For now, however, we can take our leave of spiritlessness, of the self-satisfied Golden Age "Christian gentleman," SK's favorite target.

Another low form of despair that warrants attention is "despair over something earthly," a sub-form of the despair of weakness (the desire not to be oneself), and it often results in driving the despairing person back into unconsciousness or spiritlessness, a condition to which it is closely related. A person in despair over something earthly can grope inwardly for a while, or may turn outward, SK writes, toward busy activity,

> toward, as it is called, Life, Reality, the active life . . . for many years happily married, an active and industrious man, father, and citizen, perhaps even a great man; in his house the servants call him "Himself"; in the city he is among the notables; his behavior is that of a respectable person, or with the respect of one who is, as far as one can see, a person. In Christendom he is a Christian (in just the same sense that he would be a heathen in heathendom, and in Holland a Dutchman), one of the cultured Christians [de dannede Christne]. [p. 168]

By means of "shrewdness" he has conquered—repressed and rendered unconscious—the despair which had flickered into consciousness, but his shrewdness is really a dangerous and profound "stupidity," for it lulls him away from consciousness and self-awareness. Though this form of despair originally contained a glimmer of consciousness, SK apparently feels that we should group it in the general category of spiritlessness, for he labels it "the most common form of despair" [p. 169], a term he elsewhere reserves for spiritlessness proper.

The various reflective types of despair become rarer as they become more reflective. Most people, SK continues, do not even attempt to live as spirit, and to be concerned for one's soul, to wish to exist *qua* spirit, is seen by the world as a waste of time that should be punished by law, or as madness, as treason against humanity, to be met with disdain and mockery. Quiet, respectable, unconscious or faintly conscious despair, on the other hand, is the mode, and those who practice it "are Christians, reassured by the priests concerning their salvation" [ibid.]. Most people live their whole lives without surpassing the spiritual state of childhood and youth—immediacy with a bit of reflection—and they usually come to regard despair (by which they mean the beginnings of a consciousness of despair) as a quality of youth, which one outgrows in order to become what the world calls "mature." But even this leaving childishness for the "maturity" of the bourgeois philistine is really a loss [pp. 170–71].

In order definitively to take leave of spiritlessness, one must look at the more intense variants of the "weak" (but conscious) form of the sickness, namely the self that is no longer spiritless, but is shut up or "encapsulated" [indesluttet] within itself. Such a self refuses to call upon the help of forgetfulness in order to slip back into spiritlessness and become "a man and a Christian like other men and Christians; no, the self is too much self for that" [p. 174]. Such encapsulation can take a myriad of forms, but, SK points out, it is quite capable of taking on the incognito of respectability just like its counterpart, the spiritless bourgeois philistine, though the differences between the two outwardly similar types are instructive. This more intensified type of despairing person plays the role of the respectable citizen less convincingly—at any rate to himself.

> Our despairing person is thus encapsulated enough to be able to hold every extraneous person—i.e., everyone—away from his self, while, externally, he is entirely a "real person." He is an educated man, a husband, father, even an unusually capable official, a respectable father, pleasant to be with, very sweet to his wife, carefulness itself with his children. And a Christian?—well, yes, he is that, too—however, he prefers to avoid talking about it, even if he is happy to see, with a certain wistful joy, that his wife occupies herself edifyingly with godly things. He goes to church very rarely, because it seems to him that most of the priests don't know what they are talking about. [p. 175]

Thus, as can be seen from this middle level of consciousness of the sickness, the more consciousness one has of one's condition, the less the church and the official ideology of Christian culture satisfy, though, by the same token, the greater is the real but unfilled spiritual need that is opened up.

The final and highest level of consciousness that the sickness takes is that of defiance, in which the self defiantly and despairingly wills to be itself in defiance of the power which established it. Such a self wishes to "create itself" [at skabe sig selv, p. 179],[9] and its proud and conscious defiance of its own ultimate ground can take two forms, both of which are Promethean. The active form is that of the stealer of fire, sheer Byronic energy, the absolute ruler of oneself, the inhabitant of the realm of pure possibility, a realm that never becomes anything actual or concrete. One is in fact absolute ruler over nothing, and the splendid structures one builds are only "castles in the air" [p. 180]. The alternative, suffering type of defiance—Prometheus chained to the rock— is a proud unwillingness to shoulder the burden of temporality and positivity that is one's lot, a despairing superiority to the world with its strife and duties. Thus the defiant Promethean, according to whether he is "active" or "suffering," tries to abandon the eternal or the temporal component of the self [p. 181], while SK explains that the healthy individual, on the other hand, meets his or her responsibilities both to eternity and to time [cf. pp. 181–82n.]. As we have seen in our examination of other works, and as we will shortly see in our examination of SK's view of health and politics in *The Sickness Unto Death*, both parts of the human synthesis are indispensable, even though the eternal part ought to occupy a superior position; it is just as much a form of despair to desert the world for "eternity" as it is to attempt to forget the eternal for the world. SK's presentation of these two forms of Promethean defiance is symmetrical.

In ascending order of consciousness, the three basic forms[10] of the sickness unto death are thus *spiritlessness, encapsulation*, and *defiance* [Aandløshed, Indesluttethed, and Trods], and they correspond to distinct social types. Spiritlessness, or unconscious self-satisfaction, is the special characteristic of the philistine bourgeoisie, whereas defiance is the property of the highly self-conscious oppositional type, the romantic genius-rebel. These two types correspond to the extremes of unconsciousness and hyperconsciousness that we have seen clearly delineated earlier, in *A Literary Review*, as the rebel of Revolutionary age and the self-satisfied burgher of the "present age." Encapsulation and the despair in which one consciously wills not to be oneself have a mediating, or middle, position between these two extremes, and a typical representative is the respectable and dutiful Christian who sees the hollowness of respectability and fears the emptiness of his or her Christianity without having anything definite to substitute for these things. This troubled individual is perhaps SK's ideal reader. Let us turn both to an examination of the way in which humanity's sickness demonstrates itself in social behavior and to an examination of our potential. That is, let us investigate, in the final section of this chapter, the notions of politics and health contained in *The Sickness Unto Death*.

D. POLITICS AND HEALTH

The other works we have examined so far were all composed prior to the great revolutionary wave that swept over Denmark and Europe in the spring months of 1848. However, as has been mentioned, *The Sickness Unto Death* was written during these cataclysmic events, and it thus gave SK an opportunity to set forth his version of what was happening to Christendom, his diagnosis, and also the beginnings of a proposed cure.

> The fundamental misfortune of Christendom [SK writes] is really Christianity; that is, that the doctrine of the God-Man . . . by having been preached again and again, has been taken in vain, that the qualitative difference between God

and humanity has been pantheistically abolished, first aristocratically, speculatively, then by the mob in the streets and alleys. [p. 227]

Elitist intellectual circles—i.e., such speculative philosophers and theologians
as Heiberg and Martensen—have compromised Christianity by abusing the
Christian notions of God and the God-Man in order to deify their own aristocratic-conservative notion of a compound Christian-bourgeois culture. This
disrespect for the distance present within the nearness of God and humanity
in Christianity has carried over from the elite conservative circles to liberals
and to street revolutionaries. "Of course," SK continues, "a good number of
the philosophers who participated in spreading this doctrine of the superiority
of the generation to the individual turn away in disgust when their doctrine
has sunk so low that the mob has become the God-Man" [p. 228]. The elitist
conservatism of the leading circles does not change the fact that the present
development is their creation. SK thus charges that the very same leading spirits
who had made such a career out of taunting—and being idolized by—the philistine bourgeoisie, laid the groundwork for the ensuing rampage of spiritlessness under the banners of the deification of the people. It is our familiar symbiosis of the "refined," ideology-producing portion and the philistine or
spiritless, ideology-consuming portion of the Christian bourgeoisie. Without
naming individual names, SK is in effect charging Heiberg, Martensen, *et al.*
with having made possible the success of Orla Lehman and the rabble behind
him.

    According to SK, what has happened in the political arena of Christendom
is merely the analogue to what has happened in the religious sphere, namely,
that "the doctrine of the God-Man has made Christendom impudent" [ibid.].
Instead of having limited what humanity claims as its rightful sphere, the
Christian doctrine of the God-Man—speciously interpreted by modern speculative philosophy and theology—has fuelled an all-consuming pride and ambition, so that the age sees a God who comes close to humanity as weak, like
a king who has been obliged to grant a constitution, and people secretly whis-
per: "Well, he really *had* to" [ibid.]. The speculative interpretation of the doctrine of the God-Man has overlooked or minimized the significance of the
absolute and qualitative distinction between God and humanity that lies at the
center of the closeness of God to humanity and has thus made Christian culture
impertinent in relation to God. It makes no difference that the cultivated aristocrats who started this misinterpretation of the relation of God to humanity
did so in the name of refinement and the status quo, because their handiwork,
in SK's opinion, formed the intellectual and spiritual climate that nurtured the
revolutionary forces of levelling and mob rule. The speculative abuse of the
God-Man in order to deify humanity became the most powerful weapon in
the arsenal of "the tyranny of the fear of people." The conservative misuse of
the God-Man has led to the revolutionary notion that the voice of the people

is the voice of God, and now it is believed that when "the public, the highly honored, cultivated public, or the people" commits a crime in collectivity, it is no longer a crime but "God's will" [p. 232].

The only way out of political and religious chaos, in SK's opinion, is a firm rejection of both camps, both the aristocratic Hegelianism of the "cultured" class and the will-o'-the-wisp notion of absolute, deified, popular sovereignty favored by the "philistine" class. All forms of philosophical or political abstraction must be eschewed, and every person must confront his or her own concrete individuality and responsibility as an ethical and religious individual. "If order is to be maintained in existence . . . attention must first and foremost be given to the fact that every person is an individual person and becomes aware of being an individual person" [p. 227]. Each person must resist the temptation to be melted into an abstraction, the mass. This mass wishes to combine with the doctrine of the God-Man in order to deify the totality of humanity, for whom, by implication, anything will be permissible if it is done in the name of the people. SK's political philosophy is one of self-restraint and priorities, of political modesty and self-control.

From the very beginning, SK continues, Christianity has protected itself from impertinence and presumption with the doctrine of sin, whose category is the category of individuality, which cannot be speculatively thought [p. 228]. Sin and the individual person do not admit of being thought, and speculation, knowing this, belittles them. The doctrine of sin brings with it the realm of the ethical, with its concentration upon reality and the individual, whereas speculation cannot hold fast to concrete individuals, but merely to abstractions. "The dialectic of sin is diametrically opposed to the dialectic of speculation" [p. 229]. The individual and the doctrine of sin as the responsibility (and the sickness) of the individual are Christianity's mode of protecting itself against any impertinent familiarity that would abuse the closeness established between humanity and God by the God-Man.

For God, every individual sinner exists in his or her full individuality, and God has no trouble keeping track of it all. It is not as a simple equality via the abstract middle-term of the human race, but as a sinful individual, and in fear and trembling, under pressure and in humiliation, that one ought to feel one's relatedness to God, SK writes. Unlike animals, where the example is less than the species, with humanity it is the individual who is greater than the race, "and this definition is again dialectical, signifying that the individual is a sinner, but also that it is perfection to be an individual" [p. 230n.]. Thus the doctrine of sin not only splits the mass into individuals but also strengthens the qualitative difference between God and humanity, for in no way is a human so absolutely different from God than in being a sinner "before God." The two things—God and humanity—which Christianity holds together, can be seen all the more clearly, because of their proximity, to be qualitatively different [p. 231].

Thus, humanity is separated from God by the chasm of sin, and God is separated from humanity in his ability to forgive sin. Right here, in the heart of the religion that has most taught the equality of God and humanity, SK stresses, is also to be found, in its most concentrated form, the possibility of offense, which is necessary to keep us from confusing God and humanity [ibid.]. For, as we have seen, without the possibility of offense, the doctrine of the God-Man would simply be the deification of humanity and would give us total license. "Christianity's doctrine is the doctrine of the God-Man, of the kinship between God and humanity, but, be it noted, such that the possibility of offense is, if I dare say so, the guarantee by which God ensures that humanity cannot come too near him" [p. 235].[11]

Therefore, the possibility of offense, which speculation has done so much to minimize with its notion of mediation, must be re-emphasized as a corrective both of religious and of political confusion. In SK's view, these confusions are threatening to create an all-engulfing Leviathan, a monster more terrible than any of the properly pagan cultures, precisely because it derives its power and its presumption from its distortion of Christianity's unparalleled claims. The clergy of Christendom are afraid to accentuate the fact that Christianity is "inconceivable" [ubegribelig]—which is synonymous with the possibility of offense—and they dare not stress the pure and simple command to believe [p. 238n.]. Instead, the theologians set out to "prove" the perfection of Christianity, and thereby—like the lover who, in setting out to "prove" his love, proves only that he dissembles—they demonstrate their fraudulence [p. 214]. For no proof, no argumentation, not even Christ's love, can take away the fact that Christianity contains at its core a moment of absurdity, which one must accept in faith or reject, in offense, as untruth. "The fact that there is an infinite qualitative difference between God and humanity—*there* is the possibility of offense which cannot be taken away" [p. 237]. Christ can do all in his approach to us; he can take on the guise of the humble servant, etc., but he cannot take away the possibility of offense, and even if he could, he would not want to [pp. 235–36]. "These words: 'Blessed is he who is not offended in me' are a part of the proclamation of Christ" [p.237]. To reject them straightforwardly as untruth is the highest form of sickness, according to SK, the sin against the Holy Spirit for which there is no help. The possibility of this highly conscious form of the sickness unto death is the irreducible core of Christianity, and without this possibility, its opposite, faith, which is the only genuine state of human health, would be rendered impossible.

By producing an emasculated version of Christianity, which seeks to circumvent intellectual embarrassment and the real dangers of this highest and most conscious form of offense, Christendom has also ruled out the alternative form of the highest consciousness, which is health. As a result, society has been tranquilized into a state of semi-consciousness and has been sent careening down the road of political disaster. Here, and with increasing intensity in the future, SK saw his task as the opposite of this tranquilization—namely, to call attention to the qualitative differences which lie at the heart of Christianity, to stress the possibility of offense, and, in effect, to make Christianity *dis*respectable, so that the Golden Age juggernaut of philosophically and theologically sanctioned Christian culture would come to a halt. That task and the task of rebuilding on that wreckage were not, however, essential parts of *The Sickness Unto Death*, but of its projected sequel, *Fundamental Recovery*.

The Sickness Unto Death does, however, contain an incidental description of the healthy condition and of the place of social obligation in the healthy individual. In discussing the self as a synthesis of infinitude and finitude, SK writes that

> the self is the conscious synthesis of infinitude and finitude, which relates itself to itself, whose task is to become itself, which can only be done in relation to God. To become oneself is to become concrete.[12] But to become concrete is neither to become finite nor to become infinite, because that which must become concrete is indeed a synthesis. The development must thus consist in coming infinitely away from oneself in the infinitization of the self, and in coming infinitely back to oneself in finitization. [p. 143]

The self must both be out of the world and in it simultaneously; it must abstract itself *and* return. This is quite in keeping with the prioritarian vision of Matthew 6:24–34, which was a major theme in the *Christian Discourses*. The self must be

> to the same degree concrete and abstract, so that the more infinite it becomes in purpose and determination, the more entirely present and simultaneous it becomes with itself in that little part of the task that can be done right now; so that, in becoming infinite, it [the self] in the strictest sense comes back to itself; so that when it is *farthest away* from itself . . . [it] is at the same instant *nearest* to itself in doing that infinitely small part of the work that can be done even today, even in this hour, even in this instant. [p. 145]

This is the health of the ordinary Christian, of the "citizen" who, in seeking *first* the Kingdom of God *also* turns to the task immediately at hand, to ethical participation in the world—i.e., to "all these things" of Matthew's Gospel. Such a hypothetical, healthy individual realizes himself or herself both as finite and as infinite, as temporal and as eternal.

However, what about the case of the exceptional individual who is called to witness specifically to the transcendent and absolute priority of the divine? This is the problem with which the *Two Ethico-Religious Essays* somewhat inconclusively concerned themselves. It is the problem of the Christian who does not find wholeness in any form of integration with the world and its problems. Instead he finds it in inexorable opposition to the world; it is the case of the saint rather than that of the citizen.

The Sickness Unto Death contains an apparently autobiographical digression about "the poetic-existence with a religious tendency" [p. 189], which would ordinarily not be of particular interest to the present work, with our non-biographical approach to SK's work. However, in discussing what might well be his own case, SK raises an issue that is of much more than personal significance. Indeed, SK's treatment of this question clarifies a great deal about the posture which his authorship takes toward social responsibility (and toward participation of the individual in "the world") *and* about his scornful rejection of the deceit that he saw as underlying Christian culture. This rejection of the fundamental presuppositions of Christendom takes on an increasing importance in SK's work. Indeed, the polemic against Christendom ultimately displaces SK's attempt to arrive at any final answer to the question of whether an exceptional suffering individual ought to seek ethical integration into the world *or*, instead, can justifiably see himself as called upon to resist the world in all its forms in order to martyr himself, in one way or another, by witnessing to the absolute transcendence of the religious sphere.

In discussing the condition of a person who feels that he might be one who is called to the saint-martyr role—and thus called to resist any form of integration in the world—SK writes,

> His collision is really this: Is he the one who has the call? Is the thorn in the flesh [i.e., his inconsolable suffering] an expression of the fact that he will be used for the extraordinary? Is it in God's order that he has become the extraordinary? Or is the thorn in the flesh something under which he must humble himself in order to achieve that which is universally human? [p. 190]

Thus, the choice for the individual who feels himself or herself exceptional in his or her suffering is whether to regard this sense of exceptionality as a hidden form of pride and therefore to humble himself or herself under the same ethical norms that hold for others in the world *or* to regard this sense of a call to exceptionality and to solitary witness as a true call to accept "authority." If one chooses ethical participation in the world (under the "prioritarian" rubric, to be sure), one implicitly labels one's tendencies toward martyrdom as hubris or masochism, but one also risks the possibility of being in bad faith to the Absolute, which has indeed singled out others in the past, so why not in the present instance? Is the struggle to accept the universal ethical norms of the world really a flight away from accepting solitary opposition to the world as one's appointed role? Is the rejection of pride really a form of cowardice? On the other hand, is the choice of solitary suffering a heroic witness to God's absolute transcendence, or is it pride and dementia? If such suffering was ever justifiably assumed by individuals in biblical times or the intervening centuries, how can one reject its possibility now?

The dilemma of how the person who feels he or she has a "thorn in the flesh" is to interpret these sufferings can thus be seen to be the same dilemma that underlay the problem of "authority" in the *Two Ethico-Religious Essays*. In both cases, what appears to be an abstruse discussion of the personal fantasies of some tormented individual—perhaps SK himself—is actually a theoretical rumination on the question of Christianity's claim upon the individual. On the one hand, Christianity requires the individual to be a citizen who— even while "having all things as though he has them not"—lives a socially and politically engaged life in accordance with universal ethical norms. On the other hand, Christianity may also assert its absolute claim and command the individual to resist social integration and be, in short, not "citizen" but "saint." How is one to deal with the potential conflict between the roles of "citizen" and "saint?"

But here, again, as in the *Two Essays*, after having turned up the tension to the highest degree possible, SK does not resolve it but breaks the spell by pointing out that, in any case, the absurdly shallow and hypocritical situation of present-day Christendom makes it impossible even to discuss this question intelligently. SK does indeed seem to lean in the direction of solidarity with his fellows and of finding the hankering after sainthood a bit suspect. However, before he can resolve the problem—and immediately after his statement about the "collision," within the individual, of the positions I have labelled the saint and the citizen—SK continues:

> But enough of this. I can say with the emphasis of truth: to whom am I speaking? Such psychological investigations to the Nth degree—who concerns themselves about them? The insipid pictures that are painted by the priests are more easily understood; alas, they resemble anyone and everyone, people as they are for the most part: spiritually understood, nothing. [pp. 190–91]

The argument summarized above applies both here and to the choreography of the authorship as a whole: The difficult, perhaps unanswerable question of authority—but which is not for this reason unaskable or unworthy of being asked—is moot until all unseriousness in the hybrid bourgeois culture of "Christendom" has been disposed of.

In this apparently autobiographical fragment, SK thus turns away from his discussion of the personal (and general) problem of the potential conflict of worldly responsibility with the transcendent authority of religion, to the immediate task at hand: an attack on the actual state of Christendom in order to alter the situation and make discussion possible. The movement here is thus in miniature that of the later authorship, generally, and the "attack on the Church," in particular: a meditation upon a profoundly important hypothetical conflict, interrupted by the cold truth that such meditation is useless in the actual present context; this, in turn, is followed, finally, by a concrete, practical-political intervention in the form of a polemic calculated to change that actuality. The political implications of SK's authorship are striking both in their similarities to, and in their differences from, those of another great critic of

Hegel, namely Karl Marx: One must both talk about life and change it, for the talk makes change necessary, and the change makes talk possible. "Health" requires *both* consciousness *and* action.

24. Training in Christianity

O

A. INTRODUCTION: THE HISTORICAL SETTING AND STRATEGIC PLACEMENT OF *TRAINING IN CHRISTIANITY*

Even before he had completed writing *The Sickness Unto Death* in May 1848, SK had already begun work on its much more radically critical companion piece, *Training in Christianity* [*Indøvelse i Christendom*] [SV XII, pp. 1–239], which, like *Sickness*, was also authored (officially) by Anti-Climacus. *Training in Christianity* was completed by the early part of December 1848, but (presumably because of its polemical nature) SK delayed in publishing it for nearly two years, until September 1850, a much greater delay than for any other of the major pieces published in his lifetime. *Training* is the major turning point in SK's career from the time of the conclusion of the properly pseudonymous authorship (with the *Concluding Unscientific Postscript*) until his death. It marks the beginning of a relentless and single-minded campaign against "Christendom," in which SK no longer takes time to discourse in detail upon ethics or Christian love or the psychology of the individual but moves steadily into an increasingly open posture of conflict with the established Church and the Golden Age notion of Christian culture. *Training in Christianity* marks the beginning of the rapid transformation of SK's work from the criticisms of a reformer into the angry zeal of a Samson, culminating in the "fight against the Church" [Kirkekamp] which marked the last year of his life.

Training in Christianity was seen by SK as a "dialectical" or pivotal book, a book that could be taken either as a declaration of war against the marriage of religion and culture or as a stern and loving corrective, an ultimate warning. As we shall see, the book was an ultimatum. The "author" was Anti-Climacus, while the "editor" was Søren Kierkegaard. The intent of this pseudonymity was not to obscure the actual facts of authorship, which were obvious enough, but to allow for the proper sort of "dialectical distance" between SK's own position as an "ordinary" person and the radical critique permissible for an author who was not embarrassed to wield "the ideal." We must bear in mind the distinction between the "ideal" position articulated in *Training* and SK's own position for two reasons: first, in order that we can see the book as the *ultimatum* it was when it was published in December 1850; and second, in order that we can see how the same book was transformed into a *weapon* when SK dissolved that distinction in the heat of the attack on Christian culture four and a half years later, in May 1855.

The only place in *Training* where SK speaks officially in his own name is the "Editor's Foreword," where he explains that the pseudonym Anti-Climacus "has forced the requirement for being Christian up to its highest ideal" [p. xi]. "The requirement ought indeed to be spoken, presented, and heard, however. From the Christian standpoint the requirement ought not be diluted or suppressed instead of making an admission and a confession with respect to oneself. . . . The requirement ought to be heard," SK explains, in order that we might learn how properly to make use of grace and avoid abusing it [ibid.]. *Training in Christianity* was a sort of time bomb that could only be defused with an "admission" or "confession" by the officials of Christian culture (presumably Bishop Mynster himself) that the religion preached officially in Denmark was a domesticated, mild form of "the Christianity of the New Testament." Without some sort of show of honesty and humility by the established Church, there was the very strong implicit threat that sterner measures would have to be taken. As we shall see, the implication of SK's position on the mutual delimiting of politics and religion, which we have been following up to now, becomes clear and explicit in *Training in Christianity*: either an honest "admission" that religion had compromised itself by becoming too closely intertwined with the social-political order or a radical divorce between the social-political realm and the realm of religion, carried out by whatever means necessary.

It was no accident that SK decided to make such a drastic escalation of his criticism of the marriage of Christianity and culture at this particular time. SK's decision to issue the "ultimatum," *Training in Christianity*, and to intensify greatly his insistence upon respect for the proper boundaries between politics and religion was made in the context of a specific historical development, namely the long process of peasant self-awareness and self-possession in cultural, political, economic, and religious matters, which culminated in the revolutionary events of 1848 and the democratic constitution of 1849.

As we have seen in part one of the present work, it was Denmark's peculiar fortune to be the only European nation that did not surrender the revolutionary changes made in 1848 to the tide of reaction that followed in the next few years. In some measure this resistance to reaction was due, of course, to the fact that the urban liberal class which had taken over the reins of government had successfully identified itself with the nationalist cause and the patriotic war against the Germans for the retention of Slesvig and the "ancient boundaries" of Denmark. Thus, the easy victory of constitutionalism and of universal male suffrage was facilitated in part by the existence of an external enemy. However, what was far more important was that the peasant mass—"the common man" who constituted some 70–80 percent of the Danish population—had embarked on a long-term project of economic self-improvement, the acquisition of literacy, and the quest for adulthood in religious and political affairs. This movement for peasant "adulthood" far surpassed liberal nationalism in breadth, depth, and tangible accomplishments. As has also been shown in the present work, the latest and most self-conscious phase of the rise of the rural masses can be dated from the land reforms of the 1780's, and the process of remaking Danish economic and political life continued until the early years of the present century. The peasant movement was thus a profound sea change in Danish life, which both antedated and outlived the liberal nationalist movement of mid-nineteenth-century Denmark. The revolutionary changes of 1848 and the democratic constitution of 1849 were far more the accomplishments of the peasant "common man" than of liberal nationalism, which was merely their immediate precipitator.

After 1848–49 it was clear that the state and all its accoutrements, including the Church, the university, the theatre, and all the other official taste-making organs, were, formally at least, no longer the property of the Crown or of a small aristocratic circle of the elect, but were *res publicæ*, the property of the people as a whole. The "common man" could now be held accountable for the functioning of "his" official institutions, and it is especially important in this regard that we remember the great importance attached to this change particularly as pertaining to the Church, the name of which, as we have seen, was officially changed from the "State Church" to the "People's Church" [Folkekirke].

This chapter and the chapters that follow will chart SK's decision to turn from internal criticism to open warfare against an Establishment that deliberately confused the categories of religion with those of politics and society. His decision can best be understood as having been conditioned and motivated, both in its intensity and in its particular timing, by the broad social and political changes that were being consolidated in the years immediately following 1848–49. The change of greatest importance in this connection was that which was mentioned above, namely the legal coming-of-age of the "common man," of the peasant majority, which under democratic parliamentarianism had at least nominal control over its own religious affairs and could no longer blame the failings of the Church on a small group of royal clerics and a faraway absolute regime.

If the newly liberated people was to take responsibility for its religious life, it must be made to differentiate between religion as an absolute and prior commitment of the individual to God *and* religion as a socially supportive institution. By the early 1850's, when the new regime—which claimed to speak for "the people"—came to seem increasingly stable and permanent, SK determined that the time for this distinction to be made was now. Similarly, if the liberals were ever to be compelled to respect the secularism inherent in their own political philosophy—instead of taking the easy way out by retaining the absolutist institution of the State Church and merely renaming it a "people's" institution—the time was clearly now. SK's task in the early 1850's was, in the face of radical political and social change, to teach his society that it was *now* imperative to hold politics and religion separate. The conservative partisans of the *ancien régime* had to be made to realize that the old composite state was gone forever. The liberals had to be made to respect their own secularism and the mutual boundaries of public and private, politics and religion, material and spiritual matters. And, perhaps most of all (as we shall see in the closing chapters), the newly enfranchised common man had to be made to realize that although adulthood as a *political* person implied membership in groups (i.e., the shifting parties and majorities instrumental to material life), that same adulthood as a religious person obligates one to remain, before all else, an integral individual before God.

Thus it was the political events of 1848–49 and the years immediately thereafter which forced SK to concentrate his energies as never before upon the problem of religion and politics and upon defining and delimiting the claims of the social-political realm. Now that it was the official legal property of "the people," the established Church, in claiming to represent "the Christianity of the New Testament," was capable of cutting the "common man" off from his own religious possibilities and from true Christianity far more completely than the old absolutist State Church could ever have done. The ultimatum posed in *Training in Christianity* and subsequent works demanded that the established Church admit its inadequacy and its distance from the genuine "Christianity of the New Testament" and that it grant the individual freedom of conscience in this new democratic age. If this demand for an "admission" was not met, SK made an implicit threat (which, in the event, was carried out), namely, that he would do all in his power to work for the dissolution of the established Church and for the complete divorce of society and religion. As we shall see in the final chapters of the present work, the reason for the continuing escalation of polemic in SK's subsequent writing and in the "attack on Christendom" was not simply the failure of the Establishment to respond to the original ultimatum of *Training in Christianity* but its casual and steady motion in precisely the opposite direction: accommodation with the new political order. Meanwhile, for its part, the new political order was steadily consolidating its position and was quite happy to stabilize itself with the anomaly of a liberal-democratic state church.

B. CHRISTIANITY AS "CONTEMPORANEITY" WITH CHRIST

To return to our consideration of *Training in Christianity*, we will first examine the general tendency of the work as an ultimatum to Golden Age

Christendom; we will then turn to examine its specific discussion of politics and of the proper limits of politics.

In the "Invocation" or opening prayer we are told that "contemporaneity" [Samtidighed] with Christ is the condition of faith, and that, more precisely defined, it *is* faith [p. 1]. This notion of contemporaneity implies a position that has been present to some degree in what we have examined so far but which comes to dominate in the remainder of SK's authorship and to form the underpinning for his assaults on a society that he felt had improperly domesticated the absolute transcendence of religion.

The notion of faith as "contemporaneity" implies a radically dualistic notion of being,[1] in which one's life in the temporal world is a distinctly inferior form of existence, a form of death, while one's life as spirit, in the timeless realm of the eternal, is an infinitely superior and "real" form of existence and is a form of death to the world. Insofar as one is both matter and spirit, one lives on two planes simultaneously, but if one is in a proper relation to the eternal, one's life as "spirit" predominates; one is in faith and is therefore dead to the temporal world. The older prioritarian notion of the Christian as citizen, of the coexistence in the self of the temporal and the spiritual being, has been tightened so much that participation in the temporal realm as citizen becomes almost indistinguishable from martyrdom. We shall see this transformation developed in the chapters that follow.

Contemporaneity with Christ is faith, and the Christ with whom one is to be contemporaneous, SK tells us, is not the resplendent and glorious Christ of the end of time but the degraded and crucified Christ of history, who is thus both "the object of faith" [Troens Gjenstand] and "a sign of offense" [Forargelsens Tegn] [p. 2]. Blessed is he who is not offended, SK concludes. We are to

> fear nothing which can only corrupt the outer person; do not fear them who can kill the body: But fear yourself, fear what can kill faith and thereby kill Jesus Christ for you—offense, which, indeed, can be given by another, but which is, however, an impossibility unless you yourself accept it. Fear and tremble, for faith is carried in a fragile vessel of clay, in the possibility of offense. Blessed is he who is not offended in him, but believes. [p. 74]

Christ says "Come hither, all ye who labor and are heavy laden, and I will give you rest"; he invites absolutely all, making no differences or distinctions [p. 12]. His invitation to salvation is universal. Yet people flee, SK writes, as though Christ had said not "come hither" but *procul o procul este profani*[2] [p. 21]. In fact, we might say that "come hither" and *procul o procul* are the same thing, the content of Christ's message, but that the former is heard by the ear of the spirit and the latter is heard by that of the flesh.

Christ is not to be approached via "world history" or to be judged, humanly, by his life's consequences. Because he was divinity, the intrusion of the eternal in time, the consequences of Christ's life—whether they be a body of moral doctrine, the successful reign of the Church on earth, etc.—are less important than the *fact* of his existence on earth, i.e., the Incarnation; the reverse is of course the case for any mere human [pp. 29–30]. "One can learn nothing about him from history, for nothing at all can be 'known' about him. . . . [A]s God, his life, the fact that he lived and has lived, is infinitely more decisive than all the consequences of this in history" [p. 22]. Thus, Christ is only accessible in personal appropriation as both the "object of faith" and a "sign of offense."

Not only can one not get any knowledge about Christ from history, but, particularly, one cannot prove that Christ, a human, was God, for this is at odds with reason [Fornuft], and therefore can only be proven to be at odds with reason [pp. 24–25]. *Reason* can come to the understanding that all these attempts to *understand* the key to divinity as being lodged in history, etc. are unreasonable and wrong, while faith, on the other hand, can see that these efforts to limit God's absolute transcendence by assimilating him to the human categories of historical understanding (Hegelian world-historical Reason, moral principles, etc.) are mockery of God, blasphemy [p. 27].

It is most important, SK stresses, that we remember that the words of invitation ("come hither," etc.) were spoken not by the exalted but by the degraded and humbled Christ.[3] For the believer (i.e., one who is "contemporaneous" with Christ), Christ's glory is not yet come, yet exists now in faith. Nothing can be *known* of Christ's glory, it can only be *believed* [pp. 22–23]. Thus, when we remember that Christ *chose* his degradation in time, we see that "history" wastes energy (at best) in setting things straight by giving Christ honor, etc. This is because history does not know who Christ was,

> because no one *knows* that, and the person who *believes* it must become contemporaneous with him in his degradation. . . . Woe to the race which impudently dared to say: "Let us now forget the injustice he suffered. History has now made it clear who he was, and has installed him in his proper place." [pp. 31–32]

What Christ did in saving us was inseparably intertwined with the lesson he taught us about what the "truth" suffered, necessarily, in his generation and will suffer, necessarily, in every generation: "Christ freely willed to be lowly, and even though his intention was to save humanity, he also wished to express what 'the truth' must suffer in every generation"—namely, degradation, mockery, rejection, and death [p. 32]. This is SK's understanding of the message of Christianity, namely the radical dualism of "world" vs. "truth," so that what "the world" understands as life, "the truth" sees as death, and vice versa. The world is death to the truth and the truth is death to the world.

The invitation ("come hither") was spoken by the degraded Christ, and one has no right to appropriate a single word of Christ's without becoming contemporary with him in his degradation, his opposition to the world; in this way one will be unable to avoid confronting the possibility of offense against which he warned his contemporaries. But, SK continues, when the invitation is spoken by "an elegant man in silk . . . in a pleasing, melodious voice, so that it gives a delightful echo in the lovely arches, a silken man who casts honor and respect upon those who hear him," then the meaning is precisely the reverse of Christianity; it is heathendom [p. 36]. (This, of course, was a scarcely veiled reference to the style and social function of Bishop Mynster.) Being truly Christian means being an "imitator";[4] it means being an imitator not in the far-off sense of imitating someone long gone but in the contemporaneous sense, so "that your life is as much like his as is possible for a human life" [p. 101]. This is what Christianity is; it is no "doctrine"; any talk of offense with regard to a doctrine is a misunderstanding [ibid.].

Christendom has become heathendom by focusing upon the historical triumph of Christianity since Christ's death instead of upon the obligation to "follow after." But this historical triumph is not the paradigm:

> No, Christ's life here on earth, that is the paradigm; it is in a likeness with this that I and every Christian must strive to form our lives. . . . [E]very generation has to begin from scratch with Christ. . . . And therefore being a Christian in Christendom [i.e., being an "official Christian"] is as different from being a Christian in contemporaneity with Christ as heathendom is different from Christianity. [p. 102]

Similarly, SK insists—in a reference to the respectable Christianity of Bishop Mynster's "observations"—that the meaning of Christianity is that one must "*really* come to suffer with him, not make observations at the foot of the cross" [p. 160]. (Later in this chapter we will deal with SK's extended and vitriolic criticism of Mynster's "observational" Christianity.)

Building on his increasingly radical interpretation of the enmity of truth and world, SK continues, "opportunity enough will be given to you to suffer as he did, but even if no opportunity were given, what is in question in each case is of course not so much the opportunity to do so, but the willingness to suffer as he did" [p. 161]. Here, despite everything, SK is apparently hedging his bet. He leaves open the possibility, not of simple-minded integration in temporality, to be sure, but of a temporal Christian existence that does not include actual persecution or martyrdom, yet is lived in willingness to submit to such suffering. Thus, even here, in the midst of SK's darkly pessimistic *Training in Christianity*, the possibility of "prioritarianism" is held open, but it must be noted that it is a very "strict" version of the two worlds regimen, and that "dying away" is given so much emphasis that one wonders whether such a prioritarian Christian would have any desire for "all these things."

Christ's life may be depicted to us with the degradation stressed and the glory visible only in the distance as an object of faith, or it may be the glory that is stressed, with the degradation as an almost-forgotten memory. SK insists that if true Christianity is to be preached, the former alternative must be chosen; Christ's life in degradation must always remain present to us to keep us from taking the glory in vain [pp. 171–72]. In keeping with the earlier interpretation of "come hither" versus "*procul o procul*," this would seem to mean that all the eye of the flesh can see is the degradation and that the glory is never simply and straightforwardly accessible, but is visible only to the eye of the spirit. Spirit, however, suffers and must suffer in time, for the temporal and the eternal see things oppositely. Thus, there must be a painful confrontation with the possibility of offense, with a suffering renunciation of worldly ease. "Exalt- edness and degradation are related to each other like this." SK tells us: "The true degradation of Christ is not pure and simple degradation; it is simply the mirror-image of exaltedness, but the image is in this world, where exaltedness must show itself in reverse, as lowliness and degradation" [p. 183]. In other words, there are two worlds, and degradation and glory are the same reality seen with different eyes. "Christianly understood, then, degradation in this world is elevation. So Christ went on high, but his life and story on earth is, of course, what he left behind for imitation: that true elevation is degradation, or that degradation is true elevation" [pp. 236–37].[5] The reversal effected by this radical dualism means that it is "as much an essential part of 'the truth' to suffer in this world as it is to triumph in another, the world of truth" [p. 144].

Christianity, then, is "the Absolute." With its strange invitation, Christi- anity does not come into the world as "a luxury edition of mild consolations," but as something which God wishes for us not only out of Love, but also as *God*, i.e., as the unquestionable Absolute. God does not wish to be recreated by humanity as "a nice human God," SK tells us; rather, "*he* wishes to re- create humanity" [p. 59, emphasis added].

> One might also say that relatively [i.e., humanly, temporally] understood, the Absolute is the greatest of troubles. In all the tired, lazy moments in which a person is dominated by sensory things, Christianity is madness to him, because it is not commensurable with any finite Why.... There is indeed an infinite difference between God and humanity, and therefore it was clear in the con- temporaneous situation that becoming a Christian (being re-formed to equality with God), humanly speaking, is an even greater torment and wretchedness and pain than the greatest human suffering, and is, in addition, a crime in the eyes of one's contemporaries. [p. 60]

Thus, that which God wills for us in Christianity is labelled by SK as "inhuman" from every "human" point of view; it is sheer suffering to the individual, and it is seen as criminal in the eyes of others. Yet this is only the view of "rela- tivity."

When a person lives such that he knows no higher standard for his life than that of human understanding, then all of his life is relativity, laboring only for relative ends. He undertakes nothing about which his understanding cannot give a reasonable notion of what to expect, based upon the likelihood of profit and loss, answering for him the question of why and wherefore. It is otherwise with the Absolute. At first glance the understanding ascertains that this is madness. . . . [T]he understanding comes to a halt at the Absolute. The contradiction is to require the greatest possible sacrifice of a person, who must dedicate his entire life to being sacrificed—and why? Yes, there is no why. Then it is indeed madness, the understanding says. There is no why because there is an infinite why. [pp. 110–13]

SK's Christianity is radically anti-worldly, entirely removed from relativity and the relative good, and he grants that it is thus "in a certain sense quite true" that Christianity is "an enemy of humanity" [menneskefjendsk] [p. 111]. And yet, SK maintains, this "antihuman" otherworldliness is precisely true humanity, for this removal from relativity is what constitutes "the possibility of offense" without which there could be no true God-Man, who is always accompanied by this possibility [p. 114].

Modern times, however, have abolished the offense to reason that the God-Man poses, either by taking only the "doctrine" and rejecting the God-Man (Enlightenment moralism) or by resolving the offense of the God-Man into a "speculative unity" (i.e., Hegelianism) [p. 115]. "That which modern philosophy understands by faith is really what one calls an opinion. . . . Christianity is made into a doctrine [e.g., Kant's moral religion]. . . . The next step is therefore to 'conceive' this doctrine [e.g., Hegelian intellectualism]" [p. 131]. According to SK, Kant and Hegel have been sequential distortions of the "absolute" and (from a relative point of view) "antihuman" religion which is Christianity.

Despite all the efforts at domestication by modern philosophy, Christ, the God-Man, remains a "sign." What is a "sign?" "A sign is the denied immediacy, or the second being which is different from the first being" [p. 116]. Thus, he insists that "Spirit is the denial of straightforward immediacy. If Christ is the true God, then he must also be unrecognizable, cloaked in unrecognizability, which is the denial of all straightforwardness. Straightforward recognizability is precisely the characteristic of the false God" [p. 127]. Thus Christ's lack of "straightforwardness" or direct recognizability was not an accidental trait but something essential to the very definition of God, because true religion is shrouded in the unknowableness that necessarily accompanies a qualitatively higher form of being in this world. The only proper sort of human relation to such a higher form of being is not intellection but faith (or offense).

By the same token, SK continues, all of Christ's message is "indirect," even when he appears to speak "directly," for no direct speech uttered by so contradictory a figure as a "God-Man" can ever be straightforwardly and un-problematically appropriated by the human understanding. But,

> take away the possibility of offense, as they have done in Christendom, so that all of Christianity becomes straightforward communication, and Christianity is abolished. It has become an easy, superficial thing, which neither wounds nor heals deeply enough, the untrue invention of a merely human sympathy that forgets the infinite qualitative difference between God and humanity. [p. 130]

Thus, in sum, there is "an infinite qualitative difference between God and humanity." "True God" is "cloaked in unrecognizability" and exists only as "an object for faith." "Spirit," or supersensory, otherworldly being ("denied immediacy"), is "true God," knowable only indirectly, through the mode of faith. Thus, if the truth about reality is spiritual, then faith is the highest mode of human existence.

If you cannot break through the immediacy in yourself and become contemporaneous with Christ, SK writes, you will be flatteringly deceived by "the priests" that you are a Christian anyway or you will be plagued to madness by a Socratic gadfly who will remind you that you are not a Christian [p. 61]. (This latter is an obvious reference to what SK considered to be his own Socratic mission to his times.) It is Christianity's misfortune that it has had the "good fortune" to succeed in the world, which has become "knowledgeable" about Christ.

> People have become *knowing* about Christ by impermissible and illicit means, for, as we have seen, the permissible way is to be *believing*. People have mutually strengthened one another in the thought that, with the help of the outcome of Christ's life, the 1800 years, the consequences, they have come to know the result. As this gradually became wisdom, all the sap and strength was distilled out of Christianity. The paradox was relaxed. One became a Christian without noticing it and without paying the least attention to the possibility of offense. . . . In this way Christianity has become heathendom. . . . Christendom has abolished Christianity without really knowing it. The consequence is that if anything is to be done, one must attempt to reintroduce Christianity into Christendom. [pp. 33–34]

C. THE "STRUGGLING CHURCH" (*ECCLESIA MILITANS*): A POLEMICAL ALTERNATIVE TO THE CHRISTIANITIES OF GRUNDTVIG, MARTENSEN, AND MYNSTER

We have now gone beyond SK's definition of Christianity and have entered into his specific examination of the present state of established Christianity and how it got that way. First we will examine SK's antithesis of the "struggling

Church" versus the "Church triumphant," and in this connection we will also examine SK's criticism of what he viewed as Grundtvig's "domesticated Christianity." Then we will look at SK's criticism of the marriage of Christianity with "philosophy" and at his criticism of "observational" Christianity, which were directed at the alternative "domestications" of Martensen and Mynster, respectively.

SK prays that we be preserved from the foolish notion that we are members of a Church that is triumphant already in this world and that we not forget that we are in a struggling Church, a Church that can perish in only one way, namely by being flatteringly convinced that it is a Church triumphant [p. 185]. Thus, the distinction between "struggling" and "triumphant" is a distinction between two views of the same reality—the Church—in two different modes of being: time (where the Church must always be struggling) and eternity (where the Church is always triumphant). The structure of SK's argument can again be seen to rest upon the increasingly familiar dualism of two opposed modes of being. And just as the absolute distinction between the temporal and eternal modes of being is the very nerve of SK's understanding of Christianity, so, for SK, the most serious crime is the confusion of these modes. This confusion is particularly deadly because it comes "flatteringly," as a compliment, namely that the Church "triumphs"—that Christ is "glorious"—*now*. Because it comes as a compliment, this error is less likely to be recognized for the danger that it is, particularly by the "common man" who becomes increasingly important to SK in the post-1848 period.

To emphasize the duality of modes in this connection, SK reminds his reader that "[t]he entire existence of the Church on earth [is] a parenthesis or something parenthetical in Christ's life; the parenthesis began with Christ's ascension and is to be completed with his return" [p. 186]. Earthly time, in other words, is time out of divine "time," i.e., eternity.[6] "Truth," then, is a mode of being—a participation in divine time (eternity)—and is not a form of substantive knowledge. Truth is existential, not cognitional: "The existence of truth is its reduplication in you, in me, in him, that your, my, his life, as a struggling approximation, expresses the truth, is truth's existence. . . " [p. 189]. But now Christianity has changed, and after centuries of being taught, the truth has become transformed into a *knowing*, which "they continually talk of conceiving, speculating, observing, etc." [p. 190] (an obvious jibe in the direction of Mynster, Martensen, *et al.*).

If the truth is a "way," it cannot be abbreviated by one who has gone before for any who follow after, whereas if the truth is a "result," it can be summed up and acquired more easily by latecomers. This is the difference between Christian "truth" and worldly "truths" [ibid.]. Thus there is no occasion, here on earth, to "triumph," because the "truth," being a "way," can in no wise be abbreviated for us by those who have gone before [p. 192]. In this world, Christianity is a struggling and not a triumphant Church, and when it is "true Christianity, it is indeed a kingdom in this world, but not of this world, i.e., it is struggling" [p. 194]. That is to say that insofar as Christianity is "true" Christianity, it expresses the "truth," and "truth" *is* struggle: "truth" is to stand astride two modes of being, remaining in this world but not of it.

The early, struggling Church, SK continues, had the task of expressing Christianity in an environment that was opposed to Christianity, whereas the triumphant or the established Christianity of Christendom wishes to express Christianity in an environment that is "synonymous with being Christian" [p. 195]. This latter position is *prima facie* inadmissible for SK, because his Christianity *is* the assertion of an opposed, perfect realm of being in the midst of the present, imperfect realm of time; it *is* the strife of upholding the superior claim of the perfect and the eternal amid the imperfect and the temporal. As a task carried on by human beings on earth—in contrast to the delights and transports of the saved in Heaven, whatever they may be (SK devotes about as little attention to Heaven as Karl Marx does to the classless society)—religion *is* strife.

In an attempt to be a bit more precise in his terminology, SK explains that the "Church triumphant" is not exactly what exists today, but designates the post-Constantinian fusion of the political and social order with a radically otherworldly religion. It is the immediate ancestor of the present Church, which SK calls the "established Church." The Church triumphant brought about the confusion of Christianity by providing for the external recognizability of religious merit in the form of high office, honors, rewards, etc., whereas the present Danish established Church produces the same confusion by means of "hidden inwardness" [p. 196].

SK's argument seems to imply a completely undialectical Christianity of simple martyrdom and to require that all suffering be immediately recognizable as such, so he explains what he means in an abbreviated history of Christianity.[7] In its early, pre-Constantinian phase, the Church was the struggling Church, recognizable *in reverse* by the opposition it received. In the post-Constantinian era, the Church became the Church triumphant, in which Christianity was straightforwardly recognizable by the praise and honor one received. In time, however, the social situation that had made a special clergy class possible and desirable changed, and the old barriers broke down. Every class and estate wanted to join in, but this became impossible, because their daily jobs dealt with things which were indifferent to religion. There was no way for religious excellence to mirror itself straightforwardly and directly in the lives and stations of the mass of people (innkeepers, for example). This mass of "indifferent things" made the straightforward recognizability of the Church triumphant impossible, yet it did not return the situation to the opposition between the world and the Church that had characterized the struggling Church. Instead, the notion of "hidden inwardness," which prevails in the "existing established Christendom" of SK's Denmark, was substituted. Externality was permitted to continue undisturbed, and every trade and occupation was turned over to its own standards of merit.

> Thus they got rid of the external and assigned the Christian life to inwardness. A universal settling of accounts has been given and received for all of us. It is settled. We are all Christians, completely in the same sense that we are all human beings.... In the established Christendom we are all true Christians, but in hidden inwardness. The external world has absolutely nothing to do with the fact that I am a Christian. My existence as a Christian cannot be measured by its standards. If I am an innkeeper, I do not require that the fact that I am a true Christian must be recognizable in the fact that I do the best business.... [p. 198]

Thus there have been three stages in the life of the Christian Church. In classical times the Church existed in opposition as a struggling Church. In the static, hierarchical society of the Middle Ages, Christianity was preached by the Church triumphant. Finally, in modern, bourgeois, secular times (whose arrival had just been sealed and certified in 1848–49) we have established Christendom, with its universal and automatic Christianity of "hidden inwardness." The original error had been committed in the transition from the struggling to the triumphant Church, but SK clearly feels that his generation is attempting an even more compound error by solidifying the transition to established Christendom. In the modern, bourgeois established Church, the undesirable features of the Church triumphant are retained, while adding the even worse features of automatic, universal religion in "hidden inwardness," features which make the old errors worse by removing the irrational excrescences of absolutism and making a flawed system more "democratic" and stable. The turmoil of the 1840's and the revolutionary changes of 1848–49 seemed proof to SK that the modern form of the established Church was about to solidify its hold, and he felt himself confronted with a situation that was at once a great disaster and a great opportunity. *Training in Christianity* is the first installment in SK's attempt to intervene in this critical period in Church history. He is attempting to smother at birth the "Danish People's Church," the most modern and rational form of established Christendom, and to direct "the common man" back to the struggling Christianity of the first phase of the Church.

In present-day Christendom great effort has been expended to render impossible the confrontation with the possibility of offense. True Christianity, however, "places absolute emphasis upon entering into Life [i.e., the eternal], upon eternal blessedness as the absolute Good, and therefore, again, infinite emphasis upon avoiding offense" [p. 106]—but not upon avoiding confrontation with the *possibility* of offense. In Christendom

> there is no infinite opposition between that which is Christian and that which is worldly. That which is Christian [in Christendom] is related to the worldly at

most as its intensification, and most likely under the category of "Culture" [Dannelse]; but it is straightforward, a regular comparative, of which the positive is "civic justice." [Ibid.]

In Christendom, in other words, Christianity has been qualitatively assimilated to the world of Culture, the social good, finite ends, and "civic justice," of which Christianity merely represents a quantitatively higher instance. True Christianity, on the other hand, is a risky (potentially "offensive") entrance into the realm of the Absolute Good, which is infinitely and qualitatively removed from the worldly social calculus.

So long as the world exists, then, the Church must be a struggling Church in the world. If it ceases to struggle, it ceases to exist [pp. 202–203]. There are two conflicting modes of being, and until the ideal coincides with the actual— which it never can in the corruptible sphere of time—there will always be conflict. To deny this is the most dangerous lie of all. All earthly utopias are tyrannical and anathema to SK, but none more so than the Church triumphant. In summing up the situation, SK points out that, by arguing for the truth and greatness of Christianity on the basis of its historical success (i.e., "world history," etc.), "people have simply forgotten that Christianity is related essentially to eternity" and not to history [p. 203]. Again, the deepest crime is the confusion of categories and the claim that the old feud between early, struggling Christianity and the world was merely "narrow bickering": "No, love of God is hatred of the world. And the day that Christianity and the world become friends, Christianity is abolished" [p. 205].

Is there, then, no place for the notion of congregation in a struggling Church? In a clear reference to the congregational theology of Grundtvig, SK replies:

> A concept such as "congregation" with which people are so busy nowadays, is, when applied to this life, really an impatient anticipation of eternity. That which corresponds to the struggle is "the individual." . . . And even if the individuals were thousands, struggling in union, from a Christian point of view, every individual, apart from his unity with the others, also struggles by himself, and must give an account as an individual on the day of judgment, when his life, as an individual, will be tested. Therefore the congregation is really the primary property of eternity. "The congregation" is in rest what "the individual" is in unrest. Therefore "the congregation" has no home in time, but only in eternity, where it is, at rest, the gathering together of all the individuals who stood fast in the struggle and the testing. [pp. 204–205]

This statement is typical of SK's dualism: Time is "unrest"; it is no place for final concretions or ultimate structures but a tentative and imperfect realm. Eternity is "rest," the proper place for such constructions as "the congregation." SK is radically sceptical about the validity of any temporal union or construction, though we have seen him admit (for example, in *A Literary Review*) that, under proper conditions and in awareness of its merely *relative* validity, the "principle of association" can be valid for the political and social purposes of material prudence. But any temporal association that aims at ultimate significance and does not confess its own tentative nature must be openly rejected. Grundtvig's elevation of "the congregation" as the only true locus of the "living Word" is the exact opposite of SK's position here, which is of course primarily directed against Grundtvig. But SK's position is also a criticism, from a skeptical, "parenthesist" point of view, of the Hegelians, who also shared with Grundtvig the "romantic" view that history and historical constructions have some ultimate significance.

As has been mentioned, in addition to its attack upon the congregational theology of Grundtvig, *Training in Christianity* also contains a vigorous assault upon the Christianities of Martensen and Mynster, who, in SK's view, have each in their way relaxed the radicality of Christianity and have accommodated it to the world. Martensen's method is that of philosophy, or "speculation," which enables one to mediate the divine and human categories through the medium of world history, thus avoiding the confrontation with the possibility of offense.

> [O]ne only becomes a Christian in the situation of contemporaneity with Christ, and in the situation of contemporaneity every individual will take notice [of the possibility of offense]. But in Christendom we have all become Christians without noticing anything of the possibility of offense; this [possibility of offense] is, among other things, Christianity's defense against "speculative comprehension" and is fatal to such comprehension. [p. 97]

This is a direct assault on Martensen and his supporters in the Church, or, as SK goes on to call them,

> all the Messrs. speculative theological professors, without whose help and assistance, as is well known, Christianity came into the world, while it is possible, on the other hand, that, if nothing else hinders it, with their help and assistance it could be practiced out of the world. [Ibid.]

In another part of his attack on the Hegel-Martensen compromise between Christianity and the world, SK noted that had "a philosopher" [i.e., a Hegelian] actually been contemporaneous with Christ, the philosopher might have characterized him as

> "a form of pure subjectivity driven to the extreme, and a pure negation such as has never been seen before. He has no doctrine, no system . . . absolutely nothing objective or positive. . . . in thinking that God could reveal himself at all in the form of a single person, he betrays but little philosophical culture [Dannelse].

The race, the universal, the total, is God, but the race is not, however, any particular individual." [pp. 46–47]

SK continues in an even more pointedly sarcastic vein, noting that had "a cleric" (and it is clearly a Hegelian cleric with faith in the world-historical progress of the Absolute Idea) been contemporaneous with Christ, the cleric might have remarked, disapprovingly, that

> "the government of the world does not move in tumultuous leaps. The development of the world—and this is clear from the fact that it is a *development*—is not *revolutionary*, but *evolutionary*. The person who is truly the Expected One will therefore be of quite another appearance, and will come as the most splendid flowering and highest development of the established order. Thus will the person who is the Expected One truly come, and he will behave quite differently. He will acknowledge the authoritative judgment of the established order, will summon all the clergy to a council, will present the council with his result and his credentials—and then, if he receives a majority by ballot, he will be received and acclaimed as the Extraordinary One he is, the Expected One." [p. 45]

Such satire and comedy is one of SK's principal means of pointing out how the "philosophical" wing of the established order flees from every contact with the historically deflationary concept of contemporaneity, which, as he writes elsewhere, is a concept that is "rat poison against the docents." (When SK had been a student, Martensen had been his *privatdozent*.)

Grasping the matter in a somewhat more serious vein, SK attacks the Hegelian theology for its faith in progress and change and its consequent inability to "pause," to remain "stopped" or "standing"[8] in the face of the unconditionality of the divine command:

> Christianity is the Unconditional, has only one being, unconditional being; if it is not unconditional, it is abolished. What holds unconditionally with relation to Christianity is: Either/Or. This impudent talk that one must go further [gaa videre, a reference to a signal phrase in Martensen's work], that one cannot remain standing with Christianity, with faith, with that which is simple, with obedience, with this "Thou shalt"—this impudent talk has been heard long enough and loudly enough. And it has seeped through, further and further down into the people, upon whom the judgment of the highest social circles has naturally had an influence. It has penetrated, and all too easily, because every person, alas, has a natural, inborn desire for disobedience. [p. 208]

Thus, as in *The Sickness Unto Death*, not only is speculative theology and philosophy seen as subversive of the relationship to God, but it is also seen as a social poison whereby the "highest social circles" promote the spirit of rebellion and "disobedience" in "the people." As we have also seen in *The Sickness Unto Death*, this disobedience of "the people" is a rebellion not only in spiritual affairs, but against social order as well. By promoting their pernicious speculative philosophy, "the highest social circles" have created the political and social anarchy of present-day Denmark, SK argues, and now they must reap what they have sown. Closely linked to "philosophy's" crime is its false belief in "progress":

> [I]t is untruth, this talk with which people flatter the race and themselves, that the world goes forward. For the world goes neither forward nor back; it is essentially the same, like the sea, the air, in brief, like an element. It is and must be the element that can provide the test for the person who is supposed to be a Christian, who is always, in this world, a member of the struggling Church. [p. 212]

Thus, in attacking the notion of progress, SK takes up a radically anti-romantic, sceptical position with regard to history, a position that harmonizes well with his dualism of opposed modes. History is essentially meaningless. Time has no significance in itself but is the vehicle, "the element," the catalytic agent, by means of which one comes into awareness of one's true self, one's existence as an individual before God, where one exists "truly," in a trans-temporal mode of being—i.e., in "eternity." Time is the medium through which the self discovers its true, trans-temporal individuality, and it is thus the medium through which one discovers the essential nullity of time, the insignificance of history. It is only as individuals related to God and not as participants in civilization-building, history-making humanity, that human beings have their genuinely and essentially human existence.

But, in SK's view, it was not speculative theology alone that transformed the unconditional and subjective character of Christianity into an objective doctrine of progress. Bishop Mynster's "observational" religion has also had the result of objectifying and distancing the relation of the individual to Christ. The sermon, SK writes, has become "the observation" [Betragtningen], which puts the distance of objectivity between the observer and the thing observed, namely Christianity. First of all, this is impermissible because that which is observed is not merely a passive object, but the living Word of God, an active subject, which acts upon and through us. Secondly, the "observational" method opens up a chasm of impersonality between the preacher and the listener; indeed, the time is coming when "getting personal" will be eschewed in religion, just as it is in the theatre in the relationship between actor and audience. Nowadays the priest asks his listeners if he may "use these moments to make some observations," and the genuinely Christian, personal sermon will soon come to be seen as

> unseemly, uncultured [udannet] behavior—and thus of course it will not *do* to speak personally (the speaking "I") and to persons (the hearing "you"). And if this does not do, then preaching itself is abolished. But thus it is. People only

make observations. And "the observation" does not come too close ["at komme for nær" = "to come too close," but also "to offend"] either to the speaker or the listener. [p. 216]

This shift from the personal sermon to the "observation" also expresses the change from a religion which formerly produced "imitators," to the Christianity of the established Church, which produces only "admirers" of Christ. But, SK reminds us, every word which we have of Christ's is from the degraded, not the glorified Christ, and what the degraded Christ wanted was not admirers, "not adherents to a doctrine, but imitators of a life" [p. 217].

> What, then, is the difference between "an admirer" and "an imitator?" An imitator *is* or strives *to be* that which he admires. An admirer holds himself personally detached, and consciously or unconsciously fails to discover that that which is admired contains a challenge to him, that he be or at least strive to be that which he admires. [p. 220]

Christianity is sheer ethical obligation, sheer activity, nothing other than the challenge to stand in the world, as Christ did, in such a way that one relates *first* to the higher reality, the Kingdom of God; one thus proclaims the relativity and inadequacy of that which is commonly called "reality." This is imitation, and it will certainly (or almost certainly) call forth persecution, suffering, or even martyrdom at the hands of society's protectors of "reality." Imitation is thus not like admiration (which would have been appropriate had Christ come in glory rather than degradation or opposition), because admiration is the proper relation with respect to excellences and differences which one cannot hope to strive for or to achieve, such as beauty, talent, genius, riches, etc. But all these excellences are temporal, inessential, and necessarily inaccessible to most of us, whereas the possibility of excellence held open by Christ is eternal and essential and unconditionally accessible to all. SK reminds us that with respect to that which is essential to humanity, Christianity is completely egalitarian. Christianity *is* "that which is universally human" [det Almeen Menneskelige]. Christianity is

> that to which every person, unconditionally every person, can attain, to which there are attached no conditions other than those that are within the power of every person, the universally human. . . . [It is that] to which every person is obligated, and which thus stands within every person's power. In this case, admiration is completely misplaced and is generally a deception, a cleverness, which seeks evasions and excuses. [p. 221]

"Observational" religion fosters the desire to remain detached, to admire rather than imitate, to relate only via the power of the imagination to that which is desired. This "is not the invention of evil people. No, it is what one might call the flabby invention of better but weaker people" [p. 223]. But as we have seen in Anti-Climacus' other book, *The Sickness Unto Death*, it is precisely the weak, the spiritless, the bourgeois philistines, who are most dangerous to the life of the spirit. They lull themselves and others to sleep, while, on the other hand, openly evil, demonic personalities, possessed as they are of a large quantum of consciousness, promote wakefulness. The great danger at present is the sleep of the bourgeois philistine and the risk that such sleep will spread like a contagion. It is clear that, in blaming this sleep on observational religion, SK is singling out the man who was in fact the principal preacher to Copenhagen's cultured bourgeoisie, Bishop Mynster. Now that everyone is officially Christian, SK continues, there is also the related danger that the mere "admirer" will now appear to be an extra-good Christian, while the old category of excellence, the "imitator," has disappeared altogether [pp. 231–32]. Soon, even though "observations" are made on the subject of imitation itself, the most they will arouse will be an occasional admirer; nonetheless, SK repeats in concluding this attack on Mynster, only the imitator is the true Christian [p. 235].

D. THE CONCLUDING MESSAGE TO THE READER AND "THE MORAL"

In concluding our examination of *Training in Christianity*—and before looking at the specific section which deals with defining and delimiting the role of politics—we will note SK's parting charge to the reader, with its populist anticlericalism and, especially, its call for a humbling admission of the inadequacy of our official Christianity. This admission, SK asserts, is the minimal condition under which honesty, at least, may be restored to our relations with God.

SK calls for a return to what he calls "the Christianity of the New Testament," with its unconditional requirement to imitate Christ in witnessing to the absolute primacy of the eternal, even while in the midst of the world. He calls upon his reader to face squarely the fact that imitation involves dying away from the world and an unqualified willingness to suffer. This Christianity is compared to the Christianity of established Christendom, with its "admiration," its concern with objective doctrine, and its fascination with the world-historical mediation of the truth and the historical triumph of Christianity.

The reader is commanded to "judge, then, for yourself" and "examine yourself now"[9] in order to see how things fit, for as a reader you have a right to judge for yourself and examine yourself, and you have no right to let "the others" (or to let yourself) fool you into imagining that you are a Christian when you are not. The reader is further adjured to remember, in making himself or herself contemporaneous with Christ, that in Christ's day it was "godfearingness" to persecute Christ, and that all those whose job it was to guide the soul in those days warned against him [pp. 37–38]. This is an outright and undisguised call to the "common man," over the heads of the clergy, to examine his own conscience and to make up his own mind about whether the Christianity preached by the established Church (and perhaps believed in by the individual reader) coincides with "the Christianity of the New Testament." The individual person is adjured to follow the promptings of his or her own conscience and not "the others" (clearly the clergy), and at several points in the book SK calls particular attention to the spiritual untrustworthiness of professional clerics, who, in Christ's time, assured the people that it was true worship of God to exclude Christ's disciples from the synagogue and even to martyr them.

If one finds oneself weak and wanting in faith, SK counsels honesty and humility. Fearing and trembling unto despair do no good. It is best to admit forthrightly before God how things stand, even if one is only creeping forward slowly, for then one at least avoids the dishonesty which "poetically alters Christ from God into a sentimental sympathy that has been invented by people themselves. Thus Christianity, instead of drawing people up to the heavenly, is detained along the way and becomes pure and simple humanity" [p. 63]. Even if "true Christianity" is not within our reach, ordinary honesty certainly is, and this will enable us to avoid the worst crime of all, the confusion of categories that confounds the divine with the merely human.

Finally, our investigation must take careful account of the "Moral" (which concludes one large section of *Training in Christianity* but which SK evidently means for us to understand as applying to the entire volume). The "Moral" is particularly important, because, along with the Editor's Foreword at the beginning of the book, it is designed to make the book ambivalent, "strict" yet "mild." Like the entire book of which it is a part, the "Moral" is an ultimatum to Golden Age Christendom that will contain no threat if only the "established order" is honest with itself and makes a humbling admission of the difference between "official Christianity" and the "Christianity of the New Testament" that the book describes. Another reason that we must take note of the "Moral" is that, on the occasion of the publication of the second edition of *Training*, after four and one-half years of silence from the established Church regarding his challenge, SK will publicly retract not only the Editor's Foreword, but also this "Moral" and even his use of the pseudonym Anti-Climacus. Thus the "Moral" is one of the key components of SK's ultimatum, and it will be revoked when his threat is carried out.

The most important paragraph of the "Moral" must be quoted extensively in order for us to understand the tentativeness and ambivalence present even in such a polemical work as *Training*, and also for us to understand the effect of revoking the "Moral" several years later.

> And what does all this mean? It means that every individual, in quiet inwardness before God, must humble himself in relation to what it is to be a Christian in the strictest sense, and admit honestly before God where he is, so that he may

worthily receive the Grace which is offered to every imperfect being—that is, to everyone. And then, no further: then attend to his employment, happy with it, love his wife, happy with her, raise his child to joy, love his fellow man, be happy with life. If anything further is required of him, God will surely let him understand it, and will in that case help him further along. . . . [B]ut it is required of everyone that he honestly humble himself under the claims of the ideal. And therefore they must be heard, heard again and again in all their infinity. Being a Christian has become a nothing, a joke, something which everyone automatically is, something one attains more easily than the most insignificant skill. Truly, it is high time that the requirements of the ideal were heard. [p. 64]

The message is quite simply one of *honesty*, of the honest admission or confession that is the precondition for the proper reception of grace. Beyond this, one is to continue being a "Christian citizen," and if any further sacrifice is required, God will communicate it to the person concerned and grant him the strength to continue. This latter possibility is treated as a special case in the "Moral" and is not at issue. What is at issue and what stands condemned is any coming lightly to Christianity without having humbled oneself before the "Ideal." The "prioritarian" vision is very clearly maintained here, and despite all rhetoric which seems to indicate to the contrary, a strict but recognizable prioritarianism, in the sense in which it has been discussed thus far in the present work, must be deemed operative until this "Moral" is revoked, in May 1855, during the escalation of the attack on Christendom. Finally, we must bear in mind the importance not only of "grace," but also of "the worthy reception of grace." Therefore, we must remember that when this "Moral" is finally revoked it will not signal a return to a pre-Lutheran position of meritorious works but a move to a position which SK feels takes adequate account of both works and grace—while still assigning primacy to grace and denying the saving efficacy of works. Ultimately, SK will adopt the only position which he feels is equal to an optimistic and democratic age in which "the people" have been led to believe that they "own" religion along with all the other *res publicæ*.[10]

E. THE POLITICAL MESSAGE OF *TRAINING IN CHRISTIANITY*

In a sub-section of *Training in Christianity* that deals with Christ's collision *qua* human with the constituted authorities, SK treats the question of the nature of politics as such and the particular disorders and presumptions to which the properly political realm is partial.

In understanding the collision of the *human being* Christ with the established political order, the fundamental question that must be asked is: "Is the individual higher than the established order [det Bestaaende]?" [p. 81]. This is also the fundamental question facing liberal society, in which the state is denied the status of a moral being and in which the whole, consequently, is less than (or at least no greater than) the sum of its parts. Thus, in liberal society the community is ultimately subordinate to the moral, intellectual, and spiritual freedom of the individual, which the community has been established to protect. Kierkegaard, along with liberalism, answers the question in the affirmative, insisting that in moral and spiritual (i.e., non-material) matters the individual is indeed not to be subordinated to the established order. This position occasionally causes liberalism serious problems, as when society threatens to disintegrate by the centrifugal force of this individualism. This of course caused SK no such qualms, for he was essentially interested only in the religious sphere of the individual and in one's relation to the eternal; he was interested in the political sphere only to the extent of defining it and limiting it to the sphere of relative independence which was properly its own.

Viewing Christ simply as human, his collision with the established order is that of any teacher of "inwardness" who collides with "empty externality." "It is a collision that happens again and again in Christendom: It is, in short, the collision of pietism with the established order" [p. 82]. SK thus sees himself as the heir to the pietist tradition of "inwardness" vs. "externality," even though he rejected the pietist groups of his own day as embodying disguised forms of externality. What happened to Christ can "also happen in our time," SK continues.

> Why has Hegel made the conscience and the conscientious relationship in the individual into "a form of the bad" (cf. *Rechtsphilosophie*)? Why? Because he deified the established order. But the more one deifies the established order, the more natural is the conclusion: "*Ergo*, he who denies or opposes this divine thing, the established order, *ergo* he must be close to imagining that he is God." Perhaps he does not say (and if he is a witness to the truth, it is certain that he does not) anything blasphemous about himself. No, the blasphemy is really a projection of the ungodliness with which the established order is venerated as the divine, an acoustic illusion occasioned by the fact that the established order silently says to itself that *it* is the divine, which it now is able to hear via the witness to the truth—as though it were he [and not the established order] who claimed to be more than human. [pp. 83–84]

Thus, society has an innate penchant for self-deification (and perhaps never more than in the Hegelian present), though it will not admit this to itself. Therefore, when an individual collides with it for any "inward" reason, it is society's bad conscience that leads it to accuse the individual of blasphemy.

The danger of deifying the social and political order is that it creates a spiritual wasteland in which all the free space for the spirit, all transcendence and tentativeness, is vulnerable to being filled up or replaced by the civic religion of utility or *raison d'état*:

The deification of the established order makes everything worldly. The established order can be completely in the right in asserting that, with respect to worldly matters, one must adhere to the established order, that one must be satisfied with that which is relative [as opposed to Absolute], etc. But they finally come to make the God-relation worldly as well, wishing to make it conform to a certain relativity, in order that it not be essentially different from one's station in life, etc., instead of willing that this [the God-relation] must be the Absolute for every person, and that this, the individual's relation to God, be precisely that which makes every established order tentative. . . . [p. 86]

This passage remains a classical summary of SK's willingness to grant a relative independence to the political sphere, while insisting upon the disruptive, politically sceptical, other-worldly, "tentative-izing" social function of religion, which must always be on guard against society's built-in tendency to lay claim to the entire individual personality.

The protesting individual wants to secure the God-relationship as the primary component of the individual,

but the established order will not bear the thought that it is supposed to consist of anything so loose as an assembly of millions of individuals, each of whom has his own relationship to God. The established order wishes to be a whole which knows nothing higher than itself, but which has every individual under itself, and which judges every individual who finds his place in the established order. And that individual—even though he teaches the most humble, but also the most humane doctrine of what it is to be human—will then be subjected to terror by the established order and will be accused of blasphemy. [p. 87]

Thus we see SK's "liberalism" again: Society is not greater than the sum of its parts but is in fact less, a collection of individuals, each of whom, as an individual—and only as an individual—is in possession of, or is capable of being in possession of, the Absolute. The abstraction which is the "whole" is in fact less than the component parts and is dangerous because of its continuing lust for control and its obliviousness to priorities. The only real functions of the whole are within the sphere of "relativity" or "quantity," i.e., in attending merely to the practical arrangements and material interests of its members. Thus, as we have noted, SK allows that "the established order can be completely in the right in asserting that, *with respect to worldly matters,* one must adhere to the established order, that one be satisfied with that which is relative, etc." [p. 86, emphasis added].

Therefore, SK continues, the established order is in continual rebellion against God, claiming that it has a hand in "the development of the world," of "the human race," and then along comes a "Smart Alec" [Peter Næsviis] who wishes to assert that the individual is higher than the social and political order:

> It might well be that he was the "gadfly" which the establishment needed in order to keep from falling asleep, or in order not to fall into self-deification, which is worse. Every person must live in fear and trembling, and therefore no established order may be free of fear and trembling. Fear and trembling means that one is becoming, and every individual, also including the race, is and must be conscious of being in becoming. And fear and trembling means that there is a God, which no individual and no established order dare forget for an instant. [p. 84]

Society would like to live in a semi-conscious or self-deified state, unaware of its own relativity and inadequacy, unaware of the existence of a higher mode of being, desiring nothing more than to stop up the mouths of the dissident, "inward" individuals. "But God does not will this, and he uses just the opposite tactic. He uses the individual to irritate the established order out of self-satisfaction" [p. 85]. Thus it is the political task of the (suffering) "inward" individual to promote spiritual openness and tentativeness in society by keeping society in a state of annoyance and self-doubt. This was the role of the gadfly in Socrates' polis and a role that SK is obviously adopting in relation to his own city. Viewed from the merely human point of view, Christ was such a trouble-maker or gadfly. SK remarks, elsewhere in *Training*, that in his own day Christ was probably judged by "the shrewd statesman" as "a phenomenon" with whom one ought not involve oneself for fear of becoming involved in his catastrophe. What does he want? Republic, revolution, nationality, communism? Or is he against all parties? I must take every precaution to avoid him [p. 47, paraphrase]. The "inward" individual who collides with the social order has no concrete political program, and that is precisely his danger to the society; he cannot be negotiated with or co-opted away from his task, which is precisely to witness to a higher reality and thereby keep the social and political order open, tentative, and subject to doubt.

Not only will the social order impute blasphemy to this religious gadfly, but it will attempt to stir up popular sentiment against him on the grounds that he is an elitist, an individual claiming a superhuman authority for himself:

> When the individual appeals to his relation to God vis-à-vis an established order that has deified itself, it does indeed look as if he makes himself more than human. However, this is in no way the case, for he of course acknowledges that every person, unconditionally every person, has and must have for his own part the same relation to God. . . . [H]e who disavows an established order is seen by that order as one who makes himself more than human, and people are offended by him, even though he really only makes God into God and himself into a human being. [pp. 86–87]

Thus, far from breaking with the human race by asserting individuality and the primacy of the God-relation, the "inward" individual actually affirms what is truly universal and human about humanity. He lets God be God and humanity, human. He is an egalitarian and affirms that every individual has this same possibility. The important thing is that society must be understood to stand posterior to the individual grounded in the God-relation; society, however, is continually trying to forget its humble origins, its secondary, derivative nature, and to assert a primacy that subjects the individual to one or another abstraction.

In concluding this consideration of the specifically political portion of *Training in Christianity*, we will examine SK's treatment of two biblical instances of the payment of taxes, for these are clearly seen by SK as paradigmatic for defining the proper limits of the political sphere.

SK examines one classical instance of Christ and the matter of taxes, namely Matthew 22:15–22, where the pharisees are attempting to trap Christ in treason (or blasphemy) by asking him whether it is lawful to pay taxes to Caesar. (Christ's famous reply, upon inspecting the inscription on the coin and finding it to be Caesar's, is of course: "Render unto Caesar that which is Caesar's and unto God that which is God's".) SK stresses that what is important in this incident is the completely matter-of-fact and indifferent manner with which Christ approaches the "problem" of the pharisees. With his off-hand manner and simple approach to the problem, Christ thus creates

> an infinitely wide difference, which he fixes between God and Caesar—"Give God that which is God's!"—because in their worldly manner they [the pharisees] wished to make the question of whether one is permitted to give taxes to Caesar into a question concerning God. It is by such means that worldliness wishes to deck itself out as godliness, and therefore they confused God and Caesar in this question, as if the two of them had something to do with one another in a straightforward and immediate fashion, as if God were also a sort of Caesar. That is, what they actually did in this manner was secretly to take God in vain, to make him worldly. But he [Christ] posits the difference, the infinite difference. He makes giving taxes to Caesar into the most indifferent thing of all, i.e., into something one must do without wasting one word or one moment in talking about it, in order to have all the more time in which to render unto God what is God's. [pp. 158–59]

Thus again, religion and politics concern one another only as mutually delimiting categories. The relation to God is the superior moment, to which the political relation must remain subordinate; but within its sphere, politics has its own legitimate claims: *Of course* one pays one's taxes and participates in the life of the state. Danger arises only when people (for example, pharisees) attempt to confuse the categories and impute divine significance to worldly matters. But, essentially, SK sees nothing problematical in the coexistence and division between the religious and the political realms.

However, SK makes it clear that it is not always so easy to deal with the relation of religion to politics by a simple parting of the ways. In explaining another tax question in Matthew (Mt. 17:24–27, where Christ, asked about taxes, catches a fish with the tax money in its mouth), SK points out that "the question is whether he [Christ *qua* human], this individual human being, will acknowledge the established order by paying taxes" [p. 88]. SK's reply to this question is that "because paying taxes is an indifferent externality, Christ submits and avoids giving offense. *It would be otherwise in relation to an externality which impudently claimed to be piety"* [ibid., emphasis added].

In other words, all matters of the social and political sphere are matters of indifference, in which we are to submit to the various forms of social usage— *excepting* those "externalities" which transgress upon a person's religious integrity, the essential individuality which is the basis for all else. "Taxes" (the material realm generally) are the rightful domain of society. But not all externalities of the established order are so indifferent, for some tend in the direction of the corruption of the internal, the spiritual, which is a matter of conscience. One must not be so "spiritual" and "internal" that *no* affront from the "external" world of politics can rouse one to action. One must fight to preserve the boundaries and priorities of the inner person when they are threatened and disregarded by an "impudent," self-deifying society. There are times when political intervention by the religious person is called for. SK is clearly going beyond the God-Caesar dichotomy of Matthew 22 and creating a framework within which he himself could venture into the political arena in the future— in the event that an "attack on Christendom" became necessary.

25. Autobiographical Pieces, "Two Notes" Concerning "the Individual," and the "Open Letter" to Dr. Rudelbach

○

A. INTRODUCTION

In the summer and fall of 1848, while SK was writing *Training in Christianity*, he also wrote the first of his two autobiographical pieces, *The Point of View for My Activity as an Author* [*Synspunktet for min Forfatter-Virksomhed*] [SV XIII, pp. 511–82]. When it was finished, this work struck him as too personal, so he shelved it, and in March 1849 he wrote a shorter and less intimate piece, entitled *On My Activity as an Author* [*Om min Forfatter-Virksomhed*] [SV XIII, pp. 487–509], with which he was more satisfied. Even so, SK had qualms about revealing himself, and it was not published until August 1851. (The first autobiography, *The Point of View*, was not published until four years after SK's death, when it appeared in the final form in which he had prepared it, namely, with the *Two Notes* [*Tvende 'Noter'*] [SV XIII, pp. 583–612] concerning "the individual" attached as a supplement.)

The *Two Notes* are among the most specifically political pieces SK wrote, and we will consider them separately from the autobiographical works themselves. Apart from the *Two Notes*, we will consider the two autobiographical pieces as if they were one work, for their differences in intimacy and detail are important only to the biographer, and we will be examining this material only for the evidence it contains about the form and growth of SK's criticism of his society. The final portion of this chapter will examine the "Open Letter" to Dr. Rudelbach [SV XIII, pp. 436–44], published in *Fædrelandet* in January 1851, in which SK spells out his differences with the Grundtvigians and with the liberal idea of the separation of church and state, a principle which SK's developing critique had not yet led him to embrace.

B. THE RETROSPECTIVE SHAPE AND PURPOSE OF THE AUTHORSHIP

Looking back upon the whole of his authorship, from the appearance of *Either/Or* in 1843 to the present (1848–49), SK claims that the entire corpus was composed "*uno tenore*, in one breath, if I dare say, such that the authorship is religious from first to last" [p. 495]. Yet there is a certain uneasiness in SK's desire to claim the entirety of the authorship, even the "aesthetic" pseudonymous works, as part of a preconceived whole with an ulterior religious purpose, and he admits that "this is how I understand the whole thing now. In the beginning I could not see the whole of what has been my own development" [p. 500]. The wholeness now apparent in his work was not visible at the outset, because "it was Providence [Styrelsen] that educated me, and the education is reflected in the process of productivity" [p. 562]. The religious element has been present since the beginning of the "aesthetic" authorship, SK insists, and this can be seen from the *Two Edifying Discourses* [*To opbyggelige Taler*] of 1843, which accompanied the publication of *Either/Or*. In stressing that his authorship has had a continuing religious purpose, SK wishes to combat the erroneous notion that religion is something in which one takes refuge only when one grows older, a notion which has been strengthened by the lamentable fact that in their actual lives people often move from being fiery spokesmen of the aesthetic in their youth to being tired supporters of conventional religion in their old age [p. 536]. (Witness Oehlenschläger's example in this connection.)

SK insists that behind all the various voices of his authorship, the underlying religious intent was to mount a polemic to dispel the "sensory illusion" of Christendom [pp. 517–18]. "A sensory illusion is never directly abolished," and one who would approach it must do so by indirection, confessing one's shortcomings with respect to Christianity, as does Johannes Climacus in the *Postscript*. In an implicit criticism of the reforming zeal of Grundtvig and the other pietistic groups, SK insists that one must not claim to be an extraordinary Christian [p. 531]. "A certain party of the orthodox," who cohere in a tight circle, assure one another that they are the true Christians, while the others are not. Even if this were true, and these "orthodox" (obviously pietists and Grundtvigians) were the only Christians, this would be an incorrect tactic, suitable perhaps for proclaiming Christianity in the heathen context of old, but not in "Christendom," where indirection is called for [pp. 534–35]. Christendom requires "a new military science," namely the combination of openness and indirection which characterized SK's two-layered authorship [pp. 539–40].

"The world wishes to be deceived" [*mundus vult decipi*], alas, and in his duplicitous authorship SK has done so, though not for his own profit. "Others" have specialized in deceiving the world for private gain:

> The secret in the deception which pleases the world that wants to be deceived lies partly in forming a coterie and everything that this entails, joining one or another of those societies for mutual admiration whose members assist one another orally and in print, for the sake of worldly gain—and partly in hiding from the mass of people, never being seen, in order to use the effects of fantasy. [p. 545]

SK claims that he, on the other hand, pursued the policy of "breaking with all the coteries" [p. 547]. This attack on "coteries" is a clear reference to the inbred and self-ratifying nature of the Golden Age Copenhagen cultural elite, e.g., the Oehlenschläger-Mynster group of the earlier decades and, especially, the Heiberg-Martensen circle. The reference to "coteries" and the calculated use of "hiding from the people" in order to increase one's "fantasy" value has its precise parallel in the attack on the "Most High Court Preacher" in *The Crisis in the Life of an Actress*.[1] Thus, SK's method has been one of indirection with an ulterior religious intent, namely to dispel the "sensory illusion" that "Christian culture" is Christianity. In pursuit of his goal, SK has found it necessary to break with the "orthodox" (the pietists and Grundtvigians) on the one hand and the "coteries" of the Golden Age cultural elite, on the other.

SK insists that he has "willed only One Thing" as an author, and this has been "the religious," which he wished to "put into reflection" and then "to reflect out of it" again, so that the goal of the authorship has been *"to reach, to come to,* simplicity" [p. 495, SK's emphasis]. That is, SK's Christianity is not simplicity or immediacy, but *simplicity after reflection*, new simplicity, new being; one must become as a child, yet be in full possession of adulthood, voluntarily renouncing what SK elsewhere calls "worldly shrewdness." However, here "in Christendom," everything has been intellectualized or "put into reflection." Now that humanity has reached adulthood and reflection, there can be no going back, no simple forsaking of the intellect; rather, one must follow the movement of reflection all the way through until it reveals itself in its inadequacy.[2] "One does not reflect oneself into Christianity, but one reflects oneself out of everything else and becomes more and more simply, a Christian" [ibid.]. The goal is "simplicity" [Eenfoldighed]. The movement is *"to come to* the simple; the movement is *from* the Public *to* 'the individual.' *Religiously understood*, there is in fact, no Public, but only individuals" [p. 499]. In asserting this radical individualism, Kierkegaard does not intend to rule out entirely the concept of the congregation at this point, but wishes to qualify it. Thus, in an aside clearly directed at Grundtvig, SK adds that to the extent that the concept of the congregation does exist, it must not be confused with politically valid concepts such as "the public, the mass, the numerical" [p. 499n.].

In presenting Christianity, SK argues, there are two types of error. The error of "strictness" is to state the "infinite requirement" of Christianity without mentioning grace. The error of "mildness," on the other hand, is one of cheap grace; it is "taking Christianity in vain, either by ... making the 'infinite' requirement finite, or even by omitting it entirely and going *straightway* to 'grace,' which of course means that it is taken in vain" [p. 506]. SK wishes to keep Christendom from taking Luther and the meaning of Luther's life in vain [ibid.]. What is needed is *both* "concern" [Bekymring] (or "fear and trembling") *and* grace.

SK does *not* advocate "pietistic strictness," which he says is utterly foreign to him:

> No, what I have wanted to help bring about is, with the help of confessions, to bring, if possible, some more truth into these . . . imperfect existences such as we lead; and this is something, anyway, and is in any case the first condition for coming to exist as more capable beings. [Ibid.]

SK repeatedly insists that his is not the program of a pietistic or self-righteous fanatic, but that it is merely an attempt to produce the "honesty" which is the precondition for "existing capably." As SK points out later, in the "attack on the Church," the campaign for "honesty" is a campaign for "*human* honesty," and thus serves the worldliness of secular liberalism as fairly as it serves the religiousness of SK's radically dualistic Christianity. To the extent that liberalism is sincere about its own secularism and does not make transcendent claims for politics (which, after all, is contrary to the spirit of liberalism)—to this extent liberal politics is as much a beneficiary of Kierkegaardian "human honesty" as is the religiousness of "the individual"—although, of course, it is for the sake of the latter that SK has undertaken his campaign for honesty.

According to SK, the traditional tactic has been to get as many people as possible to subscribe to Christianity, even if one were not sure that it really was Christianity to which they were subscribing. SK's tactic, he explains, has been to state "Christianity's requirement" in its "full ideality," even if it should prove so lofty that not a single person could accept it [pp. 505–506]. His tactic has not been to provide an "apology" for Christianity but to prepare *us* for an apologizing or humiliating confession when we dare call ourselves Christians. Only then, only after such a humiliation and confession before the "Ideal," can grace be accepted properly. This, of course, recalls the point of SK's most recent book, *Training in Christianity*, and SK makes it very clear how the relation between that book and the established Church is to be understood.

> To the extent that an established Church has self-understanding, it will in like measure also understand the most recent book, *Training in Christianity*, as an attempt to find an ideal standpoint for the Established order . . . (which is, by the way, expressed straightforwardly in the "Foreword," which expresses my understanding of the book). [p. 507]

What SK says is thus as much of a threat as an offer of support. *If* the established Church has "self-understanding"—a key condition—it will see *Training in Christianity* as a form of ideal support, an attempt to help the Establishment save itself by offering it, by means of an "admission" or "confession," a chance to reach out beyond its present mediocrity to "an ideal standpoint." This moderate and charitable attitude is not very visible in *Training* itself, SK admits, for that book is technically by the pseudonym Anti-Climacus, but it is present in the

Foreword of the book, which tenders the olive branch and is signed by SK in his own name. (Thus we must note again the vital significance when, in May 1855, SK publicly retracts the accommodating Foreword and insists on letting *Training* stand on its own as a bitter attack on the established order. This retraction presumably reflects SK's view that by May 1855 the establishment had shown that it lacked the "self-understanding" necessary to accept *Training* as an ideal form of support.)

SK is sure that he will be accused of being a "misanthropic traitor" who has committed "crimes against humanity," and he admits that this is true insofar as he has loved God in a Christian way and has not expended his energies in saying that

> the world is good, loves the truth, and wills the Good, that the requirement of the times is the truth, that the race is truth or even that it is God, and that the task is thus (in Goethean-Hegelian fashion) to satisfy the present. On the contrary, I have striven to express that the world, if it is not evil, is mediocre; that "the requirement of the times" is always stupidity and foolishness; that, in the eyes of the world, the truth is a ridiculous exaggeration or an odd excrescence; that the Good must suffer. I have striven to express that it is misunderstanding and heathenism to use the category "race" with reference to being human, particularly as the expression for that which is most high. This is because a human being differs from an animal race not merely with its generic advantages, but with respect to its peculiarly *human* characteristic, namely, that every individual in the race (not an outstanding individual, but every individual) is greater than the race. This is inherent in the God-relationship—and it is Christianity whose category is the individual, precisely the category that has been so ridiculed by our great Christian age—because it is so much higher to relate oneself to God than it is to relate oneself to the race or through the race to God. [p. 572n.]

SK's radically dualistic world-view thus links "Goethean" humanism (as for example in Mynster's Olympian calm) to "Hegelian" pantheism (Martensen's intellectualism) and rejects them in favor of a thoroughgoing individualism in which the whole is persistently subjugated to the sum of its parts, or, indeed, to any one of them. Earlier, we saw this theological variant of the well-known liberal principle developed in *Training in Christianity*, and it is worth noting that here the point is developed by SK in a context which makes it clear that it is directed not at the new liberal forces in society but at the conservative "Goethean-Hegelian" cultural synthesis of the Golden Age, a synthesis with which the post-1848 liberals now seemed dangerously close to striking a bargain.

C. 1848 AND THE SIGNIFICANCE OF THE NEW POLITICAL SITUATION TO THE LIFE OF THE SPIRIT

It is in these autobiographical pieces that SK makes his most important and extensive comments about the significance of the events of 1848. Since it is the contention of the present work that the revolutionary social transformation which came to expression and consolidation in 1848–49 was the shaping and driving force behind the final phase of SK's authorship, the more important of SK's remarks on 1848 will be cited at length. SK is first of all proud of the fact that, although his view of "the mass" [Mængden] might have seemed exaggerated before 1848, people will now have to grant that he was right, and if anything, not insistent enough. Similarly, SK is proud of his invention (or his recovery of the Socratic invention) of "the single individual" [den Enkelte], the antidote to "the mass." Finally, SK is proud that *Christian Discourses* did not have to be altered when he read the proofs during the spring of 1848, and it even reads as though it had been written after, not before, the revolution [pp. 554–55]. (Of course, however, as the present work attempts to document, 1848 did have an impact, even though it did not force SK to alter the proofs of *Christian Discourses*. The revolution did not cause an about-face, but it did occasion an enormous tightening of SK's Christian categories, and an intensification of his critique from that of a reformist to that of a radical.)

SK writes of 1848:

> If the mass is what is evil, if chaos is that which threatens, then there is only salvation in one thing, to become the individual. The saving thought is "this individual" . . . . The events of recent months, which have been of world-historical significance and have overturned everything, have brought into the world spokesmen of new-born, fantastic, and, of course, confused ideas, while on the other hand, everyone who has, in various ways, been a spokesman in the past has been reduced either to silence or to the embarrassment of being forced to purchase a brand-new suit of clothing. Every system has been exploded. In the course of a couple of months, the past has been ripped away from the present with such passion that it seems like a generation has gone by. . . . Not even the dissolution of ancient civilization was as great as the world-historical catastrophe that has loomed up, and that is the absolute *tentamen rigorosum* for everyone who *was* an author. [p. 555]

There can be no question, then, that SK saw 1848 as one of the major turning points of history. Only by neglecting social and historical elements has Kierkegaard scholarship missed the point that his entire authorship is informed and guided by his vision of politics and society and that the concluding, polemical phase of his authorship must be understood as an expression of the requirements of that vision in the post-1848 world.

"The threads of intelligence broke in '48; the whine which heralds chaos was heard!," SK writes. There were errors on both sides, by the rulers and the ruled, on the way to 1848. The rulers depended exclusively upon mere worldly shrewdness, while

> the guilt of the lower classes was the desire to dispense with all government. . . .
> The punishment is that that which is coming to be most bitterly missed is

precisely government. In our century, as never before, the human race and individuals . . . have been liberated from all the nuisances (if you wish to call them that) that stem from the fact that something stands, and must stand, unconditionally firm. . . . Indeed the human race will come to feel, as never before, the truth in the fact that what the race and every individual in it needs is for something to stand—and for something to *have to stand*—unconditionally firm. They need what divinity, the Loving One, invented in Love, the Unconditioned, for which humanity, which is clever unto its own corruption, has substituted the much-admired notion of "to a certain degree." Ask the sailor to sail without ballast—he capsizes. Let the race, let every individual in the race, attempt to exist without the Unconditioned—it is, and remains, chaos. . . . [E]ven the greatest of events and the most strenuous life [is] chaos or like sewing without fastening the end of the thread—until the end is again made fast by bringing forth the Unconditioned, or by having the individual, even if at great remove, at any rate relate to something Unconditioned. A person cannot simply live in the Unconditioned, breathe only the Unconditioned; he will perish . . . but, on the other hand, no one can "live" in the deeper sense without relating to the Unconditioned. . . . If—to stay with my theme, the religious—if the human race, or a large number of individuals in the race, have grown out of the childlike stage in which another person can represent the Unconditioned for them—well, even so, for this very reason the Unconditioned cannot be dispensed with. Indeed, it is all the less possible to dispense with it. [pp. 508–509]

Thus SK's meaning is that in 1848 the mass of humanity rebelled against all forms of unconditional social and political authority. The danger is that this rebellion is being extended to the very idea of the Unconditioned itself (i.e., God) and that the human race has entered a stage of chaos and will surely capsize like a sailor sailing without ballast. Politics, our collective human existence, needs boundaries or it is in despair; the boundary, the "knot on the end of the sewing thread," is religion, the *individual* relation to God. We cannot live purely in the Unconditioned itself; we are too weak and need to create mediate forms of political and social authority. But neither can we live without the idea of Unconditional Authority at all. We need politics and culture, but they must have limits. If humanity has become too mature to endure the "childlike" state of the absolutist regime in which particular people were regarded as representative of the Unconditioned, fine; let the people now create new forms of social and political authority. SK makes no call to turn back the clock. He is no reactionary. But, he insists, let these new forms—democratic representative government, etc.—remain mindful that there *is* an Unconditioned. In fact, in a state of political "adulthood" it is even more important for every individual to cling fast to the notion of an Unconditioned Being who stands outside the boundaries of our temporal social life. The fact that, in prerevolutionary days, the true Unconditionality of God was too closely identified with the earthly institutions of "unconditional" subjection and fealty is not an excuse for making the opposite error and rejecting the notion of an absolutely transcendent God as the anchor of our personal existence and the limit of our social life. As we pass into maturity we must not reject the reality of the Unconditioned along with the unreal and metaphorical images of unconditionality that formerly characterized our common culture. We ought not seek to regress and become reactionary inhabitants of the lost childhood world of absolutist Christendom. On the contrary, we must attack the notion of a Christian cultural compromise as very dangerous, and in embracing the popular sovereignty of the post-1848 era, we must also accept the built-in limitations on politics and culture that liberal secularism also contains. We must realize the relativity of all culture in the absolute limit of the Unconditioned.

Thus, politics and religion define and delimit one another for SK. We will see the depth and radicality of this insight come to maturity in the course of the 1850's, as the revolution becomes consolidated and SK moves correspondingly closer to his "attack on Christendom." This concludes our discussion of the political view contained in the autobiographical pieces themselves, and in the remainder of this chapter we turn, first, to an examination of the "Two Notes" concerning "the individual," which SK appended to the first autobiographical sketch, and secondly, to a look at the January 1851 "Open Letter" to Dr. Rudelbach.

D. THE "TWO NOTES" CONCERNING "THE INDIVIDUAL"

In the Foreword to the highly political "Two Notes," SK writes that

> in these times, everything is politics. The difference between this totally political point of view and that of religion is as wide as the heavens (*toto coelo*), just as their beginning and end points differ *toto coelo*, because the political view begins on earth and remains there, while the religious, tracing its beginnings from on high, wishes to transfigure and then lift the earthly realm up to heaven.
>
> An impatient politician, who peruses these pages hurriedly, will certainly find little which edifies him; so be it. But if, on the other hand, he would generously allow himself a little patience, I am convinced that he, too, will take note—even from the brief hints contained in these pages—that the religious is the transfigured reproduction of what the politician, to the extent that he really loves being human and loves humankind, has thought in his happiest moments, even though he will find the religious impractical because it is much too high and too ideal. [p. 589]

If Feuerbach ("theology is anthropology") or Marx felt that they were inverting Hegel, SK certainly seems to be inverting Feuerbach in these lines.[3] Religion is the transfigured fulfillment of the dream of politics, SK tells us, and this should be clear to every "patient" politician. The implication of this is that the true and proper task of politics is not to usurp the sphere of religion by attempting the impossible but to be aware of its own earthbound nature and to remain within it, dealing with practical and material matters, without claiming any finality or *telos* within itself. Genuine humanity and genuine happiness are in the sphere of religion. In effect, then, "anthropology is theology."

SK's Foreword to the "Two Notes" continues:

> But even though "impractical," the religious is eternity's transformed rendering of the fairest dream of politics. No politics has been able to, no politics can, no worldliness has been able to, no worldliness can, think through or realize the idea of human equality [Menneske-Lighed, a pun on Menneskelighed = humanity, which is also an intended reading] to its final consequence. By looking at the [logical] categories, one can see that it is eternally impossible to realize complete equality within the medium of "worldliness" [Verds-Lighed, also a pun, which can be read as meaning "worldly equality" or "worldliness"]—that is, the medium whose essence consists in differences. Because if complete equality is to be attained, "worldliness" must depart utterly from the scene, and when complete equality is achieved, "worldliness" has come to an end. But is it not something of an obsession on the part of "worldliness," to wish to force a total equality—in the midst of worldliness! Only the religious can, with the help of eternity, carry out human equality [Menneske-Lighed, which also means humanity] to its final consequences, the godly, the essential, the non-worldly, the true, the only possible human equality. And therefore—let this be said to its glory—the religious is the only true humanity [Menneskelighed, which also means human equality]. [pp. 589–90][4]

Religion, then, is the proper sphere for the ideal and absolute yearnings for equality which in recent times have improperly—and, as we shall see, dangerously—found expression in politics and in political vocabulary.

In concluding the Foreword SK asks to be granted

> yet another word; allow me this. What the times *require*—yes, who could finish totalling it up, now that worldliness has caught fire by means of a self-combustion caused by the worldly friction of worldliness upon worldliness?[5] On the other hand, what the times *need*, in the deepest sense—this can be said quite entirely in one word, they need eternity. The misfortune of our time is precisely that it has become only "time," temporality which impatiently wishes to hear nothing about eternity. In addition, our times well-meaningly or in rage, even want to make the eternal completely superfluous by means of a conjured-up imitation, which can never, in all eternity, succeed, because the more one thinks that one can harden oneself to be able to dispense with the eternal, the more one needs it deep down. [p. 590]

Thus, however much they feel themselves able to dispense with spiritual ballast, what the times need is "eternity," i.e., a parallel but superior and transcendent mode of being, a form of absolute Unconditionality, as SK termed it in the autobiographical pieces. And, if the times do not get "eternity" in the proper religious way, but attempt to repress or do without it, it will return in demonic form as a "conjured-up imitation," an artificial eternity, which will haunt us and which is extremely dangerous. The repressed returns. The proper sphere of politics is modest, unassuming, non-utopian; it has no need to repress the legitimate and delimiting claims of eternity. SK's message is one of political openness, but it is opposed to the attempt to capture transcendence within political forms, as in the dream of a temporal attainment of *total* equality. SK's politics remain pragmatic, open, modest, but they have also become increasingly fierce in their insistence on the need to contain society's claims to omnipotence; that is, SK's politics come increasingly to define themselves negatively as anti-totalitarian. Politics must not attempt closure.

The first of the "Two Notes" deals with the principle of majoritarianism and its proper and improper application. According to one view, SK writes, truth is wherever "the mass" [Mængden] is. According to another view—his own—SK writes, wherever "the mass" is there is untruth, and truth is the property only of *individuals*. Even if what the mass holds to be true is identical to that which is espoused as true by every individual *qua* individual, it is untrue when held by the mass, at least insofar as this is done "such that 'the mass' has any *decisive*, voting, clamorous, audible significance whatsoever" [p. 592]. This point, made in the way in which SK makes it, is of great assistance in showing that SK was a classical liberal in his schematic understanding of politics (if not in his merely personal opinions on day-to-day affairs). SK's point here—like his understanding of politics generally—draws the line as it is drawn in the classical liberal view, where the majoritarian principle is seen as an *instrument*. Classical or Rousseauian democracy, on the other hand, views the whole, the community, as significant in its own right, as the primary moral being, greater than the mere sum of its parts, i.e., greater than the personal interests and private views of each individual. It is precisely the liberal (as opposed to the Rousseauian-democratic) view that the whole is not greater than the sum of its parts, that the community does not have status as a moral being.

The famous conflict in Rousseau between the "will of all" and the "general will" develops precisely around the fact that the community is claimed to be a moral being. If the correct course of action for the community *qua* moral entity were "x," and if every individual *qua* private individual and for his or her private reasons (but not as a member of the moral whole) were to will course of action "x," the latter action, while apparently identical with the former, would not (according to Rousseau) be a moral action, would not be an instance of the general will, but would be merely an instance of the will of all. Such an action would not be a "democratic" expression of the state as a moral being but merely the "liberal" expression of the state as a neutral instrumentality, the sum of individual private interests (in this case unanimous).

The important point to be made here is that SK makes the same distinction as Rousseau and recognizes the same boundary between "liberalism" and "democracy"; between "the will of all" and "the general will"; between that which is held to be true by an individual *qua* individual and that which he or she holds *qua* member of the group. And for SK, it is possible for a given position to be right when held by the individual *qua* individual but wrong when held *qua* member of the group "such that the mass had any decisive significance." SK and Rousseau make the same distinction between the group as the mere sum of individual interests and the group as a supposed moral entity. Further, in allowing the individual to be wrong when he or she believes something in one role, but right when he or she believes this same thing in his or her other role, SK and Rousseau both use the same heuristic device to illuminate the crucial distinction between two forms of the individual's relation to the group. Thus, SK and Rousseau draw the same boundary between "liberalism" and "democracy": "Democracy" sees the state as a moral community and as the primary locus of the self, whereas "liberalism" sees the state as a mere instrumentality which serves the material interests of *individuals*, which remain the only entities of ultimate significance. Most important of all, of course, is that even though SK and Rousseau agree on all this, they make value judgments which are *diametrically opposed*. For the "democrat" Rousseau, the individual truly "lives" only to the extent that he or she partakes of the community. For the "liberal" SK, on the other hand, the community is a pragmatic association—which, depending upon the era and the degree of "adulthood" enjoyed by "the common man," may or may not find it prudent to adopt some appropriate form of majoritarianism—in which the individual can truly "live" only to the extent that he or she develops an individualized and all-transcending, absolute relation to "eternity." Seen in this light, Rousseau is the classical democrat, who values the individual only in relation to the community, and SK is the socially sceptical liberal, who values the community only in relation to the individual.[6]

Majoritarianism does, however, have a *relative* validity, SK admits:

> I have indeed never denied that with respect to all temporal, earthly, worldly purposes, the mass can have its validity, even decisive validity . . . [*But*] from an ethical-religious point of view, the mass is untruth, when it is supposed to be the deciding instance as to what "the truth" is. [p. 592n.]

Thus, any form of majoritarianism in the realm of the spirit is inappropriate, whereas the majoritarian principle may be legitimately employed with respect to limited, temporal matters.

> That which is at times partially and at other times completely valid in politics and similar fields becomes untruth when it is transferred to areas of mind, spirit, religiosity. And for the sake of a caution that is perhaps exaggerated, I ought to

add just this: By "truth" I always mean "eternal truth," but politics and the like
do not have to do with "eternal truth." [pp. 595–96]

Thus, again, it is clear that SK's anti-majoritarianism is not a conservative
political position, nor is he opposed to the principle of popular sovereignty
when applied to temporal matters of material prudence. Rather, SK's position
defines boundaries and leaves the temporal, material world open to any properly modest politics. SK's position is thus tailor-made for liberal secularism
insofar as this latter takes seriously its own modest pretensions and its secularism.

SK's position remains rigorously individualistic but is steeped in a religious
egalitarianism that keeps it from becoming elitist. SK explains in a footnote
that when he speaks of the evils of "the mass," he is using a purely formal
conception; he is not employing the term in its everyday social sense as "the
masses" versus "the better sort," but rather in the sense of *any* numerical
grouping, which could as easily be "a number of noblemen, millionaires, great
dignitaries, etc." [p. 593n.]. SK's "egalitarian individualism" becomes especially
clear in the following:

> "[T]he mass" is untruth. With respect to eternal, godly, Christian matters, it is
> just as Paul says, "Only one reaches the goal." . . . Only one reaches the goal,
> that is to say that everyone can do so, and everyone ought to become this one,
> but only one reaches the goal. — Where there is a mass, therefore, or where the
> fact that there is a mass is *given decisive significance* [emphasis added], *there*
> what is being worked for, lived for, striven for, is not the highest goal, but only
> one or another earthly thing. This is because the eternal can only be worked
> for decisively where there is One, and everyone who is willing to let God help
> him can become this One. "The mass" is untruth . . . . The mass as an ethical
> or religious court of appeal is untruth, while it is eternally true that everyone
> can be the One. This is the truth. [pp. 592–95]

To regard "the mass" as a "court of appeal" with regard to ethical-religious
Truth is to deny God and one's "Neighbor," whereas to honor every person,
every individual, unconditionally, is true fear of God and love of one's Neighbor. "And 'the Neighbor' is the absolutely true expression for human equality
[Menneske-Lighed]. If everyone truly loved his neighbor as himself, complete
human equality [Menneske-Lighed] would be unconditionally achieved" [p.
597]. And, as we know from the Foreword to these "Two Notes," *complete*
human equality is the promise of eternity, which is unrealizable in politics. We
must beware of demonic, pirated editions of the eternal and watch out for the
return of the repressed.

What, then, does all this about the proper and improper use of the majority
mean to the religious reformer? First of all, SK tells us, no "witness to the
truth," *qua* religious personality, ought dare involve himself with the mass but

should instead try to break it up into individuals. He must especially guard against allowing himself to be confused with a politician [p. 595]. This seems clearly to be directed against Grundtvig's political movement, where the boundaries between political and religious reform were very unclear. Nor ought he to seek the help of the mass even to break up the mass, for the end does not justify the means. SK seems to be signalling his supporters that they must not expect him to lead a mass movement in support of his notions, for that would be a contradiction in terms [p. 598].

The second of these quite specifically political "Notes" deals less with the problem of majoritarianism but rather concentrates first upon the crucial importance of the category of "the individual" and then gives yet another proposed etiology of the present revolutionary and chaotic state of affairs. SK writes that

> the situation of these times . . . [makes it clear that we have an enormous responsibility to combat] an immoral confusion that wishes, with the assistance of "humankind" or of fantastical social categories, to demoralize the individual philosophically and socially; it is a confusion that wishes to teach ungodly disdain with respect to that which is the first condition for all religiosity, namely, being an individual person. [pp. 602–603]

" 'The individual' is the category of the spirit through which—in the religious sense—time, history, and the race must pass" [p. 604].

Whether the category of the individual is applied in the interest of "the established order" or "catastrophically," in conflict with that order, "'the individual' is the category of the spirit, of the awakening of the spirit, as opposite to politics as is indeed possible" [p. 607]. The category of the individual has as little interest in the world, earthly reward, or honor as it has in revolutionary changes in the external ordering of society. Christianity itself stands and falls with the category of the individual, for without this category, "pantheism has won an unconditional victory" [p. 608]. The category of the individual was first used by Socrates to dissolve heathendom, and it will be used a second time in Christendom to help make the people (the "Christians") confront Christianity [pp. 609–10].

SK insists that the origin of the modern confusion lies precisely in the neglect of the Christian category of the individual. All doubt, all disobedience to God

> has its final refuge in temporality's illusion, that we are quite a few in numbers, or that we are the entirety of the human race, and can come in the end to overawe God, and even become Christ. And pantheism is an acoustic illusion that confuses *vox populi* with *vox dei*, an optical illusion that forms a cloud-image from the fogs of temporality, a mirage, cast by its own reflection, which claims to be the eternal. [p. 609]

Here again, SK warns against the demonic, the "conjured-up imitations of the eternal" that intrude themselves into modern politics.

> [E]very rebellion against obedience in social life, every rebellion against the worldly regime in the political sphere, is connected to and derived from this rebellion of the race against God in the matter of Christianity. This rebellion, this misuse of the category of "the race," does not, by the way, recall the [open] uprising of the Titans, but is *reflection's* rebellion, the sneaking rebellion, continued from year to year, generation to generation. [p. 608]

Here, as in *The Sickness Unto Death*, SK argues that what has happened is that a pantheistic intellectual revolt against the absolute transcendence of God began in the circles of the "cultured" and has then spread, via the liberal philistine bourgeoisie, to political and social rebellion in the streets, for which the pantheistic revolt of the cultured elite is thus responsible.

In the parallel etiology in the autobiographical pieces, however, SK puts forth an apparently different sequence: Humanity, having lost faith in unconditional political and social authority, now thinks it is so great that it is able to abolish *all* unconditionality, *all* authority, divine as well as human, and is able to live entirely without "the idea of the Unconditioned" at all.

Thus the one etiology proceeds from intellectual revolution against God to social revolution against human authority, whereas the other proceeds from social to religious revolt. How can these two different arguments be reconciled? A reasonable attempt at a unified description of SK's etiology of revolution is as follows: First the speculative (that is, Hegelian) cultural elite revolted in the name of "the race" [Slægten] against God's absolute and transcendent authority, but they did so with much politeness and refinement. Then the masses, given the signal by the liberal bourgeois philistines—who, for their part, looked to the pantheistic intellectual elite for models of culture—revolted against social and political authority. Finally, the most radical have revolted against the idea of God as the Unconditioned. Thus the movement has gone full circle, from the refined religious rebellion of the conservative elite, to the social and political rebellion of the liberals and the common people, to the radical rejection of religion by the most "advanced" members of this latter group.

The eleventh hour is now approaching, when "the people" or (to keep things more individualistic and within SK's preferred vocabulary) "the common man" [den menige Mand] must be warned away from the abyss. SK does not propose to turn the clock back to pre-revolutionary notions of political and social authority and legitimacy. He only wishes to try to compel society to restrict itself to its proper sphere and to insist that the forces of liberal secularization take the limits of their own secularism seriously. Liberal society must not prop itself up with outdated notions of Christian culture. This, at least, is the direction in which SK is moving in the "Two Notes," and the description of SK's position here gives us some reasonable anticipation of the point at which he will arrive by December 1854, when Bishop Mynster was dead, Martensen installed as his successor, and the shadow of reaction definitively lifted from the new political order. At that point it will be time for SK to act upon the consequences of his "liberal" position openly and decisively, no matter how radical or destructive this might seem, for in the threatened assimilation of the old conservative idea of "Christendom" to the new liberal *res publica*, nothing less was at stake than the loss of the transcendent, "vertical," religious dimension from the life of "the common man."

All this, however, carries us somewhat ahead of ourselves. Before we can assess the "attack on the Church," we must examine the "Open Letter" of January 1851, where SK reveals how far he still is from embracing fully the liberal position on the boundaries of church and state. And, after the "Open Letter," we have still to examine the two sets of discourses "Recommended to This Age." These discourses, which stem from the early 1850's, allow us to chart the final stages of SK's radicalization, as he progressed from the moderate and conciliatory position of the "Open Letter" to the radical intransigence of December 1854 and thereafter.

E. THE "OPEN LETTER" TO DR. RUDELBACH

In January 1851, Dr. A. G. Rudelbach, a scholar and publicist who had been friendly to Grundtvig's cause, published *On Civil Marriage* [*Om det borgerlige Ægteskab*], in which he argued for the institution of civil marriage as a part of the campaign of separation of church and state in which Grundtvig's party was then engaged. In support of his criticism of state religion and his call for the separation of Christianity from the state, Rudelbach pointed to the work of SK, writing that

> [t]ruly, it is precisely the highest and most profound interest of the Church in our times . . . to be emancipated from what can rightly be called *habitual* and *legally established* Christianity. . . . This is the same as what one of the most excellent writers in recent times, *Søren Kierkegaard*, seeks to emphasize, impress upon, and—as Luther says—to drive into every person who will listen. . . . But civil marriage is an important, perhaps indispensable instrument in this emancipation, a necessary part of the coordinating of all the official arrangements that signify and make possible the introduction of freedom of religion.[7]

As we have noted earlier, SK's rejoinder serves to indicate the relatively moderate public stance he was willing to take in January 1851, as well as the possibilities for further development which he left himself. In his reply—entitled "Occasioned by a Remark by Dr. Rudelbach Concerning Myself" [Foranlediget ved en Yttring af Dr. Rudelbach mig betræffende], published in *The Fatherland*, January 31, 1851—SK notes that he especially wants to make sure that Rudelbach's use of him has not misled people into thinking that he is a member of "a certain party" [p. 441], i.e., the Grundtvigians.

Rudelbach's claim that SK, like Rudelbach himself, opposes "habitual and legally established Christianity," is a half-truth at best, and thus, also half-untruth, SK insists. First of all, with respect to "the Christianity of habit," it is indeed true that SK hates it, but, SK adds, he hates it in *all* its manifestations, also those of the sectarians and "the awakened."

> And if there were no other choice, if the choice were only between *this* sort of habitual Christianity—a worldly capriciousness that lives carefree, imagining that it is Christian, perhaps without even having any impression of what Christianity is, *and* the sort of habitual Christianity found among sectarians, the awakened, the hyper-orthodox, the party-liners—if things were as bad as this, I would unconditionally choose the first. [p. 437]

SK mounts a vigorous assault upon Rudelbach as a member of the Grundtvigian group, which SK saw as "a party of the hyper-orthodox." SK serves notice here, as earlier and later in his authorship—but not in the final attack on the Church, where he clearly and uncompromisingly rejects both the Establishment and the Grundtvigian alternatives—that, if pressed, he would embrace the imperfections of the present arrangements in preference to the self-righteousness of the "sectarians." Of the two forms of perdition—mindless establishmentarianism and self-righteous reforming zeal—the former is to be preferred. The self-righteous hypocrisy and back-room politicking of the reformist zealot tend to pollute the wellsprings of reform and to downgrade and devitalize the important notion of reformation itself, a notion SK, for his own reasons, wishes to keep in reserve.

Furthermore, while it is true that SK opposes "the Christianity of habit," as Rudelbach has claimed, SK insists that nowhere in his works has he attacked "legally established Christianity" [Stats-Christendom = State Christianity], for he does not believe that the problem lies in "the external" [det Udvortes]. SK insists that his whole authorship has been "an existential corrective of the established order, aimed at increasing inwardness in 'the individual'—this is to say that I have certainly never directed a word against the doctrines and organizational arrangements of the established order" [p. 441]. (All this is technically true, but only by means of the maieutic fiction of allowing "Anti-Climacus" to be the "author" of *Training in Christianity*, a fiction which, as we now know, was to be withdrawn in May 1855 in the heat of the "attack on Christendom." We will see shortly that, even within this article itself, SK carefully reserves the right to intervene in "the external" under certain circumstances, and the story of SK's progress from January 1851 to the onset of the "attack" in December 1854 is largely the story of his inspection of the political and social scene in order to ascertain whether those circumstances were indeed present.)

Politics is itself an area of relative freedom, in which alternative social solutions are possible, always provided, of course, that they maintain an honest inner awareness of their tentative and secondary nature. SK does not present himself as a reactionary authoritarian or a conservative dogmatist; there is no *prima facie* case against liberalism and representative government:

> I can understand that a politician would believe that free institutions are ben-eficial to the state, because politics is an external thing which, by its very nature, not having any life in itself, must take its life from forms. From this comes politics' faith in forms. But that Christianity, which has its life in itself, is to be saved by means of free institutions, this is in my opinion, a complete misun-derstanding of Christianity which, when it is true and in true inwardness, is infinitely higher and freer than all institutions, constitutions, etc. [pp. 439–40]

This is another of SK's classic statements of the difference between the *relative* good of politics (which does not possess its end in itself) and the *absolute* Good of religion (which does possess its end in itself). Politics is left to itself. Matters of "free institutions" and "constitutions, etc." are matters of choice for poli-ticians, and as a purely political matter, SK can "understand" the liberal point of view.

But, SK reminds his readers—in a statement that could serve as a motto for the present work as a whole—"*there is nothing that makes me so uneasy as anything that even merely smacks of this disastrous confounding of politics and Christianity*" [p. 438, emphasis added]. This confusion of religion and politics will lead to a reformation, SK admits, but a bad reformation, in which the mediocre is replaced by worse, to the great acclamation of the general public. On the other hand,

> Christianity is inwardness, making inward. If, in any given age, the [external political] forms under which Christianity must be lived out are not the most perfect, and if one can make them better, then in God's name do so. But, *es-sentially,* Christianity is inwardness. Just as it is the human's advantage over the animal to be able to live in every climate, so is it Christianity's excellence, precisely because of this inwardness, to be able, according to its strength [in the individual], to be able to live under even the most imperfect of forms. Politics is this external being, this tantalizing busyness with changing the externalities. [p. 439]

Christianity and politics delimit one another and are (or ought to be) connected only at their common boundary. Christianity *can* live under various political circumstances, even the most unfavorable, "according to its strength" in the inwardness of the individual. If a change for the better in the external forms can be effected, it is permissible, even laudable, to do so, but only if this does not challenge the "essential inwardness" which is Christianity. Thus, while condemning the politicking of such groups as Rudelbach's Grundtvigians, SK leaves open the door for a possible later political sally of his own, if by so doing he could improve the external "forms" within which Christianity must operate. But it must be stressed that, when they confuse politics and Christianity, Christianity's "friends" are more dangerous than her avowed enemies.

Citing Acts 5:29 ("We ought to obey God rather than men"), SK grants that Christianity does indeed know of instances when the external arrangements of the established order are such that Christianity ought *not* acquiesce in them. Christianity is not indifferent to *all* externality. But, SK adds, when confronted with such serious problems, the Apostles did not take political counsel, did not discuss how they might mobilize a tactical political majority for freedom of conscience by allying themselves with forces with whom they were usually at odds [p. 441]. (This is a clear reference to the Grundtvigians' strange bedfellows in the post-1848 period, e.g., their alliance with their old opponent, H. N. Clausen.) The Apostles knew no party spirit, for each was an individual bound to God [p. 442]. The Apostles chose not to politick, but to stand as solitary witnesses for the truth, to be martyred, to suffer for the truth.

Similarly, Luther did not have "knowledge of the numerical situation"; he did not try to arrange a majority for freedom of conscience—of all things!—but acted and let others decide whether or not to follow his lead. If Luther could look upon today's Denmark, SK concludes, he would say "this situation is not really dangerous. The only dangerous thing—and it would be very dangerous—would be if such stuff [i.e., the reforming campaign of the Grundtvigians] were called Reformation and seriousness" [p. 443n.].

Thus, an honest challenge to external political conditions is sometimes permissible and requires a risk-taking, suffering individual who stands up for what he or she believes and who does not try to prepare his or her ground—in a case of conscience!—by mobilizing a floating, tactical majority, as Grundtvig did in the Rigsdag over such issues as the church constitution, parish bonds, priest-freedom, civil marriage, etc. We must especially note, in concluding this chapter, that although SK deprecates present-day reformers in comparison to the Apostles of the book of Acts and in comparison to Luther, the very existence of these examples of conscientious intervention by religious individuals in the world of "the external" does show that there *are* times when such action is called for.

26. Two Series of Discourses "Recommended to the Present Age"

○

A. *FOR SELF-EXAMINATION*

In 1851–52 SK composed two sets of discourses "recommended to the present age," namely *For Self-Examination* [*Til Selvprøvelse*] [SV XII, pp. 291–370] and the "second series" of these discourses, *Judge for Yourselves!* [*Dømmer Selv!*] [SV XII, pp. 371–481]. These two works, although not developing anything new in the theological or theoretical sense, are essentially popularizations of the radical critique contained in *Training in Christianity*. They are particularly interesting to us in that, on the one hand, the two sets of discourses continue the line of thinking in *Training*, while on the other hand, the second set of discourses, in particular, reflects a significant deepening of SK's critique of Christian culture and represents a halfway stage between the caution of the "Open Letter" to Rudelbach and the abandon of the "attack on Christendom."

The first set of discourses, *For Self-Examination*, was written in the summer of 1851 and published in September of that year. It went through several editions in SK's lifetime and was, until the pamphleteering campaign of the "attack," his most widely sold work. The second set of discourses, *Judge for Yourselves!*, was written in the period from September 1851 until sometime early in 1852, but it should be noted that this significantly more radical work, though it lay ready for press, was never published in SK's lifetime. It thus marks a development in SK's evolution as a writer which, in the early 1850's, he apparently regarded as too radical to be published, but which, by 1854–55, had already been surpassed by the far more heady material of *The Moment*. Let us examine these two sets of discourses from 1851–52 in their order of composition, in order to note both the new elements and the elements of continuity with the earlier works that they contain in their criticism of the social-political synthesis of Christendom.

For Self-Examination[1] is a set of three discourses, the longest and most important of which is, significantly, based upon a text of James, the Apostle whose stress upon works has often been held to be inimical to the grace theology of Lutheranism. As will be noted in the course of examining this work, the increasing emphasis upon James leads also to a shift in the interpretation of Matthew 6:24-end and a corresponding de-emphasis of the possibility of seeing bourgeois social integration as a legitimate form of prioritarianism. In the post-1848 period, SK's assessment of the social and political state of Christendom led him to an increasingly revisionist position with respect to James and "works." SK's growing feeling that traditional Lutheran grace was being taken in vain led him to see that the normal form of Christian interaction with the social order is opposition and witness—and not the prioritarian integration which shrouds its differences with the world in hidden inwardness as a solely private matter between the individual and God.

James tells us (Jas. 1:22-end) that we must be "doers and not just hearers of the Word" and that we must look into the mirror of the Word, see ourselves deeply and remember what we see, remaining obligated to translate our vision into action, into deeds. SK points out that God's Word is indeed a mirror of the soul and that in reading God's Word one must treat it as a mirror in which one sees oneself. We must not waste time observing the mirror (as in the obfuscations of biblical criticism) [pp. 315–19]; in fact, the sort of scholarship that examines the mirror of the Word is really a method of protecting *ourselves* from the Word [pp. 322–23]. Rather, having looked in the mirror, we must move straight to action. If one does not read God's Word such that one is immediately obligated, then one has not read *God's* Word [pp. 318–19]. In other words, God's Word is not an objective something that is accessible to neutral cognition but is a challenge to action that exists only in being appropriated and acted upon by the individual; Christianity is not cognition, but sheer activity. Similarly, preaching should not be an art-form that differentiates between those of greater and lesser rhetorical talent but should, "in unity with the Holy Spirit, center all attention upon only one thing, that one must do that which has been spoken of" [p. 303]. *Or*, if one does not proceed directly to action, then one must come forward "instantly [with a] humbling admission" of one's weakness and inadequacy [p. 320]. This is, of course, the principal theme of *Training in Christianity*. In that work, as in this, what SK demands is "honesty" [Redelighed]. It is more honest [redelig], in fact, to *hide* the Bible so that one will not be confronted with it, than it is to deal with it in a way that does not obligate one to act [ibid.].

Reading the Bible obligates one to become a subjective personality, SK insists, and not merely an impersonal intellect, the product of "culture" [Dannelse] and refinement. When you read the Bible, SK insists, "you must read a fear and trembling into your soul, so that, with God's help, you will succeed in becoming a person, a personality, saved from that terrible monstrosity into which all of us humans—created in God's image—have been transformed, an impersonal, objective something" [p. 331]. We have protected ourselves from seeing ourselves in the Bible by saying that it is "vanity" to be "subjective," whereas on the other hand, "refined" [dannede] and "serious" people "transform the Word into an impersonal thing (the objective, an objective doctrine, etc.)," to which one relates oneself objectively [p. 324]. Refined and serious people view it as "unrefined" [udannet] and "vain" to bring one's personality into play [ibid.]. All this is of course another assault on the Golden Age cultural elite, particularly the Heiberg-Martensen group, which is the obvious representative of "the impersonality or objectivity so praised in our century as culture [Dannelse] and seriousness" [p. 327].

SK's diatribe against the objectivity and impersonality of the "culture" elite reaches one of its highest points in this work, and it will be useful to cite a portion of it at some length, so that its "populist," almost rabble-rousing quality in addressing itself to the common man can be appreciated:

> [H]ow profoundly clever and cunning it is when the world's refinement, in Christendom, making use of what is undeniably true—that the selfishness that continually brings up its "I" and its personality is vanity—that, making use of this fact, they have transformed the seriousness in the relationship to God's Word into vanity, so that people free themselves from seriousness and from the efforts of seriousness, and thereby guarantee themselves respect as serious and cultured people. O, depth of cunning! They make God's Word into something impersonal, something objective, a doctrine. . . . And they relate themselves impersonally (objectively) to this impersonal thing. And at the height of the world's refinement, at the head of the cultured public and of scholarly learning, they defiantly claim that this is seriousness and culture. They pity those personal (subjective) wretches, if possible, into the dunce's corner! O, depth of cunning! For it is only too easy for us humans to preserve this impersonality (objectivity) in relation to the Word of God; it is really an innate genius which we all have, something which we receive gratis along with original sin, for this praised impersonality (objectivity) is neither more nor less than lack of conscience. And it is clear that lack of conscience makes life easy and full of enjoyment—though, naturally, not so that this is obvious, which would be foolish, stupid, imprudent, like the crimes that are reported to the police—no, no, in moderation, to a certain degree, and therefore with taste and refinement. But that is too much, to make this into seriousness and culture! [pp. 327–28][2]

Further on in *For Self-Examination*, SK points out that not only is such impersonal and un-Christian refinement and culture [Dannelse] just as bad as the crude impiety of the mob, but, in a way, it is worse. SK takes the most extreme of examples in his indictment of "Dannelse," namely the crucifixion of Christ and the fact that Christ was condemned by the most "refined" [dannet] of Roman procurators. "O, human 'culture,' what is your real difference from that which you most abhor, unrefinedness [Udannetheden], and the crudeness of the mob? You do the same as they do, but you pay attention to form, you do not do it with unwashed hands—o, human 'culture' " [p. 348]. In fact, as we have seen elsewhere and as we see again in *For Self-Examination*, the refinement that claims to abhor the crowd and the public is in fact intimately related to the crowd and is dependent upon it for its survival.

In earlier works we have seen how SK traced the revolt of the crowd back to the circles of the "Dannede." In the present work he sets up the familiar antithesis between the individual who struggles quietly with his religious scruples and "the crowd, or the highly honored, cultivated [dannede] public," whose *proper* concern is not religious matters but such things as "public transportation and street-lighting" [p. 310]. Two points of particular interest emerge here. First is the reminder that "the public" *does* have a legitimate area of its own, namely such matters of material prudence as public transportation, etc. Secondly, we should note the close relation SK draws between the "cultured" and "the crowd," as in the phrase, "the crowd, or the 'cultured' public." The impersonality of the crowd is a form of the impersonality of culture. This impersonality is a suitable attitude in relation to such public affairs as transport and street-lighting, but is wholly inappropriate as a mode of relating to the mirror of the Word of God, which must obligate the reader, quite personally, either to action or to an "instantaneous humbling admission."

As a final example of SK's determination to twit and tease the "refined public" for its lack of even an elementary understanding of true Christianity, we may note SK's teasing reference to a book that was noted in part one of the present work, namely *The Spirit in Nature* [*Aanden i Naturen*], the recently published (1850) masterpiece of popularizing *Naturphilosophie* by H. C. Ørsted, the eminent Danish physicist, who had long been the darling of "the cultured public." After dwelling at length upon the miraculousness of Christ's ascension, SK sums up by saying that it was "an ascension that defies all natural laws, defies the spirit [Aanden]—though, of course, only the nature-spirit [Natur-Aanden]!—in Nature [i Naturen]" [p. 354]. This open mockery of Ørsted's respected *Spirit in Nature* is but one of the more flagrantly "populist" attempts by SK to sharpen the antithesis between the dominant notions of "culture," on the one hand and subjectively appropriated Christianity (which he also polemically terms "New Testament Christianity") on the other.

The most common tendency with respect to Christianity is not naked unbelief but rather that it is *taken in vain*, accepted lightly. The cure for this is to insist upon death as "the middle term," to insist upon "dying-away" as the precondition of faith. "There is nothing, no definition of that which is Christian, unless Christianity first posits death, dying-away, as the middle term, in order thereby to insure Christianity against being taken in vain" [pp. 359–60]. Christianity has been called "the mild consolation," SK notes, but some consolation it is, preceded by death to the world! Here SK returns to the radically dualistic understanding of Christianity which, as we have seen, underlay the polemical *Training in Christianity*, and which, as we will see shortly, underlies the entire closing phase of the authorship. The life that Christianity gives is a *new* life but not an *immediate* one:

a new life, literally a new life, because—take note—death, dying-away, intervenes; and a new life, on the other side of death, Yes, that *is* a new life. . . . Death intervenes, that is the teaching of Christianity: You must die away; it is precisely the life-giving Spirit that kills you; that is the first utterance of the life-giving Spirit, that you must go into death, that you must die away—thus it is, in order that you not take Christianity in vain. The life-giving Spirit, that is the invitation. Who would not gladly accept it! But die first, that is the stopping point! . . . Thus, first death, first you must die away from every merely earthly hope, every merely human confidence; you must die away from your selfishness, or from the world, because it is only through your selfishness that the world has power over you. If you have died away from your selfishness, you have also died away from the world. But there is, of course, nothing to which a person clings so firmly—indeed, with his whole life!—as to his selfishness! [pp. 360-61]

Thus, the message of the Word is that one must die first, and only then does the life-giving Spirit come. And the new life that the Spirit brings is faith.

Faith is against the understanding; faith is on the other side of death. And when you died or died away from yourself, from the world, then you also died from all immediacy in yourself, also from your understanding. That is, when all confidence in yourself or in human assistance, and also all immediate confidence in God, when all likelihood [Sandsynlighed] is extinguished, when it is as dark as in the dark night—this is of course also the death we are describing—then the life-giving Spirit comes and brings faith. [p. 365]

There is a radical dichotomy between the this-worldly concerns of the understanding and other-worldly concerns, for which the organ is faith. There is no simple ascent or progress from the one realm to the other. There is no simple progress from Creation to Redemption, from the first to the second birth. The other-worldly does not build upon the worldly, but rather, the worldly, if it is to be properly used and understood at all, must follow and not precede the other-worldly. SK's order of things is "First death, then life" [p. 364]. Nothing could be more opposed, not only to speculative theology (which is the principal target of *For Self-Examination*) but also to the optimistic Grundtvig's maxim, "Human first, and then Christian, that is life's order." No, the unchanging substratum for SK is precisely the reverse: "First death, then life."

SK's message for the age, therefore, is to place renewed emphasis upon James' call for works, that we be "doers of the Word," for only thus can we be led to experience the true depth of our inadequacy and thereby become able to receive Christianity's grace properly, and not in vain. SK's view of the history of Christianity is one of a dialectic of grace and works; in some ages the one element is overstressed or taken in vain, in others it is the other. The task is continually to put the two elements into their proper relationship to one another, and for SK this relationship is one of grace *plus* works, though recognizing the superiority of the former element and without the imputation of any merit to the latter. It is a sort of revisionist Lutheranism. Each age must have what it needs. "Times are different," SK points out,

> there was a time when the Gospel, 'grace,' had been transformed into a new law, stricter with people than the old law had been. . . . Everything had become works, and just as trees have unhealthy growths, these works were corrupted by unhealthy growths, very often simply hypocrisy, imagined meritoriousness, idleness. It was precisely there that the problem lay, not so much in the works. For let us not exaggerate; let us not permit the errors of a past time to lead us into new error. No, take this unhealthiness and untruth away from works, and let us then retain works in honesty, in humility, in gainful activity. [p. 306]

In this bygone time, when works were overemphasized and merit was attributed to them, Luther came along and boldly called for setting James aside. This was very risky, SK insists, and a terrible sacrifice for Luther. And further, we must not forget that Luther's "life expressed works," even while he downgraded the message of the Apostle James [p. 307]. Thus, when he served as a corrective, Luther was not a one-sided one. But, SK asks, what has happened to the Lutheran appeal for grace over works? Just what one might expect to happen over time, for there is a worldliness in every person that would like to be a Christian at "a bargain price." Thus, with respect to works and faith, people tend to want either to have *merit* for the performance of good works *or*, if faith and grace are to be stressed, then to be *free of works* altogether [ibid.]. This sort of attitude proclaims that "'if it is to be works and, despite everything, faith as well, then it is indeed madness.' Yes, it certainly is madness; so, too, was true Lutheranism, for of course, it was Christianity" [p. 308].

SK claims that Luther said—or would have said in today's works-less Christianity—that to preach the Gospel is to let "faith's unrest" manifest itself in one's daily life, in the streets and not simply in the "quiet hours" [stille Timer, a by-now-familiar code for Mynster's Golden Age Christianity] in church or in books [p. 309]. "Faith, that restless thing, must be recognizable in one's life" [p. 310]. SK does not scruple to call upon Luther as the perennial reformer, even to the point of having Luther—who, as we know, could not abide James— call for a renewed emphasis on James and on works, in view of the present situation in Christendom. SK writes, of Luther,

> Don't you think he would say: "The Apostle James must be brought forth a bit, not for works *against* faith, no, no, but neither was that the Apostle's intention, but *for* faith, in order, if possible, to cause the need for 'Grace' to be deeply felt in true, humble inwardness, and in order, if possible, to keep Grace—and the notion that faith and Grace are the only salvation, the only redeeming thing— from being taken entirely in vain, from becoming a hiding place for a very refined worldliness." [p. 314]

We must never forget, SK concludes, that works are the "minor premise" [Undersætning] which is implicitly present in the Lutheran formula. Faith and Grace remain the "major premise" [Oversætning], and are not dethroned by the presence of works—but both premises are present [ibid.].

We will conclude our investigation of *For Self-Examination* by looking at SK's account of his own role. He insists that he has not worked for outward tumult but for an "inward transformation," opposing both "external spectacle" and "deathly silence."

> I have worked against it [this deathly silence], and worked to awaken unrest in the direction of making-inward. Let me define exactly where I am, so to speak. There is among us an extremely honorable, venerable old man, the leading cleric of this Church [i.e., Mynster]. That which his "sermon" has willed is identical to what I want, except that I wish to be one note stronger, which comes from the peculiarity of my personality and from what these peculiar times require. There are some among us who claim to be Christian in the strictest sense [e.g., Grundtvigians and other "awakened" pietist groups], to be Christian as opposed to us others. I have not been able to adhere to them. . . . Basically, I am a part of the average, and it is here that I have worked for unrest in the direction of making-inward. [p. 311]

Thus SK claims, despite everything, to be a sort of moderate reformer, not exclusive and self-righteous like the various Grundtvigian and pietist groups, but a centrist like Mynster, "except one note stronger."

Yet, finally, there is a gulf separating SK from Mynster, namely SK's continuing insistence that we make a humbling "admission" of the inadequacy of our "Christianity" in comparison with that of the saints and martyrs of the early Church. We ought, SK insists, to set aside time each day to contemplate our imperfection in comparison with the greatness of those who dared all for faith, and we ought to contemplate the unfairness in the fact that we should all inherit the same salvation [p. 313]. SK says that *this* sort of contemplation, which emphasizes the importance of works and prepares one for the proper reception of grace, is an example of what he means by "a movement that is unrest in the direction of making-inward" [p. 314], and this is very far indeed from Mynster's Christianity.

By the time of the composition of *For Self-Examination* in 1851, SK cannot have been unaware of the great difference between himself and Mynster on the issue of an "admission," and we must thus interpret his claim to be very like Mynster "except one note stronger" as a tactical position that he adopts for popular consumption. In part, SK makes this claim in order to differentiate himself from the Grundtvigian and other pietist reformers. For the rest, SK makes this claim in order to prepare the way for the furious assault on "Christendom" that would ensue if Mynster ultimately failed to make some sort of statement and if the existing conservative-liberal Christian cultural compromise

continued to thrive and consolidate its position. Still, in spite of what he knew
to be Mynster's attitude toward the thesis of *Training in Christianity,* in general,
and toward his call for an "admission," in particular, SK felt bound to reiterate
that call, perhaps in the faint hope that the old man would come around
somehow and bring the entire non-Grundtvigian Christian community with
him, or perhaps only for the record.

> Ah, we who call ourselves Christian, we are, Christianly understood, so pam-
> pered, so far from having died away from the world—which, however, Chris-
> tianity requires of them who wish to call themselves Christians—that we hardly
> even have a conception of that sort of seriousness; we still cannot do without
> and abandon the mitigations of artifice; we cannot stand the true impression of
> reality. So, now, let us at least be honest and admit it. [pp. 303-304]

Thus, in comparison with *Training in Christianity, For Self-Examination* does
exhibit a certain progress in extending the limits of polemic, but the latter work
still remains a popularization of the former, and it remains within the basic
framework in which an all-out assault on the social and political "externals"
of Christendom is held in abeyance pending a possible "admission."

B. *JUDGE FOR YOURSELVES!* (PART ONE)

If *For Self-Examination,* the first of the two series of discourses "recommended to the present age," is largely concerned with restoring James to what
SK saw as his rightful place in Lutheran Christianity, then *Judge for Yourselves!,*
the second set of these discourses, constitutes a major re-interpretation of our
key scriptural locus in Matthew.[3] Taken together, *For Self-Examination* and *Judge
for Yourselves!* constitute a landmark in SK's rethinking of Lutheranism in the
post-1848 world. *Judge for Yourselves!* consists of two rather lengthy discourses;
let us first examine the one that most concerns itself with a reinterpretation of
Matthew and then turn our attention to the other, in which SK deals quite
explicitly with the specifically post-1848 social and political developments that
give special urgency to his case.

The first of the two discourses is entitled "Christ as Exemplar, or 'No One
Can Serve Two Masters,'" the latter title taken, of course, from the now-
familiar Matthew 6:24-end, upon which the discourse is constructed. Like SK
himself, SK's readers have presumably now come to know Matthew 6:24-end
quite well, but this time we will be exposed to the "strict" side of prioritarianism, namely that one must really strive to seek *first* the Kingdom of God,
and that no one can serve two masters. Accordingly, SK presents us with a
Christianity characterized by a thoroughgoing dualism of parallel worlds: The
"world" and the Gospel talk of two completely different worlds. This world
talks only of this world, whereas the Gospel talks of "a discovery that is

mortally dangerous for 'this world': another world. The Gospel speaks eternally and about this other world of eternity" [p. 425].

If this is the way that being is structured, then "the highest" mode of existence must be in keeping with this. "The highest thing is, while remaining unconditionally heterogeneous to the world by serving God alone, to remain in the world, in the middle of reality, before everyone's eyes, and to direct attention to oneself" in so doing [p. 440]. Thus, Christianity is a stance, a posture, in which one bravely and openly bears witness to another world, a higher reality, while remaining in the midst of this world and the present reality, in spite of the suffering and persecution that is sure to follow as a consequence of having insisted upon allowing the Eternal mode to penetrate the temporal. This is "serving only one master," namely Eternity, and it is quite different from the social integration of the bourgeois Christian "citizen."

This, according to SK, is also what Christ does par excellence. He serves only one master and uses all his powers to guarantee that in earthly terms he amounts to nothing. Christ insists upon three things: first, upon standing in the middle of the world; second, upon proclaiming, in the midst of the world, that "my kingdom is not of this world"; and, third, upon focusing all attention on this contradiction. "It is as if it were an attempt to drive the human race from its senses; that is, he wishes to force upon them, or force them into, the definition of being 'Spirit' " [p. 445]. In other words, in witnessing to the unseen but higher reality of which we, as human beings, also partake, Christ was attempting, in his apparently absurd and contradictory behavior, to compel us to become aware of what we truly are.

What is provocative in Christ's behavior is his insistence upon being nothing (which normally would deserve obscurity) and upon being the focus of attention. It is madness. It is "just as insane as wishing to establish, in the middle of this world, a Kingdom that is not of this world" [pp. 445–46]. This provocative madness, if held seriously, becomes a war of life and death between Christ's reality and that of the world. They are like fire and water; only one may win. One can serve only one master. Thus, when the mob cried out for Barabbas, who had committed crimes only against individual people, it knew what it was doing in preferring him to Christ, who had launched "an attack against the entire human race and against what it is to be human!" [p. 447]. This radically dualistic Christianity, which preaches the "offensive" eschatological penetration of the superior element of eternity into time, does not lend itself to bourgeois social integration—though it remains possible, in a higher and more risk-filled, oppositional way, to be both a Christian and a good "citizen." This will be the message of SK's own foray into political border warfare, an assault that he saw as a good turn both to Christianity and to the social-political sphere.

SK grants that, understood in the above sense, the call to "serve one master" is quite "unreasonable" [p. 428]. SK insists that he has great respect for ordinary human honesty, and he will always respect "reasonableness" when it has the *honesty* to say quite baldly that "the Unconditioned is ridiculous" [p. 431]. "This is not what is dangerous, at least not for Christianity. . . . On the other hand, what can be dangerous is when one suppresses the truth, if not in unrighteousness, then in *ambiguity*" [pp. 431–32, emphasis added]. The principal danger for SK is always in half-truth—e.g., "to a certain degree"— and ambiguity, and never in honest rebellion and defiance. This is because, as we have seen, the former are all forms of "spiritlessness," by far the most widespread, deadly, and pernicious sort of the sickness unto death. In "Christian culture," if not in all cultures, the danger to true religion always comes from Christianity's "friends" and not from its avowed enemies. Our "enlightened, free-spirited, cultured [dannede] times" wish to modify, to soften the unreasonable demand to serve only one master [p. 428]. Our times wish to act according to the human understanding, whose principle is

> to a certain degree, in moderation . . . both/and . . . . And we therefore demand a Christianity that can be brought into harmony with the rest of our existence, in keeping with the change that—with the increase of enlightenment and culture and the liberation from all lower forms of oppression—has come over the human race, or at least over the most important segment of the race, the cultivated public. [Ibid.]

Thus, it is again "culture," the "*cultivated* public," that feels that our age has become so enlightened and progressive that it must have a more reasonable, domesticated Christianity.

Christianity, as we have seen, places opposites together. Christ, the glorious, lived in poverty and degradation. There was a star over his birth but a cross at the end. Both the star and the cross are real, "and no eye sees the cross and the star bound together in a higher unity. . . . It is not the star that one bears (a later invention!); alas, one bears the cross!" [p. 434]. This is an attack upon the Hegelian speculation, which sees the Christian opposites bound together in a synthetic "higher unity." And this is at the same time a broader blow directed at the entire status-seeking Christian *haute bourgeoisie*, for whom there was no higher reward than to be awarded the "Knight's Cross" [Ridderkorset], worn by all the luminaries—Mynster, Heiberg, Martensen, both Ørsteds, etc.—and which was, literally, a large and glorious star containing a cross. Both the Hegelian "higher unity" and the unity of the entire Christian social order of the Golden Age are the targets of SK's attack.

"Reasonableness," SK asserts, would rather *compromise* the juxtaposed extremes of Christianity, and it would even be willing to dispense with them for the sake of a Christianity the human race could live with. Bourgeois respectability would of course like to dispense with the cross, but it would even be willing to dispense with the star at Christ's birth, in order thus to have him "born into a legitimate marriage and at least into a presentable, well-off, bourgeois family. Christianity, however, is not like that; it always has the things of Heaven at its disposal, but not the least scrap of earthly things" [p. 434]. Bourgeois respectability is spiritual death, as is bourgeois avarice, and SK taunts the Christian and respectable middle class by reminding his readers that Christ was and became "nothing," and never possessed anything [p. 437].

In sum, worldly "reasonableness" is diametrically opposed to the Unconditioned, to the Unconditional requirement of Christianity, for "nothing is more offensive to reasonableness than the Unconditioned" [p. 429]. In wishing to abolish the absolute and Unconditional demand, we really wish to abolish God himself but will not admit this [p. 438]. Christ expresses the Unconditioned, the absolute requirement "to serve only one master," and it is thus perfectly in keeping with reasonableness to require Christianity abolished. But what is inexcusable and dishonest is to require Christianity changed or modified so that it is "reasonable." To this Christianity can never agree. People can take it or leave it; it will not force itself upon anyone. But "reasonableness is a rebellion against the Unconditioned" and wishes, covertly, to substitute some modified form of Christianity—for example, the Kantian-moralistic or the Hegelian-intellectualistic forms—while preserving appearances unchanged [p. 430]. And "reasonable" people will no longer allow genuine Christianity in church, but will "tolerate" a priest "who, in a seemly fashion, observes decorum [and] limits himself to declaiming in quiet hours" [p. 431]—a not very veiled reference, once again, to the poor Mynster, darling of the respectable.

SK traces four stages in the historical devolution of Christianity to its present state. The first phase is that of "suffering for the teachings," which is clearly a reference to the climate of straightforward persecution that surrounded the early Church of saints and martyrs [p. 468]. The next phase SK describes is characterized by "the struggle of an anguished conscience, fear and trembling," and describes the religious scruples that characterized the Lutheran Reformation [ibid.]. The third phase is described as "a quiet enjoyment of life, observing civic justice, while thinking often about God, so that the thought of him is included somewhat, but without ever coming to feel the impact of Christianity as a stumbling block, without really noticing that Christianity is offensive to the Jew in me and foolish to the Greek in me" [p. 469]. This is clearly a description of the polite, domesticated Mynsterian Christianity of the Golden Age. The fourth and final stage, "the most general sort of Christianity, is a worldly life, avoiding great crimes (more, indeed, out of shrewdness than for the sake of conscience), a secret seeking after the pleasures of life—and then, once in a while, a so-called pious mood" [ibid.]. This last and most degenerate phase clearly refers to the present, post-revolutionary "People's Church," in which being Christian has become merely another attribute implicated in being a normal citizen of the liberal-democratic constitutional monarchy of Denmark.[4]

What is particularly worth noting, however, is that the story of Christianity, thus told, is not simply a steady downward progress. It is true that the second, "Lutheran" phase (with anguished consciences and fear and trembling) is seen as a falling-off from the true "imitation" of the "early Church," but the "Lutheran" phase is praiseworthy nonetheless. On the other hand, the third, "Mynsterian," phase ("quiet enjoyment" combined with obliviousness to the genuinely Christian, or "offensive," elements of Christianity) is not seen, in its turn, as an understandable falling-off in relation to the Lutheran phase. Rather, the Mynsterian phase is portrayed as simply vile and hypocritical and (as we know from other passages) is seen as responsible for the complete degeneration of Christianity in the final "People's Church" phase. The domestication of Christianity has led to its ultimate undoing. The polite Christianity of the third phase made possible the empty Christianity of the fourth, and it is no accident— if my assignment of names to the various stages is correct—that Bishop Mynster, the typical representative for the third phase, presided over the transition to the empty "People's Church" of the modern, post-1848 era.

Thus, what we have now, SK explains, is "bourgeois philistinism" and "spiritlessness," which has changed the original, ideal Christian scale of measure into something trivial, so that a mediocre local pastor "thinks that he is suited to indicate the scale of measure and the model" for Christianity [p. 467] ["model" here = "Mynster," an outrageous pun, see accompanying note].[5] "It is bourgeois philistinism to situate oneself like this in supposed Christianity so that one actually abolishes Christianity" [ibid.]. Thus, Bishop Mynster stands accused of having accepted the leadership of the philistine bourgeoisie, of having allowed his own shrunken Christianity to be used as a "model" [Mynster], and thus of having presided over the abolition of Christianity. A new cultural ideal has been substituted for Christianity, and what is perhaps the worst feature of this reign of "good taste" is that it still persists in calling itself "Christianity."

SK points out that the human race, rather than imitate Christ in dangerous provocation of the world and in the suffering that is sure to follow, has preferred to re-define Christianity to mean the adherence to the Golden Mean, to "decorum," to "taste and culture" [pp. 456–57]. Naturally, when Christianity comes so cheaply, a certain spiritual idleness follows, and Christianity's elevated conceptual vocabulary of suffering, Imitation, etc. no longer seems applicable to such a domesticated religion. Christian terminology seems laughable, exaggerated, and "people finally become bored with Christianity, because the pressure of 'Imitation,' of the ideal, of Christ as Exemplar, is lacking" [p. 468].

What do the times *need*, then, as opposed to what they *want* or "require?" SK replies with the familiar answer of *Training in Christianity*: The times need

> 'Imitation,' to which corresponds Christ as Exemplar [i.e., as contrasted with the traditional Lutheran emphasis upon Christ as Redeemer]; this must again be

brought into play if there is to be meaning in Christendom; as has been mentioned, it must be done in such a way that draws upon the lessons of earlier times. [pp. 458–59]

In other words, in restoring works to their rightful place we must not give up the Lutheran insistence upon their inefficacy and insufficiency for salvation. We must learn from the earnestness of mediaeval piety while rejecting mediaeval "externality" and notions of merit. "The Middle Ages understood Christianity as meaning action, life, the re-formation of existence" [p. 460], SK notes, and it is this active, "ethical" element in mediaeval piety that he seeks to preserve. Further, SK continues, let us never forget that Luther did not abolish the imitation of Christ or suffering for the truth but only the notion of merits and of trafficking in merits. Luther, in fact, was himself a sacrificing witness to the truth in his own life [p. 461].

If mediaeval Christianity, in its zeal for action and works, was "monastic-ascetic," our Christianity, in its concentration upon intellectualizing and objective doctrine, is "professorial-scientific" [p. 462]. But, SK notes, "Christianity came into the world without professors, and anyone who has an eye for Christianity will see clearly that no one is so capable of practicing Christianity out of the world as 'the professor' " [pp. 462-63].[6] "And therefore imitation must be brought into play" [p. 463], SK concludes, because the cure for too much sterile talk is the obligation to *act*. The "professor" pales when the alternative of "imitation" is posed. "Ethics" finds "scholarship" too light in the scales. In Luther's time, "when 'the cloister' [was] the deviation, Faith [had to] be brought into play" [p. 464]. By the same token, SK understands his present stress upon imitation to be a tactical, corrective measure for the current historical circumstances. And SK again cautions that even while "imitation must be kept in mind," it must be done "in such a way that we have learned the lesson of past errors" [ibid.].

Imitation must be at least posited as an alternative in order to serve as a stark reminder and drive away the optimistic confusions of the present:

> The mildest way in which it [imitation] can be brought to bear is as a possibility—or what one would call dialectically—just so that it pressures doubt into silence and holds existence in order.... This is the most lenient way in which "imitation" can be brought to bear. It is only "the professor" who must be shaken off, the self-importance of scholarship which must be rebuffed. At the same time, everyone is spared. However far back he may be, however far from being able to be called an imitator of Christ, everyone who wishes to relate himself in seemly fashion to Christianity is spared. No one (this ought to have been learned from the errors of a long-gone age) is to be made anxious to venture out beyond his capabilities. Under "Grace" everyone breathes freely and openly. I suggest nothing further than this. ... But I have some anxiety, because the matter of meritoriousness can come back so easily, and I am most of all afraid

of that. . . . And therefore I go no further with imitation than to the point of letting it serve as a pressuring possibility, which can pressure doubt into silence and push in the direction of humiliation. It is a lenient form, I admit. I do not intend to make Christianity more lenient in secret. No, I proclaim as solemnly as possible that this is what I am doing. . . . imitation must be brought to bear in order to press us into humility. It is quite simple. Everyone must be measured against the Exemplar, the ideal. [pp. 464–66]

Thus, imitation is to stand as the ideal, as an occasion for SK's all-important "admission." This is the only means of keeping us from taking Luther in vain, from seeking "cheap grace," and it must be accomplished without returning to the pitfalls of meritoriousness or of efficacious works. Only *after* we have been weighed and found wanting, only after we come to live, as Luther did, in fear and trembling, only then can we properly ask for and receive grace. This is the "strict" meaning of Matthew 6:24-end. No one can serve two masters. Christ is the Exemplar. What is regarded as normal by Christianity is imitation, not the docile, latter-day Lutheran-bourgeois citizen of the two regimes.

The closing message of the discourse "Christ as Exemplar or 'No One Can Serve Two Masters' " thus calls for a humiliation that is appropriate to SK's radically dualistic scheme of being. SK demands that if a person is unable to perceive and live within the "real," higher world of "the truth," then at least he must make a humbling admission. This is the honesty demanded by "Providence," and it is the precondition for having any dealings with Providence, Love, or Grace [pp. 472-73].

C. *JUDGE FOR YOURSELVES!* (PART TWO)

The other discourse which constitutes *Judge for Yourselves!* is entitled "Becoming Sober" (based on I Peter 4:7, "Therefore be sober"). Better than any other writing of SK's later period, "Becoming Sober" clearly delineates the profound opposition between the parallel but heterogeneous modes of "the Spirit" and "the world," as well as spelling out, quite clearly, the social and political reasons why Christendom's confusion of these two realms must be combatted "now," in the post-1848 world—that is, *"in our time."* This discourse illuminates better than any other document how SK's growing understanding of the political and social implications of 1848 enabled him to make the transition from the relatively moderate public stance of the "Open Letter" of January 1851 to the revolutionary iconoclasm and open intransigence of the "attack," which began in December 1854—all the while remaining within the theoretical framework of *Training in Christianity*.

SK points out that the "world" called the Apostles "drunk" while Peter told the world to "be sober," and SK uses the opportunity to stress the diametrically opposed views taken by the realms of World and Spirit:

> [T]he worldly mind sees Christianity as drunkenness, and Christianity sees the worldly mind as drunkenness. . . . [T]he difference between that which is worldly and that which is Christian is not that one is of one opinion, the other of another; no, the difference is that they always have diametrically opposed opinions. . . . [p. 380]

The World is straightforwardly and immediately what it is, but Christianity (as Spirit) is such that every category first presents itself as its opposite. As we have seen elsewhere in SK, Christianity is immediacy, but a *new* immediacy, an immediacy *after* distance. It is the opposite of straightforward accessibility and recognizability. Thus, as SK writes here, Christianity gives life, but only after making one die away. Christianity fills one with "Spirit," but only after making one sober [p. 381].

The sobriety of Christianity appears as drunken foolishness to the worldly shrewdness that relies upon "probability" (which is one of SK's favorite attributes for describing the bourgeois-philistine outlook).[7] "Christianly understood, letting go of probability, and daring with confidence in God, precisely this is being sober. . . . On the other hand, Christianly understood, reasonableness, caution, shrewdness [are] . . . drunkenness!" [p. 386]. In addition to such obvious crimes as murder, robbery, etc., Christianity also recognizes "still another sort of plague: cowardly shrewdness and spineless cleverness, wretched toiling after probability . . . [which is] from the Christian point of view, the most dangerous plague" [p. 385]. The worldly person can never let go of probability, but

> he who has never let go of probability has never involved himself with God. . . . [T]his must stand fast, that this, precisely this, is Christianity: to dare to let go of probability in confidence in God, and that one, if one wishes to be a Christian, can be excused from this daring only by means of humility and admissions! [pp. 383–85]

Sobriety, then, is not merely the only true state of spiritual health, it is also the state of being one's only true self, a state that one is under obligation to achieve, or, failing that, at least to exhibit honesty in admitting one's weakness. "[T]o become sober is *to come to oneself, in self-knowledge and before God, as nothing before him, yet infinitely, unconditionally, obligated to him*" [p. 386, emphasis in original]. Only before God can one achieve the transparency of sobriety. All other forms of coming to oneself are dizziness and emptiness. Only in realizing one's nothingness before God can one become cold sober. Finally, one must understand that one is completely and unconditionally obligated to him, for only via the Unconditional can one escape the half-way commitments, the "to a certain degree," which characterize the so-called sobriety of the world [p. 388].

Thus SK's Christianity is radically dualistic in its insistence upon the existence of a higher reality and upon the imperfection of the lesser world. This lesser reality deals only in approximations, probabilities, "to a certain degree," and thus, when applying its mode of understanding to the realm of the Spirit— of which absoluteness and unconditionality are the hallmarks—the lesser realm of approximations is not merely relatively untrue but is absolutely and unconditionally false. It is this confusion of categories that causes the worst drunkenness of all, the drunkenness that is sure that it is sober. Therefore we need the Unconditional as an absolute standard of sobriety. "The Unconditioned is the only thing which makes one entirely sober" [p. 389].

> Christianity believes that it is precisely the Unconditioned, and only the Unconditioned—or the impression, the pressure of the Unconditioned—that is capable of making a person entirely sober when he . . . unconditionally surrenders himself to the power of the Unconditioned; and, on the other hand, this "to a certain degree," this is precisely what is intoxicating, narcotizing, which makes one heavy and sleepy, and lazy and slack. [pp. 388–89]

In concluding his discussion of drunkenness and sobriety, SK asserts that

> this is Christianity's opinion. It is not the Unconditioned that makes us drunk, but it is the Unconditioned that makes it clear that we *are* drunk, which we ourselves certainly know, and this is why we shrewdly hold only to finite things and slink along next to the tall buildings [i.e., like a drunk who is afraid to reveal his drunkenness by walking across an open plaza], remain in the alleyways, and never dare to venture forth into the infinite. And it is Christianity's view that it is precisely the Unconditioned that makes us sober, after having first made it apparent that we are drunk. [p. 395]

With the Christian call to "sobriety" in mind, SK asks the reader to look at how Christendom has failed its radical calling, how it has perverted, modified, and tempered the requirement to "seek *first* God's Kingdom." SK writes:

> [I]f I became *contemporary* with someone whose life expressed the fact that he sought *first* the Kingdom of God, expressed the fact that he was unconditionally related to the Unconditioned, or that he was "Spirit"—lost, alienated from all temporal, finite, earthly matters, dead to them—I could not bear him. I would be constantly driven to distraction. I would be tempted to call him, the only sober person, drunk. [pp. 393–94]

Here, again, SK explicitly links his position with a "strict" interpretation of Matthew 6:24-end, and it is now clear that "seeking first God's Kingdom" cannot be a form of "hidden inwardness." Christendom has failed to keep faith with Christianity's absolute and infinite requirement. It has become mired in an endless series of compromises. "We have gotten the finite and the infinite, the temporal and the eternal, the highest and the lowest, mixed together so that it is impossible to say which is which—that is, the situation is an impenetrable ambiguity" [p. 402].

In order to explain how things have gotten so bad, SK compares the situation to a mismanaged bank or business enterprise for which he is now conducting an audit. In the first three hundred years of Christianity, doctrine *was* practice, and Christianity claimed many suffering "witnesses to the Truth," who remade the world and stored up, as it were, an enormous "operating capital" [Drifts-Capital] [p. 407]. But then, after its suffering centuries, Christianity became a power in the world and began to become distorted as people sought to find accommodation with the world in order to avoid suffering. Clever deceptions became the mode. Now, as auditor to Christendom, it is SK's sad, sobering duty to report to the stockholders that

> [t]he 300 years' worth of diligently acquired operating capital is used up, my ladies and gentlemen. Nothing more can be tortured out of it by means of new deceptions, because the shrewdness to see through such deceptions has become just as great as the deceptions themselves. The operating capital is used up, that is the situation. . . . Christianity has reached the point where it must be said: "Now I must begin anew." [p. 408]

SK's primitivism forces him to find the fatal flaw of "Christian culture" or "Christendom" as far back as the Constantinian settlement, and his view of politics and society leads him to conclude that now, finally, in the situation emerging out of 1848, we are confronted with a fundamentally new form of political authority and social order. According to SK, the novelty of the post-revolutionary era presents us with both a challenge and an opportunity. The post-1848 world is a challenge because the forces of democracy and of liberal constitutionalism must not be allowed to make their peace with and amalgamate with the old hierarchic-aristocratic Church-State complex. It is at the same time an opportunity, in SK's view, because the dawning of the age of liberal secularism was the first radically new departure in 1,400 years, a new departure that would allow Christianity to re-assume its rightful oppositional role to the established culture of "the world."

Continuing his "report to the stockholders," SK writes that ever since Christianity's era of open suffering came to an end with the Constantianian settlement, people have continually given one another "assurances" that they *would* suffer if it were required of them. But now these "assurances" have become a form of evasion; they no longer suffice. SK is compelled to report that

> this assurance fund, this cash, which a bank must always possess in order to be a bank, and which was owned by Christianity's bank—it is used up, my ladies and gentlemen! Instead of drawing upon the bank, a new bank must first be

formed with that which serves as cash—actions, actions of character. If I cannot do that, well then, there is one thing I can do, one thing I must do, and this alone I will do: I will at least refrain from giving "assurances" in order to lie my way into something. . . . If I am not capable—and I certainly am not in any sense—of being a hero, well, at least I will refrain from giving the appearance that this is because of circumstances. . . . Thus, the time of assurances is past—assurances, which are the most dangerous of all hypocritical inventions, more dangerous than pharisaic self-righteousness, because there is at least always something in living so strictly, but assurances are nothing at all, while they lie their way to that which is most high. [pp. 413–14]

By this point in his career, SK is so determined to warn against the perils of "assurances" which make cheap grace available, that he is even able to see pharisaical works-righteousness as a relative good by comparison. As we have seen elsewhere—and even in this same book, *Judge for Yourselves!*—SK stresses that his work ought only to be understood as a "corrective" to present-day Lutheranism and that "the errors of the past with respect to merit" must not be repeated. Still, we must interpret his relative praise of the Pharisees and his deliberate resurrection of the epistle of James as quite a "corrective" indeed to Lutheranism. SK's position might be better interpreted as a partial departure from Lutheranism as traditionally understood, a departure he felt was justified by the extraordinary risk and challenge presented to Christianity by the social and political realities of the new, post-1848 Denmark. The traditional Lutheran position—the accommodationist-prioritarian interpretation of Matthew and the notion of "hidden inwardness"—would no longer suffice in post-absolutist Denmark.

In the past, the great and true Christian went forth "to proclaim Christianity in poverty, in degradation—the true preaching," SK claims [p. 406]. For his own part, however, he admits that although he is far below the "true Christians," he is at least humble and honest enough to admit it, so that he is happy to have a good conscience [ibid.]. The unconditional, existential determinant of Christianity is that one must die, one must die away from the world, SK repeats, but the official proclaimers of Christianity sell this message as an ordinary ware, the proceeds of which go to the support of their careers. SK lampoons them with great hilarity: "'You must die away from the world—that will be ten dollars.' 'What? Ten dollars? To whom?' 'To me. It's my way of earning a living, my career, to proclaim that people must die away from the world'" [p. 409]. In this manner, SK claims, an enormous and cumbersome layer of civil service, with large salaries, regular promotions, honors, titles, etc. has been introduced between God—with his bitter message of dying away from the world—and the human race.

SK finds that the 1,000 professional priests [Levebrøds-Præster = daily-bread priests] are more a proof of the absence of Christianity than of its presence. To the person who asks whether there can be a paid clergy at all and who wishes to know how the ordinary preacher is to live, SK replies that a paid pastor should live

> humbly before God—and, further, in the childlike happiness and satisfaction that it is the most honest thing in the world (I am completely convinced) that a man works for a living. I would do the same thing. I would, bravely, before God, and with a good conscience, earn my bread by preaching Christianity, for example. But, but, but, my congregation must not have occasion to let me understand, *sub rosa*, that this is my way of earning a living, because I myself intend to say straightforwardly and with such good cheer and confidence that it will be a pleasure: This is my way of earning a living. It is not for the sake of Christianity that I have taken this job, it is for my own sake. In truth, it is not at all dangerous for the congregation to come to know what it knows already, namely that I, too, am a human being who has to live on something. Nor is it dangerous that the congregation should come to know the truth, that I am not so strong in the faith, so alive with the Spirit, that I could bear to proclaim Christianity in poverty (which is undeniably what is most dear to Christianity). . . . The dangerous thing is if I self-importantly heap scorn upon earning a living while I privately take very good care of it. [p. 405]

SK writes that he does not insist that priests should live on air:

> By no means, not in the slightest. But on the other hand, it is Christianity's view that a person can and must hold things separate from one another, make it *clear* when he is working for his own advantage and when for the cause, idea, Spirit, the higher things, so that he at all costs avoids mixing them up or letting them fuse together. . . . It is the view of Christianity that in working for an idea, to seek in addition one's own advantage—in serving the truth, to seek in addition one's advantage—is nonsense and the road to hypocrisy. [p. 403]

What is important for SK, then, is the familiar drawing of boundaries and the avoiding of confusions between what is this-worldly and materially and socially advantageous on the one hand and what is other-worldly on the other. SK wishes to force an either-or situation upon those who prefer to have a both-and. One must either proclaim Christianity in poverty and degradation *or* admit, in good conscience, that one cannot.

Thus, the priest has a right to a fair salary, but the congregation has a right to demand that the priest's claim to a special "Christian worthiness" [christelig Værdighed] be set aside [p. 406]. The clergy, on the other hand, wants both the comfortable career and the special "Christian worthiness." SK insists that the priest must choose

> either a strenuous life, strained in self-denial and the forsaking of things . . . and then the claim to Christian worthiness, *or* the mild form, in which a priest's life is no more strained than anyone else's, and, thus, abandonment of the claim to Christian worthiness. To have both at one time is untruth. [pp. 406–407]

The priest must "make the admission," and the matter will be closed. "This will be the end of the affair, that we soberly come to make the confession of what we are and what Christianity is" [p. 407]. With the insistence upon the "admission" of our inadequacy in comparison to the "ideality" of Christianity, we are again on the familiar terrain of *Training in Christianity*, and yet, the call for an end to claims of "Christian worthiness" presages a new emphasis, namely upon the secularization, the de-sacralization, of human society, of "the world."

What begins, in *Judge for Yourselves!*, as a call for an end to the confusion of social standing with genuine "Christian worthiness," will become in the final year of SK's life and activity, a call first for "an admission" from the established Church; then for a boycott; and finally for the complete dis-establishment of religion, the total divorce of the worldly and spiritual realms. The motive force behind this increasing anticlericalism and this call for secularization and dis-establishment is precisely SK's sense of the profound and unprecedented character of the new social and political realities that were becoming dominant in the post-1848 climate.

As mentioned at the outset of this portion of the chapter, the special importance of the "Becoming Sober" discourse is that it permits us to document quite specifically that *it was SK's perception of these social and political developments that underlay his decision to launch his all-out "attack on the Church."* In other historical circumstances it seems clear that SK would have been able to content himself with remaining an internal critic. But "in our time"—i.e., in the liberal-democratic epoch with its "People's Church," which threatened to assimilate Christianity to the *res publicæ*—nothing would suffice but an all-out attack, conducted with the freedom permitted an outsider. Thus, the language cited in the paragraphs which follow is crucial to the development of the historical argument of the present work.

"A priest *in our time*," SK writes, "cannot truthfully make a claim for any sort of worthy respect other than that which can be made by any other man in his field of activity, i.e., in proportion to his capability" [p. 404, emphasis added]. What SK is referring to, clearly, is that during the previous half-century or more, and culminating in the events of 1848–49, there has been a revolution in the consciousness of the average congregation. With the rise of the peasantry to power, "the common man" has become much more capable of raising questions, both religious and political, and of thinking for himself. The ecclesiastical arrangements that had sufficed for Christianity under absolutism are no longer adequate for the present. In the mind of "the common man," the institutional failings of the established Church under absolutism were always those of "the others." This is no longer possible now that "the common man," "the people," *own* the "People's Church"—now that "the people," in law and theory, at least, are responsible for the "Christianity" which is foisted upon them.

With particular reference to what he saw as the contradictory insistence of the clergy on being treated both as "Christian worthies" and on receiving comfortable livings and guaranteed careers, SK writes that

> there have been times when this way of proclaiming Christianity was less of-fensive—even if it was not completely praiseworthy, which it never is—times, namely, when the congregation was less knowing, less aware of the relationship between a striving for that which is infinite and a striving for that which is finite. . . . As things now are, preachers of Christianity cannot come to any open-ness or good conscience vis-a-vis the all-too-knowing congregation without mak-ing it apparent which is which, whether it is the finite or the infinite which they will. [pp. 410–11]

Thus, just as childlike trust and credulity correspond to the earlier phase of absolutist society and to "Christendom," so do radical self-criticism and hon-esty correspond to the mature self-possession presupposed by democracy. Otherwise Christianity will become the more-or-less open laughing-stock of the people. Similarly, "hidden inwardness" might be sufficient for aristocratic-absolutist times, but when it became apparent after 1849 that democracy had really come to stay, it was clear to SK that something stronger, "the ideal of imitation," with its consequent "humbling admission," was the appropriate mode of existence for Christianity in a popular-democratic culture.

It is difficult to overstress the enormous importance of this social-historical component in understanding SK's work, particularly the more-or-less "inex-plicable" last years that culminated in the attack on the Church. Now that the apolitical Golden Age was over and public life had come to claim its own in Danish society, the drawing of boundaries between politics and religion came to assume an increasingly important place in SK's thought. SK began as an essentially apolitical and conservative elitist, who at the most might have found congenial the role of internal reformer. It took SK's deepened understanding of the social developments that were consolidated in the years following 1848 to transform him into a revolutionary critic of "the established order" [det Bestaaende = both the established Church and the entire established order of things]. Only through such an understanding of the social and political changes of his times could SK have adopted his ultimate "liberal" goal of seculariza-tion—though, perhaps, from motives that were the opposite of those which fired most liberals—the goal namely, of "a free church in a free state."

There can be no question that it was his growing post-1848 sense of his nation's social, political, and religious *coming-of-age* which prompted SK to demand an immediate "admission" or confession of inadequacy on the part of official Christianity. The clergy must respond to the present situation

> *either* by letting go of finitude and finite advantages *or* by confessing that this way of proclaiming Christianity is not really Christianity. This situation is like

that in relation to modesty: Modesty is one thing with respect to a very little child, and it is something else as soon as it is clear that the child has grown and become knowing. To wish, after knowledge has been acquired, and after it must be assumed that both [adult and child] have knowledge and that each knows that the other is knowing—to wish, after all this has happened, to preserve the first sort of modesty would not only not be modesty, but would be an extremely corrupted and corrupting immorality. . . . The dangerous situation is, when the congregation is knowing, and when the preacher is knowing, and when each knows that the other knows—then, not to say it, to wish to keep things in a higher, more ceremonious tone, the untruth of which is a shared secret: This is what is dangerous and demoralizing. [p. 411]

SK's language about childhood and maturity is not mere metaphor or analogy. He himself explains that his talk about modesty is quite literally about the coming-of-age of the congregation, that is, of "the people" as a whole.[8] The old untruths, tolerated during the childhood of the people when their political, cultural, and religious needs were aristocratically administered by others, no longer suffice. In SK's view, the danger is that the people, now that they have become the "all-too-knowing congregation," will react with cynical disdain. And this disdain will not be directed only at the clergy, because official Christianity is no longer the property of an aristocratic elite trained to serve an absolute regime in far-off Copenhagen, but is the property of "the people" collectively, "the People's Church." Therefore, the danger is that popular scorn and cynical disdain will be directed at Christianity itself.

The advent of popular sovereignty, coupled with the retention of the old Church-State apparatus of the absolutist regime, raises the possibility that state power and "mature" cynicism by the hitherto uncorrupted "common man" can combine to block off the "vertical" or transcendent dimension of existence for the ordinary person. Hitherto, it was always possible for the common man (for example, in the many "awakenings") to differentiate between "his" Christianity and "their" Church, and to reject the latter while retaining the former. For the future, however, this "People's Church" would be the common man's own institution. In these circumstances, SK demanded and hoped for an "admission" by the Church that its Christianity was not "the Christianity of the New Testament." He had not yet arrived at the position of demanding disestablishment.

In any event, it would no longer be possible for "the common man" to reject "their" Church while retaining "his." The tremendous growth of the moral and political power of the state which had been facilitated by the introduction of popular sovereignty, made it possible, for the first time, for the "horizontal" community, the social realm, to do a highly effective job of snuffing out the "vertical" or transcendent relationship of the individual to God. This was SK's vision of the politics of his time, as it is reflected in his works, and he saw it as his religious and political task to define the proper limits of the community and of religion sharply enough to prevent this "public-ization," this one-dimensional heathenization, of human life from taking place. SK's scepticism about society, his denial of independent moral standing to the community, even under popular sovereignty, and his desire to restrain the state from exercising control over the individual in matters not properly political but private and religious, once again prompts us to see him as more appropriately labelled a classical "liberal" than anything else.

All these considerations, then, underlie SK's call for "an admission," a call which he insisted was motivated by nothing so base as self-righteousness, nor so lofty as religious duty alone, but by the demands of simple *human honesty*.

> Thus, one of the two: *Either* there must be a real renunciation of worldly things in order, in sacrifice and suffering, to proclaim Christianity—this is the higher form—*or* one may guarantee oneself the earthly, temporal things, but also make the confession that this sort of preaching is not really Christianity. This first form is something that no person has the right to demand of another, but has the right to demand of *himself*. We people do have the right to demand the second form of one another. [p. 412]

The first alternative, religious self-sacrifice, is thus a private matter between the individual and God. No one has the right to ask another to be a saint or martyr or to insist that the other person oppose the norms of society for the sake of something "higher"—though one has a religious duty to examine *oneself* before God in this matter. The second alternative, however, to make a "confession" of the spuriousness of one's so-called Christianity, is required both by religious duty and by the human honesty that enters into all true "horizontal," social, political relationships. It is the *social* quality of honesty that enables one to demand it of others where one cannot demand *private*, religious self-sacrifice. And it is the social property of honesty which thus makes it not only "good religion," but also "good politics" to demand an "admission" from the People's Church. Thus, as we shall shortly see, when SK fights his open campaign against the Establishment, he does so in the name, not of Christianity, but of "human honesty"—that is, as an act that is "horizontal," social, politically responsible. Human honesty, then, becomes politics' only real protection against itself, against the overweening ambitions of the social realm to overrun its own proper boundaries and snuff out the transcendence of the private, "vertical" realm, to the detriment both of true religion and of the true politics that build upon human honesty.

Thus, SK calls for an admission,

> a confession that this way of proclaiming Christianity, which, in worldly fashion, is the preacher's living and his career (arranged, given norms, guaranteed, etc. all in a worldly fashion)—that this is not really Christianity, regardless of how accurately he preaches the doctrines, "the sound doctrines" . . . . [T]his whole

arrangement with the 1,000 priests is not really Christianity, but a milder doctrine, which is, in comparison to real Christianity, a whole quality milder. [p. 410]

Here we can see how much more radical SK is in *Judge for Yourselves!*, which constitutes the "second series" of discourses "recommended to the age," than in *For Self-Examination*, which constituted the "first series." In speaking up for Christianity in the "first series," SK is very conciliatory and notes that his message is the same as Bishop Mynster's, though it is "one note stronger." Here, on the other hand, in the "second series," SK is much more severe with the official Christianity that Mynster unblushingly represented and calls it "not really Christianity" but "a whole quality milder." As in the "Open Letter" to Rudelbach, SK at this point is still able to make his peace with the idea of an established Church, and he is still opposed to a revolution in "external" things, but the gulf between SK and those "external" things has become much wider. Nonetheless, SK pins his hopes (publicly and officially, at least) on the ability of the Establishment to respond to the call for simple honesty, noting that no honest person can call his position too strict [p. 418].

In concluding the discourse "Becoming Sober," SK suddenly shifts his fire from the main body of the established Church to the reformer Grundtvig, who derived much of his power from the fact that he was, in spirit, only half in the established Church and was repeatedly able to bargain for concessions by threatening to pull his followers out. Of these hyper-orthodox Grundtvigians and other pietists, SK writes,

> I know well that in every age, and in my own time, there live people who make the claim of being Christians in the strict sense. I have not been able to join them. No, what has seemed truer to me has been to accept a milder form, a leniency—but then to admit that this is not really Christianity . . . . I know full well that I am not sober, for only "Spirit" is sober. But I do not at any rate become completely mentally confused, drunk in the sensory illusion that this mild doctrine, that this, is true Christianity. [Ibid.]

Now that we are aware of insobriety, of our spiritual bankruptcy, we have reached what SK here, as elsewhere, calls a "stopping place," and, in order for our pause to be sobering and true, we must not let it be turned into some kind of revolution or overturning of mere "externals."

> Above all, we must keep watch to avoid the most frightful of all confusions, when people decide to reform but, be it noted, in such a way that to reform becomes a pleasure, a profit, etc., instead of involving the making of sacrifice and the willingness to suffer in the highest sense. [pp. 408–409]

This pejorative language about revelling in reformation rather than sacrificing for it is quite typical of SK's transparent references to Grundtvig. What is remarkable in the present instance is that, in a book that as a whole is almost exclusively directed against the staunchest supporters of the established ecclesiastical arrangements, SK finds it necessary and desirable to single out the Grundtvigian reform movement for special criticism, as if to point out his own willingness to remain a friendly ally of the Church if it would only make the requisite "admission."

The criticism of Grundtvig reaches its high point in the "Moral" appended to the end of the entire work *Judge for Yourselves!* To prevent the reader from getting the incorrect impression, SK reminds us in this "Moral" that, bad as it is, the existing ecclesiastical structure is better than false reform. "Dabbling at reform is more corrupting than the most corrupt Establishment, because to reform is the highest thing, and dabbling at reform is thus the most corrupting thing of all" [p. 479]. If reformation is indeed the highest, then counterfeit reformation is the lowest, SK insists. Presumably this is because, as noted earlier in the present work, SK believes that a false reformation not only cannot succeed in its announced intent but that it can also make people cynical about reformations and destroy the possibility of reform itself—and the possibility of reform ought always to stand as our saving hope.

If there is no truly selfless and self-sacrificing reformer among us, SK continues, then let us hold to the imperfect institutions we have, individually admitting to ourselves how far from Christianity we are.

> The evil thing in our time is not the established order with its many errors. No, the evil thing in our time is precisely this wicked pleasure, this trifling about wanting to reform, this fakery of wishing to reform without being willing to suffer and make sacrifices. . . . Nowadays, [instead of a courageous one-man reformation such as that Luther started] we have a mess, as though in a dance hall, where all wish to reform. This cannot be an idea from God, but is an impudent invention of human beings, which is why, instead of fear and trembling and many struggles of conscience, there is Hurrah, Bravo, acclamation, balloting, shouting, hubbub, spectacle—and false alarm! [pp. 479–80, emphasis in original]

Concluding as it does a work aimed almost entirely at "the established order with its many errors," SK's language (and his deliberate emphasis) seems harsh indeed. This "Moral" must be understood as reflecting SK's fear that "the people" were more in danger of being seduced and disappointed by the reforms promised by the Grundtvigians than they were of being taken in by the established order. (The popular tone and common language adopted by SK in both of these sets of discourses "recommended to the present age" indicates that they were intended by him for "the people.") SK clearly fears that a discredited reformation will cripple Christianity's self-healing vigor.[9]

Seen in this light, the assault on Grundtvig at the close of *Judge for Yourselves!* is in fact anything but a mere afterthought in a book that is principally devoted to criticizing the pillars of the established order. For SK's "reform" to have the intended effect, it had to be clearly differentiated in the mind of the popular reader from the "reform" intended by Grundtvig. SK's diagnosis of the ills of the established order, his plan of action, and his assault differed radically from Grundtvig's. However, the verbal similarity of the term "reform" and the common target of the established order might have obscured for many the enormous differences between the programs proposed by SK and by Grundtvig (as it had done for the Grundtvigian Rudelbach in 1851 and as it would do for the establishmentarian Martensen in 1855). It was evidently for the purpose of dispelling this confusion that SK found it necessary to include an assault on Grundtvig in *Judge for Yourselves!*

SK's emphasis upon the radical dualism of God's Kingdom and the kingdom of "the world" leads to a careful division. On the one hand, empiricism, pragmatism, and freethinking "agnosticism" about ultimate social truths are properly characteristic of the natural sciences and politics. On the other hand, our relation to the Kingdom of God must be marked by strict orthodoxy, humility, and obedience. There is no way to infer any positive worldly values, social systems, historical concretions, etc. from the "other" and "higher" world. For SK, when they are properly related to each other, politics and religion delimit and define one another negatively; there are no positive inferences of political *content* to be made from Christianity. For Grundtvig, on the other hand, in spite of his supposed rejection of the mediating pantheism of romanticism, the Kingdom of God has direct, concrete, and specifiable significance for us in our social activities. Furthermore, for Grundtvig there is a reciprocal action as well: Our cooperation in the task of building society and our participation in human history prepare us to become full Christians. We live, says Grundtvig, according to the order: Creation, then Redemption. For Grundtvig, the temporal is the anteroom of the eternal. For SK, in contrast, the temporal is related to the eternal as its distortion, indeed, as its opposite. For SK, what is Caesar's is Caesar's, and what is God's, God's. The state is secular. There can be no Christian state, no Christian society.

27. The Attack on Christendom

O

A. FROM 1850 TO DECEMBER 1854: THE PREPARATIONS

During the early 1850's SK waited in vain for the "admission" he sought from Bishop Mynster on behalf of the official Church. SK had sent Mynster an inscribed copy of *Training in Christianity* when it was published,[1] and he awaited some form of public response. Nothing ever materialized, however, beyond a vague and unsatisfactory private conversation with Mynster[2] and a rather annoying bit of public praise that the aged bishop bestowed upon SK for his opposition to the Grundtvigian style of reformation in the "Open Letter" to Rudelbach.[3] (What was particularly annoying in Mynster's praise was the fact that, even while he was turning SK's criticism of Rudelbach to his own advantage, the bishop could not resist twitting SK by deliberately linking his praise of SK as "a gifted author" with praise of SK's old adversary M. A. Goldschmidt as "one of our most talented authors.")[4]

Beyond the evasive conversation and the praise from Mynster (which SK saw as a calculated insult), there was no further response regarding the position SK had taken in *Training*, much less any acknowledgment of the shortcomings of official Christianity. During the next several years, then, SK continued to note both the silence of official Christianity to his pleas for "honesty," and, at the same time, the alacrity with which the old State Church adapted itself to the new realities of the increasingly well-entrenched liberal-democratic forces. An open clash between SK's conception and the official conception of the proper limits of religion and society became more and more unavoidable. Still, throughout the early 1850's, SK nourished the faint hope that Mynster might make some kind of concession before he died, while at the same time SK was storing up polemical material for use in the event that he did not.

Bishop Mynster, of course, never made the slightest concession to SK's view and died on January 30, 1854. This was the signal to SK that he must wage his long-contemplated "attack" on Christendom, and the question from this point onward was merely one of timing. Martensen's sermon of Sunday, February 5, 1854, the Sunday immediately preceding Mynster's burial, grandly characterized Mynster as "a witness to the Truth" [Sandhedsvidne], one "of the whole series of witnesses to the Truth which extends through time like a chain, from the days of the Apostles to our own day."[5] Given SK's criticisms of Bishop Mynster, his lifelong animosity to Martensen, and, particularly, his own specially developed use of the term "witness to the Truth," Martensen's eulogy could not fail to irritate and, indeed, to outrage him. SK saw in Martensen's eulogy not only the canonization and ratification of Mynster's misunderstandings about Christianity and the Church but also a rather undisguised bid by Martensen to position himself as the leading candidate to succeed Mynster as Primate of the Danish Church. SK, therefore, immediately wrote a polemical reply to Martensen's sermon, taking issue both with its characterization of Mynster's achievement and with its self-serving character, which promoted Martensen's ambitions.

However, SK did not immediately publish his reply to Martensen, partly because he did not want to be encumbered with a lawsuit by Martensen for having attempted to interfere with Martensen's chances for the episcopal chair, and partly because he did not wish to be involved in a libel or blasphemy suit brought by the extremely conservative A. S. Ørsted ministry which was then in power. A lawsuit by either Martensen or the government would likely have been a long-drawn-out affair and would have obscured the broader and deeper intent of SK's assault, namely to alter the entire ordering of boundaries between the spiritual and the political realms. Thus SK spent most of 1854 writing pieces that he would use in the campaign when it finally came, and he waited, first, for the bishopric question to be settled, and second, for the Ørsted ministry to be replaced by a liberal regime which took a more generous view of freedom of the press.

Notwithstanding the objections of King Frederick VII,[6] Martensen was invested as bishop on April 15, 1854, having narrowly defeated the liberal Clausen for the post, and in early December 1854 the Ørsted ministry fell after a protracted crisis during which it had attempted to tamper with the liberal-democratic constitution of 1849 and return to a form of modified absolutism. As discussed in chapter 7, in the constitutional crisis of 1854, bourgeois liberals and democratic peasants compromised the differences which had divided them since the victories of 1848–49, and the Rigsdag elections of early December 1854 demonstrated that the forces of representative and parliamentary government were wise enough to unite and strong enough to resist any attempt at reaction.

Thus, the resolution of the constitutional crisis of 1854 spelled the end of the Ørsted ministry, which had stood between SK and his projected campaign against Christendom. Of equal or greater importance, however, is the fact that the outcome of the crisis was a signal that the new social order had withstood its most severe challenge. SK had been correct in seeing the trend toward *res publica* as something permanent, as the dawn of a new era for Christianity and for the state, a new era which demanded new tactics. A new, liberal ministry took office on December 18, 1854, and on the same day SK opened his "attack on Christendom" in the columns of the liberal daily *The Fatherland* [*Fædrelandet*], which was Denmark's leading serious newspaper. The simultaneity of the beginning of SK's attack and the installation of a new liberal ministry was thus anything but a coincidence.

B. THE STRUCTURE OF THE ATTACK

SK's attack on Christendom had two distinct phases. The *Fatherland* phase (in which SK campaigned almost exclusively in the columns of that newspaper) lasted from December 18, 1854 to May 26, 1855. The *Moment* [*Øieblikket*] phase (when SK campaigned almost exclusively through his own magazine, *The Moment*, which he published himself and which had a rather wide circulation) lasted from May 26, 1855 until SK's death. [All the writings constituting the attack are contained in SV XIV, pp. 1–364]. We will consider the development of SK's culminating attack in each of these two phases.

In the first, *Fatherland*, phase, a development can be seen in SK's tactics and stated objectives as he took increasing note of the unwillingness of the official Establishment to meet any of his demands or even to engage in a dialogue with him. Thus, the *Fatherland* phase displays a movement through several stages. It began with the examination of the concept of the "witness to the Truth," with the concomitant criticism of Martensen and Mynster, and the continuing call for an "admission." It moved to a more generalized anticlericalism and the bald assertion that "the Christianity of the New Testament does not exist." Next came the hint of a popular call for a boycott of "official Christianity," followed by an even more trenchant and populist anticlericalism. This culminated on May 16, 1855 in the retraction of the Foreword and the "Moral" of *Training in Christianity*, which had hitherto held in abeyance the severe criticism contained in that book. Finally came the popular call for a complete boycott of all official ecclesiastical activities. Because the first, *Fatherland*, phase of the attack shows this chronological development, our detailed examination of this phase of the often misunderstood (or "inexplicable") attack will also proceed chronologically.

The second phase of SK's attack, which is voiced principally through *The Moment*, does not, however, display this chronological development of tactics and objectives, except for the fact that it is here, in his own magazine, that SK is finally able to make the transition from the implicitly temporary position of a boycott to the call for the permanent, legal, and final separation of Church and state.[7] This was a rather radical position in Denmark at that time, and not even most liberals or Grundtvigian democrats had had the courage to put it forth, consonant though it might have been with their principles. It makes sense, then, to examine the second phase of the attack structurally, as a whole, in order to show the total shape of SK's final critique.

C. DECEMBER 18, 1854 TO MAY 26, 1855: THE *FATHERLAND* PHASE

The beginning thrust of SK's attack was primarily an assault on Martensen for his characterization of Mynster as a witness to the Truth, and also, necessarily, an assault on the reputation of Mynster himself. In the beginning, SK seems to have had hopes of using this issue of Mynster and witnesses to the Truth to generate debate about the difference between "New Testament Christianity" and the "Christianity" of the official Church, thereby inducing the Church to engage in fruitful self-criticism. This failed to happen, and SK's attack then moved through the progressive phases of broadening and deepening as noted above, until it articulated the final message, first of boycott and then of the complete separation of Church and state. Let us turn to the development of the attack in its successive stages.

In the opening article of the campaign, which appeared in *The Fatherland,* December 18, 1854, SK notes that Martensen has called Mynster a "witness to the Truth," one of the "holy chain" of such witnesses. SK asks: What, then, was Mynster's "preaching" about? If we look first, SK replies, at Mynster's sermons and writings, we will see that

> Mynster's preaching distorts, covers up, fails to mention, and omits some of the most decisively Christian tenets, things that seem inconvenient to us humans, things that will make our lives strenuous, hinder us in the enjoyment of life— the part of Christianity about dying away, about voluntary renunciation, about hating oneself, about suffering for the teachings, etc. [p. 6]

If, on the other hand, SK continues, we define one's "preaching" as one's life, as what one's life expresses—and this is what Christianity wants, SK insists, in order to protect itself against characterless teachers instead of witnesses— then "Bishop Mynster's preaching of Christianity was not in character. . . . [O]utside of the quiet hours [in church] he was not in character, not even in the character of his sermons, which as noted, compared with the New Testament are a serious watering-down of Christianity" [ibid.]. This want of character in Mynster's conduct could be seen by anyone, SK asserts. Referring to what he saw as Mynster's all-too-flexible and ready attitude to deal with the new regime or with anyone who came into power, SK points out that "in 1848 and after, this became apparent even to blind admirers" of the late Bishop [ibid.].

As SK notes in the article itself, the main body of his article was written in February 1854 but was held until the present date for publication. The article as published also includes a more personally polemical "Postscript" that was written in the fall of 1854. In the "Postscript" SK stresses his profound dissatisfaction, not merely with the fact that Mynster was not in his "preaching" a witness to the Truth, but also with Mynster as a person. SK finds himself unhappy with Mynster, not simply because he was not a witness for the Truth (there was no great danger in that), but because, in addition to all the other advantages that he derived (in the grandest style) from preaching Christianity, he also had the pleasure—by declaiming in the quiet hours on Sunday and by covering himself with worldly shrewdness on Monday—of putting on the appearance of being a person of character, a man of principles, a man who stands firm when all else vacillates, a man who does not fail when all others fail, etc. However, the truth was that he had a very high degree of worldly shrewdness, but was weak, pleasure-mad, and great only as a declaimer. [p. 10]

The fact that Mynster was a royal official does not in itself constitute the weakness of his message; rather, the weakness consists in the fact that he used his office to authorize his sort of message as the true Christian message and thereby made the *true* Christian message seem to be a sort of exaggeration [p. 7n.]. Thus Mynster's crime was one available only to the head of an established religion: he used the strength of his office to make "true" religion that much less accessible to the ordinary person.

Therefore, neither Mynster's sermons nor his life were that of a witness to the Truth, in SK's opinion, and if Mynster is now to be held up as a witness to the Truth, "a protest must be made" [p. 6].

Thus, the main body of the article denies that Mynster had been a witness to the Truth and takes Martensen to task for having characterized him as such. The "Postscript," on the other hand, is a more personal assault on Mynster's character and reputation. There is a certain tension between these two sections, which will be illuminating to examine. The clarification of this tension will be of considerable help in providing a better understanding of the social and political realities that occasioned and shaped the attack on the Church.

The main body of this first installment of the attack was written, as noted, in February 1854, and is primarily to be understood not as an attack upon Mynster himself, but upon *Martensen's* eulogy of the late Bishop, which SK quite understandably saw as a self-serving fabrication, designed to canonize the Mynsterian tradition and thus to ease the way for the "Mynsterian" Martensen to succeed to the bishopric in preference to the liberal Clausen. Toward the end of 1854, however, when the more bitterly personal assault in the "Postscript" was written, Martensen's installation as Bishop was an accomplished fact. The danger now was that Martensen's account of Mynster's career would be converted from the tactical apology of a would-be bishop to the official version. That is, the danger for SK was that Martensen would continue to find a way to make the Mynsterian tradition of aristocratic gentility at least reasonably acceptable to liberal constitutionalism and that the all-too-stable Christian cultural compromise characteristic of the Golden Age would be continued into the liberal-democratic age.

By the latter part of 1854, SK felt that to prevent this from happening it was necessary not only to rebut Martensen's characterization of Mynster as a witness to the Truth but also to debunk Mynster's reputation as such, and thus settle accounts, not simply with Martensen, but with the entire Mynster era of the Church, which was already beginning to bask in the glow of hagiography. A further impetus which must have prompted SK to write and publish not only the main body of the article but also the "Postscript" was the political and cultural maturity of "the common man," which had been guaranteed and consolidated by the outcome of the long struggle over the liberal-democratic constitution that had raged during 1854. In the absence of other political developments, the ecclesiastical victory of Martensen would by itself have put a great deal of pressure on SK to launch his attack, and in the absence of Martensen's promotion to the primacy of the Danish Church, the social and political developments that were definitively consolidated in the course of 1854 would have put an even greater pressure upon him. Therefore, when in the course of 1854, both Martensen and liberal-democratic constitutionalism were successful in their quests, it became impossible for SK to limit the opening of the assault to a mere attack upon the characterization of Mynster as a witness to the Truth—for, after all, who *is* a witness to the Truth any more? It was now imperative to attack Mynster's reputation as such, and the entire, revered, Mynsterian period of Danish Christendom. Therefore SK wrote and published the "Postscript." This, in my view, is the social-political explanation of the tension contained within the opening article of SK's attack.

In the second article of the attack (*The Fatherland*, December 30, 1854) SK pursues his quarry of Mynsterian Christendom further, and begins by defining what he means by "a witness to the Truth" and by "Christianity." As a concept, the "'witness to the Truth' is related to the fact that Christianity is heterogeneity with this world, which is why the 'witness' must always be recognizable by his heterogeneity with this world, by renunciation, by suffering . . ." [p. 17].

SK's radically dualistic conception of Christianity as heterogeneity thus spells the end of any theology of "hidden inwardness." Witnessing to the Truth is a suffering and demanding form of heterogeneity with the world, and it does not prosper well "in addition" to something else, SK continues. To wish to take all worldly goods and advantages and then "in addition" to be a witness to the Truth is "what one might Christianly call a devil of a way to be a witness to the Truth" [ibid.]. Thus, in effect, seeking *first* God's Kingdom leaves one neither the time nor the desire for anything "additional."

It is not necessary to be a martyr to be a witness to the Truth, SK claims, but witnessing to the Truth always involves suffering; it is thus possible to differentiate between those who proclaim Christianity as "suffering witnesses to the Truth" and those who "proclaim Christianity in such a way that the proclaimer is a royal official, a person of rank, and in which the proclamation is one's own dazzling career, rich in pleasures" [p. 16n.]. SK leaves no doubt that this latter was the case with Bishop Mynster. As he writes in his next article (*The Fatherland*, January 10, 1855),

Mynster's preaching is to New Testament Christianity as Epicureanism is to Stoicism, or as cultivation, refinement and culture [Dannen] are to fundamental transformation and radical cure. Bishop Mynster's sermons no more carry Christianity to the point that is everywhere present in the New Testament, the break, the deepest, the most incurable break with this world, than . . . his life resembled a break with the world in the least way. [p. 24]

It can be seen that SK's attack has broadened from a mere assault upon Martensen's portrayal of Mynster as a witness to the Truth to an attack on the entire conception of Christianity for which Mynster stood. As SK wrote in his second article, "In my writings I have pursued my task, which is, in my existence and in my activity as an author, a continual attack upon the entire Mynsterian understanding of the message of Christianity" [p. 21].

In the fourth article (*The Fatherland*, January 29, 1855), SK expresses his anger at what he felt was a lack of serious ecclesiastical response to his challenge to Mynster's status as a witness to the Truth, and he points out that if Mynster is allowed to pass as such a witness, then so is every priest in the country "who is not guilty of a breach of civil justice" [p. 26]. Insofar as there has been no "admission" forthcoming from the clergy as a whole, SK argues, it must be assumed that the entire clergy, whose position with respect to being witnesses to the Truth does not differ qualitatively from Mynster's, is also laying claim to witnessing. In sum, the refusal of the clergy to make the requisite admission, and the unseriousness which greeted SK's charges, now leads him to broaden his attack further, from an attack upon Mynsterian Christianity to an anticlerical assault upon the clergy in general, upon the entire official establishment.

The New Testament, SK continues, tells us to proclaim Chirst in poverty and degradation "for nothing" [Matthew 10:8]. Thus, the only way in which the present Christian practice of a paid, established clergy can be defended (if, indeed, it can be at all) is with the means to which SK alluded under his pseudonym Anti-Climacus in *Training in Christianity*, namely by a humble admission of the difference between New Testament Christianity and the official version. But the Church has refused to breathe a single word regarding this demand, and not only that, not only have we not had an admission from the Church, but on the contrary, a position has been articulated that equates being a priest with being a witness to the Truth. *This* position cannot be regarded as simply a very mild or watered-down version of the radical Christianity of the New Testament, concerning which a humbling admission might be appropriate. No, SK insists,

from the Christian point of view, as soon as what we call a priest is in addition to mean a witness to the Truth, the entire religious establishment becomes an impudent disrespect . . . . [I]t is an open falling-away from the Christianity of the New Testament . . . an attempt to make a fool of God, to make a fool of him, as if we did not understand what he is talking about in his Word. So, when God says that we should proclaim his teachings without pay, we understand it to mean that preaching is of course a way of making a living, the most secure way to earn one's daily bread, with regular promotions. When he says to preach his Word in poverty, we understand it to mean to draw thousands in salary. When he says to preach his Word in degradation, we understand it to mean to make a career, to become an "Excellency." We understand being a stranger in this world to mean becoming a royal official, a person of rank. We understand abhorrence for the assistance and use of worldly power to mean making ourselves secure through the use of worldly power. We understand suffering for the teachings to mean using the police against others [a reference to the arrests of pietists and to the enforced baptism of the children of Baptists urged by Mynster and the official clergy]. We understand forsaking all things to mean that we get everything, all the finest refinements after which the heathen vainly thirsted—and in addition are witnesses to the Truth. [pp. 27–28]

It is important to note the rhetorical pyrotechnics and the rabble-rousing tone that now begin to assert themselves increasingly in SK's style, as he moves almost entirely away from the scholarly or devotional manner in order to set about addressing "the common man." SK thus points out provocatively that he would rather commit all sorts of heinous crimes than participate, politely and cleverly, in "making a fool of God" as they do in the official Church. It would even be better, he concludes, to mock God quite openly [p. 28]. In this incendiary prose, we have the beginnings of a call for a general boycott of official Christianity.

In a series of articles published in *The Fatherland* on March 20, 21, and 22, 1855, SK resumes his campaign after a silence of almost two months. In an article that he ominously prefaces with the citation of Mark 13:2 ["Do you see these great buildings? There will not be one stone left upon another"], SK again calls for an "admission" [p. 34]. SK has implicitly raised the stakes again and hints that, in the absence of the sort of admission he has demanded, the entire structure of the Establishment will lie in ruins. After comparing the state of Danish Christianity to the mediocrity and the foolishness of "the parlor of the bourgeois philistine" [p. 36], SK goes on to give "the authentic description of a priest [as] a half-worldly, half-spiritual, entirely ambivalent royal official, a person of rank," and he asks his readers to remember the biblical warning [Mark 12:38, Luke 20:46] to "beware of them who like to walk about in long robes" [p. 37]. There is a steady rise in the level of anticlericalism and of humorous invective.

What, then, is to be done?, SK asks. His reply to his own rhetorical question is that a threefold response is called for. First, we must admit that the official Christianity is untrue, that the Christianity proclaimed throughout the land is not the radical Christianity of the New Testament. Second, we must at least *ask* ourselves the question of whether perhaps the human race has so deteriorated from the effects of generation upon generation of mild "Christianity" that it is no longer capable of producing Christians in the New Testament sense. And finally, SK writes, while *we* are perhaps satisfied with the sort of degenerate religiosity of which we are capable, we must await God's judgment as to whether even an honestly admitted dilution of Christianity is acceptable to him [pp. 39–40].

In the next three articles (in *The Fatherland*, March 26, 28, 30, 1855) SK takes his most provocative public stand thus far, insisting that "the Christianity of the New Testament . . . does not exist at all" [p. 41]. In an article entitled "A Thesis—Only a Single Thesis," SK points out that whereas Luther had 95 theses, he has only one, namely that *"the Christianity of the New Testament does not exist at all. There is nothing here to reform"* [p. 45, emphasis added]. All that we have is a long-continued "Christian crime" to be investigated, a crime committed with stealth over a long period of time, during which, under the name of the perfectibility of Christianity, the human race has tried to dupe God out of Christianity by getting Christianity to become exactly the opposite of what it is in the New Testament [ibid., paraphrase]. As for himself, SK insists that he is no reformer, no seer, no deep thinker, nor even, according to the definitions of the New Testament, a Christian, but rather "an unusually talented police detective" whose job it is to clear up this criminal case [p. 46].

Now, it is precisely "because Christianity is Spirit, the sobriety of Spirit and the honesty of Eternity, [that] nothing is more suspicious to its police officer's gaze than all these fantastical entities: Christian states, Christian countries, a Christian people, and—wonder of wonders!—a Christian world!" [p. 43]. SK concludes that "in the final analysis, the basic confusion in Christendom, both in Protestantism and Catholicism, lies precisely in the concept of the Church, or in the concept of Christendom" [p. 48]. When Christianity came into the world, SK explains, the task was "the extensive," that is, to work for spreading the faith as broadly as possible. Now, however, in "Christendom," where "a false diffusion" characterizes Christianity, the task is just the opposite, to counter extensiveness with intensiveness [p. 48n.]. This state of universal Christianity and universal mediocrity has been achieved in Protestantism, and especially, SK tells us, in "Denmark, in the regular, *gemütlich* Danish mediocrity" [p. 48]. Who would believe, looking at "Christian" Denmark, that Christ preached suffering, sacrifice, and death? But we are tranquilized as neither Jew nor heathen ever managed to be, SK asserts, tranquilized with the eternal reassurance of our right to enjoy this life [p. 49].

And how has all this been achieved, SK asks? He replies with the simplistic, rhetorical assertion that the clergy has been the motive force in European history and has promoted the conversion of entire states, from the top down, in order the better to support the careers and worldly needs and ambitions of the clergy as a class. Thus the clergy has always treated the king as more important than the beggar, SK continues; but

O, my God, my God, my God! No! If Christianity sees that there is any difference for God, then it is the beggar who is infinitely more important than the king, infinitely more important, because the Gospel is preached for the poor! But look, for the priests, the king is infinitely more important than the beggar. [p. 50]

SK's anticlericalism has become so strong that he is willing to flirt with a populist interpretation of Christianity in order to engage the attention of "the common man." All the thousands in money, which buy silk and velvet finery for the clergy, SK continues, it is "blood money!" For blood money is what Judas took when he sold Christ's blood, and this money for the clergy is also blood money, "which is earned with the blood of Christ and by betraying Christianity and transforming it into worldliness" [ibid.].

SK's tone has become very strident and harsh, and he ends the piece with a deliberately rabble-rousing incitement to rebellion against ecclesiastical authority:

And you, you thoughtless mass of humanity. . . . Ah, not only are you deceived, but you want to be deceived! What good does all honest love and all unselfishness do? You not only are deceived—if that were all, then something good could certainly be achieved—but you want to be deceived! [p. 51]

The next article (published in *The Fatherland*, March 31, 1855) is perhaps the most important of the entire series for demonstrating SK's understanding of his attack as a secular, "political" act, however religious its motivations must have been. The article is entitled "What Do I Want?," to which SK immediately replies: "Very simply, I want honesty" [p. 52]. He insists that he represents neither "Christian strictness" (as opposed to, say, the "mildness" of Mynster) nor, for that matter, "Christian mildness." "By no means, I am neither mildness nor strictness. I am human honesty" [ibid.]. We must note the adjective "human," as opposed to "Christian," for just as SK, at this point in his career, was no longer willing to refer to himself publicly as a Christian, so was he insistent upon presenting his campaign for reordering the boundaries of the spiritual and the social realms as a *human* campaign.

The untruth and *dis*honesty of official Christianity is that it refuses to reveal honestly and "recklessly" [hensynsløst] what the real Christian requirement is [p. 53]. (SK, on the other hand, must be seen as the "reckless" proponent of human honesty, whatever its cost, for he knows that whenever it is relentlessly pursued—as in the progress of his whole authorship—it will lead the individual to confront Christianity in any event.)

Now there are about 1,000 paid teachers of Christianity in Denmark, SK continues. They are well paid, have families, etc., none of which is wrong from a human point of view, and in fact SK would increase their salaries if he could. *But*, it is dishonest for them to pretend to teach *Christianity* in anything other than poverty. Let us pay them, SK concludes, but let us not "ambush" [snigmyrde = literally, "sneak murder"] Christianity by refusing to take the next step and reveal the real requirements of Christianity [pp. 53–54].

All SK demands, then, is *honesty*, and it has become clear that up to the present the Establishment has shown no will to be honest of its own accord [p. 54]. If the generation wishes, in all honesty, openly to state that it will not submit to God's power, and "honestly, genuinely, unreservedly, openly to make a straightforward revolt against Christianity," then, SK says, "strange as it may sound, I will go along with it," because wherever there is "honesty," he will go along [ibid.]. But one thing SK will not do, he will not for any price take part in official Christianity, which by silence and artifice pretends to be the Christianity of the New Testament [p. 55].

Thus SK announces, for himself at least, the existence of a boycott, pending some show of "honesty" or an "admission" of inadequacy by the official Church. There has not as yet been any completely unambiguous call for a general boycott, much less a call for the permanent disestablishment of religion. SK feels constrained to reiterate that he campaigns in the name of human honesty, not of religion: "I will dare this for honesty. On the other hand, I do not say that it is for Christianity that I dare. Assume, assume this, assume that I quite literally became a sacrifice. I would not be a sacrifice for Christianity, but because I wanted honesty" [ibid.]. It is of great importance to note the *secular* character of the terrain on which SK chose to make his attack. The terrain is *human* honesty, and it therefore places SK squarely in the social-political sphere with those against whom he contends. In the coming world of secular liberalism, he takes up a position plainly within the boundaries of human, social-political discourse but insists upon an *honest* secular liberalism, one which respects its own principles and limitations.

Anticlericalism dominates the four articles published in *The Fatherland* between April 11 and May 10, 1855, and there is a marked increase in stridency as the month goes by. At the beginning of this period SK notes that Christianity, which came into the world as a truth for which one died, has now become a truth upon which one lives and supports one's family [p. 59]. He tempers this criticism, however, by adding that none of this is written out of any animosity toward the clergy as a class, for they are just as capable, respectable, etc. as any other class; they make themselves contemptible only when they accept the appellation "witnesses to the Truth" [p. 60]. Two weeks later, SK is rather more bitter, and writes of "Christianity, the Christianity of the New Testament, about which people are anxious and afraid; and this is why industrious priests, under the name of Christianity, have invented a candy which tastes splendid, and which people are delighted to purchase" [p. 68]. Christianity, *real* Christianity, is existential unrest, and "the industrious priests" are accused of pandering to humanity's basest fear, the fear of self-knowledge, by dispensing the tranquilizer of state religion, the people's opiate. Thus, on this argument, SK is not exaggerating when he claims that "New Testament Christianity" and the official Christianity dispensed by "the priests" are not simply different from one another, but *opposites.*

Finally, by the end of this month of increasing anticlericalism, SK proclaims that the official silence with which the ecclesiastical establishment has greeted his attack shows that "what concerns the clergy is their bread and butter"; it is now apparent that "official Christianity is, aesthetically and intellectually, something ridiculous, something unrespectable, [and] from a Christian point of view, something which gives offense" [p. 70]. The priests are the most dishonest class in society, SK concludes, more dishonest than merchants and usurers, for at least *they* are honest about their profit-taking [p. 71]. The development of SK's anticlericalism in this first (*Fatherland*) phase of the attack has run its full course; SK's vocabulary knows no greater contempt than that marshalled in the May 10, 1855 number of *The Fatherland.* The time has come for a qualitative escalation of the attack, from invective to some form of action.

Parallel with this anticlerical invective, SK had also been raising more and more doubts as to whether—in view of the radically other-worldly nature of Christianity—there is *any* justification for the existence of an established Church at all. SK points out the contradictions involved:

> By virtue of a royal license—a royal license is of course something that is related to a kingdom of this world—to wish to have any authority about that which concerns a kingdom that is not only a kingdom of another world, but is a kingdom whose passion, unto life and death, is exactly that it does not want to be a kingdom of this world, is . . . laughable. . . . [T]o call upon the authority of one's *royal* license is, from a Christian point of view, really to acknowledge about oneself that one is faithless to the kingdom that refuses at all costs to be a kingdom of this world—or one acknowledges that one's Christianity is a playing at Christianity. [p. 62]

A bit later in this period (mid-April to mid-May 1855), when an opponent raises the issue of whether SK ought perhaps to be expelled from the Church for his opinions, SK makes light of the terrors that such an inconsequential punishment would hold for him, but then turns his attention to what he considers to be the real question involved: "Can one be a royally authorized teacher of Christianity? Can Christianity (New Testament Christianity) be preached by royally authorized teachers? Can the sacraments be administered by them? Or is there not a self-contradiction contained in this?" [pp. 67–68]. Implicit in SK's questions, of course, is an answer in the negative, but he apparently felt it was still necessary to continue a bit longer to wait and hope for some form of official "admission"—if only, perhaps, to complete the education of the public, "the common man," about the futility of such hoping and waiting.

As long as SK was still officially awaiting some sign of compromise or recognition, the columns of an ordinary newspaper, which can facilitate debate and print replies, were clearly the proper place to publish. However, after SK could publicly discount the likelihood of a positive or constructive reply, the proper vehicle for continuing the attack would logically be his own journal. By mid-May 1855 SK knew that it was time to make the transition from the columns of *The Fatherland* to the pages of *The Moment*, and his journalistic activity of the last two weeks of May was designed to terminate the first phase of the attack while alerting his readers to the new, higher, stakes in his campaign and referring them to its continuation in the pages of his new journal.

The major turning point of the entire attack came in the publication, in the May 16, 1855 number of *The Fatherland*, of the article entitled "To the New Printing of *Training in Christianity*." This very important piece has already been referred to several times in the present work. SK explains that his earlier idea had been that the established Church could only be defended by poetically bringing judgment to bear upon it (via the pseudonym Anti-Climacus). Having had the truth brought to its attention, the Church could then defend itself by judging itself, by admitting what the Christian requirement was and then admitting that it did not live up to this requirement. Now, however, things have changed, SK states. He has challenged the Church, and it has not responded as he had hoped. "Now," SK writes, "I am quite certain of two things: first, that the established order is untenable from a Christian point of view; that every day that it exists is, from a Christian point of view, a crime; *and*, that one may not call upon grace in this way,"—that is, in the fashion of the established Church, without first having been truly humbled [p. 81]. Therefore, he concludes, were *Training in Christianity* to be published in revised form today, it would appear without the pseudonymity which had placed a dialectical distance between the author and the book, and without either the "Moral" or the thrice-repeated Foreword that had made the book only a *hypothetical* critique of the official Church. Thus, what SK had originally regarded as a sort of ultimatum that could serve as the last defense of the Establishment now becomes an attack on it. The ultimatum has not been answered, and therefore, in SK's view, the time is past for waiting patiently for an "admission" and for pretending to be engaged in a dialogue or a debate.

From this point onward, waiting for an "admission" is no longer an issue, and the attack on the notion of Christian culture can now proceed as an assault, pure and simple, proceeding from the pages of SK's own pamphlets. If the various forces that made up the established order would not speak out in favor of a reordering of the boundaries between that which is social and that which is spiritual, then SK would have to do so on his own. Waiting for an "admission" was clearly no longer a suitable posture for SK, and in the end only an insistence upon the total secularization of society would suffice.

SK's long-delayed boycott call appeared in the form of an independently published pamphlet on May 24, 1855, eight days after the article "revising" *Training in Christianity*. The pamphlet, entitled *This Must Be Said, So Let It Be Said*, was published bearing the date "December 1854," i.e., the date of the very beginning of the attack, and the reader is left to make the obvious surmise that it has been held in readiness until the official Church demonstrated its failure— as SK had expected—to be forthcoming with an "admission." Now the pamphlet is published as the capstone of the *Fatherland* campaign. The message of the tract is simple: Boycott.

> Whoever you are, whatever your life might be, my friend, by ceasing to participate (if you do) in public worship as it presently is (with its claim to being the Christianity of the New Testament) you will continually have one sin fewer, and a great sin: You are not taking part in making a fool of God. [p. 85]

This is followed by a later section dated "May 1855," in which "the official worship of God" is labelled "a falsity, a fake" [p. 86]. "The common Christian" [den menige Christen] is addressed in a friendly tone, and SK allows that ordinary people have certainly participated in official worship *bona fide* until now, believing that it was New Testament Christianity, for the fakery runs deep, indeed so deep, SK continues, that there are even some priests who are *bona fide*. SK explains that the fakery has been the gradual product of centuries, so that the Christian faith has come to be the opposite of what it was. Now, however, the official lies have been exposed, and now we are responsible for ceasing to participate in official Christianity and thus for putting a stop to the attempt "to make a fool of God" [ibid.]. This is the highly explicit and popularly worded call for "the common man" to walk out of the official Church, the call toward which the entire *Fatherland* campaign had been building.

Two days after the publication of *This Must Be Said*, SK published his last piece in *The Fatherland* and took the occasion once again to make it clear that it is "the common man" with whom he is seeking to make contact. SK bemoans the fact that his opponents have acted unworthily and have not responded in dignified fashion but have instead attempted to sabotage his influence by deliberately depicting him to "the common man" as a "screecher." This smear, SK notes, was for example the theme of an anonymous article in *The Daily News* [*Dagbladet*], which did its best to put the judgment of "nonsense" into the mouth of "the common man" [den menige Mand] [p. 98]. Therefore, SK now fights back and appeals directly to "the common man," over the heads of the "demoralized priests" and the "corrupted gentlefolk" [p. 99]. Is it not true, SK asks "the common man," that you can understand the difference between the genuinely other-worldly sacrifice required by New Testament Christianity and a comfortably arranged familial life, with regular promotions, which is based upon describing how other people once upon a time lived in this other, self-sacrificing way? [ibid.].

SK concludes this, his last appeal to "the common man" through the ordinary medium of the daily press, by returning to his oft-used theme of clerical venality, and points out that the question of the established order can now be seen to be not a religious but solely a financial consideration. It is a question in which the 1,000 royal appointees [the official clergy] are shareholders, and that is why they have remained silent [p. 100]. With this final, highly incendiary and populist riposte, the *Fatherland* campaign came to an end on May 26, 1855, having served its purpose for SK by stating the issue to "the common man" as one involving the entire re-definition of the boundaries of Christianity and "the world" and the consequent destruction of "Christendom." The first issue of *The Moment* appeared the same day.

D. MAY 26, 1855 AND AFTER: THE LAST PHASE, *THE MOMENT*

As stated in the introduction to this chapter, *The Moment* [*Øieblikket*] was the organ for SK's final formulation of his long-planned attack on Christian culture, and as the ten numbers of *The Moment* display little or no internal development in their critique of Golden Age Christendom, the *Moment* phase of SK's attack will be examined as a synchronous unit rather than developmentally.

In SK's special conceptual vocabulary, the name "*The Moment*" refers to the point of contact of time and eternity, or "the breakthrough of eternity" into time [p. 349]. "The moment" is the eschatological penetration of the eternal realm of the reality of Spirit into the temporal realm of "the World." "The moment" is equally accessible to every individual; it is freedom.

At the very beginning of his new undertaking, in the first number of *The Moment*, SK explains his role—or what he calls the "mood" [Stemning] of the undertaking—in terms which he admits borrowing from Plato's *Republic*. Plato wrote that a state will be ruled properly only when those who rule do not *desire* power, SK notes. It is the same with other tasks in life. When one is compelled by "something higher" and against one's own desire, one achieves "true seriousness." Such is the case in the present enterprise, SK continues. His merely personal desires oppose activism in the present "moment," and he would prefer to hold the present at a distance, as in his poetic work. But it is precisely because SK is forced to do so by "something higher," and against his own desire, that his enterprise represents "true seriousness" [pp. 105–106]. Thus SK invokes Plato and declares his radically dualistic posture openly at the outset of his new venture. The world is divided between "desire" and the "true seriousness" that comes from following the promptings of "the higher" against the wishes of desire. The statement is a fuller expression of the point made against Grundtvig in the "Moral" appended to *Judge for Yourselves!*, where the same Platonic requirement—that service to something higher can be genuine only when one disregards one's personal desires—was applied to those who derive satisfaction and enjoyment from their claim to be religious reformers.[8]

In another number of *The Moment* SK explains that his task is specifically *Socratic*. He refuses to call himself a Christian, he notes, which is a fact that must be emphasized in this "Christian world," where "being Christian is something that everyone naturally is" [p. 351]. It is precisely this notion of being "naturally" a Christian which SK's dualistic, anti-immediate Christianity combats. Thus, SK repeats

> I am not a Christian, and unfortunately [for SK's opponents] I can make it apparent that the others are not either—indeed, that they are even less so than I. This is because they imagine themselves to be, or they lie their way into being it [Christian]. . . . The only analogy I hold before myself is Socrates. My task is a Socratic task, to revise the definition of being Christian. I myself do not call myself a Christian (keeping the ideal free), but I can make it apparent that the others are even less so. [pp. 351–52]

The analogy is to Socrates, who, in his famous "ignorance," was less ignorant than his neighbors, because he admitted it. The same Socratic vocation held, *mutatis mutandis*, for SK, who, although not claiming the Socratic "ignorance," did claim to be "not a Christian."

In accordance with this Socratic and Platonic standpoint, SK's Christianity is "unnatural," the enemy of all immediacy, and demands "dying away." It is not a religion of "humanity" in the popular sense of the term. "Being a Christian in the New Testament sense is just as different, in the upward direction, from being human, as, in the downward direction, being an animal is different from being human" [p. 270]. Christianity does not, then, differ from "humanity" simply as a quantitative amplification of it but is qualitatively removed from the ordinary human sphere.

Yet Christianity's extraordinariness, although difficult of attainment, is the most rigorously egalitarian proposal available to humanity. This is most clearly demonstrated by the difference between a "genius" and a "Christian." The genius is "Nature's extraordinary one," which no ordinary person can become, whereas a Christian is "freedom's extraordinary one, or more accurately, freedom's ordinary one, except that he occurs very rarely" and is what *everyone* can become [p. 192]. The message of Christianity, of the appearance of Christ in the form of a humble servant, is that "this extraordinary thing is the ordinary, is accessible to everyone—but, however, a Christian is something even rarer than a genius" [ibid.]. We have again SK's familiar accentuation of the absolute and perfect *equality* of all with respect to the only essential thing about truly human life, namely access to the higher reality of Eternity. God is no respecter of persons.

As a Christian, one is "completely foreign to this life," SK insists, even though one stands suffering "in the middle of the reality of this life" [pp. 270–71]. One must be both "foreign" and in the midst of the created, painful reality of "the world." As in earlier works (most notably *The Sickness Unto Death*), one must avoid immersing oneself exclusively in the world and time, while on the other hand one must not flee suffering temporality and take refuge in eternity alone. One must live life as a balance of finitude, necessity, and temporality on the one hand and infinitude, possibility, and eternity on the other. As in the *Phaedo*, one is a foreigner in the world, but one is also "on duty for the gods," and one may not leave one's station voluntarily. The Christian task, like the Platonic task, is to witness the existence and perfection of another plane of being while remaining rooted in the midst of the imperfection of "the world," and this vocation necessarily involves a collision of modes which will cause one to suffer.

Therefore, SK insists, if one has the courage, one will discover what it is to be a Christian, namely, "to become a Christian is to become, humanly speaking, unhappy in this life. The situation is, the more you involve yourself with God, and the more he loves you, the more you will become, humanly speaking, unhappy in this life, the more you will come to suffer in this life" [p. 226]. And this thought is a sudden and baleful illumination of

> the whole lusty commerce of the merry, child-rearing, career-making priest guild, and like a stroke of lightning, shines through this fantastical delusion, the masquerade, the social playing, the tomfoolery of "Christendom," Christian states, countries, a Christian world—the stronghold of all sensory delusions! [Ibid.]

By means of Christendom, Christian culture, the material world of time and of the senses has made a comfortable peace with the supersensory world of religion. "This world" is a world of deception, of illusion, which is suddenly and disastrously illuminated and dispelled by the divine lightning of a higher reality—one thinks of the appearance of the Commendatore at Don Giovanni's banquet. What discomfort is caused by the catastrophic discovery that one's "reality" is merely the play of shadows on the wall of the cave of time!

SK insists that he, at any rate, has had the mummery of "this world" illuminated and dispelled for himself, and he now imparts his vision to others, though without calling himself a Christian: "No, I am still far behind" [pp. 226–27n.]. SK feels that at least he has the advantage of honesty and will tell the truth about what he knows Christianity to be, refusing to varnish it—as do the priests, who have taken oaths on the New Testament!—in the hope of gaining millions of "Christians" [ibid.]. The cave sequence in the *Republic* can stand as a metaphor for SK's understanding of his entire work: he is a reporter of another world, and his greatest love is neither to leave the cave for the sunlight nor to devote himself to organizing gainful activities for the blind within the cave. Rather, having seen the light, he returns to the cave to make his report in spite of the mockery and unbelief with which he will be greeted.

Christianity deals with a world entirely different from that of "humanity." Therefore, SK points out, when Christianity requires that one must love one's enemy, one could say in a sense that it has good reason to require this, because God indeed wishes to be loved, and "God is, speaking merely humanly, a person's most frightful enemy, your mortal enemy. He wishes, of course, that you shall die, die away; he hates precisely that in which you naturally have your life, that to which you cling with all your joy of living" [p. 189]. God loves us and wants to be loved by us—out of Love. Yet, "speaking merely humanly," it is frightful to be loved by and to love God, and we must remember that "the minor premise in the statement 'God is Love' is 'he is your mortal enemy' " [p. 190].

One's natural and spiritual selves are thus totally divided against one another. It is as though it were a struggle between two different people and the question was who one would become. This is SK's interpretation of Christianity, and it is this complex and anti-worldly vision which he has set himself the task of conveying to "the common man." SK writes,

> all religion in which there is any truth at all, and particularly Christianity, has as its purpose a total transformation of the person, and wishes, in renunciation and self-denial, to take away from a person all things, and precisely those things to which he is immediately attached, in which he immediately has his life. . . . Becoming . . . Christian in the New Testament sense is calculated to break the individual free of the context to which he clings with the passion of immediacy, and which in immediate passion clings to him. [p. 262]

Thus, in SK's view, the aim of all religion, and especially Christianity, is total personal transformation by means of a break with the "immediacy" in which the "natural" person reposes. As SK puts it in *The Moment*, it is a matter of "Eternity" versus "nature" in us. Just as we "naturally" want what will nourish the joys of living, so we need—if we are to live, not naturally, but for "the eternal"—a dose of "world-weariness" [p. 328].

But this break with "desire," with one's "natural" self, with one's "immediacy," seems too difficult for people, SK continues, so the human race has invented a "most highly respected social class, the priests. Their task is to reverse the entire relationship, so that that which people desire becomes religion—though one must call upon God's name and pay a certain sum to the priests" [p. 262]. We pay priests to pervert religion into its opposite, so that we can be "religious" and yet remain in immediacy, doing as we like. Thus, as SK points out in an article in *The Moment* entitled "The Difficulty of My Task," it is easy to see that New Testament and official Christianity do not resemble one another. SK's special problem stems from the fact that the priests have gotten people to believe that they must find the truth—Christianity—*pleasing*, whereas for genuine New Testament Christianity, the truth is the truth whether or not it pleases; indeed, "it is the truth precisely because it does not please" [p. 183]. Christianity does not "please"; it tears us out of our natural immediacy.

Therefore, as SK points out in another *Moment* article, "The task has a double direction" [pp. 119–20]. *First* there is a "sensory illusion"—a mental confusion and deception within the *individual* as to what Christianity is—and this error must be dispelled. This is the personal and subjective task. But *secondly*, there is also an enormous *governmental and social* apparatus, the 1,000 civil servants (i.e., clergy) "with the instinct of self-preservation," who are interested in keeping people from finding out what Christianity really is and from finding out that they are not really Christians [p. 119]. As for this second sort of deception, "*the state of course has it in its power to dispel it. And this is the other half of the task, to work in the direction of getting the state to take this sensory deception away*" [p. 120, emphasis added]—i.e., the task is to work for the disestablishment of official religion.

Thus, there are two principal parts to our task, in SK's view: working on the deception within oneself and working to combat the social and political structures that surround and bewitch us. As SK himself says, it is like a disease for which, even while we work on it psychically, we must also take *physical* remedies [ibid.]. Both the subjective and the objective elements are needed. Of course, what is rather revolutionary for SK is the "objective" emphasis, the active intervention in the field of politics and social institutions that he found necessary in this final stage of his career. SK asks the reader to read and re-read this piece carefully. The message of the article is compound: self-criticism, criticism, transformation. SK, who had often been cast (or had cast himself) in the role of "subjectivist," is here justifying his intervention in the "objective" world, and the clear implication of his position is that one ought to intervene in the "objective" sphere precisely by demanding that the state exercise its above-mentioned "power to dispel" the "sensory deception" of official Christianity.

The most urgent implication of the otherworldly and "unnatural" character of SK's "New Testament Christianity" is that one must come to a total break with Christendom. In one of the final issues of *The Moment*, SK writes:

> Avoid the bewitchment of the priests at all costs. Believe me, or just look, unprejudiced, at the New Testament for a moment, and you will see that Christianity has not come into the world in order to reassure you in your natural condition while it guarantees the priest a blossoming and satisfying way of earning a living. Rather, it has come into the world, forsaking everything, in order—by means of the terrors of eternity—to tear you out of the peace and tranquility in which you naturally exist. [p. 324]

The "awakening" message of Christianity is designed to combat one's "natural" state. The divine unrest of Eternity is pitted against the foolish repose of Nature.

It is generally agreed, SK writes, that Mynster and Grundtvig are the two greatest spirits that Danish Christendom has produced in recent decades. They are the best that Christian culture can achieve, and SK proceeds to examine them in order to discover what part of their contribution has been specifically and genuinely Christian in nature. SK concludes that Mynster's seriousness, at bottom, extends no further than to

> getting through this life happily and well in a humanly honorable fashion, [while the New Testament's view is] not to want to slip through this life happily and well, but precisely to take care to collide with this world in deadly earnest. . . . There is thus a world's, a heaven's, difference between the Mynsterian view of life (which is really Epicurean, the enjoyment of life, the lust for life, belonging to this world) and the Christian view, which is that of suffering, of enthusiasm for death, of belonging to the other world. [pp. 220–21]

On the other hand, SK continues, we could take Grundtvig as the best representative our age can muster. Grundtvig is even regarded as "a sort of Apostle" [p. 221]. But what has he really done? He has fought for the right to express himself on religious matters and for the right of others to adhere to him. Thus, he has fought for civic freedom in religious matters, SK concludes. That is very good. But, SK continues, had Grundtvig achieved what he wanted, he would have allowed the entire "sensory illusion" of the official Church to continue existing and would not have fought against the "*lèse majesté*" of allowing this falsified Christianity to continue. He would have allowed others to persist in their illusions, for he was *only* interested in civic freedoms. "Measured with this scale," SK concludes, "G. can never really be said to have fought for Christianity. He has really only fought for something earthly, civic freedom for himself and his adherents" [p. 222].

It could of course also be said of SK himself that, in fighting for "human honesty" and the separation of Church and state, he, too, fights only in the civic and not in the religious sphere. However, what seems to be the important distinction from Grundtvig in this connection is that, unlike Grundtvig, SK has openly proclaimed that *he* fights "merely" in the name of human honesty and has disclaimed any especially Christian status. Grundtvig, on the other hand, claimed to fight in the name of Christianity and allowed himself to be portrayed as a great reformer and even as "a sort of Apostle," while he was, in SK's view, in fact only a campaigner in the human sphere of civic freedom. In SK's opinion, it is because of this contradiction, this confusion of categories, this desire to appear to be more than he was, that Grundtvig must be rejected.

Thus, SK concludes, when one examines the two leading representatives of modern Christendom—men who are accounted "seriousness and wisdom" (Mynster), on the one hand, and Apostolic courage and enthusiasm (Grundtvig), on the other—they can be seen to be merely Epicureanism and civil libertarianism, respectively. Measured against the goals of the original Christianity of the New Testament, both of them appear only luke-warm, indifferent. "The times are so deeply sunken in indifferentism that they have no religion at all, are not even in a state of religion" [p. 222].

SK demands in *The Moment* that we must have a little honesty, a little "light in this matter" [p. 111]. Let it be made clear to all what Christianity really is, so that they can honestly choose to be Christians, "and let it be said loudly to the whole people: It is infinitely dearer to God in Heaven that you . . . honestly admit that you are not and do not wish to be Christian, than this loathesome situation, in which to worship God is to make a fool of him" [ibid.]. Thus, honest atheism is preferable to dishonest "Christianity," and SK makes it clear once again that throughout the entire attack on Christendom his stance is that of a campaigner for *human honesty* and not specifically for Christianity. SK clearly feels that any "honest" person, Christian or not, must agree with him.

Humankind, however, has a penchant for dishonesty. "Spiritually understood, a person in his natural state is sick. He is in error, in self-deception, and therefore desires most of all to be deceived" [p. 239]. The "poet" is one of the greatest of deceivers, and therefore is greatly beloved of the natural self. There are very few in each generation, SK continues, who really are so hard-boiled as to will *not* to have the Good, and, similarly, there are very few serious and honest enough to will to realize the Good in themselves [ibid.]. A "human being" is thus a cowardly and dishonest creature, on the whole, who wishes neither to cast the Good so far away as the first few nor yet to have it so close at hand as the latter few [p. 240]. SK is clearly describing, yet again, the common and banal state of "spiritlessness" dealt with in *The Sickness Unto Death* and elsewhere: the multitude who lack the courage either of open defiance or of faith. SK continues, explaining that this prevalence of cowardliness and dishonesty is why the "poet" is so popular, because he appeals precisely to hypocrisy. This the poet does by taking the Good—which, if it became reality, would occasion terrible suffering—and allowing the Good to be the occasion for the finest sorts of enjoyment. The poet takes the notion of forsaking the world, for example, which in reality is painful, and transforms it into an enjoyable emotion which one cultivates in "quiet hours" [ibid.]. But it is not quite the poet who is the most dangerous person, for

> [t]he poet, of course, calls himself only a poet. *What is far more dangerous is for the person who is only a poet, by being what is called a priest, to put on the appearance of being something far more serious and true than the poet, and yet only be a poet. This is hypocrisy in the second degree.* [pp. 240–41, emphasis in original]

It hardly needs saying that SK's target here is the "poet-priest" of the "quiet hours," Mynster, or more accurately, the entire edifice of Golden Age "Mynsterian Christianity," which had effected a compromise of Christian doctrine with human sensibilities and good taste. For SK, *honesty* is the paramount virtue here. The few who openly reject the Good pose no great danger; rather, it is the mediocre and hypocritical many who are truly subversive.

This theme of honesty versus hypocrisy is also developed in SK's incendiary pamphlet *What Christ Judges About Official Christianity* [*Hvad Christus dømmer om officiel Christendom*], which was published separately during the opening weeks of the *Moment* phase of the campaign. SK writes:

> The difference between the freethinker and official Christianity is that the freethinker is an honest man who straightforwardly *teaches* that Christianity is poetry, fiction. Official Christianity is a falsification that ceremoniously assures us that Christianity is something quite different from fiction. Official Christianity ceremoniously rages against the freethinker and by this means conceals the fact that in reality official Christianity itself makes Christianity into poetry, abolishing the imitation of Christ, so that one is only able to relate to the Exemplar via the power of imagination. [pp. 141–42]

Once again, it is clear that SK has taken his stand on the secular, *human* terrain of honesty, a virtue accessible to all, regardless of their religious convictions. Honesty is the precondition of all moral universals and of all proper politics and social interaction, and it is thus within the social-political realm and not in the lofty, transcendent realm of religion, that SK has chosen to campaign. His attack on Christian culture must be seen as an intervention into the political arena, the sphere of ordinary human discourse, where universal ethical norms, the ordinary rules of "human honesty," constitute the standard. This point is of great importance to the present work. Thus SK is able to welcome "freethinkers" as honest people, while spurning hosts of official and putative Christians,[9] because the former have exercised scrupulous respect—perhaps at great personal cost—for the boundary between "the World" and "Eternity," while the latter, feeling no constraints of honesty, have thoroughly confused and muddied this boundary. The irony, in SK's view, is that the respectable opinion of the world execrates the freethinker, who is honest in his faithfulness to the world, while it admires and lionizes the hypocrite.

As SK writes in a *Moment* article, the most admired "Christian" is not the one who openly seeks earthly success, for that is vulgar and impious and shows a lack of taste and breeding; nor is the most admired "Christian" the one who is truly pious and self-denying, for that involves pain and suffering and is thus too threatening. No, the most admired teacher of "Christianity" is the one who is clever, who is very pious and *"in addition"* has glory and success [pp. 312–13]. This is the hypocrite, and there is no one to whom God is more opposed, SK writes, for "according to God's definition, the task of life is precisely to be reformed, because every person is a born hypocrite by nature" [p. 313]. But there is nothing "the world" so admires as the finer forms of hypocrisy.

Hypocritical humanity needs and wants the Church to serve as its hypocritical protector. In his attack SK seeks to demonstrate that the principal function of the Church is to use a debased form of religion to guard against, to innoculate against, New Testament Christianity. In an article in *The Moment* entitled "A Rebellion in Defiance/A Rebellion in Hypocrisy," SK points out that when there is a force that does not please "humanity," and it can be overcome with superior force at humanity's disposal, then humanity revolts in defiance. But when the force cannot be overcome by humanity's superior force, humanity revolts by hypocrisy, as in the present case of Christianity and its degeneration into Christendom [p. 203]. The Church thus serves as the most "ambivalent" of places, SK continues. "It is not ambivalent to make a fool of God, but it is ambivalent to do so under the guise of worshipping him, . . . [just as] it is ambivalent to abolish Christianity under the guise of spreading it" [p. 205]. Thus again, honest rebellion is preferable to the dishonest embrace of "Christendom," which is hypocritical rebellion.

In another piece, entitled "The Truth About 'The Priest's' Significance to Society," SK carries this argument still further. Given the radically otherworldly goal of Christianity, SK points out, the problem then becomes for "humanity" ("the human race," "society") to protect itself against Christianity, which, as we have seen, is the deadly enemy of merely natural human being. Now, "society" reasons that it would be unwise to reject Christianity outright, for then one becomes involved with it. (Here, again, one notes SK's preference for the honest atheist over the hypocritical "Christian.") It is smarter for society to employ "perjurers" who can render Christianity harmless. Therefore, the "perjurers" ("priests," as SK explains) are employed, their numbers being in accordance with the size of the population. "'We,' society says, 'we are only laymen; we cannot occupy ourselves with religion like this; we rest quietly in confidence in the priest, who is, of course, obligated by his oath upon the New Testament' " [p. 268]. The priests are thus *experts,* whom society engages deliberately in order to shield it from the painful realities of life and from the existential choices posed by Christianity. Then society is able to wash its hands of the most important problems of life, saying that the priest is the expert, after all, and is bound by the New Testament, and should know. Now, SK continues, the comedy is complete, for the priests express precisely the opposite of Christianity.

> This is "the priest's" significance to society, which from generation to generation consumes a "necessary" quota of perjurers in order, under the name of Christianity, to be completely secured against Christianity, to be completely secure in being able to live in heathendom, safe, and even refined by the fact that this is Christianity. [p. 269]

In the final number of *The Moment,* SK raises this point again, in an article entitled "'The Priest' as Breakwater." It is the priest's task to protect society by allowing society to say:

> "We have no responsibility. We are common folk. We do what the priest says. He has taken an oath. We dare not judge the priest. . . ." All "humanity's"

shrewdness is directed toward one thing, toward being able to live without responsibility. The significance of the priest for society ought to be to do everything to make every person eternally responsible for every hour that he lives, even in the least things he does, because this is Christianity. But, his significance for society is to guarantee hypocrisy, while society pushes off the responsibility from itself onto "the priest." [pp. 359–60]

According to SK's critique, official Christianity also performs a more mundane task for society, namely the promotion of such socially useful ends as conformity, familial solidarity, and sentimentality about childhood. When a young man without religion fathers a child, he feels that because "everyone" has a religion, the child must have religion, and so, as the child's father, must he. Whence originates, SK concludes, the official evangelical Lutheran religion [p. 244]. Similarly, a merchant, whose motto is "Everyone is a thief in his chosen profession," regards this axiom as his religion, but he realizes that it is advantageous to adopt the reigning religion of whatever country he finds himself in, and hence goes and takes Lutheran communion—the body and blood of Christ!—a couple of times a year [p. 246]. Lutheran Christianity covers up embarrassment and makes one socially respectable, and these are the real reasons, SK insists, for the establishment and survival of official Christianity.

Nor ought one to overlook the social need for family solidarity as a bastion of support of established Christianity, SK continues:

> The Christianity of "the priests" addresses itself to using religion (which, alas, exists for precisely the opposite purpose) to cement families together more and more egoistically, and for arranging family festivities, beautiful, glorious family festivities, for example, infant baptism and confirmation. And these festivities— compared, for example, with trips to the park and other familial joys—have a special sort of captivation, in that they are "in addition" religious. [p. 263]

Children are brought up to be "Christian," as it is called—that is, "they are filled up with children's sweets," which the parents sample, too, so that they can become sentimental about their youth and about Christianity, which they can never really recapture, because they believe that one must be a child to be a Christian [p. 255]. Sentimental nonsense about childhood and Christianity is thus another exploitation of Christianity, which is used as a sort of cement to help bond together the progression of family-nation-state-civilization.[10]

Official Christianity is thus a contagious sentimentality that is transmitted from one generation of children to the next via the agency of bathetic adults. When a man is mature, SK argues, he says to himself, " 'I am really too old to become a Christian now. . . . That is something one must become in one's childhood or not at all. But now that I have children, they will be raised Christian' " [p. 252]. The Christianity of Christendom is built on the assumption that one can only become a Christian as a child and that one must be a Christian from childhood or not at all. This, SK argues, is the opposite of New Testament Christianity, which addresses itself to the unintoxicated adult.

> The truth is that one cannot become a Christian as a child. . . . Becoming a Christian presupposes (according to the New Testament) a completely human existence—what, in the natural sense, one might call a man's maturity—in order to become a Christian by breaking with everything to which one clings in immediacy. Becoming a Christian presupposes (according to the New Testament) a personal consciousness of sin and of oneself as a sinner. [p. 253]

Here again we note the radical emphasis on "breaking with everything to which one clings in immediacy," the forceful break with the world of comfortable appearance, a break that is necessarily painful and impolite. Christianity, a religion of mature daring and sober renunciation, has become a sentimentally remembered phase of childhood, in which everyone wishes he or she could have remained but which is, alas, outgrown and bequeathed to the next generation of children, who likewise outgrow it and pass it on. "Christianity" is never retained by the children as they mature, because it is never taken seriously by the adults. Thus, SK concludes, the nonsense of "Christianity" is poured into child after child, generation after generation, a Christianity that is for children and upon which adults look back in wistful sentimentality. The only future for such children is either to remain embedded in such nonsense all their lives or to tear themselves out of it painfully and to make the terrible decision: Either God is God or their parents are liars [p. 266, paraphrase].

It is clear—both from the general tone of the closing phase of SK's career and (especially) from his view that the social and political developments of his Denmark constituted the coming-of-age of "the common man"—that with respect to Christianity, SK saw an analogy between the families he discusses in the polemics summarized in the preceding pages and the "family" of Denmark as a whole.[11] "Childhood" in religious, as in political and social matters, has now come to an end for Danish society. It is now time for "the common man" to choose whether to accept the cultural compromise of his parents *or* to accept "God as God"—which would necessarily entail the realization that his "parent," i.e., the officially Christian society of the Golden Age, has lied to him.

Is there, then, a proper sphere for the state, for society, for politics, at all? And if so, what is it? In his attack on Christendom SK insists, as he had done earlier, that politics has its own relatively independent sphere of existence, which, when properly respected, is legitimate and not inimical to the true interests of Christianity. What must be guarded against, of course, is any expansionist attempt by society to confuse the boundaries of politics and religion, for, as SK carefully notes in his attack, not only is such a confusion of boundaries a disregard of the prerogative of religion, but it is bad politics as well. "Good religion" and "good politics" can coexist successfully.

The idea of the state, SK writes in one *Moment* article, seems to be as follows: It is the task of the state, in civilization, to see to it that various things that people need are available to them in a comfortable manner and at a reasonable price. This is the case, for example, with piped water, roads and highways, street illumination, and public safety. *But,* society tends to argue, Why isn't this also the case with "eternal blessedness?" Of course, society grants, it will cost money—everything does—but by procuring it in bulk it will be possible to provide it more reasonably, more securely and splendidly, than if everyone had to do it separately [p. 121, paraphrase]. Here SK objects strenuously. With respect to things of this world, comfort, convenience, and economy are of course important considerations. With respect to such properly social-political matters of material prudence as piped water, for example, SK would much prefer to receive them in the most "comfortable" way. But, with respect to the eternal, the mode of acquisition is not a matter of indifference. No, SK continues,

> the eternal is not really a something, but is the way in which it is obtained. The eternal is obtained in only one way . . . in the difficult way of eternity, which Christ characterizes with the words, "Narrow is the way and strait is the gate which leads to life, and few are they who find it." [p. 122]

The difference, then, between politics and religion is the difference between the manipulation of *objects* in the material world for the sake of convenience and comfort and the posture of a *subject,* the self, in relation to eternity. There is nothing wrong with society's desire for prudent arrangements of material matters, but this political approach must not be extended to the vertical, or religious dimension.

In a subsequent article on the proper limits of religion and politics, SK cites I Peter 2:17, "You must fear God and honor the King," and continues:

> *If possible* [emphasis added], a Christian should be His Majesty's best subject. But, *from a Christian point of view,* the King is not the proper authority—he is not and can not and must not and will not be the proper authority—in relation to a kingdom that will not for any price be of this world, if it be a matter of life and death will not be of this world. . . . In its own exalted divine seriousness, Christianity has always granted the King his seriousness. It is only this disgusting play-Christianity that has [in claiming that Christianity is dependent upon an official clergy and upon "royal protection"] committed treason both against the New Testament and against the King, by placing the worthiness and seriousness of his royal existence in a confusing light. [pp. 125–26]

Politics *qua* politics is acceptable, then, and it is important to note that for SK the "treachery" represented by official Christianity not only sabotages religion, but politics as well. It is "treason against the King."

Pursuing this same theme in a later article, SK asks, "Is it defensible for the state to receive an oath [from a priest], which not only is not kept, but the swearing of which is a self-contradiction?" [p. 157]. Christianity, SK insists, is a kingdom not of this world, but the *state* receives an oath from the teacher of Christianity (the priest) in which the teacher swears fealty to the *New Testament*, which is the opposite of the state [pp. 157–58]. Thus, if the priest really is an imitator of Christ, which his oath upon the New Testament obligates him to be, then his status as a royal official is a hindrance, for at the same moment that he moves to fulfill his oath, he must destroy his status as a royal official. The whole thing, SK concludes, is "a self-contradiction! And how corrupting, both of the state and of Christianity!" [p. 158]. Thus, again, politics can be seen to have its legitimate sphere, and indeed, has an interest in seeing religion's true boundaries respected, for the corruption of religion is also the "corrupting of the state." SK's arguments in favor of an independent existence for Christianity and a secularization of politics and culture are clearly built upon the ordinary human ground of "honesty," which protects the integrity both of religion and of politics.

Since both religion and politics can only be preserved by a scrupulous protection of their differing modes of being, then, for SK, the final judgment regarding the official established clergy must necessarily be one of *total* rejection:

> With the clerical estate it is not like it is with the other estates, where there is nothing wrong with the estate in and for itself. No, the clerical estate is, from a Christian point of view, evil in and for itself. It is a corruptedness, a human selfishness, which turns Christianity in precisely the reverse direction from that in which Christ turned it. [p. 213]

And there is not a single exception among the clergy, SK insists. They are not like other classes, with some good and some bad representatives [p. 269]. This is because the clergy is a class which by definition violates the *boundary* between the religious and the social-political spheres. The notion of an official clergy is thus wrong as such and is to be rejected *in toto*. To talk about good priests and bad priests completely misses the point SK is trying to make, for his opposition to the clergy, he feels, is nothing personal but a matter of principle.

In another article based on the evangelical admonition to "Beware of those who like to walk in long robes" [Mark 12:38 and Luke 20:46, SK's second use of this text in his attack], SK interprets the evangelists as opposing all uniformed clergy—that is, all officially constituted clergy *per se*—for they are part of the "official worship of God," which Christ did not want [p. 213]. Further, the long robes, splendid buildings, etc., which are a part of an official ecclesiastical establishment, are a falsification of the New Testament, SK insists, because these things aim at seducing the masses who, alas, "only all too easily allow themselves to be bewitched by sense impressions" [ibid.].

SK's principled opposition to an established clergy provided him with a major portion of the popularly oriented (indeed, almost rabble-rousing) anti-clerical material of the ten numbers of *The Moment*. SK's acerbic anticlericalism formed a continuing, attention-getting counterpoint to his views concerning New Testament Christianity and the boundary between that Christianity and the proper social-political sphere, which he boldly tried to present to "the common man" of the new Denmark. Some representative samples of this anticlericalism follow below.

In a short novella entitled "First God's Kingdom," SK makes his final, polemical use of Matthew 6:24-end. The familiar biblical passage is used as the text on which SK's young priest, Ludvig From [= Louis Pious]—who has in fact sought first everything *other* than God's Kingdom, e.g., success, marriage, a job, a better-paying parish—bases his first sermon, which was judged an enormous success by his bishop [pp. 248–50]. The moral of the tale, SK tells his "common man," in case he has failed to get it already, is to stay as far away from the official Establishment as possible. For further information, SK here, as elsewhere in *The Moment*, refers his reader to his boycott pamphlet *This Must Be Said* [p. 250].

What the priest means by a "Christian," SK explains in another article, is "a good shearing sheep, a presentable mediocrity to whom eternity is closed" [p. 211].

SK asserts that if one studies the "glorious ones," the genuine witnesses to the Truth, one concludes that "Christianity is the truth," whereas if one observes the priest, one concludes that "profit is the truth" [p. 336]. Therefore, SK continues, the priest must be stopped in the same way in which one stops a thief, by shouting "Stop! Thief!," for the priest steals from the "glorious ones" and he deceives "the simple people, the mass of humanity, who do not have the ability to see through the priest's practices" [p. 337]. Here, as everywhere in his anticlericalism, we can see that SK's final message is in principle classically "liberal"—in its definition of the task of politics; in its determination to maintain the boundaries between politics and religion; and in its insistence upon the secular nature of "society." However, the *style* of expression SK gives this message to "the common man" is markedly "populist."

SK writes thusly to "the common man":

> In the splendid cathedral, the high, well-born, highly honored, and worthy Geheime-General-Ober-Hof-Prædikant, the chosen darling of the important people, steps before a select circle of the select, and *movingly* sermonizes on a text chosen by himself, namely, "God has chosen the lowly and the despised of the world [I Corinthians 1:28]," *and no one laughs!* [p. 217]

Did St. Paul have an official position?, SK asks. No. Did he make a lot of money? No. Was he married at least? No. Well, then, SK concludes, St. Paul was no serious man! [p. 218]. SK thus mocks, for the edification of "the common man," the virtues of position, money, and marriage, which were cherished by the bourgeois philistine entourage of Mynsterian Christianity.

SK asks "the common man" whether it is the same teaching when Christ says, "Sell all that you have and give it to the poor," and when the priest says, "Sell all that you have and give it to me" [ibid.].

SK acidly remarks that "one cannot live on nothing . . . yet the priests perform this magic: Christianity absolutely does not exist, and yet they live off it" [p. 219].

In a short piece entitled "The Theatre/The Church," it is noted that one of the signal differences between the theatre and the Church is that the theatre is honest enough to warn you in writing that you will not get your money back [pp. 235–36].

In another piece, entitled "The Priest's Worship," SK again links his anticlericalism with his populist appeal. Let us imagine, he writes, that the one thing that God had forbidden us was to take a trip to the park. Then the priests would find a way of blessing the carriages and the horses, for a fee, so that all could go to the park as a part of their divine worship. Money would enter into it such that the things most pleasing to God would be accessible only to "millionaires" [p. 358].

In another, genuinely gutter-level piece, entitled "That the Priests are Cannibals, and in the Most Disgusting Fashion," SK argues that, as one stores food in a good season, so are all the suffering witnesses to the Truth stored up in a sort of ecclesiastical salt barrel, and their cries of "follow me" are to no avail, for the priest simply commands, "Be quiet and be eaten. You will feed me and my family" [p. 334, paraphrase]. There are three reasons, SK argues, that the priest is actually worse than the savage cannibal: (1) The cannibal is wild, whereas the priest is a learned, "cultured" [dannet] man; (2) the cannibal eats only his enemies, but the priest eats those whom he says are his friends; (3) the cannibal acts out of a sudden passion and then returns to more decent ways, whereas the priest is a deliberate, planning cannibal and makes this his nourishment for his whole life [pp. 334–35]. In the beginning, SK admits, the priest has perhaps a troubled conscience because of the cries of the eaten, but in time the priest hardens himself and no longer hears anything. He no longer has his earlier blush of embarrassment at being called a disciple of Christ [p. 335].

It was, however, in the separately published pamphlet, *What Christ Judges About Official Christianity*, that the anticlericalism of the latter phase of SK's attack reached its high-water mark, for SK here marshalls Christ's own words of condemnation as the ultimate escalation in the war against Christendom. The text cited is Matthew 23:29–33 [cf. also Luke 11:47–48], where Christ speaks against the hypocritical scribes and pharisees who tend and build "the graves of the prophets" and who boast that had *they* been alive in the days of the martyred prophets, *they* would not have put them to death. What the scribes and pharisees actually show in their proud lamentations over the departed prophets is their own lack of modesty or genuine contrition, which proves only that they indeed would put the prophets to death today, given the opportunity. Christ therefore becomes angry and calls the hypocritical clergymen of his day "serpents," "vipers' brood," etc. In SK's understanding of things, this is precisely the situation of Christendom. Instead of "suffering for the teachings" and following after Christ, as Christ commanded, the official Church "builds the graves of the prophets" and "plays Christianity," while offering a fine career with regular advancement, plenty of opportunities for rank and title and at the same time pretending to renounce the things that it enjoys—even while preaching the forsaking of worldly things [pp. 145–46]. Worst of all, SK continues, the Church will not *admit*, as SK has asked so many times, that it preaches a watered-down Christianity, that it, in effect, would have "killed the prophets" [p. 146]. SK concludes that, in Christ's own words, this clerical hypocrisy, which has its deepest roots in the "natural self" and in the desire to be "comfortable" and to arrange the worship of God most conveniently, is a form of "blood-guilt" [pp. 146–47].

SK ends this inflammatory argument with the populistic opinion that if Christ came back today, he would judge "the teachers" just as he did in the past, but would allow "the congregation" to be excused on the grounds that it had been misled [p. 147]. The reader of these words, SK admits, is probably shocked and horrified at what SK writes, never having seen the biblical passage in print or heard it from the pulpit. Why, the words "vipers' brood, serpents!" Terrible! Words one would never hear "in the mouth of any cultured person [Dannet]! And to let him repeat them several times, it is so frightfully clumsy! And to turn Christ into a person who uses violence!" [p. 148]. Christ has thus been enrolled by SK into the ranks of the war against culture [Dannelse], for it is precisely culture which has domesticated and emasculated Christianity and which has misled the people into thinking that religion must be expressive of good taste and moderation. Finally, SK predicts that if the teachers and cultivated leaders of Christendom were contemporary with the prophets, they would kill them: "That is, they would secretly have the people do it and bear the guilt, as in fact happened" [ibid.]. (SK is clearly referring, in particular, to the crucifixion of Christ, which in SK's view showed the same pattern as the political events leading up to and culminating in 1848: The cultured elite, who blaspheme in their pantheistic speculation, have secretly egged on the people and then recoil in self-righteous horror at the results, even while they scramble to solidify their position and reap what benefits they can.)

The elucidation of the populist nature of SK's anticlericalism is best concluded with a typical example of his call for "the common man" to boycott and dissociate himself completely from the official institutions of Christendom: "Whoever you are, consider this: Flee from the guidance of the priests at all costs. . . . You cannot learn anything true about the truth Which Suffers—i.e., about Christianity—from the professionals. Flee them, they are fooling you out of eternity . . ." [p. 310].[12]

However, in addition to the call for boycott and individual dissociation from Christendom, which is omnipresent in *The Moment*, there is also a clear and unambiguous call for a permanent and general solution to the problem, namely a divorce or separation between religion and the state, the disestablishment of Christianity. SK entitles one article, "Is It Defensible for the state— the Christian state!—to Make, If Possible, Christianity Impossible?" [p. 109]. "The factual situation in the country," SK explains, "is really this: Not only does Christianity, the Christianity of the New Testament, not exist, but, if possible, it is being made impossible" [ibid.]. If the state deliberately employed 1,000 civil servants whose business it was directly to hinder Christianity, it would not be as pernicious or as dangerous as this, SK maintains, where 1,000 civil officials are hired to proclaim Christianity and have a pecuniary interest in having people call themselves Christians [pp. 109–10]. Nothing is so opposed to the essence of Christianity as having people take their Christianity lightly, yet this is what the priest fosters for the sake of his livelihood [ibid.].

In another article, SK goes even further in his critique of the system that retains the "1,000 priests" and directly embraces separation as the only solution. To show how wrong everything is in Christendom, all that need be done is for the state to turn the preaching of Christianity into a voluntary, private matter—"*and this is the only true Christian requirement, and also the only reasonable thing*" [p. 161, emphasis added]. We will soon see whether there really are one and one-half million Christians and whether there is need for 1,000 priests. Perhaps none of those presently employed will be capable of taking over the positions which do become available [ibid.].

"If the State Truly Wishes to Serve Christianity," SK entitles a subsequent article, "Then Let It Abolish the 1,000 Paid Positions" [p. 164]. By creating 1,000 paid positions, with no personal risks, SK argues, the "Christian" state has managed to corrupt Christianity in a way that no heathendom could have. Imagine, SK continues, the corrupting effect upon poetry of 1,000 state-paid official poets! The same, but worse, is the case with religion [pp. 164–65].

When we need the help of a physician, SK argues, the state does not need to force us to understand it, so why, with the help of police and legal barriers,[13] does the state force people to recognize their spiritual needs [p. 162]? This argument for the disestablishment of religion is clearly based on the classical liberal values of secularism and of individual responsibility and initiative, which are destroyed by clumsy social-political intervention in the private sector, the realm of the individual. State intervention kills daring and promotes a safe mediocrity. SK's publicly articulated view of the relation between religion and the social-political sphere has come a long way since his disavowal of Rudelbach's January 1851 attempt to enlist his support for civil marriage—but then the political evolution of Denmark in the post-1848 period was also very marked and rapid!

SK's most potent image in his call for the secularization of the state and the disestablishment of Christianity is drawn from the cholera epidemic that ravaged Copenhagen in 1853. In a hospital, SK writes, they try all kinds of remedies, but still the patients die like flies, because the poison is in the building itself. So, too, in the case of Christendom. We try new hymn books, altar rituals, etc.,[14] when the sickness is in the structure itself, the established Church. Let the whole thing fall down in a heap, SK insists; close "these boutiques," the only ones left open by the strict Sunday closing laws, and "let us again worship God in simplicity, instead of making a fool of him in splendid buildings" [p. 170]. What is needed in our characterless time, SK concludes, is to practice "the divorce, the separation between the infinite and the finite, between striving for that which is infinite and that which is finite, between living *for* something and living *off* something" [p. 174]. *"What Christianity needs is not the smothering protection of the state. No, it needs fresh air . . ."* [p. 170, emphasis added].

Thus—at the close of his career, by virtue of his understanding of the political and social ferment that had resulted in popular sovereignty, in the "People's Church," and in the coming to adulthood of "the common man"— SK is finally brought to embrace the liberal principle of "a free Church in a free state," or in his words, the principle of "fresh air."

SK, in sum, feels that in his campaign for the dissolution of Christendom and in his call for the individual to refuse to participate in public worship he has done his part, which is to make "the common man," his reader, "aware." SK writes that, until his attack, "the common man" may have believed what the civic officials told him, he may have had ignorance as an excuse for his actions. But now: "You yourself bear the responsibility for how you act . . . you have been made aware!" [p. 251]. In the final number of *The Moment* which SK managed to ready for the press before his death, he pleads with "the common man" to flee these priests, who only want to divert your attention from finding out what true Christianity is, and to change you into a paying member of the State Church by confusing you and befogging you with nonsense and "sensory deceptions." Pay your Church taxes, SK advises; in fact, pay them double, so that it is clear to the keepers of Christendom that what concerns them—money—does not concern you, for you are concerned with what interests you infinitely, Christianity [p. 357, paraphrase].

In this same last number of *The Moment*, SK makes a final egalitarian approach to "the common man," whose coming to "adulthood"—in the view of the present work—was the social and political presupposition that motivated the entire latter portion of SK's authorship. The political situation which SK saw developing around him led him to formulate and to express his politics in the way that he did. In his final piece, SK writes:

You common man! The Christianity of the New Testament is something infinitely high, though not high in such a way that it addresses itself to the differences between people with respect to talent and the like. No, it is for all. . . . You common man! I have not cut my life off from yours. You know that I have lived in the streets, am known by everyone, am possessed of no class egoism. So, if I belong to anyone, I must belong to you, you common man. . . . [pp. 356–57]¹⁵

Epilogue: The Response to the Attack
on Christendom

O

A lengthy account of the response that greeted SK's attack on Christendom is beyond the scope of the present work, but a number of notable points will be mentioned here. The newspapers, with the exception of *The Fatherland*, were generally quite negative or obtuse in their reception of SK's critique. The conservative *Berling Times* [*Berlingske politiske og Avertissementstidende*] was the vehicle for much of the respectable criticism of SK's views, but criticism was also very widespread on the "left," as for example the petit-bourgeois *Copenhagen Post* [*Kjøbenhavnsposten*], the semi-respectable *Courier* [*Flyveposten*] and the *Daily News* [*Dagbladet*], which hovered between liberalism and populism. The openly democratic papers such as the *People's Paper* [*Folkeblad*] and the *Morning Post* [*Morgensposten*] revelled in the attack, on the other hand, and used it to make political hay of their own.[1]

As might be expected, the clerical establishment generally greeted SK's criticisms with opposition or silence, with the only supporting voices being those of well-known "characters" within the Church. The liberal Clausen saw only a "sickly, ecstatic excitement" in SK's attack,[2] and SK's lone academic supporter was a philosophy professor, Rasmus Nielsen, whose support was of such a half-way, compromising nature that he appeared foolish and was publicly written off by SK and privately mocked by Martensen.[3] The intellectual elite in general was shocked and uncomprehending. F. C. Sibbern, SK's former philosophy professor, wrote in March 1855 that he could only see a "sectarian" in SK, "whose attack stands alongside those brought by the Baptist and Mormon preachers."[4] The conservative jurist and politician A. S. Ørsted was deeply offended by SK's attack upon his friend Mynster's Christianity and devoted several pages of his very valuable memoirs to correct "the injustice of this accusation."[5]

The response of the Heiberg circle can be gauged from a remark by Johanne Luise Heiberg in a letter of July 9, 1855 to her husband. Fru Heiberg greatly admired SK, and her remarkable memoirs,[6] first published posthumously in

1892–93, are notable for their irenic silence regarding the entire last year of SK's life; in the July 1855 letter, however, Fru Heiberg finds it necessary to append the remark "unfaithful beast" to a chance reference to SK.[7] It seems clear that the breach of faith that so offended the Heibergs was not so much SK's break with established religion—we have examined Heiberg's careless treatment of Christianity—as his offense against the good taste of the Golden Age and the solidarity of the cultured class.

In thoughtful liberal circles, however, the disapproval and misunderstanding of SK's actions was not quite unanimous. One of those who saw more deeply was Fru Hansine Andræ, the very intelligent and politically shrewd wife of C. G. Andræ, a brilliant mathematician and liberal politician who became the Finance Minister and the constitutional wizard of the liberal ministry that in December 1854 had replaced the reactionary Ørsted government. Fru Andræ's political diaries from the mid-1850's are one of the primary sources of insight into the thinking of the highest liberal circle of the period, and she takes a somewhat different view of the seriousness of SK's task than did most of the more prominent conservatives and "recognized" intellectual figures of the time. On October 8, 1855, when SK lay in the hospital with his terminal illness, she wrote in her diary:

> Søren Kierkegaard lies in the hospital . . . very sick—paralysis of the legs as a consequence of tuberculosis of the spine marrow. This awakens concern doubly at this time, because, with his writings against Mynster, Martensen, and the clergy—or, perhaps to express it better, against the whole outer form of the worship of God—he has aroused a great sensation, and it is certain that his writings, which have a large readership, including many theologians, will sooner or later have a revolutionary impact upon matters concerning the Church.[8]

Thus, at least some intelligent citizens—in this case the very canny Fru Andræ, who was not without important literary connections of her own—were able to see more deeply and to discern, perhaps even with a degree of sympathy, the true import and intention of SK's "liberal" attempt to sort out religion and culture and to dissolve the old Christian cultural synthesis. Fru Andræ's diary proves that not everyone was obligated to see SK as a minor figure or as a misanthropic crackpot, but that, on the contrary, he could be understood and respected, even by "respectable" people, during his attack on the Church.

Of equal, or even greater interest, perhaps, are the responses of two of the principals of the attack, Martensen and Grundtvig. In letters to a friend, Martensen complains of the "unbelievably fanatical" and "moblike" character of SK's attack,[9] and several weeks later he reports with relief that his wife and his friend Paulli (who was Mynster's son-in-law) have listened to Grundtvig's sermons and have determined that Grundtvig has decided not to lend any support to the Kierkegaardian rebellion.[10] (The fact that Martensen could have felt that it was "not quite clear from the beginning"[11] whether or not Grundtvig might make common cause with SK only shows how far from understanding his adversaries' intentions Martensen was.)

The new Primate was beset with other troubles at this time, which he may have felt were not unrelated to SK's attack on the established Church. Specifically, the new liberal government made it possible for the Rigsdag to erode the financial resources of the Church, and thus, when the cabinet minister Knuth visited Martensen to discuss SK's unseemly behavior, the Bishop took the occasion to speak up for the preservation of ecclesiastical control over the tithe taxes.[12]

In his memoirs from 1883, Martensen discusses SK's attack at length and finally endorses Sibbern's view that in his attack SK "had here revealed himself as a philistine"[13]—which was perhaps the worst epithet the Golden Age had at its disposal. In Martensen's view, SK's attack seemed to have greatest appeal not only for freethinkers, who hated the Church, but, alas, also for peasants, for "women, who had devoted themselves fanatically to Mynster," and for sectarians.[14] In Martensen's view, SK's criticisms were "Mephistophelean" and self-contradictory, in that "he restricted himself strictly to individuals, in spite of the fact that he now addressed them *en masse*," and the net result, in Martensen's opinion, is that SK "has contributed in no small measure to the spread of unbelief here in this country."[15]

Grundtvig's response to SK was even more remarkable and no less bound up with ulterior church-political considerations. Grundtvig seems to have wanted to use SK as a bogey with which to scare the traditionalist clerical opposition into accepting the Grundtvigian program of the "loosening of parish bonds" (i.e., free choice, not geographical assignment, in determining one's parish), a reform measure which was finally passed in April 1855, in the midst of SK's furious and frightening attack.

Grundtvig's sermons during the 1854–55 church year—which spanned the whole period of SK's attack—have been unearthed and published by Professor P. G. Lindhardt of Aarhus University.[16] In these sermons we can see very clearly that Grundtvig spent much of the year making quite specific responses each Sunday to the journalistic assaults that SK had published during the preceding few weeks. After an initial hesitation during the period in which SK appeared to be principally settling up accounts with Mynster, who was an old adversary of Grundtvig's as well,[17] Grundtvig replied very strongly when SK began to broaden the attack into an assault upon the entire clergy.[18] In his Palm Sunday 1855 sermon[19] (the one which so pleased Martensen's wife and Mynster's son-in-law Paulli), Grundtvig replied to SK's attack upon the notion of a "Christian world," and in his Good Friday sermon later that same week,[20] Grundtvig's argument is continued and his notion of gradual Christian growth [Væxt] is stressed in opposition to the radical duality of SK's thought. The sermons of April 22[21] and 29[22] defended, as against SK's otherworldliness, the permissibility of having many of one's specifically Christian joys and sorrows in common with "the World." On June 17[23] Grundtvig replied to SK's *What Christ Judges*, advising his congregation not to fear Christ's judgment, for Christ will be mild and understanding. On July 29[24] Grundtvig struck out at those who label the clergy "deliberate misleaders," and "wolves in sheep's clothing" and in turn labelled such critics dangerous and "false prophets." On September 16[25] Grundtvig replied to SK's specific assault upon the Grundtvigians, and on the following Sunday[26] he attacked those who would make Christ "inhuman" in his strictness.

The aftershocks of SK's assault continued to be felt by Grundtvig and his movement for many years. Both SK's and Grundtvig's criticisms, however much they differed in their radicality and in their final vision, shared a strong distaste for the official Golden Age ecclesiastical establishment. To a certain extent, therefore, Grundtvig's followers were able to turn SK's attack to account by opening their ranks to those whom SK had driven away from the mainstream establishmentarianism of Mynster and Martensen. However, SK's populist appeal and his closeness to the peasant pietist tradition gave his attack a credibility and an attractiveness among much of what the Grundtvigians considered their primary public. Rightly or wrongly interpreted, SK's criticisms were seized upon by the more anticlerical and fundamentalist wing of the peasant pietist movement, the Inner Mission, which eventually was adroitly guided back into more safely clerical channels by Vilhelm Beck, the ultra-conservative pietist who himself claimed to have been "awakened" by reading SK's *Moment* in his student years.[27] From the early 1860's onward, Beck's Inner Mission cut deeply into the success of Grundtvigianism.

As has been noted earlier, SK was also instrumental in the conversion *from* religion of such "moderns" as Georg Brandes and Harald Høffding, and Ibsen's powerful drama *Brand* is clearly modelled on the stormy closing phase of SK's career.[28] Thus, both the "right" and the "left" in the Danish culture of succeeding decades could trace their origins to SK's attack on the cultural synthesis of Golden Age Christendom, while the great, though mutually antagonistic, "center" streams of "social Christianity," represented by Grundtvig and Martensen, felt themselves fundamentally immune to SK's criticisms.

As a final, comical note, yet another possible "response" to SK's attack upon Mynster's Christendom might be added to round out this sketch. The dramatist and historian of the theatre, Thomas Overskou, reports in his very lively and readable memoirs[29] that in the spring of 1856, several months after SK's death, table-tipping and séances had become the pastime of the Copenhagen bourgeoisie, even including such normally sober and respectable people as the Heibergs and Bishop Martensen. The "apparatus" or instrument of communication used by the spirit during these sessions, Overskou reports, was a small, four-legged table, perhaps "a piece of dollhouse furniture," with a pencil bound, point-down, to one of its four legs. The dollhouse table was then placed upon a large pad of paper on an ordinary dining table. Each of those participating in the séance then formed part of "a chain," by placing his or her little finger upon this little table or "apparatus," diagonally across the little finger of the person next to him or her. The other hand was held away from the "apparatus," and both arms were to be kept off the dining table. The spirit was supposed to communicate with those present by acting through the combined little fingers of the participants, thus causing the apparatus to move, writing its reply on the paper below.[30] (The mental image of all these great and learned people placing their little fingers on a jury-rigged dollhouse table is irresistibly amusing.)

At one particular séance at the Heibergs, the spirit was asked, "Who is the cleverest man in Denmark?" and duly replied "Heiberg!"[31] A bit later—perhaps because, like the others present, she had been made nervous by SK's recent attacks upon the reputation of the late, respected Bishop Mynster—Fru Heiberg asked the telling question, "Is Bishop Mynster happy and glad in the place where he now is?"[32] The spirit answered, "Glad," and this rather disconcerted those present, as they were not accustomed to distinguishing between the generally synonymous terms "happy" and "glad." What might it mean, they speculated? Is Mynster "glad" but not "happy?" And if so, why? The spirit was consulted again, and the question this time was "Is Bishop Mynster *happy* where he is?"[33] This time the spirit answered unequivocally, "No," and much perplexity ensued, finally to be dispelled by the consultation of expert opinion, which arrived at the complex interpretation that "the deceased can be *glad*—perhaps in viewing the glory of God—and yet not be happy—perhaps because of feelings of his own imperfections."[34] Thus, in the spring of 1856, did the cultural elite of Golden Age Christendom express and purge its fears concerning the blessedness of its departed Bishop Mynster.

Notes

INTRODUCTION

1. Walter Lowrie, *Kierkegaard* (Oxford: Oxford University Press, 1938), pp. 365–66. Lowrie also claims that it was a surfeit of liberalism and popular sovereignty, of which SK is supposed to be the antithesis, that was to blame for the communism and fascism of the 1930s!

2. The best example of the Marxist approach is Georg Lukács. Lukács apparently had an infatuation with Kierkegaard prior to the First World War, but he eventually came to view Kierkegaard simply as a symptom of the illness and irrationality of bourgeois society. In *Der junge Hegel* [*Georg Lukács Werke*, vol. 8 (Berlin: Luchterhand, 1948)] Lukács discerns a dangerous anti-Hegelian philosophical trend which turns away from the real world to "eine religiöse Wirklichkeit . . . eine Sphäre der mystischen Pseudo-wirklichkeit, die entweder vollständig inhaltslos ist—eine Nacht, in der alle Kühe schwarz sind, wie Hegel später in der 'Phänomenologie' spottet—oder ein irrational-istischer Behälter, der mit beliebigen reaktionären Inhalten willkürlich gefüllt werden kann" [ibid., p. 283]. Lukács finds this tradition rooted in the anti-Hegelianism of Schelling, "die die Vorläuferin einer ganzen Reihe von späteren reaktionär-irrationalistischen Philosophien von Kierkegaard bis Heidegger geworden ist" [ibid.]. Thus, as Lukács elsewhere remarks, Kierkegaard is "einer der Stammväter und Klassiker der modernen Dekadenz" [*Essays über Realismus, Georg Lukács Werke*, vol. 4, p. 478] because he is a reactionary-irrationalist philosopher, a link in the destructive chain which runs from Schelling to Heidegger and through Heidegger (as Lukács points out elsewhere) to Hitler! In a later book, *Die Zerstörung der Vernunft* [*Georg Lukács Werke*, vol. 9] Lukács enlarges upon his Kierkegaard criticism, though without changing this fundamental position.

3. See Valter Lindström, *Efterföljelsens teologi* [The Theology of Imitation] (Stockholm: Diakonistyrelsens Bokförlag, 1956), pp. 128–29, 153–54, *et passim* for the classic presentation of the "slippage" theory. This theory is also embraced by N.H. Søe in G. Malantschuk and N. H. Søe, *Søren Kierkegaards Kamp mod Kirken* [Søren Kierkegaard's Fight Against the Church] (Copenhagen: Munksgaards Forlag, 1956), where Søe also writes: "In my view, Kierkegaard would have had a much stronger position in Danish intellectual life if he had died a year or two earlier" (p. 72). For a full discussion of the various interpretative attempts to deal with (and discount) Kierkegaard's attack on Christendom, see Kresten Nordentoft, *"Hvad siger Brand-Majoren?": Kierkegaards Opgør med sin Samtid* ["What Does the Fire Chief Say?": Kierkegaard's Settling-Up with His Times] (Copenhagen: G. E. C. Gad, 1973), pp. 11–24.

1. HISTORICAL BACKGROUND AND THE RISE OF THE PEASANTRY TO 1820

1. Jens Vibæk, *Reform oq Fallit, 1784–1830* [Reform and Bankruptcy, 1784–1830], vol. 10 of *Danmarks Historie* [History of Denmark], John Danstrup and Hal Koch, eds. (Copenhagen: Politikens Forlag, 1964), p. 92.

2. During the period covered by the present study, Danish agricultural land was measured according to an ancient system which measured its productive capacity rather than its surface area. The fundamental unit was a "Tønde Hartkorn," which means, literally, "a barrel of grain." Depending upon the quality of the land in question, this unit could mean anything from a fairly small parcel, on the very best agricultural land, to many acres on poor, unproductive soil.

3. Fridlev Skrubbeltrang, *Den danske Bonde. 1788–1938* [The Danish Peasant, 1788–1938] (Copenhagen: Landbrugsudstillingen [Agricultural Exhibition], 1938), p. 10.

4. Hugo Matthiessen, *Det gamle Land* [The Ancient Countryside] (Copenhagen: Gyldendal, 1942), p. 13.

5. Skrubbeltrang, *Den danske Bonde*, p. 10.

6. Vibæk, *Reform oq Fallit*, p. 58.

7. Skrubbeltrang, *Den danske Bonde*, p. 23.

8. Ibid., p. 10.

9. Until the reforms of the late eighteenth and early nineteenth centuries, the Danish word for "peasant"—"Bonde"—was used indiscriminately to refer both to the generally better-off copyholder [Fæstebonde] group and the worse-off cottager [Husmand] group, but this blanket label made social sense because there was a great deal of mobility and intermarriage between the two groups, which had not yet hardened into classes. In the course of the nineteenth century, the bulk of the copyholders became "self-owners" [Selvejere] or "farmers" [Gaardmænd], whereas the cottagers remained in their old position of dependency, which was in fact rendered worse by their increasing social immobility and isolation. The general term "peasant" [Bonde] still continued to apply to both groups, but now it was a substantial misrepresentation of social reality, and the general term was invoked when a sentimental-bucolic or polemical, anti-estate owner sense was intended. In actual practice, after the reform period, the term "peasant" generally concealed more than it revealed, for it obscured the deep differences in class interest between the new class of self-owner farmers and the cottagers. However, for the present study, "peasant" will be retained in order to accentuate the basic rural-urban division in Golden Age Denmark.

10. Vibæk, *Reform oq Fallit*, p. 90.

11. Skrubbeltrang, *Den danske Bonde*, pp. 60–64.

12. Ibid.

13. Ibid., p. 72.

14. Ibid., p. 73.

15. Ibid.

16. Fridlev Skrubbeltrang, *Husmænd i Danmark gennem 300 Aar* [Cottagers in Denmark During 300 Years] (Copenhagen: Schultz, 1942), p. 13.

17. Ibid., p. 46.

18. Ibid., p. 55.

19. Cf. Skrubbeltrang, *Husmænd*, chapter V, *passim*.

20. Frederik Bajer, *Nordens politiske Digtning, 1789–1804* [Scandinavian Political Poetry, 1789–1804] (Copenhagen: C. A. Topp's Forlag, 1878), p. 66.

21. Ibid., p. 65.

22. Vibæk, *Reform og Fallit*, p. 378.

23. Ibid., p. 462.

24. Ibid., p. 437.

25. Adolph Frederik Bergsøe, *Den danske Stats Statistik* [Danish State Statistics], vol. I (Copenhagen: 1844), p. 364.

26. Roar Skovmand, *Folkestyrets Fødsel, 1830–1870* [The Birth of Popular Government, 1830–1870], volume 11 of *Danmarks Historie* [History of Denmark], John Danstrup and Hal Koch, eds., (Copenhagen: Politikens Forlag, 1964), p. 86.

27. Ibid.

28. Ibid., p. 17.

29. Bergsøe, *Statistik*, vol. I, p. 444.

2. RELIGIOUS CURRENTS UNTIL 1820

1. See the discussion in Marie Mikulová Thulstrup, *Kierkegaard og Pietismen* [Kierkegaard and Pietism] (Copenhagen: Munksgaard, 1967).

2. See the discussion in Hal Koch, *Danmarks Kirke gennem Tidende* [The Danish Church Through the Ages], 2nd ed. (Copenhagen: Gyldendal, 1960), chapter III, "Subjektivismens gennembrud i pietismen og oplysning" [The Breakthrough of Subjectivism in Pietism and Enlightenment], as well as F. E. Jensen, *Pietismen i Danmark* [Pietism in Denmark] (Copenhagen: O. Lohse, n.d.), *passim*.

3. "Af døbte vrimle Stand og Land, men hvor er Troens Brand?", in J. L. Balling and P. G. Lindhardt, *Den Nordiske Kirkes Historie* [The History of the Scandinavian Church], 2nd rev. ed. (Copenhagen: Nyt Nordisk Forlag-Arnold Busck, 1967), p. 152.

4. The Herrnhut movement (known in English as the Moravian Brethren) in Germany founded a congregation which they called a "Brüdergemeine," or "Congregation of Brothers"; as we will see, the Herrnhut movement in Copenhagen adapted this term directly, calling their own congregation the "Brødremenighed."

5. See J. Lundbye, *Herrnhutismen i Danmark* [Herrnhutism in Denmark] (Copenhagen: Karl Schønbergs Forlag, 1903), pp. 115ff.

6. Ibid., p. 85.

7. Ibid.

8. Ibid., p. 127.

9. *Søren Kierkegaards Samlede Værker* [The Collected Works of Søren Kierkegaard], A. B. Drachmann, J. L. Heiberg, H. O. Lange, eds., 1st ed., vol. I (Copenhagen: Gyldendal, 1901), p. 44.

10. Lundbye, *Herrnhutismen*, p. 210.

11. Ibid., p. 201.

12. F. E. Jensen, *Pietismen i Jylland. Studier over jydske Menighedstilstande, særlig paa Landet, omkring Midten af det 18. Aarhundrede* [Pietism in Jutland: Studies in the Conditions in Jutland Congregations, Particularly in the Countryside, in the mid-18th Century], No. 5 of *Teologiske Studier* [Theological Studies] published by *Dansk Teologisk Tidsskrift* [Danish Theological Journal], Section II (Copenhagen: G. E. C. Gad, 1944), p. 166.

13. Lundbye, *Herrnhutismen*, p. 187.

14. Ibid., p. 75.

15. Balling and Lindhardt, *Den Nordiske Kirkes Historie*, p. 147.

16. Lundbye, *Herrnhutismen*, p. 89.

17. See Wolfdietrich von Kloeden, "The Development of Kierkegaard's View of Christianity," in *Bibliotheca Kierkegaardiana*, Niels Thulstrup and Marie Mikulová Thulstrup, eds., vol. I (Copenhagen: Reitzels, 1978), ch. 2 (B. H. Kirmmse, trans.), pp. 81–107, and Sejer Kühle, *Søren Kierkegaard. Barndom og ungdom* [Søren Kierkegaard: Childhood and Youth] (Copenhagen: Aschehoug, 1950), p. 10.

18. Kühle, *op. cit.*, p. 17.

19. The great Danish Church historian Hal Koch makes this point very forcefully in his *Danmarks Kirke Gennem Tidende* and in his volume, entitled *Tiden 1800–1848* [The Period 1800–1848], vol. VI of *Den Danske Kirkes Historie* [History of the Danish Church], Hal Koch and Bjørn Kornerup, eds. (Copenhagen: Gyldendal, 1954).

20. See Balling and Lindhardt, *Den Nordiske Kirkes Historie*, p. 158, and the discussion in Koch, *Danmarks Kirke Gennem Tidende*.

21. Balling and Lindhardt, *op. cit.*, p. 159.

22. See Adam Oehlenschläger, *Erindringer* [Memoirs], vol. II (Copenhagen: Höst, 1850), p. 14.

3. THE PEASANT AWAKENINGS OF THE 1820'S AND AFTER

1. P. G. Lindhardt, *Vækkelser og kirkelige Retninger i Danmark* [Awakenings and Ecclesiastical Currents in Denmark], 2nd ed. (Copenhagen: 1959), p. 10.

2. See the amusing portraits in the uncompleted novel of rural life by Hans Egede Schack, *Sandhed med Modification* [Truth, With Modification], Carl Dumreicher, ed. (Copenhagen: Dansk Kautionsforsikrings-Aktieselskab, 1954).

3. See the relevant chapters in Koch, *Tiden 1800–1848*.

4. See Lindhardt, *Vækkelser*, chapter II, part 3, *passim*.

5. Cited in Roar Skovmand, *De folkelige Bevægelser i Danmark* [The Popular Movements in Denmark] (Copenhagen: Schultz, 1951), p. 14.

6. Lindhardt, *Vækkelser*, chapter II, part 5, *passim*.

4. THE RISE OF LIBERALISM IN THE 1830'S

1. Skovmand, *Folkestyrets Fødsel*, pp. 142–43.

2. Ibid., p. 146.

3. Harald Jørgensen, *Trykkefrihedsspørgsmaalet i Danmark, 1799–1848* [The Question of Freedom of the Press in Denmark, 1799–1848] (Copenhagen: Munksgaard, 1944), pp. 177–92.

4. Skovmand, *Folkestyrets Fødsel*, p. 158.

5. Skovmand, *De folkelige Bevægelser*, p. 18.

6. Skrubbeltrang, *Den danske Bonde*, p. 199.

7. Skovmand, *Folkestyrets Fødsel*, p. 165.

8. *Søren Kierkegaards Papirer* [The Papers of Søren Kierkegaard], P. A. Heiberg, V. Kuhr, E. Torsting, eds., 2nd augmented ed. with N. Thulstrup; Index by N.J. Cappelørn, vol. I (Copenhagen: Gyldendal, 1968), I B 1 and 2, pp. 157–78. (See the explanation of the standard system of abbreviated notation below, chapter 17, note 2.)

9. *Søren Kierkegaards Samlede Værker* [The Collected Works of Søren Kierkegaard], A. B. Drachmann, J. L. Heiberg, H. O. Lange, eds., 1st ed., vol. XIII (Copenhagen: Gyldendal, 1906), pp. 9–39.

10. P. Munch, "Embedsstanden" [The Civil Service Class], in Institute for Historie og Samfundsøkonomi, *Fra Stænder til Folk* [From Estates to People] (Copenhagen: Gyldendal, 1943), p. 13.

11. Ibid.

12. Ibid., p. 12.

5. THE PEASANT MOVEMENT TO THE LATE 1840'S

1. Skrubbeltrang, *Den danske Bonde*, p. 79.

2. Ibid., p. 100.

3. Ibid., p. 104.

4. Hans Lund, "Gaardejerne" [The Farm Owners], in *Fra Stænder til Folk*, p. 55.

5. Skovmand, *Folkestyrets Fødsel*, p. 92.

6. Ibid., p. 94.

7. See Sigurd Jensen's excellent study, *Fra Patriarkalisme til Pengeøkonomi* [From Patriarchalism to Cash Economy] (Copenhagen: Gyldendal, 1950), which deals in detail with this development. The previous paragraph in the present work is a condensation of Jensen's principal argument.

8. Skrubbeltrang, *Den danske Bonde*, chapter VI, *passim*.

9. Johannes Lehmann, ed., *Den unge Orla Lehmann* [The Young Orla Lehmann] (Copenhagen: Dansk Kautionsforsikrings-Aktieselskab, 1957), p. 65. The entire speech is contained on pp. 65–74.

10. The Danish word "Almue" has many meanings, conveying both "common people" and "peasantry," because those groups were for many centuries virtually synonymous in Denmark.

11. Skovmand, *Folkestyrets Fødsel*, p. 189.

6. THE NATIONAL QUESTION IN SOUTHERN JUTLAND

1. Skovmand, *De folkelige Bevægelser*, p. 24.

2. *Samlede Digte af Carl Ploug* [Collected Poetry of Carl Ploug], 5th ed. (Copenhagen: Forlagsbureauet i Kjøbenhavn, 1876), pp. 23–24.

3. Ibid., p. 112.

4. Erich Henrichsen, *Mændende fra 48* [The Men of '48] (Copenhagen: G. E. C. Gad, 1911), p. 123.

7. 1848 AND AFTER

1. Skovmand, *Folkestyrets Fødsel*, p. 234; see pp. 221–301 for a clear exposition of the complexities surrounding 1848–49 and the constitutional and national problems in Denmark.

2. Ibid., p. 277.

3. Ibid., p. 317.

4. Henrichsen, *Mændene fra 48*, p. 123.

5. H. J. H. Glædemark, *Kirkeforfatningsspørgsmålet i Danmark indtil 1874* [The Church Constitution Question in Denmark Until 1874], (Copenhagen: Munksgaard, 1948), p. 3.

6. Ibid., Conclusion, *passim*.

7. Monrad was a very curious personality. He was a liberal in politics but his theological position was not far from that taken by his conservative colleague Mynster. Furthermore, in his philosophical preferences he was a Hegelian, a taste which he shared with his esteemed opponent, Martensen. (See the discussion in Svend Hauge, *Studier over D. G. Monrad som religiøs Personlighed* [Studies of D. G. Monrad as a Religious Personality] (Copenhagen: G. E. C. Gad, 1944), p. 251. It was this Hegelianism which particularly seems to have been Monrad's inspiration in drafting the portions of the 1849 Constitution which dealt with the Church. The very term "People's Church" [Folkekirke] is Monrad's own invention, and in Monrad's use of it the word was meant to imply a Hegelian sense of religion's function in the life of a people. Thus, Monrad writes in his notes that "the spirit does not give its whole fullness to any single individual, but to [their] totality." This in turn makes necessary a Church, in order that the people, organically arranged, can "feel the pulse-beat of the spirit." In "pursuing its elevated

task," Monrad continued, the Church "promotes the well-being of the State" (P. G. Lindhardt, *Tiden 1849–1901* [The Period 1849–1901], vol. VII of *Den Danske Kirkes Historie* [History of the Danish Church], Hal Koch and Bjørn Kornerup, eds. (Copenhagen: Gyldendal, 1958), p. 61; see also Asger Nyholm, *Religion og Politik. En Monrad Studie* [Religion and Politics: A Study of Monrad] (Copenhagen: Nyt Nordisk Forlag / Arnold Busck, 1947), pp. 99–121. As the designer of the ingeniously vague notion of the "People's Church"—a phrase which won acclaim across the entire political spectrum, it might be noted—Monrad served in Denmark's first constitutional cabinet as the first "Kultus-minister" and was subsequently elevated to a bishopric by the arch-conservative Myns-ter, who found himself quite able to live and negotiate with the new regime, with the "People's Church," and with Monrad himself—a pliability (some might call it oppor-tunism or lack of principle) which earned Mynster the special contempt of Søren Kier-kegaard in the early 1850s.

8. Skovmand, *Folkestyrelsens Fødsel*, pp. 410–11.

9. Ibid., p. 410.

8. THE SOCIAL ORIENTATION AND INTELLECTUAL ORIGINS OF THE GOLDEN AGE

1. See the humorous, but apparently accurate sketch contained in P. M. Møller's *Statistisk Skildring af Lægdsgaard i Ølsebymagle* [Statistical Sketch of a District Official's Farm in Ølsebymagle]: "The farm has only one public library, which is arranged on a green wall cabinet in the parlor. It consists of the new evangelical hymnal, Rasmussen's *ABC*, and Birch's *Bible History*" (P. M. Møller, *Efterladte Skrifter* [Posthumous Writings], 3rd ed., vol. II (Copenhagen: Reitzel, 1856), p. 198). See also Svend Møller Kristensen, *Digteren og Samfundet* [The Poet and the Society] 2nd ed., vol. I (Copenhagen: Munks-gaard, 1965), pp. 20–22. I am indebted to Møller Kristensen's excellent study for much of the information in the first portion of the present chapter concerning the social composition of the readership of the Golden Age.

2. Møller Kristensen, *op. cit.*, pp. 20–23.

3. Ibid., p. 37.

4. Ibid., p. 25.

5. Ibid., p. 34.

6. Ibid., p. 33.

7. Ibid., pp. 58–59; cf. pp. 50–54.

8. Ibid., p. 59.

9. Trivial literature, i.e., street ballads, pietist tracts, and pot-boiler adventure nov-els, usually translations, were aimed at the lower and lower-middle classes, and sold much more widely.

10. Møller Kristensen, *op. cit.*, p. 61.

11. Ibid., pp. 61–62. The priests were virtually the only mediators of culture to the countryside and the provincial towns. Hans Christian Andersen, who grew up in the provincial town of Odense, made his first acquaintance with literature when he borrowed books from the libraries of two old women, both of them widows of pastors.

12. Henrik Steffens, *Indledning til philosophiske Forelæsninger* [Introduction to Phil-osophical Lectures] (Copenhagen: Gyldendals Trane-Klassikere, 1968), p. 5.

13. Ibid., p. 6.

14. Ibid., pp. 109–10.

15. Ibid., p. 114.

16. Ibid., p. 126.

17. H.C. Ørsted, *Aanden i Naturen* [The Spirit in Nature], 3rd ed., vol. 1 (Copenhagen: Höst, 1856), p. 141.

18. Ibid., pp. 93ff.
19. Ibid., pp. 135ff.
20. Steffens, *op. cit.*, pp. 134–35.
21. Ibid., pp. 141–42.
22. Ibid., p. 143.

9. THE "RARE FEW": ADAM OEHLENSCHLÄGER AND THE FIRST GENERATION OF THE GOLDEN AGE

1. "Guldhornene" [The Golden Horns], is reprinted in its original 1802 version in F. J. Billeskov Jansen, ed., *Den danske Lyrik, 1800–1870* [The Danish Lyric: 1800–1870], vol. I (Copenhagen: Reitzel, 1961), pp. 30–32.
2. Ibid., p. 30.
3. Ibid., p. 31.
4. Ibid.
5. Ibid.
6. Ibid., p. 32.
7. Ibid.
8. Ibid., p. 31.
9. "Hakon Jarls Død" [The Death of Hakon Jarl], in F. J. Billeskov Jansen, ed., *op. cit.*, vol. I, pp. 32–33.
10. Ibid., pp. 32, 33.
11. Ibid., p. 33.
12. The earlier version of the poem cycle is found in *Poetiske Skrifter,* I–II (Copenhagen: Schubothe, 1805), vol. I, pp. 419–80. There are at least four different versions of the poem cycle extant (not counting the German translation), and I have chosen to compare the original 1805 version, which occasioned such commotion, with a version which was published in 1846 in *Oehlenschlägers Digterværker* [Oehlenschläger's Poetical Writings], vol. 15 (Copenhagen: Høst, 1846), pp. 203–53. This latter version was probably the last which Oehlenschläger saw through the press.
13. Oehlenschläger, *Erindringer*, vol. III, p. 52.
14. Oehlenschläger, *Poetiske Skrifter* (1805), vol. I, p. 421.
15. Ibid., p. 424.
16. *Oehlenschlägers Digterværker*, vol. 15, p. 207.
17. *Poetiske Skrifter* (1805), vol. I, p. 426.
18. *Oehlenschlägers Digterværker*, vol. 15, p. 211.
19. *Poetiske Skrifter* (1805), vol. I, pp. 437 and 443–46; and *Oehlenschlägers Digterværker*, vol. 15, pp. 212 and 221–23.
20. *Poetiske Skrifter* (1805), vol. I, p. 464.
21. *Oehlenschlägers Digterværker*, vol. 15, p. 241.
22. *Poetiske Skrifter* (1805), vol. I, pp. 473 and 474; and *Oehlenschlägers Digterværker*, vol. 15, p. 247.
23. *Poetiske Skrifter* (1805), vol. I, p. 476, and *Oehlenschlägers Digterværker*, vol. 15, p. 248.
24. *Poetiske Skrifter* (1805), vol. I, p. 479.
25. *Oehlenschlägers Digterværker*, vol. 15, p. 253.
26. *Poetiske Skrifter* (1805), vol. I, pp. 456–57.
27. *Breve til og fra Adam Oehlenschläger, 1809–1829* [Letters to and From Adam Oehlenschläger, 1809–1829], Daniel Preisz, ed., vol. I (Copenhagen: Gyldendal, 1953), pp. 75–76.
28. Ibid., pp. 73–74.

29. Ibid., p. 74.

30. Ibid.

31. Ibid., p. 75.

32. Ibid., pp. 79–80.

33. Fr. Schmidt, *Dagbøger* [Diaries], cited in Møller Kristensen, *op. cit.*, vol. I, p. 142.

34. See Oehlenschläger, *Erindringer* [Memoirs], vol. II, p. 14, where Bishop Balle's objections to the Jesus-Nature poem are particularly lamented in view of Oehlenschläger's enthusiasm for the Bishop. Oehlenschläger maintains that any mistake in understanding the genuine identity of views between himself and Bishop Balle must rest upon an unfortunate misunderstanding on the Bishop's part.

35. Cited in Møller Kristensen, *op. cit.*, vol. I, p. 144 (emphasis added).

36. Oehlenschläger, *Erindringer*, vol. II, p. 121.

37. Ibid., vol. II, pp. 121–22.

38. Ibid., vol. IV, p. 285.

39. Ibid., vol. IV, p. 296.

40. *Oehlenschlägers Digterværker*, vol. 16, pp. 9–13.

41. Ibid., p. 10.

42. H.C. Ørsted, *Samlede Skrifter* [Collected Writings], vol. IX, p. 90, cited in Møller Kristensen, *op. cit.*, vol. I, p. 214.

10. PIETY AND GOOD TASTE: J. P. MYNSTER'S RELIGION AND POLITICS

1. Mynster, *Meddelelser om mit Levnet* [Communications About My Life], 2nd printing (Copenhagen: Gyldendal, 1884), p. 24. These memoirs of Mynster, written when he was in his 60's and 70's, are the principal source for much of what is known of Mynster's early life.

2. Mynster's youthful friendship with Steffens is discussed in Børge Ørsted, *J. P. Mynster og Henrich Steffens* [J. P. Mynster and Henrik Steffens], 2 vols. (Copenhagen: Nyt Nordisk Forlag-Arnold Busck, 1965).

3. *Meddelelser*, p. 153.

4. Ibid., p. 154.

5. Ibid.

6. Ibid.

7. Ibid., pp. 155–57.

8. Ibid., p. 163.

9. K. Olesen Larsen, *Søren Kierkegaard læst af K. Olesen Larsen* [Søren Kierkegaard Read by K. Olesen Larsen], vol. I, Kirkehistoriske Studier [Studies in Church History], published by the Institute for Danish Church History, 2nd Series, No. 24 (Copenhagen: G.E.C. Gad, 1966), p. 105.

10. Ibid., vol. I, p. 90.

11. Ibid., vol. I, p. 96.

12. Ibid., vol. I, p. 117.

13. Mynster, *Prædikener* [Sermons], vol. II (Copenhagen: 1815).

14. Ibid., vol. II, p. 10.

15. Ibid., vol. II, p. 11.

16. Ibid., vol. II, p. 12.

17. Ibid., vol. II, p. 288.

18. Ibid., vol. II, p. 289.

19. Ibid., vol. II, p. 290.

20. Ibid., vol. II, pp. 291–94.

21. Ibid., vol. II, p. 295.

22. Ibid., vol. II, p. 295–96.

23. Mynster, *Kirkelige Lejligheds-Taler* [Occasional Church Addresses], vol. I (Copenhagen: Reitzel, 1854), pp. 127–28.

24. Ibid., vol. I, p. 128.

25. Ibid., vol. I, p. 129.

26. Ibid., vol. I, p. 132.

27. Mynster, *Prædikener paa alle Søn- og Hellig-Dage i Aaret* [Sermons for Every Sunday and Holiday in the Year], vol. I (Copenhagen: Gyldendal, 1823), p. 79.

28. Ibid., vol. I, p. 80.

29. Ibid.

30. Ibid., vol. I, p. 81.

31. Ibid., vol. I, p. 82.

32. Mynster, *Betragtninger over de christelige Troeslærdomme* [Observations Upon the Doctrines of the Christian Faith], 3rd printing, vol. I (Copenhagen: Deichmanns, 1846), p. 311.

33. Ibid., vol. I, p. 341.

34. Ibid.

35. *Meddelelser*, p. 166.

36. Ibid.

37. *Breve fra J. P. Mynster* [Letters from J. P. Mynster] (Copenhagen: Gyldendal, 1860), p. 68 (emphasis added).

38. Ibid., p. 70.

39. *Breve til og fra Adam Oehlenschläger, 1798–1809* [Letters to and from Adam Oehlenschläger, 1798–1809], H. A. Paludan, Daniel Preisz, and Morten Borup, eds., vol. I (Copenhagen: Gyldendal, 1945), pp. 93–94.

40. Ibid., vol. I, p. 95.

41. *Breve fra Mynster*, p. 72.

42. *Af efterladte Breve til J. P. Mynster* [From Extant Letters to J. P. Mynster] (Copenhagen: Gyldendal, 1862), p. 12.

43. *Breve til og fra Oehlenschläger, 1798–1809*, vol. I, pp. 126–27.

44. Mynster, *Blandede Skrivter* [Miscellaneous Writings], vol. III (Copenhagen: Gyldendal, 1853), pp. 349–54.

45. *Af efterladte Breve til J. P. Mynster*, p. 13.

46. *Breve til og fra Oehlenschläger, 1798–1809*, vol. I, p. 147.

47. Ibid., vol. I, p. 155.

48. Ibid., vol. I, p. 171.

49. C. L. N. Mynster, ed., *Nogle Blade af J. P. Mynster's Liv og Tid* [Some Pages From J. P. Mynster's Life and Times] (Copenhagen: Gyldendal, 1875), p. 19.

50. *Breve til og fra Oehlenschläger, 1798–1809*, vol. I, p. 192.

51. Ibid., vol. II, p. 185.

52. For another discussion of this entire episode, see B. Ørsted, *J. P. Mynster og Henrich Steffens*, vol. I, pp. 332–45.

53. *Breve fra Mynster*, p. 85.

54. *Af efterladte Breve til J. P. Mynster*, p. 19 (emphasis in original).

55. Mynster, *Betragtninger*, vol. I, p. 22.

56. Mynster, *Kirkelige Lejligheds-Taler*, vol. II, p. 394.

57. Ibid., vol. II, p. 398.

58. Ibid., vol. II, p. 397.

59. Niels Munk Plum, *Jakob Peter Mynster* (Copenhagen: G. E. C. Gad, 1938), p. 93.

60. *Meddelelser*, p. 187.

61. Ibid., p. 231.

62. Ibid., pp. 231–32.
63. Ibid., pp. 236–37.
64. Ibid., p. 246.
65. Ibid., p. 249.
66. Ibid.
67. *Nogle Blade*, p. 99.
68. Ibid., p. 100.
69. Ibid.
70. Ibid., p. 99.
71. Ibid., p. 101.
72. Ibid., p. 103.
73. Ibid., p. 104.
74. Ibid., p. 105.
75. Ibid., pp. 106–107.
76. Ibid., p. 107.
77. *Kirkelige Lejligheds-Taler*, vol. I, pp. 202–12.
78. *Meddelelser*, p. 229.
79. *Kirkelige Lejligheds-Taler*, vol. I, pp. 205–206.
80. Ibid., p. 207.
81. Ibid., p. 210.
82. *Breve fra Mynster*, p. 151.
83. *Betragtninger*, vol. II, p. 260.
84. *Breve fra Mynster*, p. 151.
85. *Meddelelser*, p. 250.
86. *Nogle Blade*, p. 341.
87. See Mynster, *Blandede Skrivter*, vol. I, pp. 370ff.
88. *Meddelelser*, p. 278.
89. After his appointment to the theological faculty of the University, Martensen fulfilled the expectations which Clausen and Mynster had had of him. In the latter 1840s it became Martensen's turn to uphold the alliance of gentility and social comportment—which at times made for such strange bedfellows in church politics—by cooperating with Clausen in the exclusion from the faculty of A. G. Rudelbach, who, all agreed, was one of the most formidable Danish theologians of his time but who had unfortunately been a long-time associate of Grundtvig. See Clausen's memoirs, *Optegnelser om mit Levneds og min Tids Historie* [Notes on the History of My Life and Times] (Copenhagen: G. E. C. Gad, 1877), pp. 311–13, for Clausen's account of his successful cooperation with Martensen in this endeavor. J. C. Lindberg's extraordinary career (and much else of interest) is expertly presented in Kaj Baagø, *Magister Jacob Christian Lindberg. Studier over den grundtvigske bevægelses første kamp* [Jacob Christian Lindberg, M. A.: Studies of the Grundtvigian Movement's First Battle] (Copenhagen: G. E. C. Gad, 1958).
90. Cited in Plum, *Mynster*, p. 106.
91. *Meddelelser*, p. 239.
92. *Nogle Blade*, p. 404.
93. Collected in Mynster, *Blandede Skrivter*, vol. II, pp. 73–144.
94. Ibid., vol. II, p. 144.
95. *Meddelelser*, p. 240.
96. Ibid., p. 241.
97. Mynster, *Blandede Skrivter*, vol. II, p. 143.
98. *Meddelelser*, p. 252.
99. *Kirkelige Lejligheds-Taler*, vol. I, pp. 243–44.
100. Ibid., vol. I, pp. 297–304.

101. *Meddelelser*, p. 266.
102. Ibid.
103. Ibid., p. 267.
104. *Kirkelige Lejligheds-Taler*, vol. I, pp. 259–60.
105. *Meddelelser*, p. 243.
106. Ibid., pp. 277, 279.
107. Ibid., p. 241.
108. Ibid., p. 253.
109. *Kirkelige Lejligheds-Taler*, vol. I, p. 250.
110. Ibid., vol. I, p. 302.
111. Ibid., vol. I, pp. 256–57.
112. *Meddelelser*, p. 287.
113. Ibid.
114. Ibid.
115. Ibid., p. 289.
116. Ibid., p. 278.
117. Ibid., p. 279.
118. Ibid., pp. 249–50.
119. Ibid., p. 288.
120. Cited in Hal Koch, *Tiden 1800–1848*, p. 304.
121. *Meddelelser*, p. 279.
122. Ibid., p. 284.
123. Ibid.
124. Ibid., pp. 289–90.
125. Ibid., p. 259.
126. Ibid., p. 286.
127. Ibid., p. 291.
128. Mynster, *Blandede Skrivter*, vol. I, p. 464.
129. Mynster worked on his *Outline of Christian Dogmatics* in 1826–30, i.e., just prior to the composition of his popular *Observations*. He worked on the *Outline* again in 1850 but decided not to publish it in deference to Martensen's *Christian Dogmatics*, which had been published in 1849 and which Mynster valued very highly. Mynster's book can be found in the posthumously published volume VI of his *Blandede Skrivter*, pp. 1–400.
130. Mynster, *Blandede Skrivter*, vol. VI, pp. 311–12.
131. Ibid., vol. VI, pp. 315–16.
132. Ibid., vol. VI, p. 321.
133. Ibid., vol. VI, p. 322.
134. Ibid.
135. *Kirkelige Lejligheds-Taler*, vol. I, p. 426.
136. Ibid., vol. I, p. 425.
137. Mynster, *Prædikener holdte i Aarene 1846 til 1852* [Sermons Given in the Years 1846 to 1852], 2nd ed., vol. II (Copenhagen: Gyldendal, 1854), p. 74 (emphasis added).
138. Ibid., vol. II, pp. 17–18.

11. JOHAN LUDVIG HEIBERG

1. *Johan Ludvig Heibergs Prosaiske Skrifter* [Johan Ludvig Heiberg's Prose Writings], vol. VI (Copenhagen: Reitzel, 1861), pp. 1–112. See also Heiberg's critique of Oehlenschläger's *Væringerne i Miklagaard* [The Varangians in Constantinople] (1827) and Heiberg's *Svar paa Hr. Prof. Oehlenschlägers Skrift* [Reply to Hr. Prof. Oehlenchläger's Writing] (1828), both in *Prosaiske Skrifter*, vol. III, pp. 169–284.

2. Cf. the discussion in Paul Rubow, *Dansk litterær Kritik i det nittende Aarhundrede indtil 1870* [Danish Literary Criticism in the Nineteenth Century Until 1870] (Copenhagen: Levin & Munksgaards Forlag, 1921), chapters 3, 4, and 5.

3. Heiberg's works were performed 155 times at the Royal Theatre between 1825 and 1830; see Arthur Aumont, ed. *J. L. Heiberg og hans Slægt paa den danske Skueplads* [J. L. Heiberg and His Family on the Danish Stage], ed. (Copenhagen: Jørgensen, 1891), pp. 11–40.

4. One typical such journal was *Perseus*, which survived only from 1837 to 1838. It had only 133 people on its subscription list, but these, however, included H. N. Clausen, H. C. Ørsted, J. P. Mynster, Oehlenschläger, and Søren Kierkegaard, virtually every one of the Golden Age principals with whom we are dealing in the present work excepting Martensen, who presumably received his issue from Heiberg himself, and Grundtvig, who was too far removed from these circles even to want to follow along (see Morten Borup, *Johan Ludvig Heiberg*, vol. II (Copenhagen: Gyldendal, 1948), p. 174.

5. Cf. Hans Brix, *Fagre Ord* [Fair Speech] (Copenhagen: Gyldendals Uglebøger, 1963), pp. 156-60.

6. *Heibergs Prosaiske Skrifter*, vol. I, p. 436.

7. Ibid., vol. I, pp. 381–460.

8. Ibid., vol. I, p. 435.

9. Ibid., vol. I, p. 384.

10. Ibid., vol. I, p. 387.

11. Ibid., vol. I, pp. 388–89.

12. Ibid., vol. I, p. 390.

13. Ibid., vol. I, p. 391.

14. Ibid., vol. I, pp. 394–95.

15. Ibid., vol. I, pp. 395–97.

16. Ibid., vol. I, p. 392.

17. Ibid., vol. I, pp. 402–403.

18. Ibid., vol. I, p. 385.

19. Ibid., vol. I, pp. 408 and 414–15.

20. Ibid., vol. I, p. 400.

21. Ibid., vol. I, p. 396.

22. Ibid., vol. I, p. 420.

23. Ibid., vol. I, p. 398.

24. Ibid., vol. I, p. 412.

25. Ibid., vol. I, p. 413.

26. Ibid., vol. I, p. 409.

27. Ibid., vol. I, p. 407.

28. Ibid., vol. I, pp. 416–17.

29. Ibid., vol. I, p. 392.

30. Ibid., vol. I, p. 391.

31. Ibid., vol. I, p. 421.

32. *Johan Ludvig Heibergs Poetiske Skrifter* [Johan Ludvig Heiberg's Poetical Writings], vol. IX (Copenhagen: Reitzel, 1862), pp. 109–18.

33. Cited in Borup, *Heiberg*, vol. II, p. 192.

34. *Heibergs Poetiske Skrifter*, vol. IX, p. 109.

35. Ibid., vol. IX, p. 118.

36. Ibid., vol. X, pp. 163–324.

37. Brix, *Fagre Ord*, p. 178.

38. H. L. Martensen, "Nye Digte af J. L. Heiberg" [New Poems by J. L. Heiberg] (review), *Fædrelandet* [The Fatherland], nr. 398–400 (January 10–12, 1841).

39. *Heibergs Poetiske Skrifter*, vol. X, p. 170.

40. Ibid., vol. X, p. 172.
41. Ibid., vol. X, p. 173.
42. Ibid., vol. X, p. 174.
43. Ibid., vol. X, p. 175.
44. Ibid.
45. Ibid., vol. X, p. 176.
46. Ibid., vol. X, pp. 176–77.
47. Ibid., vol. X, p. 177.
48. Ibid., vol. X, p. 178.
49. Ibid., vol. X, pp. 178–79.
50. Ibid., vol. X, pp. 180–81.
51. Ibid., vol. X, p. 181.
52. See Brix, *Fagre Ord*, p. 182.
53. *Heibergs Poetiske Skrifter*, vol. X, p. 319.
54. Ibid.
55. Ibid., vol. X, p. 320.
56. Ibid., vol. X, pp. 322–23.
57. Ibid., vol. X, p. 324.
58. Borup, *Heiberg*, vol. II, p. 185.
59. *Heibergs Poetiske Skrifter*, vol. X, p. 185.
60. Ibid., vol. X, pp. 188–89.
61. Ibid., vol. X, p. 195.
62. Ibid., vol. X, p. 205.
63. Ibid., vol. X, p. 206.
64. Ibid., vol. X, p. 217.
65. The Danish word for "fundament" is *Grund,* which also means "reason."
66. *Heibergs Poetiske Skrifter*, vol. X, p. 219.
67. Ibid., vol. X, p. 221.
68. Ibid., vol. X, p. 239.
69. Ibid.
70. Ibid., vol. X, pp. 240–41.
71. Ibid., vol. X, p. 242.
72. Ibid., vol. X, pp. 242–43.
73. Ibid., vol. X, p. 244.
74. Ibid., vol. X, p. 262.
75. Ibid., vol. X, p. 263.
76. Ibid.
77. Ibid., vol. VIII, pp. 147–264.
78. Ibid., vol. VIII, p. 178.
79. Ibid., vol. VIII, pp. 177–82.
80. Ibid., vol. VIII, p. 186.
81. Ibid., vol. VIII, p. 188.
82. Ibid., vol. VIII, pp. 182–83.
83. *Heibergs Prosaiske Skrifter*, vol. VI, pp. 171–260.
84. Ibid., vol. VI, p. 195.
85. Ibid.
86. Ibid., vol. VI, p. 200.
87. Ibid., vol. IV, pp. 378–402.
88. Ibid., vol. IV, pp. 401–402.
89. Ibid., vol. IV, p. 402.
90. Ibid., vol. VI, pp. 263–83.
91. Ibid., vol. X, pp. 328–49.

92. Ibid., vol. V, pp. 93–132.
93. Ibid., vol. VI, p. 265.
94. Ibid., vol. VI, p. 266.
95. Ibid., vol. VI, p. 265.
96. Ibid., vol. VI, p. 276.
97. Ibid., vol. IV, pp. 416–59.
98. Ibid., vol. IV, p. 422.
99. Ibid., vol. IV, p. 423 (emphasis added).
100. Ibid., vol. VI, p. 270.
101. Ibid., vol. VI, p. 271.
102. Ibid., vol. X, pp. 338–39.
103. Ibid., vol. X, p. 340. Rather perversely, Heiberg attempts to apply this anti-liberal, statist doctrine to French politics, claiming that it was just such an excess of atomism and lack of state authority which characterized the Terror, whereas the relative absence of atomistic and individualistic tendencies and the presence of an overarching notion of state authority is said to explain the comparatively better political constellation which characterized the July 1830 Revolution! See *Heibergs Prosaiske Skrifter*, vol. VI, p. 272.
104. *Heibergs Prosaiske Skrifter*, vol. X, p. 328.
105. Ibid., vol. VI, p. 269.
106. Ibid., vol. X, pp. 336–37.
107. Ibid., vol. VI, pp. 269–70.
108. Ibid., vol. X, pp. 329–30.
109. Ibid., vol. X, p. 332.
110. Ibid., vol. X, p. 333.
111. Ibid., vol. X, p. 329.
112. Ibid., vol. X, pp. 334–35.
113. Ibid., vol. X, p. 335.
114. Ibid., vol. VI, p. 266.
115. Ibid., vol. X, p. 336.
116. Ibid., vol. X, p. 337.
117. Ibid., vol. X, p. 340.
118. Ibid., vol. X, pp. 343–44.
119. Ibid., vol. VI, p. 267.
120. Ibid., vol. VI, p. 278. Heiberg does not fail to include the Hegelian theodicy's favorite escape clause. In this period, Heiberg writes, the dissolution of the people into the public takes place with increasing briskness, which would lead to very dark prospects indeed if we could not rely upon that which "Hegel has fittingly called 'the cunning of Reason,' " which will ensure that "even the present struggle against the Idea paves the way for its [the Idea's] advance" (*Heibergs Prosaiske Skrifter*, vol. X, p. 345). However, such cosmic optimism as idealism provides must not be used in vain; it must not make us complacent in our tasks of working upon ourselves and combatting the "politicizing public," because, as Heiberg explains, "Reason prefers to work honestly and only uses cunning in emergencies" (ibid.).
121. *Heibergs Prosaiske Skrifter*, vol. X, p. 344.
122. Ibid., vol. V, p. 99.
123. Ibid.
124. Ibid., vol. V, p. 100.
125. *Heibergs Poetiske Skrifter*, vol. VIII, pp. 212–13.
126. *Heibergs Prosaiske Skrifter*, vol. V, pp. 97–98.
127. Ibid., vol. V, p. 98.
128. Ibid., vol. V, p. 101.

129. *Heibergs Poetiske Skrifter*, vol. VIII, pp. 204–18.
130. Ibid., vol. VIII, p. 205.
131. Ibid., vol. VIII, p. 217.

12. H. L. MARTENSEN

1. Martensen, *Af mit Levnet* [From My Life], vol. I (Copenhagen: Gyldendal, 1882), p. 95.
2. Ibid., vol. I, p. 99.
3. Ibid., vol. I, pp. 101–104.
4. Ibid.
5. Ibid., vol. I, pp. 105–106.
6. See the discussion in Hal Koch, *Tiden 1800–1848*.
7. Skat Arildsen, *H. L. Martensen: hans Liv, Udvikling, og Arbejde* [H. L. Martensen: His Life, Development, and Work] (Copenhagen: G. E. C. Gad, 1932), pp. 197–201.
8. *Af mit Levnet*, vol. II, pp. 4–6.
9. Cited in Arildsen, *H. L. Martensen*, p. 200.
10. Martensen, *Grundrids til Moralphilosophiens System* [Outline of the System of Moral Philosophy], 2nd printing (Copenhagen: Reitzel, 1864), p. iii (not numbered).
11. Ibid., p. 1.
12. Ibid., pp. 41–42.
13. Ibid., pp. 2–3.
14. Ibid., p. 3.
15. Ibid., p. 2.
16. Ibid., p. 3.
17. Ibid., p. 22.
18. Ibid., p. 41.
19. Ibid., p. 4.
20. Ibid., p. 74.
21. Ibid., p. 75.
22. Ibid., pp. 75–76.
23. Ibid., p. 74.
24. Ibid., p. 76.
25. Ibid.
26. Ibid.
27. Ibid., p. 77.
28. *Af Mit Levnet*, vol. II, p. 3.
29. See the discussion in Arildsen, *H. L. Martensen*, p. 242.
30. Ibid., p. 225.
31. Martensen, *Den christelige Dogmatik* [Christian Dogmatics], 4th printing (Copenhagen: Reitzel, 1883), pp. iii–iv.
32. Ibid., p. 84.
33. Ibid., pp. 84–85.
34. Ibid., pp. iv–v.
35. Ibid., p. v.
36. Ibid., p. vi.
37. Ibid., p. 5.
38. Ibid., p. 3.
39. Ibid.
40. Ibid., p. 6.
41. Ibid., p. 5.

42. Ibid., pp. 66–67.

43. Ibid., p. 7.

44. Ibid.

45. Ibid., p. 28.

46. Arildsen, *H. L. Martensen*, p. 226 (emphasis added).

47. *Den christelige Dogmatik*, pp. 71–72.

48. Ibid., p. 91.

49. Ibid.

50. Ibid., p. 89.

51. Ibid., pp. 68–69.

52. Ibid., p. 82.

53. Ibid., pp. 15–16.

54. Ibid., p. 16.

55. Ibid., p. 19.

56. Ibid., p. 21.

57. Ibid., p. 259.

58. Ibid., p. 268.

59. Ibid., p. 266.

60. Ibid., p. 455.

61. Ibid., p. 86.

62. Ibid., p. 88.

63. Ibid., p. 95.

64. Martensen, *Lejlighedstaler* [Occasional Addresses] (Copenhagen: Gyldendal, 1884), p. 39.

65. *Den christelige Dogmatik*, p. 9.

66. Ibid., pp. 214–15.

67. Ibid., p. 454.

68. *Af mit Levnet*, vol. II, p. 5.

69. Ibid., vol. II, p. 6.

70. Ibid., vol. II, pp. 4–5.

71. Ibid., vol. II, p. 6.

72. Ibid., vol. II, pp. 26–27.

73. Ibid., vol. II, p. 24.

74. *Breve og Aktstykker vedrørende Johan Ludvig Heiberg* [Letters and Documents Concerning Johan Ludvig Heiberg], Morten Borup, ed., vol. II (Copenhagen: Gyldendal, 1948), p. 298.

75. *Af mit Levnet*, vol. II, p. 41.

76. Ibid., vol. II, p. 43.

77. Ibid., vol. II, pp. 44–45.

78. *Lejlighedstaler*, p. 404.

79. Ibid., p. 406.

80. Ibid., p. 403.

81. Ibid., pp. 406–407.

82. Martensen tells us in his memoirs that although Ørsted had started out as a Kantian adherent of a merely rational moral religion, he had "more and more devoted himself to Mynster," until "his moral view . . . was transfigured into the Christian view of Providence" (*Af mit Levnet*, vol. III, pp. 10–11). As we have seen in chapter 10, Mynster's "providential" religion was sufficiently flexible to enable the officially Christian culture of the Golden Age to claim A. S. Ørsted, one of its most illustrious sons, for the Church.

83. *Lejlighedstaler*, pp. 392–93.

84. Ibid., p. 400.

85. *Af mit Levnet*, vol. II, p. 70.

86. Ibid., vol. II, p. 74.

87. Ibid., vol. II, p. 75.

88. Ibid., vol. II, p. 8.

89. Ibid., vol. II, pp. 77 and 81.

90. Ibid., vol. II, pp. 71–72.

91. Ibid., vol. II, p. 72.

92. Ibid., vol. II, p. 90.

93. Cited in Carl S. Petersen and Vilhelm Andersen, *Illustreret dansk Litteraturhistorie* [Illustrated History of Danish Literature], vol. III (Copenhagen: Gyldendal, 1921), p. 563.

94. *Af mit Levnet*, vol. II, p. 10.

95. Ibid., vol. II, p. 94.

96. Ibid., vol. II, p. 96.

97. Ibid., vol. II, p. 75.

98. Ibid., vol. II, pp. 83–84.

99. Ibid., vol. II, p. 82.

100. Bjørn Kornerup, ed., *Biskop H. Martensens Breve* [Bishop Martensen's Letters], published by the Society for Danish Church History, vol. I, *Breve til Gude, 1848–1859* [Letters to Gude, 1848–1859] (Copenhagen: G. E. C. Gad, 1955), pp. 12–13.

101. Ibid., vol. I, p. 35.

102. Ibid.

103. Ibid., vol. I, p. 36.

104. Ibid., vol. I, p. 37.

105. Ibid., vol. I, p. 36.

106. Ibid., vol. I, p. 38.

107. Ibid.

108. Ibid., vol. I, p. 35.

109. Ibid., vol. I, p. 37.

110. Ibid.

111. *Af mit Levnet*, vol. III, p. 1.

112. Martensen, *Prædikener* [Sermons], 4th collection (Copenhagen: Reitzel, 1854), pp. 225–38.

113. Ibid., pp. 231 and 235.

114. *Biskop H. Martensens Breve*, vol. I, pp. 45–46.

115. Ibid., vol. I, p. 111.

116. *Af mit Levnet*, vol. III, p. 140.

117. Ibid., vol. III, p. 144.

118. Ibid., vol. III, p. 143.

119. Ibid., vol. II, p. 86.

120. Ibid., vol. II, p. 96.

121. Ibid., vol. II, p. 94.

122. Ibid., vol. II, pp. 106–107.

123. Ibid., vol. II, p. 120.

124. Ibid., vol. II, p. 121.

125. Ibid., vol. II, p. 122.

126. *Den christelige Dogmatik*, p. vi.

127. *Af mit Levnet*, vol. II, p. 124.

128. Ibid., vol. II, p. 125.

129. Ibid., vol II, p. 107. Martensen's criticisms of the merely negative content of liberal individualism eventually led him in the direction of Christian socialism. He noted that the events of 1848 showed that "this strange revolution was not only political, but

social," involving at its core "the fourth estate." "The social problem is the question of rich and poor, of labor and capital, of the needs of society, and of a more equal and just distribution of life's earthly goods" (*Af mit Levnet,* vol. II, p. 127). Within its womb the liberal revolution of 1848 also bore *"an antithesis to liberalism,* which, when it is revealed, must lead to struggle, for liberalism wants individualism, [and] socialism wants society and solidarity" (ibid.). Martensen continues in this vein, noting that "our present social culture is to be compared not to a tree, which spreads its branches on every side, but to a pyramid, at whose narrow top only a few of the favored are to be found, while its broad base is formed by a swarm of people who possess nothing and who suffer, who are left entirely on their own and are therefore ready for every sort of self-help. . . . [T]his can be helped neither by charitable nor police measures, but only by *statecraft"* (ibid., vol. II, pp. 129–30). "From this time forth, the social problem continues as a sort of undercurrent in society. . . . [E]very time it begins its progress, liberalism puts up a fantastic resistance, because liberalism does not wish to allow itself to be deprived of its mastery over capital, its free competition, its stock market speculations and swindles, etc. It is being increasingly confirmed that liberalism will dissolve society into sheer individuals [Enkelte] with their individual interests, which for many are mere pecuniary interests. Socialism, when it is understood according to its true meaning, wishes to hold society together in solidarity, to subordinate the individual to society. . . . With us, however much we have changed ministries, and however much we talk about men of the Right and men of the Left, everything goes on in the old uniformity of liberalism, and they know and understand nothing which does not appear in the worn-out categories of liberalism. Perhaps a new revolution, a new 1848, is needed to bring people to understand what they cannot learn upon reflection. Time will show whether we have the right to say: When the new 1848 dawns, when liberalism and socialism battle one another in full consciousness, then a new era will break forth in world history, and society will cloak itself in a new form" (ibid., vol. II, pp. 128–31). Thus, in the 1870s and 1880s the conservative Martensen emerged as a pioneer of Christian socialism, basing his new position on his old statist and anti-liberal arguments, namely the moral value of the community, the need for authority, and the immoral chaos of social individualism.

It is interesting to note that in his *Den christelige Ethik* [Christian Ethics], 2nd printing, vol. III, *Den almindelige Deel* [The General Section] (Copenhagen: Gyldendal, 1871), pp. 275–300, the aging Martensen made another extensive socialist and communitarian argument, of which the arch-individualist villain was Søren Kierkegaard. Martensen, apparently, saw the thesis of the present work as clearly as I do, namely that the "conservative" Søren Kierkegaard is a 20th-century fiction: SK was the enemy of Martensen, because he was a liberal!

It is also interesting to note that Martensen was not the only Golden Age mainstream luminary to espouse the "social" side of 1848 in opposition to its "liberal" side. In the spring of 1848 Adam Oehlenschläger wrote: "Here in the city the officials smile a bit at the promise 'to find work for workers,' which they regard as impossible. But it seems to me that when people *can* work, and *want to* work, and cannot *live* without work, and yet cannot *get* work, then the arrangements of the state have made them into legitimate pillagers and rebels" (*Erindringer,* vol. IV, p. 285). We should note, however, that Oehlenschläger's "socialist" opinions remained private sentiments and that the sympathy Martensen proclaimed in his 1883 memoirs for the masses whom the 1848 liberals abused did not find expression at the time in anything other than righteous horror at the liberals for having unleashed such a monster and for having raised such unsatisfiable expectations.

130. *Af mit Levnet,* vol. II, p. 126.
131. Ibid., vol. III, p. 110.
132. Ibid., vol. II, p. 31.

133. *Biskop H. Martensens Breve*, vol. I, p. 120.
134. *Af mit Levnet*, vol. II, pp. 108–109.
135. Ibid., vol. II, p. 132.
136. Ibid., vol. III, p. 133.
137. Ibid.
138. Ibid., vol. III, pp. 98–99.
139. Ibid., vol. III, p. 100.

13. N. F. S. GRUNDTVIG AND HISTORY'S FLOCK: NATIONAL POPULAR CULTURE IN THE SERVICE OF RELIGION

1. N. F. S. Grundtvig, *Udvalgte Digte* [Selected Poems], Introduction and Notes by Steen Johansen (Copenhagen: Reitzel, 1963), pp. 9–11.
2. Ibid., pp. 10–11.
3. N. F. S. Grundtvig, *Værker i Udvalg* [Selected Works], Georg Christensen and Hal Koch, eds., vol. I (Copenhagen: Gyldendal, 1940), pp. 140–47.
4. Ibid., vol. I, p. 147.
5. Ibid., vol. I, pp. 250–60.
6. Ibid., vol. I, pp. 259–60.
7. Ibid., vol. I, p. 255.
8. Ibid., vol. I, p. 257.
9. Ibid., vol. I, p. 331.
10. Ibid., vol. VII, p. 367.
11. Ibid., vol. I, pp. 309–11.
12. Ibid., vol. I, p. 310.
13. Ibid.
14. Ibid., vol. I, pp. 310–11.
15. In both the absolutist and the liberal phases of his political development, Grundtvig shunned the urban elitist stance which corresponded to his own changing position; thus, in his first phase he avoided the aristocratic absolutism of Mynster or Heiberg, whereas in his second phase he avoided the elitist sort of liberalism typified by Clausen.
16. Grundtvig, *Værker i Udvalg*, vol. I, pp. 335–480.
17. H. C. Ørsted's reply to Grundtvig's Chronicle was entitled "Imod den store Anklager" [Against the Great Accuser], and Grundtvig's polemical rebuttal of Ørsted's piece was entitled "Imod den lille Anklager" [Against the Little Accuser]. This should serve to indicate the bitter tone of the disagreement which severed Grundtvig's relations with the leading cultural circles of the Golden Age.
18. Grundtvig, *Værker i Udvalg*, vol. II, pp. 241–71.
19. Ibid., vol. II, p. 246.
20. Ibid., vol. II, p. 271.
21. Ibid., vol. II, p. 254.
22. Ibid., vol. II, p. 243.
23. Ibid., vol. II, p. 246.
24. Ibid., vol. II, p. 264.
25. Ibid.
26. Ibid., vol. II, p. 267.
27. Ibid., vol. II, p. 269.
28. Ibid., vol. II, p. 270.
29. Ibid., vol. VII, pp. 188–93.
30. Ibid., vol. VII, p. 188.

31. Ibid., vol. VII, pp. 194–96.
32. Ibid., vol. VII, p. 195.
33. Ibid., vol. VII, p. 193.
34. Ibid., vol. VII, pp. 174–87.
35. Ibid., vol. VII, p. 177.
36. Ibid., vol. VII, p. 185.
37. Ibid., vol. VII, p. 179.
38. Ibid., vol. VII, p. 183.
39. Ibid., vol. II, pp. 24–50.
40. Ibid., vol. II, p. 31.
41. Ibid.
42. Ibid., vol. II, p. 32.
43. Ibid., vol. II, p. 34 (emphasis added).
44. Ibid., vol. II, p. 35.
45. Ibid.
46. Ibid., vol. II, p. 38.
47. Ibid., vol. II, p. 36.
48. Ibid., vol. II, p. 38.
49. Ibid., vol. II, p. 43 (emphasis added).
50. Ibid., vol. II, p. 44.
51. Ibid., vol. II, pp. 51–92.
52. Ibid., vol. VII, pp. 289–313.
53. Ibid., vol. VII, p. 290.
54. Ibid., vol. VII, p. 291.
55. Ibid., vol. VII, pp. 289–91.
56. Ibid., vol. VII, p. 313.
57. Ibid., vol. VII, p. 370.
58. Ibid., vol. VII, pp. 366–480. The quoted phrase appears on pp. 366 and 373.
59. Ibid., vol. VII, p. 372.
60. Ibid., vol. VII, p. 373.
61. Ibid., vol. VII, p. 375.
62. Ibid., vol. VII, p. 374.
63. Ibid., vol. VII, p. 373.
64. H. N. Clausen, *Catholicismens og Protestantismens Kirkeforfatning, Lære og Ritus* [Catholicism and Protestantism: Their Church Constitutions, Doctrines, and Rites] (Copenhagen: Andreas Seidelin, 1825.
65. Ibid., p. 309.
66. Ibid., p. 323 (emphasis in original).
67. Grundtvig, *Værker i Udvalg*, vol. II, pp. 317–49.
68. Ibid., vol. II, p. 340.
69. Ibid., vol. II, p. 318.
70. Ibid., vol. II, p. 334.
71. Ibid., vol. II, p. 317.
72. Ibid., vol. II, p. 318.
73. Ibid., vol. II, p. 320.
74. Ibid., vol. II, p. 330.
75. Ibid., vol. II, p. 326.
76. Ibid., vol. II, p. 341.
77. Ibid., vol. II, p. 337.
78. Ibid., vol. II, p. 336.
79. Ibid., vol. II, p. 337.
80. Ibid., vol. II, p. 336.

81. That Jesus actually spoke the exact words of the Apostles' Creed is not stated directly in the 1825 *Reply*, but in the years which followed, Grundtvig insisted that the fact that the Creed was directly inspired by Jesus was "about certain" (*Kirkelige Oplysninger* [Churchly Information], in *Værker i Udvalg*, vol. III, p. 438). In any event, Grundtvig attributes a directly divine origin and a much earlier date to the Apostles' Creed than scholarship has been able to establish.

82. *Værker i Udvalg*, vol. III, pp. 359–447.

83. Ibid., vol. VI, pp. 1–273.

84. Ibid., vol. III, pp. 367–68.

85. Ibid., vol. III, p. 440.

86. Ibid., vol. III, pp. 219–93.

87. Ibid., vol. III, pp. 313–58.

88. Ibid., vol. III, p. 318.

89. Ibid., vol. III, p. 316.

90. Ibid., vol. V, pp. 378–94.

91. Ibid., vol. V, p. 379.

92. Ibid., vol. V, p. 380.

93. Ibid., vol. V, p. 386.

94. Ibid., vol. V, p. 389.

95. Ibid., vol. V, p. 393.

96. Ibid., vol. V, p. 394.

97. Although he had been impressed with Grundtvig's daring in the 1820s, Søren Kierkegaard lost respect for Grundtvig when the latter allowed himself to be bought off with moderate concessions in the 1830s. Kierkegaard came to regard Grundtvig as a master of bluff and theatrics who was vehement in his criticism but at the same time very careful to look out for his own interests and to feather his nest within the State Church. See the excellent discussion of this in P. G. Lindhardt's volume VII of *Den Danske Kirkes Historie*, entitled *Tiden 1849–1901* and in Lindhardt's *Vækkelser*, chapter II, part 2.

98. Mynster, *Meddelelser*, p. 270.

99. Grundtvig, *Værker i Udvalg*, vol. VI, pp. 274–390.

100. The curious reader may want to know that the first five congregations were the Hebrew, Greek, Latin, Anglo-Saxon, and German congregations; the seventh, Grundtvig wagers "ten to one," will be India! (*Værker i Udvalg*, vol. VI, p. 381).

101. Grundtvig, *Værker i Udvalg*, vol. VI, pp. 283–84.

102. Ibid., vol. VI, pp. 337–38.

103. Ibid., vol. VI, p. 354.

104. Ibid., vol. VI, p. 352.

105. Ibid., vol. VI, p. 349.

106. Ibid., vol. VI, p. 347.

107. Ibid., vol. IV, pp. 1–126.

108. Ibid., vol. IV, pp. 8–10.

109. Ibid., vol. IV, pp. 140–44.

110. Ibid., vol. IV, p. 140.

111. Ibid., vol. IV, p. 143.

112. Ibid., vol. IV, p. 144.

113. Ibid., vol. IV, pp. 149–65.

114. Ibid., vol. IV, p. 151.

115. Ibid., vol. IV, p. 154.

116. Ibid., vol. IV, p. 158.

117. Ibid., vol. IV, p. 159.

118. Ibid., vol. IV, pp. 164–65.

119. Ibid., vol. VIII, pp. 123–25.
120. Ibid., vol. VIII, pp. 123–24.
121. From "The King and the People," ibid., vol. VIII, p. 151.
122. Ibid., vol. VIII, p. 152.
123. From "Farewell to King Frederik," ibid., vol. VIII, p. 159.
124. Ibid., vol. VIII, pp. 149–50.
125. Ibid., vol. VIII, pp. 113–15.
126. Ibid.
127. Ibid., vol. V, pp. 243–51.
128. Ibid., vol. V, p. 244.
129. Ibid.
130. Ibid., vol. V, pp. 245–46.
131. Ibid., vol. V, p. 246.
132. Ibid.
133. Ibid., vol. V, p. 247.
134. Ibid.
135. Ibid., vol. V, p. 248.
136. Ibid.
137. Ibid., vol. V, pp. 248–49.
138. Ibid., vol. V, pp. 250–51.
139. Ibid., vol. V, pp. 278–85.
140. Ibid., vol. V, pp. 279–80.
141. Ibid., vol. V, p. 283.
142. Ibid.
143. Ibid.
144. Ibid., vol. V, p. 285.
145. Ibid., vol. V, pp. 280–81.
146. Ibid., vol. V, p. 281.
147. For a full and excellent discussion of this, see P. G. Lindhardt, *Vækkelser*, chapters II and III.
148. Grundtvig, *Værker i Udvalg*, vol. V, pp. 295–300.
149. Ibid., vol. V, p. 297.
150. Ibid., vol. V, p. 298.
151. Ibid.
152. Ibid., vol. V, p. 299.
153. Ibid., vol. V, pp. 299–300.
154. Ibid., vol. V, p. 300.
155. Ibid., vol. V, pp. 369–78.
156. Ibid., vol. V, p. 371.
157. Ibid., vol. V, p. 372.
158. Ibid., vol. V, p. 373.
159. Ibid.
160. Ibid., vol. V, p. 374.
161. Ibid.
162. Ibid., vol. V, pp. 377–78.
163. Ibid., vol. V, p. 375.
164. Ibid.
165. Ibid.

14. H. N. CLAUSEN AND ORLA LEHMANN: THE LIBERAL ALTERNATIVE TO THE GOLDEN AGE MAINSTREAM

1. H. N. Clausen, *Optegnelser om mits Levneds og min Tids Historie*, p. 340.

2. Ibid. It does not seem to have occurred to Clausen that such a rural activist would doubtless have incurred the wrath of the local constabulary and could easily have been arrested for purposes of harassment on trumped-up charges, precisely in order to provide the basis for an attack upon his reputation.

3. Clausen, *Optegnelser*, p. 341.

4. Quoted in Clausen, *op. cit.*, p. 341.

5. Ibid., pp. 340–41.

6. Emil Aarestrup, *Digte* [Poems], Hans Brix, ed. (Copenhagen: G. E. C. Gad, 1930), p. 208.

7. See the discussion in Lindhardt, *Vækkelser*, chapter III, part 2. We also ought to note the irony of Grundtvig being elected to represent rural Præstø against the elitist "learned gentlemen" of the capital. Grundtvig himself had served in Præstø as his first parish in 1821–22, and the reason that his stay in Præstø had been so brief was that what young Grundtvig had really wanted in 1821 was a Copenhagen parish. Thus, as soon as the parish of Our Savior became available to him, Grundtvig left his rural Præstø congregation and set out for the capital! Grundtvig's election in place of Hans Hansen and H. N. Clausen was scarcely a victory of country over city.

8. Quoted in P. Munch, "Embedsstanden," in *Fra Stænder til Folk*, pp. 16–17.

9. Ibid., and Lindhardt, *Vækkelser*, p. 54 (emphasis added on last word).

16. SØREN KIERKEGAARD: LIFE AND LITERARY CAREER TO FEBRUARY 1846

1. The method of the present work is nonbiographical, because I feel that the biographical approach to understanding SK's writings has been seriously overworked, contributing to what Howard Hong has labelled the recurrent "genetic fallacy" in the interpretation of SK's work. (Hong's remarks were made at a meeting of the Søren Kierkegaard Society in Copenhagen in 1973.) Rather, the present work studies the historically specifiable forces working in SK's environment and in particular the various religious and political-cultural alternatives which he could choose or reject. The aim of the present work is thus not that of the psychologizing biographer who wishes to penetrate the motives and the moment of SK's choices themselves. On the contrary, the plan of this study is first to depict carefully the most important historical materials available to SK, which has been done in part one, and then to give a detailed examination of SK's result, his choices, his religious and political alternative to official Christian society. Thus, my intent is to avoid psychological reductionism or the hagiographic accumulation of the details of SK's personal life, details that are meaningless unless one means to fit them into an overall "explanation" of the relation between SK's private life and his remarkable, public literary career. It is not my intent to provide such an "explanation"; rather, it is my contention that such "explanations" are in principle elusive and unattainable, and even if they were not so, are of no real use.

In view of the above position, and in view of the overwhelming (and unproductive) biographical bias of much SK research, my biographical account of SK will be brief and will focus on historically specifiable influences rather than on events—or surmises about events—in SK's private life. The popular and widely-read English language SK biographies by Walter Lowrie, *Kierkegaard* (Oxford: Oxford University Press, 1938 [2nd ed. Harper Torchbooks, 1962]) and *A Short Life of Kierkegaard* (Princeton: Princeton University Press, 1942 [2nd ed., 1965]), lean very heavily upon the ingenious but unproven work of P. A. Heiberg, *Søren Kierkegaards religiøse Udvikling: Psykologisk Mikroskopi* [Søren Kierkegaard's Religious Development: Psychological Microscopy] (Copenhagen: Gyldendal, 1925) and Frithiof Brandt's clever but discredited historical sleuthing, *Den unge Søren Kierkegaard* [The Young Søren Kierkegaard] (Copenhagen: Levin & Munksgaard, 1929). Lowrie's biographies and the heavily biographical introductions and critical apparatus which he supplied for his numerous English translations have been very influential in shaping the reception accorded SK in the English-speaking world, and in the present writer's view this influence has been unfortunate. The insoluble riddle of SK's personal life—including such matters as his relationship to his father, his possible youthful visit to a bordello, and his broken engagement to Regine Olsen—has consistently made its unnecessary presence felt in the understanding of his works. (The English-speaking world is of course heavily indebted to Lowrie for his extensive and pioneering work as a translator of SK. Much of the broad interest in SK worldwide was stimulated by Lowrie's labors. My criticism of the biographical approach pursued by Lowrie and others is not meant to detract in the least from my gratitude for Lowrie's work as a translator and as a promoter of the study of SK's work.)

The best biographical work which opposes this trend is the excellent work of Sejer Kühle, who successfully dismantled Frithiof Brandt's fictions and went on to write the definitive work on Kierkegaard's early years, *Søren Kierkegaards Barndom og Ungdom* [Søren Kierkegaard's Childhood and Youth] (Copenhagen: Aschehoug, 1950). Also very valuable is the work of Jørgen Bukdahl, *Søren Kierkegaard, hans Fader og Slægten i Sædding* [Søren Kierkegaard, His Father, and the Family in Sædding] (Ribe: Dansk Hjemstavns Forlag, 1960) and the provocative *Søren Kierkegaard og den menige Mand* [Søren Kierkegaard and the Common Man] (Copenhagen: Gyldendals Uglebøger, 1970), which has been particularly useful in the present work. Among the almost unbelievable myriad of other biographical SK studies, Carl Weltzer's *Peter og Søren Kierkegaard* [Peter and Søren Kierkegaard], 2 vols. (Copenhagen: G. E. C. Gad, 1936) deserves special mention as a storehouse of biographical information and documents, as do the various perceptive pieces by K. Olesen Larsen which have been collected in *Søren Kierkegaard Læst af K. Olesen Larsen* [Søren Kierkegaard Read by K. Olesen Larsen], 2 vols. (Copenhagen: G. E. C. Gad, 1966), and the various articles and introductory essays by the great Danish Church historian P. G. Lindhardt, whose Kierkegaard-related work includes *Konfrontation* [Confrontation] (Copenhagen: Akademisk Forlag, 1974). All of these biographical works have been very useful in preparing the present study, and I remain indebted to them.

2. On the fortune which SK inherited from his father, see Frithiof Brandt and Else Rammel, *Søren Kierkegaard og Pengene* [Søren Kierkegaard and Money] (Copenhagen: Levin & Munksgaard, 1935).

3. *Søren Kierkegaards Papirer*, V A 3. (See explanation of abbreviated reference system, chapter 17, note 2.)

4. The student address is reprinted in *Søren Kierkegaards Papirer* I B 1–2.

5. *Søren Kierkegaards Samlede Værker*, vol. XIII, pp. 9–39. These three political articles, which SK acknowledged as his own in signing the third of them, were not in fact his first appearance in print, for he had published a satirical, anonymous letter in December 1834.

6. Ibid., vol. XIII, pp. 41–92.

7. Ibid., vol. XIII, pp. 93–393.

8. Ibid., vols. I and II.

9. Ibid., vol. III, pp. 169–264.

10. Ibid., vol. III, pp. 53–168.

11. Ibid., vol. IV, pp. 273–428.

12. Kresten Nordentoft, a leading scholar in this area, was of this opinion; see his *Kierkegaard's Psychology*, trans. B. H. Kirmmse (Pittsburgh: Duquesne University Press, 1978), *passim*.

13. *Kierkegaards Samlede Værker*, vol. XI, pp. 111–241.

14. Ibid., vol. IV, pp. 171–272.

15. Ibid., vol. VI.

16. Ibid., vol. VII.

17. Ibid., vol. VII, p. 131.

18. Ibid., vol. VII, p. 192.

19. Ibid., vol. VII, p. 332.

20. Ibid., vol. VII, p. 252.

17. A LITERARY REVIEW

1. *Kierkegaards Samlede Værker*, vol. VIII, pp. 1–105. Because each of the remaining chapters of the present work usually deals in detail with a single work by SK, and because the many references would make for great inconvenience if they were put in the form of notes, a simplified form of reference will be incorporated within the text itself. The first reference to or quotation from the work under discussion will be followed by a note in brackets which reads "SV," for *Søren Kierkegaards Samlede Værker*, followed by the roman numeral of the volume number, and then by the page or pages under discussion. Thus, the above note would appear incorporated in the text of the present work as [SV VIII, pp. 1–105]. All later references in any given chapter to the SK book under discussion will also be noted in square bracket form, but "SV" and the volume number will be omitted as unnecessary. Thus, a subsequent reference, in this same chapter, to SK's *A Literary Review* will merely read [p. 68], i.e., the material in question is to be found in *Kierkegaards Samlede Værker*, vol. VIII, p. 68. The few instances in which more than one SK work is discussed in detail in the same chapter (chapters 25–27) will not disturb this system of reference because in each of those instances the closely-related works under discussion are all to be found in the same volume of the *Samlede Værker*. Any reference to a work of SK's which is not under detailed discussion in a given chapter will be noted separately in the normal fashion.

2. References to *Søren Kierkegaards Papirer* will be given in square brackets in the text in accordance with the standard abbreviation, in which "Pap." indicates *Kierkegaards Papirer*; the roman numeral indicates the volume number; the arabic numeral indicates the tome number, if applicable (some volumes are published in up to six tomes); the capital letter "A," "B," or "C" indicates the section of the volume ("A" for journal entries, "B" for drafts of published material, "C" for notes on reading); the next arabic numeral is a serial number indicating the cited material's placement in the section; and, finally, a page number is given if the matter in the serial number entry extends over two or more pages and only a specific page is referred to. Thus, a typical reference to material on page 274, serial number 97, section B, of tome 4, of volume VI of *Søren Kierkegaards Papirer* would appear in the text as [Pap. VI 4 B 97, p. 274]. Every reference to the *Papirer* will carry full information in the square brackets, and therefore if "[p. 22]" occurs a sentence or two after a reference to the *Papirer* it does *not* refer to the *Papirer* but to the volume of the *Samlede Værker* which contains the principal work under discussion in a given chapter.

3. "Purity of heart is in willing one thing" [Hjertets Reenhed er at ville Eet] is a reference to a theme of SK's which will be central in his next work. *A Literary Review* was not to be, any more than several earlier and later attempts, the conclusion of SK's enormous authorship.

4. Cf. the similar interpretation in *The Sickness Unto Death* [SV XI, pp. 227–28, discussed in chapter 23 of the present work], where SK blames the aristocratic and conservative speculative idealists for having paved the way for mob rule and the revolutions of 1848.

5. Here SK develops the themes of "authority" and "recognizability," which occupied him especially at this time, as he was studying the strange case of the "authoritative" Pastor Adler. The *Two Minor Ethico-Religious Essays*, which were published in 1849, carry this theme further, and it comes to the fore again in SK's attack on the Church. The political significance both of the *Two Essays* and of the attack will be dealt with in chapters 21 and 27, respectively.

18. *EDIFYING DISCOURSES IN VARIOUS SPIRITS*

1. SK develops his concept of "the individual" [den Enkelte] in "Purity of Heart," and later on, in 1849, when he thought he might publish that work in a second edition, he prepared two draft prefaces which dealt further with the concept of the individual. These prefaces, which belong with "Purity of Heart" and deserve to be read as a further development of one of the principal themes of that discourse, were never published in SK's lifetime but were published later as "Two Notes Concerning the Individual," along with the autobiographical piece *The Point of View for My Activity as an Author*. Because of their dates of composition, we will deal with them in chapter 25 of the present work, in connection with *The Point of View*.

2. SK uses a wonderful word-play here, as "Brydning," in keeping with the optical metaphor, means "refraction," but it also means "struggle."

3. A reference to the asocial Ishmael (cf. Genesis 16:12) and more pointedly to the freebooter Goldschmidt's *Corsair*, SK's antagonist, which displayed this same Ishmaelic slogan proudly on its masthead as its program.

4. SK thus briefly opens once again the way to an alternative possibility—besides that which I have called the "prioritarian citizen"—for the Christian individual to relate himself to "the world," namely as martyr-Apostle. However, one cannot assume this role without divine "authority," and it is at this point in SK's authorship an open question as to how far one can go in relating oneself critically to "Christendom" without claiming such authority and the role of saint or Apostle. Thus, here, as subsequently, the question is left to the individual's "self-examination" [Selvprøvelse, which figures in the title of one of SK's later, more polemical pieces, *For Self-Examination*, which will be examined in chapter 26].

5. This same theme—mockery transformed into honor—is also the theme for the most scathing of SK's assaults on Christendom in *Christian Discourses* [SV X, pp. 222–32, cf. the discussion of this in chapter 22 below].

6. SK's discussion of the "struggling" vs. the "triumphant" view is taken up again in the more polemical *Training in Christianity*; see chapter 24 below.

7. Cf. SV VIII, p. 397: "[T]he greatest fault of the age is that it does not respect Eternity's blessedness."

8. As time goes by, SK is less hesitant about applying "heathen" to modern Christendom, and his polemical tone becomes stronger; see especially the discourses on "The Worries of the Heathen" in *Christian Discourses*.

9. "The Difference Between a Genius and an Apostle" is one of the *Two Minor Ethico-Religious Essays* which SK published in 1849. It was a salvaged fragment from "The Big Book on Adler," a study of the problem of "authority" which SK worked on at the same time as the *Edifying Discourses in Various Spirits*.

19. WORKS OF LOVE

1. SK often calls Christian love merely *Kjerlighed*, just as he usually calls the worldly form simply *Elskov*, corresponding to the biblical distinction between *agape* and *eros*. As English lacks the two distinct words for these two forms of love, I am forced to use the adjectives "romantic" (or "poetic" or "worldly") love, and "Christian" (or "genuine") love, which will also occasionally be expressed simply by writing "Love" with a capital "L."

2. Also in this "revisionistic" vein are the first of the *Two Discourses at the Communion on Fridays* [*To Taler ved Altergangen om Fredagen*] [SV XII, pp. 261–90] (1851), which is based on Luke 7:47 ("He who has loved little is forgiven little") and the first discourse of *For Self-Examination* (1851), which is based on the epistle of James, who stresses good works and whom, significantly, Luther himself did not favor.

3. I am indebted for this insight to a lecture given by Lektor Paul Müller of the University of Copenhagen before the Søren Kierkegaard Society in 1973.

4. SK reserved a full-scale investigation of the nature of sin for his subsequent book, *The Sickness Unto Death*, and it will be dealt with in chapter 23 when we examine *The Sickness Unto Death*. For the purposes of understanding *Works of Love*, an ordinary orthodox understanding of sin as radical separation from God is sufficient.

5. Cf., for example, the following, from *A Literary Review*: "The principle of association . . . at most is valid with respect to material interests" [SV VIII, p. 99].

6. The reason that "the loving person" can make the optimistic assumption that the basis of Love is already present in his Neighbor is that, according to an equally optimistic (but much overlooked) tenet of SK's anthropology, in absolutely every individual "Love is present, like the sprout in the seed" [Kjerlighed er tilstede, som Spiren i Kornet] [SV IX, p. 210]. A proper emphasis upon this *fundamental optimism* in SK is necessary if he is to be seen as something other than a pessimistic misanthrope. I gratefully acknowledge having received this insight (along with much else) from Kresten Nordentoft's excellent *Kierkegaard's Psychology*, see especially pp. 347–86.

7. *Kierkegaards Samlede Værker*, vol. I, p. v.

8. "Offense" is here to be understood as that in Christianity which gives offense or is a stumbling-block to the natural categories of human reason. The term is more fully developed in SK's subsequent "Anti-Climacus" writings—*The Sickness Unto Death* and *Training in Christianity*—and it will be dealt with in detail in chapters 23 and 24 in the discussion of those works. Cf. also chapter 23, note 3.

9. There are also alternative forms of despair in which one neglects the temporal element of the self-synthesis; see the full discussion of them in chapter 23 on *The Sickness Unto Death*.

10. The "Two Notes Concerning the Individual," which were written simultaneously with *Works of Love* and which were to serve as prefaces to an intended second edition of *Edifying Discourses in Various Spirits*, correspond precisely to this view, in dethroning—but not banishing—the fleshly and in putting it under the dominion of self-denial and Love of Neighbor, with God as "middle term." Likewise, both *Works of Love* and the "Notes Concerning the Individual" stress that worldly love and the temporal sphere in general see people according to their *differences*, while genuine love and the Eternal disregard differences and see only *equality*. Both pieces conclude that universal, perfect equality cannot be realized within the political sphere, but only within the religious.

21. TWO MINOR ETHICO-RELIGIOUS ESSAYS

1. SK's book on Adler has been posthumously published in various forms. It is included in the Danish edition of the *Papirer* [Pap. VII 2 B 235–70]. An excellent annotated

edition was recently published as *Nutidens religieuse Forvirring: Bogen om Adler* [The Modern Religious Confusion: The Book on Adler], Julia Watkin, ed., (Copenhagen: Reitzel, 1984). Walter Lowrie published a translation, *On Authority and Revelation: The Book on Adler, or a Cycle of Ethico-Religious Essays* (Princeton: Princeton University Press, 1955), and a new translation, entitled *The Book on Adler*, is forthcoming as volume XXIV in the new Princeton University Press edition of *Kierkegaard's Writings*.

2. "Self-examination" = "Selvprøvelse"; cf. also the earlier use of the word in SV VIII, p. 402, discussed above in chapter 18 on *Edifying Discourses in Various Spirits*, where SK also raises the question of whether one ought to consider confessing Christ as an "Apostle" to heathen Christendom and where SK also drew back, inconclusively, from the issue by leaving it to "the individual's serious self-examination." "Self-examination" also figures in the title of another of SK's disquieting, polemical books, *For Self-Examination* (1851).

3. We have already seen how Martensen, himself half-German and with strong intellectual ties to Germany, had been offered the bishopric of his native Slesvig in order to soothe national tensions, and how he turned down this task of national reconciliation because he saw it as containing too many headaches.

4. Soon after finishing "The Worries of the Heathen," SK makes the point even more damningly in *The Sickness Unto Death*, that heathendom, in its properly "spiritless" sense, is the exclusive property of Christendom.

5. Indeed, in the previous essay H. H. pointed out that a demonic person could imitate the martyr and force the age to put him to death [SV XI, p. 84].

22. CHRISTIAN DISCOURSES

1. As will be seen in more detail in what follows, it was especially Section 3, "Thoughts Which Stab in the Back," which SK feared might get him into difficulties, but he did confess that "there is perhaps much hypochondria in this fear" [Pap. VIII 1 A 602, p. 278].

2. I Corinthians 7:30–31: "[Let] those who buy [be] as though they had no goods, and those who deal with the world [be] as though they had no dealings with it. For the form of this world is passing away." Cf. the formulation of this which SK puts in the mouth of Judge William in *Either/Or*, vol. II, where "the eternal man . . . will preserve intellectual gifts, but in his innermost heart he will know that he who has these things is as he who has them not" [SV II, p. 188]. In *Works of Love* SK again refers to this biblical passage—"one who has earthly goods . . . must be as one who has them not" [SV IX, p. 30]—which is obviously of paramount importance to him. The Pauline notion of being *in* the world but not *of* it, of "having all things as though you had them not," stands at the very center of SK's thought. It should also be noted that the "form" of SK's world did indeed appear to be "passing away," so there was perhaps an even better fit between the Pauline verse and SK's situation.

3. SV IX, p. 133, discussed above in chapter 19 on *Works of Love*.

4. The theme of the "spiritlessness" of the "philistine bourgeoisie" of Christendom receives full treatment by SK in *The Sickness Unto Death*, cf. chapter 23 below.

5. "Hyggelig, rolig, Gud! er din Bolig," in *Sang-Værk til den danske Kirke* [Song Works for the Danish Church], vol. I (Copenhagen: Wahl, 1837).

6. Cf. SV IX, p. 190, discussed in chapter 19 above.

7. SV XI, pp. 227–28, discussed in chapter 23 below.

8. Cf. chapter 19, note 6.

23. *THE SICKNESS UNTO DEATH*

1. I will hereafter use "SK" as the author of *Sickness*, with the warning that the "real" author is Anti-Climacus, whose radically absolute views SK did not, at this time at any rate, dare to set forth as his own.

2. "Edifying" = "opbyggelig," which literally means "upbuilding," i.e., that which builds up one's soul in the personal, Christian sense.

3. "Offense" is understood in the sense that the individual recoils from and rejects or "takes offense" at God's approach, as when Christ says "Blessed is he who is not offended in me" [Matt. 11:6] or when St. Paul writes, "I preach Christ crucified, an offense to the Jews and a foolishness to the Greeks" [I Corinthians 1:23]. Cf. also, chapter 19 note 8.

4. "Only to a certain degree" [kun til en vis Grad, SV XI, p. 208], is a favorite SK pejorative, as in "willing the Good to a certain degree."

5. Cf. the Foreword to *The Sickness Unto Death*, SV XI, p. 118. Anti-Climacus' other book, *Training in Christianity*, follows the development in the opposite direction, i.e., the way of faith.

6. *The Sickness Unto Death* in fact forms a parallel to Hegel's *Phenomenology of Spirit*. In SK's book, as in Hegel's, the self is described as it passes through successively more adequate levels of self-knowledge until it finally comes to know itself as self-conscious spirit and in its factual relation to God.

7. Unlike the English word "philistine," the Danish "Spidsborger," which is usually translated "philistine," contains a built-in indictment of the bourgeoisie [= Borgerskab] and the respectability which being bourgeois implies. "Spidsborger" itself is allied to the German "Spiessbürger," and originally meant a free citizen [= Borger] wealthy enough to be allowed to be a part of the militia for the defense of the city, and as such to be permitted to carry a spear [= Spyd]. Thus a Spidsborger was a respectable, spear-carrying member of the middle class, and came in time to be a term of contempt. I have therefore chosen to convey the word's full meaning by translating it as "bourgeois philistine" rather than simply as philistine. The specifically class-related sense of the term SK uses is of interest to the present work.

8. It is suggestive to note that Kierkegaard's category of "spiritlessness," which is a form of opposition or resistance to "Spirit," is very similar to the metaphysical definition of fascism as "resistance to transcendence" given by Ernst Nolte in *Three Faces of Fascism*, Leila Vennewitz, trans. (New York: Holt, Rinehart, and Winston, 1966), pp. 429–54 *et passim*. It is further interesting to note that the social class to which Kierkegaard has typically related "spiritlessness" is the "philistine bourgeoisie," while fascism, of course, has been classically associated with the middle and lower-middle class.

9. "At skabe sig" is a pun which means both "to create oneself" and "to put on an act" or "to show off."

10. For the sake of simplicity some of the variations and sub-forms included in SK's rather baroque (but tripartite) presentation have been omitted.

11. "To come too near" = "at komme for nær," which means both "to come too close" and "to give an affront" (Fornærmelse).

12. SK here uses "concrete" in the ordinary sense of "particular" but also in its original sense of something "grown together."

24. *TRAINING IN CHRISTIANITY*

1. SK's dualism recalls that of Plato, and the Platonic dualism of the world and eternity is no less radical and polemical than SK's. We ought not to be deceived by the genial tone of the *Phaedo* or the *Symposium* or by the apparent step-wise gradualism of

the latter work. They are just as polemical as *Training in Christianity* or *Judge for Yourselves!*, and the gap, for example, in the *Symposium* between the worldly notions of the beautiful and the face of Beauty itself is as absolute as any of SK's distinctions between a worldly good (which becomes an evil if held absolutely) and the Good itself. Similarly, in the *Phaedo*, as in SK's later work, life is to be a "rehearsal" of death [*Phaedo* 66c-68b] (cf. "dying away"), and the proper "tendance" of the soul—not any physical, social, or intellectual pursuits—ought to lay first claim upon one's life. And, finally, although the properly-lived life is subject to this radical duality, this does not imply any sort of withdrawal from the daily activities of the world. Socrates tells us that we have been placed here at our posts by the gods and must not "desert" but, rather, maintain a constant critical involvement with the life of the polis, questioning, vexing, and defying it when it threatens to transgress its proper limits.

2. "Away, away, ye unclean," Virgil, *Aeneid* 6, 258.

3. Bonhoeffer also stresses the crucial importance of a suffering, degraded God, which he finds to be the key to Christianity's uniqueness. Furthermore, although he differs from Kierkegaard on other key points, Bonhoeffer, like Kierkegaard, proceeded from the "suffering God" to a position of radical "secularity." "Here is the decisive difference between Christianity and all religions. Man's religiosity makes him look in his distress to the power of God in the world: God is the *deus ex machina*. The Bible directs man to God's powerlessness and suffering; only the suffering God can help. To that extent we may say that the development towards the world's coming of age outlined above, which has done away with a false conception of God, opens up a way of seeing the God of the Bible, who wins power and space in the world by his weakness. This will probably be the starting-point for our 'secular interpretation.' " [Dietrich Bonhoeffer, *Letters and Papers From Prison*, Eberhard Bethge, ed., enlarged edition (New York: Macmillan, 1972), p. 361.] See also Bonhoeffer's *The Cost of Discipleship* (New York: Macmillan, 1963).

As the present work seeks to demonstrate, the events which culminated in 1848–49 served the same purpose in Kierkegaard's thinking as the interwar period did in Bonhoeffer's: They symbolized "the world's coming of age," and they gave the signal for a radical reinterpretation both of Christianity and of "the world."

4. "Imitator" = "Efterfølger," literally "follower after," but "Imitator" as in *The Imitation of Christ* more perfectly expresses SK's meaning in English.

5. SK's concern with "reversedness" is particularly strong in the period after 1848, as for example in the discourses entitled *"The Chief Priest"* - *"The Publican"* - *"The Woman Who Was a Sinner"* [*"Ypperstepræsten"* - *"Tolderen"* - *"Synderinden"*] [SV XI, pp. 245–80], written in the late summer of 1849 and published in November of that year, where SK writes "Humiliation is elevation" [SV XI, p. 268].

6. SK's discussion of human time as a "parenthesis" in the "real" time of eternity parallels his discussion of "pauses" and "interruptions" at the beginning and toward the end of "Purity of Heart." There we learn that sin—the "busyness" of the temporal world—is an "interruption" of the eternal relationship to God and that the "pause" or "interruption" of our life by confession or repentance is an interruption within this interruption. Thus, the God-relation is in the highest sense a continuation in much the same sense that in *Training*, "Truth" is contact with eternity within the "parenthesis" of human history. See chapter 18 above.

7. Yet, even while considering SK's argument for the inadequacy of "hidden inwardness," we must also remember that his remarks are given a certain tentative nature by his own statement, cited above, that what matters for a true Christian is having a proper posture toward the world, not the actuality of suffering itself but the willingness to do so. Thus SK can be "strict" without being heavy-handedly literalistic.

8. See note 6, above.

9. "Examine yourself now" [prøv Dig nu selv] and "judge, then, for yourself" [døm saa selv] are phrases nearly identical with the titles of the two books, *For Self-Examination* [*Til Selvprøvelse*] and *Judge for Yourselves!* [*Dømmer selv!*], which SK wrote in 1851–52. These two works continued in the same populist, anticlerical vein as *Training in Christianity* but with continually increasing radicality in their social criticism.

10. It ought also to be noted that immediately after publishing this apparently "strict" book in the fall of 1850, SK wrote *An Edifying Discourse* [*En opbyggelig Tale*] [SV XII, pp. 241–59], which he published on December 20, 1850, and which may thus be said to "accompany" *Training* and to balance its message. This short *Discourse* is clearly designed to keep SK's audience from placing an overly "strict" construction on the call for imitation contained in *Training*, for in this little work SK stresses that "his [Christ's] death changes everything infinitely. It is not as though his death abolished the significance of the fact that he is also the exemplar, no, but his death becomes the infinite comfort, the infinite headstart with which the striving individual begins, namely that atonement has been made" [SV XII, p. 258]. In other words, in this little discourse, the first work composed and published after the appearance of *Training in Christianity*, SK stresses that the emphasis on Christ as exemplar and the obligation to imitate him must not blind us to the overriding soteriological importance of Christ as atoner. However "strict" SK appears to be in *Training*, he continued to insist that grace precedes and lays the groundwork for works, and not the reverse.

25. AUTOBIOGRAPHICAL PIECES, "TWO NOTES" CONCERNING "THE INDIVIDUAL," AND THE "OPEN LETTER" TO DR. RUDELBACH

1. Cf. chapter 20 above, where it is documented that this attack is directed at Martensen, whereas the attack on "coteries" is directed at "Mynster, Heiberg, Martensen, and suite."

2. We shall shortly see how the same principle also holds for politics. Now that "the common man" has achieved political adulthood and democracy has become the order of the day, there is no turning back. There is no point in rejecting democracy *per se* or in trying to pretend that these are other than democratic times. The task is to illuminate popular sovereignty in such a way as to show its inadequacy for any *ultimate* purpose, i.e., for anything other than purely instrumental uses in the realm of "politics" proper, of "material prudence." Like reflection, democratic politics must not be rejected out of hand but must be made to demonstrate its inadequacy for any transcendent purpose. SK is neither an irrationalist nor a reactionary.

3. It is impossible, of course, to prove that SK had Feuerbach in mind when he wrote the foregoing, but we ought to note that, like Marx, he was an avid reader of Feuerbach and purchased *Das Wesen des Christentums* in 1844.

4. SK had for a time considered publishing these *Two Notes* together with a third short essay and this introduction, entitling the entire work *Three Notes Concerning the Individual*. The third of these *Notes* was separated from the present two, however, and was published as the Foreword to *Two Discourses at the Communion on Fridays*, which was written in December 1849 and published in 1851 on the same day as *On My Activity as an Author* (which, in the Kierkegaardian scheme of things, the communion discourses were to "accompany"). This third "Note" on the individual thus ended up as part of the "accompaniment" to the one autobiographical sketch, whereas the other two "Notes" were appended to the longer autobiographical piece. In this third "Note," as in the present Foreword to the *Two Notes*, SK also lays great stress upon the importance of equality as the heart both of humanity and of Christianity. SK writes of "this view of life, which is the idea of humanity [Menneskelighed] or of human equality [Menneske-

Lighed]: Christianly understood, every person (the individual), unconditionally every person, still again, unconditionally every person, is equally near to God. And in what way is each near and equally near? In being loved by him. Thus there is equality, infinitely, between people" [SV XII, p. 267].

5. Note that it is therefore both sides which are at fault in the social explosion, not simply the lower classes.

6. If classical liberalism has now become wedded to democracy, it is of course not from any faith in the wisdom or moral superiority of the community, but because of progressive disillusionment with any alternative means of organizing society. To sceptical, individualistic liberalism, democracy is a tool, not a faith; it is something into which liberals have entered by the back door. As Thiers rather modestly put it in mid-nineteenth-century France, "a republic is the form of government which divides us least," and as Churchill put it in our own century, "democracy is the worst form of government, except for all those other forms of government that have been tried from time to time." The contrast of SK with Grundtvig is thus striking. Grundtvig was a "natural-born" democrat who backed into the liberal institutions of representative government through historical necessity, while SK was a "natural-born" liberal (in the sense of being an individualist and an "agnostic" about social truth) who came by necessity to accept a limited and instrumental form of democracy.

7. Cited in SK's "Open Letter" as printed in SV XIII, p. 436.

26. TWO SERIES OF DISCOURSES "RECOMMENDED TO THE PRESENT AGE"

1. The expression "for self-examination" had by 1851 become a stock phrase in SK's polemical vocabulary. Cf. earlier references in chapter 18, note 4; chapter 21, note 2; and chapter 24, note 9.

2. It should be reiterated that For Self-Examination had by far the widest circulation of any of SK's writings until the "attack." His readership must certainly have extended considerably beyond the narrow social spectrum normally thought of as the literate public.

3. It ought to be noted that a transitional interpretation of Matthew 6:24-end was given in the three "godly discourses" entitled The Lily of the Field and the Bird of Heaven [Lilien paa Marken og Fuglen under Himlen. Tre gudelige Taler] [SV XI, pp.1–46], written in March and April 1849 and published in May 1849 as an "accompaniment" to the publication of the pseudonymous Two Ethico-Religious Essays, which themselves had been composed in 1847 and have been discussed in an earlier chapter of the present work. In The Lily and the Bird, SK offers us an interpretation of the key Matthew passage which is strict enough to avoid a permissive, "Protestant" concentration upon "all these things [which] shall be added unto you." The problem for SK is how to avoid a distortion of Lutheranism which merely nods in the direction of seeking first God's kingdom, and then, in its concentration upon "all these things," gets on with the "real" Protestant business of commerce and citizenship. Thus, in The Lily and the Bird of 1849 SK shifts from his earlier prioritarian interpretation of Matthew to a view which sees Christ's talk of "all these things [which] shall be added" as a form of parental condescension, as when a father promises a child dessert if the child finishes the main course, a course which the loving parent knows will satisfy and obviate all other hunger [SV XI, pp. 22–23]. In Matthew, SK argues, Christ, speaking as our nutritionist-parent, has had to appeal to the child in us by holding before us the prioritarian hope of enjoying both God's Kingdom and "all these things" of the world. But, SK argues, in understanding Matthew we must come to leave our childish expectations behind and realize that God's Kingdom can only be sought when it is sought first and that the satisfaction of this search will

render meaningless and unnecessary all seeking after worldly success. Here, in SK's "transitional" interpretation of Matthew, as in the discourses of *Judge for Yourselves!* which are under discussion, the theme of "childhood's end" is of great importance: The emergence of "the common man" from centuries of tutelage requires that we be stricter with ourselves and eschew interpretations—the ossified "two kingdoms" regimen of orthodox Lutheranism, for example—which have made it possible to domesticate Christianity into a new form of paganism. The alternative danger, of course, is that, in his zeal to avoid the worldliness which Protestantism's "cheap grace" has brought into being, SK risks ending up in a rehabilitation of works. It is precisely this middle course which SK attempts to define in the present discourses and the subsequent "attack," where "the common man" is told that he must come fully into his maturity, seeing the vanity of worldliness and the priority of grace as well as both the importance and the inefficacy of works. Quite a task for "the common man," but these, SK says, are the requirements of our new "maturity!"

4. With minor modifications, this is a somewhat stronger variant of the schematic history of Christianity—as "ecclesia militans," "ecclesia triumphans," and "hidden inwardness"—which SK put forth in *Training in Christianity* and which was discussed in chapter 24 above.

5. The Danish word for "model" is "Mønster," and this was the spelling which was current in SK's own time. However, in denigrating the mediocre local pastor who is foolishly exalted as a "model" for others, SK deliberately makes a pointed reference and a wonderful pun by using the antiquated spelling of the word: "Mynster"!

6. It is interesting to note that in a passage in *Training in Christianity*, discussed in chapter 24 above, SK expresses the same thought, in virtually identical language, when he says of the "professors" that "with their help and assistance it [Christianity] could be practiced out of this world" [SV XII, p. 97].

7. See, for example, *The Sickness Unto Death* [SV XI, pp. 153–54]; also, see above, chapter 23.

8. In the middle of our own century, Dietrich Bonhoeffer has also directed attention to the modern world's "adulthood" or "coming-of-age" as a pivotal fact which necessitates a fundamental reinterpretation of Christianity: "You would be surprised, and perhaps even worried, by my theological thoughts and the conclusions they lead to. . . . What is bothering me incessantly is the question of what Christianity is, or indeed who Christ really is, for us today. The time when people could be told everything by means of words, whether theological or pious, is over, and so is the time of inwardness and conscience—and that means the time of religion in general. We are moving towards a completely religionless time. . . . How do we speak of God—without religion, i.e. without the temporally conditioned presuppositions of metaphysics, inwardness, and so on? How do we speak (or perhaps we cannot now even 'speak' as we used to) in a 'secular' way about 'God'?" [*Letters and Papers From Prison*, pp. 279–80]. "The attack by Christian apologetics on the adulthood of the world I consider to be in the first place pointless, in the second place ignoble, and in the third place unchristian. Pointless, because it seems to me like an attempt to put a grown-up man back into adolescence, i.e. to make him dependent on things on which he is, in fact, no longer dependent, and thrusting him into problems that are, in fact, no longer problems to him. Ignoble, because it amounts to an attempt to exploit man's weakness for purposes that are alien to him and to which he has not fully assented. Unchristian, because it confuses Christ with one particular stage in man's religiousness. . . . The question is: Christ and the world which has come of age . . . " [ibid., p. 327]. "[T]he world's coming of age is no longer an occasion for polemics and apologetics, but is now really better understood than it understands itself, namely on the basis of the gospel and in the light of Christ" [ibid., p. 329].

9. As we will see, SK's particular distaste for those who "enjoy" being reformers is shown in the first number of *The Moment* to be a specifically Platonic prejudice, borrowed from Socrates' assertion in the *Republic* that only those who do not wish to do so are fit to rule. So, too, the only true reformers must be those who take no pleasure in it.

27. THE ATTACK ON CHRISTENDOM

1. For the copy of *Training in Christianity* dedicated to Mynster, which has only recently come to light, see N. J. Cappelørn, "Fire 'nye' Kierkegaard-dedikationer" [Four 'New' Kierkegaard Dedications], *Kierkegaardiana*, No. IX (1974), pp. 260–66. It is interesting to note that we know of several other dedication copies of *Training*, one of which was presented to the liberal leader H. N. Clausen, and another was given to Dr. Rudelbach only a month or two before SK's "Open Letter," which differed sharply with the construction Rudelbach placed upon the authorship as a whole and upon *Training* in particular.

2. For SK's conversation with Mynster, see Pap. X 3 A, 563–64. According to SK's account, Mynster had allowed it to be rumored to SK that he was very displeased with *Training* and saw it as "a profane trifling with the Holy." However, when SK went to Mynster to hear the criticism personally, Mynster adopted a friendly, evasive tone, in which he stated that, even though, in his opinion, "the book will not do any good," "every bird must sing with its own voice." In the end, SK had to content himself with neither a full criticism nor, of course, the hoped-for "admission," and he counted himself lucky to avoid a lawsuit by the powers that be.

3. See Mynster's pamphlet *Yderligere Bidrag til Forhandlingerne om de kirkelige Forhold i Danmark* [Further Contributions to Discussions of the Ecclesiastical Situation in Denmark] (Copenhagen: 1851), reprinted in Mynster, *Blandede Skrivter*, vol. II, pp. 23–61.

4. Ibid., vol. II, pp. 60–61.

5. H. L. Martensen, "Prædiken i Christiansborg Slotskirke den 5te Februar 1854, Søndagen før Biskop Mynsters Jordefærd" [Sermon in Christiansborg Castle Church, February 5, 1854, the Sunday Preceding Bishop Mynster's Burial], reprinted in Martensen, *Lejlighedstaler*, pp. 17–31; see especially p. 20.

6. Cf. the discussion in chapter 12 above.

7. I concede that it can be argued that the phase of the attack contained in *The Moment* does contain a development, namely a development of neurotic excesses, perhaps indicative of SK's private resentments and sexual conflicts. However that may be, it is the subject for a psychological biography or an imaginative reconstruction of SK's inner life—of which there are many—and not for an assessment of the content and development of the social thought of the writer and public person Kierkegaard.

8. Cf. SV XII, pp. 478–80, and the discussion in chapter 26 above.

9. Thus, among the most legitimate of SK's first-generation descendants in Danish culture are not the churchmen, not even the Inner Mission churchmen, who attempted to turn SK's views to the task of the internal reform of the People's Church, but such brazen freethinkers as Hans Brøchner and Georg Brandes.

10. This point was made quite well, and without embarrassment, by one of SK's opponents during the attack, who had complained to the newspapers: "How would things have gone with the human social order, with civilization, if Christianity had not been adopted by the State, if there had not been an official Christianity and Christendom? . . . He [SK] gives no regard to the conditions necessary for the state or for human society. . . . He does not bother himself with what would become of the society which

gave up Christianity, even if this were an accommodated version of Christianity" (in *The Copenhagen Post* [*Kjøbenhavnsposten*], Year 29, No. 109 (May 12, 1855), reprinted in R. Nielsen, ed., *S. Kierkegaards Bladartikler med Bilag samlede efter Forfatterens Død* [S. Kierkegaard's Newspaper Articles, With a Supplement Collected After the Author's Death] (Copenhagen: Reitzel, 1857), pp. 272–73.)

11. It is common Danish usage to refer to "Familien Danmark" [the family, Denmark].

12. This is perhaps the best place to note that, even in the midst of the apparently intemperate anticlerical tirades which characterized the final phase of his attack on Christendom, SK was still conscious of the need to orchestrate his authorship carefully and to demonstrate to the common reader that his war against the abuses of Christian culture was not a fundamental change in his life or an act of gross impiety. Thus, in early September 1855, in the midst of this final phase of the attack, SK published his last discourse, *The Unchangingness of God* [*Guds Uforanderlighed*] [SV XIV, pp. 277–94], which had been written more than four years earlier, but which he saved until this occasion. In it SK writes: "We will speak, then, if possible, both in fear and in pacification, of Thee, Thou Unchanging, or of Thy Unchangingness" [p. 286]. The "unchangingness" of external things (when they appear such), SK explains, is only illusory. The world of appearances is sheer change. But God is unchanged in the tumult of everything. He is unchanging clarity, the Father of Light, eternally unchanged, a clarity in which there is no darkness [ibid., paraphrase]. Perhaps SK also wishes to show that he, too, has striven to be unchanging in his devotion to God, even in the midst of apparent change and tumult. Yet another reason, perhaps, for SK to stress God's unchangingness at this time is that it was particularly important to remember this divine attribute in the face of revolutionary times, when all else in Denmark was changing. The point, at any rate, of publishing *The Unchangingness of God* at this particular time seems to have been to convey to the common reader the rather subtle message that SK's task was a dialectical one, that his attack was not mere destructiveness or *Schadenfreude*, but rested upon a base which SK felt to be constructive.

13. SK is here referring to the legal harassment of lay pietism and of Baptists and to the fact, mentioned in Part I of the present work, that the confirmation certificate issued by the priest to the confirmed was that person's basic document of legal citizenship and adulthood, without which one could not take most jobs, hold office, etc.

14. SK is referring to Mynster's repeated and unsuccessful attempts to introduce a new hymnal and altar ritual.

15. As an amusing historical footnote, it might be added that in this same final piece SK also predicted his own posthumous fate: "My dear reader, you can see that this does not lead straight to profit. This will happen only after my death, when the oath-bound professionals will take my life, too, as an addition to their salt-barrels" [SV XIV, p. 356]. This is precisely the role which SK was destined to play posthumously in the Established Church of Denmark. Although SK refused on his deathbed to accept the sacrament from "a civil servant," his remains were laid out in the Church of Our Lady in Copenhagen, the principal church of the capital, and were given official burial at a service at which his own partisans were forbidden to speak. Latterly, a statue of SK has been unveiled as a part of the monumental circle of bronzes surrounding Frederik's Church ("The Marble Church"), the Sacre-Coeur of Copenhagen, where he stands serenely in the company of Grundtvig, Mynster, and Martensen.

EPILOGUE

1. The standard (and rather chatty) treatment of the journalism of the period is Chr. Kirchoff-Larsen, *Den danske Presses Historie* [The History of the Danish Press], vol.

III (Copenhagen: Berlingske Forlag, 1962). Much of the press reaction to SK's attack itself can be found in R. Nielsen, ed., *S. Kierkegaards Bladartikler,* and the rest must be sought out individually in the Royal Library and the library of Copenhagen University. A sampling shows that the conservative *Berling Times* published Martensen's single article of reply (*Berlingske Tidende,* 1854, No. 302, Thursday, Dec. 28, 1854), whereas the *Copenhagen Post* (*Kjøbenhavnsposten,* 1854, No. 300, Sunday, Dec. 23, 1854) refused to take SK seriously and proposed an acrostic, the solution of which indicated that SK was a "fool" [Nar], and the *Courier* (*Flyveposten,* 1854, No. 301, Wednesday, Dec. 27, 1854) likewise felt that in his attack SK had shown that he was truly a man "without seriousness."

2. H. N. Clausen, *Optegnelser om mit Levneds og min Tids Historie,* p. 448.

3. *Biskop H. Martensens Breve,* vol. I, pp. 131, 134, 135, *et passim.*

4. F. C. Sibbern, *Breve til og fra F. C. Sibbern* [Letters To and From F. C. Sibbern], C. L. N. Mynster, ed., vol. II (Copenhagen: Gyldendal, 1866), p. 224; cf. pp. 224–26.

5. A. S. Ørsted, *Af mit Livs og Min Tids Historie* [From the History of My Life and Times] (Copenhagen: Arne Frost-Hansens Forlag, 1951), pp. 394ff.

6. Johanne Luise Heiberg, *Et Liv gjenoplivet i Erindringen* [A Life Relived in Recollection], Aage Friis, ed., 4th ed. rev., 4 vols. (Copenhagen: Gyldendal, 1944).

7. Aage Friis, ed., *Fra det Heibergske Hjem: Johan Ludvig og Johanne Luise Heibergs indbyrdes Brevveksling* [From the Heiberg Home: The Correspondence Between Johan Ludvig and Johanne Luise Heiberg] (Copenhagen: J. H. Schultz Forlag, 1940), p. 346.

8. Hansine Pouline Andræ, *Geheimraadinde Andræs politiske Dagbøger* [Madame Privy Councillor Andræ's Political Diaries], Poul Andræ, ed., vol. I (May 1855-March 1856) (Copenhagen: Gyldendal, 1914), p. 111.

9. *Biskop H. Martensens Breve,* vol. I, p. 136.

10. Ibid., vol. I, pp. 142–43.

11. Ibid., vol. I, p. 143.

12. Ibid., vol. I, p. 138.

13. Martensen, *Af mit Levnet,* vol. III, p. 13.

14. Ibid., vol. III, p. 15.

15. Ibid., vol. III, pp. 21, 19, and 18. Martensen thus finds SK's universal application of individualism self-contradictory and impossible to believe. This is a parallel to Martensen's political views, where, as we have seen, he finds it impossible for "the common man" to do what, under absolutism, "the rare few" can do, namely, to serve as an "authority" to himself, i.e., to legislate for himself, to will for himself the moral law which he wills for all of society. Kierkegaard, on the other hand, insists that what is essential to being human is something which absolutely every individual must be presupposed to possess. If the ability to be an authority for oneself is so important as to be essential to humanity, then it must be presupposed to be in everyone's possession. This forms a precise parallel to SK's assertion that, in the religious sphere, absolutely everyone can be an individual before God. If, on the other hand, these abilities are not essential attributes of being human, but merely the possessions of the rare few, a part of Golden Age "Culture," then they are nothing to become so exercised about. By allowing every individual to come into open, conscious possession of the whole of his or her birthright, by giving every individual complete power of disposition—for better or for worse—over *all* in him or her that is "essential to being human," the fateful developments of the post-1848 era have presented humanity with an unprecedented challenge, SK feels. It is no longer possible for an individual to hide from his or her own "essential" self by citing the interposition of intermediate forms of authority, which have always cut off all but the rare few from a true apprehension of themselves. Now humanity has been put on its own—free to choose glory or perdition—and if, in Martensen's view, people in freedom have chosen perdition, then Martensen is of course

correct when he remarks, à propos of SK's celebration of this freedom, that "he [SK] has contributed in no small measure to the extension and strengthening of unbelief here in this country."

Kierkegaard would probably not take exception to this last statement of Martensen's except to point out that it would be better to substitute the word "honesty" for "unbelief," for he was merely celebrating the freedom and honesty which would make it possible for the "unbelief"—or "despair," to use the terminology of The Sickness Unto Death—which was already present to make itself known, to make itself clearly conscious to itself. And, SK might have added, consciousness of despair is the necessary first step away from "spiritlessness" and toward recovery. Who, after all, is the real "philistine"— the social cosmetologist, who puts a nice face on the inner truth of despair, or the "radical surgeon" who (to use SK's term) "holds open the wound of negativity?"

16. P. G. Lindhardt, Konfrontation [Confrontation] (Copenhagen: Akademisk Forlag, 1974).

17. Grundtvig, for example, had refused to attend the burial services for Mynster, and this snub by one of Copenhagen's and Denmark's great spiritual leaders to a deceased colleague and superior was seen by many as evidence of a shocking resentment.

18. Lindhardt, Konfrontation, pp. 54–57.

19. Ibid., pp. 79–81.

20. Ibid., pp. 84–87.

21. Ibid., pp. 95–98.

22. Ibid., pp. 98–100.

23. Ibid., pp. 128–30.

24. Ibid., pp. 144–47.

25. Ibid., pp. 159–61.

26. Ibid., pp. 162–64.

27. For a discussion of the early years of the Inner Mission, of the role of Vilhelm Beck, and of the influence of anticlerical polemics upon this movement, see P. G. Lindhardt, Vækkelser, Part III, chapter 3, "Indre Missions første Tid" [The Early Days of the Inner Mission]. Lindhardt's particular strength consists in being faithful to the religious content of the various pietist groups while showing the social and economic forces which helped cause them to divide and cluster in the manner that they did.

28. In spite of the great poetic liberties Ibsen allows himself in his play, Brand seems to me a powerful, sympathetic, and permissible version of the radical Kierkegaard of the attack on Christendom, and thus I cannot agree with Lowrie when he objects to Ibsen's play as "an example of illegitimate interpretation of S. K." (Lowrie, Kierkegaard, p. 10).

29. Thomas Overskou, Af mit Liv og min Tid [From My Life and Times], ed. with notes by Robert Neiiendam, vol. II, 1819–1873 (Copenhagen: Nyt Nordisk Forlag / Arnold Busck, 1962).

30. Ibid., vol. II, p. 194.

31. Ibid., vol. II, p. 195.

32. Ibid.

33. Ibid., vol. II, p. 196.

34. Ibid.

Select Bibliography

WORKS BY KIERKEGAARD

Kierkegaard, Søren. *Breve og Aktstykker vedrørende Søren Kierkegaard* [Letters and Documents Concerning Søren Kierkegaard]. ed. Niels Thulstrup. 2 vols. Copenhagen: Munksgaard, 1953–54.

———. *Samlede Værker* [Machine-Readable Text]. ed. Alastair McKinnon. (*Søren Kierkegaards Samlede Værker* on computer discs. Customized software also available.) Montreal: Inter Editions, 1987.

———. *Kierkegaard's Writings*. ed. and trans. with introductions and notes by Howard V. Hong, Edna H. Hong, Henrik Rosenmeier, Reidar Thomte, et al. 26 vols. projected (11 vols. published as of December 1989). Princeton: Princeton University Press, 1978– .

———. *Søren Kierkegaards Papirer* [The Papers of Søren Kierkegaard]. eds. P. A. Heiberg, V. Kuhr, and E. Torsting. 16 vols. in 25 tomes. 2d augmented ed. by N. Thulstrup. Index by N. J. Cappelørn. Copenhagen: Gyldendal, 1968–78.

———. *Søren Kierkegaards Samlede Værker* [The Collected Works of Søren Kierkegaard]. eds. A. B. Drachmann, J. L. Heiberg, and H. O. Lange. 14 vols. 1st ed. Copenhagen: Gyldendal, 1901–1906.

———. *Nutidens Religieuse Forvirring. Bogen om Adler* [The Modern Religious Confusion: The Book on Adler]. ed. Julia Watkin. Copenhagen: Reitzel, 1984.

———. *Søren Kierkegaard's Journals and Papers*. trans. with notes by Howard V. Hong and Edna H. Hong, assisted by Gregor Malantschuk; index prepared by Nathaniel J. Hong and Charles M. Barker. 7 vols. Bloomington and London: Indiana University Press, 1967–78.

BIBLIOGRAPHIES, GUIDES TO LITERATURE ON KIERKEGAARD, CONCORDANCES

Deuser, Hermann. *Kierkegaard. Die Philosophie des religiösen Schriftstellers. Erträge der Forschung*. Darmstadt: Wissenschaftliche Buchgesellschaft, 1985.

Henriksen, Aage. *Methods and Results of Kierkegaard Study in Scandinavia: A Historical and Critical Survey*. Copenhagen: Munksgaard, 1951.

Himmelstrup, Jens. *Søren Kierkegaard. International Bibliografi* [International Søren Kierkegaard Bibliography]. Copenhagen: Nyt Nordisk Forlag / Arnold Busck, 1962.

Jørgensen, Aage. *Søren Kierkegaard-litteratur, 1961–1970. En forløbig bibliografi* [Literature on Søren Kierkegaard, 1961–1970: A Preliminary Bibliography]. Århus: Akademisk Boghandel, 1971.

———. "Søren Kierkegaard-litteratur, 1971–1980" [Literature on Søren Kierkegaard, 1971–1980]. *Kierkegaardiana*, No. XII (1982): 129–229.

Kabell, Aage. *Kierkegaard-Studiet i Norden* [Kierkegaard Studies in Scandinavia]. Copenhagen: Hagerup, 1958.

Lapointe, Francois. *Søren Kierkegaard and His Critics: An International Bibliography of Criticism*. Westport, Connecticut: Greenwood Press, 1980.

McKinnon, Alastair. *The Kierkegaard Indices*. vol. I *Kierkegaard in Translation*; vol. II *Konkordans til Kierkegaards "Samlede Værker"* [Concordance to Kierkegaard's *Samlede Værker*]; vol. III *Index Verborum til Kierkegaards "Samlede Værker"* [Index Verborum to Kierkegaard's *Samlede Værker*]; vol. IV *Computational Analysis of Kierkegaard's "Samlede Værker"*. Leiden: Brill, 1970–75.

Thulstrup, Niels. "Theological and Philosophical Kierkegaard Studies in Scandinavia, 1945–53." *Theology Today* XII, 3 (October 1955).

(Jørgensen's bibliographies are available on computer disc from Mr. Stephane Hogue, c/o SKDB, Department of Philosophy, McGill University, 855 Sherbrooke Street West, Montreal, P. Q., Canada H3A 2T7. Additional general bibliographical material can be found in volume 1 of *Søren Kierkegaard's Journals and Papers* and in Thompson, Josiah, ed. *Kierkegaard: A Collection of Critical Essays* (Garden City, New York: Doubleday (Anchor paperback), 1972). Topical bibliographical material can be found in the individual volumes of *Søren Kierkegaard's Journals and Papers* and *Kierkegaard's Writings*.)

NEWSLETTERS AND PERIODICALS FOR KIERKEGAARD RESEARCH

International Kierkegaard Newsletter. ed. Julia Watkin, Stenagervej 15, 2900 Hellerup, DENMARK (published every autumn).

Kierkegaardiana. Published by the Søren Kierkegaard Society of Copenhagen. Copenhagen: 1955–   . (Current publisher is Reitzel. Published every two or three years. 14 vols. have appeared as of 1988.)

Søren Kierkegaard Newsletter. ed. C. Stephen Evans, Department of Philosophy, St. Olaf College, Northfield, Minnesota 55057, USA. (Published twice a year).

PRIMARY WORKS BY AUTHORS OTHER THAN KIERKEGAARD

Aarestrup, Emil. *Digte* [Poems]. ed. Hans Brix. Copenhagen: G. E. C. Gad, 1930.

Andræ, Hansine Pouline. *Geheimraadinde Andræs politiske Dagbøger* [Madame Privy Councillor Andræ's Political Diaries]. Vol. I, May 1855-March 1856. ed. Poul Andræ. Copenhagen: Gyldendal, 1914.

Andreasen, Uffe. ed. *Romantismen, 1824–40* [Romanticism, 1824–40]. Copenhagen: Gyldendal, 1974.

Billeskov Jansen, F. J. *Den Danske Lyrik* [The Danish Lyric: 1800–1870]. 2 vols. Copenhagen: Reitzel, 1967.

Clausen, H. N. *Catholicismens og Protestantismens Kirkeforfatning, Lære og Ritus* [Catholicism and Protestantism: Their Church Constitutions, Doctrines, and Rites]. Copenhagen: Andreas Seidelin, 1825.

———. *Optegnelser om mit Levneds og min Tids Historie* [Notes on the History of My Life and Times]. Copenhagen: G. E. C. Gad, 1877.

Grundtvig, N.F.S. *Sang-Værk til den danske Kirke* [Song Works for the Danish Church]. Vol. I. Copenhagen: Wahl, 1837.

———. *Udvalgte Digte* [Selected Poems]. introduction and notes by Steen Johansen. Copenhagen: Reitzel, 1963.

———. *Værker i Udvalg* [Selected Works]. eds. Georg Christensen and Hal Koch. 10 vols. Copenhagen: Gyldendal, 1940–49.

Gyllembourg, Thomasine ["'Forfatteren til 'En Hverdags-Historie'," pseud.]. *To Tidsaldre* [Two Ages]. *Skrifter* [Writings], vol. 11, collected and edited by Johan Ludvig Heiberg, 1–198. Copenhagen: Reitzel, 1851.

Heiberg, Johan Ludvig. *Breve og Aktstykker vedrørende Johan Ludvig Heiberg* [Letters and Documents Concerning Johan Ludvig Heiberg]. ed. Morten Borup. 5 vols. Copenhagen: Gyldendal, 1946–50.

———. *Fra det Heibergske Hjem. Johan Ludvig og Johanne Luise Heibergs indbyrdes Brevveksling* [From the Heiberg Home: The Correspondence Between Johan Ludvig and Johanne Luise Heiberg]. ed. Aage Friis. Copenhagen: J. H. Schultz Forlag, 1940.

———. *Fra J. L. Heibergs Ungdom* [From J. L. Heiberg's Youth]. eds. Julius Clausen and P. Fr. Rist. Copenhagen: Gyldendal, 1922.

———. *Johan Ludvig Heibergs Poetiske Skrifter* [Johan Ludvig Heiberg's Poetical Writings]. 11 vols. Copenhagen: Reitzel, 1862.

———. *Johan Ludvig Heibergs Prosaiske Skrifter* [Johan Ludvig Heiberg's Prose Writings]. 11 vols. Copenhagen: Reitzel, 1861–62.

Heiberg, Johan Ludvig, et al. *Heibergske Familiebreve* [Heiberg Family Correspondence]. ed. Morten Borup. Copenhagen: Gyldendal, 1943.

Heiberg, Johanne Luise. *Et Liv gjenoplivet i Erindringen* [A Life Relived in Recollection]. ed. Aage Friis. 4 vols. 4th rev. ed. Copenhagen: Gyldendal, 1944.

Hertz, Henrik. *Stemninger og Tilstande. Scener og Skildringer af et Ophold i Kjøbenhavn* [Moods and Situations: Scenes and Sketches from a Stay in Copenhagen]. Copenhagen: Reitzel, 1839.

Høffding, Harald. ed. *Udvalgte Stykker af Dansk Filosofisk Litteratur* [Selections of Danish Philosophical Literature]. Copenhagen and Kristiania (Oslo): Gyldendal, 1910.

Martensen, Hans L. *Af mit Levnet* [From My Life]. 3 vols. Copenhagen: Gyldendal, 1882–83.

———. *Biskop H. Martensens Breve* [Bishop H. Martensen's Letters]. ed. Bjørn Kornerup. 2 vols. Copenhagen: G. E. C. Gad, 1955–57.

———. *Den christelige Dogmatik* [Christian Dogmatics]. 4th printing. Copenhagen: Reitzel, 1883.

———. *Den christelige Ethik* [Christian Ethics]. 3 vols. 2d printing. Copenhagen: Gyldendal, 1871.

———. *Grundrids til Moralphilosophiens System* [Outline of the System of Moral Philosophy]. 2d printing. Copenhagen: Reitzel, 1864.

———. *Jacob Böhme. Theosophiske Studier* [Jacob Böhme: Theosophical Studies]. Copenhagen: Gyldendal, 1881.

———. *Katholicisme og Protestantisme. Et Leiligheds skrift* [Catholicism and Protestantism: An Occasional Piece]. Copenhagen: Gyldendal, 1874.

———. *Lejlighedstaler* [Occasional Addresses]. Copenhagen: Gyldendal, 1884.

———. *Meister Eckhart. Et Bidrag til at oplyse Middelalderens Mystik* [Meister Eckhart: A Contribution to the Elucidation of Mediaeval Mysticism]. Copenhagen: Reitzel, 1840.

———. "Nye Digte af J. L. Heiberg" [New Poems by J. L. Heiberg] (review). *Fædrelandet* [The Fatherland], nos. 398–400 (January 10–12, 1841).

———. *Prædikener. Første Samling* [Sermons: First Collection]. Copenhagen: Reitzel, 1847.

———. *Prædikener. Anden Samling* [Sermons: Second Collection]. Copenhagen: Reitzel, 1849.

———. *Prædikener. Tredie Samling* [Sermons: Third Collection]. Copenhagen: Reitzel, 1852.

———. *Prædikener. Fjerde Samling* [Sermons: Fourth Collection]. Copenhagen: Reitzel, 1854.

———. *Prædikener, holdte i Aarene 1854 til 1858* [Sermons Given in the Years 1854 to 1858]. Copenhagen: Gyldendal, 1858.

———. *Prædikener, holdte i Aarene 1859 til 1863* [Sermons Given in the Years 1859 to 1863]. Copenhagen: Gyldendal, 1863.

———. *Prædikener, holdte i Aarene 1864 til 1869* [Sermons Given in the Years 1864 to 1869]. Copenhagen: Gyldendal, 1869.

———. *Prædikener paa alle Søn- og Helligdage i Aaret, forhen trykte og utrykte* [Sermons for Every Sunday and Holiday in the Year, Previously Published and Unpublished]. Copenhagen: Gyldendal, 1875.

Mynster, C. L. N., ed. *Nogle Blade af J. P. Mynsters Liv og Tid* [Some Pages From J. P. Mynster's Life and Times]. Copenhagen: Gyldendal, 1875.

Mynster, Jakob Peter. *Af efterladte Breve til J. P. Mynster* [From Extant Letters to J. P. Mynster]. ed. C. L. N. Mynster. Copenhagen: Gyldendal, 1862.

———. *Betragtninger over de christelige Troeslærdomme* [Observations Upon the Doctrines of the Christian Faith]. 2 vols. 3d printing. Copenhagen: Deichmanns, 1846.

———. *Blandede Skrivter* [Miscellaneous Writings]. ed. J. H. Paulli (for vols. 4–6). 6 vols. Copenhagen: Gyldendal, 1852–57.

———. *Breve fra J. P. Mynster* [Letters from J. P. Mynster]. ed. C. L. N. Mynster. Copenhagen: Gyldendal, 1860.

———. *Efterladte Prædikener* [Posthumous Sermons]. ed. C. L. N. Mynster. Copenhagen: Gyldendal, 1875.

———. *J. P. Mynsters Visitatsdagbøger* [J. P. Mynster's Journal of Pastoral Visitations]. ed. Bjørn Kornerup. 2 vols. Copenhagen: Munksgaard, 1937.

———. *Kirkelige Lejligheds-Taler* [Occasional Church Addresses]. ed. F. J. Mynster. 2 vols. Copenhagen: Reitzel, 1854.

———. *Meddelelser om mit Levnet* [Communications About My Life]. ed. F. J. Mynster. 2d printing. Copenhagen: Gyldendal, 1884.

———. *Prædikener* [Sermons]. vol. 1. 3d printing. Copenhagen: Gyldendal, 1826. (originally published 1809).

———. *Prædikener* [Sermons]. vol. 2. Copenhagen: 1815.

———. *Prædikener holdte i Aarene 1846 til 1852* [Sermons Given in the Years 1846 to 1852]. 2 vols. 2d ed. Copenhagen: Gyldendal, 1854.

———. *Prædikener holdte i Aarene 1852 og 1853* [Sermons Given in the Years 1852 and 1853]. ed. F. J. Mynster. Copenhagen: Gyldendal, 1855.

———. *Prædikener paa alle Søn- og Hellig-Dage i Aaret* [Sermons for Every Sunday and Holiday in the Year]. 2 vols. Copenhagen: Gyldendal, 1823.

———. *Taler ved Præste-Vielser. Første Samling* [Sermons from Ordinations of Priests: First Collection]. Copenhagen: Reitzel, 1840.

———. *Taler ved Præste-Vielser. Anden Samling* [Sermons from Ordinations of Priests: Second Collection]. Copenhagen: Reitzel, 1846.

———. *Taler ved Præste-Vielser. Tredie Samling* [Sermons from Ordinations of Priests: Third Collection]. Copenhagen: Reitzel, 1851.

Møller, Poul Martin. *Efterladte Skrifter* [Posthumous Writings]. 6 vols. 3d ed. Copenhagen: Reitzel, 1855–56.

Nielsen, R., ed. *S. Kierkegaards Bladartikler med Bilag samlede efter Forfatterens Død* [S. Kierkegaard's Newspaper Articles, With a Supplement Collected After the Author's Death]. Copenhagen: Reitzel, 1857.

Oehlenschläger, Adam. *Breve til og fra Adam Oehlenschläger, 1798–1809* [Letters To and From Adam Oehlenschläger, 1798–1809]. eds. H. A. Paludan, Daniel Preisz, and Morten Borup. 5 vols. Copenhagen: Gyldendal, 1945–50.

——. *Breve til og fra Adam Oehlenschläger, 1809–1829* [Letters To and From Adam Oeh-lenschläger, 1809–1829]. ed. Daniel Preisz. 4 vols. Copenhagen: 1953–58.

——. *Oehlenschlägers Digterværker* [Oehlenschläger's Poetical Works]. 17 vols. Copen-hagen: Høst, 1844–46.

——. *Oehlenschlägers Erindringer* [Oehlenschläger's Memoirs]. 4 vols. Copenhagen: Høst, 1850–51.

——. *Oehlenschlägers Poetiske Skrifter* [Oehlenschlägers Poetical Writings]. ed. F. L. Liebenberg. 32 vols. Copenhagen: Selskabet til Udgivelse af Oehlenschlägers Skrifter, 1857–62.

——. *Poetiske Skrifter* [Poetical Writings]. 2 vols. Copenhagen: Schubothe, 1805.

Overskov, Thomas. *Af mit Liv og min Tid* [From My Life and Times]. ed. with notes by Robert Neiiendam. 2 vols. Copenhagen: Nyt Nordisk Forlag / Arnold Busck, 1961–62.

Ploug, Carl. *Samlede Digte af Carl Ploug* [Collected Poetry of Carl Ploug]. 5th ed. Co-penhagen: Forlagsbureauet i Kjøbenhavn, 1876.

Schack, Hans Egede. *Sandhed med Modification* [Truth, With Modification]. ed. Carl Dumreicher. Copenhagen: Dansk Kautionsforsikrings-Aktieselskab, 1954.

Sibbern, F. C. *Breve til og fra F. C. Sibbern* [Letters To and From F. C. Sibbern]. ed. C. L. N. Mynster. 2 vols. Copenhagen: Gyldendal, 1866.

——. *Gabrielis' Breve* [Gabrielis' Letters]. ed. Poul Tuxen. Copenhagen: J. Jørgensen and Co., 1927.

Steffens, Henrik. *Indledning til philosophiske Forelæsninger* [Introduction to Philosophical Lectures]. Copenhagen: Gyldendal (Traneklassiker), 1968.

Ørsted, A. S. *Af mit Livs og min Tids Historie* [From the History of My Life and Times]. Copenhagen: Arne Frost-Hansens Forlag, 1951.

——. *Blandede Skrifter i Udvalg* [Selected Miscellaneous Writings]. ed. Troels G. Jørgensen. Copenhagen: Gyldendal, 1933.

——. *Moralfilosofiske Skrifter i Udvalg* [Selected Writings on Moral Philosophy]. ed. Troels G. Jørgensen. Copenhagen: Gyldendal, 1936.

Østed, H. C. *Aanden i Naturen* [The Spirit in Nature]. 2 vols. 3d ed. Copenhagen: Höst, 1856.

SECONDARY WORKS

Andersen, Vilhelm. *Den danske Litteratur i den nittende Aarhundredes første Halvdel* [Danish Literature in the First Half of the Nineteenth Century]. vol. III of Carl S. Petersen and Vilhelm Andersen, *Illustreret dansk Litteraturhistorie* [Illustrated History of Danish Literature]. Copenhagen, Kristiania (Oslo), London, Berlin: Gyldendal, 1924.

——. *Den danske Litteratur i den nittende Aarhundredes anden Halvdel* [Danish Literature in the Second Half of the Nineteenth Century]. vol. IV of Carl S. Petersen and Vilhelm Andersen, *Illustreret dansk Litteraturhistorie* [Illustrated History of Danish Literature]. Copenhagen, London, Berlin: Gyldendal, 1925.

——. *Tider og Typer af dansk Aands Historie: Goethe* [Periods and Types in Danish Intellectual History: Goethe]. 2 vols. Copenhagen and Kristiania (Oslo): Gyld-endal, 1915–16.

Andreasen, Uffe. *Poul Møller og Romantismen* [Poul Møller and Romanticism]. Copen-hagen: Gyldendal, 1973.

Arildsen, Skat. *H. L. Martensen. Hans Liv, Udvikling, og Arbejde* [H. L. Martensen: His Life, Development, and Work]. Copenhagen: G. E. C. Gad, 1932.

Aumont, Arthur. *J. L. Heiberg og hans Slægt paa den danske Skueplads* [J. L. Heiberg and His Family on the Danish Stage]. Copenhagen: Jørgensen, 1891.

Baagø, Kaj. *Magister Jacob Christian Lindberg. Studier over den grundtvigske bevægelses første kamp* [Jacob Christian Lindberg, M. A.: Studies of the Grundtvigian Movement's First Battle]. Copenhagen: G. E. C. Gad, 1958.

Bajer, Frederik. *Nordens politiske Digtning, 1789–1804* [Scandinavian Political Poetry, 1789–1804]. Copenhagen: C. A. Topp's Forlag, 1878.

Balling, J. L. and Lindhardt, P. G. *Den nordiske Kirkes Historie* [The History of the Scandinavian Church]. 2d rev. ed. Copenhagen: Nyt Nordisk Forlag / Arnold Busck, 1967.

Banning, Knud. *Degnekristne* [Lay Preachers]. Copenhagen: G. E. C. Gad, 1958.

Bell, Richard, ed. *The Grammar of the Heart: New Essays in Moral Philosophy and Theology*. San Francisco: Harper and Row, 1988.

Bergsøe, Adolph Frederik. *Den danske Stats Statistik* [Danish State Statistics]. vol. 1. Copenhagen: Trykt paa Forfatterens Forlag, 1844.

Billeskov Jansen, F. J. *Romantik og Romantismen* [Romance and Romanticism]. vol. III of *Danmarks Digtekunst* [The Art of Danish Poetry]. Copenhagen: Munksgaard, 1958.

———. *Studier i Søren Kierkegaards Litterære Kunst* [Studies in the Literary Art of Søren Kierkegaard]. Copenhagen: Rosenkilde og Bagger, 1951.

Borup, Morten. *Johan Ludvig Heiberg*. 3 vols. Copenhagen: Gyldendal, 1947–49.

Brandes, Georg. *Danmark* [Denmark]. vols. I and II of *Samlede Skrifter* [Collected Writings]. Copenhagen and Kristiania (Oslo): Gyldendal, 1919.

Brandt, Frithiof. *Den unge Søren Kierkegaard* [The Young Søren Kierkegaard]. Copenhagen: Levin and Munksgaard, 1929.

Brandt, Frithiof and Rammel, Else. *Søren Kierkegaard og Pengene* [Søren Kierkegaard and Money]. Copenhagen: Levin and Munksgaard, 1935.

Bredsdorff, Elias. *Goldschmidt's Corsaren. Med en udførlig redegørelse for striden mellem Søren Kierkegaard og "Corsaren"* [Goldschmidt's *The Corsair*, With a Detailed Account of the Conflict Between Søren Kierkegaard and *The Corsair*]. [Århus]: Sirius, 1962.

Brix, Hans. *Analyser og Problemer. Et Udvalg* [Analyses and Problems: A Selection]. Copenhagen: Gyldendal (Uglebøger), 1965.

———. *Danmarks Digtere. Fyrretyve Kapitler af dansk Digtekunsts Historie* [Denmark's Poets: Forty Chapters in the History of the Art of Danish Poetry]. Copenhagen: Aschehoug Dansk Forlag, 1962.

———. *Fagre Ord* [Fair Speech]. Copenhagen: Gyldendal (Uglebøger), 1963.

———. *Tonen fra Himlen. Billeder af den kristelige Lyrik* [Music from Heaven: Pictures of Christian Lyrical Poetry]. Copenhagen: Gyldendal (Uglebøger), 1964.

Bukdahl, Jørgen. *Søren Kierkegaard, hans Fader og Slægten i Sædding* [Søren Kierkegaard, His Father, and the Family in Sædding]. Ribe: Dansk Hjemstavns Forlag, 1960.

———. *Søren Kierkegaard og den menige Mand* [Søren Kierkegaard and the Common Man]. Copenhagen: Gyldendal (Uglebøger), 1970.

Bukdahl, Jørgen K. *Om Søren Kierkegaard. Artikler i Udvalg* [On Søren Kierkegaard: Selected Articles]. ed. Jan Lindhardt. Copenhagen: Reitzel, 1981.

Cappelørn, Niels Jørgen. "Fire 'nye' Kierkegaard-dedikationer" ["Four 'New' Kierkegaard Dedications"]. *Kierkegaardiana*, no. IX (1974): 260–66.

———. "Kierkegaards eigener 'Gesichtspunkt': Vorwärts zu leben, aber rückwärts zu verstehen." *Neue Zeitschrift für Systematische Theologie und Religionsphilosophie*, 17. Band, Heft 1 (1975): 61–75.

Christensen, Villads. *Søren Kierkegaards Motiver til Kirkekampen* [Søren Kierkegaards Motives in the Attack on the Church]. Copenhagen: Munksgaard, 1959.

Clausen, H. P. "Den sociale problemstilling ved udforskningen af de gudelige vækkelser" [Explorations in the Religious Awakening Movement: Social Issues]. *Kirkehistoriske Samlinger* [Church History Miscellany] 7, vi (1965–68): 137–67.

Clausen, H. P.; Myer, P.; and Pontoppidan Thyssen, A. *Kulturelle, politiske og religiøse bevægelser i det 19. Århundrede* [Cultural, Political, and Religious Movements in the Nineteenth Century]. Århus: Universitetsforlag, 1973.

Collins, James. *The Mind of Kierkegaard*. Chicago: Henry Regnery, 1953. Reprint. Chicago: Henry Regnery (Gateway paperback), 1965.

Connell, George. *To Be One Thing: Personal Unity in Kierkegaard's Thought*. Macon, Georgia: Mercer University Press, 1985.

Crites, Stephen. *In the Twilight of Christendom: Hegel vs. Kierkegaard on Faith and History*. Chambersburg, Pennsylvania: American Academy of Religion, 1972.

Deuser, Hermann. *Dialektische Theologie: Studien zu Adornos Metaphysik und zum Spätwerk Kierkegaards*. Munich and Mainz: Kaiser / Grünewald, 1980.

———. "Kierkegaard in der Kritischen Theorie." *Text & Kontext* Band 15 (1983): 101–13.

———. *Søren Kierkegaard: Die paradoxe Dialektik des politischen Christen. Voraussetzungen bei Hegel: Die Reden von 1847/48 in Verhältnis von Politik und Ästhetik*. Munich and Mainz: Kaiser / Grünewald, 1974.

Dewey, Bradley. *The New Obedience: Kierkegaard on Imitating Christ*. Washington, D.C.: Corpus, 1968.

Diem, Hermann. *Kierkegaard: An Introduction*. trans. David Green. Richmond, Virginia: John Knox, 1966.

———. *Kierkegaard's Dialectic of Existence*. trans. Harold Knight. Edinburgh: Oliver and Boyd, 1959. Reprint. Westport, Connecticut: Greenwood Press, 1978.

Dunning, Stephen N. *Kierkegaard's Dialectic of Inwardness: A Structural Analysis of the Theory of Stages*. Princeton: Princeton University Press, 1985.

Dupré, Louis. *Kierkegaard as Theologian: The Dialectic of Christian Existence*. New York: Sheed and Ward, 1963.

Eller, Vernard. *Kierkegaard and Radical Discipleship*. Princeton: Princeton University Press, 1968.

Evans, C. Stephen. *Kierkegaard's "Fragments" and "Postscript": The Religious Philosophy of Johannes Climacus*. Atlantic Highlands, New Jersey: Humanities Press, 1983.

Feldbæk, Ole. *Denmark and the Armed Neutrality, 1800–1801: Small Power Policy in a World War*. Copenhagen: Akademisk Forlag, 1980.

Fenger, Henning. *Kierkegaard, The Myths and Their Origins: Studies in the Kierkegaardian Papers and Letters*. trans. George C. Schoolfield. New Haven and London: Yale University Press, 1980.

Gardiner, Patrick. *Kierkegaard*. Oxford and New York: Oxford University Press, 1988.

Geismar, Eduard. *Søren Kierkegaard: Hans Livsudvikling og Forfattervirksomhed* [Søren Kierkegaard: The Course of His Life and His Work as an Author]. 2 vols. Copenhagen: G. E. C. Gad, 1927–28.

Glædemark, H. J. H. *Kirkeforfatningsspørgsmålet i Danmark indtil 1874* [The Church Constitution Question in Denmark Up to 1874]. Copenhagen: Munksgaard, 1948.

Grimsley, Ronald. *Kierkegaard: A Biographical Introduction*. New York: Scribners, 1973.

Gustafson, Berndt. *I den Natt. Studier til Søren Kierkegaards förfallsteori* [In the Same Night: Studies in Søren Kierkegaard's Theory of Degeneration]. Stockholm: Diakonistyrelsens Bokförlag, 1962.

Hannay, Alastair. *Kierkegaard*. London, Boston, Melbourne: Routledge and Kegan Paul, 1982.

Hansen, Knud. *Revolutionær Samvittighed. Essays og Taler om Søren Kierkegaard og Karl Marx* [Revolutionary Conscience: Essays and Addresses on Søren Kierkegaard and Karl Marx]. Copenhagen: Gyldendal (Uglebøger), 1965.

Hansen, Søren Gorm. *H. C. Andersen og Søren Kierkegaard i dannelseskulturen* [Hans Christian Andersen and Søren Kierkegaard in the Culture of "Refinement"]. Copenhagen: Medusa, 1976.

Hauge, Svend. *Studier over D. G. Monrad som religiøs Personlighed* [Studies of D. G. Monrad as a Religious Personality]. Copenhagen: G. E. C. Gad, 1944.

Heiberg, P. A. *Søren Kierkegaards religiøs Udvikling: Psykologisk Mikroskopi* [Søren Kierkegaard's Religious Development: Psychological Microscopy]. Copenhagen: Gyldendal, 1925.

Henningsen, Bernd. *Politik eller Kaos?* [Politics or Chaos?]. Copenhagen: Berlingske Forlag, 1980.

Henrichsen, Erich. *Mændene fra 48* [The Men of '48]. Copenhagen: G. E. C. Gad, 1911.

Himmelstrup, J. *Sibbern*. Copenhagen: J. H. Schultz Forlag, 1934.

Høffding, Harald. *Danske Filosoffer* [Danish Philosophers]. [Copenhagen and Christiania (Oslo)]: Gyldendal, 1909.

———. *Mindre Arbejder. Anden Række.* [Lesser Works. Second Series]. Copenhagen: Gyldendal, [1905].

———. *Søren Kierkegaard som Filosof.* [Søren Kierkegaard as a Philosopher]. Copenhagen: P. G. Philipsens Forlag, 1892.

Høirup, Henning. *Grundtvig's Syn paa Tro og Erkendelse. Modsigelsens Grundsætning som teologisk Aksiom hos Grundtvig* [Grundtvig's View of Faith and Knowledge: The Principle of Contradiction as a Theological Axiom in Grundtvig]. Copenhagen: Gyldendal, 1949.

Holm, Kjeld; Jacobsen, Malthe; and Troelsen, Bjarne. *Søren Kierkegaard og Romantikerne* [Søren Kierkegaard and the Romantics]. Copenhagen: Berlingske Forlag, 1979.

Holm, Søren. *Filosofien i Norden før 1900* [Philosophy in Scandinavia Before 1900]. Copenhagen: Munksgaard, 1947.

———. *Græciteten* [Greekness]. Copenhagen: Munksgaard, 1964.

———. *Søren Kierkegaards Historiefilosofi* [Søren Kierkegaard's Philosophy of History]. Copenhagen: Festskrift udg. af Københavns Universitet, 1952.

Holmgaard, Otto. *Exstaticus. Søren Kierkegaards sidste Kamp, derunder hans Forhold til Broderen* [Søren Kierkegaard's Last Battle, Including his Relationship With His Brother]. Copenhagen: Nyt Nordisk Forlag / Arnold Busck, 1967.

Institutet for Historie og Samfundsøkonomi. *Fra Stænder til Folk* [From Estates to People]. Copenhagen: Gyldendal, 1943.

Jensen, F. Elle. *Pietismen i Danmark* [Pietism in Denmark]. Copenhagen: O. Lohse, n.d.

———. *Pietismen i Jylland. Studier over jydske Menighedstilstande, særlig paa Landet, omkring Midten af det 18. Aarhundrede* [Pietism in Jutland: Studies of the Conditions in Jutland Congregations, Particularly in the Countryside, in the mid-18th Century]. Copenhagen: G. E. C. Gad, 1944.

Jensen, Sigurd. *Fra Patriarkalisme til Pengeøkonomi* [From Patriarchalism to Cash Economy]. Copenhagen: Gyldendal, 1950.

Johansen, H. C. *En Samfundsorganisation i opbrud, 1700–1870* [The Break-up of Social Organization, 1700–1870]. vol. IV of *Dansk Socialhistorie* [Danish Social History]. Copenhagen: Gyldendal, 1979.

Johansen, Steen. ed. *Erindringer om Søren Kierkegaard* [Søren Kierkegaard Remembered]. Copenhagen: Reitzel, 1980.

Johnson, Howard A. and Thulstrup, Niels. eds. *A Kierkegaard Critique*. New York: Harper and Brothers, 1962.

Jørgensen, Carl. *Søren Kierkegaard. En biografi* [Søren Kierkegaard: A Biography]. Copenhagen: Nyt Nordisk Forlag / Arnold Busck, 1969.

Jørgensen, Harald. *Trykkefrihedsspørgsmaalet i Danmark, 1799–1848* [The Question of Freedom of the Press in Denmark, 1799–1848]. Copenhagen: Munksgaard, 1944.

Kirchoff-Larsen, Chr. *Den danske Presses Historie* [The History of the Danish Press]. vol. 3. Copenhagen: Berlingske Forlag, 1962.

von Kloeden, Wolfdietrich. "The Development of Kierkegaard's View of Christianity." *Bibliotheca Kierkegaardiana*. vol. 1, ch. 2, eds. Niels Thulstrup and Marie Mikulová Thulstrup. trans. Bruce H. Kirmmse. Copenhagen: Reitzel, 1978.

Koch, Hal. *Danmarks Kirke gennem Tidende* [The Danish Church Through the Ages]. 2d ed. Copenhagen: Gyldendal, 1960.

———. ed. *Et Kirkeskifte. Studier over brydninger i dansk kirke- og menighedsliv i det 19. Århundrede* [A Church Transformed: Studies of Conflict in the Life of the Danish Church and its Congregations in the Nineteenth Century]. Copenhagen: G. E. C. Gad, 1960.

———. *Tiden 1800–1848* [The Period 1800–1848]. vol. 6 of *Den danske Kirkes Historie* [History of the Danish Church]. eds. Hal Koch and Bjørn Kornerup. Copenhagen: Gyldendal, 1954.

Kühle, Sejer. *Søren Kierkegaards Barndom og Ungdom* [Søren Kierkegaard's Childhood and Youth]. Copenhagen: Aschehoug, 1950.

Larsen, Jørgen. *H. N. Clausen. Hans Liv og Gerning* [H. N. Clausen: His Life and Work]. Copenhagen: G. E. C. Gad, 1945.

Lehmann, Johannes, ed. *Den unge Orla Lehmann* [The Young Orla Lehmann]. Copenhagen: Dansk Kautionsforsikrings-Aktieselskab, 1957.

Lindhardt, P. G. *Konfrontation* [Confrontation]. Copenhagen: Akademisk Forlag, 1974.

———. *Søren Kierkegaards Angreb på Folkekirken* [Søren Kierkegaard's Attack on the People's Church]. Århus: Aros, 1955.

———. *Tiden 1849–1901* [The Period 1849–1901]. vol. 7 of *Den danske Kirkes Historie* [History of the Danish Church]. eds. Hal Koch and Bjørn Kornerup. Copenhagen: Gyldendal, 1958.

———. *Vækkelser og kirkelige Retninger i Danmark* [Awakenings and Ecclesiastical Currents in Denmark]. 2d ed. Copenhagen: Reitzel, 1959.

Lindström, Valter. *Efterföljelsens teologi* [The Theology of Imitation]. Stockholm: Diakonistyrelsens Bokförlag, 1956.

Lomholt, Esbern. *Med Syvtallet* [With the Fire Poker]. Copenhagen: Rosenkilde og Bagger, 1959.

Lønning, Per. *Samtidighedens Situation. En Studie i Søren Kierkegaards Kristendomforståelse* [The Situation of Contemporaneity: A Study in Søren Kierkegaard's Understanding of Christianity]. Oslo: Forlaget Land og Kirke, 1954.

Lowrie, Walter. *Kierkegaard*. Oxford: Oxford University Press, 1938.

———. *A Short Life of Kierkegaard*. Princeton: Princeton University Press, 1942. Reprint. Princeton: Princeton University Press (paperback ed.), 1965.

Lundbye, J. *Herrnhutismen i Danmark* [Herrnhutism in Denmark]. Copenhagen: Karl Schønbergs Forlag, 1903.

Mackey, Louis. *Kierkegaard: A Kind of Poet*. Philadelphia: University of Pennsylvania Press, 1971. Reprint. Philadelphia: University of Pennsylvania Press (paperback ed.), 1972.

———. *Points of View: Readings of Kierkegaard*. Tallahassee: University Presses of Florida / Florida State University Press, 1986.

Malantschuk, Gregor. *The Controversial Kierkegaard*. trans. Howard V. Hong and Edna H. Hong. Waterloo, Ontario: Wilfred Laurier University Press, 1978.

———. *Fra Individ til den Enkelte* [From the Individual to "the Single Individual"]. Copenhagen: Reitzels, 1978.

———. *Frihed og Existens. Studier i Søren Kierkegaards Tænkning* [Freedom and Existence: Studies in the Thought of Søren Kierkegaard]. eds. Niels Jørgen Cappelørn and Paul Müller. Copenhagen: Reitzel, 1980.

———. *Kierkegaard's Thought*. eds. and trans. Howard V. Hong and Edna H. Hong. Princeton: Princeton University Press, 1971.

———. *Kierkegaard's Way to the Truth: An Introduction to the Thought of Søren Kierkegaard.* trans. Mary Michelsen. Minneapolis: Augsburg, 1963.

Malantschuk, Gregor and Søe, N. H. *Kierkegaards Kamp mod Kirken* [Kierkegaard's Attack on the Church]. Copenhagen: Munksgaard, 1956.

Matthiessen, Hugo. *Det gamle Land* [The Ancient Countryside]. Copenhagen: Gyldendal, 1942.

McCarthy, Vincent. *The Phenomenology of Moods in Kierkegaard.* The Hague: Martinus Nijhoff, 1978.

McKinnon, Alastair. ed. *Kierkegaard: Resources and Results.* Waterloo, Ontario: Wilfred Laurier University Press, 1982.

Michelsen, William. *Tilblivelsen af Grundtvig's Historiesyn: Idehistoriske Studier over Grundtvigs Verdenskrönikker og deres litterære Forudsætninger* [The Genesis of Grundtvig's View of History. Grundtvig's *Chronicles of World History* and Their Literary Background: Studies in the History of Ideas]. 2 vols. Copenhagen: Gyldendal, 1954.

Møller Kristensen, Svend. *Digteren og Samfundet* [The Poet and the Society]. vol. 1. 2d ed. Copenhagen: Munksgaard, 1965.

Mullen, John Douglas. *Kierkegaard's Philosophy: Self-Deception and Cowardice in the Present Age.* New York: New American Library (Mentor paperback), 1981.

Müller, Paul. "Betingelsen for meddelelsen af det kristelige hos Søren Kierkegaard" [Kierkegaard's Prerequisite for the Communication of Christianity]. *Dansk teologisk Tidsskrift* [Danish Theological Journal] 36. Årgang (1973): 25–43.

———. "Grundprincipperne i Søren Kierkegaards meddelelsesdialektik og deres anvendelse i forfatterskabet" [The Fundamental Principles of Søren Kierkegaard's Dialectic of Communication and Their Use in His Authorship]. *Dansk teologisk Tidsskrift* [Danish Theological Journal] 41. Årgang (1978): 123–33.

———. *Kristendom, Etik og Majeutik i Søren Kierkegaards "Kjerlighedens Gjerninger"* [Christianity, Ethics, and Maieutics in Søren Kierkegaard's *Works of Love*]. Copenhagen: København Universitets Institut for Religionshistorie, 1976.

———. *Meddelelsesdialektikken i Søren Kierkegaards "Philosophiske Smuler"* [The Dialectic of Communication in Søren Kierkegaard's *Philosophical Fragments*]. Copenhagen: Reitzel, 1979.

———. *Søren Kierkegaards Kommunikationsteori* [Søren Kierkegaard's Theory of Communication]. Copenhagen: Reitzel, 1984.

———. "Tvivlens former og deres rolle i erkendelsen af det historiske. En studie i Søren Kierkegaards erkendelesesteori" [The Forms of Doubt and Their Role in Historical Knowledge: A Study of Søren Kierkegaard's Theory of Knowledge]. *Dansk teologisk Tidsskrift* 37. Årgang (1977): 177–216.

Nielsen, Harry A. *Where the Passion Is: A Reading of Kierkegaard's "Philosophical Fragments".* Tallahassee: University Presses of Florida, 1983.

Nordentoft, Kresten. *"Hvad siger Brand-Majoren?". Kierkegaards Opgør med sin Samtid* ["What Does the Fire Chief Say?": Kierkegaard's Settling-Up With His Times]. Copenhagen: G. E. C. Gad, 1973.

———. *Kierkegaard's Psychology.* trans. Bruce H. Kirmmse, Pittsburgh: Duquesne University Press, 1978.

———. "Noget om Kierkegaard, Freud, og Marx" [Something About Kierkegaard, Freud, and Marx]. *Kredsen* [The Circle] (Århus) 41. Årgang, no. 1 (1973): 1–8.

———. *Søren Kierkegaard. Bidrag til kritikken af den borgerlige selvoptagethed* [Søren Kierkegaard: Contribution to the Critique of Bourgeois Self-Absorption]. Copenhagen: Dansk Universitets Press, 1977.

Nyholm, Asger. *Religion og Politik. En Monrad Studie* [Religion and Politics: A Study of Monrad]. Copenhagen: Nyt Nordisk Forlag / Arnold Busck, 1947.

Olesen Larsen, Kristoffer. *Søren Kierkegaard Læst af K. Olesen Larsen* [Søren Kierkegaard Read by K. Olesen Larsen]. eds. Vibeke Olesen Larsen and Tage Wilhelm. 2 vols. Copenhagen: G. E. C. Gad, 1966.

Ørsted, Børge. *J. P. Mynster og Henrik Steffens* [J. P. Mynster and Henrik Steffens]. 2 vols. Copenhagen: Nyt Nordisk Forlag / Arnold Busck, 1965.

Perkins, Robert L. ed. *The Sickness Unto Death. International Kierkegaard Commentary*, vol. 19. Macon, Georgia: Mercer University Press, 1987.

———. ed. *Two Ages. International Kierkegaard Commentary*, vol. 14. Macon, Georgia: Mercer University Press, 1984.

———. ed. *Thought: A Review of Culture and Idea*, vol. LV, no. 218 (September 1980) (special Kierkegaard issue).

Petersen, Teddy. *Kierkegaards polemiske debut. Artikler, 1834–36 i historisk sammenhæng* [Kierkegaard's Polemical Debut: The Articles of 1834–36 in Their Historical Context]. Odense: Odense Universitets Forlag, 1977.

Plekon, Michael. "Introducing Christianity into Christendom: Reinterpreting the Late Kierkegaard." *Anglican Theological Review* 64 (1982): 327–352.

———. "Kierkegaard and the Interpretation of Modernity." *Kierkegaard-Studiet* (Osaka) no. 11 (1981): 3–12.

———. "Kierkegaard, the Church, and Theology of Golden Age Denmark." *Journal of Ecclesiastical History*, vol. 43. no. 2 (April 1983): 245–266.

———. "Moral Accounting: Kierkegaard's Social Theory and Criticism." *Kierkegaardiana*, no. XII (1982): 69–82.

———. "Prophetic Criticism, Incarnational Optimism: On Recovering the Late Kierkegaard." *Religion* 13 (1983): 137–153.

———. "Protest and Affirmation: The Late Kierkegaard on Christ, the Church, and Society." *Quarterly Review* vol. 2, no. 3 (Fall 1982): 43–62.

———. "Towards Apocalypse: Kierkegaard's Two Ages in Golden Age Denmark." *Two Ages: International Kierkegaard Commentary*, vol. 14. ed. by Robert L. Perkins. Macon, Georgia: Mercer University Press, 1984, pp. 19–52.

Plougman, Vera. *Søren Kierkegaards Kristendomsforståelse* [Søren Kierkegaard's Understanding of Christianity]. Copenhagen: Gyldendal, 1975.

Plum, Niels Munk. *Jakob Peter Mynster som Kristen og Teolog* [Jakob Peter Mynster: Christian and Theologian]. Copenhagen: G. E. C. Gad, 1938.

Pojman, Louis P. *The Logic of Subjectivity: Kierkegaard's Philosophy of Religion*. University, Alabama: University of Alabama Press, 1984.

Pontoppidan Thyssen, A. *Vækkelsernes frembrud i Danmark i første halvdel af det 19. Århundrede* [The Outbreak of Awakenings in Denmark in the First Half of the Nineteenth Century]. 6 vols. Copenhagen: G. E. C. Gad, 1960–74.

Roberts, Robert C. *Faith, Reason and History: Rethinking Kierkegaard's "Philosophical Fragments."* Macon, Georgia: Mercer University Press, 1986.

Rohde, H. P. *Gaadefulde Stadier paa Kierkegaards Vej* [Mysterious Stages on Kierkegaard's Way]. Copenhagen: Rosenkilde og Bagger, 1974.

Rubow, Paul. *Dansk litterær Kritik i det nittende Aarhundrede indtil 1870* [Danish Literary Criticism in the Nineteenth Century Until 1870]. Copenhagen: Levin og Munksgaards Forlag, 1921.

Scharling, C. I. *Grundtvig og Romantikken, Belyst ved Grundtvigs Forhold til Schelling* [Grundtvig and Romanticism, Illustrated by Grundtvig's Relation to Schelling]. Copenhagen: Gyldendal, 1947.

Schørring, Jens Holger. *Teologi og Filosofi. Nogle Analyser og Dokumenter vedrørende Hegelianismen i dansk Teologi* [Theology and Philosophy: Some Documents Concerning Hegelianism in Danish Theology]. Copenhagen: Institut for Kirkehistorie / G. E. C. Gad, 1974.

Skjoldager, Emanuel. *Den egentlige Kierkegaard. Søren Kierkegaards Syn på Kirken og de kirkelige Handlinger* [The Real Kierkegaard: Søren Kierkegaard's View of the Church and of Ecclesiastical Acts]. Copenhagen: Reitzel, 1982.

———. *Hvorfor Søren Kierkegaard ikke blev Grundtvigianer* [Why Søren Kierkegaard Did Not Become a Grundtvigian]. Copenhagen: Reitzel, 1977.

Skovmand, Roar. *De folkelige Bevægelser i Danmark* [The Popular Movements in Denmark]. Copenhagen: Schultz, 1951.

———. *Folkestyrets Fødsel, 1830–1870* [The Birth of Popular Government, 1830–1870]. vol. 11 of *Danmarks Historie* [History of Denmark]. eds. John Danstrup and Hal Koch. Copenhagen: Politikens Forlag, 1964.

Skubbeltrang, Fridlev. *Den danske Bonde. 1788–1938* [The Danish Peasant, 1788–1938]. Copenhagen: Landbrugsudstillingen, 1938.

———. *Husmænd i Danmark gennem 300 Aar* [Cottagers in Denmark During 300 Years]. Copenhagen: Schultz, 1942.

Sløk, Johannes. *Da Kierkegaard Tav. Fra Forfatterskabet til Kirkestorm* [When Kierkegaard Remained Silent: From the Authorship to the Attack on the Church]. Copenhagen: Reitzel, 1980.

———. *Søren Kierkegaard*. Copenhagen: G. E. C. Gad, 1960.

———. *Kierkegaard—Humanismens Tænker* [Kierkegaard: Humanism's Thinker]. Copenhagen: Reitzel, 1978.

———. *Kierkegaards Univers. En ny guide til geniet* [Kierkegaard's Universe: A New Guide to the Genius]. [Viby]: Centrum, 1983.

Smith, Joseph H. ed. *Kierkegaard's Truth: The Disclosure of the Self*. New Haven and London: Yale University Press, 1981.

Sørensen, Villy. *Digtere og dæmoner. Fortolkninger og vurderinger* [Poets and Demons: Interpretations and Evaluations]. Copenhagen: Gyldendal (Uglebøger), 1973.

———. *Mellem Fortid og Fremtid: Kronikker og Kommentarer* [Between Past and Future: Newspaper Articles and Commentaries]. Copenhagen: Gyldendal (Uglebøger), 1969.

Sponheim, Paul. *Kierkegaard On Christ and Christian Coherence*. New York: Harper and Row, 1968.

Swenson, David F. *Something About Kierkegaard*. ed. Lillian Marvin Swenson. Minneapolis: Augsburg, 1945. Reprint. Macon, Georgia: Mercer University Press, 1983.

Taylor, Mark C. *Journeys to Selfhood: Hegel and Kierkegaard*. Berkeley, Los Angeles, London: University of California Press, 1980.

———. *Kierkegaard's Pseudonymous Authorship: A Study of Time and the Self*. Princeton: Princeton University Press, 1975.

Thompson, Josiah. *Kierkegaard*. New York: Alfred A. Knopf, 1973.

———. *The Lonely Labyrinth: Kierkegaard's Pseudonymous Works*. Carbondale and Edwardsville, Illinois: Southern Illinois University Press, 1967; London and Amsterdam: Feffer and Simons, Inc., 1967.

———. *Kierkegaard: A Collection of Critical Essays*. Garden City, New York: Doubleday (Anchor paperback), 1972.

Thulstrup, Marie Mikulová. *Kierkegaard og Pietismen* [Kierkegaard and Pietism]. Copenhagen: Munksgaard, 1967.

Thulstrup, Marie Mikulová and Thulstrup, Niels. eds. *Bibliotheca Kierkegaardiana*. 16 vols. Copenhagen: Reitzel, 1978–88.

Thulstrup, Niels. *Kierkegaard's Relationship to Hegel*. trans. George L. Stengren. Princeton: Princeton University Press, 1980.

Toftdahl, Hellmut. *Kierkegaard først—og Grundtvig så* [Kierkegaard First—And Then Grundtvig]. Copenhagen: Nyt Nordisk Forlag / Arnold Busck, 1969.

Troels-Lund. *Bakkehus og Solbjerg* [Hill House and Sun Mountain]. 3 vols. 2d ed. Copenhagen: Gyldendal, 1972.

Vedel, Valdemar. *Guldalderen i dansk Digtning* [The Golden Age in Danish Poetry]. Copenhagen: Gyldendal (Uglebøger), 1967.

Vibæk, Jens. *Reform og Fallit, 1784–1830* [Reform and Bankruptcy, 1784–1830]. vol. 10 of *Danmarks Historie* [History of Denmark]. eds. John Danstrup and Hal Koch. Copenhagen: Politikens Forlag, 1964.

Walker, Jeremy. *The Descent Into God*. Kingston, Ontario and Montreal: McGill-Queens University Press, 1985.

———. *To Will One Thing: Reflections on Kierkegaard's "Purity of Heart"*. Montreal: McGill-Queens University Press, 1972.

Weltzer, Carl. *Peter og Søren Kierkegaard* [Peter and Søren Kierkegaard]. 2 vols. Copenhagen: G. E. C. Gad, 1936.

———. *Grundtvig og Søren Kierkegaard* [Grundtvig and Søren Kierkegaard]. Copenhagen: i Commission hos Gyldendal, 1972.

Westphal, Merold. *Kierkegaard's Critique of Reason and Society*. Macon, Georgia: Mercer University Press, 1987.

Index

BRUCE H. KIRMMSE is Professor of History at Connecticut College. As a Fulbright and a Danforth Fellow, he lived in Denmark for several years. He is the author of numerous articles on Kierkegaard and translator of *Kierkegaard's Psychology* by Kresten Nordentoft.

MANAGING EDITOR: TERRY CAGLE
BOOK AND JACKET DESIGNER: SHARON L. SKLAR
PRODUCTION COORDINATOR: HARRIET CURRY
TYPEFACE: PALATINO WITH MERIDIEN DISPLAY
COMPOSITOR: IMPRESSIONS, INC.
PRINTER: MALLOY LITHOGRAPHING